WOMEN WELFARE AND EMPOWERMENT IN INDIA

Vision for 21st Century

Women Welfare and Empowerment in India

Vision for 21st Century

Edited by

Dr. Rameshwari Pandya
Faculty of Home Science,
The M.S. University of Baroda,
Gujarat

NEW NC CENTURY

New Century Publications
New Delhi, India

NEW CENTURY PUBLICATIONS
4800/24, Bharat Ram Road,
Ansari Road, Daryaganj,
New Delhi - 110 002 (India)

Tel.: 011 – 2324 7798, 4358 7398, 6539 6605
Fax: 011 – 4101 7798
E-mail: indiatax@vsnl.com
www.newcenturypublications.com

Editorial office:
34, Gujranwala Town, Part-2,
Delhi - 110 009

Tel.: 27247805, 27464774

First Published – **July 2008**

ISBN: **978-81-7708-172-5**

Published by New Century Publications and printed at Salasar Imaging Systems, New Delhi

Designs: W & P Graphics Pvt. Ltd., New Delhi

PRINTED IN INDIA

Dedicated to My Mother
A symbol of strong and empowered woman

FOREWORD

Since the UN Declaration of the International Decade for Women (1980-1990), greater interest is noticeable in issues related to welfare, development and empowerment of women worldwide. Health, education and employment are deemed to be crucial areas for women's empowerment. History, geography and socio-economic settings of a region play significant role in the development and empowerment of women anywhere in the world. Though belatedly, it has been realised that women make significant contribution to the overall development of a nation. The role and status of women in a society is determined by a complex mix of economic, social, religious, cultural and political factors.

I am pleased to see in this book the contributions of academicians, researchers and extension personnel who are directly/indirectly engaged in activities related to development of women. These experts hail from different parts of India and their experiences and findings are extremely relevant to understand the problems of Indian women and to find appropriate solutions to them.

Issues addressed in the book are well-categorised into 6 Theme Parts, viz.

- Health, Nutrition and Fertility of Women
- Education and Training of Women
- Employment of Women
- Self-help Groups (SHGs) and Empowerment of Women
- Problems of Rural Women
- Women, Media, Politics and Human Rights

I am confident that the information provided in this book will be of great value to those interested in women studies and also to government and non-government agencies engaged in ameliorating the conditions of women at the grassroots level.

I also take this opportunity to congratulate Dr. Rameshwari Pandya for her painstaking efforts to make the useful information contained in this book accessible to a wide audience.

Baroda
January 2008

Professor Prerna Mohite

ABOUT THE BOOK

In India, policies and programmes of the government at different levels cover various dimensions and strategies of gender development. Over the years, efforts have been made to empower women socially, economically and politically. However, due to lack of synergy and coordination, the achievements are not satisfactory. It is imperative that an integrated policy and strategy be formulated to address economic, social and political issues related to women along with the requisite programmes and schemes.

Though India has created protective legislations for women, the enactments have not been easy to implement. The vastness of the country, the scattered nature of women workers, their lack of education and legal literacy, the indifferent attitude of government bureaucracy have all contributed to the continuing vulnerability of women. This is true not only of rural unorganised women, but also of urban women workers. Although the Constitutional commitments to women find reflections in the planning process, legislations, policies and programmes of the Central and State Governments yet the current socio-economic status of women is unsatisfactory in terms of almost all important indicators of human development.

This book has emerged from the research papers contributed by social scientists and academicians from different parts of India, focusing on specific gender-related issues. The volume will provide valuable information and inputs to academicians, researchers, NGOs, and government agencies and functionaries. It contains 42 research contributions related to women issues. These contributions have been categorised into the following 6 Theme Parts. (a) Health, Nutrition and Fertility of Women, (b) Education and Training of Women, (c) Employment of Women, (d) Self-help Groups (SHGs) and Empowerment of Women, (e) Problems of Rural Women and (f) Women, Media, Politics and Human Rights.

EDITOR'S PROFILE

Dr. Rameshwari Pandya graduated from Lady Irwin College, University of Delhi. She secured her B.Sc., B.Ed., M.Sc., M.Ed. and Ph.D. degrees from The M.S. University of Baroda, Vadodara, Gujarat. She is the recipient of Shrimati Leela Ben Shah Gold Medal for her academic excellence.

Presently, she is a senior faculty member in the Faculty of Family and Community Science, The M.S. University of Baroda. She has published more than 70 research papers in professional journals of repute and has to her credit the following books: *Women in India: Issues, Perspectives and Solutions*; *Imbibing Value Education: Various Perspectives*; *Facets of Women's Development;* and *NGOs for Development: Indian Perspectives*. She has successfully completed several projects and is currently handling a major project titled *Promotion of Communal Harmony* funded by Indian Council of Social Science Research (ICSSR), New Delhi.

EDITOR'S NOTE ON THE BOOK

Women in Indian Society

In the 2001 Census, the sex ratio in India stood at 933 females per 1,000 males. There are many reasons for excess of male over female population. The lack of pre-natal and post-natal care has been the major cause of high death-rate among women in reproductive age. The preference for male child persists even to this day and is reflected in better food and other amenities of life provided to boys in preference to girls. Similarly, there is evil practice of sex selective female abortions. It is noteworthy that in Western countries, the sex ratio favours the feminine population.

Again, according to 2001 Census, women (495.7 million) comprise 48.3 per cent of the country's population. Most women workers in the country are employed in the rural areas, primarily as labourers. In the urban areas, women workers are mainly employed in the unorganised sector comprising household industries, petty trades, manual services, and building and construction.

In India, the work participation rate of women is less than half that of men. Among women, widows are the most vulnerable sections of the society. Several studies have pointed out that female widowhood in India tends to be associated with economic deprivation. The multiple roles of women and the meagre ability to access resources and available assets are areas of concern. It is important to emphasise that women require adequate security and protection to be self-reliant.

Over the years, efforts have been made to empower women: socially, economically and politically. However, due to lack of synergy and coordination, the achievements are not satisfactory. It is imperative that an integrated policy and strategy be formulated to address economic, social and political issues related to women along with the requisite programmes and schemes.

Constitutional Rights of Indian Women

The Constitution of India recognises the right of women to employment and includes a number of Articles to give directions to the state policy. Article 14 lays down the equality before law of all citizens of the country, and Article 15 prohibits discrimination on grounds of sex, religion, race etc. Article 16 (1) and (2) emphasise equal opportunities for all in the matter of employment and prohibits discrimination in employment.

Article 15 (3) of the Constitution empowers the state to make special provisions for women and children within the framework of the fundamental rights. Articles 39 and 42 specifically refer to women and children. They direct the State to secure health and strength of all workers (men, women and children) and to prevent the abuse of children for economic gains. Humane and just conditions of work and maternity benefits are assured to women by Article 42.

Though India has created protective legislation for women, the enactments have not been easy to implement. The vastness of the country, the scattered nature of women workers, their lack of education and legal literacy, the indifferent attitude of government bureaucracy have all contributed to the continuing vulnerability of women. This is true not only of rural unorganised women, but also of urban women workers. It is noteworthy that nearly 80 per cent women work in the unorganised sector and out of them nearly 60 per cent are self-employed. Though the Constitutional commitments to women find reflections in the planning process, legislations, policies and programmes of the Central and State Governments yet the current socio-economic status of women is unsatisfactory in terms of almost all important indicators of human development.

Problems of Women

Employment: In a labour-surplus country like India, the working class is destined to be one of the weaker sections of society. Society being male-dominated, female labour receives poor recognition and value. It is not that there are no statutory provisions. In fact, the Constitution of India provides equal rights and opportunities to both the genders. In addition, there are specific provisions for protection and welfare of working women in many of the labour laws. However, most of these statutes do not cover the units in small and informal sectors which are the predominant workplaces of women. Even where they are covered by the statutes, the poor enforcement practically nullifies the provisions. Paradoxically, the very laws which are meant for working women are sometimes turned against their interests by unscrupulous employers. If the employers find it difficult to bypass these provisions, they get rid of the women workers and thus strike at the economic base of their livelihood. All these factors need to be studied in depth while drafting policies and legal provisions for the working women.

For the reasons mentioned above, union leaders and others interested in the welfare of women must acquire sound knowledge of existing provisions of labour. Although women's development is an integral part of our general developmental plans yet government action alone can neither be adequate nor effective unless women themselves become more aware of their rights and the corresponding responsibilities. Every woman is a working woman, whether she works at home or outside it. Many women work to earn money. Working women must know that they have some basic rights which are given by the law. Some of these constitutional rights include the following. First, every woman must get wages because every person must be paid for his or her work. Second, a person must be paid at least the minimum wage which is fixed by the government. Third, every woman must be paid the same wage as is given to a man if she does the same/similar kind of work. This means that a woman must be paid wages equal to a man's wages, not less. Fourth, women workers must be given special benefits during their pregnancy, after delivery, or after an abortion.

Rural women are mainly employed in agriculture, its allied activities and agro-based enterprises. There exists a glaring gender bias in terms of ownership, nature of work assigned, wage payment, freedom in choice of work etc. Though the women contribute a significant proportion of agricultural production, they are discriminated against, ill-paid and their role is largely neglected. It underscores the need for an appropriate legal-institutional framework to reduce gender disparity in agriculture sector and to ensure sustainable development.

Health and Education: Women, nearly half of the total population, are lagging behind in access to the existing health care and educational opportunities in the country. A proper level of awareness, along with a conducive environment, needs to be developed for this purpose. Promotion of health, education and awareness will significantly contribute to women development. Formation of Self-help Groups (SHGs) among poor women, provision of micro credit financing to them would be a great support which will help them to start micro enterprises to generate income and overcome poverty.

From Gender Gaps to Gender Parity

Gender equality is a component as well as an instrument of development. No country can be deemed developed if half of its population is severely disadvantaged in terms of basic needs, livelihood options, access to knowledge, and political voice. Gender equality is an instrument of development because without it national goals of development will be difficult to achieve as, for example, poverty alleviation, population planning, family welfare and environmental sustainability.

Ensuring gender parity has become a great challenge for the modern world. Gender equality forms part of development strategy in many countries of the world including India. When both men and women have equal access to services and resources, enjoy equal rights, and get equal opportunities to develop skills and capabilities then the development of the country is fast and balanced.

In spite of considerable efforts towards advocacy and awareness of gender equality and launching of various programmes for welfare of women, gender discrimination in India remains pervasive in many dimensions of life. Though the nature and magnitude of discrimination against women vary from country to country, in no part of the world gender parity has been achieved completely in legal, social and economic terms. Gender gaps are widespread in respect of access to and control of resources, economic opportunities, and political voice. Women are still exploited, discriminated against and subjected to harassment and violence.

Recent Initiatives for Women

In India, policies and programmes of the government at different levels cover various dimensions and strategies of gender development The Ninth Five Year Plan (1997-98 to 2001-02) adopted the strategy of Women's Component Plan, under which not less than 30 per cent of funds/benefits were earmarked in all the women-related sectors, for women-specific programmes. The Tenth Five Year Plan (2002-03 to 2006-07) also undertook schemes to further strengthen the process of Women's Component Plan. In order to address the welfare issues relating to women, a Task Force on Women and Children was constituted by the Government of India in August 2000 under the Chairmanship of Shri K.C. Pant. In its report submitted in April 2002, the Task Force, *inter alia*, recommended the setting up of an Inter-Ministerial Standing Committee in the Department of Women and Child Development, composed of official and non-official experts, to review and monitor gender mainstreaming in Government. The Task Force also reviewed the whole gamut of legislations concerning women and recommended amendment of 22 laws to make them more effective.

Several women welfare programmes have been launched by successive governments in recent years. The important among these are the following.

Under the Support for Training and Employment (STEP), marginalised and assetless women are provided training for new technologies in agriculture, dairying, horticulture, fisheries, handicrafts, handlooms etc. and organised into groups and provided with necessary infrastructure, managerial and marketing support for productive activities on a sustainable basis. Since the inception of the Programme in 1987, 134 such projects have been implemented benefiting more than 6 lakh women throughout the country.

Under the Women's Economic Programme, now named *Swavalamban*, employment-linked training is provided to women in various traditional and non-traditional trades. Annually more than a thousand projects are sanctioned to train about 50,000 women.

Since its inception in 1993, *Rashtriya Mahila Kosh* (RMK) has sanctioned credit worth Rs. 113.50 crore to benefit more than 4.28 lakh women through

1,046 NGOs spread over the country. Apart from its core activities, the RMK has been catalytic in the development of several new organisations dealing with micro credit across the country, both in the public sector and voluntary sector. Funds from RMK flow to the needy women through the intervention of Women Self-help Groups (SHGs).

Under the Short Stay Homes Scheme, the Government is implementing a National Plan of Action for the rescue, rehabilitation and reintegration of women and girls trapped in commercial sex. The new scheme of *Swadhar* was launched for providing a comprehensive package of food, shelter, health cover, counselling and skill training to women and girls in difficult circumstances. Major States have formulated Action Plans and comprehensive project proposals synergising the efforts of the Central Government and non-government organisations.

After the success of the pilot project *Swa-shakti* under which more than 12,000 SHGs were formed in 10 States, the Government launched a new scheme *Swayamsidha* on November 29, 2001. Under the programme, 53,100 SHGs comprising of 9,29,250 women beneficiaries, have been formed in 650 blocks throughout the country.

In order to address the phenomenon of domestic violence, which is widely prevalent but remains largely invisible in the public domain, the Protection from Domestic Violence Act, 2006 was enacted by the Parliament. The Act envisages that the Protection Officer would assist the victim of domestic violence to be secure from violence and help her to access shelter homes, health care and legal advice.

In order to study the problems of self-employed and unorganised women workers, the Government of India had appointed a commission known as National Commission for Self-employed Women. After an arduous study of their problems and discussions with various voluntary organisations working for women, the Commission came out with a number of useful and important recommendations to improve the condition of women workers in general and rural and unorganised women in particular. Several of these recommendations refer to amendments in the existing laws.

Agenda for Action

If we are serious about improving the economic status of poor women working in the informal sector of the economy, we have to devise concrete strategies which can help to enhance the ownership of and control over productive assets by these women. Perhaps it will be the single most important intervention towards their empowerment and economic well-being. Some of the assets that women can be given are plots of land, houses, tree pattas, livestock licenses, bank accounts, membership of organisations and identity cards.

Improvement in the social and economic conditions of women calls for fundamental changes in the laws regarding the rights of women, particularly widows, to property. Though belatedly, the Indian society has awakened to the need to make women equal partners in the socio-economic development of the country.

The Present Volume

The volume has emerged from the research papers contributed by social scientists and academicians from different parts of India, focusing on specific gender-related issues. The volume will provide valuable information and inputs to academicians, researchers, NGOs, and government agencies and functionaries. It contains 42 research contributions related to women issues. These contributions have been categorised into the following 6 Theme Parts.

Part I: Health, Nutrition and Fertility of Women
Part II: Education and Training of Women
Part III: Employment of Women
Part IV: Self-help Groups (SHGs) and Empowerment of Women
Part V: Problems of Rural Women
Part VI: Women, Media, Politics and Human Rights

Acknowledgements

I place on record my deep appreciation and gratefulness to the contributors for their worthy contributions. This work, which is replete with new concepts and practices, will appeal to all categories of readers, particularly academicians, researchers, legislators, government officials, and non-governmental organisations engaged in ameliorating the socio-economic conditions of half of the human race.

Thanks are also due to my friends and colleagues for their opinions and suggestions. I would like to especially thank Professor Prerna Mohite, Dean Faculty of Family and Community Sciences, The M.S. University of Baroda for writing foreword for the volume and for supporting and motivating me. For the support and co-operation extended to me by my family, I can simply say thanks. Finally, I express my appreciation for my publisher Mr. Sandeep Sury for showing patience and understanding at various stages of the publication of this work.

Vadodara Rameshwari Pandya
June 2008

CONTRIBUTORS

Avani Maniar Department of Extension and Communication, Faculty of Family and Community Sciences, The M.S. University of Baroda, Vadodara.

Varsha Parikh Department of Extension and Communication, Faculty of Family and Community Sciences, The M.S. University of Baroda, Vadodara.

Neerja Jaiswal Department of Home Management, Faculty of Family and Community Sciences, The M.S. University of Baroda, Vadodara.

Uma Iyer Professor, Department of Food and Nutrition, Faculty of Family and Community Sciences, The M.S. University of Baroda, Vadodara.

Shruti Shah Department of Food and Nutrition, Faculty of Family and Community Sciences, The M.S. University of Baroda, Vadodara.

Shonima Venugopal Department of Food and Nutrition, Faculty of Family and Community Sciences, The M.S. University of Baroda, Vadodara.

Kavita Sharma Department of Food and Nutrition, Faculty of Family and Community Sciences, The M.S. University of Baroda, Vadodara.

Rajul Jain Department of Food and Nutrition, Faculty of Family and Community Sciences, The M.S. University of Baroda, Vadodara.

Bhamini Mehta Department of Human Development and Family Studies, Faculty of Family and Community Sciences, The M.S. University of Baroda, Vadodara.

Shagufa Kapadia Professor and Head, Department of Human Development and Family Studies, Faculty of Family and Community Sciences, The M.S. University of Baroda, Vadodara.

Mini Sheth Department of Food and Nutrition, Faculty of Family and Community Sciences, The M.S. University of Baroda, Vadodara.

B. Suguna Department of Women's Studies, Mahila Visvavidyalayam, Tirupati.

G. Sandhya Rani Department of Women's Studies, Mahila Visvavidyalayam, Tirupati.

Shalini Sharma Assistant Professor of Sociology, Department of Human Development and Sociology, Punjab Agriculture University, Ludhiana.

Simran K. Sidhu Associate Professor of Sociology, Department of Human Development and Sociology, Punjab Agriculture University, Ludhiana.

Indira Mallaya Department of Human Development and Family Studies, Faculty of Family and Community Sciences, The M.S. University of Baroda, Vadodara.

Bhagyashree Hakim Department of Human Development and Family Studies, Faculty of Family and Community Sciences, The M.S. University of Baroda, Vadodara.

Rameshwari Pandya Department of Extension and Communication, Faculty of Family and Community Sciences, The M.S. University of Baroda, Vadodara.

Richa Kapoor Department of Extension and Communication, Faculty of Family and Community Sciences, The M.S. University of Baroda, Vadodara.

Y. Bhaskaracharyulu Professor and Head, Department. of Adult and Continuing Education, Andhra University, Visakhapatnam.

D. Pulla Rao Associate Professor, Department of Cooperation and Applied Economics, Andhra University, Visakhapatnam.

Y. Nirmala Research Scholar, Department of Adult and Continuing Education, Andhra University, Visakhapatnam.

Manisha Pathak-Shelat Faculty of Journalism and Communication, The M.S. University of Baroda, Vadodara.

Mumtas N.S. Department of Education, Farook Training College, Calicut.

K. Thangamani Professor and Head, Home Science Extension Education, Avinashilingam University for Women, Coimbatore.

Darshini Durkal Department of Extension and Communication, Faculty of Family and Community Sciences, The M.S. University of Baroda, Vadodara.

Om Raj Singh NIPCCD, Siri Institutional Area, Hauz Khas, New Delhi.

Tejpreet Kaur Kang Associate Professor, Department of Human Development and Sociology, College of Home Science, Punjab Agriculture University, Ludhiana.

Trupti T. Shah Department of Business Economics, Faculty of Commerce, The M.S. University of Baroda, Vadodara.

Saraswati Raju Iyer Assistant Professor, Department of Sociology and Social Work, Acharya Nagarjuna University, Nagarjuna Nagar, Guntur.

V. Girija Devi Department of Home Science, Government College of Women, Thiruvananthapuram.

Harnek Singh Professor, Department of Human Development and Sociology, Punjab Agriculture University, Ludhiana.

Muninder Sidhu Professor, College of Home Science, Punjab Agriculture University, Ludhiana.

Gaganpreet Kaur Research Fellow, College of Home Science, Punjab Agriculture University, Ludhiana.

D. Padmavathi Associate Professor, Department of Women's Studies, Mahila Visvavidyalayam, Tirupati.

Ravi Prakash Yadav University Department of Industrial Relations and Personnel Management, T.M. Bhagalpur University, Bhagalpur.

Raginideep Department of History, M.U. Bodh Gaya.

Puja Roy Department of History, Patna University, Patna.

Habilslade O. Ogale Department of Bank Management, Alagappa University, Karaikudi.

Praveen Devgan Faculty of Education, Dayalbagh Education Institute, Agra.

Manjari Acharya Reader, Post-graduate Department of Home Science, Sardar Patel University, Vallabh Vidyanagar, Gujarat.

Rupal N. Thakkar Research Scholar, Post-graduate Department of Home Science, Sardar Patel University, Vallabh Vidyanagar, Gujarat.

Tinku Paul Research Officer, *Sahyog*, Allahabad.

D.S. Dhillon Professor and Head, Department of Extension Education, Punjab Agriculture University, Ludhiana.

Minaxi Pathak Professor and Head, Department of FRM, Faculty of Home Science, Assam Agricultural University, Jorhat, Assam.

Jabir Hasan Khan Department of Geography, Aligarh Muslim University, Aligarh.

Md. Mustaquim Research Scholar, Department of Geography, Aligarh Muslim University, Aligarh..

Rekha Bhagat Professor, Indian Agricultural Research Institute, Pusa, New Delhi.

Surya S. Research Scholar, Indian Agricultural Research Institute, Pusa, New Delhi.

Varsha H. Patil Computer Engineering Department, K.K. Wagh College of Engineering, Nashik.

Vidya R. Khapli Computer Engineering Department, K. K. Wagh College of Engineering, Nashik.

Smriti Bhosle Head, Department of Sociology, L.J.N.J. College, Ville Parle (East), Mumbai.

Madhur Bala District Health Educator, Nahan.

O.P. Monga Professor and Chairman, Department of Sociology, Himachal Pradesh University, Shimla.

Anuradha Mathu Department of Extension and Communication, Faculty of Family and Community Sciences, The M.S. University of Baroda, Vadodara.

H.R. Sudhindra 107, Shantharanga, Akshayanagar, Begur Hobli, Bangalore.

Babita Shukla Department. of Extension and Communication, Faculty of Family and Community Sciences, The M.S. University of Baroda, Vadodara.

Mausumi Majumdar Freelance Journalist, B-6, Academic Staff Quarters, G.B. Pant Social Science Institute, Allahabad.

Poonam Tiwari Faculty of Home Science, G.B. Pant University of Agriculture and Technology, Pantnagar.

CONTENTS

Part II: Education and Training of Women

Part III: Employment of Women

Part VI: Women, Media, Politics and Human Rights

Part I: Health, Nutrition and Fertility of Women

1

Tribal Women of Gujarat: HIV/AIDS Awareness and Education

Avani Maniar

HIV/Aids and its Prevalence

Human Immuno-deficiency Virus (HIV) is a lent virus that belongs to the retroviruses group that may cause HIV infection/AIDS, a health condition in which a person is affected by a series of diseases because of poor immunity. HIV by itself is not an illness and does not instantly lead to AIDS. An HIV-infected person can lead a healthy life for several years before he/she develops AIDS. AIDS is a health condition that results from the deficiency in the body's immunity following HIV infection. HIV attacks the human body by breaking down its immune system that is meant to fight diseases. Over a period of time, the immune system weakens and the body loses its natural ability to fight diseases. At this stage, various diseases affect the infected person.

Acquired Immune-deficiency Syndrome (AIDS) has emerged as one of the most serious public health problem in the developing countries and also a major problem in India. It has spread wide across nation, caste, creed, sea and racial boundaries. 2006 has been a pivotal year in the AIDS response. The number of people living with HIV rose to almost 40 million, the highest number ever, however declines in infection rates were observed in some countries, as well as positive trends in young people's sexual behaviours. Prevention efforts were shown to be working, highlighting the need to scale up, expand and adapt prevention programmes to address the different drivers of the epidemics. According to the latest figures published in the UNAIDS/WHO 2006, AIDS Epidemic Update, an estimated 39.5 million people are living with HIV. There were 4.3 million new infections in 2006 with 2.8 million (65 per cent) of these occurring in sub-Sharan Africa and important increases in Eastern Europe and Central Asia, where there are some indications that infection rates have raised by more than 50 per cent since 2004. In 2006, 2.9 million people died of AIDS-related illnesses. Although the HIV prevalence rate is still low in South-East Asia, it is one of the most rapidly growing HIV/AIDS epidemics globally. Because of the largest population base and presence of several factors that enhance the spread of HIV, including poverty, gender inequality and social stigma, the South-East Asia region is likely to increasingly suffer the brunt of the epidemic. An estimated 7.2 million people are living with HIV/AIDS in South-East Asia (2006); it is the second highest number of cases in the world after sub-Saharan Africa.

India and HIV/AIDS

India has among the highest number of persons living with HIV/AIDS in the world today, although the overall prevalence remains low. Some states experience a generalized epidemic with the virus transmitted from high-risk groups into the general population. A major challenge is to strengthen and decentralize the program to the state and district levels to enhance commitment, coverage and effectiveness. There are more than 5.1 million individuals infected with HIV in this country of over 1 billion people (UNAIDS 2003). The total number of AIDS cases in 2002 was estimated to be about 550,000. Seven states—Andhra Pradesh, Goa, Karnataka, Maharashtra, Manipur, Mizoram, and Nagaland—already have generalized epidemics, as indicated by a 1 per cent of higher prevalence rate among pregnant women in prenatal clinics. These seven states represent 22 percent of the population. India has the highest number of HIV-infected persons in the region (5.2 million). The majority of HIV infections in the region occur through unsafe sex between men and women

Table 1.1: State-wise HIV/AIDS Affected People

State	HIV +	State	HIV +
Tamil Nadu	52,063	Orrisa	641
Andhra Pradesh	15,099	Punjab	454
Maharashtra	14,325	Assam	372
Gujarat	6,873	Pondicherry	302
Karnataka	4,345	Himachal	302
Manipur	2,946	Jharkhand	258
Delhi	2,759	Bihar	155
West Bengal	2,397	Mizoram	106
Chandigarh	1,934	Uttranchal	79
Kerala	1,769	Andaman & Nicobar	37
Uttar Pradesh	1,751	Arunachal Pradesh	13
Madhya Pradesh	1,729	Meghalaya	8
Rajasthan	1,153	Tripura	5
Nagaland	736	Jammu & Kashmir	2
Haryana	655	Daman Diu	1
Goa	657		

Table 1.1 reveals that Tamil Nadu has the highest number of registered HIV positive patients i.e. 52036 and Daman Diu the lowest with 1 registered patient infected by HIV/AIDS. 13 states have thousands of HIV infected patients and the other 11 with hundreds of patients. Maharashtra and Andhra Pradesh have more than 14000 infected patients. Even Gujarat ranks on the fourth position with 6873 HIV infected patients. The number of infected persons is going on increasing. This is due to lack of knowledge of HIV/AIDS. It is very difficult for a country to come out from such a dreaded situation. The only alternative is to make people aware about HIV/AIDS and its bad effects. This will not solve the problem but at least stop the growing generation from being infected from HIV/AIDS. So there is a need to create awareness amongst the high-risk groups. The UNICEF and Government of India have taken up a project titled "HIV Prevention among Young People and Children" which places an increased emphasis on HIV/AIDS. This project supports the national objectives to prevent HIV infections among young people. The project intends to reach all out of school young people in Valsad, Vadodara and Surat districts of Gujarat who have never enrolled or dropped out of school. Through "Peer Education" all out of school young people will be equipped with accurate knowledge on prevention and protection against HIV/AIDS. They are the ones who are most vulnerable to HIV/AIDS because of adverse social and environmental factors that they face. Peer outreach in focused vulnerable communities has been shown to be an effective way to develop skills among young people.

Deepak Charitable Trust (DCT) a corporate based NGO of Vadodara has undertaken this project in collaboration with UNICEF. The project by DCT is one of the efforts to prevent HIV/AIDS. DCT was established in 1982 has mission of creating an enabling and sustainable environment among rural communities. DCT is working in the area of maternal and child health and has well trained professionals to implement community development projects in the district of Vadodara. It has undertaken the "HIV Prevention among Young People and Children" in 2 talukas of Vadodara district. The goal of this project is to contribute to reduction of HIV/AIDS in Gujarat by reaching young people specially those in vulnerable communities through peer outreach, inter personal communication and strengthening youth friendly service delivery. Two peer educators per village will be trained to establish contact with all out of school young people in their village and equip them with accurate knowledge on and skills on prevention and protection against unsafe sexual behavior. The peer educators will organize Inter Personal Communication (IPC) activities to impart this knowledge amongst youth. The focus area population is two block of Vadodara district Jetpur Pavi and Kavant.

The students of Department of Extension and Communication, Faculty of Family and Community Sciences have a course of field experience in their curriculum and in the course they work in rural areas of Vadodara district on various developmental issues. One of the objectives of the course is to train the students to develop Information Educational Communication (IEC) material to bring about desirable changes amongst the rural target group. Since Deepak Charitable Trust's project aimed at preparation of IEC material for teaching the tribal youth about HIV/AIDS, the objective of the department and DCT coincided and they both decided to work together for the project.

Socio-economic Data of Villages

Jetpur Pavi of Vadodara district was selected for the HIV prevention programme. It is about 80 kilometers away from Baroda city. There are about 217 villages in this taluka but the students worked in only 9 villages namely Bhilwaniya, Chimli, Moti Amrol, Shivjipura, Kevda, Muvada, Motibej, Sakhandra and Lodhan. These villages are scattered on a large area. They appear as a cluster of mud-plastered walls shaded by a few trees, set among a stretch of green or dun-colored fields, with a few people slowly coming or going, oxcarts creaking, cattle lowing, and birds singing-all present an image of harmonious simplicity. At slack seasons, village life appears to be sleepy, but usually villages are humming with activity. The work ethic is strong, with little time out for relaxation, except for numerous divinely sanctioned festivals and rite-of-passage celebrations. The taluka and villages can be further described under following headings:

Housing: The village dwellings are built very close to one another in a nucleated settlement, with small lanes for passage of people and sometimes carts. Village fields surround the settlement and are generally within easy walking distance. In hilly tracts of these villages dwellings are more spread. Most of the houses are mud houses, but 2-3 concrete houses are also constructed. The mud houses are nicely made with "Lipan". The kitchen and the rooms are well arranged. Cleanliness inside the house is seen. The houses are very well managed. The family consisted of 7-12 members.

Education: The total literacy rate in Jetpur Pavi in 2001 was 48.9 per cent. The male literacy was 64.1 per cent and female literacy rate was 32.8 per cent. There is discrimination in educating a girl child.

The males are educated till 7-10 std., but majority of the females are illiterate. There is a Government school till primary section and one anganwadi in each village.

1.2: Population of the Villages Covered

Name	TRU	TOTP	TOTM	TOTF	PSC
Jetpur Pavi	Total	225894	116158	109736	5463
Jetpur Pavi	Rural	225894	116158	109736	5463
Jetpur Pavi	Urban	0	0	0	0
Muvada	Rural	3115	1607	1508	82
Bhikhapura	Rural	1543	797	746	137
Vadoth	Rural	957	517	440	63
Kevada	Rural	404	202	202	0
Shivajipura	Rural	607	313	294	0
Moti Bej	Rural	3331	1670	1661	116
Lodhan	Rural	1174	604	570	0
Moti Amrol	Rural	5120	2618	2502	109
Muldhar	Rural	1754	904	850	0
Sakhandra	Rural	1922	1014	908	14
Chimli	Rural	1265	653	612	0
Bhilvaniya	Rural	665	330	335	0

Contd...

Name	TRU	MSC	FSC	PST	MST	FST
Jetpur Pavi	Total	2795	2668	175183	89810	85373
Jetpur Pavi	Rural	2795	2668	175183	89810	85373
Jetpur Pavi	Urban	0	0	0	0	0
Muvada	Rural	44	38	2183	1123	1060
Bhikhapura	Rural	73	64	839	424	415
Vadoth	Rural	33	30	500	265	235
Kevada	Rural	0	0	404	202	202
Shivajipura	Rural	0	0	607	313	294
Moti Bej	Rural	56	60	3185	1596	1589
Lodhan	Rural	0	0	1113	577	536
Moti Amrol	Rural	61	48	4928	2514	2414
Muldhar	Rural	0	0	1753	903	850
Sakhandra	Rural	5	9	1779	941	838
Chimli	Rural	0	0	1247	644	603
Bhilvaniya	Rural	0	0	360	184	176

TOTP – Total Population; TOTM – Total Population (Male); TOTF = Total Population (Female), PSC = Population (Scheduled class); MSC = Population (Scheduled class Males); FSC = Population (Scheduled class Females); PST = Population (Scheduled tribe); MST = Population (Scheduled tribe Males); FST = Population (Scheduled tribe Females)
Source: Census 2001

Population

- The total population of the taluka is 2, 25,294 from which 1, 16,158 are males and 1,09,736 are females. In that 5463 is the scheduled class population and 1,75,183 is scheduled tribe.

- The average population per village is 1066.
- From all these villages, Moti Amrol had the highest population of 5120 and Kevda the lowest with 404.
- In all the villages the male population was more than the female except in Kevda with equal male-female population of 202 each.
- In one village named Bhilwaniya, the females were 5 more than males.
- Kevda, Shivjipura, Lodhan Muldhar, Chimli and Bhilwaniya have only scheduled tribe population.

Road and Transportation: There are packka roads to reach the villages and there are RCC roads in some of villages. To reach the interior part of the village there are kachha roads. The villagers have to walk long distances to buy things from local market.

Water and Sanitation: Sanitation is never perceived as a priority especially in rural areas where open space is readily available. They don't have proper drainage facility. There are many hand pumps in almost every village. The water facility is good and easily available to them.

Occupation: Agriculture and cattle rearing is the main occupation of the people. The crops like cotton, maize, tuver dal, sugarcane, amla etc. are grown. Work is the first priority for these people. They work for the whole day. Even women are engaged in the agricultural work.

Objectives of the Project

- To develop IEC material on HIV/AIDS for tribal adolescent girls and women.
- To develop understanding for HIV/AIDS amongst tribal adolescent girls and women.
- To implement the designed IEC material amongst the tribal adolescent girls and women.
- To evaluate the effectiveness of IEC material for teaching concepts related to HIV/AIDS.

Steps Followed in Implementation of the Project

To achieve the planned objectives, certain steps were followed which were as follows:

Analysis of Data: Peer educators who were trained in the training programmes organized by DCT, conducted FGDs with their peers in their villages. The tribal adolescents discussed about various issues related to sex and the practices, which they followed in their villages. Questions related to their leisure time activities, addiction, age of marriage, STDs, HIV/AIDS and use and importance of condom were included. The target group consisted of both males and females. Qualitative data collected on the issues was given to the students of the department of EC. Students interpreted 26 FGDs which were students critically analyzed. The qualitative FDGs data was then transformed in a tabular form.

Finding referred to the views of the people on the particular issue. They were written as it appeared in the FGD. Inference referred to the interpretation of the finding. The students interpreted the views of the people and then according to the interpretation, messages were designed.

Following trends emerged by interpreting the FGDs:

- The FGDs gave a clear picture about the existing knowledge and practices of the people.
- Both men and women were unaware of STDs and HIV/AIDS.
- The women had not even heard the word AIDS.
- Social evils and superstitions prevailed in the villages.
- Misconceptions on menstruation, use of condom, marriage age, etc. also prevailed there.
- They had incomplete knowledge of the topics that were covered in the FGDs. So there was a need felt to make people aware and remove the existing misconceptions from their minds.

According to the knowledge and need of the people, the issues of constructive utilization of leisure activity, correct marriage age effects of addiction, menstrual cycle and care during menstruation, HIV/AIDS, STDs, use and importance of condom, bad effects of pornographic material, etc. were identified as topics which require intervention from the Development agency. Hence on the above mentioned topics it was decided to design IEC material.

Designing of IEC Material: The steps followed of designing the IEC material was as follows:

- For designing the messages, the students collected rich information from various authentic sources. The information was collected from NGOs, dermatologists, gynecologists, books, internet, etc.
- After referring different material, the content for each issue/topic was finalized. But only deciding the content part was not enough. The FGD results interpreted that there were more number of illiterates in the villages.
- There was a need to incorporate simple messages along with appropriate visuals/illustrations. Illustrations attract the attention and gives idea at a glance. A topic can be understood well by seeing the picture rather than reading something. It helps to actually visualize the things and have better

understanding. The people were illiterates so the write-ups were of least importance. So appropriate visuals were selected.

- The visuals were selected which villagers could relate to their situations.
- The content and its visuals were put on teaching material/aid. Large colourful visuals with bold write-ups were incorporated in the teaching aid.
- The various teaching materials used were charts, flip book, flash cards, leaflets, brochures, flex, etc. Each aid has its specific purpose.
- A logo was also designed. It emphasized on the four ways of transmission of HIV/AIDS. It had specific purposes that whenever the people see that logo they could easily understand the causes of HIV/AIDS. It had a bright colour combination that would easily attract the attention of the people. It was printed on all the teaching aids so that they can see and relate.

The communication strategies decided to teach the various issues related to HIV/AIDS were as given in Table 1.3.

Leisure Activity: A flipbook was designed on utilization of leisure time activity. Flip book helps to create awareness amongst the people. It helps to maintain a sequence. Activities like mehandi, toran and photo frame making, reading newspaper or magazines, etc was included. These activities were decided according to the target group as they can relate themselves to it. Colourful visuals were selected to attract the target group.

Addiction: A bottle shaped flipbook was designed on addiction to relate with addictive things. The ill effects of addiction and how it leads to HIV/AIDS were included very skillfully. It was full of colourful visuals with less of write up. It was designed keeping in mind their daily practices.

Marriage Age: Flash cards were designed on correct marriage age. They helped in better understanding of the topic and maintain continuity in it. It was in a story form, so that a story goes on with colourful picture. This would be more effective. The ill effects of early marriage were covered through this story. Colourful, bold, large visuals with no write-ups were included. The characters, customs, traditions and practices followed by the villagers were included so that they can relate and better understand the topic.

Menstruation: Flash cards were designed on menstruation. It helped in better understand the topic and maintain continuity in it. Colourful, bold, large visuals with no write-ups were included. The complete menstrual cycle and care during menstruation was included. The idea of sex determination was also included.

STDs: Charts were designed on STDs. There were different topics to be covered like what is STDs, its symptoms, precautions, and effects if not cured. Each topic was to be covered separately. So one topic was covered on one chart.

Large, bold visuals with some write-ups were included.

HIV/AIDS: A flipbook was designed on HIV/AIDS. It included large, related visuals with key words. A puppet show was designed to better understand the topic. The script included the local concepts, characters, and practices of the people so that they can relate themselves. A pamphlet was also designed complementary to the puppet show. This was to be distributed so that the people can refer to it later.

Table 1.3: Communication Strategies

S.N.	Topic / content	Objectives	Strategies
1	Leisure activities	To create awareness of different leisure activities amongst adolescent girls and women.	Flip chart Skit
2	Marriage Age • Correct marriage age • Effects of early marriage	To create awareness amongst adolescent girls and women regarding appropriate age for getting married.	Flash cards
3	Pornography • Correct sources of sex education.	To create awareness amongst adolescent girls and women regarding the correct sources of sexuality.	Chart
4	STDs • Meaning • Symptoms • Problems if not treated	To create awareness amongst adolescent girls and women regarding STDs and its effects.	Charts
5	HIV / AIDS • Meaning • Transmission • Symptoms • Precautions • Misconceptions	To create awareness amongst adolescent girls and women regarding HIV / AIDS and their effects on human life.	Flip book Puppet show Leaflet Skit
6	Addiction	To develop understanding amongst adolescent girls and women regarding addiction and its effect on health.	Flip chart
7	Condom • Steps to use Condom Benefits	To create awareness amongst adolescent girls and women regarding steps of using condom and its benefits.	Demonstration Train(steps) Flex
8	Menstruation • Process • Care • Sex determination • Physical change	To create awareness amongst adolescent girls and women regarding the menstrual cycle and its care.	Flash cards Brochure

Implementation of Communication Strategies

The designed IEC material was to be implemented in the field. The steps following in the implementation were as follows:

1. Rapport Building: Rapport building with the group is of utmost importance. The peer educators (PEs) and outreach workers (ORWs) from Deepak Charitable Trust, working in the villages were informed about the visit of the students to the villagers. They informed the villagers and helped the students to gather the target group. The villages where the peer educators (PEs) and outreach workers (ORWs) were not available, the students themselves went door to door and gathered the group. Then a warming up session was arranged in which the group shared their views with the students. A very informal discussion was held. Some games like passing the parcel, one-minute game, etc. were played with the group. Through games the students came to know the target group and build rapport with them.

2. Pre-testing: After the group settled, pretest was conducted to test the basic knowledge of the target group regarding the topics like effects of addiction, HIV/AIDS and its precautions, STDs, menstruation, importance of condom and effects of early marriage. A questionnaire was designed as a pre-testing tool, which had different sections on addiction, HIV/AIDS, STDs, menstruation, condom, marriage age etc. The questionnaire gave an idea about the knowledge/awareness level of the group on the above issues. It consisted of 30 questions in all. All the questions were close ended i.e. with 4 options each. Marks were allotted to each question and the total marks were 40. This questionnaire helped the students to gather lot of information from the target group. The target group was illiterate and hence questionnaire as a technique was not appropriate. So, the interviews were conducted and the answers given by women, were written down by the students.

3. Teaching: The actual activity was started with some skits and puppet shows to generate interest and gather attention of the girls and women. Then the content of various issues was covered with the help of IEC materials like charts, flash cards, flip book, demonstrations, leaflets, games, skits, puppet shows, etc. Simple issues were taken first so that the women feel comfortable. Everything was in a good logical sequence from simple to complex. Women were illiterate so it was necessary to keep in mind their understanding level. Interesting, easy topics were covered first and then preceded to difficult ones. Topics like marriage age, leisure activities and addiction were dealt first and then menstruation, and HIV/AIDS and STDs topics were covered.

4. Summarising and Evaluation: At the end of the session a post-test was conducted to check the gain in knowledge on the above-mentioned issues.

Evaluation was also done through observation, question-answer session and discussion.

Village-wise Results

The effectiveness of the communication strategies can be measured through various evaluation techniques. A questionnaire was designed to check the knowledge of the people. Pre test and post test was conducted with the target group. And the results showed good gain in knowledge of the people. The target group consisted of women of 15 – 35 years of age.

The results were classified into two:

- Village wise gain in knowledge.
- Area wise gain in knowledge.

Table 1.4 (a) Chimli

S N.	Topic	Maximum score	Pre test (N=11)		Post test (N=9)		Gain in knowledge
			Average score	per cent	Average score	per cent	per cent
1	Addiction	4	2.17	54.54	3.11	77.77	23.23
2	HIV / AIDS	7	0.58	8.33	3	42.85	34.52
3	STDs	11	1.83	16.66	5.44	49.49	32.83
4	Condom	6	0.5	8.33	4	66.66	**58.33**
5	Menstruation	6	2.66	44.44	2.77	46.29	01.85
6	Marriage Age	6	1.33	22.22	3.88	64.81	42.59
	Total	40	9.73	24.32	22.22	55.56	31.24

Chimli: In the village Chimli the total gain in knowledge was 31.24 per cent. The maximum knowledge gain was with respect to the content on 'condom and its usage (58.33 per cent)'. The least gain in knowledge was for the section on 'menstruation (1.85 per cent)'. This shows that in village Chimli condom related IEC material was effective and menstruation related material proved least effective.

Moti Amrol: In the village Moti Amrol the total gain in knowledge was 43.75 per cent. The maximum knowledge gain was with respect to the content on 'STDs (54.24 per cent)'. The least gain in knowledge was for the section on 'menstruation (26.11 per cent)'. This shows that in village Moti Amrol STDs related IEC material was effective and menstruation related material proved least effective.

1.4 (b) Motiamrol

S.N.	Topic	Maximum Score	Pre test (N=10)		Post test (N=15)		Gain in knowledge
			Average score	per cent	Average score	per cent	per cent
1	Addiction	4	1.1	27.5	2.53	63.33	38.83
2	HIV/AIDS	7	0.7	10	4	57.14	47.14
3	STDs	11	0.9	8.18	6.83	62.42	54.24
4	Condom	6	0.7	11.6	3.53	58.88	47.28
5	Menstruation	6	2.9	48.33	4.46	74.44	26.11
6	Marriage Age	6	2.6	43.33	5	83.33	40.00
	TOTAL	40	8.9	22.25	26.4	66	43.75

Table 1.4 (C) Shivjipura

S.N.	Topic	Maximum Score	Pre test (N=6)		Post test (N=17)		Gain in knowledge
			Average score	per cent	Average score	per cent	per cent
1	Addiction	4	3	75	3.11	77.94	02.94
2	HIV/AIDS	7	0.66	9.42	4.76	68.06	39.08
3	STDs	11	1.5	13.64	6.88	62.55	48.92
4	Condom	6	0.66	11.11	4.05	67.64	56.53
5	Menstruation	6	3.33	55.5	4.29	71.56	16.06
6	Marriage Age	6	2.16	36.11	4.52	75.49	39.38
	Total	40	11.5	28.75	27.23	68.08	39.33

Shivjipura: In the village Shivijipura the total gain in knowledge was 39.33 per cent. The maximum knowledge gain was with respect to the content on 'condom and its usage (56.53 per cent)'. The least gain in knowledge was for the section on 'addiction (2.94 per cent)'. This shows that in village Shivijipura condom related IEC material was effective and addiction related material proved least effective.

Lodhan: In the village Lodhan the total gain in knowledge was 22.33 per cent. The maximum knowledge gain was with respect to the content on 'HIV/AIDS (35.72 per cent)'. The least gain in knowledge was for the section on 'menstruation (13.09 per cent)'. This shows that in village Lodhan HIV/AIDS related IEC material was effective and menstruation related material proved least effective.

Table 1.4 (d) Lodhan

S.N	Topic	Maximum Score	Pre test (N=14)		Post test (N=14)		Gain in knowledge
			Average score	per cent	Average score	per cent	per cent
1	Addiction	4	1.85	46.43	2.8	70	23.57
2	HIV/AIDS	7	2	28.57	4.5	64.29	35.72
3	STDs	11	3.93	35.71	6.21	56.49	20.78
4	Condom	6	2.15	35.71	3.42	57.14	21.43
5	Menstruation	6	3.93	65.48	4.71	78.57	13.09
6	Marriage Age	6	3.86	64.29	4.79	79.76	15.47
	Total	40	17.71	44.28	26.64	66.61	22.33

Table 1.4 (e) Motibej

S.N	Topic	Maximum score	Pre test (N=14)		Post test (N=13)		Gain in knowledge
			Average score	per cent	Average score	per cent	per cent
1	Addiction	4	2.57	64.29	3.15	78.85	14.56
2	HIV/AIDS	7	0.14	2.04	5.15	73.63	71.59
3	STDs	11	0.07	0.64	7.15	65.03	64.69
4	Condom	6	0.28	4.76	3.85	64.1	59.34
5	Menstruation	6	2.07	34.52	4.77	79.49	44.97
6	Marriage Age	6	2.29	38.1	4.53	75.64	37.54
	Total	40	7.43	18.57	28.62	71.54	52.97

Motibej: In the village motibej the total gain in knowledge was 52.97 per cent. The maximum knowledge gain was with respect to the content on 'HIV/AIDS (71.59 per cent)'. The least gain in knowledge was for the section on 'addiction (14.56 per cent)'. This shows that in village Motibej HIV/AIDS related IEC material was effective and addiction related material proved least effective.

Table 1.4 (f) Kevda

S.N	Topic	Maximum Score	Pre test (N=15)		Post test (N=13)		Gain in knowledge
			Average score	per cent	Average score	per cent	per cent
1	Addiction	4	2.2	55	2.8	70	15.00
2	HIV/AIDS	7	0.53	8.8	2.84	47.33	38.50
3	STDs	11	2.4	21.81	5.92	53.84	32.03
4	Condom	6	0.73	12.16	2.92	48.71	36.55
5	Menstruation*	6	2.83	47.22	3.6	60	12.78
6	Marriage Age	6	2.2	36.66	4.46	74.35	37.70
	Total	40	10.14	25.35	21.69	54.22	28.87

Kevda: In the village Kevda the total gain in knowledge was 28.87 per cent. The maximum knowledge gain was with respect to the content on 'HIV/AIDS (38.50 per cent)'. The least gain in knowledge was for the section on 'menstruation (12.78 per cent)'. This shows that in village Kevda HIV/AIDS related IEC material was effective and menstruation related material proved least effective.

Table 1.4 (g) Bhilwaniya

S.N	Topic	Maximum Score	Pre test (N=24)		Post test (N=20)		Gain in knowledge
			Average score	per cent	Average score	per cent	per cent
1	Addiction	4	1.63	40.75	2.55	63.75	23.00
2	HIV/AIDS	7	0.73	10.53	4.85	69.28	58.75
3	STDs	11	0.84	7.65	8.1	73.64	65.99
4	Condom	6	1.63	27.19	4.7	78.33	51.14
5	Menstruation	6	3.42	57.02	5.15	85.84	28.81
6	Marriage Age	6	3.42	57.02	5	83.33	26.31
	Total	40	11.68	29.21	30.35	75.87	46.66

Bhilwaniya: In the village Bhilwaniya the total gain in knowledge was 46.66 per cent. The maximum knowledge gain was with respect to the content on 'STDs (65.99 per cent)'. The least gain in knowledge was for the section on 'addiction (23.00 per cent)'. This shows that in village Bhilwaniya STDs related

IEC material was effective and addiction related material proved least effective.

Table 1.4 (h) Sakhandra

S.N	Topic	Maximum Score	Pre test (N=12)		Post test (N=7)		Gain in knowledge
			Average score	per cent	Average score	per cent	per cent
1	Addiction	4	2.58	64.58	3.86	96.43	31.80
2	HIV/AIDS	7	1.25	17.86	4.29	61.22	43.36
3	STDs	11	3.25	29.55	7.43	67.53	37.98
4	Condom	6	1.67	27.78	3.29	54.76	26.98
5	Menstruation	6	2.67	44.44	3	50	05.56
6	Marriage Age	6	2.67	44.44	4	66.67	22.23
	Total	40	14.08	35.21	27	67.5	32.40

Sakhandra: In the village Sakhandra the total gain in knowledge was 32.40 per cent. The maximum knowledge gain was with respect to the content on 'HIV/AIDS (43.36 per cent)'. The least gain in knowledge was for the section on 'menstruation (5.56 per cent)'. This shows that in village Sakhandra HIV/AIDS related IEC material was effective and menstruation related material proved least effective.

Table 1.4 (i) Muvada

S.N	Topic	Maximum Score	Pre test (N=17)		Post test (N=15)		Gain in knowledge
			Average score	per cent	Average score	per cent	per cent
1	Addiction	4	2.52	63.23	3.06	76.66	13.43
2	HIV / AIDS	7	1.35	19.32	3.2	45.71	26.39
3	STDs	11	3.17	28.87	5.33	48.48	19.61
4	Condom	6	1.47	24.5	3.06	51.11	26.11
5	Menstruation	6	4.58	76.47	4.8	80	03.53
6	Marriage Age	6	3.24	53.92	4.93	82.22	28.30
	Total	40	21.65	54.13	24.73	61.83	07.70

Muvada: In the village Muvada the total gain in knowledge was 7.70 per cent. The maximum knowledge gain was with respect to the content on 'marriage

age (28.30 per cent)'. The least gain in knowledge was for the section on 'menstruation (3.53 per cent)'. This shows that in village Muvada marriage age related IEC material was effective and menstruation related material proved least effective.

Table 1.5 shows total village-wise gain in knowledge to the respondents:

Table 1.5: Village-wise Gain in Knowledge

S.N	Village	Total Gain in Knowledge (per cent)
1	Motibej	52.97
2	Bilwaniya	46.66
3	Moti Amrol	43.75
4	Shivjipura	39.33
5	Sakhandra	32.40
6	Chimli	31.24
7	Kevda	28.87
8	Lodhan	22.33
9	Muvada	7.70

Table 1.5 gives the data of village wise total gain in knowledge of the target group. It depicts that the maximum gain in knowledge was observed in Motibej (52.97 per cent) and the minimum in Muvada (7.70 per cent). All the villages had a gain in knowledge, which ranged from 20–50 per cent except Muvada.

Table 1.6 gives area-wise results.

Table 1.6: Area-wise Results

(per cent)

S.N	Village	Men.	Marriage Age	Condom	STDs	HIV/ AIDS	Addiction
1	Motibej	44.97	37.54	59.34	64.69	26.39	14.56
2	Bhilwaniya	28.81	26.31	51.14	65.99	58.75	23.00
3	Moti amrol	26.11	40.00	47.28	54.24	47.14	38.83
4	Shivjipura	16.06	39.38	56.53	48.92	39.08	2.94
5	Lodhan	13.09	15.47	21.43	20.78	35.72	23.57
6	Kevda	12.78	37.70	36.55	32.03	38.50	15.00
7	Sakhandra	5.56	22.23	26.95	37.98	43.36	31.80
8	Muvada	3.53	28.30	26.11	19.61	26.39	13.43
9	Chimli	1.85	42.59	58.33	32.83	34.52	23.23

Table 1.6 reveals the area wise gain in knowledge of the target group. On the content of "menstruation (44.97 per cent) and condom (59.34 per cent)" maximum gain in knowledge was observed in Motibej. On the content of "marriage age" maximum gain in knowledge was in Chimli village (42.59 per cent). In the content of STDs (65.99 per cent) and HIV/AIDS (58.75 per cent)" the maximum gain in knowledge was in Bhilwaniya village. There was a maximum gain in knowledge on the content of "addiction (38.83 per cent)" in Moti amrol.

Table 1.7: Effectiveness of Communication Strategies

S.N.	Topic/content	Strategy	Effectiveness of different strategies
1	Leisure activities	Flip chart Skit	Effective as it was full of colourful visuals. Effective due to live performance.
2	Marriage Age • Correct marriage age • Effects of early marriage	Flash cards	Effective due to colourful related visuals without write-up which was in story form.
3	Pornography • Correct sources of sex education.	Chart	Not used much because target group were women and they don't use this material. This topic should be dealt with boys/males.
4	STDs • Meaning • Symptoms • Problems if not treated	Chart	Not so effective because of more write-ups.
5	HIV/AIDS • Meaning • Transmission • Symptoms • Precautions • Misconceptions	Flip book Puppet show Leaflet Skit	Effective with clear explanation and related examples. Long puppet show was boring. If the puppet show is short then it would be effective. Less effective as it had write-ups. It was meant for individuals than for group. Effective due to live performance.
6	Addiction	Flip chart	Effective because of good colourful related visuals.
7	Condom • Steps to use Condom • Benefits	Demonstration Train(steps) Flex	Effective as a live demonstration was there so that the people can visualize. Effective as large, bold pictures. Effective due to good, funny visuals.
8	Menstruation • Process • Care • Sex determination • Physical change	Flash cards Brochure	Effective due to good visuals. The brochure had small visuals and write-ups. If it would be in larger size then it would be effective.

On the basis of the observations and the reactions of the participants, Table 1.7 records the conclusions regarding the effectiveness of communication strategies:

Suggestions

Suggestions to Improve the IEC material

- Folk media like Bhavai, Drama and Puppet show would be more effective for imparting messages on different topics like HIV/AIDS, superstition, family planning because as it is in drama or Bhavai, it attracts the attention of audience easily.
- Besides HIV/AIDS other issues can be included like marriage age, menstruation, addiction, pornography, farming practices, irrigation practices, knowledge regarding seeds, care during pregnancy.
- Short duration sessions should be conducted for long term to impart detail knowledge about different topics.
- Training sessions for the peer educator should be conducted for longer period of time as in-depth knowledge about the subject is required for them to impart proper knowledge.
- More and more interactive sessions should be conducted to seek the attention and participation of audience.

Suggestions for New IEC material

- More and more colourful visual should be incorporated in IEC material like Flip chart, flash card, charts and posters.
- Demonstration method can be used to make the sessions more effective and impart better understanding to the target group.
- Visuals should be realistic and bigger in size.
- The individuals who will handle the material should have complete knowledge of the issue. Explanation should be supplementary to the teaching material. Examples related to the existing situation should be quoted.
- Simple language should be used to design messages. If possible the local language should be used for the better understanding of the subject matter.

2

Reproductive Health of Adolescent Girls

Varsha Parikh

Adolescence is the period of transition from childhood to adulthood and is characterized by efforts to achieve goals related to the expectations of the mainstream culture, and by spurts of physical, mental, emotional and social development (WHO 1986). Adolescence is also defined as the developmental period from 10 to 20 years of age during which biological, psychological and social changes occur (Kurz and Rao Gupta 1991).

World interest in adolescent health issues has grown dramatically in the past decade beginning with the 'International Year of Youth' in *1985* and the 'World Health Assembly' in 1989, when discussion focused on the health of youth. The reasons for this interest are varied. Firstly, 30 per cent of the population comprises adolescents, which makes them a formidable group (Kurz and Johnson-Welch, 1994). Secondly, adolescence is a period of transition from childhood to adulthood, marked by profound changes in the body, mind and social relationships (Ghosh 1992). Adolescence is a key period in which many behaviors are formed. Adolescence also represents an opportunity to influence the development of adult health and nutrition behaviours that are being formed (Kurz and Rao Gupta 1991). There is enough research evidence to suggest that adolescent girls in India are a vulnerable group and need to be included in health research and programs. From the day of her birth, a girl is viewed as a burden and liability. In India, she is taught to make to do with the leftovers when she is hungry and work through sickness and pain. As a young girl, the cause of her malnutrition is not so much the lack of food as lack of access to enough food (Government of India and United Nations Children's Fund 1988, Rajkumar 1995).

Nutritional requirements increase due to rapid growth taking place during adolescence and when this is coupled with inadequate dietary intake, the result is small body size and nutritional deficiencies, especially of micronutrients such as iron and vitamin A. The onset of menarche further predisposes the underprivileged girls to anemia (Kashyap and Gopaldas 1988).

Many studies have reported a very low mean nutrient intake by the underprivileged adolescent girls. Satyanarayana et al (1981) reported inadequate nutrient intake among lower income group adolescent girls of Hyderabad, the values being 70-80 per cent of the well-to-do girls. Other studies have reported that large proportions of lower income group girls are in a negative energy balance (Kanani et al 1992).

The reproductive health needs of adolescents in India are largely unmet. This is of concern since adolescents are currently estimated to be almost one quarter of India's population. Moreover, adolescents contribute a significant proportion of all births occurring in the country; 10-15 percent of all births annually occur among women in their early teens (Census of India 1991). Despite legal prohibitions, early marriage continues to be the norm and the pressure to prove fertility immediately after marriage results in early pregnancies. (Jejeebhoy 1996),

Data from several studies show that Indian adolescent girls and boys in rural and urban areas are poorly informed about menstruation, sex and reproduction (Bhende *1995,* Abraham 1996, Mutatkar and Apte 1996). Early sexual activity without sufficient knowledge of the anatomy and physiology also exposes Indian adolescents to the risk of unwanted pregnancies and sexually transmitted infections (STIs), including HIV. The alarming increase in HIV prevalence in India underlines the need to focus attention on the sexual and reproductive health needs and concerns of adolescents (United States Bureau of Census 1994).

Background and Objective of the Project

The Baroda Citizens Council (BCC), an urban community development organization in Baroda implemented project on reproductive health of women. While working on this project, it was realized that there was a critical need for programs for adolescent girls. Women in the communities also expressed this need. Therefore, in the later years focus shifted to reproductive health issues of adolescent girls in three urban slums of Baroda while health services for women continued. These slum communities were Akota, Ramdevnager, near Gotri and Rampura, near Akota. Major objective of the project, was to study the perceptions of young women and adolescent girls regarding adolescent growth and development, nutritional needs and reproductive health issues.

Profile of the Slum Communities

Adolescent girls from three different communities, Akota, Ramdevnagar-Gotri and Rampura were enrolled in the study. Akota with 850 households, situated within city limits had a predominant population of Muslims (80 per cent), Ramdevnagar-Gotri situated on the outskirts of the city with its *650* households had 95 per cent of Hindu population. Rampura situated near the main city, adjacent to Akota village, had a mixed population of Hindus and Muslims comprising about 500 households. In Akota, most of the people were self-employed as building contractors, automobile drivers, mechanics, and small-scale businessmen. Other occupations included daily wage labour and employment in industries and government offices. Basic amenities like electricity and potable water were available to all the households. However, water facility in terms of an individual tap in the household was available to about 70 per cent of houses. The rest of them fetched water from the nearby community hand-pumps. The main health care services used by the people in this area were provided by the government hospital situated at a distance of about 3 to 4 kilometers and local health practitioners, both indigenous and allopathic, in and around the community.

On the other hand, in Ramdevnagar-Gotri, people were employed in the nearby industries or small offices, construction labour and daily wage labour. Some were self employed (vegetable/fruit vendors). About 30 per cent of the women also worked; most of them as domestic servants. Majority *(95 per cent)* of the households availed of electricity facility. Drinking water was obtained from community taps and hand-pumps. Water for other domestic purposes like cleaning utensils and washing clothes was used from a pond located in the middle of the slum that is normally filled by rain water. The health care services used by the people were the government health centre (1/2 km away) and local health practitioners, both indigenous and allopathic.

In Rampura, the economic status of the residents was comparatively poorer as people were employed as daily wage labourers, mill workers or involved in small-scale business activities. In terms of basic amenities, only about *50 per cent* of the families had electricity facility, 40 per cent had individual toilet facility; drinking water facility was in the form of a community stand post. Although health care facilities were available nearby, they were not availed by the women except for emergency. The main ethnic groups were the Vaghri and Dhobi communities.

Methodology

To achieve the research goals, various qualitative and participatory research methods were used in this study. Table 2.1 gives an overview of these methods. The qualitative methods included Semi-Structured Interviews and Focus Group Discussions with adolescent girls whereas the participatory research methods consisted of Body Mapping and Venn Diagramming sessions as described below.

Focus Group Discussions (FGDs) were carried out with the adolescent girls initially to build rapport with them and also to find their perceptions regarding their health and diet.

Semi-Structured Interviews (SSIs) were conducted with adolescent girls in the three slum communities to gain an understanding regarding their socio-economic status and menstrual history. Information regarding the girls' perceptions of physical and behavioural changes during adolescence, general health, diet, marriage and family life was also obtained through the interview.

The Body Mapping (BM) exercises were conducted with groups of 13-15 adolescent girls per session, to elicit information regarding their perceptions of anatomy and the functions of various organs in the body.

Venn Diagrams (VD) was carried out with three groups of adolescent girls to seek information regarding their sources of health information, sexuality and reproductive health.

The most useful data were obtained from SSIs, which are primarily reported here. The other methods, the Body Maps and Venn Diagrams gave additional insights especially as regards reproductive health. FGDs served to build rapport with the girls initially and to give a broad understanding of health related perceptions of girls.

Table 2.1: Qualitative and Participatory Methods Used in the Study

Method	Informants	Number	Purpose/Information
Focus Group Discussions (FGDs)	Adolescent Girls	10	Rapport building with the girls (initial stage). Perceptions regarding health and diet.
Semi-Structured Interviews (SSIs)	Adolescent Girls	147	Socio-economic status of the girls and information regarding menstruation. Perceptions regarding physical and behavioural changes during adolescence, general health and diet, marriage and family life.
Body Mapping Exercises	Adolescent Girls	03	Perceptions of girls regarding various organs in the body and their functions.
Venn Diagrams	Adolescent Girls	03	Sources of health information, sexuality and reproductive health

Results and Discussion

In all the following tables Area A refers to Akota community, Area R refers to Rampura community whereas Area G refers to Gotri, Ramdevnagar community.

I. Socio-economic Profile of the Respondents

Table 2.2 presents the socio-economic profile of the respondents. It can be seen that almost half of the respondents were Muslims and little more than half were Hindus.

Age wise distribution of girls also showed same picture, where 45 per cent of the girls were in the age group of 10-14 years and a little over half (55 per cent) were in the age group of 15-20 years.

The average family size was six. Fifty four percent of the families had an average monthly income ranging from Rs. 1,001- 2,500. Majority of them had per capita income in the categories of below Rs. 200 and between Rs. 201-400 indicating their poor economic status. Fifty seven percent of the girls were currently studying, out of which only 38 per cent had reached the secondary school level and 53 per cent were at primary school level. The main reason for dropout from school, as reported by girls, was that they were not interested in studying (47 per cent). Other reasons included parents' discouragement, financial problems, long distance from school, and illness of self/family member, household responsibilities and refusal of schools to give admission.

About 40 per cent of the mothers were non-literate and 40 per cent had completed primary school education. In case of fathers, 43 per cent had completed secondary school whereas 40 per cent had completed primary school education. Very few fathers (5 per cent) were non-literate. Qualitative data collected through other methods such as focus group discussion, body mapping, Venn diagram also highlighted that parents' discouragement was the major factor for the girls' discontinuation of education. The mothers of the school dropouts were observed to be interested in training them for household tasks rather than educating them. As quoted by one mother, *"Ladki ko padhake kya karna hai, aakhir use`ghar hi to sambhalna hai!"* (What is the use of educating her, after all she has to look after house only).

II. Perceptions of Adolescent Girls Regarding Physical and Behavioral Differences between Younger and Older Girls

Table 2.3 reveals that most of the girls (88 per cent) reported **that** as compared to the older girl (14-15 years of age), the younger girl (7-8 years of age) was shorter and lighter. More than one-third (43 per cent) of the girls said that the younger girls looked more like children. Breast development was another response, which they thought could be useful for differentiating between a younger and an older girl. As far as behavioural differences were concerned, the girls responded that a younger girl played more and was carefree (43 per cent), stubborn (33 per cent), innocent (27 per cent) and did less/no work at home (18 per cent), whereas the older girl was understanding and mature (62 per cent) worked at home (38 per cent), behaved appropriately (13 per cent), did not fight and she was also reserved or shy (7 per cent).

Table 2.2: Socio-economic Profile of the Adolescent Girls (N=148)

	Perceptions	Area A	Area R	Area G	Total
		N= 70	N=33	N=45	N=148
		Percentage Values			
I.	Religion				
	a) Muslims	77	36	04	46
	b) Hindu	23	64	96	54
II.	Age (years)				
	a) 10-14	43	45	49	45
	b) 15-20	57	55	51	55
III	Family Composition				
	Average Family Size	07	06	05	06
IV	Family Income per month				
	a) <=Rs. 1000	19	44	39	31
	b) 1001-2500	60	44	54	54
	c) >=2501	21	12	07	15
	d) No response	10	03	09	08
V	Educational Status				
a.	a) Currently studying	44	45	84	57
	b) Drop out: Studied up to	53	55	16	42
	i) Secondary school (std.X)	51	22	14	38
	ii) Primary school (Std. VII)	49	61	71	53
	c) Non-literate	05	00	00	01
b.	Reasons for drop out				
	a) Girl not interested in studying	49	50	29	47
	b) Parents discouraged education	30	22	43	29
	c) Financial problem	14	11	29	15
	d) Long distance from school	22	00	14	15
	e) Others (household responsibilities, did not get admission in school, illness of self/family members)	38	28	33	36
VI	Education of Parents				
a.	Mothers				
	a) Completed secondary school	15	03	13	12
	b) Completed primary school	45	26	42	40
	c) Non-literate	40	71	45	40
	d) No response	14	06	16	13
b.	Fathers				
	a) Above secondary school level	07	00	08	06
	b) Completed secondary school	54	32	37	43
	c) Completed primary school	37	57	50	40
	d) Non-literate	02	11	05	05
	e) No response	23	33	16	19

When asked about the physical changes which took place in their bodies after the age of 14-15 years, 93 per cent of the girls reported an increase in height while more than three-fourths (78 per cent) reported an increase in weight too. Breast development was reported by nearly one-third of the respondents and a few girls mentioned acne on face (15 per cent) and appearance of pubic hair (7 per cent).

Table 2.3: Perceptions of the Adolescent Girls Regarding Physical and Behavioral Differences between Younger and Older Adolescents (N=148)

No.	Perceptions	Area A	Area R	Area G	Total
		N= 70	N=33	N=45	N=148
		Percentage Values			
1	Physical differences between a 7-8 year old and 14-15 year old girl				
a.	As compared to the older girl, the younger girl				
	i) Has less height	79	91	100	88
	ii) Has less weight	76	30	81	67
	iii) Looks more like a child	66	21	19	43
	iv) Has a clear face (no acne/pimples)	31	15	07	20
	v) Does not have pubic hair	09	00	02	05
	vi) Does not menstruate	18	09	00	10
	vii) No response	04	00	04	03
b.	The older girl				
	i) Has more height	78	91	100	87
	ii) Has more weight	75	33	81	67
	iii) shows breast development	70	21	14	42
	iv) Has a acne/pimples on her face	31	16	03	20
	v) Has pubic hair	08	00	02	04
	vi) No response	04	00	04	03
2.	Behaviour difference between a 7-8 year old and 14-15 year old girl				
a.	The younger girl				
	i) plays and is carefree	64	20	23	43
	ii) is stubborn	27	20	50	33
	iii) Has more freedom/does what she wants to do	20	00	05	11
	iv) Does speak whatever she likes to, without thinking	08	16	10	10
	v) Is innocent	23	20	40	27
	vi) Does less work/doesn't do any work	23	24	08	18

Contd...

b.	The older girl				
	i) is understanding and mature	42	95	60	62
	ii) works in the home	56	13	32	38
	iii) does not go to play	18	-	04	10
	iv) is reserved / shy	06	08	-	07
	v) Others (behaves appropriately doesn't fight)	18	08	08	13
	vi) No response	06	24	13	13
3.	Physical changes observed in self after 10-12 years of age				
	i) Increase in height	89	100	92	93
	ii) Increase in weight	77	69	86	78
	iii) Breast development	74	17	22	45
	iv) Acne / pimples on the face	25	07	06	15
	v) Appearance of pubic hair	12	00	03	07
	vi) No response	19	12	20	21
4.	Emotions experienced regarding these changes				
	i) Did not feel anything	51	62	53	54
	ii) Felt a sense of shame	18	10	17	16
	iii) Felt grown up	19	07	03	12
	iv) Others (felt happy, fearful)	12	17	23	16
	v) No response	19	12	33	22
5.	Perceptions of adolescent girls regarding importance of adolescent period				
a.	10-14 year old girls				
	i) Good learning period	15	00	00	10
	ii) Girls get married	00	00	14	02
	iii) Physical development takes place	00	00	14	02
	iv) It's time when girls get spoilt	03	00	00	02
	v) Any other (development of thinking, important decisions are taken, completion of education)	00	00	00	00
b.	15-20 year old girls				
	i) Good learning period	59	00	00	40
	ii) Girls get married	09	22	14	12
	iii) Physical development takes place	03	44	00	14
	iv) It's time when girls get spoilt	06	11	28	08
	v) Any other (development of thinking, important decisions are taken, completion of education)	30	33	28	30
	vi) No response / Not applicable	50	72	83	66

More than half of the respondents (54 per cent) stated that they did not feel anything regarding these changes taking place in their physique. A few girls felt a sense of shame (16 per cent); and 12 per cent reported that they felt grown up.

Table 2.4: Perceptions of Girls Regarding General Health, Diet and Selected Food Practices (N=148)

	Perceptions	Area A N= 70	Area R N=33	Area G N=45	Total N=148
		Percentage Values			
1.	Descriptions of a 'healthy person'				
	A healthy person is one who :				
	i) Does not fall sick often	67	61	58	63
	ii) Can work properly and does not get tired soon	50	39	73	55
	iii) Feels energetic	40	18	78	47
	iv) Is active	29	09	38	27
	v) Has appropriate height and weight	19	33	11	20
	vi) Others (is energetic)	42	03	64	41
2.	Reasons to -				
a.	Believes herself to be healthy				
	i) Does not fall sick often	74	38	24	48
	ii) Can work properly	14	33	24	22
	iii) She is fat	12	21	22	17
	iv) Eats properly	12	00	16	11
	v) Eats fresh foods	09	08	08	09
b.	Believes herself to be unhealthy				
	i) often falls sick	37	56	25	39
	ii) Feels very weak and tired	33	44	25	34
	iii) Gets body pain and headache	48	00	13	32
3a.	Dietary practices necessary for good health				
	i) Eat nutritious food	79	50	33	58
	ii) Eat at regular intervals	25	50	71	45
	iii) Avoid spicy / oily food	31	09	05	18
	iv) Eat non-vegetarian food	23	13	00	13
	v) Fresh, clean, light food is good	21	00	22	10
b.	Nutritious foods are				
	i) Vegetables	76	69	85	77
	ii) Legumes and sprouts	63	31	67	57
	iii) Milk with routine diet	49	31	09	33
	iv) Properly cooked food	31	41	27	32
	v) Non vegetarian food	43	31	07	29
	vi) Fruits	22	13	16	10

Contd...

	vi) Tasty food	18	06	02	10
	vii) Less spicy and oily food	15	06	04	10
	viii) Fresh and light food	00	00	22	07
c.	The health of a weak girl can be improved by				
	i) Taking regular meals	47	41	79	55
	ii) Taking nutritious meals	46	38	54	46
	iii) Taking complete meals	41	66	14	38
	iv) Taking 'Shakti-ni-dava' (tonic)	37	28	21	30
	v) Consulting good doctor	40	00	14	23
	vi) Doing regular exercise	06	06	19	10
	vii) Others (be happy, fruits, fresh foods)	19	06	21	17
	viii) No response	04	03	00	03
4a.	Foods and their health giving properties				
	Green leafy vegetables	65	81	82	74
	Milk & milk products	40	30	03	20
	Legumes	35	30	13	30
	Animal foods	26	14	34	28
	Cereals	14	19	08	13
b.	Foods and their harmful effects				
	i) Stale food	54	56	32	48
	- Vomitting / diarrhoea	45	47	00	36
	- headache	19	47	83	40
	- constipation	13	27	25	19
	- malaria / sickness	03	07	00	03
	ii) Too much spicy / oily food	47	22	47	42
	- cough, vitamins gets destroyed	44	33	11	31
	- burning sensations inside body	15	17	11	14
	- others	41	50	78	57
	iii) Uncovered food	28	15	16	21
	- diarrhoea	31	00	33	27
	- spreads germs in body	44	50	16	50
	- others (acidity, gastric pain)	25	50	00	23
	iv) Too many sweets	16	04	16	13
	- diabetes	78	00	50	63
	- hot for body	33	100	50	44
	v) Too much salty food	09	00	00	04
	- blood gets converted into water	40	00	00	40
	- increase Blood pressure	20	00	00	20
	vi) No response	19	18	16	18

Though two-thirds (66 per cent) of the girls could not respond the importance of adolescent period, interesting responses were obtained from some of the older girls. Forty percent of them responded that 'Adolescence is a good learning period', whereas 30 per cent of them mentioned about the development in thinking capacity, decision making and completion of education at this stage.

III. Perceptions Regarding Health and Nutrition

As presented in Table 2.4, nearly two-thirds **(63 per cent) of the** girls described **a** healthy person as one who didn't fall sick often; a little more than a half said that one who could work properly was healthy and nearly half of the girls stated that a healthy person felt energetic.

As stated by one of them *"Tandurast hoy to badhu kaam fatafat kari shakay ane thaki pan najaway"*. (A healthy person can work faster, and does not get tired).

Forty eight percent of the girls believed themselves to be healthy, as they did not fall sick often. More than a one-third of the girls thought that they were not healthy, as they often fell ill or felt weak and tired during working or got body pain and headache.

A little over half (58 per cent) of the girls believed that eating nutritious food at regular intervals was good for health *("Paushtik khorak khavathi tandurasti vadhe chhe")*. A majority (77 per cent) of the girls stated vegetables as nutritious food. A little over half mentioned legumes and sprouts as nutritious foods, whereas almost one-third (33 per cent) of the girls also said that milk taken with routine diet, well-cooked food and non-vegetarian foods were nutritious. To improve health of a weak girl, suggestions given by girls included taking regular meals and consuming nutritious and complete meals. Nearly a third (30 per cent) of them also recommended *'Shakti nii* dava' (health tonics).

Table 2.4 further presents the health giving properties and harmful effects of different foods. Majority (74 per cent) of the girls responded that green leafy vegetables helped maintain one's health *("Shaakbhajithi sharir saru rahe chhe)* and protected against illness, increased iron in body and were also good for the eyes. The knowledge level regarding other food products and their health giving properties was quite low. One third of the girls stated that legumes gave protein, vitamins, energy; animal foods gave fat, energy, protein, vitamins; milk and milk products gave vitamins, energy, minerals and sharpened intelligence also *"Dudhmathi sharirne shakti male chhe"*. Harmful foods were stale food; spicy or deep fried foods or eating too many sweets or uncovered food.

Three-fourths (76 per cent) of the girls mentioned that their mothers were the decision-makers regarding the foods to be cooked, where as the mother mostly purchased major food items like cereals, pulses, vegetables, fruits, sugar and jaggary, sometimes by the father. Nearly one third (30 per cent) of them said that they sometimes purchased cereals, pulses, legumes, vegetables.

With regard to fasting, 34 per cent girls fasted regularly, usually on Thursdays. The frequency of fasting increased during festivals, as 91 per cent of the girls kept a fast during *'Ramzan'* (Muslims) or *'Gaurivrat'* (Hindus). The food intake during fasting decreased in a majority (80 per cent) of the girls. In case of Hindu girls, the food mainly consisted of starchy foods and cereals (e.g. sweet potato), while the Muslim girls fasted the whole day long without even taking any water and ate only after the sunset.

IV. Perceptions about Menarche

It is evident from Table 2.5 that three-fourths of the girls (78 per cent) reported that they attained menarche between the age of 13-15 years, which is similar to the mean age reported in other studies for underprivileged girls approximately at 13 years (Baxi 1991). In the present study data collected during medical check-up also support that girl in these slum communities attained menarche between the ages of 13-15 years.

About one-third of the older girls said that they were apprehensive / anxious at onset of menarche, pointing to the need for creating awareness regarding menarche and giving emotional support. About one-fourth of them said 'they did not feel anything and therefore, accepted *it'*. As many as 62 per cent of the girls informed their mothers at the onset of menarche and a few informed sisters or friends. But in one area, though *50 per cent* of the girls said that they informed their mothers, 25 per cent of the girls said that they informed their elder sister. Data regarding advice given by others at onset of menstruation showed that half of the girls *(50 per cent)* were told that "bad blood comes out of body during menstruation". This was supported by the data collected through other qualitative methods. Thus, it is not surprising that the girls believed the same. Regarding reasons for menarche, about one-third of the girls (30 per cent) thought that menarche occurred 'to remove bad blood from the body' *"Sharirinathi kharab lohi bahar nikdi jaay chhe"*, whereas 33 per cent of the girls said that they had not given any thought to the reasons for menarche, and a few girls (13 per cent) related menarche to a woman's reproductive function. Nearly all the girls (99 per cent) reported that they use a pad made out of old clothes. The cloth was washed and dried to be used again.

About half of the girls did not answer clearly regarding the change in behavior of family members after the girl started menstruating. The rest however reported that they were not allowed to go out alone, not allowed to play like they did earlier or not allowed to mix with boys. They even reported that their style of dressing had changed.

Table 2.5: Information about Menarche among the Adolescent Girls (N=148)

	Perceptions	Area A N=70	Area R N=33	Area G N=45	Total N=148
		Percentage Values			
1.	Girls menstruating at present	69	61	44	59
2.	Age at onset of menarche (years)				
	a) 12	15	10	00	10
	b) 13	29	20	40	29
	c) 14	27	15	25	24
	d) 15	23	40	15	25
	e) >15	06	15	20	12
3.	Feelings at the time of menarche				
a.	10-14 years				
	a) Felt apprehensive / anxious	19	05	10	14
	b) No feeling,	00	00	00	00
	c) Aware about it hence expecting it	00	05	00	01
	d) Others (did not like it, cried , was unhappy)	08	00	00	04
b.	15-20 years				
	a) Felt apprehensive / anxious	40	30	35	36
	b) No feeling, aware about it hence expecting it	25	25	30	26
	c) Aware about it hence expecting it	08	10	15	10
	d) Others (did not like it, cried , was unhappy)	08	25	10	12
4.	Who was informed about onset of menarche				
	a) Informed mother	50	75	80	62
	b) Informed elder sister	25	05	05	16
	c) Informed friend	10	05	15	10
	d) Did not tell anybody	08	05	00	06
	e) any other (aunt , bhabhi, teacher)	06	10	00	06
5.	Advise given at the onset of menstruation				
	a) Explained that bad blood comes out of body during menstruation	52	85	10	50
	b) Did not explain anything but gave clothe for using as a pad	06	10	45	15
	c) Informed that every girls gets it when she is 13-14 years old	02	05	10	05
	d) Did not give any advice	02	00	20	06
6.	Perceptions of girls regarding the occurrence of menstruation				
	a) Hs never thought about it	33	30	35	33
	b) It removes bad blood form body	25	60	10	3
	c) Does not have any idea about it	15	00	20	13
	d) Menstruation should occur only then a woman can conceive	10	00	30	13

Contd...

	e) Any other (when girls became 13-14 years old, it happens naturally)	17	10	05	13
7.	Activities followed by the adolescents during menstrual period				
	a) avoid religious activities	94	90	80	90
	b) have to eat in separate utensils	13	10	60	23
	c) avoid kitchen activities	15	15	60	25
	d) avoid sleeping on same bad as before	10	15	65	24
	e) Any other (sit in a dark corner all alone, avoid household chores)	06	10	90	26

As regards activities followed by the adolescents during menstrual period, 90 per cent of the girls said they avoided religious activities, followed by one-fourth of the girls who said that they had to eat in separate utensils, avoid kitchen activities/household chores, avoid sleeping on the bed but sleep on the floor; sit in a dark corner all alone.

V. Perceptions of Girls Regarding Marriage and Family Planning

Presented in Table 2.6 are the perceptions regarding marriage and family planning, which only a few girls responded in this section. More than half of the girls reported that ideal age for marriage of girls is 18-20 years and for boys is 20-22 years and above. As regards the desirable gap between marriage and birth of the first child, more than one-third said there should be either one year or 2-3 years.Nearly two-thirds of the girls could not! did not specify which parent (father or mother) was responsible for the sex of the unborn child. However, 37 per cent of them believed that both father and mother were responsible for the sex of the unborn child and 35 per cent said that mother was responsible.

Majority of the girls reported to have some knowledge about contraceptives, which, they received mainly through the mass media (TV/radio), school or sister/relatives. Data gathered through Venn diagrams also showed varied sources of information for general health and nutrition i.e. mother, friend, neighbourhood women, school, books and doctors. The fact that breast-feeding has a protective effect for delaying the next pregnancy was known to only 3 per cent of girls. Most of adolescent girls (80 per cent) perceived that breast milk had important nutritional benefits and 35 per cent girls felt it conferred immunity in the child.

Most of the girls (88 per cent) did not have any knowledge about Sexually Transmitted Diseases (STDs) and Acquired Immuno Deficiency Syndrome (AIDS). Among the girls who could respond, the major cause of AIDS was believed to be having sexual relationship with an AIDS patient, followed by vertical transmission from mother to child (56 per cent).

Table 2.6: Perceptions of Girls Regarding Marriage and Family Planning (N=148)

	Perceptions	Area A	Area R	Area G	Total
		N=70	N=33	N=45	N=148
		Percentage Values			
1	Ideal age for marriage (years)				
a.	a) For girls				
	i) <18	13	23	04	13
	ii) 18-20	59	59	85	65
	iii) 20-22	28	18	11	22
	iv) >22	00	00	00	00
	b) For boys				
	i) <18	00	00	00	00
	ii) 18-20	07	04	19	09
	iii) 20-22	54	46	70	56
	iv) >22	39	50	11	35
b.	No response / Not applicable	13	33	40	25
2a.	Desirable gap between marriage and birth of first child				
	i) < 1 year	07	00	13	06
	ii) 1-2 years	20	29	31	25
	iii) 2-3 years	43	47	31	42
	iv) After 3 years	20	24	25	27
	v) No response / Not applicable	36	48	65	48
b.	Desirable spacing of children				
	i) One year	29	31	75	39
	ii) 2-3 years	45	46	13	39
	iii) > 2 years	20	23	00	16
	iv) Does not know	04	00	06	04
	v) Any other	02	00	06	03
	vi) No response	36	48	65	48
3.	Sex of the unborn child decided by				
	i) Both	24	00	67	37
	ii) Mother	38	50	27	35
	iii) Father	38	25	00	23
	iv) Nature's discretion	00	25	07	05
	v) No response / Not applicable	70	88	67	75
4.	Information regarding various kinds of family planning methods				
	i) Oral pills	59	83	60	64
	ii) Condoms	18	33	90	42
	iii)IUD's	41	20	10	30

Contd...

	iv)Family planning operation	06	40	05	15
	v) Any other	12	00	00	00
	vi) No response / Not applicable	70	88	67	75
5.	Sources of above information				
	i) TV / Radio (Mass media)	59	50	30	58
	ii) school	00	00	70	21
	iii) Brother / Sister	23	17	00	15
	iv) Neighbours / relatives	18	33	00	15
	v) No response / Not applicable	76	81	77	78
6.	Awareness about AIDS				
	AIDS is caused by :				
	i) Having sexual relationship with AIDS patients	75	75	100	83
	ii) Vertical transmissions from mother to the child	62	00	83	56
	iii) Giving blood of AIDS patient to a healthy individual	25	00	17	17
	iv) Any other (Shaving)	62	00	100	61
	v) No response / Not applicable	89	88	87	88

Many of them (61 per cent) also mentioned shaving as a means of transmission of AIDS but they could not explain how. The girls had superficial and often incorrect knowledge regarding HIV and AIDS. The present study has highlighted several important issues pertaining to awareness and perceptions of adolescent girls in the areas of health, nutrition, sexuality and reproductive health.

Firstly, though the girls do possess some information about these topics, their knowledge is superficial, not precise and often incorrect. For example, though the girls do know of the importance of a nutritious diet for normal adolescent growth and development, and also that fruits and vegetables, and other protective foods need to be taken, they are not sufficiently aware of the functions of various foods and deficiencies arising from lack of adequate intake; especially nutritional deficiencies relevant in adolescence like iron deficiency anemia. Though the girls have some awareness of reproductive health issues, most of them do not have adequate and correct knowledge about several important areas such as physiology of menstruation, desirable age of childbearing, contraceptives and family planning and STDs/HIV/AIDS.

Secondly, these adolescent girls in the slums, not surprisingly, had access to multiple sources of information for health issues such as mass media (TV, radio), school, peers, relatives, neighbourhood women, books. These multiple channels should be adequately used for educating adolescents.

Thirdly, family members (especially mother) played a crucial role in influencing development of adolescent girls though the responsibilities they assigned to the girls at home; the food they cooked and its nutritive value, or inadequate emotional support they gave to the girls and the health information (or lack of it) they passed on to their daughters. It is evident that health awareness strategies will be ineffective for adolescents unless they involve the family as well.

Emerging Need for Information on Reproductive Health Issues

All the girls expressed a need for information on all reproductive health issues. Based on the responses of the adolescent girls the following reproductive health needs have emerged:

- Importance of maintaining proper genital hygiene during menstruation.
- Identification and role of various reproductive organs (both male and female)
- Significance of the menstrual cycle in a girl's life and how it occurs as a cyclic process.
- Common problems during menstruation.
- Means of safe sex and knowledge of birth control measures
- Causes and symptoms of STIs and HIV/AIDS.
- Beliefs and Misconceptions associated with menstruation, STIs and HIV/ AIDS
- Counseling of teachers and parents to have a more open and empathetic attitude towards adolescent reproductive health.

Suitable Means of Solving Reproductive Health Problems

All the respondents reported that adolescents should be given information regarding reproductive health. They also felt that their parents should be sensitized towards discussing reproductive health issues with them. All the adolescent girls in groups were also in favor of opening a special centre where adolescents could be given this information. They suggested that a centre could either be opened at a health centre or in the school or at a sewing center like the one they were attending as they could easily come there.

Recommendations

- It is clear from this study and from reported literature globally that several issues need to be addressed in adolescent programs such as early marriage, vulnerability to STDsIHIV/AIDS, lack of formal education, family problems and others.
- The common thread running through all these is the need for spreading awareness and promoting favourable attitudinal changes among the girls with

regard to meeting their health and nutritional needs at present and preparing for their future roles of womanhood and motherhood.

- Awareness generation activities need to be multi-channeled and be integrated into other health and development programs for adolescents. According to a multi-country survey by the International Center for Research on Women (1994), successful strategies for working with adolescents (including educational strategies), were those that sought active participation from adolescents, showed interest in adolescents' concerns and focused on counselling; peer counselling; group based and individual counselling.
- Equally important is the attitude of the health care system and service provider working for the adolescents, who requires to be sensitised to provide need of the adolescents.
- The rights of adolescents to privacy, confidentiality and respect must be ensured through appropriate training and sensitization of those working with the youth.
- Both boys and girls should be included in programs, especially to sensitize boys to their own needs and to take greater responsibility for their families' health needs in future- especially those of women and children.
- Education is the single most important factor that can positively influence over all development. The school, therefore has an important role to play in not only imparting values, discipline, respect for time but also in imparting knowledge on sexual and reproductive health and importance of responsible sexual behaviour. Whereas, the voluntary organisations should come forward and address the needs of out of school adolescents.
- Most policy documents tend to look at adolescent boys and girls separately. Girls are considered as future wives and mothers hence early marriage, teenage pregnancy and child survival is linked to girl's education where as programmes for adolescent boys mostly stem from. concerns related to sexual behaviour, adolescent crime and perhaps in few instances with livelihood training. But issues concerning early marriage, teenage pregnancy or eve teasing and other forms of abusive behaviours can not be checked unless both the sexes are involved in all the programmes. There is enough evidence to show that working with one group to the exclusion of the other group does not lead to sustained impact. Therefore, in all the programmes both boys and girls should be included.
- Adolescents should be provided with the opportunity to participate in decision-making processes and activities that affect their lives and future. Privacy and confidentiality are essential prerequisites to address adolescent

issues especially with regard to matters relating to reproductive and sexual health, relationships and emotions.

- There is no government policy specifically for adolescents. It is the National Youth Policy that caters to the adolescents as well. The Draft National Youth Policy 2001 provides a comprehensive overview of youth issues and concerns and comes closest to the policy on adolescents, it makes a distinction between the age of adolescence (13-19) and the age of attainment of maturity (20-30) thereby making a distinction between these different phases and highlights several areas of concern for adolescents.
- By marking the age of adolescence, the policy has given a special focus on adolescent health, education including non-formal education as well as their nutritional requirements and has also facilitated advocacy efforts for focus on adolescents in government programmes. However, the need for a specific policy that would bring about focused development strategy and cater to the special needs of the adolescents in a comprehensive manner together for boys and girls cannot be overlooked. It is also felt that a nodal department to coordinate and monitor the policies and interventions for adolescents needs to be urgently created.
- Involvement of the adolescents during the formulation of policy and programmes should be ensured. Brand Ambassadors from adolescent groups could be created from among the various classes in the schools who could voice their opinion and concerns. More surveys are needed to understand adolescent behaviour in a broader context of social, family, and gender relations especially in the changing social, economic and cultural scenario so that intervention programmes could be planned accordingly.
- The idea of introducing "Life Skills Education" for the adolescents in schools is a welcome step. The Child Development, Adolescent and Health Centre of the Vidyasagar Institute of Mental Health and Neurosciences (VIMHANS) has prepared the module after having tested it in 82 schools through the medium of workshops. This module which provides a check-list for various learning disabilities, speech and language disorders, common childhood emotional and behavioural problems and easy rectification measures that can be carried out in the classrooms will be useful to the teachers, peer trainers and counsellors working with children as this will enable them to identify children's problems at an early stage.

So, it can be concluded that healthy girl child grows into healthy adolescent girl which ultimately grows into healthy women. Healthy women contribute to the empowered family, community and nation as a whole.

References

Advocates for Youth, "Passages—A World's Eye View of Adolescent Issues", Washington, D.C, U.S.A. 1995.

Baxi M., "Intervention Research to Combat Anemia in Adolescent Girls—A Qualitative and Quantitative Approach", M.Sc. Dissertation, Department of Foods and Nutrition, M.S. University of Baroda, Baroda. 1991.

Baroda Citizens Council, "Perceptions of Underprivileged Adolescent Girls of Vadodara on General Health, Nutrition and Reproductive Health", Gujarat, India.

Ghanekar J., "Nutritional Status and Perceptions of Disadvantaged Adolescent Girls in Slums" M.Sc. Dissertation, Department of Foods and Nutrition, M.S. University of Baroda, Baroda. 1995.

Jejeebhoy S., "Adolescent Sexuality and Reproductive Behaviour: A Review of the Evidence from India. International Center for Research on Women. 1994.

Kanani S J, Bhargava J, Mair K, Parikh A and Sanghani S., "Nutritional Status of Adolescent Girls in Baroda (India) with a Focus on Growth, Department of Foods and Nutrition, M.S. University of Baroda, Baroda. (Unpublished document). 1992.

Kashyap P and Gopaldas T., "Impact of Haematinic Supplementation on Sub-maximal Work Capacity in Underprivileged School Girls (8-15 years).

Kurz K M and Johnson-Welch C., "The Nutrition and Lives of Adolescents in Developing Countries: Findings from the Nutrition of Adolescent Girls Research Programme. International Center for Research on Women, Washington D C, U.S.A. 1994.

Kurz K and Rao Gupta, "Nutrition of Adolescent Girls in Developing Countries, International Center for Research on Women, Washington, D C, U.S.A. 1991.

Kumar Rachana, "Problems of the Adolescents: Implications for Interventions, Social Welfare, New Delhi. 2004.

Poplinsky N L., "Addressing Needs and Opportunities: A Survey of Programmes for Adolescents, International Center for Research on Women, Washington, D C, U.S.A. 1994.

Rajkumar M., "Gender Issues in Primary School Health Programmes. National Workshop on School Health, British Council and Sehat, New Delhi. 1994.

Satyanarayana K, Naidu A N and et al., "Effect of Nutritional Deprivation in Early Childhood on Later Growth: A Community Study without Intervention. 1981.

United States Bureau. Census of United States, United States. 1991.

World Health Organisation. Young People's Health: A Challenge for Society. Report of a WHO Study Group on Young People and Health for All by the Year 2000, WHO, Geneva. 1986.

3

Fertility and Health of Rural Women

Neerja Jaiswal

Introduction

Today population concerns are among the most complex and controversial issues. There is, however, little disagreement that rapid population growth not only negates the gains of development, but it is also seriously undermining the habitability of this planet. India is the second largest populous country in the world. With a rapid growth of population, it is difficult to imagine the gains of economic development and better quality of life. Fertility which is directly related to population growth is affected by number of factors such as cultural preferences of diverse roots and strengths, family structures that distribute power over fertility decisions in various ways, customs and taboos related to sexual behavior, child birth and child bearing, varying and rapidly changing economic conditions, and increasing government concerns and activism in many countries.

An exhaustive review of population policies in various developing countries indicates that although a large number of countries (89) of the Third World actively support family planning, their major concern is with arresting population growth. The concern for women is secondary, and women are viewed narrowly and objectified as targets of, rather than participants in the program of such countries. Women, who are the chief characters in the bearing and rearing of children, have virtually no voice in the regulation of their fertility, particularly in the Third World Countries.

Indian rural population which constitutes the bulk of our nation is characterized by strong family orientation. The family is the source of physical and emotional support and fulfills most social needs. Their relative isolation, low income, low level of education, narrower outlook has made them lag far behind the developmental process. But it is important that they should realize that their decisions regarding fertility have significance outside the immediate family circle, and in fact extend even beyond the confines of their community to the nation as a whole.

As used by the demographers, the term *fertility* refers to childbearing. It is contrasted with fecundity which is the term used to refer to the capacity to bear children. Thus, a fertility rate refers to the relative frequency with which births actually occur within a population (Bouge, 1971).

Rarely any country has achieved a high standard of living and better quality of life, without experiencing a significant decline in fertility. On the other hand, the reverse is also the case, no country has achieved a low birth rate in the absence of significant economic growth and or social change. Controlling population growth is not a technical matter. It is a human problem, involving human decisions and motivations.

Socio-economic approaches as well as various incentives and disincentives have been imposed as valuable components of a total package of population planning. But what is essential is to create a continuing climate to change the values, goals and attitudes of female and male population education which develops awareness and understanding of the dynamics of population changes emphasizing how such changes can be influenced and be influenced by the quality of life at both the society and the family level will prove to be quite beneficial.

Last but of utmost importance is the high status of women, within the family and society. Since women bears the major responsibility of bearing and rearing the children, if gains decision making power related to her family building process, the problem of high fertility can be tackled easily.

Rationale of the Study

Human fertility is a complex process responsible for the biological maintenance of the society. The levels of fertility vary across the different societies. A high level of fertility persists among the developing country while it is low in the developed countries. The unprecedented increase of the population of the developing countries is causing much alarm in the world because of its threat to the world resources and human survival in the long run. The proportion of couples effectively planning their family size is very low in most of the developing countries. The investigator felt that an understanding of the factors associated with the low fertility levels is indispensable to regulate the high fertility level in the developing countries and specially India with very high rates of natural increase. Thus, the following study was conceived.

Moreover the research on fertility in most developing countries has concentrated more on fertility control than on the familial and interpersonal aspects of fertility behaviour.

Simple awareness and availability of family limiting methods may not effectively control fertility unless people are properly motivated to reduce fertility. This transformation in attitudes and behaviour regarding fertility calls for highlighting the relevance of different psychological, modernization, socio-economic and demographic variables affecting fertility behaviour to evolve an integrated effective plan for limiting fertility. Therefore, fertility along with the above stated variables was chosen for the present research.

At the same time there has been a single minded interest in individuals or respondents alone. Thus an attempt has been made in the present study which will focus on both the partners regulating the fertility behaviour and not only the women alone.

Reviewing of literature highlighted that not a single study has been undertaken in the selected locale that motivated the investigator to undertake the present investigation with the following objectives:

Objectives of the study are as under:

- To explore the effects of fertility on the health of the woman in the family.
- To determine the role and the nature of assistance provided by the health care centers in fertility transition.
- To find out the opinion of the respondents regarding the family size, sex of the child and their fertility control behaviour.

The study was limited to 50 households (i.e. 50 married couples) of Bhathuji village, Chhani, district Vadodara.

Hypotheses of the Study:

1. There exist an association between the fertility and the following psychological variables: (a) preference for the son, (b) infant mortality.
2. There exist an association between the fertility and the following variables: (a) planning of the family size, (b) inter-spouse communication, (c) income of the family, (d) occupation of the respondent, (e) educational status of the respondents and (f) type of the family.

The research designed in the study was descriptive in nature. The sampled size of the study constituted 100 respondents i.e. 50 males and 50 females from 50 households of 'Bhathuji' village, Chhani, district Vadodara. The samples were selected purposively based on the willingness of the samples to participate in the study. Data was collected through survey method by personally interviewing the male and female respondents separately on a structured, semi-structured and open ended interview schedule to avoid any pressurized and biased responses. Data was further coded and tabulated and statistically analyzed.

Findings and Discussion

Demographic Data: Age of the Respondents: The findings highlighted that a higher percentage of the male respondents (40 per cent) were in the age group of 26 to 30 years at the time of the interview. Little more than one-half of the female respondents (56 per cent) were younger (20 to 25 years) as compared to the male respondents. The mean age of the female respondents was 26.06 years and that of male respondents as 28.88 years.

Age at Marriage plays an important role in fertility transition. The trend which is followed in the locale where the present study is conducted is that marriage takes place quite early as they believe that if the male and female child is grown up and if somehow their marriage is delayed, it is then difficult to get the marriage partner. Thus, child marriages were found to be more prominent in their community. Comparatively a larger percentage of the male respondents (40 per cent and subsequently 32 per cent) were married between the age of 18 to 20 years and 15 to 17 years which is quite low as prescribed by our constitution stating the marriage age as 21 years for boys and 18 years for girls. Nearly one-half of the female respondents (48 per cent) were married at the age of 12 to 14 years. It was the custom of the community that immediately after marriage the girl is not sent to her husband's house until she gains puberty at the onset of menstruation cycle when she becomes capable of bearing children. The mean age at marriage of male respondents and female respondents was found to be 16.84 years and 15.62 years respectively.

Age at Entry into Parenthood: It was found that 27.66 per cent husbands and equally the same percentage of the wives entered into parenthood between the age of 21 and 22 years and 19 to 20 years respectively. It was very surprising to note that equally 23.40 per cent wives started their reproductive span from the age of 15 to 18 years. Onset of fertility behaviour at such an early age in case of wives as compared to husbands was in itself a threat to child and mother mortality leading to population explosion. The mean age at the entry of parenthood for females was 17.87 years and that of males as 21.34 years. Three couples did not experience as one of them was newly married. In case of second couple, the wife was expecting their first child and in case of third couple the wife experienced four miscarriages and was unable to bear children due to some genetic defect.

All the male and female respondents were **Hindus** and belonged to **scheduled caste**. Majority of the couples (68 per cent) were having **nuclear families.**

The educational status of husbands was found to be comparatively better than their counterpart. One-half of the males were illiterate as compared to 82 per cent of the females.

Occupation of the Respondents: The male respondents were found engaged in petty occupations like vegetable selling, carpentry work, basket making, rag picking, agricultural labourer, auto industry helper, auto mechanic and as skilled labourers. The highest percentage (46 per cent) of the male respondents were working as agricultural labourers in the nearby banana farms on daily wages. This was the easiest occupation which they could secure on the basis of their capabilities. Another attraction in this occupation was that besides getting the daily wages, they were given four-six bananas in the lunch as free lunch for them. Otherwise only one meal was affordable to them and that too a simple dinner in a day. Only 4 per cent were engaged as auto industry helper on salary basis 28 per cent of the respondents were low grade self employed like Vegetable vendors, Carpenters and Basket Weavers.

Vegetable vendors and Basket weavers had to travel 12-14 kms. to market their products at Vadodara. Carpenters were found to sell their products in Southern India (Madras) and in some parts of Madhya Pradesh like Indore, where they used to travel with their ready products, in groups, on hired trucks, while being away from their families for 5 to 6 months. One respondent owned his own auto repairing centre for trucks and large vehicles and was earning better than other respondent.

Majority of the female respondents (98 per cent) were not found to be engaged in gainful employment. They were simply playing the role of traditional house wife of rearing the children, performing the household tasks and bearing the children. The wives of the low grade self- employed males (Carpenters and Basket weavers) were assisting their husbands in their profession. Only one female respondent was working as rag and scrap picker. A probe about the use of their leisure time for productive revenue earning occupation highlighted that the respondents despite of their willingness were not able to use it productively. The major constraints reported to do so were the lack of funds, availability of raw material and their ignorance about the marketing potential. The respondents reported that not a single government programme was in operation in this particular village.

Monthly Income of the Respondents: The analysis of the findings revealed that the economic status of the households was very pathetic .Two- third of the households were having their monthly income of Rs. 500 or less. Nearly one-fourth of the households had their monthly income ranging between Rs. 501- Rs. 1,000. The monthly income of 4 per cent households was above Rs. 1,000. Majority of the households were having only one bread earner. Majority of the male respondents were daily wage earners as compared to 12 per cent who were drawing seasonal income (carpenters). 4 per cent of the respondents were salaried workers and one respondent was self employed in his own business.

Fertility Data

Size of the Family: Nearly one-half (52 per cent) of the households were having medium sized family with four to six members in the family. Approximately one-fourth of the households had a large sized family with ≥7 family members. The total number of family members in the households were 251 (on an average 5.02 in each household) with almost the same number of male female sex ratio.

Ever Born Children in the Family: 40.43 per cent of the families experienced the death of only one child as compared to 34.04 per cent families with zero infant mortality. The infant mortality was higher among 4.25 per cent of the families with five and more child death. The male and female sex ratio of ever born children was 4:5.

Ever Living Children in the Family: Most of the families (35.56 per cent) were having two ever living children. An equally 24.44 per cent were having one and three ever living children in the families. Only 4.44 per cent families were found to be having five and more ever living children. The total ever living children in 50 households were 107 with a mean of 2.37 in each family. The male female ratio of ever living children was 0.91:1.

Miscarriages and Abortions among Female Respondents: The findings highlighted that 2.08 per cent females experienced two and four miscarriages respectively. Only 6.25 per cent females experienced one miscarriage and the majority of the female respondents did not experience any miscarriages during their reproductive span.

Delivery Place, Expenditure and Assistance: The data regarding the place of delivery revealed that majority of the female respondents had their deliveries in their homes only. A comparatively higher percentage of them (44.68 per cent) were assisted in delivering their children by their neighbors followed by their mother-in-law (38.29 per cent). A proportionately very less percentage (14.89 per cent) got their children delivered under the specialized supervision of a doctor. Majority of the female respondents incurred no expenditure on their deliveries (93.61 per cent).

Inter-spouse Communication Regarding Family Size: Planning of the family size plays a crucial role in fertility as it directly shows how responsible and aware the couples are towards the welfare of their families. Proportionately a very small number of the couples (10 per cent), were found to have had planned their family size before begetting the children as compared to 90 per cent of the couples. Inter-spouse communication about fertility matters is indicative of woman's status in regulating her fertility behavior. Only 30 per cent of the couples had inter-spouse communication about the fertility matters compared to larger proportion of the couples who were non-communicative about such matters with each other.

Health Data

Perceived Health Status Resulting from Fertility Behavior: Only 44.68 per cent of the female respondents perceived their health status resulting from pregnancies as compared to slightly more than one-third of the female respondents (34.04 per cent) who perceived their health as poor. Most of the respondents had an average birth weight of their children as compared to one-fourth of them who reported low birth weight of their children at the time of delivery. Of the respondents who perceived their health status as poor, majority of them reported to avail medical help during their illness. The others were least concerned about their health. Most of the respondents (58.82 per cent) visited government hospital as compared to slightly more than one-tenth (11.76 per cent) who approached the private doctors due to their complicated cases which were declined to be treated in government hospital.

Nature of Health Problems: Further probing into the nature of health problems of the female respondents due to their fertility behavior came to light that they were suffering from tuberculosis, permanent stomach ache, anemia, low body immunity causing frequent fever and high susceptibility to infectious diseases, general weakness, permanent body aches especially backache, aches in hands and legs, and low stamina. The children of the respondents were found suffering from general weakness, frequent fever and coughing due to low immunity, small pox, liver problems, pre-mature births and iron deficiency as a result of fertility behavior of the female respondents.

Concern about the Wife's Health in Increasing the Family Size: Enquiring the concerns of the husbands about the health of the wife's while increasing the size of the family highlighted that surprisingly 98 per cent of the respondents responded that they do care the health of their wife's. One husband who was having a second wife, was not concerned about his wife's health. He opted to go for a third marriage if his second wife will also be unable to bear children or dies while delivering the child.

Existence of the Health Centre: As reported by the respondents there existed neither any health centre nor any private medical practitioner in the village. The respondents had to approach the government hospital named 'Samuhik Arogya Shala' located about 5-6 kms from the village at 'Chhani Jakat Naka'.

Nature of Assistance Provided by the Health Centers: Few respondents who used to consult doctors at the government health centers during the family illness reported to have free medication facilities but were not very happy and satisfied as according to them the medicines provided were not very effective in curing illness. Moreover they were dissatisfied with the long ques and the time spent at the hospital for seeking medical help. The awareness regarding the vaccination of the children was reported to be poor among the respondents. Occasional visits of the medical personnel from the hospital to vaccinate the children was not the regular feature. Since the vaccinations were provided free of charge, the respondents got their children vaccinated but never took them to the hospital on their own for the purpose.

Role of Health Centre: The health centre was found to be playing a very passive role in creating awareness among the families about the fertility limiting methods and its importance. Only in very few cases (17.02 per cent) of deliveries which were taken up by the doctors at the hospital, the respondents were found to be operated for controlling the fertility. The lure associated behind the operation was only the monetary benefits of Rs. 130/- associated with it and not the fertility control.

Desired Sex Ratio of the Children in the Family: A higher percentage of the male respondents (46 per cent) and female respondents (56 per cent) stated two children, a son and a daughter as an ideal sex in the family with their contradictory responses when they were asked about the desired number of children and their sex in the family. Most of them then preferred three children with two sons and one daughter. Preference for the sons was more among the couples with an expectation that son provides financial assistance, an old age support, support during illness and provides family lineage, which is not possible in case of daughters. A higher percentage of the couples (40 per cent husbands and 40 per cent wives) desired to go for a maximum of three conceptions for the sake of having son in the family.

Preference for Second Wife for the Sake of Son: The findings reported that there was a strong emotional bonding between the couples. Majority of the male respondents preferred to compromise without a male sex in the family rather than bringing a second wife and go on taking trials at the cost of their wives for the sake of having son in the family.

A probe about the opinion regarding the usage of the family planning method by the couples it was found that more than one-half of the couples (56 per cent) opined that it should not be used. Further enquiring the reason, majority of them reported that since children are god's gifts they do not have any other option but to accept them.

Fertility Limiting Behavior: Majority of the couples were unaware about the fertility limiting methods. Very few (8 per cent) who were aware about it had gained knowledge from their colleagues, friends and hospitals. Majority of the respondents reported that they had not adopted any fertility limiting method. The adoption status among women was higher than their counterparts among the couples who had adopted the same. The three methods being adopted by the respondents, were the sterilization method, the rhythm (calendar) method and pills for limiting their family size, the sterilization method being the most popular one.

The findings of the hypothesis testing revealed that the fertility was found to be significantly associated (chi square 5.06 at 0.05 level) with the infant mortality (psychological variable) in the family, rather than the preference for son by the male and the female respondents. Thus, higher the infant mortality among the families the higher was their fertility behavior. The fertility was also found to be significantly associated with the income of the family (socio-economic status variable, chi square 7.89 at 0.05 level) and the type of the family (demographic variable, chi square 15.75 at 0.05 level). Thus the fertility was found to be highly dependent on the type of the family whether it be joint or nuclear and on the income of the family. The higher the income the higher was fertility and vice versa among the families.

Conclusion

Human fertility is a complex process responsible for the biological maintenance of the society. But when it goes beyond the limit it becomes deterrent to the overall development of the nation. At micro level the first and the most important victim of high fertility is the woman herself, who is pivotal personality around which the family revolves thereby affecting the family too. Thus, the need of the hour is to undertake action oriented projects at micro level by the NGO's, Social Workers and the Extension Workers, to create awareness about the benefits of fertility transition and develop an educative and motivational values and attitudes among the family members about the same. This will somehow help to utilize the woman's health resource in a better manner ensuring development of all the family members and subsequently a better quality of life of the family.

References

Adams A. and Castle S., Gender Relations and Household Dynamics, in Sen G., Germain A. and Chen L., eds., Population Reconsidered: Health, Empowerment and Rights,

Ahmed, Alia. Women and Fertility in Bangladesh. New Delhi. Sage Publications, 1991.

Bledsoe, C., Constructing Natural Fertility: The Use Of Western Contraceptive Technologies in Rural Gambia. Population and Development Review, 20(1):81-113. 1994.

Bogue, D.J.A Model Interview for Fertility Research and Family Planning Evaluation. Community and Family Study Center. University of Chicago. 1970.

Bogue, D.J. Demographic Techniques of Fertility Analysis. Community and Family Study Center. University of Chicago. 1971.

Bongaarts, J. and Watkins, S. Social Interactions and Contemporary Fertility Transitions, Population and Development Review, 22(4): 639-682. 1996.

Boulay, M. and Valente, T.W.: The Relationship of Social Affiliation and Interpersonal Discussion to Family Planning Knowledge, Attitudes and Practice. International Family Planning Perspectives. 25(3):112-118 & 138. 1999.

Caldwell, J.C. and Caldwell, P. The Role of Marital Sexual Abstinence in Determining Fertility: A Study of the Yoruba in Nigeria. Population Studies, No. 31, pp. 193-213; 1977.

Caldwell, J.C. and Caldwell, P. The Cultural Context of High Fertility in Sub-Saharan Africa. Population and Development Review. 13(3):409-437. 1987.

Das Gupta, M. Kinship Systems And Demographic Regimes, in: Kertzer, D. and Fricke, T. (eds). Anthropological Demography: Towards a New Synthesis. Chicago, IL, USA: University of Chicago Press. pp. 36-52. 1997.

Godley, J. Kinship Networks And Contraceptive Choice In Nang Rong, Thailand, International Family Planning Perspectives. 27(1):4-10. 2001.

Hill, A. (ed). Population, Health and Nutrition in the Sahel: Issues in the Welfare of Selected West African Communities, Boston, MA, USA: KPI. 1985.

Kohler, H. Behrman, J. and Watkins, S. The Density of Social Networks and Fertility Decisions: Evidence from South Nyanza District, Kenya, Demography. 38(1):43-58. 2001.

Malhi P., Influence of Gender Preference for Children on Fertility Behaviour: A Comparative Study of Men and Women in Haryana. The Journal of Family Welfare. 41(2): 53-60. 1995.

Madhavan, Sangeetha, Adams, Alayne, and Simon, Dominique. Women's Networks and the Social World Of Fertility Behavior. International Family Planning Perspectives. 29:2. 2003.

Montgomery, M. and Casterline, J. Social Influence, Social Learning and New Models of Fertility. Population and Development Review. 22 (Suppl.):151-175. 1996.

Page, H.J. and Lesthaeghe, R. (eds). Child-Spacing in Tropical Africa: Traditions and Change, New York: Academic Press. 1981.

Ryder, N. Fertility And Family Structure, Population Bulletin of the United Nations, No. 15, pp. 15-34; 1983.

Steele, F. Amin, S. and Naved, R. Savings/Credit Group Formation and Change in Contraception. Demography. 38(2):267-282. 2001.

Velkoff, Victoria A. and Adlakha, Arjun. Women's Health in India. International Programs Center. 1998.

World Bank. A New Agenda for Women's Health and Nutrition. World Bank, Washington D.C. 1994.

4

Adolescent Nutrition

Uma Iyer, Shruti Shah, Shonima Venugopal and Kavita Sharma

The term adolescence meaning "to emerge" or "achieve identity" is a relatively new concept, especially in development thinking. The origins of the term from the Latin word, 'adolescere' meaning "to grow", to "mature" indicate the defining features of adolescence. Adolescence is defined as a transient stage, between childhood and adulthood and a formative period during which many life patterns are learned and established. Adolescents are tomorrow's adults and 85 per cent of them live in developing countries. There are 1.2 billion adolescents aged 10-19 years in developing nations, making up one-fifth to one-quarter of the country's population. Traditionally, preschool age children and women of reproductive age have been targeted as nutritionally vulnerable group in developing countries, whereas in developed countries, the focus tends to be on nutrition related chronic diseases of the ageing population. Adolescents are in between group, with some nutritional problem commonalities with children and adults.

India is one of the few countries where males significantly outnumber females and this imbalance has increased over time. One reason for the adverse juvenile sex ratio is the increasing reluctance to have female children. Social neglect of women and girls is the other contributing factor. Health of women is an important factor in determining the overall health of the society.

Adolescence is considered a nutritionally vulnerable period of life for several reasons. First, is the greater demand for nutrients because of the dramatic increase in the physical growth and development. Second is the change of lifestyle and food habits of adolescents that affect both nutrient intake and needs. Third are those with special nutrient needs during pregnancy and illness. Fourth, adolescence can be the second opportunity to catch up growth if environmental conditions especially in terms of nutrient intake are favorable. Finally, psychological changes and development of their own personality can impact on their dietary habits during a phase when they are very influenceable

Adolescents are overlooked in most health programmes as they are basically considered a healthy group. In general, adolescent mortality rates are lower than for other age groups, such as 0-4 years. However, the pervasiveness of gender discrimination in India, lower nutritional status of females, early marriage and high fertility, and early child bearing (leading to maternal mortality) contribute to a wide difference in nutritional status and mortality rates in adolescent females and males. In the older adolescent age group, female mortality is significantly greater than male mortality (1.9 vs. 1.3) as female adolescents begin to experience problems of early pregnancy, the effects of malnutrition and anemia.

India, like many other developing countries, is experiencing rapid urbanization characterized by a double burden of disease in which chronic diseases become more prevalent while infectious diseases remain undefeated. Large shifts have occurred in diet and in physical activity patterns in adolescents. Modern societies seem to be converging on a diet high in saturated fats, sugar, and refined foods but low in fibre often termed the 'western diet' and on lifestyles characterized by lower levels of physical activity. These changes are reflected in nutritional outcomes, such as changes in average stature, body composition and morbidity.

The main nutritional problems are micronutrient deficiency, particularly, iron deficiency anemia and depending on the context, under-nutrition or obesity and their associated co-morbidities. Chronic Under-nutrition that results in stunting is responsible at adolescence for delayed growth and maturation, magnified obstetric risk, and reduced work capacity. Under-nutrition persisting through childhood may have significant effect on cognitive development, school achievements and later health.

Elevated blood pressure, dyslipidemia, and a higher prevalence of factors associated with insulin resistance and type 2 diabetes appear as frequent co-morbidities in the overweight and obese pediatric population. Obesity in childhood, particularly, in adolescence, is a key predictor for obesity in adulthood.

Iron deficiency anemia (IDA) is an important public health problem resulting in considerable morbidity and mortality in women and young children. In NFHS II, the prevalence of anemia was 56 per cent in women of age 15-19 years. The prevalence of mild, moderate and severe anemia was 36.2, 17.9 and 1.9 per cent respectively. It adversely affects the cognitive performance, behavior and growth of infants, pre-school and school children. Further, it reduces the use of energy sources by muscle and hence the physical capacity and work performance of adolescents and adults; Immune status is compromised and morbidity from infections is seen in all age groups.

Nutritional vulnerability may in certain respects be lower in adolescence than early childhood, but adolescence provides a window of opportunity to prepare nutritionally for a healthy adult life. Some nutritional problems originating earlier in life can potentially be corrected, in addition to addressing the current ones. It may also be a timely period to shape and consolidate healthy eating and lifestyle behaviors, thereby preventing or postponing the onset of nutrition related chronic diseases in adulthood. Furthermore, there is very little data on adolescent nutrition to back up programmes depicting the problems of over-nutrition and under-nutrition especially with regard to adolescent girls. In view of these factors, it is important to investigate research on two contrasting themes – severe malnutrition and obesity in adolescents as a means of strengthening programmes. Most of the studies in India have focused on under-nutrition in low socioeconomic group but there is dearth of data on the dual burden in urban areas. The present study focused on the formative research on adolescent nutrition in both boys and girls, which would help to plan action-oriented research to address issues related to adolescents

With this background a study was planned with the following objectives:

- To study the nutritional status of adolescents (10-18 years) of urban Vadodara with respect to Under-nutrition, Over-nutrition and Iron deficiency anemia
- To study the effect of dietary practices and activity pattern on the prevalence of the under-nutrition and over-nutrition.
- To map the prevalence of dyslipidemia among adolescent children.

Material and Methods

The adolescent children were selected from the school of urban Vadodara. One school was purposively selected. All the children from 5th -12th standard in the age group of 10 -18 years were enrolled for the study.

Experimental Plan

The study involved 2 phases

- Collection of general information along with anthropometric measurements to study the nutritional status of adolescent's in the age group of 10-18 years in a school set up.
- To find the risk factors associated with the nutritional deficiencies and excesses.

The general information was collected from all the enrolled children (n=671), which included religion, education and occupation of parents, socio-economic status, and general habits. The data was obtained using a pre-tested questionnaire. Anthropometric measurements such as height, weight, waist and hip measurements were recorded using standard procedures. The prevalence of under-nutrition and over-nutrition was ascertained using various standards. They were International Obesity Task Force standards as given by Cole et al, CDC standards, Must et al standards and Agarwal standards. For risk factor analysis, all the children who were willing to participate and gave information pertaining to diet and activity were included in the study. Out of 671 children information could be collected on 414 children. Out of 414 children, 191 were normal, 137 were underweight, 54 were overweight, and 10 were obese. A structured questionnaire was used to obtain the general dietary information and the dietary profile of the children, which included breakfast consumption pattern, frequency of consuming soft drinks, fast foods, ice creams, chocolates etc. Dietary intake was taken using "24- hour dietary recall method". The nutritive value of foods consumed was calculated from the raw ingredients using the values given in "Nutritive Value of Indian Foods" by Gopalan. General activity information was obtained using a structured questionnaire and the seven days activity profile of the children was taken using self-administered pre tested questionnaire. The 24-hour dietary recall and seven days activity pattern were done on a sub sample of 392 children. The lipid profile was done on 269 children. Biochemical analysis included hemoglobin and lipid profile tests. Fasting blood samples were tested for Total Cholesterol (TC), High-density lipoprotein cholesterol (HDL-C), Triglycerides (TG), and fasting blood glucose levels (FBS). Serum levels of FBS, TG, TC and HDL-C were enzymatically assayed using commercially available kits while LDL-C was calculated by Freidwald's formula. Hemoglobin levels were estimated using cyanmethemoglobin method.

Statistical Analysis include standard deviation, Chi square and percentile and Z score values for height for age, weight for age and weight for height was calculated in Epi Info 6. For others, frequency distribution was computed. All tests were considered significant at $p<0.05$ levels.

Results and Discussion

General Profile of the Subjects: In all 671 children, were enrolled for the study of which 376 were boys and 295 were girls. Majority (96 per cent) of the children were Hindus with per capita income of Rs. 1000 and above. Most of the fathers were employed and mothers were housewives. The mean BMI was 17.4 and 18.2 for boys and girls respectively. Waist Circumference and Waist Hip Ratio (WHR) for boys was 68 cm and 0.86, while for girls it was 62 cm and 0.78 respectively (Table 4.1).

Prevalence of Under-nutrition: The prevalence of underweight was 34 per cent, with 41.2 per cent of boys and 24.7 per cent of girls being underweight using Must et al standards. According to Agarwal standards, the prevalence of under-nutrition was low (19 per cent) with 19.9 per cent of boys and 17.6 per cent of girls being underweight. The prevalence of underweight and wasting was higher in boys as compared to girls. Thus, under-nutrition is also a problem even in middle and high-income group adolescent children, both boys and girls and is not confined to lower income group.

Table 4.1: Anthropometric Profile of Subjects (Mean ± SD)

Variables	Boys	Girls	Total
N	376	295	671
Height (m)	1.6 ± 0.1	1.5±0.1	1.5±0.1
Weight (kg)	44.0 ± 12.8	42.4±11.03	43.2±11.9
BMI (kg/m²)	17.4 ± 3.4	18.2±3.8	17.8±3.6
WC (cm)	68.3±9.2	62.4±8.15	65.3±8.7
WHR (cm)	0.9±0.1	0.8±0.1	0.8±0.1

WC = Waist Circumference; WHR = Waist Hip Ratio; BMI = Body Mass Index

Prevalence of Overweight and Obesity: The prevalence of overweight and obesity was 8.2 per cent and 1.5 per cent by IOTF standards, 6.9 per cent and 2.8 per cent by CDC standards, 7 and 1.5 per cent by Must et al standards, and 9.4 per cent and 3.0 per cent by Agarwal standards. The prevalence of overweight and obesity varied with the type of standards used. The highest prevalence of overweight and obesity was obtained with Agarwal standards (Indian standards), as the cutoff values were lower as compared to other standards. In general it was seen that the prevalence of overweight and obesity was higher in girls than boys. Thus, over-nutrition was found to coexist with under-nutrition in adolescent children. Waist Circumference was markedly increased in both overweight (20.2 per cent) and obese children (34.2 per cent) while in underweight it decreased by 9.7 per cent as compared to normals. High waist circumference values may act as an independent risk factor placing the subjects at a high risk of CVD later in life and therefore, needs to be monitored. This observation highlights the need to monitor growth in girls during adolescent period..

Income: In the risk factor analysis, it was observed that the prevalence of overweight and obesity increased with the increase in the per capita income of the parents. Thus, per capita income had an influence on the prevalence of overweight in these children. A study reported that the families' social class during subject's childhood had a long term influence on BMI and the mean BMI at birth was highest in offspring from the highest social class.

Dietary Intake and Food Habits: Faulty food habits are one of the causative factors for obesity. When the nutrient intake of the children was studied it was seen that the mean calorie intake and protein intake was comparable between the normal, overweight and obese children (Table 4.2). The mean fat intake ranged from 54 -76 g. The per cent calories' coming from fat was on the higher side (35 per cent) as against the recommended value of 15-25 per cent. Also, a strong positive correlation was found between energy intake and fat intake (r= 0.87). Through 24-hour recall method, it was observed that 16% of the children used to consume more than 100% of energy (Table 4.3). Other nutrients except iron nearly meet 70 per cent of RDA. Only 35 per cent of the RDA for iron was met for children. When the per cent RDA for iron was looked into, it was found that 82 – 90 per cent of the children had iron intake <50 per cent of RDA (Table 4.4).

Only 31 per cent of the children had breakfast before coming to school. The trend remained similar for normal, underweight, overweight and obese children. A strong need is felt to address the problem of skipping breakfast. The most popular food items consumed by the children were Potato wafers (36.5 per cent), Samosa (25.8 per cent), Puff (24 per cent) and Noodles (22.7 per cent). The soft drinks consumed were Sharbat (24.7 per cent) and Pepsi (23.5 per cent). The frequency of consumption of fast foods, soft drinks, chocolates, ice-creams and sweets revealed that most of these food items were consumed by the children at least once a week thus contributing to the energy intake. Further, looking into the fast food consumption trends and empty calorie intake, attempts need to be made to sensitize the children regarding good food habits.

Table 4.2: Mean Nutrient Intake of the Children (Mean ± SD)

Variables	N	Un	Ow	Ob	Total
Calories (kcal)	1707±652.6	1902±595	1726±588	1304±664	1768.1±633.3
Proteins (g)	45.3±16.27	49.4±15.87	45.6±16.97	37.5±19.52	46.62±16.44
CHO (g)	225.5±93.92	254.6±124.01	233.2±83.54	156.5±64.29	235.1±105.0
Total fat (g)	65.6±26.76	76±29.67	68.5±27.42	53.9±35.02	69.3±28.52
Crude fibre (g)	4.6±2.46	5.0±2.06	5.1±2.43	4.11±1.70	4.8±2.31
Iron (mg)	10.8±4.92	11.6±5.39	14.02±17.24	8.73±4.19	11.5±8.04
Vitamin C (mg)	53.8±71.53	62.12±54.01	55.74±52.56	45.6±51.92	56.8±62.8
β-carotene (µg)	2349±2740	2226±1627	1900±1355	1728±1510	2227±2222

N = Normal; Un = Underweight; Ow = Overweight; Ob = Obese

TV Viewing: When the duration of TV viewing was looked into it was found that majority of the children used to watch TV for approximately 2 hours (Table 4.5). The duration of time spent on TV by overweight and obese children were more than the normal children and needs to be curtailed. A study reported that boys and girls who watched 4 or more hours of television each day had greater body fat and BMI than those who watched less than 2 hours per day.

Table 4.3: Per cent RDA from Energy

per cent RDA from Energy	N (191)	Un (137)	Ow (54)	Ob (10)	Total
<50	24 (13)	9 (7)	5 (9)	5 (50)	43 (11)
50-75	80(42)	50 (36)	21 (39)	3 (30)	154 (39)
75-100	65 (34)	48 (35)	21 (39)	0 (00)	134 (34)
>100	22 (12)	30 (22)	7 (13)	02 (20)	61 (16)

Table 4.4: Per cent RDA from Iron

per cent RDA From Iron	N (191)	Un (137)	Ow (54)	Ob (10)	Total
<50	168(88)	123(90)	44(81)	9(90)	344 (88)
50-75	17(9)	8(6)	7(13)	1(10)	33 (8.4)
>75	6(3)	6(4)	3(6)	-	15 (4)

Value in Parenthesis indicate Percentage

Table 4.5: Duration of Time Spent on T.V (Mean ± SD, Hours/day)

TV Viewing	N	Un	Ow	Ob	Total
Boys	1.82±0.88	1.94±1.43	2.02±1.33	2.98±0.82	1.90±1.15
Girls	1.64±0.84	1.77±0.75	1.56±0.67	2.37±1.37	1.70±0.82
Total	1.76±0.87	1.88±1.23	1.81±1.01	2.6±1.17	1.83±1.04

Lipid Profile: When the lipid profile in adolescent children was studied, the Triglyceride (TG) and Total Cholesterol (TC) values were higher in girls than boys (Table 4.6). The lipid profile was higher in 13-15 years girls than boys. A study carried out among school children in Riyadh reported that mean levels of TG and TC/HDL-C ratio were higher among girls than boys in the 12 –15 year age group. Since under-nutrition and over-nutrition affects the lipid profile, the data was analyzed in relation to these factors. The lipid profile of underweight children was comparable with the normal children except for the serum TG levels, which were lower in underweight boys. Higher BMI had an influence on lipid profile. But the trend was different when overweight children were compared with normal. The TC, TG, Low density lipoprotein (LDL-C), Very Low Density Lipoprotein (VLDL-C) and Non HDL-C were higher in overweight boys than healthy boys. In case of girls, such a trend was not seen (Table 4.7).

Table 4.6: Lipid Profile of the Children (Mean ± SD, mg/dl)

Variables	Boys	Girls
FBS	83±16.5	83±6.6
TG	121±45.4	134±43.6
HDL-C	49±11.4	49±12.0
LDL-C	98±34.1	99±34.9
TC	162±37.3	170±37.3
VLDL-C	24±9.1	27 ±8.8
NON-HDL	125±36.3	126±31.8

Table 4.7: Lipid Profile of the Children In Relation to Under-nutrition and Over-nutrition (Mean±SD, mg/dl)

Variables	Normal		Underweight		Overweight		F TEST
	Boys	Girls	Boys	Girls	Boys	Girls	
N	64	83	67	30	6	14	264
FBS	83±6	83±7	84±7	82±7	80±5	81±5	0.53
TC	165±35	172±39	159±38	162±33	216±30	160±40	3.2**
TG	126±46	133±44	110±41	130±47	170±49	153±36	4.35***
HDL-C	50±12	47±13	50±11	51±12	47±13	49±10	0.49
VLDL-C	25±9	27±9	22±8	26±9	34±10	31±7	4.39***
LDL-C	99±30	101±37	92±35	91±32	142±31	88±15	2.64*
NON-HDL-C	126±31	129±35	116±38	118±28	170±39	121±9	2.67*
TC/HDL-C	4±0.8	4±1.3	3±0.9	3±0.9	5±1.9	4±0.6	3.03*
LDL/HDL-C	2±0.6	2±1.1	2±0.8	2±1.0	3±1.6	2±0.3	2.76*

Prevalence of Dyslipidemia: Based on National Cholesterol Education Programme (NCEP) classification, the prevalence of dyslipidemia was obtained. Both hypercholesterolemia and hypertriglyceridemia was seen in children. This calls for screening of dyslipidemia among children to avert later coronary events. About 31 per cent of children had Hypertriglyceridemia (i.e. Triglycerides>150mg/dl) and 19 per cent of children had Hypercholesterolemia (i.e. Total Cholesterol>200mg/dl). Further, among these children 12 per cent of children had low levels of HDL-C levels (i.e.<40 mg/dl) and 2.6% of children had both hypercholesterolemia and hypertriglyceridemia. The trends were similar in both boys and girls. These findings are alarming, in that they predict an unfavorable cardiovascular disease incidence for this population in the foreseen future. This calls for screening for dyslipidemia among children to avert later coronary events.

About 1/5th of the adolescent children were anemic (22 per cent). The prevalence of anemia was lower in boys (15 per cent) than in girls (28.8 per cent) (Table 4.8). All the anemic boys had mild anemia while 80 per cent of anemic girls had mild anemia and the remaining 20 per cent had moderate anemia. The maximum prevalence of anemia was seen in the age group of 13-15 years in both boys and girls as compared to 10-12 years and 16-18 years. Malnutrition was looked into in relation to anemia. Anemia was seen in both over-nutrition and underweight. Anemia was present in 19 per cent of normal, 25 per cent of underweight, 14.3 per cent of overweight and 60 per cent of obese children. These findings suggest that guidelines for screening for iron deficiency anemia may need to be modified to include children with elevated BMI. Since only mild degree of anemia was seen, awareness should be created to improve iron status as well as its bioavailability.

Table 4.8: Frequency Distribution of Haemoglobin Levels in Children

Hb(g/dl)	Boys		Girls	
	N	per cent	N	per cent
>12	119	85	94	71.2
11-11.99	16	11.4	21	15.9
10-10.99	5	3.6	9	6.8
9-9.99	-	-	6	4.5
8-8.99	-	-	2	1.5

From our study it is evident that in urban areas a dual picture is emerging with the problems of excess (overweight and obesity) coexisting with underweight and anemia. Further, the dual burden with anemia among girls places them at risk in future. The consequences of anemia in terms of poorer pregnancy outcome are well known. In addition to a higher risk of low birth weight, prematurity, stillbirth, neonatal infection and maternal mortality, anemia in pregnancy may be associated with a higher risk of hypertension and heart disease in the offspring of anemic mothers. Also the long-term health risks and disadvantages of overweight and obesity are well documented. High prevalence of dyslipidemia in adolescent girls at this age also highlights the need for monitoring and correcting the condition to avert later consequences.

Conclusions

Results from our study calls for a comprehensive nutrition screening to assess the nutritional profile of the adolescent children with the focus on the girl child as monitoring and intervening at this stage may go a long way in maintaining the health to avoid any later consequences. Since, at adolescent stage under-nutrition coexists with over nutrition, there is a need to monitor body mass index (BMI) regularly in schools because the growth in this age group is rapid. Attempts should be made to develop a nomogram of BMI for adolescent population for rapid screening. As skipping of breakfast was a common feature among children, attempts need to be made to develop good breakfast habits. High intake of fat coupled with fast foods calls for inculcating good habits early in life. The prevalence of overweight along with dyslipidemia at adolescent stage highlights the urgency for screening these populations for health promotion. Both under-nutrition and over-nutrition are at risk for iron deficiency anemia. Since only mild degree of anemia was seen, intervention strategies should focus on improving the bioavailability of iron.

Based on these observations, we propose that Nutrition Health Index Card should be developed for each adolescent child, which takes into consideration anthropometric measurements, dietary information and biochemical parameters. Each adolescent child especially girls should have his/her Nutritional Health Index Card to assess and monitor the nutritional status throughout the adolescent period. It is widely recognized that women's health interventions are highly cost-effective. According to the World Bank, improving health care for women offers the biggest return on health care spending for any demographic group of adult's along with other multiple pay offs such as well being and productivity of women, significant benefits for families, communities, and national economies. (www.worldbank.org). Policy adopted by school regarding nutrition health index card would help to optimize the health of adolescent children and may serve as a guiding tool for later eventualities.

References

Delisle H, Chandra M V and De Benoist B. Should Adolescents be Specifically Targeted for Nutrition in Developing Countries? To Address to Problems and How? 2000.

Alaimo K, Olson CM, Frongillo EA. Food insufficiency and American School aged children's cognitive, academic, and psychosocial development. *Pediatrics;* 108:44-53. 2001.

Grantham- Mc Gregor SM, Walker SP, Chang S. Nutritional Deficiencies and later behavioral development. *Proc Nutr Soc;* 59: 257-65. 2000.

Cole T J, Bellizzi M C, Flegal K M and Dietz W Z. Establishing A Standard Definition For Childhood Overweight and Obesity Worldwide: International Survey. *BMJ*; 320: 1240 – 56. 2000.

Kuczmarski R J, Ogden C L, Grummer – Strawn LM et al. CDC growth charts, United States. *Adv Data*; 314:1-27. 2002.

Must A, Dallal G E and Dietz W H. Reference Data for Obesity: 85th and 95th Percentile of BMI and Triceps and Skin Fold Thickness. *Am J Clin Nutr;* 53: 839 – 46

Agarwal D K and Agarwal A K (2003) The Growth- Infancy To Adolescence. CBS Publishers and Distributors, New Delhi. 1991.

Gopalan C, Rama B V and Balasubramanian S C. Nutritive Value of Indian Foods. National Institute of Nutrition, ICMR, 1999.

Raabo E. Methods of Enzymatic Analysis by GOD/POD method. *Scand J Clin. Lab. Invest*; 12:402. 1969.

Mc Gowan MW, Artiss JD, Stanberg DR and Zak BA. Peroxidase coupled method for the colorimetric determination of triglyceride. *Clin. Chem.*; 29:538. 1983.

Glueck J, Stockbridge and Hardy. Estimation of total cholesterol by CHOD-PAP method. *Clin. Med*; Vol 114/2: 142-151. 1989.

Warnick JR, Maryfield CB, Benderson JB Chen JS and Albert JJ. HDL Cholesterol quantification of phosphotungstate Mg+2 and by dextran sulphate Mn+2 polythene glycol precipitation both with enzymatic cholesterol assay compared with lipid research method. 1982.

Laitinen J, Power C and Jarue Lin M R. Family Social Class, Maternal BMI, and Age at Menarche as Predictors of Adult Obesity. *Am J Clin Nutr*; 74:287 – 94. 2000.

Andersen RE, Crespo CJ, Bartlett Sj, Cheskin LJ, Pratt M. (1998) Relationship of physical activity and television watching with body weight and level of fatness among children. *JAMA,* Vol 279; No 12: 938-942. 1998.

Al – Shehri S N, Saleh Z A, Salama M M and Hassan Y M. Prevalence of Hyperlipidemia among Saudi School Children in Riyadh. *Ann Saudi Med*, Jan-Feb; 24 (1): 6 - 8. 2004.

5

Counseling Mothers in Child Feeding Practices

Kavita Sharma, Rajul Jain and Uma Iyer

Malnutriton in Young Children

'One out of three children begin life with a significant disadvantage. Only one in 10 children grow normally' (UNICEF 1995). Malnutrition is implicated in more than half of all child deaths worldwide. Its survivors are left crippled, vulnerable to illness and intellectually disabled. Yet the worldwide crisis of malnutrition has stirred little public alarm (UNICEF 1998).

According to current estimates, about 70 per cent of all childhood mortality in developing countries is due to five major conditions: diarrhoeal diseases, acute lower respiratory tract infections, malaria, measles and malnutrition. Evidence shows that malnutrition even in its milder forms can increase the likelihood of mortality from a number of different disease entities and may be associated with up to 56 per cent of all childhood mortality (Pelletier et al 1995). In India, malnutrition in children is a major concern, as about 53 per cent of children under-five years are underweight and 52 per cent are stunted (UNICEF 2000).

Malnutrition contributes to 60 per cent of the 10 million deaths globally that occur every year among children less than five years of age. Moderately and severely malnourished children are five to eight times more likely to die than are adequately nourished children. The commonest immediate causes of death in these children are infections. Even children with mild malnutrition (who form the majority of children in a typical rural Indian community), have a greater risk of death than children who are normally nourished. The total number of child deaths attributable to mild and moderate malnutrition is far greater than those attributable to severe malnutrition. Of children that survive, malnutrition causes long-term ill effects on growth, health, and mental and educational development. Malnutrition thus leads to decrease in productivity over the entire life of children who survive malnutrition (CARE 2003).

Every fourth child worldwide is affected by Protein Energy Malnutrition (PEM), with 150 million children being underweight and 182 million stunted. The profile of malnutrition in India is one where the distribution of children's age-standardized weight is dramatically to the left of the global reference standard, suggesting a major under-nutrition problem. Whether under-nutrition is measured as the prevalence of underweight, stunting or wasting, it is clear that the nutritional situation in India is amongst the worst in the world (Table 5.1). India's prevalence of underweight (47 per cent) compares to Bangladesh (48 per cent) and Nepal (48 per cent), but is much higher than all other countries within South Asia and far higher than the averages for other regions of the world. High prevalence combined with India's large population means that of the 150 million malnourished children aged under five in the world, more than a third live in India (UNICEF 2003).

Table 5.1: Underweight, Stunting and Wasting in India Compared to Other Regions

Region	Percent of under-five (2000)		
	Underweight	Stunted	Wasted
Latin America and Caribbean	6	14	2
Africa	24	35	8
Asia	28	30	9
India	47	45	16
Bangladesh	48	45	10
Bhutan	19	10	3
Maldives	45	36	20
Nepal	48	51	10
Pakistan	40	36	14
Sri Lanka	33	20	13
All developing countries	22-27	28-32	7-9

Source: ACC/SCN/2004

In India, nearly half of the children below 3 yrs. of age remain underweight or stunted. The National Family Health Survey (NFHS) in its early report reflected that overall prevalence of malnutrition in 0-2 years age group was more than 50 per cent. Not much improvement is seen in the scenario as, the recent NFHS-II (1998-99) shows 46.7 per cent underweight children among less than two years age group.

The death rate among infants is highest at birth, with 60 per cent of deaths occurring within the first month of life. It is estimated that 33 per cent of the children born in India, as against 5-7 per cent in developed countries weigh less than 2.5 kg at birth. Consequently simple diarrhoeal and other gastro-intestinal disorder and common respiratory infections become major killer of infants. Those who survive are caught up in a vicious circle of disease and malnutrition (UNICEF 1981).

Malnutrition runs in an intergenerational cycle. The underweight girl children grow into malnourished adolescent girls who are likely to be malnourished mothers. Percentage of women who are malnourished is very high and they give birth to low birth weight children (Gupta et al 2001).

Along with the availability of food and the prevention of disease, there is one other major determinant of whether a young child will be malnourished or not; exactly how the infant is fed is crucial to growth in the early months of life. First of all, a child of this age needs to be exclusively breasted. Breast milk not only meets all the child's nutritional needs but also offers considerable protection against disease (both because of inherent immunological properties and because it minimizes the chances of infection through unclean water and contaminated foods) (Ramalingaswami 2003).

Childhood mortality is caused primarily by poverty, but is exacerbated by ignorance in the family and the community of the basic dietary needs of the child, particularly during weaning phase (UNICEF 1981). Since human development proceeds rapidly for the first eighteen months of life, the nutritional status of pregnant and breastfeeding mothers and the young children is of paramount importance for a child's later development (UNICEF 1998). During this period faulty infant feeding practices, such as delayed initiation of breast-feeding, pre-lacteal feeds, early introduction of top feeds and untimely and inadequate introduction of complementary foods and not primarily poverty leads to malnutrition (Aneja et al 2001).

For bringing a change in the infant feeding practices, a shift in practices and perceptions, which are deeply ingrained, is required. Nutrition communication programs, if effectively implemented, may be able to improve targeted behaviours. Counseling mothers on appropriate infant and young child feeding (IYCF) practices would be a step towards empowering them to take follow the correct practices and improve the nutritional status of their children. However before any such interventions are formulated and implemented, it is important to know the prevailing practices related to infant and young child feeding (IYCF) and the current nutritional status of the children.

Infant and Young Child Feeding (IYCF) Practices: The Current Scenario

Initiation of Breast feeding: Breastfeeding should start as soon as possible ideally within half an hour from birth, as at this time the baby's suckling reflex is strongest and the baby is more alert. Early initiation stimulates breast milk production and stimulates far better milk flow from mother's breast to the baby.

But sadly the practice of early initiation of breastfeeding is low. It has been reported to be 12-13 per cent (Daxini and Kanani 2005, and Sharma and Kanani, 2005, Sharma 2006, Sharma 2006a, Sharma 2007).

Colostrum Feeding: For the first 72 hours after delivery the breasts secrete colostrum, which provides the infant with crucial nutrition needed at this hour (Gupta 2000). As compared to mature milk, colostrum contains large quantities of protective substances, has more protein, vitamin A, vitamin K and enhances the development and maturation of the baby's gastrointestinal tract. Though, secreted in small quantities (30-90ml/day), colostrum suffices the calorific needs of a new born in the first few days of life. So, colostrum is all that a baby needs for the first few days (UNICEF 1994). However, avoidance of colostrum and introduction of other foods at a very early age are very widespread (Dixon 1992). Studies have reported the practice of feeding colostrum by only 29-61 per cent mothers (Daxini and Kanani 2005, Sharma and Kanani 2005, Kanani and Gadre 2003, Sharma 2006, Sharma 2007). Even where colostrum had been given to a good number of children (75.6 per cent in Shivpuri), in most of these cases, breast feeding was initiated only 2 days after the birth of the child or at times after 3 days, thus, depriving the child of much of the colostrum (Sharma 2006a).

Pre-lacteal Feeding: Feeds such as water, honey, gripe water, tea, animal powdered milk, given to a baby before lactation is established, are referred to as prelacteal feeds. Giving prelacteal feeds result in infection and failure of successful breastfeeding (UNICEF 1994). Furthermore, the use of prelacteal feeds may predispose mothers to continue such practices even after milk production has been established, which can interfere with the maintenance of breastfeeding (Blomquist et al 1994). In spite of this the practice of colostrums is very common. Studies have reported the prelacteal feeding to be 40 per cent - 94 per cent (Daxini and Kanani 2005, Sharma and Kanani, 2005, Srivastava and Sandhu, 2005, Sharma 2006, Sharma 2007), In a study done in Shivpuri district of Madhya Pradesh, prelacteals were given to a large number of children (65.8 per cent). Giving water before 6m of age, in most cases right from birth seemed to be the norm (Sharma 2006). In this study, more than four-fifths of the children were given plain water before they were six months of old. In most of the cases water was reported to have been given from the time of the birth itself. This itself is a constraint to exclusive breastfeeding.

Exclusive Breast Feeding: For the first six months of life, an infant does not require any other food or drink when exclusively breastfed. But exclusive breastfeeding, during the first 6 months of life is distinctly uncommon in India (5-15 per cent) and other developing countries. Instead, the most common practice is to continue breastfeeding in combination with water, other fluids or breast milk substitutes. Recent scientific research (Truong Si Anh et al 1995) makes it clear that young infants do not require anything other than breast milk not even water. Breast milk has enough water in it to meet the hydration requirements even under extremely hot and dry summer conditions of the country. Feeding anything other than breast milk, including water, is not only unnecessary but also increase the risk of diarrhoea, risk of premature termination of breast milk intake (Sachdev 1991).

Exclusive breast feeding for the first 6 months of life, protects infants from diarrhoea, whereas, non breastfed infants have thirty times greater risk of attacks of severe diarrhoea (Sur et al 2001). Exclusive breast fed infants have significantly higher proportional weight gain than the early weaned infants. Exclusive breastfeeding for first six months of life not only fulfils the necessary conditions for good health, nutrition and care but also protects the child against infections and makes them less susceptible to gastrointestinal tract and respiratory infections (UNICEF 1995).

The low birth weight babies who are exclusively breastfed have significantly better weight gain than normal birth weight babies. Thus, it can be suggested that low birth weight babies are more benefited in the form of weight gain, when exclusively breastfed as compared to those who are not exclusively breastfed (Sur et al 2001).

Although exclusive breastfeeding is advised till about six months of age. The NFHS-I data revealed that about 51 per cent of the lactating mothers in the country practice exclusive breastfeeding at 3 months of age. This prevalence has not shown a significant improvement over last six and half years as shown by NFHS-2 results (UNICEF 2000). The data shows that only 19.4 per cent are exclusively breastfed at six months and 54.2 per cent at 3 months of age. It means half the babies born in India are subjected to faulty feeding practices within a short period of three months despite all the efforts made in this direction. Studies have reported the practice of exclusive feeding for less than 3 months to vary from 27.7 per cent (Sharma 2007) to 74 per cent (Sharma 2006) to 80 per cent (Daxini and Kanani 2005) and 84 per cent by (Sharma and Kanani 2005). Bottle-feeding rate also remains the same 14.5 per cent below 12 months of age (Gupta et al 2001).

Introduction of Complementary Foods

At 6-11 months of age malnutrition among infants is about 43 per cent, which could be due to inadequate breastfeeding, not exclusive breastfeeding and inappropriate complementary foods. At two years this percentage goes up to about 63 per cent, which could again be due to inadequate food or inappropriate practices (BPNI 2003). The faltering of growth begins at 4-6 months and continues up to 24 months. The malnutrition incidence is highest in very young children, i.e. six months to twenty-four months. This onset of faltering and malnutrition coincide with the introduction of complementary foods to a child's diet (UNICEF 1995).

Breast milk is all that a baby needs until the age of 4-6 months. By 4-6 months, a mother's milk production reaches a maximum and plateaus at this volume. However, baby's growth and development continues to occur at a rapid pace during the first year of life. In order to maintain the optimum rate of growth and development, the baby at this stage needs foods in addition to mother's milk and not instead of it. This process of supplementing breast milk with fluids and foods, complementary feeds is commonly called weaning. The period starts from the time that fluids and foods other than breast milk are first introduced till the baby is no longer dependent on his mother's milk. This period, called 'the period of complementary feeds' is commonly referred to as the 'weaning period' (UNICEF 1994).

The dilemma regarding the age when complementary foods should first be given to exclusively breastfed infants is referred to as 'weanling dilemma'. From the standpoint of physiological maturation and nutritional need, giving foods other than breast milk to the infant before about four months is usually unnecessary and may entail risks, like increasing the infant' vulnerability to diarrhoea and other diseases. Moreover, because of the effect on the infant's feeding behaviour and breast milk secretion, any other food or drink given before complementary feeding is required, may interfere with maintenance of breastfeeding (Sachdeva 1994).

On the other hand, by around six months of age breastfed infants require complementary feeding along with breast milk and are fully developed functionally to cope with it. Traditionally the period between 4-6 months of age has been seen as suitable for infants to begin to adapt to different foods, food textures and mode of feeding (Akre 1989). Introduction of foods other than breast milk before four months of age into the young infant's diet decreases the frequency and intensity of suckling and as a consequence, breast milk production also decreases. Under these circumstances the food given will not be so much a complement to breast milk as a partial replacement (Akre 1989).

During the second half of infancy, when significant amounts of complementary foods are usually introduced into the diet in addition to breast milk, children in less developed countries are at greater risk of nutritional deficiencies and secondary functional disturbances than at any other time in postnatal life. During the weaning period these infants frequently consume less food energy and other nutrients, and display reduced linear and weight growth velocities compared with their counterparts in more affluent countries (Brown 1999).

It is frequently assumed that nutritional inadequacies during the weaning period can be ascribed to one or more of the following three phenomena: insufficient food availability in the household, suboptimal child-feeding behaviours, and the frequent occurrence of infections, which may interfere with nutrient intake and utilization (Brown 1999).

When foods are introduced early the baby runs the risk of recurrent infection, which is likely to result in malnutrition and allergy (UNICEF 1994). Whereas, late introduction of complementary foods lead to insufficient caloric intake resulting in inadequate weight gain as breast milk alone is not sufficient to provide the much needed nutrition (Gupta et al 2001). The baby runs the risk of sub optimal growth and malnutrition, and the baby is unwilling to accept foods when the foods are introduced late (UNICEF 1994). Despite this, in India only one-third infants are introduced appropriate complementary foods between 6-9 months.

In studies carried out in urban slums of Vadodara, only 24 per cent to 32 per cent mothers introduced top milk at the appropriate age of 6m, with a mere 20 per cent to 26 per cent introducing complementary foods at this age. The type of complementary foods given were non-nutritious, like dal water, rice water or biscuits. Thus not only was complementary feeding not introduced at the appropriate age, but the food given was inadequate and inappropriate (Sharma 2006, Sharma 2007).

IYCF Practices and Nutritional Status

Data on the relationship between various infant feeding practices and prevalence of under-nutrition show a strong correlation between the two. The age of introducing solid foods has been found to significantly affect the nutritional status of the children (Sharma 2006a). Children who were started on solid foods at 6 months of age had a significantly better nutritional status as compared to those to whom solid foods were introduced either before they were 6 months old or after the age of 6 months. Those children who were not fed solid foods had a higher prevalence of malnutrition as compared to those who were fed frequently.

Therefore the possible etiological factors found for the causation of protein energy malnutrition amongst young children are inappropriate IYCF practices, specifically, non-feeding of colostrum, lack of exclusive breastfeeding in first six months of life, late introduction of semi-solid and solid foods, dilution of top milk accompanied by faulty weaning practices by mothers (Aneja et al 2001).

It has been found that, nutrition education can positively effect changes in the attitudes and practices of mothers and is an extremely valuable tool in alleviating the malnutrition, which may occur as a result of improper feeding practices (Agarwal et al 1989).

Role of Nutrition Communication in Effecting Behaviour Change

The ultimate aim of nutrition education should be to produce nutritionally literate decision makers who are motivated, knowledgeable, skilled, and willing to choose appropriate nutrition alternatives (Lewis, 1976). In order to be effective, nutrition education must communicate clear messages with a specific behaviour-change goal for target groups (Guthrie, 1978 in Valdecanas, 1985).

Nutrition education and communication programmes have evolved from a one-way flow of communication, that is, a mere dissemination of information to persuade target groups to change food beliefs, attitudes, and habits.

Nutrition education and communication is a mechanism for interaction among participants, and as a resource, applying a co-ordinated, multi-sectoral and interdisciplinary effort, toward improving and sustaining the nutritional status of the most vulnerable groups, children and women.

While formulating a nutrition education intervention it is important to do so in the context of the socio-cultural, economic, political, and technological environments, which include food and nutrition issues. Nutrition education interventions, requires that the various causes and effects of nutrition issues and problems be addressed in a concerted manner. Thus, a systematic analysis of the nutrition and health-related needs of a community should be the base for developing an effective nutrition education programme. Thus, UNICEF's "Triple A" Approach, consisting of *Assessment, Analysis and Action* (UNICEF, 1992), needs to be used. Therefore, the first step would be a situational analysis that would help in assessing the problem (Assessment), i.e., formative research is required which would help in documenting the existing knowledge, attitude and practices. The next step would be to identify (Analyze) pertinent issues that need to be addressed through nutrition education. Once this is done, then the nutrition communication program can be formulated (Action).

Nutrition communication has been defined as an as persuasive communication that attempts to change communication knowledge, attitudes and practices (Gillespie 1981), a process, which through education, communication and education related research, tries to promote the nutritional well being of people (Gussow and Centento 1984). It is also stated as an umbrella term which covers a wide range of information and education interventions for influencing nutritional status, including nutrition education and social marketing (Lediard

1991).

For a good nutrition communication it is important to understand the beliefs, attitudes, social pressures and other factors that could influence the IYCF practices and child health. It is essential to understand beliefs that influence people. If the mother believes that performing a behaviour will lead to unfavourable outcomes, one should try to find out why. The mother is more likely to be convinced if the benefits of the behaviour can clearly be shown in an observable demonstration. Social pressures on the person or subjective norms can create various obstacles, hence influencing the opinions of the leaders in the family and community is also required for an effective behaviour change. Investigator should avoid targeting behaviours that are complicated, and include those behaviours for change process that are realistic and are critical to improve health of the participating groups. Enabling factors are those factors in the environment that make the behaviour change possible or feasible, such as adequate time, availability of health/ nutrition services, income, water supply, housing and sanitation. One should make sure that the required enabling factors, which support change, are available and that social pressures from the family or community are facilitative rather than obstructive for the target group.

Steps in Nutrition Communication Strategy Development

Careful planning is required to develop the nutrition communication strategy, which should include the following elements:

1. Formative Research: The aim of formative research is to provide a reasonably valid estimate of the prevalence of the problem and the behavioural dimensions contributing to the problem. Achteberg (1994) has suggested that formative research needs to be carried out foe the development of sound effective nutrition education material each and every time a new intervention program is initiated.

2. Behaviour Analysis: According to Rasmuson et al (1988), planning of nutrition communication must be based on a thorough analysis of the behavioural dimensions of the health problem. A detailed profile provides of the recommended behaviour pattern, listing of all discrete practices in the sequence in which they should ideally occur and the consequences of each behaviour must be constructed. Behaviour analysis provides the tools to build this list with the necessary specificity. The behaviour profile provides a broad range of potential objectives for the communication program. Once behavioural objectives are established, a planner must chose which practices the communication program can realistically address.

3. Creative Strategy Development: After the main focus of the program is decided (including cognitive and behavioural objectives), its message design and media/ channel for transmitting the message needs to be developed. A participatory approach involving the target group is again found to be most useful. Manoff (1986) has given several message design factors for developing messages, summarized below:

- Content factors: These factors include understanding the problem, identification of target audience, detecting resistance points (which must be countered and neutralised), solution of the problem including required actions.
- Design factors: The single idea – each message is more effective when it is confined to a single idea, directed at a special problem at a specific target audiences. Such messages are more likely to be absorbed, concentrated upon, and reacted to.

Language and cultural relevance- the style and expression employed must be suitable.

Distinctive message style – the sounds, look, attitude and the key language terms should be consistent from message to message. Such treatment has a cumulative effect.

Low fatigue index – a message that is interesting and captivating as well as instructive has a low fatigue index. For that a variety of visual aids and message approach needs to be developed.

- Persuasive factors: a message must be given for the reason why it is desirable. Emotions always affect decisions; therefore, empathy with the audience is essential. The audience must sense an emotional assurance that someone cares and understands the problem, and is concerned. Action capability is the compatibility between what the message expects in terms of action and what the audience is capable of doing despite limitation of income, time, food availability.
- Memorablilty factors: idea reinforcement – to fix the new idea and to persuade its adoption calls foe idea reinforcement. Theme music can be a potent reinforcement device. A repeated reference key message or phrases maximises awareness. Hornik (1985) suggested that for delivery of educational message use of many channels will be more effective than using a single channel.
- Minimising distractions – more details should not be included than what the audience needs to know. Every element must be essential to the message. The time and attention of the audience must not be trifled with.

4. Message Approach: Message approach plays a significant role in any communication strategy. Certain media are better suited for certain messages, audience and circumstances. Suitability of a media mix depends on the skills and attitudes of the audience in relation to the available media; size and attitudes of the audience in relation to the available media; size and dispersion of the audience; nature of the stimuli; local resources (both financial and technical), mature of responses we desire from the audience and the nature of reinforcement we want to be able to give (Anderson 1988).

Nutrition education and communication are now recognised as a primary form of intervention in national food and nutrition programmes.

The definitions of counseling given by Good (1945), Pepinsky and Pepinsky (1954) and Wrenn (1951) are: Good defined counseling as the "...individualized and personalized assistance with personal, educational, vocational problems, in which all pertinent facts are studied and analyzed, and a solution is sought, often with the assistance of Specialists, school and community resources, and personal interviews in which the counselee is taught to make his on decisions". According to Pepinsky and Pepinsky, "Counseling is a process involving an interaction between a counselor and a client in a private setting, worth the purpose of helping the client change his/her behavior so that a satisfactory resolution of needs may be obtained". To Wrenn, "Counseling is a dynamic and purposeful relationship between two people in which procedures vary with the nature of students' needs, but in which there is always mutual participation by the counselor and the student with the focus upon self-clarification and self-determination by the student". A recent and much accepted definition is: "Counseling denotes a professional relationship between a trained counselor and client. This relationship is usually person-to-person, although it may sometimes involve more than two people. It is designed to help clients to understand and their self determined goals through meaningful resolution of problems of an emotional or interpersonal nature" (Burks and Stefflré, 1979).

By imparting proper counseling one can improve on existing inappropriate infant feeding practices. The tools for counseling need to be focused on the mother as most decisions about infant feeding methods are made during prenatal period (Goodline and Fried 1984). Support from spouse or significant others involved in rearing the child also enhances the mothers ability to continue breastfeeding significantly longer than those without lactation support systems. All entities developing parent education material need to include information on how the father and family can support breastfeeding (Littman 1994).

Impact of Counseling on IYCF

Findings of a study on infant feeding practices of low income African

American teen mothers illustrate how cultural factors affect health practices and suggest culturally tailored interventions. Bentley (1999) found that maternal grandmothers are often primary decision-makers regarding infant feeding and that teen mothers usually follow grandmother's advice, even when it contradicts the advice of medicinal professionals. So grand mothers are targeted for educational intervention regarding the nutritional qualities of breast milk or formula and the risk of early introduction of solid foods. It is suggested that the intervention should incorporate developmental expectations of infant feeding behavior, alternative ways to manage baby crying and sleeping, and clarify the differences between adult and infant nutritional needs.

Another experimental intervention to promote breastfeeding among mothers in former Soviet Republic of Belarus, was carried out to assess the effects of the Promotion of Breastfeeding intervention trial (PROBIT). The PROBIT sites were randomly assigned to receive either an experimental intervention (n=16) modeled on the Baby friendly Hospital initiative (BFHI) of the WHO and UNICEF, or a control intervention (n=15). The experimental group was counseled with early initiation and maintaining breastfeeding and lactation and postnatal feeding. The control group continued the usual infant feeding practices. The result indicated decreased risk of gastrointestinal tract infection by 40 per cent and atopic eczema by 46 per cent in the first year of life for the breastfed babies. The breastfeeding promotion intervention, succeeded in increasing the duration and exclusivity of breastfeeding in the first year of life. Infants from the intervention sites were significantly more likely than control infants to be breastfeed to any degree at 12months (19.7 per cent v/s 11.4 per cent), were more likely to be exclusively breastfeed at 3 months (43.3 per cent v/s 6.4 per cent) and at 6 months (7.9 per cent v/s 0.6 per cent) (Kramer 2001).

Adetegbe et al (1998) assessed the impact of breastfeeding counseling programme on the prevalence of exclusive breastfeeding in rural communities of Nigeria, as breastfeeding promotion is an important intervention for control of infant diarrhea. Mothers (n=161) who had infants less than 3 months of age were indexed and were randomized into two groups. The study group (n=82) received individual focused feeding counseling, while the controls had routine advice for diarrhea. The results showed marked increase in exclusive breastfeeding prevalence for intervention group at day 7 (49 per cent vs. 6 per cent control; $p<0.0001$) and day 21 (46 per cent vs. 8 per cent; $p<0.0001$). Moreover, diarrhea recurrence at day 21 was less in the intervention group (12 per cent) than the controls (18 per cent). Thereby it can be concluded that focused breastfeeding counseling can increase exclusive breastfeeding and reduce the prevalence of diarrhea in rural communities. In a study by Landzani et al (2000), in Sovenga,

Northern province a nutrition education program was undertaken by trained local women who initiated breast-feeding on the day of birth improved significantly in the experimentals ($p<0.01$). The introduction of solid foods to infants on the first day of life decreased from 26.5 per cent to 6.3 per cent in the experimental subjects.

Research has shown that breastfeeding improves general health, growth and development of infants and significantly reduces the risk of several health problems both during early life and later years. Lower income women have been less likely to breastfeed than higher income women. Educating low-income women about the advantages of breastfeeding their babies increases the number who breastfeed (Weimer 1998).

Agarwal and Udipi (1989) assessed the impact of nutrition education to the mothers on infant feeding practices in urban families or poor socio-economic status in Bombay. The nutrition education covered the following topics, the importance of breastfeeding, supplementary and weaning foods, balanced diet, diet during pregnancy and lactation, immunization, sanitation and hygiene including safe water for drinking. The results indicate significantly higher number of mothers (18 per cent) who received higher education fed colostrum to their infants than those who did not receive any education (5 per cent). A larger percentage of non-intervened mothers (76 per cent) introduced milk and other solid foods in addition to breast milk to their infants at 3-5 months of age in contrast to 12 per cent of the intervened mothers.

Another study undertaken to empower mothers with knowledge about appropriate IYCF practices (Sharma 2007); indicated that if timely and appropriate counseling is imparted to the mothers, the infant feeding practices can be significantly improved. The mothers who received counseling on the correct IYCF practices had better practices compared to mothers who did not receive any counseling. After intervention 60 per cent mothers who had received counseling initiated breastfeeding immediately or within half an hour of birth of the child. No mother in the group not counseled initiated breastfeeding within half an hour of the birth of the child. Prelacteals were received by only 28 per cent infants in the intervened group as compared to 95 per cent in the control group. Seventy two percent mothers in the experimental group as compared to only 18 per cent in the control group fed colostrum to the infant.

The rate of the exclusive breastfeeding practiced for first six months of life by the counseled mothers was 100 per cent whereas only about 23 per cent mothers who were not counseled reported that they would practice exclusive breastfeeding for six months of life. When the impact of counseling was seen in the top milk feeding practices only 4 per cent mothers in the counseled group as compared to

37 per cent mothers in the group not counseled gave top milk before the six months of age. No counseled mother compared to all mothers not counseled practiced dilution of top milk. Majority of the infants of the mothers who were counseled (88 per cent) as compared to only 26.3 per cent infants in the not counseled group received complementary feeding at six months of age. The differences in the practices of the counseled mothers compared to those who did not receive any counseling can be regarded as the impact of counseling given to them (Sharma 2007).

In another study (Sharma 2006) a positive impact of counseling was seen on the IYCF practices of the mothers of slums of urban Vadodara. After an intervention of inter-personal counseling was given, 27 per cent of the counseled mothers and only 11.5 per cent of the mothers not counseled initiated breastfeeding within one hour after birth. 34.4 per cent and 40.7 per cent infants from both the groups received prelacteal feeds. All (100 per cent) the mothers who were given counseling and 41 per cent of the mothers not counseled fed colostrum. Rate of exclusive breastfeeding for first six months was 59.4 per cent in the counseled group, while none of the mothers in the group not counseled about the correct IYCF practices practiced exclusive feeding for first six months. Average incidence of morbidity was 0.60-episodes/ child/ month with duration 1.39 days for infants whose mothers received counseling and 0.93 episodes/ child/ month with duration 2.03 days for the infants whose mothers were not counseled. The differences seen could be due to exclusive breastfeeding.

After six sessions of counseling only 33 per cent gave top milk before six months of age while 96 per cent of the mothers not counseled top milk before six months of age. 23 per cent of the counseled mothers and 56 per cent of the mothers not counseled practiced dilution of top milk and all (100 per cent) infants and 20 per cent infants from both the groups respectively received complementary feeding at 6 months of age. These differences in the practices could be attributed to the counseling given to the mothers (Sharma 2006)

Therefore it can be suggested that nutrition education can positively effect changes in the attitudes and practices of mothers and empower them to take better care of their infants and young children.

Conclusions

Malnutrition can start before birth and can persist throughout life. Many babies are born with low birth weight and micronutrient deficiencies. Poor feeding practices during the first two years of life have immediate and often long term negative consequences on growth and development (AED 1999). There is an urgent need, therefore, for developing appropriate strategies to bring about a change in the deeply rooted perceptions regarding the infant feeding practices.

Health and nutrition education can be recommended as an extremely valuable tool in alleviating the malnutrition in infants, which may occur as a result of inappropriate infant feeding practices followed by the mothers.

Hence at community level, sustained efforts in awareness and education are necessary if related behavior is to be influenced. Sustained per natal counseling can have positive effects on breast-feeding practices. It is only through sustained intervention, that one can influence the attitudes and beliefs of the target population, which are critical elements of behavior change (Agarwal and Udipi 1989).

References

ACC/SCN. United Nations Administrative Committee on Coordination/Standing Committee on Nutrition). Fifth Report on the World Nutrition Situation: Nutrition for Improved Development Outcomes. Geneva: ACC/SCN. 2004.

Achteberg CL. Qualitative Research : What do we know about teaching good nutrition habits. Journal of Nutrition 124 : 18088-18125. 1994.

Anderson JE. The ABC model for developing communication to change behaviour. In: Effective communications for Primary Health Care. Edited by Anderson JE and Vayasevai A. Report of the Asian Regional Workshop, Bangkok, Thailand. 1988.

AED. Recommended Feeding and Dietary Practices to improve Infant and Maternal Nutrition. The linkages Project, 1825 Connecticut Avenue NW Washington, DC. 1999.

Agarwal M and Udipi AS. The impact of nutrition education on child feeding practices among low income urban Indian women. Food and Nutrition Bulletin 11 (3).

Aneja B, Singh P, Tandon M, Pathak P, Singh C, Kapil U. (2001) Etiological factors of malnutrition among infants in two urban slums of Delhi. Indian Pediatr 2001; 38: 160-165. 1989.

Bentley M. Infant feeding practices of low income African American adolescent mothers : An ecological multigenerational perspective. British Journal of Science and Medicine 49 : 108-110. 1999.

Blomquist H.K. et al. Supplementary feeding in the maternity ward shortens the duration of breastfeeding. Acta Pediatric 83: 1122 – 1126. in Complementary feeding of infant and young children. Report of a technical consultation supported by WHO, UNICEF 1995. 1994.

BPNI & UNICEF. Department of Women and Child Development in collaboration with BPNI & UNICEF. The state consultation on Infant and Young Child Feeding. 2003.

BPNI. Introducing solids (complementary feeding). 2003.

Brown. The importance of dietary quality versus quantity for weanlings in less developed countries : A framework for discussion. Food and Nutrition Bulletin 13 (2) : 23-29. 1999.

Burks H and Stefflre B. Theories of Counselling, 3rd edition, McGraw-Hill Company, New York. 1979.

CARE. India and Linkages India. PROFILES for India 2003.

Daxini M and Kanani S. Health systems research for improving quality of implementation of nutrition services in NGO implemented ICDS in rural Vadodara. Department of Foods and Nutrition, The M.S. University of Baroda, Baroda. 2005.

Dixon G. Colostrum Avoidance and early infant feeding in Asian societies Asia pacific Journal of Clinical Nutrition 1 : 225 – 229. 1992.

Gillespie AH. Applying Communication theory to nutrition education research. Journal of Nutrition Education 13 (1) : 529-532. 1981.

Gussow JD and Centento I. Nutrition education in changing world. A conceptualization and selective review. World Review of Nutrition and Dietetics 44 : 1-56. 1984.

Goodline LA and Fried PA. Infant feeding practices : Pre and post natal factors affecting choice and method and duration of breast feeding. Canadian Journal of Public Health 75 (6) : 439-444. 1984.

Gupta A. Report: promoting and supporting breastfeeding for optimal nutrition during infancy. Breast Feeding Promotion Network of India (BPNI). 2000.

Gupta A, Kushwaha KP, Sobti CJ, Jindal T. Report: Guideline for the nutrition professional – breastfeeding and complementary feeding. Breast Feeding Promotion Network of India (BPNI). 2001.

Gupta A, Sobti CJ. Faulty feeding practices and malnutrition: The link. WHO/UNICEF. 2001.

Guthrie. In: Valdecanas OC (1985) Changing concepts in nutrition information, education and communication. Ph J Nutr, 38(2): 43-50, Manila, Philippines. 1978.

Hornik R. Nutrition education: A state of the art review. Nutrition Policy Discussion Paper 1. Rome, FAO. (ACC/SCN Secretariat). 1985.

Kanani S and Gadre S. A study of care giving behaviours related to young child (6-18months) feeding among the urban poor in Vadodara. Department of Foods and Nutrition, The M.S. University of Baroda, Baroda. 2003.

Kramer MS. Innovative intervention program increases duration and degree of breast feeding in Belarus. JAMA 285 :413-420. 2001.

Landzani R, Steyn NP and Nel JH. An evaluation of effectiveness of nutrition advisors in3 rural areas of Northern Province. South African Journal of Clinical Nutrition 90 :811-816. 2000.

Lediard, M. From nutrition marketing to social marketing. Presentation at the International Nutrition Planners Forum Conference. Paris, UNESCO. 1991.

6

Gender Differences in Experiencing Childlessness

Bhamini Mehta and Shagufa Kapadia

The present research was conducted to understand an issue which has come to the fore in scientific research quite recently. Although the issue of infertility may seem to be a relatively recent concern, it has been referred to even in the ancient scriptures. The concept of the earth signifying the womb, and the seed the sperm has contextualized infertility in the gendered notions of reproduction and child bearing, especially with women bearing the societal brunt of being childless (Dube, 1986). The paper is based on a research aimed at understanding the experiences of involuntary childlessness among the middle-upper middle-income groups, residing in the urban locality of Baroda city. It focuses on the experiences and consequences of childlessness or infertility in women and men, and highlights the societal and familial beliefs about infertility and childlessness.

Infertility: A Cultural Perspective

The value of children in terms of both socio-psychological (continuing family lineage, enriching familial and marital bonds, instinctive desire to have children) and economic dimensions (support in old age) cannot be overstated. Bearing and rearing children serves critical cultural functions in hierarchical societies and confers power on women, which is otherwise not available to her.

The role of perpetrator of the human race, a role which forms a major dimension of the process of enculturation since childhood, determines the self, especially in relation to marriage. The conceptualization of self in the process of formation of identity is enmeshed with the biological givens inherited through centuries, and also the social and cultural influences that form the roots of an individual. Cultural ideologies across the world emphasize motherhood as an important and desirable part of a woman's identity, fostering privileges and reverences on her thereafter. The classical psychoanalytic assumptions too, link adult female identity to motherhood, invariably classifying all women without children as different. In a study by Alexander et al. (cited in Izzard & Barden, 2001) it was found that women without children were marginalized and made to feel different and incomplete, when faced with the cultural notions of self and gender. Social pressure for having children is manifest in most of the cultures.

For instance, in Central Africa infertile women experience social ostracism even when the incidences of secondary infertility for women are higher than primary infertility (Pearce, 1999). Similarly Thai women too are said to experience stress, low self-esteem, and feelings of incompleteness on facing infertility; further fostered by societal blame and certain acceptable activities for men such as having minor wives or visiting prostitutes for pleasure (Boonmongkon, 2000). Similarly in Egypt infertile women, irrespective of their backgrounds face stigmatization, ostracism as well as marital dissolution (Inhorn, 2000).

Significance of Parenthood in India

In most cultures marriage is associated with two aspects - one is the cordial relation between the husband and the wife, and the second is the blessing of children. In societies such as India, the reproductive role of women is highly emphasized and the onset of puberty is greatly rejoiced, often accompanied by celebrations that declare her fertility and mark her capability for future motherhood (Dube, 1998).

Importantly, a woman's status is determined by whether or not she fulfils her roles and responsibilities towards the family and the society, through her significant role of procreation. Even the unborn child in the womb of the mother plays a role in acquiring a higher status and acceptance of the woman in the community. It bestows a positive identity on her and she is recognized as fully adult and complete in the true sense on attaining motherhood (Jung, 1989). It often solidifies the marital bond and accords the woman with a position of considerable power (Riessman, 2000). The roots of such behavior lie in the religious tradition that indicates the birth of a child, especially a male, as the essential step towards the family's salvation. There are religious texts that enforce this feeling by describing the varied sufferings of childless souls after death (Kakar, 1978). As such, motherhood and womanhood are terms used simultaneously.

In case a woman is unable to conceive, she is stigmatized and rebuked by the family and the society. The woman may be ill treated or burdened with domestic chores in the family (Nene, Coyaji, Rao & Apte, 2002). The plight of a childless woman is sad; she always lives in peril of being deserted or divorced. The incidence of physical violence experienced by childless women is high. Singh, Dhaliwal and Kaur (1996) in their study of 129 childless couples seeking treatment from a primary health center in Raipur, Ambala district, Haryana found that violence was manifested in physical forms such as physical assault and frequent quarrels; psychological forms such as taunting by husband; and threat of second marriage by the husband. The woman might even force her husband for a re-marriage, just for the sake of an heir. Sayeed (2000) found that amongst childless couples with a low standard of living, the incidence of second marriages was high, and at the same time literate women had higher conjugal harmony as compared to those who were non-literate. In a community-based study of 332 women in the Ranga Reddy district of Andhra Pradesh, Sayeed (1999) found that the childless women were purposely kept away from certain ceremonies. These women hid their face from the world and refrained from any social activities.

In such societies, contemplating the idea of infertility in men is rare. However, even men are pressured to prove their virility. The father's blood not only contributes to the shaping of the child, but also gives the child a name, lineage and clan (Dube, 1986). Men too experience negative consequences of infertility, especially in the context of inter-spousal relationships. Bharadwaj (2000) highlights the distinction between "stigma" and "blame". He says that women may be primarily blamed for not having children, but stigma essentially "penetrates and attaches itself to a married body" (p.75).

Infertility: A Gendered Notion

In India, women are symbolized as the image of procreation. Motherhood is considered as a source of power for women that determines the strength of her marital bond (Gupta, 2000), and infertility is viewed as a deviance from the cultural norms and renders the woman helpless; it also provides ground for divorce, negotiable with woman's education and class structures or the husband taking in other wives. Similar practices are also reported in other cultures (Mariano, 2000; Sayeed, 2000; Skramstad, 2000). A study in Mozambique also revealed that childless persons suffer more from community's ideology regarding childlessness rather than the childless state per se (Mariano, 2000). Hence one needs to understand childlessness not only in terms of reproductive health in a physical sense, but more so as a social concern. Thus, "reproductive impairment is a medically diagnosed physiological characteristic of individuals whereas the socially constructed phenomenon of infertility involves a complex set of beliefs and values within a specific social structure" (Griel cited in Pearce, 1999, p.70).

In most societies that are patriarchal, the woman is almost always the one who is blamed for infertility in a couple (Lwanga cited in Odegaard, Folkvord, Sundby, Mbizvo & Jacobus, 2002). Researches related to infertility in men are few and affiliated to determining the medical and etiological factors associated with male fertility rather than psychological implications. Papreen et al. (2000) in their study in Bangladesh reported that infertility in men was attributed more to physical, physiological and psychosexual disorders, whereas more of supernatural causes were associated with infertility in women. Although infertility is mainly perceived to be associated with females, Gujjarappa, Apte, Garde and Nene (2002) reveal in their study on male perspective on infertility, that all men were aware that there could be 'defects' in men as well. Despite this awareness, men were reluctant to seek treatment, as they feared disgrace in the society. At times clandestine arrangements may be made to hide male infertility and to avoid dire consequences for the family's lineage (Pearce, 1999). They reported that infertile men had no worth (*tuchha*) in the society and were referred to as '*namard*', which means 'lacking in masculinity'. Similarly Papreen et al. (2000) found in their research among the urban slum population in Bangladesh that men were targets of societal ostracism on revelation of male infertility. They were not preferred for employment, have a lower status and cannot hold important positions in the community. In the same vein, Nene, Coyaji, Rao & Apte's (2002) research at the KEM hospital, Pune, including 40 couples from middle class families experiencing infertility, 12 men reported humiliating comments, use of sarcastic language, constant arguments and compensatory demands from their wives.

One way of coping for men is to transfer the blame on women. Also the society makes it easier for men, as women usually hold themselves responsible for childlessness (Khan et al, 1998). Papreen et al. (2000) in their study in the urban slums of Dhaka found that the women held themselves responsible for not having children and continued visiting faith healers, even on receiving medical evidence of their husband's infertility.

Thus, in a culture where much importance is accorded to parenthood and virility, one can imagine the boundless problems that infertility is likely to entail for both women as well as men.

Research Questions

- What is the cultural concept of parenthood; motherhood and fatherhood?
- What are the psychosocial problems experienced by women and men facing childlessness?

Objectives

- Assess the cultural and gender construction of motherhood and fatherhood as perceived by couples experiencing childlessness.
- Find out gender differences in the perceptions of childlessness and the problems faced.

Definition of Terms

- Psychosocial problems: Psychosocial problems imply the social and psychological experiences of the childless individuals as a result of the prevailing ideology of infertility in the Indian society, as well as their own understanding of the societal perceptions of infertility.

- Involuntary Childlessness: It is a condition experienced by individuals due to either self or spousal infertility.
- Childless individual: An individual experiencing childlessness due to self or spousal infertility.

Research Design and Methodology: The design of the study was essentially descriptive with an ethnographic approach. The ethnographic approach was adopted to capture the cultural realities bearing on involuntary childlessness as construed by the participants. It was felt that the qualitative nature of the research would help cull out the lived experiences of individuals experiencing childlessness. The effort has thus been to retain verbatim responses of the participants wherever possible.

Study Area: The focal group of the study comprised individuals from the urban middle/upper middle social class of Vadodara, a cosmopolitan city in the state of Gujarat, with a population of 1.5 million. The city has significant cultural variation and people of different communities and religions have settled here. It is difficult to define the middle/upper-middle class, as it constitutes a large part of the population with a range of incomes. These families do not even share a similar lifestyle, which is, in fact, determined by the caste group to which they belong, the locality in which they reside, and their own attitudes and values. In Vadodara, the middle/upper-middle income groups are the educated majority, and most of them are employed by the industries, educational sectors and/or the private firms. Each family owns at least one two-wheeler, which is either shared by the family or, in many cases, owned individually. Most women, irrespective of whether they are employed outside the home or not, own two-wheel vehicles or at least know how to ride one; this greatly facilitates their mobility.

Methodology

Participants: The participant groups comprised individuals from the middle/upper middle-income group experiencing involuntary childlessness. Men and women (not necessarily husband and wife) who were childless either due to self or spousal infertility formed the two groups.

Individuals with a family income of at least Rs. 8000 per month and education up to standard 12 were included. The participants from the group seeking treatment had been married for at least one year, whereas the group not seeking treatment would have been married for at least eight years; they had sought treatment at some point of time, either for their own or for their spouse's infertility. The study participants were selected on the bases of specific criteria mainly in order to maintain the homogeneity of the group.

There were 40 individuals, 20 women and 20 men seeking treatment for infertility and 15 individuals, 10 women and 5 men who had sought treatment earlier and had currently discontinued it, not intending to restart the process.

Method of Data Collection: In-depth individual interviews were used for data collection to elicit a holistic perspective of the perceptions and experiences related to infertility and childlessness.

The following were the main domains included in the interview schedule for the interviews with individuals experiencing involuntary childlessness: meaning of parenthood, meaning of infertility, explanations for infertility, spousal reaction/support, family reaction/support and societal reaction/support.

The schedules were prepared in English and then translated into Hindi and Gujarati, to be used according to the convenience of the participants. However, most of the participants preferred to respond in English. The schedules were pre-tested with one doctoral student from the department and one individual representing society. This was done in order to check the validity of the empirical questions.

Ethical Considerations: The ethical considerations were refined and finalised in consultation with the team of researchers/NGO representatives (researcher from Population Studies, a director of an NGO and a Lecturer from the Social Work Faculty), who formed the Ethics Committee of the project. The ethical considerations followed were taking informed consent, seeking prior permission to record interviews, ensuring protection of autonomy, rights and dignity of the participants throughout the process, assuring confidentiality, giving them the right not to answer any question or to leave the research at any point of time as well as privacy at the time of data collection.

All information and records provided by the participants were kept confidential by assigning codes for recording the data. During the interviews, if the participant did not feel like responding to any particular question, he or she had the right to say so. The recorded interviews were subsequently erased. Additionally an NGO working for women was approached to establish linkages for referrals in case a need for counselling was felt during the interviews.

Process of Data Collection

- Group presently seeking treatment: The first group of individuals who were childless was selected through practising gynaecologists. A few gynaecologists were approached and oriented to the research. Their help was requested in seeking consent from their clients who were willing to participate in the study. Handouts describing the nature of the study and assurance of complete confidentiality were given to them to be handed over to their clients. Most gynecologists had requested their receptionists or assistants to introduce the researcher to the willing participants.

- Group presently not seeking treatment: The second group of individuals who were childless was identified by the snowball method. They were briefed about the study orally, as well as given a handout describing the nature of the study. They were assured of complete confidentiality. Written consent was obtained from each individual.

The interviews were then carried out as per the convenience of the participants, either at the clinics or at their homes. The duration of each interview was approximately half an hour to one hour. Majority of the interviews with the group presently seeking treatment were clinic-based.

Data Analysis: The data was analysed qualitatively. Frequencies were calculated for the socio-demographic variables and a few other domains where it was felt necessary.

Microanalysis was done to formulate the initial categories. Coding was done at three levels. Open coding which was essential to make sense of the vast amount of data, which was qualitative in nature. This helped to code the data in the initial phase, following which axial coding was done to draw specific categories and sub-categories and selective coding was done to finally evolve categories that addressed the research questions and the objectives of the research.

Results and Interpretations

About the Participants: The age of the treatment seeking participants was in the range of 20 to 49 years, education from higher secondary to post graduation, income ranging from 8,000 to above 25,000 per month, duration of marriage between one to fifteen years, representing the nuclear as well as joint families with most of the women not employed outside the home. The non treatment seeking group was also between 20 to 59 years of age, with all of them being in the 35 plus age range except for one woman who was 28 years, education from higher secondary to post graduation, income ranging from 8,000 to 25,000 and above per month, duration of marriage between 8 – 15 years and above, representing the nuclear as well as joint families and more number of women employed outside the home.

Motherhood and Fatherhood: The groups had varied ideas about motherhood. The women were of the opinion that marriage is a preceding step to attaining motherhood. The woman gains the meaning of her life and her identity on giving birth to a child. Fatherhood is viewed more in terms of responsibility related to financial support and physical security. What became evident here was that for a woman her identity and her sense of life revolved around a child, whereas fatherhood was seen as something detached to the body and the meaning of self. Yet when it concerned the identity of the child the man and his family come into the picture, as providing the material for the woman to regenerate a being characterizing the husband's family.

> "Every girl thinks of becoming a mother. It gives a sense of completeness"
> "A lady is known by the fact that she has given birth to a child"
> "Fathers have the major responsibility to provide financial security"
> "The sperm in a man is a microchip, which contains contributions of the husband, his father, his mother and their family and the mother develops this sperm"

Importance of Parenthood: The participants in the study described parenthood in different words (see Tables 6.1). They indicated their feelings in terms of the self, the family as well as the society. They described it as a goal of marriage and family living; personal desires were cited and children were seen as bringing immense joy and happiness to the life of a married couple. They responded that every married couple would desire to have a child of their own; a child through whom their unattained wishes would be fulfilled, a child who would reflect their joys and sorrows, and importantly, strengthen the marital bond. They also opined that the family too shares the jubilation, with the child binding the family cohesively. Along with this there is the question of identity and status. The society bestows higher status on parents and the feeling expressed was that of easing social pressure on attaining parenthood. What also emerged as determining factors for attaining parenthood were certain customs and beliefs prevalent in the society such as continuity of the family lineage.

One woman participant felt that "*ma banavanu to mahatvanuj che ne*" (it is important to become a mother). While yet another woman felt that "*mara lagna ne char varsh thai gaya che to have badak hoi to saru. Have khali lage che*" (its now four years since I got married, so I feel that now I should have a child to curb the feeling of emptiness). This denotes the ideology of parenthood, thus implying the impact of childlessness, discussed in the succeeding section. Whereas men in the non-treatment seeking group were found to use more of rationalizing statements when asked about parenthood and the importance of children for them. They gave examples of children not caring for their elderly parents, "there are examples where children ditch their old invalid parents", and the experience of loneliness when the daughter leaves the parents after marriage, "suppose you have a daughter and she leaves you after 25 years.

Table 6.1: Importance of Parenthood

Category	Trt. Skg. Grp.		Non-Trt. Skg. Grp.		Total n	Illustrative Verbatim
	M	W	M	W		
	n=20	n=20	n=5	n=10		
Personal reasons						
Gives purpose to life	4	12	2	8	26	A child is important *Unse he to zindagi chalti hai, Unke siva to life hi nahin hota hai.* (There is no life without them)
Innate desire	4	6	1	1	12	A child gives you the desire to live
Support during old age	4	1	1	2	8	What about my future???
Happiness	3	2	-	-	5	Arrival of a child is a joyous occasion.
Increases social network	-	-	1	1	2	We think that if we have children then we would have a wider circle than what we have.
Achievement of unfulfilled desires through children	1	-	-	-	1	I had a dream of going abroad to study, but unfortunately it did not happen. So I think when I have a child, I will educate him abroad. The things I could not do, I will do for him.
Family and marital reasons						
Important for spouse	-	5	-	-	5	My husband says even if we have to spend lots of money a child is a must
A complete family	1	3	-	1	5	*Bachha hai to parivaar pura lagta ha.* (The child makes the family complete)
Strengthens marital bond	-	2	-	3	5	A child strengthens the relation between the husband and the wife, the life changes.

Trt.Skg.Grp. = Treatment seeking group
Non-Trt.Skg.Grp. = Non-treatment seeking group
M = Men
W = Women
Note: The total number of responses may not be equal to n because of either multiple responses given by the participants or no response.

The desire for a child is just a psychological blockage". The idea of a child representing the parental identities is also recognized. This is more evident in the treatment seeking group.

The group also talked of the importance of having a child for the family. They described this in terms of grand-parenting a child rather than the notions of continuing the family lineage for their parents.

Childlessness: A Void in Marriage

The importance of having children was indicated through expression of feelings that accompany the absence of children - depression and incompleteness (see Table 6.2). Even men reported feeling incomplete, and these were the men who had also reported being persistent with their treatment and changing a number of doctors for the same. A general "bad feeling" which participants were unable to translate in words, was reported.

Interestingly one employed woman, expressed being sarcastic with her husband during her moments of frustration. Men on the other hand did not reveal their feelings, but instead talked of their wives feelings of depression, tension and her crying for the want of a child. Here, societal orientation to masculinity was evident where men are not allowed to verbalize their feelings, unlike women who may cry in front of strangers, and thus, relieve themselves. Men did not talk of frustration in their life at all. One of the men who reported the problem of azoospermia shared that his wife would at times get angry with him (they were still undergoing treatment during the phase of the current research), and also justified her feelings of anger. In this case the woman was working, they were residing in a nuclear family and it was a late marriage, factors that were likely to enhance her bargaining power, in addition to the fact that male infertility was the cause of childlessness.

In the non-treatment seeking group, acceptance of the state of childlessness was linked with their attribution of their state to destiny. Yet, a feeling of helplessness also came through, as expressed by men.

The women were more articulate in expressing their feelings when they talked of the psychological trauma and stress of not being able to conceive, and the feelings of depression during menstruation when they again faced failure, leading to long hours of isolation and crying. This, they reported, aggravated at a later age when, after undergoing treatment for a long time they could not conceive, and their hopes started dwindling with their advancing age. Women also talked about their feelings in the absence of a child. They reported reviewing their status at times leading to negative thoughts of denial, loneliness and tension. They felt that at the level of the society, the societal attitude was either of sympathizing with their state, making the person a target of gossip or calling 'her' names such as *vanjan* (infertile), indicating that usually women are targeted. This has implications on the woman's reproductive capacity and "womanhood".

Table 6.2: Feelings Regarding Childlessness

Category	Trt. Skg. Grp.		Non-Trt. Skg. Grp.		Total n	Illustrative Verbatim
	M n=20	W n=20	M n=10	W n=5		
Feelings of Self						
Incompleteness	1	12	1	2	16	I am feeling as though I am missing something in my life.
Denial	-	5	-	-	5	
Helplessness	-	-	3	-	3	When I am all alone at home, I keep thinking about my state and cry
Acceptance of status	-	-	2	1	3	You have to accept certain facts of life. I have taken this for granted. I am practical
Feelings of Spouse						
Tension	1	-	-	-	1	For me it does not matter but I have seen her crying many times
Loneliness	1	-	1	-	2	She used to feel very upset and very lonely. While I was pre-occupied with my career
Optimism	2	-	-	-	2	She is very supportive she says *thai jase* (it will happen)
PMS (pre-menstrual symtoms)	2	-	-	-	2	She feels blue around her menstruation

Trt.Skg.Grp. = Treatment seeking group
Non-Trt.Skg.Grp. = Non-treatment seeking group
M = Men
W = Women
Note: The total number of responses may not be equal to n because of either multiple responses given by the participants or no response.

'Self' within a Larger Context: Child a Must

Marriage connotes the beginning of one's reproductive life. It provides the individual with the opportunity to prove one's fertility/virility. Society confronts couples who are unable to fulfill their social responsibilities. They report being isolated during certain occasions like '*shrimant*' (baby shower) or social gatherings such as a child's birthday party. They even felt that they were being treated as deviants, digressing from the norm. Men on the other hand reported their wives being subjected to societal queries. They viewed society as interfering with their personal lives and especially expressed that they detested persons posing questions to their wives, as they feel that these happenings had a negative psychological effect. A few men reported negative comments on their masculinity, which they found to be derogatory; these were the men who had been diagnosed as having the problem. Women too reported isolating themselves and withdrawing from social gatherings because of this.

Family and Childlessness

Most of the participants reported that the family was supportive. Women reported the natal family to be very supportive at each stage of the treatment as well as later. They described the family as encouraging, thus helping them to move ahead with the treatment (Table 6.3). Yet another reason for terming the family as supportive was also because they did not inquire about details of the treatment.

A few women from joint families reported that relatives posed inquisitive questions about their motherhood and asked them to "hurry up". Their sexual lives, for example use of contraception, were also discussed by their relatives. These women talked about identity as related to a child and a torturous life without a child.

Table 6.3: Family Attitude towards Childlessness

Categories	Trt. Skg. Grp.		Non-Trt. Skg. Grp.	
	M	W	M	W
	n=20	n=20	n=5	n=10
Family is supportive	6	13	3	2
Inquisitive	2	7	1	2
Not supportive	-	-	1	6

Note: The total number of responses may not be equal to n because of either multiple responses given by the participants or no response.

Women and a few men from the non-treatment seeking group reported isolation, neglect and rude behaviors by their family members, which in a few cases led them to establish nuclear households. The importance of the support of the family was seen in the report of a woman describing how the family ostracized her and her husband, and favored her brother-in-law and his children. She reported intense feelings of loneliness and depression and long hours of crying in isolation at a secluded place - a temple. She even shared about her disrupted personal and social life because of the family's negative attitude towards them. Women have also described their families as aggravating conditions by blaming the woman for the problem, for not supporting her husband and for suggesting that they adopt a child much against his wishes. Some families were hesitant to agree for adoption due to property matters and the feeling that the property should rightfully go to their biological grandsons from their other sons. Two men talked about how their family had created problems for their wives' which resulted into, her developing a negative self-concept.

Marital Relationships

Marriage and parenthood are intricately linked. Children are thought to bind and strengthen the marital bond. Thus, the importance of a child for an individual is likely to influence one's perceptions and attitudes towards the marital relationship. The participants reported minor conflicts between the couple, but they did not attribute the cause to childlessness. They described it as part of their marital lives. Where the husband was the source of the problem, women shared that they verbally abused their husbands, expressing their grief over not being able to conceive and having to face social inquiries due to the husbands' infertility. There are men who reported requesting their wives to disclose to the family that the problem was/lied with him (the husband), yet the wives did not, thereby bearing the brunt themselves. Marital conflicts were also reported where the husband had expressed intense desire for a child but the wife did not echo his sentiments and the age difference between the two was also greater.

> "She used to always be tensed during intercourse she was more interested to conceive than to enjoy it or take it as a normal act"
> "Sometimes we have some fights, mein *usko thoda suna bhi deti hoon ke tere kaaran mujhe bachha nahin ho raha hai mujhe. Mein usko esa pinch karke bolti hu ke kaise life ho gaya hai na?* (Sometimes I tell him that its because of you that I am not able to conceive. I tell him in a pinching way)"
> "In fact we have come closer as we are working towards solving a common problem"

In one such instance, the wife reported the husband forcing her to undertake treatment which led to disputes. Women also reported disputes over financial matters related to treatment. Men did not report any tensions or discords in their relationship because of childlessness, but they expressed their sexual lives being disturbed on account of coordinating it with the treatment procedures. They also sensed their wives being sexually disturbed because of the concern over conception. A few men also reported coming closer to each other because of this.

In the non-treatment seeking group, women reported disturbances in the marital life during the phase of treatment due to non-compliance on part of the husband in situations where male infertility was the cause. Women also talked of discord due to lack of support from the husband for the treatment and also for not consenting to adoption.

Concluding Comments

A child holds importance everywhere, irrespective of the culture or society. In India, through the child a woman gets her identity and her sense of completeness, confirming the belief that a woman is incomplete without the child and that she does not have an identity of her own. The power, respect, and position that she gets in the family and also in the society depend upon her reproductive capacity.

India being a patrilineal society, where men are the main actors in continuing the family lineage, male infertility can have serious repercussions on the man. The participants of the present research have echoed similar views. Men and women both felt that a child is necessary because it gives purpose to their lives by making it meaningful. The utmost significance of a child for one's sense of self, for smooth marital relationship and to enhance higher status in the family is evidenced in the finding that women from the non-treatment seeking group, who are in their mid 40s and 50s, still hope for this miracle to occur. This feeling is shared by almost all women, irrespective of age, employment or education. The desire to be a mother is always within the woman; but stronger than her desires are the pressures on her to bear a child from society and family. In the Indian society, especially in the middle/upper middle class, women are generally dependent upon men for financial security, Hence the child is also wanted to achieve a sense of security for old age.

Childlessness has its impact on both men and women. Both feel bad about their childless state. Childlessness affects the woman more, leaving her with feelings of loneliness and insecurity. Although men feel upset about their state, they do not report or express their feelings much, as cultural norms do not allow them to express their emotions openly.

Since children are seen as the one who strengthen the bond between the husband and the wife, childlessness can have a huge impact on the marital relationship as well. However, factors, the extent of understanding between them, whether the woman is employed or not and also their personal views about the importance of a child, determine the nature and extent of impact.

References

Bharadwaj, A. Infertility and gender: A perspective from India. In F.V. Balen, T. Gerrits & M. Inhorn (Eds.), *Social science research on childlessness in a global perspective*. Proceedings of the conference 8-11 November 1999 Amsterdam, The Netherlands (pp. 65-78). Amsterdam: University of Amsterdam. 2000.

Boonmongkon, P. Living through infertility: From loss to resolution over the life course of Thai women. In F.V. Balen, T. Gerrits & M. Inhorn (Eds.), *Social science research on childlessness in a global perspective.* Proceedings of the conference 8-11 November 1999 Amsterdam, the Netherlands (pp.28-34). Amsterdam: University of Amsterdam. 2000.

Dube, L. Seed and Earth: The symbolism of biological reproduction and sexual relations of production. In L. Dube, E. Leacock and S. Ardener (Eds.), *Visibility and power: Essays on women in society and development*. Delhi: Oxford University Press. 1986.

Dube, L. On the construction of gender: Hindu girls in patrilineal India. In K. Chanana (Ed.), *Socialization, education and women: Explorations in gender identity*. New Delhi: Orient Longman. 1998.

Gujjarappa, L., Apte, H., Garda, L., & Nene, U. *The unseen side of infertility: A study of male perspective on infertility in rural Western Maharashtra, India*. Paper presented at the International Conference on Socio-Medical Perspective of Childlessness, Goa, India. 2002.

Gupta, J.A. *New reproductive technologies: Women's health and autonomy, Indo-Dutch studies on development activities*. New Delhi: Sage. 2000.

Inhorn, M. Egyptian mothers of test tube babies: Gender, Islam, and the globalization of new reproductive technologies. In F.V. Balen, T. Gerrits & M. Inhorn (Eds.), *Social science research on childlessness in a global perspective*. Proceedings of the conference 8-11 November 1999 Amsterdam, The Netherlands (pp.149–159). Amsterdam: University of Amsterdam. 2000.

Izzard, S., & Barden, N. *Rethinking gender and therapy. The changing identities of women.* Philadelphia: Open University. 2001.

Jung, A. *Unveiling India: A woman's journey*. New Delhi: Penguin Books. 1989.

Kakar, S. *The inner world: A psycho-analytic study of childhood and society in India.* Delhi: Oxford University Press. 1978.

Khan, M.E., Kumar, N., Patel, B. C., Sikri, S., & George, P. *Infertility: Its causes and consequences - Indian scenario.* Paper presented at the International Conference on 'Reproductive health' by Indian society for the study of reproduction and fertility and UNDP/UNFPA/WHO/World Bank, Bombay, India. 1998.

Mariano, E. Conceptions about woman's childlessness and land's infertility in a Rhonga community in the South of Mozambique. In F.V. Balen, T. Gerrits & M. Inhorn (Eds.), *Social science research on childlessness in a global perspective.* Proceedings of the conference 8-11 November 1999 Amsterdam, The Netherlands (pp.136–139). Amsterdam: University of Amsterdam. 2000.

Nene, U. Coyaji, K., Rao, V. N., & Apte, H. *Infertility - A label of choice in the case of "Sexually dysfunctional couples."* Paper presented at the International Conference on Socio-Medical Perspective of Childlessness, Goa, India. 2002.

Odegaard, O. N., Folkvord,S., Sundby, J., Mbizoo, M. & Jacobus, A., *Male Infertility in Zimbabwe*. Paper presented at the conference of the IIPS India, Sujeevan Trust India and University of Amsterdam on Socio-Medical Perspective of Childlessness, Goa, India. 2002.

Papreen, N., Sharma, A., Sabin, K., Begum, L., Ahsan S. K., & Baqui, A. H. Living with infertility: Experiences among urban slum populations in Bangladesh. *Reproductive Health Matters, 8* (15), 33-44. 2000.

Pearce, T. O. She will not be listened to in public: Perceptions among the Yoruba of Infertility and Childlessness in Women. *Reproductive Health Matters, 7* (13), 69-79. 1999.

Reissman, C. K. Stigma and everyday resistance practices: Childless women in South India. *Gender & Society, 14* (1), 111-135. 2000.

Sayeed, U. Childlessness in Andhra Pradesh, India: Treatment-seeking and consequences. *Reproductive Health Matters, 7* (13), 54-64. 1999.

Sayeed, U. *Consequences of childlessness for women in Andhra Pradesh: Special reference to marital stability*. Paper presented at the Workshop on Reproductive Health in India: New Evidence and issues, Pune, India. 2000.

Singh, A., Dhaliwal, L.K., & Kaur, A. Infertility in a primary health centre of North India: A follow-up study. *The Journal of Family Welfare, 42* (1), 51-57. 1996.

Skramstad, H. Are foster children a solution for infertile Ghanian women? In F.V. Balan, T. Gerrits, & M. Inhorn (Eds.), *Social science research on childlessness in a global perspective* (pp.15-27). Amsterdam : University of Amsterdam. 2000.

7

Women and Child Health

Mini Sheth

Women and children constitute roughly 2/3rd of India's total population. The development of women has always been the central focus of the developmental planning since independence. The shifts in policy approaches in the last 50 years from the concept of welfare in the 70's to development in the 80's and now to empowerment in the 90's are fully reckoned with. Women, who are primarily responsible for the childcare need to be empowered with the basic knowledge on care practices in order to reduce the rates of infant mortality and child mortality.

Food Safety Education to Reduce Childhood Diarrhea

Diarrhoeal diseases are one of the major causes of childhood mortality and morbidity. Amongst the leading five causes of under five mortality, diarrhoeal illnesses alone account for an estimated death of 2 million children each year in the developing countries.

Such high diarrhoeal mortality and morbidity rates could be brought down to a great extent if the key causes of diarrhoea are controlled. The causes being contamination of weaning food due to poor personal hygiene, poor environmental sanitation, poor feeding practices, improper storage of food, dirty pots and utensils and fatuous customs, pets and animals. Along with these factors, low literacy level of parents, poverty, high birth order of the child and overcrowding predisposes the child to higher risk.

The World Health Organization regards illness due to contaminated food as one of the most widespread health problems in the contemporary world. Food safety especially in the weaning groups is one of the major concerns that have posed a threat to health of the children. Millions of children in the world die each year from diarrheal diseases, hundreds of millions and more suffer from frequent episodes of diarrhea and consequent impairment of nutritional status. Apart from food contamination, transmission of infection occurs by the direct contact, highly favored by the habits and customs of the people. Improper storage and handling of cooked food is equally responsible for food borne illnesses as during storage especially at ambient temperature (28-38°C) the risk of multiplication of pathogenic organisms increases. A study on 'Hazards analysis and critical control points of weaning foods fed to children under the 2 years of age belonging to low socioeconomic groups residing in urban slums of Vadodara' was undertaken by Sheth et al in 2006. *The findings showed that t*he environmental sanitation for 40 per cent of the households was poor and other 40 per cent households were rated as average. The aspects that were looked for during spot observation and in depth observation were the presence or absence of flies both inside and outside the house, infant defecation both inside and outside the house, overall cleanliness of the house, practice of garbage dumping outside the house and presence of pooled water outside the house. The personal hygiene of the mothers in five households was rated as poor that was indicated by dirty finger nails, practice of not washing hands prior to food preparation and feeding and unclean dress appearance. At the time of the survey, 6 out of 10 children were suffering from upper respiratory tract infection, 5 from diarrhea and 2 children complained of vomiting.

Salient features of the weaning foods fed to the children indicate that no special weaning foods were prepared for the children, although all the raw foods were washed 2-3 times before coking, hands of both mother and child were not washed prior to cooking and feeding; Mothers did not wash her hands in between and prior to preparation of food indicating chances of cross contamination from raw to cooked foods; same knife without washing was used for both raw and cooked foods, unclean cloth was used for wiping hands and utensils, sometimes mothers own dress was used for this purpose. Finger feeding was found to be a popular practice and children were fed generally in between the preparation of foods. Consumption of spilled food from the floor was a common practice. Most of the families fed leftover and overnight stored foods to the children. The overnight foods were occasionally warmed but not heated to boiling point before feeding. All the cooked food was kept at ambient temperatures and milk feeding bottles were not washed with soap and water before use. Only when the mothers felt that the bottles were greasy they used soap and water to wash them but none of the mothers sterilized them. The critical control points identified were high initial contamination of raw foods, poor environmental sanitation and personal hygiene of the mothers, feeding of the overnight moist food stored at ambient temperatures and insufficient steaming of these foods before feeding (Sheth et al 2000).

The weaning food samples collected from the families had high counts of coliform organisms in the range of 4.1log CFU/ml for *rice and potato vegetable* stored overnight to 3.6 log CFU/ml for rice and dal stored overnight followed by increase in counts of other pathogenic organisms including *S.aureus* (log 5.2 in overnight stored rice and log 6.1 for overnight stored chapattis) and *Bacillus cereus (log 5.7* CFU/ml *for overnight stored rice to log 6.3* CFU/ml in overnight stored chapattis*).*

These microorganisms almost doubled during overnight storage of moist cooked foods. (Coliforms are the group of organisms of the intestinal origin and are suppose to be absent in sound foods; *S aureus* if present in amounts > log3 CFU/gm are likely to produce toxins that cause food poisoning and *Bacillus cereus* are the spore forming organisms that are heat resistant and the spores usually survive the normal cooking temperatures and are known to cause food poisoning*).* Spices mixtures and mop samples collected from these families also revealed very high counts for all the organisms studied. The mop cloth that is handled often by the mothers to clean the defecation is rarely washed and disinfected and was found to be at an easy reach of the children in many houses.

Considering that food contaminated by improper handling and poor personal and environmental hygiene being responsible for a great proportion of diarrheal diseases, health education in food safety must receive high priority. Food handlers, specially mothers need to be educated on how to protect their infants and children from food borne hazards, particularly when the prevailing conditions mean that the risk of food contamination is high. The goal of the educational efforts ought to be beyond mere transfer of information. What is envisaged is to motivate and bring about sustained behavioral changes amongst the community members.

Few studies have been done which have solely focused on education as intervention and have shown reduced diarrheal morbidities amongst children. Hence considering the future implications of this cost effective strategy, a study was undertaken with the objective of assessing the effectiveness of food safety education in reducing diarrheal morbidity in children less than two years of age in urban slums of Baroda, India (Sheth et al 2006).

Strategies Developed: Prior permission was obtained from the Community Development Project Officer (CDPO) of the Integrated Child Development Services (ICDS) to work with the subjects in the community. A pre tested, structured questionnaire was used to collect information on socio-economic status (SES) and diarrhoea profile of children. The personal hygiene and environmental sanitation of the households were evaluated through observation using a 4-point scale, which ranged from poor to excellent. The environmental sanitation scores were based on the observation regarding the cleanliness of the house, presence of flies inside and outside the house, presence of feces in and around the house, water accumulation or open sewage outside the house. The personal hygiene scores were calculated on the basis of observations made on mothers in terms of cleanliness of fingernails, dress, physical appearance, hair neatness and bathing habits. Knowledge concerning several aspects of diarrhea was elicited before and after the intervention using interview schedule.

The hand rinse of children and mothers, mop, rice samples (fresh, leftover and stored overnight) were analyzed for coliforms, Total Plate Count (TPC), and Staphylococcus aureus. For determination of coliforms, dehydrated VRBA-Violet Red Bile Agar and for IPC estimation, agar powder, peptone and beef extract (Hi-Media) were used in standard proportions. Staphylococcus aureus were determined using Baird Parker Agar base (Hi-Media). The microbial analysis was carried out under aseptic condition. The colonies were counted and the counts were reported as per ml or g of sample.

Food safety education was imparted to mothers of children 6-24 months (Group 1, n=30) over a period of one month in five sessions. Group 2 did not receive any food safety education. Each session lasted for about 40-45 minutes. The messages imparted were (a) Washing hands with soap and water before and after various activities like feeding, cooking, eating and after defecation, cleaning child's nose, sweeping/mopping. (b) Not feeding leftover/overnight stores foods especially to young children and if necessary to food leftover foods, reheated to boiling point (c) Keeping the surroundings clean. The contents of each of the session were as follows:

Session 1

Theme: General introduction followed by session on causes of diarrhea.

- Basic information on diarrhea and importance of food safety.
- Information on diarrhea causing micro organisms and its sources.

Session 2

Theme: Washing hands

- Feedback of the previous session.
- Importance of hand washing.
- Flashcards showing the activities before and after which hand washing was essential.
- Chart showing merits and demerits of washing hands.
- Narration of a story "Hai! Who Daawat!" (Oh! That terrible feast!) followed by questions based on it.

Session 3

Theme: Avoidance of feeding leftover food

- Feedback of previous session.
- Importance of feeding fresh foods.
- Hazards of feeding leftover foods.

- Chart depicting the correct consumption of leftover foods.
- Role-play based on consequences of feeding leftover food.

Session 4

Theme: Keeping the surrounding clean.

- Feedback of the previous session.
- Puppet show based on the consequences of poor environmental sanitation
- Flashcards explaining the correct and wrong practices on ES

Session 5

Theme: Summarizing the messages imparted in the previous sessions.

- Feedback from the participants.

These messages were imparted using a combination of three or more aids such as charts, posters, flash cards, role play, story telling, puppet show and lectures. Various thematic slogans were used for conveying all the messages. The tools used for imparting the messages were designed keeping various points in mind such as the use of local language, clarity, unambiguity of the messages, maximum community participation, easy to operate, simple and relevant to the community, attractive enough to fascinate and stimulate action. Attempt was made to make learning real, practical and fun through seeing, hearing, discovering and doing.

The post intervention data was collected after a period of two months.

Chi square test was used to find out the differences in diarrheal morbidities and knowledge, attitude and Practices (KAP) of mothers before and after food safety education intervention.

Major Findings and Discussion

The high incidence if diarrhea in the community is often due to poor knowledge about hygiene and sanitation that emerged as risk factors for its wide spread prevalence in children from low-income communities. This is also supported by studies carried out by other investigators that revealed mothers belonging to Low Income Group (LIG) and lack of knowledge about hygiene as responsible factors for poor child feeding practices.

The educational level and socio-economic data of the households under study are depicted in Table 7.1. As can be seen, most of the families were nuclear consisting on average 4-6 members. Almost 50 percent of the mothers were illiterate whereas only 21 percent of the fathers were illiterate. Most of the families were non-vegetarians and majority (68 per cent) of them used common tap with municipal water supply for drinking and other household purposes. The monthly family income (from all sources) of majority of the households ranged between Rs. 1000 to Rs. 1,500. Forty two percent households did not have individual toilets and resorted to open defecation.

Table 7.1: Educational Level and SES Characteristic of the Families

Characteristics	Group 1 (n=34)	Group 2 (n=31)
Family Type		
Joint	14 (41)	11 (35)
Nuclear	20 (59)	20 (65)
Family size		
3	7 (21)	9 (29)
4-6	16 (47)	20 (65)
7-10	11 (32)	2 (6)
Birth order of children		
1st	13 (38)	10 (32)
2nd	8 (24)	10 (32)
3rd	10 (29)	7 (23)
4th	2 (6)	3 (10)
5th	1 (3)	1 (3)
Educational level		
Mother: Primary education	14 (41)	8 (26)
Completed H. Sc.	3 (9)	9 (29)
Illiterate	17 (50)	14 (45)
Father: Primary education	15 (44)	13 (42)
Completed H. Sc.	12 (35)	9 (29)
Illiterate	7 (21)	9 (29)
Family income/month		
Rs. 500-1000	7 (21)	9 (29)
Rs. 1000-1500	17 (50)	18 (58)
Rs. 1500-2500	8 (24)	4 (13)
Rs. 2500-3500	2 (6)	-
Type of food consumed		
Vegetarian	8 (24)	5 (16)
Non-vegetarian	26 (76)	26 (84)
Source of drinking water		
Individual tap	11 (32)	5 (16)
Common tap	23 (68)	26 (84)
Toilet facilities		
Individual toilet	20 (59)	18 (58)
Open defecation	14 (41)	13 (42)

Figures in parenthesis indicate percentages

Seventy percent children in Group 1 and seventy percent in Group 2 suffered from diarrhea of varying intensity. However, after food safety education intervention 33 percent reduction in the prevalence of diarrhea was seen in children of Group 1, which was statistically significant, whereas the occurrence of diarrhea in Group 2 remained more or less the same. This was supported by an increase in KAP of the mothers about causes of diarrhea and its preventive measures.

Before the intervention, only 27 percent of the mothers could relate both increased frequency of stools and thin watery stools as diarrhea whereas after Food Safety Education Intervention (FSEI), the percentage of mothers who could clearly define diarrhea increased to 73 percent. As regards to etiology of diarrhea, only a few mothers (23 per cent) in Group 1 attributed microbes in food as a responsible factor. However, after the intervention, 87 percent mothers held microbes in food to be a major etiology factor of diarrhea. Such observations were not noted in Group 2. Feeding leftover foods to the child, not washing hands before feeding/ cooking and keeping the house dirty were not considered as important factors for causing diarrhea by majority of the mothers in the Group 1 before the intervention. In contrast, after the intervention, a distinct positive change was seen amongst the mothers of Group 1 in these responses. The other sources of diarrhea reported by a majority of the mothers before and after the intervention were evil eye and teething.

The environmental sanitation (ES) and personal hygiene (PH) scores of the subjects are portrayed in Table 7.2. As can be seen, before FSEI, most of the households in both the groups had average ratings for ES and PH. However, after FSEI, there was a statistical significant improvement in the ES and PH scores of Group 1 household as most of them improve on ES and PH.

Table 7.2: Scores and Ratings of Environmental Sanitation and Personal Hygiene of the Households before and after the Food Safety Education Intervention

Ratings/ Scores	Environmental Sanitation				Personal hygiene			
	Group 1(n=30)		Group 2 (n=30)		Group 1(n=30)		Group 2 (n=30)	
	Pre	Post	Pre	Post	Pre	Post	Pre	Post
Excellent (18-20)	2 (7)	4 (13)	1 (4)	0	3 (10)	6 (20)	3 (10)	3 (10)
Good (16-17)	6 (20)	14 (47)	7 (23)	3 (10)	8 (27)	12 (40)	9 (30)	7 (23)
Average (14-15)	16 (53)	10 (33)	13 (43)	15 (50)	11 (36)	9 (30)	11 (36)	12 (40)
Poor (<14)	6 (20)	2 (7)	9 (30)	12 (40)	8 (27)	3 (10)	7 (23)	8 (27)

Figures in parenthesis indicate percentages

Before the intervention, 47 percent mothers in Group 1 were unaware of the association between environmental sanitation and their child's health. But after the intervention, 80 percent mothers became aware of this association. Most of the mothers attributed their child's well being to the absence of flies and mosquitoes prior to FSEI. After intervention, in addition to this there was an increase in the mothers' knowledge regarding the absence of micro organisms from the surrounding environment (such as garbage dumped outside the houses) and its association with child's health. In Group 1, only 37 percent households used a dustbin before the intervention while the rest of the households disposed the wastes just outside the house or far away from the house. However, after the intervention, a statistically significant improvement in this practice was seen as 70 per cent of the households used a dustbin to dispose the household's wastes.

The reduction in diarrheal morbidity in the present study can be attributed to mothers becoming aware of the importance of ES and PH. An improved knowledge, attitude and practice towards hygiene and sanitation were evident after FSEI. An improvement in ES scores after intervention in indicative of its success. Seventy percent of the mothers started keeping a dustbin near their houses instead of throwing wastes just outside their house, which was a breeding place for flies and mosquitoes prior to intervention. Studies have shown that education on ES and PH can reduce diarrheal morbidities'. The traditional beliefs such as "evil eye" and teething" probably existed due to the low literacy levels of the mothers (58 per cent mothers were illiterate). Such observations have also been made by Vishwanathan and Rhode. The prevalence of these beliefs continue even after FSEI, though there was improvement in other practices. This could be probably attributed to the non-coverage of this aspect in the educational package.

As regards practice of washing hands prior to feeding, cooking and eating, more mothers became aware of its importance after the intervention. In addition, the need of washing hands to avoid microbes "Jantu/keeda" was felt by 80 percent of the mothers in Group 1 that was initially felt by only seven percent of mothers.

All the mothers in Group 1 believed in washing hands with or without soap after defecation before as well as after the intervention. The reasons attributed were, "cleanliness", "hands get dirty – they smell", "because one is supposed to wash", "to avoid disease" and "to get rid of microbes". A striking difference in the knowledge of the mothers was observed after intervention with regard to the concept of washing hands with soap after defecation. This is clearly evident as all the mothers (100 per cent) reported one of the major reasons to wash their hands with soap after defecation was to get rid of pathogenic microbes.

With regard to washing hands after cleaning child's nose, 33 per cent of the mothers in Group 1 washed their hands before intervention. The major reason attributed by most of the mothers was "hands get dirty". None of the mothers knew that washing hands after cleaning child's nose could remove microbes. Whereas after the intervention, 60 percent of the mothers in Group 1 became aware of this fact.

With respect to washing hands after sweeping/moping, before FSEI none of the mothers knew that washing hands with soap after these activities could remove pathogenic microbes from their hands. After intervention, 63 percent mothers became aware of this fact.

With regard to washing their child's hands prior to giving food, most of the mothers (47 per cent) were not very particular. However, after the intervention 87 percent of the mothers in Group 1 became particular about this activity. The reason attributed by most of the mothers before the intervention was to remove soil, but after the intervention, in addition to the above stated reason, mothers washed their child's hands to get rid of microbes. The improvement in this practice was found to be statistically significant.

The agent used for washing hands by 70 percent of the household in Group 1, before the intervention was soap and water. A small number of mothers (3 per cent and 20 per cent) were also found to use ash and mud respectively. The remaining 27 per cent did not use any agent to wash their hands – they just rinsed with water. However, after the intervention all the households used soap and water to wash their hands and only 13 per cent reported the used of ash and none used mud or just rinsed with water. The improvement in this practice was statistically significant. The practice of feeding leftover foods to the child after FSEI decreased form 40 per cent to 10 per cent. Consequently there was an increase in the practice of giving leftover foods to the pets. During the intervention, emphasis was laid on the avoidance of feeding leftover foods, but at the same time, the mothers were also taught the correct methods of its consumption. Hence, after FSEI there was an increase in the percentage of mothers (from 13 per cent to 60 per cent) who became particular of consuming leftover foods only after thorough reheating to boiling temperature. A reduction from 17 per cent to 3 per cent was seen in households who ate the leftover foods without heat treatment. In relation to the perception of mother regarding how safe it is to feed leftovers to their children, 53 per cent mother prior to FSEI felt that feeding leftover food to the child was perfectly safe.

However, after the intervention none of the mothers felt that feeding cooked leftover to the child was safe and majority (57 per cent) felt that if leftovers stored at ambient temperature were fed to the child it would cause diarrhea and other problems. The number of mothers who believed in avoiding feeding of cooked leftover foods (kept at ambient temperature) to the child increased from 8 to 30 per cent. As regards to the frequency of feeding of cooked leftover foods to children, 30 mothers in Group 1 usually fed leftovers to the children prior to intervention. But after the intervention the response in this category was nil and about 83 per cent of them reported that they have completely stopped feeding cooked leftover foods to their children.

The hand rinse samples of mothers and children of Group 1 showed a decrease on coliforms, TPC and S. aureus after FSEI. A similar trend was seen with mop samples. Whereas the microbial counts in samples of Group 2 either increased or remained unchanged with respect to all the three parameters. All the samples of rice (fresh, leftover and overnight) of Group 1 showed a reduction ion the microbial counts as regards to all the three parameters. However a rise with respect to coliforms was seen in case of fresh rice whereas in Group 2 no such changes were seen. Their changes in practice were supported by knowledge gained in several areas.

The reduction in microbial counts could be attributed to reduced initial contamination of foods and consumption of leftovers only after adequate reheating. This has also been shown by Sheth et al. All these factors account for the reduction in diarrheal episode.

Conclusion

The present study was undertaken to reduce the diarrheal morbidities in children through food safety education targeting mothers. The results indicated a 33 per cent reduction in the diarrheal morbidities of the children in the Group 1 where mothers were imparted education on "safe food" practices while diarrheal morbidities among children where mothers were not counseled remained unchanged. A significant improvement occurred in the knowledge regarding hygiene and role of microbial contamination in the causation of diarrhea along with improved perception of hand washing and avoidance of feeding leftover contaminated foods as preventive measures. This was supported by reduction in the microbial counts of most samples.

The findings of the present study has shown that specific health related instructions given to the mothers such as importance of hand washing and information on feeding freshly coked food proved to be beneficial. Hence it can be concluded that foods safety education can be successfully used as an intervention strategy to reduce diarrheal morbidities in children under two years of age.

Environmental Sanitation: Before the intervention, 47 per cent mothers in Group 1 were unaware of the association between environmental sanitation and their child's health. But after the intervention, 80 per cent mothers became aware of this association. Most of the mothers attributed their child's well being to the absence of flies and mosquitoes prior to intervention. After intervention, in addition to this, there was an increase in the mothers' knowledge regarding the absence of micro-organisms from the surrounding environment (such as garbage dumped outside the houses) and its association with child's health.

Only 37 per cent households in Group 1 used a dustbin before the intervention while the rest of the households disposed the wastes just outside the house or far away from the house. However, after the intervention, a statistically significant improvement in this practice was seen as 70 per cent of the households used a dustbin to dispose the household wastes.

Personal Hygiene: As regards to washing hands prior to feeding, cooking and eating, more mothers became aware of its importance after the intervention. In addition, the need of washing hands to avoid microbes – "Jantu/Keeda" was felt by 80 per cent of the mothers in Group 1 which was initially felt by only 7 per cent of mothers.

The agent used for washing hands by 70 per cent of the households in Group 1, before the intervention was soap and water. A small number of mothers (3 per cent and 20 per cent) were also found to use ash and mud respectively. The remaining 27 per cent did not use any agent to wash their hands – they just rinsed with water. However, after the intervention, all the households used soap and water to wash their hands and only 13 per cent reported the use of ash and none used mud or just rinsed with water. The improvement in this practice was statistically significant. Studies have shown improvements in diarrheal morbidities with implementation of food safety intervention models in community.

Perceptions Regarding Leftover Foods: Questions were asked to mother regarding the management of leftovers foods, the heat treatment given to leftovers before consumption, their perception regarding feeding leftover to their child and the frequency of feeding leftovers to the child. The responses of mothers regarding these are presented in Table 7.3.

During the intervention, emphasis was laid on the avoidance of feeding leftover foods, but at the same time, the mothers were also taught the correct method of its consumption. Hence, as seen from the Table 7.4, after FSEI, there was an increase in the percentage of mothers (from 13 per cent to 60 per cent) who became particular of consuming leftover foods only after thorough reheating to boiling temperature. A reduction from 17 per cent to 3 per cent was seen in households who ate the leftover foods without heat treatment.

Table 7.3: Responses of Mothers Regarding Diarrhea and its Etiology before and after F.S.E.I.

Diarrhea	Group 1 (n=30)		Group 2 (n=30)	
	Pre	Post	Pre	Post
1) Definition of Diarrhea	4(26.7)	3(20)	5(33.3)	10(66.7)
• Thin watery stools	7(23)	4(13)	10(33)	4(13)
• Increased frequency	9(30)	3(10)	4(13)	4(13)
• Both the above	8(27)	22(73)	10(33)	17(57)
• Does not know	5(17)	1(3)	2(7)	1(3)
• Watery greenish stools	1(3)	4(13)	4(13)	5(17)
2) Etiology of Diarrhea				
• Microbes in food	7(23)	26(87)	9(30)	9(30)
• Feeding leftover	11(36)	28(93)	5(17)	5(17)
• Not washing hands before feeding/cooking	8(27)	26(87)	3(10)	4(13)
• Keeping house dirty	9(30)	26(87)	2(7)	5(17)
• Evil eye	23(77)	22(73)	28(93)	28(93)
• Teething	27(90)	24(80)	25(83)	28(93)

Numbers in parenthesis indicate percentages. The percentages may not add up to 100 due to multiple responses.

In relation to the perception of mothers regarding how safe is it to feed leftovers to their children, 53 per cent mothers prior to FSEI felt that feeding leftover to the child was perfectly safe. However, after the intervention none of the mothers felt that feeding cooked leftover to the child was safe and majority (57 per cent) felt that if leftovers stored at ambient temperature were fed to the child it would cause diarrhea and other problems. The number of mothers who believed in avoiding feeding of cooked leftover foods kept at ambient temperature to the child as it causes diarrhea increased.

As regards to frequency of feeding leftover foods to children, 30 per cent mothers in Group 1 usually fed leftovers to the child prior to intervention. But after the intervention, the response in this category was nil and about 83 per cent of them reported that they have completely stopped feeding cooked leftover foods to their child.

The study highlighted that an improvement can be brought about in the knowledge, attitude, and practice of the mothers of children less than 2 years of age with respect to their food sanitation practices by the use of FSE package. The knowledge regarding the definition and etiology of diarrhea was quite poor before FSEI. Their attitude towards sanitation and feeding was also very casual. However after FSEI, they not only gained knowledge regarding the actual causative factors of diarrhea but many of the misconceptions regarding the causative factors were corrected. These factors included presence of microbes in and around the house, poor personal hygiene and feeding of cooked leftover foods to the young child. Such improvements in the knowledge have also been reported by other investigators (Bhatia et al, 1999; Mangala et al, 2000)· The deep rooted belief such as "evil eye" and "teething" were also considered as major etiologic factors for diarrhea. These traditional beliefs probably existed due to the low literacy levels of the mothers (58 per cent mothers were illiterate). Such beliefs in this less educated communities contribute to high diarrheal morbidity. Such observations have also been made by Vishwanathan and Rhode (1990). The prevalence of these beliefs continue even after FSEI, though there was improvement in other practices. This could be probably attributed to the non-coverage of this aspect in the educational package.

After the intervention, improvements in the percentage of mothers becoming particular about washing their hands after various routine activities could be attributed to the improved knowledge of the mothers regarding hand washing. The findings of the present study agrees with other studies which have shown that specific health related instructions given to the mothers such as importance of hand washing and information on the hygienic use of latrines are beneficial (Han et al, 1989; Hoare et al, 1999).

The improvement in the knowledge, attitude and practices of mothers regarding feeding an environmental sanitation could be attributed to them becoming aware of the hazards of feeding leftover foods and the importance of environmental sanitation.

Women Health Workers as Change Agents for Improving Child Health: Health workers (who are generally women) can play a vital role in this aspect. Anganwadi Worker (AWW) working under ICDS scheme can act as effective change agents as they can bring about a positive change in the behavior of mothers and care takers. The ICDS in India is one of the largest national nutrition programs that provide a package of nutrition and health services to the vulnerable section of the population in the lower socio-economic group. Nutrition Health Education (NHE) in the scheme is envisaged as the main plank to enhance the mother's capability to look after the nutrition and health needs for her child. Though NHE is an effective component of ICDS, most of the evaluation studies of ICDS program reveal that it is one of the weakest components in terms of implementation. The main reasons for this lapse were inability of AWW to find time for NHE during her busy work schedule, low credibility of the AWW as a health workers, extremely limited participation of ICDS supervisory staff, poor community participation and lack of planning. Similarly Seshadri and Gopaldas

(1985) observed that the time spent on NHE by the AWW was less than 10 per cent of total time spent in all activities. AWW are not well equipped to handle NHE in terms of content, educational methods and aids. The training of AWW should not only cover nutrition and health education, it should inspire the confidence in them to become agents for change.

AWW can bring about a positive change in behaviors of the community people effectively because their regular home visits enable them to establish close links with mother, thus enhancing prospects for maternal and child health. Therefore health education through AWW as change agents on a large scale is needed to raise the level of public awareness of the factors leading to spread of childhood diseases. Food safety education as an intervention through change agents is an effective and inexpensive tool in bringing about the change in attitudes of mothers and caretakers.

In view of this, another study was undertaken to bring about changes in knowledge, attitude and practices of mothers of children 6-24 months of age through FSE. Food safety education was imparted to mothers of children 6-24 months of age (Group 1) over a period of 15 days through the Anganwadi workers

Selection of Subjects: Eight anganwadi centers were randomly selected from the urban slums of Baroda. From these, 200 households (25 under each anganwadi worker (AWW) working in the ICDS set up), were purposively selected with children in the age group of 6-24 months.

Baseline Survey: The baseline data of all the 200 households was collected with respect to their socioeconomic status, diarrhea profile of the children, knowledge attitudes and practices of mothers (KAP) regarding child feeding practices and microbial detection of hand rinse samples of both mothers and children).

Diarrhea Profile: At the time of interview, mothers were asked regarding the episodes of diarrhea that the child underwent and their severity in the past one month. The WHO definition of diarrhea as well as the criteria of judging the severity of diarrhea obtained from the pediatric department of Sir Sayajirao Gaekwad Hospital of Baroda, was considered as tool for establishing the diarrhea profile. According to this, children having diarrhea were categorized into those having mild (3-4 loose watery stools in 24 hours), moderate (5-6 loose watery stools) and severe (more than 6 loose watery stools which resulted in signs of dehydration and required medical attention).

Knowledge Attitudes and Practices (KAP): Information on KAP was collected with respect to mother's knowledge on 'What causes Diarrhea', child feeding practices with an emphasis on hand washing practices, environmental sanitation and personal hygiene using a pre-tested structured questionnaire and spot observations.

Determination of Enterococci in Hand Rinse Samples of Mothers and Children: Presence of Enterococci in the hand rinse samples of 50 mothers and 50 children was done using the 'Hi media' rapid Enterococci test kit. The mothers and children were asked to rinse their hands into a broad mouth funnel with sterile water into sterile bottles containing the test medium. The change in color from yellow to dark green indicated the presence of Enterococci.

Training of the AWW: Food safety education was imparted to 8 anganwadi workers in two sessions using calendars and pamphlets, role play and charts encompassing the key messages of causes of diarrhea, washing hands, keeping the households and surroundings clean and not to feed the leftovers foods stored at ambient temperatures to children. Food safety material (calendars and leaflets) was distributed to them to be further distributed to the mothers at the time of home visits. It was ensured that the anganwadi workers educated each mother regarding safe feeding practices and the consequences of severe diarrhea. Post intervention data was collected after a period of two months from the households as per the base line.

Statistical Analysis: To the data on spot observations, scores were assigned to the practices of personal hygiene and environmental sanitation and were rated as excellent, good, average and poor. The effect of intervention was determined using chi-square test. The effect of intervention on KAP of mothers regarding their knowledge on: causes of diarrhea, safe feeding practices, personal hygiene and environmental sanitation was studied using Student's t-test. In order to study the impact of intervention on diarrhea profile, percentages of children having diarrhea in varying degree of severity was calculated and compared.

KAP of Mothers Regarding the Etiology of Diarrhea, ES and PH: There was an improvement in the perceptions of the mothers regarding diarrhea, after FSEI. Most of the mothers became aware of the various etiological factors for diarrhea. Ninety per cent of them attributed not washing hands as a cause of diarrhea in children. Also 46 per cent became aware that feeding coked moist leftover foods stored at ambient temperatures for more than 8 hours is a causative factor for diarrhea in children.

The success of the present study can be attributed to the cumulative effect of improvement in all the factors such as ES, PH and feeding practices of the mothers.

All the mothers in Group 1 believed in washing hands with or without soap after defecation before as well as after the intervention. The reasons attributed were, 'cleanliness', 'hands get dirty – they smell', 'because one is suppose to wash', 'to avoid disease' and 'to get rid of microbes'. A striking difference in the knowledge of the mothers was observed after intervention with regards to the concept of washing hands with soap after defecation. This is clearly evident as all the mothers (100 per cent) reported one of the major reasons to wash their hands with soap after defecation was to get rid of microbes.

As regards to washing hands after cleaning child's nose, 33 per cent of the mothers in Group 1 washed their hands before intervention. The major reason attributed by most of the mothers was "hands get dirty". None of the mothers knew that washing hands after cleaning, child's nose could remove microbes whereas after the intervention, 60 per cent of the mothers in Group 1 became aware of this fact.

With respect to washing hands after sweeping/mopping, before FSEI, none of the mothers knew that washing hands with soap after these activities could remove pathogenic microbes from their hands. After the intervention, 63 per cent mothers became aware of this fact.

As regards to washing their child's hands prior to giving food, most of the mothers were not very particular. However, after the intervention 87 per cent of the mothers in Group 1 became particular about this activity. The reason attributed by most of the mothers before the intervention was to remove soil. But, after the intervention, in addition to the above stated reason, mothers washed their child's hands to get rid of microbes. The improvement in this practice was found to be statistically significant could be comprehended more effectively by the mothers because of their high literacy rate, that was reported to be quite low in earlier.

References

Akram, D.S. and Agboatwalla, M. A model for health intervention. J. Trol. Pediat., 1992, 38, 85-87.

Alam, N. Predictors of diarrhea in young Bangladeshi children. J. Trop. Pediat., 1999, 41, 278-281.

American Public Health Association (APHA). Recommended methods for the microbiological examination of foods. APHA Inc., N.Y., 1958.

Aneja, A., Chhikara, S., and Kaur, P. Effect of age and education on knowledge of rural women regarding health. J. Dairying Foods and Home Sci., 1998, 17, 2, 141-144.

Association of Analytical Chemists (AOAC). Official methods of Analysis Microbiological Methods, 1995, 17, 32-35.

Bhatia, V., Swami, H.M., Bhatia, M., and Bhatia S.P.S. Attitude and practices regarding diarrhea in rural community in Chandigarh. Ind. J. Pediat., 1999, 66, 499-503.

Birmingham, M.E., Lee, L.A., Ntakikiora, M., Bizimane, F. and Deming, M.S. A household survey of dysentery in Berundi, Implications for the current pandemic in Sub-Saharan Africa. Bull WHO, 1997, 75, 1, 9, 45-53.

Campbell, M.E., Gardener, C.E., Dwyer, J.J., Isaacs, S.M., Krueger, P.D. and Ying, J.Y. Effectiveness of public health interventions in food safety: A systematic review. Can. J. Public Health, 1998, 89, 3, 197-202.

Gutierrez, G., Tapier, C.R., Guiseapre, H., Reyes, H., Marting, H., and Kumati,J. Impact of oral rehydration and selected public health interventions in reduction of mortality from childhood diarrhoeal diseases in Mexico. Bull WHO, 1996, 74, 2, 189-197.

Han, A.M. and Hlaing, T. Prevention of diarrhea and dysentery by hand washing. Trans Roy Soc. Trop. Med. Hyg, 1989,83,128-131.

Hoare, K., Hoare, S., Rhodes, D., Erinoso, H.O., and Weaver, L.T. Effective health education in rural Gambia. J. Trp. Pediat. 1999, 208-214.

Kaul, M., Kaur, S., Wadhwa, S., and Chhibber, S. Microbial contamination of weaning foods. Ind. J. Pediat, 1996, 63, 1, 79-85.

Mehta, S. Infant feeding practices of women in LIG. M.Sc. dissertation. M.S. University, Baroda (unpublished thesis), 1993.

Pinfold, J.V. Analysis of different communication channels for promoting hygiene behaviors. Health Edu. Res., 199, 14, 5, 629-639.

Pisani, V. Improving personal and domestic hygiene Does it reduces diarrhoeal diseases. M.Sc. dissertation, London School of Hygiene and Tropical Medicine, 1994.

Rowland, M.G.M., Barrell, R.A.E and Whitehead, R.G. Bacterial contamination of traditional Gambian weaning foods. Lancet, 1997, 1, 136-138.

Sheth Mini , Renu Gurudasani, Vishwa Mistry, Swati Mehrotra, and Subhadra Seshadri; Food safety education as an effective strategy to reduce diarrheal morbidities in children less than two years of age, The Ind. J. Nutr. Dietetics, 2006, 43, 22-26

Sheth Mini and Monika obrah; Dirrhea prevention through food safety education, . Indian J. Pediatr, 2004, 71(10),879-882

Sheth, M., Sharma, S. and Patel, J. Hazard analysis and critical control points of weaning foods. Ind. J. Pediat, 2000, 67,6, 405-410

Vishwanathan, H and Rhode, J.E. Diarrhoea in rural India – A Nationwide study of mothers and practioners (All India summary). Vision Books, New Delhi, 1990, 17-60.

World Health Organization. Fact file diarrhoeal diseases, Dominant communicable diseases South East Asia Region DCD, SEARO. 1995.

World Health Organization. Life in the 21st century – A vision of all. The world Health Report WHO Geneva, 1998.

8

Health Status of Women

B. Suguna and G. Sandhya Rani

Among the human rights, right to health is the basic and essential right and it must not be a target of any discrimination. Women have the right to the enjoyment of the highest attainable standard of physical and mental health. The enjoyment of this right is vital to their life and well being and their ability to participate in all areas of public and private life. Health is the state of complete physical, mental social well-being and not merely the absence of disease or infirmity. Women's health involves their emotional, social and physical well-being and is determined by the social, political and economic context of their lives, as well as by biology. But the irony is that women themselves are many times denied of this basic right. This situation is due to women's vulnerability which arises from the physio-social environment in which they live in addition to various other factors.

For the past so many years, many studies have shown the importance of women's health. It is now well accepted that women's health status has got an impact on the health of the children, family and community. In spite of several studies and rapid technology advances many women still suffer preventable mortality and morbidity. While some improvements have been recorded in physical quality of life indicators, health status of women remained precarious, rather it is worsening. After numerous conferences, meetings, and symposia framed on women's health, worldwide programmes have been initiated from 1987 on wards specially to reduce the maternal mortality and morbidity. To highlight certain outcomes of inequity and discrimination, women's life span in total is found to be important. Various phases which are important due to a number of reasons include: pre-natal period, adolescence, reproductive period and elderly phase.

Women's health status is determined by many socioeconomic factors, and is one of the major determinants of health. Women's health status affects their proportion in the population, working hours, income, and their overall contribution in the work place as well in the society.

In women, nutrition forms the critical part of their overall health status. It is stated that the food intake in the lifetime comprises of the following:

- their energy output and workload
- their control over resources for house hold food security and
- their roles in the food chain etc.

Factors Affecting Women Health

Fertility: The fertility rate is high, in our country which on an average is three children per woman. It is an important contributory factor for female mortality and morbidity. In our country childbirth closely follows marriage which occurs at an young age (30 percent of Indian women are married between 15 to 19 yrs). Child birth during adolescence poses greater health risks as the girls themselves are undergoing growth and their body system is not yet fully developed. Further, the women have closely spaced pregnancies affecting health of the mother, infants and siblings.

Status of Women: This is best assessed by the autonomy they have in decision making and the access they have to the outside world. Most often, the women do not have freedom to spend money, freedom to take family decisions and to have control over their reproductive lives. This then, leads to discrimination in the allocation of household resources like food, medical care, education etc.

Education: Education empowers people to think rationally and logically. The literacy level in women remains lower than that of men because of various socio-economic and cultural factors. It is known that women's educational level and the health status is closely linked and so are the fertility levels. Education is extremely important determinant also for infant and child health. As seen in the National Family Health Survey, the proportion of underweight among children of illiterate mothers is 60 per cent, compared with 36 per cent among children of mothers who have completed middle school or higher.

Work: Women, are sometimes burdened with multiple productive functions. In addition to bearing children, they sometimes carry out strenuous Physical tasks combined with limited food intake, doing labour intensive work during their pregnancies without the needed rest, resume work before they have fully recovered. In rural homes they are also exposed to heavy smoke form kitchen fires which is extremely hazardous to their health.

Utilisation of Health Services: There can be several reasons that the health services are not properly utilized. In rural areas, especially, women may not be aware of the nearest health centres, or may not perceive the services provided to be of any benefit to them or cannot travel the distances alone. On the other hand, availability of health services is limited in rural areas. Moreover, women in urban sectors also do not realise the importance of their own health status, neither are ready to make any special efforts to keep up their health.

Cultural Factors: Preference for sons over daughters is quite deeply embedded in the Indian psyche which effects the status of women with all its consequences. Other factors also play a role, for example the belief, that reduction of food intake during pregnancy will lead to low weight foetus whose birth is easy. According to UNICEF report (1998), 58 per cent of women in Gujarat and 42 per cent in Maharashtra were reported to have reduced their food intake during the pregnancy.

Measures for Improving Women Health

Women's health has a well marked space in the overall development of a country. The care women provide to the children, determines child health and survival. To improve the status of women, they should have a predominant role in all decisions, have the education and competence to be economically independent and self-reliant.

The importance of reaching women during pregnancy for health services and care is increasingly being recognized as a critical issue for improving the maternal health, birth weight, birth outcome and child health. The population control approach based on the principle of "Health of All" emphasises reaching every resident within the geographical area with health information, services and supplies. Women with children (under two) including lactating women, need to be reached with education and counselling so that they know how to feed and care for the child, thereby contributing to better nutrition and enhanced child survival. Strengthening coordination between various government agencies and NGOs at the grassroots level is required to reach the high-risk population on health status.

Health Education: Health Education is one of the best means to empower people to adopt healthy behaviour and lead a satisfying, socially useful and productive life. People need to be aware of their potential for improving their own health through their own efforts.

Health education is a long term process concerning changes in knowledge, feeling and behaviour and hence, a very challenging task. It involves understanding people's behaviour and knowing the reasons behind that cause. Based upon the existing knowledge, attitudes and behaviour they have to be first made aware, followed by an input of necessary knowledge and skills to ultimately motivate the people to change with regard to their health. Thus it is a slow and long term process which has to be customised depending on the needs of the people, problems faced by them as perceived by them, and as perceived by health agencies, age-group, socio-economic group and the cultural background.

Adequate Nutrition through Appropriate Diet: A balanced diet is a must, at it provides all essential nutrients in the required amounts and proper proportions. Nutrients that we obtain through food have vital effects on physical growth and development, maintenance of normal body functions physical activity and health. Thus the diet must provide adequate calories, proteins, vitamins and minerals (including the micro nutrients) for health and achieving the maximum growth potential. The nutrient requirements vary depending on age, sex, work pattern, climate and the physiological stage of the person.

This is a low cost balanced diet. When possible, extra cup of milk must be given to women children and adolescents. During pregnancy and lactation, increase food. By approximately one-fourth the amount. People who are non-vegetarian may substitute part of the pulses with egg/meat/chicken/fish.

Important Physiological Stages

Adolescence: Adolescent period (teenage) is characterised by rapid increase in height and weight, hormonal changes, sexual maturation and wide swings in emotional status. Adolescent growth spurt starts at about 10-12 years in girls and two years later in boys. Development of critical bone mass is essential during this period as this forms the base for better bone health in later life. Adolescents particularly require more calcium. Though recommended dietary allowances for calcium are about 400-600 mg/day only, it is desirable to have higher quantities of calcium for adolescents to achieve high peak bone mass.

Pregnancy and Lactation: These are demanding physiological stages. In India, it is observed that diet among women form the poorer groups are essentially similar during pre-natal, pregnant and lactating period. Consequently, there is a widespread maternal malnutrition. The daily diet of a woman who is pregnant should contain additional 300 calories, 15g of protein and 10g of fat as compared to their diet before the pregnancy stage. The requirement further increases during lactation by 500 calories, 25g. Protein and fat per day. Folic acid, taken throughout the pregnancy, reduces the risk of congenital malformations and increases the birth weight. The mother as well as the growing foetus need iron to meet the higher demand for RBC (red blood corpuscles in blood) formation.

Calcium is essential, both during pregnancy and lactation. Iodine intake (though the intake of iodised salt) ensures proper mental health. Vitamin A is required during lactation to improve child survival. Nutrients like vitamins B and vitamin C need to be taken by the lactating mother. To meet the additional demand, pregnant/lactating women should eat a wide variety of foods. The quantity of food should be approximately one fourth more than what she had been consuming earlier.

Programmes for Women

Main programmes which deal with this important issue are as follows:

Reproductive and Child Health (RCH) Programme: Was launched in 1997 to provide a programme which is need based providing high quality and integrated services. This programme integrates the earlier Child Survival and Safe Motherhood Programme with the Family Welfare.

Programme along with the additional components of management of the reproductive tract infections and adolescent reproductive health. Thus, this programme addresses women's health throughout the life cycle. In the ninth five year plan (1997-2002) the Planning Commission made specific recommendations for the prevention and control of anaemia in pregnant women.

The National Nutritional anaemia Control Programme which is under the RCH programme aims at decreasing the prevalence and incidence of anaemia in women significantly during the reproductive age especially in pregnant and lactating women and preschool children. The programme focuses on provision of iron and folate supplements in the form of tablets (IFA) to high risk groups, and to pregnant and lactating women. Women receive 100mg of elemental iron and children are given 20mg iron per day. Since the absorption of iron is not too good in our Indian diets, a special emphasis on promotion of foods, rich in vitamin C is given as it helps to increase absorption.

The short duration of ingestion of IFA during pregnancy is not likely to benefit haemoglobin status. For this, we need to begin the IFA supplementation during adolescence, so that the young girl enters marital and reproductive stage in better state of health.

Integrated Child Development Services Programme (ICDS): Under the Ministry of Human Resource Development, this programme is meant for the most vulnerable groups i.e. the pre-school children, adolescents, pregnant and nursing mothers. It is the world's largest and most unique outreach programme providing a package of services comprising of immunization, health check-ups and referral services, supplementary feeding, growth monitoring and promotion, pre-school and non-formal education, nutrition and health education (NHED) and treatment of minor illness. The programme works towards convergence with other supportive services, such as safe drinking water, environmental sanitation, women's empowerment programme and adult literacy.

Special Intervention: Under ICDS is meant for adolescent girls in the age group of 11-18 years. The aim of the scheme is to meet their special needs of self-development, nutrition, health education, literacy, recreation and skill formation. The scheme was introduced in 507 selected blocks and so far 3.9 lakh adolescent girls have been covered.

Conclusion

Considering health in a broader perspective, protection of health of women (at all ages) is most important in order to build a sound and healthy nation through socio economic development. Public sector programmes providing primary health care and services for women are directed to maternal and child health. In addressing inequalities in health status and unequal access to and inadequate health-care services between women and men, Governments and other Sectors should promote an active and visible policy of mainstreaming a gender perspective in all policies and programmes, so that, before decisions are taken, an analysis is made of the effects for women and men, respectively. Primary health care network needs careful reflection. Given the importance of infrastructural facilities as a prerequisite at rendering health services to women, there is an urgent needs to improve the existing health infrastructural facilities especially in rural areas.

References

April Harding, Alexander. S. Perker, Private Participation in Health Services, The World Bank, Washington. DC 2003.

Campbell White, Thomas W. Merrick, Yazbeck, Reproductive Health, The World Bank, Washington. DC 2006.

Gulati. S.C., Rama Patnaik, Women's Status and Reproductive Health Rights, Har–Anand Publications, New Delhi, 1996.

Sapsford R., Bullock-Saxtion. J., Markwell, S. Women's Health, W.B. Saunders Company, Singapore.

9

Reproductive Health Status of Women

Shalini Sharma and Simran K. Sidhu

Women and child health received a major attention after the International Conference on Population and Development (ICPD) in Cairo 1994. Government of India being signatory to the ICPD implemented unified programme for Reproductive and Child Health (RCH), as it was considered essential to human welfare and development. A reproductive health approach means that people have ability to reproduce and regulate their fertility; women are able to undergo pregnancy and child birth safely; obstetric and gynecological disorders are addressed; the outcome of pregnancy is successful in terms of maternal and child health and their well being; and couples are able to enjoy sexual relations free from fear of pregnancy and of contracting diseases (Fathalla 1988).

It has been observed that Indians have witnessed a commendable improvement in their health during last decades with several health parameters showing upward trends. (Tables 9.1) But disturbing trends of declining state of women's health, which assumes critical significance in the context of expending population cannot be ignored. The development initiatives taken so far to benefit women can by no mean be called adequate. Even after decades of planning and socio-economic development, Indian society is still reluctant, if not vehemently opposed to give due importance to there women despite the fact that it is they who shoulder majority of the familial, social and economic responsibility.

Indian women, by and large, have a poor reproductive health status, as is evident from the NFHS data. For assessing the reproductive health of woman, the NFHS-I incorporated the following variables: antenatal care (ANC), immunization of pregnant woman, institutional deliveries and assistance at delivery. Proper ANC is crucial for the good health of both mother and child. NFHS-I data show that, among all the women who have given any live birth in the four years preceding the survey only 62.3 per cent of mothers have received various types of ANC services. All pregnant women are expected to receive doses of tetanus toxoid vaccine to be protected against tetanus. Two or more doses of this vaccine during pregnancy were received by only 53.8 per cent of all mothers.

Table 9.1: Important Health Parameters in India

S. N.	Parameter	1951	1981	1991	Current Level
1.	Crude Birth Rate (Per 1000 population)	40.8	33.9	29.5	25.0 (2002)
2.	Crude Death Rate (Per 1000 population)	25.1	12.5	9.8	8.1 (2002)
3.	Total Fertility Rate (TFR) (Per Women)	6.0	4.5	3.6	3.1 (2001)
4.	Maternal Mortality Rate (MMR) (Per 100,000 live births)	NA	NA	437 (1992-93)	407 (1998)
5.	Infant mortality Rate (IMR) (Per 1000 live births)	146 (1951-61)	110	80	63 (2002)
6.	Child (0-4 yrs) Mortality rate per 1000 children	57.3 (1972)	41.2	26.5	19.3 (2001)
7.	Couple protection rate (%)	10.4 (1971)	22.8	44.1	48.2 (1998-99) NFHS
8.	Life expectancy at birth Male Female	 7.2 36.2	 54.1 54.7	 59.7 (1991-95) 60.9 (1991-95)	 63.9 (2001-06) 66.9 (2001-06)

Source: Ministry of Health & Family Welfare and Office of Registrar General, India

The situation is not much different as for the coverage for iron and folic acid tablets is concerned which forms a prophylaxis against nutritionally induced anaemia among pregnant women. According to the NFHS-I, only 50.5 per cent of women had this coverage. Another important thrust of maternal health services is the encouragement of institutional deliveries attended by trained health professionals to ensure better health for the mother and child. The proportion of institutional births (25.6 per cent) is also very low in India.

Both international and national organizations – such as the World Health Organization (WHO), United National Population Fund Association (UNFPA), Population Association International (PAI) and Population Foundation of India (PFI) have attempted to measure the reproductive health of women with the help of certain set of indicators. The most recent index of reproductive health has been computed by PAI (2001). It puts India in moderate rank, with a score of 44.8 on a scale ranging from 0 to 100. To ensure good reproductive health, knowledge about the reproductive history that includes the age at marriage, number of children, spacing between the children, contraceptives use etc. are the necessary pre-requisites. In northern India strong preference for male child is pervasive across almost all castes and classes, the manifestations of this preference is in the form of gender discrimination & disparities in health care, food intake, education, & labour contribution from an early age. Female foeticide is the horrendous face of this discrimination Early marriage leads to women's poor health through direct and indirect mechanisms. It does so through increased fertility by exposing women to cumulative risk of pregnancy. These teenage wives and mothers often have little ability to participate in decision about child bearing and may not be able to negotiate the use of birth control. Such decisions directly influence the maintenance of their high fertility rate leading to poor health, complication of pregnancy, pre-natal and neo-natal mortality & low birth weight.

Women, particularly rural women from low socio-economic status have a little say on issues of family size, when to bear a child, spacing between children. Women by and large do not have a right to take decisions related to the choice of contraceptives to be used. Empirical evidence shows that contraceptive use contributes to fertility decline and to improvement in women's health independent of other status variables (Shen & Williamsons 1997). Female contraceptive use reflects both the demand & the supply side of contraceptives. Women's demand for contraceptives reflects their control over decisions concerning child bearing & their knowledge about family planning. On the supply side, their use of contraceptives reflects the availability, accessibility and use of governmental and non governmental educational, family planning and health services. The public health system emphasizes on permanent methods like sterilization or IUD's. But it has been observed that it is the women only who is supposed to take such precautions. In fact female sterilization accounts for 95 per cent of all sterilizations. (Office of the United Nations Resident Coordinator in India, 2001).

In addition to strong knowledge base of family planning practices, reproductive health could be measured in Antenatal, Natal and Post-natal stages, which represents three successive chronological phases of pregnancy.

Antenatal Care

The antenatal period is the care provided to a pregnant women beginning right from conception to the onset of the labour. During antenatal period medical and psychological needs of pregnant women need to be addressed. Various health promotion messages are given and women are screened for potential risk factors. ANC includes the following preventive and curative services like:

- Two doses of tetanus toxoid immunization.

- Intake of iron & folic acid tablets.
- Supplementary nutrition, nutrition and sanitation education for pregnant women.
- Clinical examination for hemoglobin (Hb), urinary tract infections (U.T.I.) and R H factors.
- High prevalence of anaemia among pregnant women indicates that there is high risk of pregnancy related complications such as high maternal mortality, low birth weight, obstetrical complications etc.
- WHO recommends four antenatal visits however it is the quality of visit rather than number which matters. So here the role of health workers, their counseling the quality of PhD's & other infrastructural facilities are of great importance.

Natal Care

Natal Care is care provided to the pregnant women at the time of delivery can be attained if following variables are:

- Place of delivery. Traditional deliveries were conducted at home in the presence of family members as it was viewed as a natural process, not requiring any medical assistance. But now it is accepted that institutional deliveries are definitely safe.
- Reproductive and Child Health (RCH) requires that 85 per cent of childbirths in India should take place in hospitals. But surveys showed dismal progress in this regard. NFHS-II states that only about 34 per cent deliveries in India take place in medical institutions. Many factors cause this problem the main being-inadequacy of infrastructure, relatively high cost and preference for home delivery (Pachauri 1996).
- Trained assistance during birth certainly has an impact on maternal health and mortality. Births that take place in non-hygienic conditions or births that are not attended by trained medical personnel are more likely two have negative outcomes in the form of maternal and infant mortality.
- The use of disposable kits during home deliveries by trained dais is highly recommended otherwise the chances of sepsis are too high.

Post Natal Care

Technically, the post natal period starts from delivery of placenta & continuous for 42 days thereafter. Once the baby is born, the prime concern is to provide postnatal care services to both the mother & her child. Postnatal care is the support (medical, psychogical) provided to lactating women after the delivery till 6 weeks to both mother & child.

This includes:

- Home visits by health workers.
- Treating health ailment reported after delivery.
- Promoting breast feeding practices.
- Intake of supplement diet.
- Infant weight, Infant immunization, health care, nutrition & sanitation practices to control neonatal and infant mortality.

Apart from these preventive and curative practices there are some socio-economic and cultural constraints that are playing havoc with the health of pregnant women. These constraints need to be urgently tackled & addressed in order to improve the overall quality of life & let the millions of women lead a fully productive life.

Cultural Constraints on Girls

Discrimination against women is pervasive in all walks of life. Gender stereotypes that are prevalent since birth extend into childhood, adulthood, during the pre and post marital phase of a woman's life. Strong favoritism for male children is reflected in the form of biased and rigid attitudes with regard to girl's bearing (female foeticide) rearing (female infanticide) & to a girl's education, training & socialization. Her physical, mental & emotional well being is not given any attention neither with in home by his so called 'own' (parents & siblings) nor outside home by state or other social institutions. She is left to the mercy of first their fathers, then husbands & finally their sons.

The overall implication of the secondary treatment, unequal access to the resources is that the women grow up maintaining 'a culture of silence'. Reproductive life is a very personal, private and secret matter in our society. Due to cultural taboos, discussion of this issue is not encouraged & sanctions forbidden. Due to this socio-cultural atmosphere women who are neither well educated, not well connected, often get wrong & faulty information abut various family planning practices. Relying on such wrong practices, often they put themselves at the risk of life. This 'Culture of Silence' that surrounds the issue of reproductive health is against the effective treatment and prevention of problems associated with reproductive health. Articulation of choices and exercising their rights is a distant dream even basic provisions are neglected due to socio-cultural taboos (Anand 2005).

Maternal Mortality

"Whose faces are behind the numbers? What were their stories? What were their dreams? They left behind children and families. They also left behind clues as to why their lives ended so early". (Surg Wadm & Punita Arora 2005).

One woman dies every five minutes in India from maternity related causes. The estimated 1,00,000 maternal deaths annually in India are, 20 per cent of the world's total of 5,00,000 presenting a grim picture (NFHS-II 1998-99). Rise in maternal mortality rate (MMR) from 407 to 500 as per the latest estimates (The Tribune 27 July, 2005) presents the grave scenario of women's health. According to the WHO, "A maternal death is defined as the death of a woman while pregnancy or within 42 days of termination of pregnancy, irrespective of the duration and site of the pregnancy, from any cause related to or aggravated by the pregnancy or its management but not from accidental or incidental causes". Maternal Mortality Ratio is the ratio of the number of maternal deaths per 1,00,000 live births. The MMR is used as a measure of the quality of a health care system.

In India, hemorrhage (25.6 per cent) ranks first as the cause of maternal death, followed by sepsis (13 per cent), toxemia of pregnancy (11.9 per cent), abortions (8 per cent) and obstructed labor (6.2 per cent), while indirect causes together total 35.3 per cent. Indirect causes such as malaria, anemia, HIV/AIDS and cardiovascular diseases complicate pregnancy or are aggravated by it.

The National Health Policy (1982) aimed at reducing the maternal mortality in India from the over 400 per 1, 00,000 live births to less than 200 per 1, 00,000 live births by the end of year 2000. But even in 2005, we are far from this target. A new scheme for the protection of women from the risk of maternal mortality called Janani Suraksha Yojana (JSY) was launched by the Prime Minister along with the National Rural Health Mission (NRHM) in April 2005. The expected outcome of NRHM covering the period 2005-2012 is spelt out in the mission documents (Bose 2007). The first outcome is to reduce the infant mortality rate (IMR) to 30 per lakh live birth & the second outcome is to reduce MMR to 100 per lakh live births (GOI 2005).

Conclusion

A cost effective package of good quality services should be developed to address the needs of specific client groups in various settings and to make these available and accessible to all, especially to the poor and the disadvantaged. Providing comprehensive reproductive health services to all is desirable goal. Since there is enormous caste, class diversity in India among regions and states, no single package of services can be recommended for nation wide implementation. Thus development of a comprehensive reproductive health service package is recommended that should include:

- Focused government intervention is of paramount importance in this effort.
- Prevention and management of unwanted pregnancy.
- Services to promote safe motherhood & child survival
- Better roads & transport facilities connecting rural to urban areas..
- Nutritional services for vulnerable groups.
- Prevention and treatment of reproductive tract infections and sexually transmitted diseases (STD's & HIV/AIDS) etc.
- Prevention and treatment of gynecological problems.
- Reproductive health service for adolescent.
- Health, sexuality and gender information, Health education and counseling of couples to make them understand the importance of various family planning & pregnancy related practices.
- Lady health workers and dais should be trained by state health department.
- Accountability of public health center's (PHC'S) in case of untoward events of maternal mortality.
- NGO's should come forward to extend help to this vulnerable section of the society.

To address reproductive health needs it is necessary to bring about a change in focus from top-down, target driven population control approach to a gender sensitive, client based approach. Also, the reproductive health programme must be designed to enhance access (physical & social) and improve the quality of services, particularly from the perspective of the user. The involvement of man is also equally important.

References

Anand Meenu, Women's Reproductive Health-Dismal Reality, *Social Welfare* 52(1), 10-17. 2005

Bosc Ashish, Speeding up Reduction in Maternal Mortality: Chasing a mirage? *Economic and Political Weekly* XLII (3), 206-208. 2007

Fathalla M, Research Needs in Human Reproduction (14) E. Diczfalury, P.D. Griffin and J. Kharina (eds), Research in Human Reproduction, Geneva: WHO. 1988

GOI: National Rural Health Mission (2005-2012): Mission Document, Ministry of Health and Family Welfare, Government of India, New Delhi, April, 28. 2005

Shen C and Williamson J B., Child mortality, Women's status, Economic Dependency and state strength: A cross-National study of less developed countries" *Social forces*; 76:667-94. 1997

Surg Wadm & Arora P., Maternal Mortality- Indian Scenario- MJAFI (61(3), 214-215. 2005

10

Empowering Older Women for Successful Ageing

Indira Mallaya and Bhagyashree Hakim

Old age population is increasing rapidly due to changing fertility and mortality regimes over the last 40 to 50 years. The size of India's elderly population aged 60 years and above, is expected to increase from 71 million in 2001 to 179 million in 2031, and further to 301 million in 2051.

India is one of the few countries in the world where males outnumber the females whose life expectancy at 60 and 70 is slightly higher than that of males. Older women are more dependent on family members for support due to substantive differences in the ages of women and men, differential life expectancy between males and females, and, differing proportion of old men and women who remarry. (Gulati & Rajan, 1999)

Old age is a developmental process wherein the individual enters the last phase of her development. Over the years, studies have focused on the not so positive side of growing old, especially for women in patriarchal societies such as India. The present context makes an effort to highlight the more productive or successful side of ageing. It then goes on to suggest strategies to help older women live their old age in an empowered manner by living life in an active and a dignified manner .Old age is also a continuous process of gaining new experiences. In other words, it is the time to add life to the years and thereby get life satisfactions. Erikson (1963), is the first developmental theorist to describe old age as a fully participatory phase, which helps broaden the social network in life. Havighurst cited in Beraon, L.B., (1996) emphasized remaining active in later life and replacing lost roles with new roles. This philosophy gave rise to the first connotation of successful ageing that emphasized old age as a 'most rewarding positive experience'. This outlook took on a domino effect and, other theorists began to perceive old age in a positive manner.

Some of their thoughts may be summed up in the following manner.

Productive ageing emerged in the 1980's.In 2004, Lupine, S.J.& Wan, N., opined that Baltes (1990), stressed the importance of reflecting areas of competences to help older persons to make accommodative shifts in the desired areas, to help maintain a positive sense of self by adaptation to changes and demands in everyday living.

Rowe and Khan (1998) expanded the definition of compensating for one's goals in accordance with loss of abilities, by suggesting three major steps of successful ageing i.e., avoiding disease, engaging in life and maintaining high physical and cognitive functions.

According to Beraon L.B., (1996), Schaie and Willis (1996), coined the term optimal ageing which involved a general strategy of being selective in one's efforts in using alternative strategies and activities to compensate for the losses associated with the ageing process. They also quoted Gibson (1995) who they said, looked at successful ageing as reaching to one's potential and arriving at a level of physical well being in old age, which is pleasing for both, self and others.

In conclusion, the philosophy of Erikson (1963), characterizes the last stage of development as working out a balance between Ego integrity versus Despair. He opined that the ability to reminiscence and reflect on one's life, gives rise to either satisfaction and happiness or dissatisfaction and unhappiness, depending on how one thinks one has lived one's life. This stage of life has been reached after having taken care of things and people, product and ideas and; after having adapted to the success and failures of existence. Thus, reminisces allow one to judge how one has lived life up to old age from, an inner perspective that could be termed as psychosocial in nature.

Psychosocial Perspective on Successful Ageing

A view on the psychosocial perspective of successful ageing may be drawn from different sources in order to focus on the key concepts having a philosophical base of human development. In the present case effort has been made to draw from theories, which provide an understanding of the key features of successful ageing. They are, Baltes' theory of selection, optimization and compensation, Erikson's eight stages of human life which cover the psychological aspects of the personality, Wenger's (1994) definition of social support networks and Neuhaus' (1982) family and friendship networks system. The latter two cover the social aspects of personality.

Thus, psychologically speaking, the development of an individual can go on till the end of life. However, technically speaking, it denotes a wider procedure concerned with expression of emotions as well as with giving information. The issues deal with reflections of self and the past, feelings with regard to the current situation and needs, about life and ideas or views from the outside.

At the core of the personality of the elders, is the perceived self-image or self-identity, which rules their behaviours and interactions with fellow human beings. Some of the crucial psychological issues emerging in old age that need attention are:

- Grandparenting issues
- Need to come to terms with one's lifetime aspirations, achievements and outcomes
- Sense of loss / bereavement
- Lifestyle changes due to disease
- Coping with pain and disability
- Fear of further physical deterioration or dependence
- Anxiety and depression
- Coping with spouse's fatality
- Boredom/loneliness
- Dissatisfaction with children
- Poor concentration and memory loss

The social component in old age, deals most with the support system in a person's social system, i.e. in the general social environment or ecology within which a person lives. This environment is made up of an informal system including family, friend and neighbours (McGuire, 1991, p.2, cited in Mallya. I, 2003). Social support consists of positive things wherein individuals provide help, guidance, care and so on, to each other. Family support refers to emotional, instrumental and financial assistance obtained from one's own family. Affirmation, feedback, money, effort and information giving, form some of the support types. The factors identifying the types of support are family size, living arrangement and communication pattern, to name a few.

Communication patterns of the elders are observed through social interaction patterns among families, friends and neighbours (Himabindu, 2002). Sibling interactions are seen to contribute to instrumental functions, such as providing goods and services.

The older persons are mostly known to interact with their peers. If it is intergenerational contact, it is within the family. Many factors affect the elders' social network, such as the size of the family and gender. Since older women outlive men, older men are still likely to be married as well as having surviving sisters. Marriage brings in a wider range of individuals as "potential support".

Wenger (1994) has evolved a model of five types of support networks, which consist of a core of family members with some friends and neighbours, averaging 5-7 members involved in support. The five types of network are a result of biology, migration and moving patterns and temperament. Different chance combination of thee factors, result in different types of networks and lifestyles. These networks would be defined as family dependent, locally integrated, local self contained, wider community based and private restricted (Wenger, 1994, pp.12, 25-26).

In urban India, the elders find help and support within families, from the neighbours and from friends, in that order, in times of crises.

A set of key features seem to emerge from the above psychological and the social perspectives that can be termed as a psychosocial perspective and psychosocial indicators of successful ageing.

These keys will provide part of the content in designing programs for older women.

Key Features of Psychosocial Perspective

- Life review and reminiscing.
- Selection of goals and selective changes in adaptive capacity.
- Occupied in life activities.
- Coping in life.
- Family roles and responsibilities.
- Peer culture.
- Socially active.
- Generational patterns of interactions.
- Social support networks which are either family-based or community-based.
- Maximizing gains and minimizing losses.
- Selection of optimal goals and canalizing them in order of priority.

Key Psychosocial Indicators

Many authors have undertaken studies on sample of older women cutting across income groups and settings, to come up with select, psychosocial indicators on successful ageing. Naik (April, 2006) came up with the following indicators.

- Cultural identity, social relations, physical powers and variety of interests emerged as values that had greater life satisfactions.
- Social interaction and integration is an important determination of successful ageing.
- Personal factor is important for good adjustment.
- Solitary and group activities that are meaningful e.g. reading, traveling and like-minded friends promote a happy feeling.
- Preplanning post retirement activities and perusal of hobbies and chosen activities, add to quality of life.
- Satisfaction is derived from social support, positive attitude to life and from perceived control.

- Outdoor exercise and remaining fully independent in daily activities, add to self worth.
- Not perceiving the self as weak and disabled even with chronic health problems contributes to successful ageing.

(Source: Naik, A., April, 2006.Successful ageing by older persons from middle income groups. Masters' dissertation, MSUB, Vadodara).

Women and Successful Ageing

India has about 65 million elderly and in about 10 years it may go up to 80 million or more. In recent years, there has been a steady increase in the average life expectancy. The women outlive men due to biological differences, apart from better medical and other facilities today. The women's crucial role within the family domain as well as their contributions to family support in various forms embracing social, psychological, emotional as well as economical are taken for granted or ignored. As the women continue to age, their contributions to society, despite their increasing age, underscore the need for their welfare Bagchi (1997). Bali (1997) has dealt with the problem of life satisfactions of older women as, has been studied by scholars like Motwani (1986), Bal Krishnan (1990), Bal Krishnan et al (1990), Chadda (1991) and Pothen (1990).

The highlights of these studies may be summed up as follows:

- There is a close relationship between life satisfaction and purposeful striving.
- Females and males differ significantly with regard to self-concept discrepancy and life satisfaction.
- Females exhibit greater hopelessness, alienation and life satisfaction, and self-esteem.
- Life satisfaction is related to locus of control, formal activity, social role, supports and religiosity as predictors of life satisfaction.
- The well being of elderly females is dependent on several factors, namely, social, economical, psychological, and health.
- Well-being is also dependent on basic needs, feelings of being wanted, useful and respected.
- The feeling of being regarded as an integral part of the family evokes a sense of pride in the women and provides them with meaning to their existence. It enhances their self-esteem and dignity.

Towards Empowering Women for Successful Ageing

The above section gave an understanding about the old age as a stage with emphasis on psychosocial functioning. One must also consider the biological, physical, areas of a women's development for meaningful intervention. However the major focus of this chapter is to use the psychosocial approach for designing program strategies for empowering women on successful ageing.

The section will cover different aspects of program development in the following order.

- Goals and outcomes of programme
- Objectives of programme
- How do older women learn?
- Participatory approach in programme
- Strategies for programme implementation
- Conclusion

It is very important to think of goals and the outcomes when one is setting out on a path of successful ageing. Some of the goals may be summed up as follows. If a programmer keeps them in mind while planning a program for older women, it will become need based and meaningful. They will lead to awareness of change in oneself and in their social relationships. These are critical in enhancing everyday life practices and well being of older women. The, goals/outcomes may be as follows:

- Maximize the life satisfactions.
- Maximize the social interactions with family and friends.
- Have a positive self-evaluation

Objectives of Programmes

- Recognize and strength ability and commitment of family to provide care to older women.
- Generate awareness on issues of old and generate enhanced measures to address them.
- Facilitate productive ageing.
- Popularize concept of lifelong preparation for old age at individual and societal level.
- Promote health care, housing and income security needs.
- Promote practices of good health and care.

How Do Older Women Learn?

Programmers should keep in mind the behaviours outlined by Hiemstra, R., 1993, regarding the learning patterns of older women (aged 55 years and older). A crucial point to be noted here is that these women (as learners) should first be helped to examine personal strengths and weaknesses in light of their educative potential. They may be assisted to complete self-inventories or self-concept measures. Such an approach empowers the women to decide about what they want from the program.

Learning Behaviours

- They engage in more learning activities, are more self-directed, and appear to have greater life satisfaction.
- They are more likely to study personal or self-fulfillment type topics.
- They are more likely to express a preference for future learning activities that are expressive (delayed gratification) rather than instrumental (immediate gratification) in nature.
- Situational (arising from one's situation in life) and dispositional (self-perceptions) barriers to learning are more likely to be expressed than are institutional ones (institutional practices and procedures).
- They are more likely to using reading and travel as educational resources.
- They seem more reflective in their thinking.
- They seem less critical (both in the sense of being discerning or being judgmental) in their thinking.
- They seem able to pull from what I call their "inner resources" to overcome obstacles to learning.
- They generally appear to have a greater margin of power over load in overcoming obstacles until permanent health decline sets in.
- They appear less self-directed but this apparently can be overcome with appropriate training and experience.
- Learn new skills, including computer skills.
- Become increasingly more self-directed.
- Be taught to use their past experiences in learning new material.

Self-inventory for Women

The following questions will induce change in the older women by providing insight and self-awareness with the help of a facilitator who will help the former, to restructure their lives.

1. Where am I today?
2. How did I get here?
3. What do I need?
4. What do I want?
5. What is the status of my affairs?
6. What am I capable of doing?

7. What are my strengths?
8. What are my weaknesses?
9. What are the opportunities for me?
10. What are my adversities? How I overcome them? How I have to let go?
11. Where do I want to go from here?
12. How do I get there?

(Source: Monk, A. A quality of life framework, 1981(pg 92). In, Ageing and retirement, edited by Mc cluskey, N.G & Borgatler, E.F., New Delhi: Sage).

Participatory Approach in Programme

A participatory approach is always welcome for participants as they take ownership for their action and above all feel empowered to conduct matters and become more confident as they go along. The programmer may act as a facilitator to set the right note and keep things on track.

Some of the approaches which have been found meaningful:

- **Involve** older women directly in defining their own needs, in designing and implementing programs that respond to these needs and in evaluating the effectiveness of these programs in relation to their health and well being.
- **Acknowledge** the full range of factors that contribute to older women's health and well being including societal attitudes, social justice and feeling of isolation.
- **Promote**, acknowledge and utilize older women's knowledge and skills and the vital role life long learning plays in increasing a person's capacity to maintain their own health and well being and to contribute to community life.
- **Encompass** the rich diversity of older women's experience and cultural backgrounds.
- **Include** one or more forms of gentle exercise, health and lifestyle information in a discussion format, peer support and social interaction.

Strategies of Programme Implementation

Herewith are some strategies outlined for empowering older women towards successful ageing. These have been put together from a review of Indian literature that deals with programmes for older women.

Reminiscing Therapy

Is a recall method that helps one to focus on the positive aspects of life so that a person can draw inspiration and fresh motivation to cope with life's challenges and come out with flying colours, to express themselves and share about past experiences. In helps to maintain memory span and keep mentally alert. An urban sample of women came up with reminisces which embraced their stages of childhood, adolescence and adulthood as well as the present stage of ageing. These behaviours had provided them with the inspiration to go on in life and feel happy in their old age abut a job well done with their lives. An overall picture of the behaviours with positive connotation is given below. It may be noted that the reminisces of the sample had both negative and positive connotations. But the positives far outweighed the negatives. The positives are grouped under the headings of major events in life and satisfactions in life.

Major Events in Life

- Major milestones were reached quite independently, such as getting a good education, getting married and having children, as well as settling them.
- Dealing with crises by using social support and coping strategies. The crises included being saved from drowning to coping with family illnesses and deaths. Thus, converting the crises into learning experiences and thereby coming out stronger from them.
- Fulfilling family goals at various stages as required, and setting a better standard of living.
- Securing scholarships to study abroad.

Satisfactions in Life

- Guiding children from own life experiences.
- Taking part in extra curricular activities, such as sports and singing.
- Traveling to new places.
- Having a well-rounded personality through parental disciplining practices.
- Transmitting knowledge to the next generation.
- Fulfilling family needs as and when required.
- Doing social service.
- Getting help for child care and so on, from family and colleagues at job.
- Developing good and sustainable qualities such as honesty and loyalty.

Thus it is clear that the sample had a good support system at home and at the job wherein the family and friends played a crucial role especially at crucial times and at crucial junctures in life, with respect to their jobs and child care.

Promoting Health Care

The systems of the elderly slow down due to advancing age and wear and tear of the bodily organs. Thus it is imperative to screen elders before there is onset of health problems/early stage of problems. General signs of failing health or related problems and chronic medical conditions may be identified by medical intervention, so that timely help may be provided to them.

Some of the problems could be eye disease or surgery, diabetes and hypertension. A general medical examination is conducted to give more emphasis on certain aspects such as hypertension, eye examination, nutrition or dietary intake, breast examination, urine examination, haemoglobin, blood examination and weight.

Physical fitness promotes a sense of wholeness or the overall well being of a person. Corbin and Lindsey (1985) in Khan, G. & Maqbool, 1998, have said that there are several kinds of knowledge and practices, which are considered important for maintaining health and promoting well being among the elderly. These may be interpreted to the older women so that they can lead empowered and active life.

- Understanding how your body works.
- Developing healthy eating habits and regular exercise.
- Getting periodic medical check-ups.
- Keeping your own medical records.
- Monitoring your health.
- Selecting personalized physical exercises and walking.
- Evaluate and modify your exercise programme.
- Being an active participant in your own health care.
- Managing anxiety and stress effectively.
- Being aware of health hazards in your life style, workplace, and environment.

Keeping physically fit involves the above mentioned self- help programmes especially suited to women's needs and interests.

Providing Psychosocial Support

Psychological issues of women need to be dealt with. The issues may be regarding the stresses and strains of being old. Or, feelings of fear of loneliness, an uncertain future and ultimate death need to be addressed.

- Giving counseling and alleviating the health and psychological problems will help them to live with confidence, respect, dignity and happiness. Counseling sessions on topics such as nutritive diets, interpersonal relationships in families, sound health practices, legal rights, psychological problems such as depression and loneliness.
- Discussion groups, to share opinions and emotions.
- Celebrate grandparents' day so that a bridge is developed between generations in a given community.

- Pets may be used for companionship and for satisfaction of caring.
- Group games physical and mental activities will increase movement and improve concentration and let off steam.

Occupational Therapy

Occupational therapy may be provided to the women wherein they earn and learn by doing group or individual activities from the food or any other cottage industry. The same will increase their sense of independence, provide functional use (cognitive and perceptual included) to their body parts; and, stimulate and motivate them to do better in life.

- Examples of occupational therapy are: Gardening potted plants, music both religious and social events with music decreases loneliness, handicrafts: sewing, knitting, crochet, lace. Other examples are recreation and entertainment programs.
- Income generating activities such as making pickles, papads, agarbatties, candles, flowerpots and vases, printing on saris.
- Leisure time activities in communities: Visits to fairs, beaches, temples or religious places for recreation and socializing.
- Hobbies and doing voluntary social service wherever children need them. Older women can give love and warmth to children in hospitals or at an orphanage.
- Volunteering for social service wherever possible.

Compiling Booklets and Handouts

It is a good idea to collect a pool of information from available research studies, the Internet, colleges or from books and write up on need-based topics for women. Simple language and a reader friendly style is always welcome. Some examples of the topics are:

- Nutritious recipes
- Special foods, which are easy to chew, swallow and digest.
- Dietary recommendations
- Household remedial tips
- General health and fitness exercises
- Legal rights for elders
- How to make a will
- How to invest money wisely
- How to identify simple signs and symptoms of health problems
- Income generating activities

Ashramadharama Perspective of Life for a Hindu

Vanaprasha (as a retiree) and Sanyasa (renunciation and preaching) are the last two stages of life according to the Hindu worldview, during which they are expected to retire from active social life and give up all their worldly goods. It entails distributing one's property and possessions and rearranging one's priorities. Reflecting on and reviewing one's life, withdrawing into oneself, and being one with god, are key features of these stages.

Core Principles of Erikson's Last 2 Stages of Psychosocial Development

Generativity vs. Stagnation: During middle adulthood, we establish our careers, settle down within a relationship, begin our own families and develop a sense of being a part of the bigger picture. We give back to society through raising our children, being productive at work, and becoming involved in community activities and organizations. By failing to achieve these objectives, we become stagnant and feel unproductive.

Ego Integrity vs. Despair: As we grow older and become senior citizens, wc tend to slow down our productivity, and explore life as a retired person. It is during this time that we contemplate our accomplishments and are able to develop integrity if we see ourselves as leading a successful life. If we see our lives as unproductive, feel guilt about our pasts, or feel that we did not accomplish our life goals, we become dissatisfied with life and develop despair, often leading to depression and hopelessness.

Strategy: Group discussion on the pros and cons of above two theories with respect to successful ageing. The principles and concepts, which are useful for leading a productive life in old age.

Conclusion

A feedback loop of theory research and practice guides a programmer to offer meaningful programs on successful ageing to older women. This is well illustrated in the present text. It is hoped that the information will prove useful to different agencies and organizations that work for older women. These women need to feel empowered if they are to be independent and feel empowered to dcal with the changing scenario of old age.

References

Bagchi, K., The plight of females in India: An overview. In, Bagchi, K. (Ed.) Elderly females in India: Their status and suffering. New Delhi: Help age India, pps.7 to 21. 2003

Bali, A.P., Elderly Females: A Silent Majority. In, Bagchi, K. (Ed.) Elderly females in India: Their status and suffering. New Delhi: Helpage India, pps.23-44. 2003

Beraon L. B Successful ageing: what does the good life look like? (Electronic version) Journal of gerontology. 1996

Gulati, L., & Rajan, S.I., The added years: Elderly in India and Kerala (Electronic version). Journal of Gerontology, 38 (6), 7 (16-724). 1999

Hiemstra, R. Older women's ways of learning: Tapping the full potential. Paper presented at the conference entitled" The enduring spirit: Woman as they age". University of Nebraska at Omaha held on April 1-3, 1993

Khan, G. & Maqbool, S. Self-help programmes for the well being of the elderly. Helpage India: Research and Development Journal, Vol. 4 (2&3) June1998, pps.16-21.

Lupine .S.J. Wan .N Successful ageing; from cell to self (Electronic version). Laboratory of human research, Douglas centre, department pf psychiatry, McGill University Canada. The royal society pp. (1421-1423) 2004

Mallya, I. Implications of international migration of children on older persons: A case study in rural Gujarat. Doctoral Dissertation, Department of Human Development & Family Studies, The M.S. University of Baroda, Vadodara, pp.1-143, (2003).

Naik, A. Views on successful ageing by older persons from middle-income group. Masters Dissertation, Department of Human Development & Family Studies, The M.S. University of Baroda, pp. 1- 60, (2006).

Prakash, I.J., Assistive technologies for improving quality of life of older people. Helpage India: Research and Development Journal, Vol. 6 (1), October 1999 –January 2000, pps.22-26.

Rajan, S.I. Demography of ageing. In, Ageing in India: Situational analysis and planning for the future. Dey, A.B. (Ed.). New Delhi: Govt. of India and WHO, 2003.

Rowe, J.W., & Khan, R.L Successful aging. New York: Pantheon. 1998

Part II: Education and Training of Women

11

Adult Education for Women

Rameshwari Pandya and Richa Kapoor

It is believed that illiteracy is the most serious human ailment and it is a great pity that Indians have entered the 21st century with most of its men and women, illiterate and poor. Adult literacy programme can be an effective mobilizing force in bringing about the much needed structural changes for which adult education needs a solid footing and a sound theory of learning.

Brief History of Adult Education

After the formation of the popular ministries in 1937, some of the states undertook adult education programme in various parts of the country. The Second World War in 1939 however, acted as a deterrent to the growth of adult education movement. Therefore, no spectacular result was achieved. However, a beginning was made and the movement was endowed with respectability and supported from various quarters. The Indian Adult Education Association, at its conference in Rewa in December 1947 recognized that education of the masses should be given the highest priority. The concepts of social education emerged in this period. The Central Advisory Board of Education at its meeting in January 1948 expressed the view that the organization of the adult education in India has become necessary. During the period 1949-52, the aim of adult education was to enable the members of their communities to work for achieving their social, economic and political development. After 1952, adult education programme became an integral part of the planned programmes. Social education organizers training centers were set up in various parts of the country, and public library movement was given a fillip. Use of radio as medium of education began to be recognized and the Ministry of Information produced a number of educational documentaries.

At the national level, in 1956, an important step in the field of adult education was the establishment of the National Fundamental Education Centre, whose functions included training and orientation of key personnel, experimentation in preparation of materials, conducting research and evaluation in the field of adult education.

Another milestone in the field of adult education was the launching in 1967-68 of the three dimensional integrated programme of farmer's training and functional literacy. This was the first time that the three central ministries, namely, Agriculture, Information Broadcasting and Education co-coordinated for imparting functional literacy to the farmers in the high yielding variety programme areas.

Yet, another effort in the field of adult education was the launching of non-formal education programmes during 1975-76 in the country for out of school youth and adults. A significant step in the field of adult education in the country was the launching of National Adult Education Programme all over the country on October 2, 1978 with an uphill task of covering ten crore illiterates in the age group of 15 to 35. Also in 1978, the universities were involved in a substantial way in the national adult education programme of Government of India.

In 1983, the UGC converted the Centre for Adult Education into full-fledged university departments of adult and continuing education. To implement the recommendations of the review committee on role of university towards the community, the UGC, in 1989, instructed that all extension programme must be conducted in area or community adopted by a university department or an affiliated college. This helped ensure development of a relationship between university, college and the community. Colleges were provided with grants to open a community education centre. This centre was to function as an extension centre of the college. In 1992, the university extension departments were asked to ensure that the communities adopted colleges for eradication of illiteracy and conducting continuing and adult education courses on a regular basis. Today, universities in the country are involved in nation-wide extension programme through Departments/centers set up and funded by UGC. These institutions are involved in programmes like literacy, post literacy, continuing education and science for people, environmental education, legal literacy and technology transfer by involving students and teachers.

Need and Significance of Adult Education

Adult education is an impelling need; the need is so imperative and over-powering that all men and women must be helped to acquire the skills and knowledge that would enable them to properly fit into the society which is fast moving. An illiterate person will face innumerable hurdles in this scientific and rapidly changing world of cut throat competition. Literacy is not only a means of liberation but also an instrument of social change. It is a tool for acquiring and sharing information on national development. Economic recession and growing burden of debt have no doubt played a major role in the decline of basic education. Literacy increases peoples' capacity to cope with the demands of living and working. Adult education is a tool to influence human thinking in a right direction. In fact, development of society depends primarily on the quality and effectiveness of its people. The importance of adult education for human resource development is being seriously recognized which is imperative for the economic development as well as for strengthening the base of democracy. The significance of universal literacy as an instrument of galvanizing and mobilizing the people, arousing community consciousness and community participation for bringing about social change is undebatable.

Changing Concept of Adult Education

According to UNESCO, the term adult education denotes the entire body of organized educational processes, whatever the content level and method may be. Through this a person regarded as an adult by the society to which he/she belongs, develop their abilities, enrich their knowledge, improve their technical or professional qualification and bring about changes in their attitude or behavior in a two fold perspective comprising of full personal development and participation in balanced and independent social, economic and cultural development. Adult education programme as envisaged in the national adult education programme is meant primarily for women and learners belonging to deprived section of the population. This does not mean that others willing to join adult education programme should be excluded but emphasis must be given to this section of the population for they constitute about 60 to 70 per cent of India's population which did not have the benefit of any type of education, formal or informal.

Role of 'Pragati Centre' in Empowering Women

The Department of Home Science Extension and Communication was started in 1953 with the objective of developing abilities in conducting and evaluating urban and rural non-formal education programme. To meet the national needs in order to contact the adult education programme, it was decided to contact Urban Basic Service (UBS) and Urban Community Development (UCD) community volunteers to bring the adult learners to the Department of Home Science Extension and Communication as they also have more or less similar objectives i.e. to encourage and guide socially and economically backward urban people to participate in the programme of their upliftment, promote equality and improve social and the physical condition through projects like literacy programme, nutrition and income generating programmes etc.

Pragati Centre was started in 1983 for conducting the adult education programme in the Department of Home Science Extension and Communication. 'Pragati' is the path towards the building of the women's skills, thought and new ideas. It also brightens the light of awareness of the women on different issues. It helps in the professional development of the third year students by providing training to plan, organize and conduct the adult education programme.

In order to conduct the adult education programme, the Department of Home Science Extension and Communication decided to contact Urban Basic Service (UBS) and Urban Community Development (UCD) community volunteers to bring the adult learners to the Department of Home Science Extension and Communication. Much of the success of adult education programme will depend upon the manner in which it is implemented and evaluated. The aim to evaluate the adult education programme of 'Pragati Centre' is not to 'prove' but to 'improve' the programme. In order to be suitable and effective, the adult education programme needs to be evaluated from time to time.

In 'Pragati Centre' the adult educators demonstrate different nutritious and delicious recipes and they deal with the different topics like dowry, health education, literacy, reproductive health, environmental education, consumer education, women's right, women's empowerment etc. with the use of different method like demonstration, workshop, discussion, puppet show, drama, educational talk etc. and materials like charts, posters, puppets, flash cards, flipcharts, films, slides, models, specimens, diagrams etc. Women take active part in each activity. Here opportunities are given to women to express their views on important family matters, like education, marriage, and employment. It changes their attitude and different patterns of role sets, which may be quite different from that of their traditional roles. It is rightly said that self-sufficiency is the 'key to stronger women'. Many of the problems, which are faced by women, existed because they were either illiterate or economically dependent on others. With a view to creating a climate where women are expected and treated as equals, it is extremely important to ensure a comprehensive curriculum for adult education.

Need for Evaluating the Adult Education Programme

Much of the success of adult education programme will depend upon the manner in which it is implemented and evaluated. Evaluation is an integral part of the adult education programme of 'Pragati Centre'. It must be a continuous process starting from the planning stage and follow-up stage. Evaluation of the adult education programme of 'Pragati Centre' is necessary not only for assessing the level of achievement of the learners but also to aid and accelerate the pace of their learning. Evaluation is a complementary process. An effort is being made to introduce a process–oriented continuous evaluation system that will help for checking carefully the different aspects of the programme of 'Pragati Centre' which is essential for bringing about the improvement in the quality and efficacy of the programme. In order to be suitable and effective, adult education programme needs to be evaluated from time to time. So, a study of an appraisal of adult education programme of 'Pragati Centre' of the Department of Home Science Extension and Communication was undertaken in the year 2003-2004 in the Faculty of Home Science, The M. S. University of Baroda.

The following are the major points which justify this study:

1. Improvement of the Programme: The adult education programme is being conducted by the Department of Home Science Extension and Communication for more than 50 years. Much of the time, efforts and money has been spent by the adult educators as well as the supervisors in conducting the adult education programme. There is a need to know the strength of the adult education programme so that educators can continue with the same in the future also and the weaknesses, which are the barriers in the success of the adult education programme, so that special efforts can be made to remove the weaknesses thus making the programme stronger and efficient. The third year students conduct the adult education programme in 'Pragati Centre' under the guidance of supervisors of the Department of Home Science Extension and Communication who help them in planning the adult education programme. Supervisors conduct meetings and discussions for the improvement of the adult education programme keeping in mind the adult learners' interest, needs and problems. Efforts can be put in, while planning the programme for better implementation under the guidance of the supervisors.

2. Usefulness of Data: This systematic study will provide authentic data, which can be presented to the policy makers, which will provide a base to show the problems in conducting the adult education programme and reasons for irregularity in attendance etc. The data can be useful to the undergraduate students as they can get an idea about what the adult learners have already learnt and what changes they want in the adult education classes or what are the new things they want to add, what are their demands, needs and problems so that they can plan the activities accordingly.

3. Proper Utilization of Funds: The Department of Home Science Extension and Communication is providing sufficient funds for the implementation of the adult education programme to educate the adult learners like giving contingency money for conducting demonstrations, workshops, dramas, expert talks and arranging educational trips. Hence, it is essential to evaluate whether proper utilization of these funds is being done or not and whether the objectives of social, economic and political awareness has been met or not? For the non-formal education, instructors go to the communities and conduct programmes but in case of the adult education programme, the adult learners come to the 'Pragati Centre' of the Department of Home Science Extension and Communication to attend adult education classes. They might be facing the problem of transportation, many times they may not be getting the bus on time or it may be expensive for them to come by auto rickshaw. Hence, the study will be helpful in understanding the problems or reasons for not attending the adult education classes.

4. Follow-up of the Programme: The adult education classes conducted in 'Pragati Centre' aims at empowering women. This study will be helpful in knowing whether the women have really gained the knowledge and have applied it in their life or just coming for the sake of attending the classes.

5. Suggestions: The manner in which the adult education programme is conducted in 'Pragati Centre' may not be according to the needs and interest of the adult learners. It may be possible that adult learners have some different needs, wants and interests. This programme is conducted for the adult learners so it is very necessary that the areas, which are covered, should be according to their needs and interests. The suggestions of the adult learners will provide a base to the adult educators and supervisors for better planning and implementation of the adult education programme in future.

Objectives of the Study

1. To develop the profile of adult learners who attended the adult education programme in 'Pragati Centre' of the Department of Home Science Extension and Communication.
2. To study the overall opinions of the adult learners regarding the adult education programme of 'Pragati Centre' of the Department of Home Science Extension and Communication in relation to the following aspects:

- Curricular aspect
- Instructors
- Physical aspect
- Methods and materials

3. To study the overall differences in the opinions of the adult learners regarding the adult education programme of 'Pragati Centre' of the Department of Extension and Communication in relation to their

- Age
- Educational level

- Regularity in attendance
- Personality Dimension
- Motivation to learn

4. To find out the reasons given by the adult learners for not attending the adult education programme of 'Pragati Centre' of the Department of Home Science Extension and Communication.
5. To obtain suggestions regarding the improvement of the adult education programme of 'Pragati Centre' of the Department of Home Science Extension and Communication from–

- Adult learners
- UBS/UCD community volunteers
- Teacher supervisors

Selection of the sample

Sample

125 adult learners (Girls and Women)

6 UBS / UCD Community Volunteers

4 teacher supervisors

Construction of the Tool and the Response System

S.N	Section	Aspects	Response system
1.	Profile of the learner	• Age • Education level • Regularity in attendance • Personality • Motivation to learn	Checklist Checklist Checklist 2 point scale 4 point scale
2.	Opinions of the adult learners	• Curriculum aspect • Instructor • Physical aspect • Methods and materials	3 point scale 3 point scale 3 point scale 3 point scale and open ended
3.	Reasons for not attending	-	2 point scale
4.	Suggestions	• Adult learners • UBS/UCD community volunteers • Teacher Supervisors	3 point scale and open ended

Plan for Statistical Analysis
Different Statistical Measure were Used for the Analysis of the Data

S.N	Purpose	Statistical Measures
1.	Background information of the respondents	Percentage
2.	Overall opinions reported by the adult learners	Percentage
3.	Overall opinion reported by adult learners according to the variables	Percentage
4.	Item wise opinions reported by the adult learners	Intensity indices
5.	Overall Differences in the opinions according to the variables	Chi-Square
6.	Reasons for not attending the adult education classes	Percentage
7.	Suggestions by the • Adult learners • Teacher Supervisors • UBS/UCD Community Volunteers	 Percentage Percentage Percentage

Background Information of the Respondents

Table 11.1 shows that sixty four per cent of the respondents were young and thirty six per cent of the respondents were old. It is also seen that more than seventy per cent of the respondents were having low level of education. Where as, nearly fourteen per cent of the respondents were highly educated. Nearly forty per cent of the respondents were introvert where as sixty per cent of the respondents were extrovert. Majority of the respondents were irregular in attending the adult education programme.

Table 11.1: Description of the Respondents Showing Their Background Related Information

S.N.	Variable	per cent
1.	Age • Young • Old	 64.0 36.0
2.	Education level • Low • Medium • High	 74.4 12.0 13.6
3.	Regularity in attendance • Regular • Irregular	 62.4 37.6
4.	Personality dimension	 14.4

	• Introvert • Extrovert	85.6

However, about eighty-five per cent of the respondents were having low motivation levels, whereas fifteen per cent of the respondents were found to be highly motivated.

It was found that majority of the girls and women had low educational level. The reasons may be that adult learners had many responsibilities at their home like taking care of siblings, cooking food etc., or may be parents had a fear in sending their daughters for further education to schools/colleges, since the atmosphere may be unsafe. Parents also might have think that if their daughter is highly educated it will be difficult for them to find a suitable match.

Attendance was not compulsory yet majority of the adult learners had regularly attended the adult education classes. This shows that the girls and women are very keen to learn and they may want to study further and increase their knowledge as the content of the programme might be interesting to them, which encouraged them to attend the classes regularly. Other reasons may be that they had a good company of friends with whom they enjoyed and regularly attended the classes.

Majority of the girls and women were found to be extrovert. The reason may be that they were very enthusiastic, active and expressive which promoted active participation in the adult education programme. It was also found the majority of the adult learners had low motivation to learn. The reason may be that they have not got the opportunity to express themselves in front of others. An opportunity for self-expression encourages and motivates a person, which gives a confidence when a person's views are appreciated by the others. Hence, it might be possible that the adult learners got a chance but they were not appreciated by others. Their past experience may be such which demotivated them to study further.

Another reason can be that in a male dominated society, females might have a fear that their freedom will be restricted if they would show their motivation and desire to learn. Another reason can be that continuous learning can motivate an adult to learn. But these are the adults who were unable to continue their education. Hence, the adults had low motivation because of long break in their education. It was found that majority of the girls and women were Hindus. However, sixteen per cent of them were Muslims. The reason may be that as Muslims follow purdah system, parents might feel secure to send their daughters to the Home Science Faculty since it is a girls' college. Secondly, the area were Home Science Faculty is situated there are many Muslim dominated areas like Nizampura, Fatehgunj, Kamatipura form where 16 per cent of Muslim girls came. It was found that majority of the respondents belonged to the joint family.

It was also found that majority of the family were, either in service or in labor. The reason may be that since they are poor and living in the urban areas, it is expensive and difficult to get a place for establishing your own business since it requires a lot of investment. There are many ups and downs a person has to face in the business, as it is very risky so it might be possible that they could not afford to take risk in business and feel secured in taking up job or earn as daily wage laborer.

Table 11.2 reveals that almost equal percentage of the respondents were from the general caste and schedule caste, whereas, fourteen per cent of the respondents were from schedule tribe. A high majority i.e. nearly seventy per cent of the respondents were Hindus, whereas, sixteen per cent of the respondents were Muslims, nearly five per cent of them being Christians and whereas only two per cent of the respondents were falling in other categories. Nearly sixty-five per cent of the respondents were living in *pucca* houses, thirty two per cent of them were living in *kacha* houses and only three per cent of the respondents were falling in the other category. A majority i.e. eighty five per cent of the respondents were having nuclear families. Majority of the adult learners had only one family member who was earning. The reason may be that there was only one male member in the family who could earn, other male member might be young and thus studying in school / college or they might be too old to go out to work. It might also be possible that female members were not allowed to go out for job. However, few women were, found to be earning. The reason may be that they had no male member in the family or male member were unable to get employment. It might be possible that women were forced to earn or may be they wanted to be independent and have their own identity.

It was found that the girls and women belonged to the low income group. The reason may be that majority of the adult learners belonged to the joint family where only one family member is earning. It might be possible that those who were earning were not much educated. Hence, they were getting low wages, as there is a lot of competition in the job market in today's world. The people who are educated even they don't get employment, and it is very difficult to survive in this competitive world. Hence, it might be possible that even if they are educated, there is a little value of that education in the job market so may be because of this reason they were getting low salary or low wages. Further, it was found that majority of the girls and women had Gujarati Medium of instruction in their schools/college. Children learn what their parents teach them. Hence, it might be possible that the parents of adult learners had low education having Gujarati background and this could be the reason that adult learners had Gujarati medium in their school/college.

Table 11.2: Distribution Showing other Characteristics Related to Background Information of the Respondents

S.N.	Variable	per cent
1.	Caste	
	• General	44.0
	• Schedule Caste	41.6
	• Schedule tribe	14.4
2.	Religion	
	• Hindu	77.6
	• Muslim	16.0
	• Christian	4.8
	• Any other	1.6
3.	Type of house	
	• Puckka house	64.8
	• Kachcha house	32.0
	• Other	3.2
4.	Type of family	
	• Joint family	14.4
	• Nuclear family	85.6

It is seen from the Table 11.3 that majority i.e. sixty seven per cent of the respondents had four to six family members. Here also, nearly twenty per cent of the respondents had seven to nine family members, ten per cent of the respondents had seven to nine family members, ten per cent of the respondents had one to three family members and only five per cent of the respondents had ten to twelve family members. Table 11.3 also shows that almost equal percentage of the respondents had three to four male members and one to two female members and one to two female members in tier family whereas, forty eight per cent of the respondents had one to two male members and almost equal percentage of the respondents had five and more male and female members in their family and remaining fifty per cent of the respondents had three to four female family members.

It can be seen from Table 11.4 that forty three per cent of the respondents were engaged in service, thirty eight per cent in labour and eleven per cent of the respondent's head of the family had business as the main occupation. It is also evident from Table 11.4 that majority of the families had only one earning member in the family, twenty eight per cent of the respondents had one to two earning members, whereas, ten per cent of the respondents had three earning members and nearly two per cent of the respondents had four earning members in the family. It was also found that majority of the adult learners were not employed as they were young and they also had low level of education which is not enough to get an employment. It might also be possible that they were capable to get an employment but as it is a male dominated society the family members may have not allowed them to get employment. Moreover, the girls and women had low level of education so it might be possible that they were getting employment, which had low status in the society. Hence, they might not have liked to be employed. It was found that only eighteen per cent people were sending their children to municipal schools where medium of instruction is Gujarati.

Table 11.3: Distribution of the Respondents Showing the Number of Family Members

S.N.	Other Characteristic	Per cent
1.	Total number of family members	
	• 1-3 members	10.4
	• 4-6 members	67.2
	• 7-9 members	17.6
	• 10-12 members	4.8
2.	Number of male members in the family	
	• 1-2 members	48.0
	• 3-4 members	41.6
	• 5 and more	10.4
	Number of family members in the family	
	• 1-2 members	40.0
	• 3-4 members	50.4
	• 5 and more	9.6

High per cent of the adult learners were employed and majority of them took employment because of their own motivation. The reason may be that they wanted to be helping hands to their parents by adding some extra income, as they might be very concerned about the income of the family. Other reason could be that the girls and women did not like to be dependent on others, as they wanted to be independent and have their own identity. Majority of the adult learners were getting low salary as they had low level of education. It was found that majority of the girls and women were working for very less hours. The reason could be that they had to reach home early and take care of home related responsibilities, which they could not afford to neglect. The demand of the job itself may not require long hours of work, however, it was found that majority of the girls and women were attending the adult education programme since one year for the reason that every year UBS/UCD community volunteers approached different slums communities so that maximum slums could be covered and maximum people could get the benefit of the adult education programme which is conducted every year in the Department of Home Science Extension and Communication, Faculty of Home Science.

Table 11.4: Distribution of the Respondents Showing the Occupation Related Information

S.N.	Other Characteristic	Per cent
1.	Occupation of the head of the family	
	• Service	43.2
	• Labour	38.4
	• Business	11.2
	• Any other	07.2
2.	Number family member earning	
	• 1 member	60.0
	• 2 members	28.0
	• 3 members	10.4
	• 4 members	1.6
3.	Total income of the family	
	• Low income group	50.0
	• Middle income group	30.4
	• High income group	19.2

However, few of the girls and women were attending the adult education programme for more than one year for the reason that they were more confident in attending the adult education classes as they were able to manage the time with other responsibilities of the house hold work. It might also be possible that they enjoyed attending the adult education classes as they had made friends while attending the programme and got used to coming to 'Pragati Centre'.

It was also found that many girls and women came on foot to the Pragati Centre to attend the programme. The reason may be to save money and also walking one to two kilometer from home to 'Pragati Centre'. However, some of them were coming by auto rickshaw. It might be possible that they were coming half way on foot and then came by shared auto rickshaw, which was not very expensive for them. Another reason of coming by auto rickshaw may be that there is no bus stand near the area where they are living or may be the females found that lot of time being wasted while waiting for the bus. Little more than one third of the adult learners were encouraged to join the adult education classes by their friends may be because they wanted a company of their friends or may be parents were not allowing them to go out alone. Another reason can be that a person enjoys more in a friendly atmosphere, they feel free and comfortable hence a company of friends was stressed by them.

Table 11.5 reveals that majority i.e. nearly eighty five per cent of the respondents had Gujarati medium, nearly nine per cent of the respondents had Hindi medium and nearly six per cent of the respondents had English medium in schools/colleges. However, point eight per cent of the respondents had other medium like Marathi, Urdu etc. in school/college.

Table 11.5 Distribution Showing the Education Related Information of the Respondents

S.N.	Other Characteristic	Per cent
1.	Medium of instruction in school/college	
	• Gujarati	84.8
	• Hindi	8.8
	• English	5.6
	• Any other	0.8

Table 11.6 shows that a majority, i.e. nearly sixty one per cent of the respondents were unmarried, whereas nearly thirty eight per cent of the respondents were married and nearly two per cent of the respondents were separated.

Table 11.6: Distribution of the Respondents According to the Marital Status

S.N.	Other Characteristic	Percentage
1.	Marital Status	
	• Unmarried	60.8
	• Married	37.6
	• Separated	1.6
	• Widowed	-

Table 11.7 shows that a majority, i.e. nearly eighty two per cent of the respondents were unemployed whereas, eighteen per cent of the respondents were employed.

Table 11.8 reveals that thirty per cent of the girls and women had less than one kilometer distance from home to 'Pragati Centre', twenty six per cent of the respondents had one to two kilometers distance, six per cent of the respondents had three to four kilometers, twenty per cent of the respondents had five to six kilometers and nearly seventeen per cent of the respondents had more than six kilometers distance from home to 'Pragati Centre'.

Table 11.7: Distribution of the Respondents Showing the Employment Status of the Respondents

S.N.	Other Characteristic	Percentage
1.	Not employed	81.6
2.	Employed	18.4

Table 11.8: Distribution of the Respondents Showing the Distance and Mode of Transportation

S.N.	Other Characteristic	Per cent
1.	Distance from home to 'Pragati Centre'	
	• Less than 1 km	30.4
	• 1-2 kms.	26.4
	• 3-4 kms.	6.4
	• 5-6 kms.	20.0
	• More than 6 kms.	16.8
2.	Mode of transportation	
	• On foot	51.2
	• By auto rickshaw	36.0
	• By bus	9.6
	• By cycle	1.6
	• By own vehicle	1.6

Table 11.9 reveals that thirty five per cent of the girls and women were encouraged by their friends, twenty seven per cent of the respondents were encouraged on their own, four per cent of the respondents were encouraged by their family members, whereas, nearly ten per cent of the respondents were encouraged by local leader and four per cent of the respondents were encouraged by their relatives to join the adult education classes.

Table 11.10 shows that only eight per cent of the respondents had faced opposition in the family to join the adult education classes. Fifty per cent of the respondents faced opposition by their family members, thirty per cent of the respondents faced opposition by their husband, whereas ten per cent of the respondents faced opposition by their relatives and others like local leaders and friends. It was interesting to find that high majority of the girls and women had not faced any opposition in the family to join the adult education classes may be because their family members know that the classes are conducted in Home Science Faculty where there are only females which made them feel secured to send their daughters. In spite of the fact that majority of the girls and women belonged to low income group, yet they are not restricted or discouraged to go ahead to attend the classes as there was no fee or expense to join the classes.

Table 11.9 Distribution of the Respondents Showing the Person Who Encouraged in Joining the Adult Education Classes

S.N.	Other Characteristic	Per cent
1.	Person who encouraged in joining the adult education classes	
	• Friends	35.2
	• Your own wish	27.2
	• Local leader	24.0
	• Relatives	9.6
		4.0

Table 11.10: Distribution of the Respondents who Opposed the Participation in the Adult Education Programme

S.N.	Other Characteristic	Per cent
1.	• Not faced opposition	92.0
	• Faced	8.0
2.	Person who opposed (N=10)	
	• Family members	50.0
	• Husband	30.0
	• Relatives	10.0
	• Others	10.0

Aspect-wise Opinion Regarding Adult Education Programme

The findings of the study revealed that overall majority of the girls and women had high opinion regarding the adult education programme may be because the programme was so well planned and executed by the instructors and teacher supervisors which resulted in an effective adult education programme. Another reason can be that attitude towards a particular thing affects the response towards it. Acceptance of anything to a great extent depends upon the attitude of people towards it. Hence, it might be possible that the girls and women had a positive attitude towards the adult education programme, which might be a major factor in having high opinion regarding the adult education programme.

The other findings of the education aspect of the programme revealed that girls and women had high opinion for the knowledge, which was useful in day-to-day life and adult education programme helped in increasing the literacy level of the learners. This finding shows that the girls and women got benefit through the adult education programme in terms of increase in knowledge. The reason may be that the content of the adult education programme was of interest to all. So, it can be said that the success of the adult education programme is largely dependent on the content, which is selected by the teacher supervisors and instructors. Hence, the needs and interest of the adult learners should be kept in mind while selecting the content of the adult education programme. Further, it was also found that girls and women had moderate opinion about the adult education programme since it taught many things besides the content, like discipline, handling different situations. The instructors should give more opportunities to adult learners to handle different situations.

The findings of the "Self-development aspect" of the programme revealed that girls and women had moderate opinion about it. That means the adult learners were concerned for their self-development to moderate level which is a very positive sign of development, in spite of having low education, low income and coming from poor family, still they showed the wish and willingness for their self-development. It is an in built wish, which was found in the girls and women. The reason could be many, may be they understood that this is a rapidly changing world towards development. To survive in this world a person has to accept and adopt change. Hence, they wanted to be in line of fulfilling the demand. So there is a change in their attitude, actions and beliefs so as to be a good citizen of a nation and could contribute to the family indirectly by developing themselves in spite of having low education status.

Another reason could be that the adult learners had interacted with those who were concerned for their development and who had high ambition in their life or could take correct decision in life. The adult learners might be influenced with those people and wanted to be like them. As the girls and women were concerned for their self-development to a moderate level, it can be said that the instructors still have a scope to encourage them for their development to a great extent by improving delivery of instructions, actions, ideas, thoughts and experiences. The instructors should make the adult learners realize that a person should be capable enough to face the problems and handle different situations of life and that can be done by realizing the need and concern for their "self development".

Further, the findings of the "health aspect" of the programme revealed that the girls and women were concerned to a great extent to find out about new recipes, trying out new recipes and also keeping a check on the nutritive value and diet of the family members. The probable reason everybody wants to look good and healthy. As community people of slum areas are malnourished as often fall sick so, may be they wanted to take precautions by giving nutritious diet to their family members. Another reason could be that they like to serve new recipes to their family members as they may want to break the monotony of daily routine diet. This finding of the study implies that the girls and women like to learn new recipes. Hence, the instructors should keep in mind while selecting the items for food demonstration in the adult education programme that it should be attractive, of low cost and should have good amount of nutritive value.

The findings of the "creativity aspect" of the programme revealed that girls and women had moderate opinion regarding creativity. The reason may be that as majority of the learners belonged to the low income group so they could not afford to buy the raw materials for making creative articles as it may be little expensive for them to make samples. They might have thought to generate income by making creative articles but they may not have skills to make such fine articles, which could be sold in the market, as a lot of practice is required and knowledge about marketing for self-employment is must. Hence, the instructors must keep in mind that:

- Product should be of low cost
- Product, which is in demand, should be produced,
- Instructors should develop skills of adult learners for making creative articles,
- Knowledge about marketing strategies should also be provided.

The instructors might have studied the psychology and characteristics of adult girls and women. They have knowledge regarding how to deal with adults in different situations. It might also be possible that, as the instructors were the students of final year (B.Sc), they were getting training under teacher supervisors to conduct the adult education programme. Hence, they might have given good performance, as they wanted to show their capabilities, talents and potentials. Shukla (1985) also found that instructors gave good performance and they used clear and loud voice and took personal interest in women learners. They went to women personally and spoke to them in a pleasant and soft voice and shared good rapport with the learners.

Further, it was found that majority of the girls and women had high opinion regarding the "Physical aspect" of the programme as it has a well planned and maintained lab where all the required facilities like gas, wash basins, utensils, comfortable chairs, desks, lights, fans etc. are available. Another reason could be that the available facilities made girls and women comfortable in the environment where they see many new faces and learnt many new things. It was found that the adult learners had high opinion regarding the "method and materials" aspect of the programme. The reason may be that teaching materials were very effective in catching attention which may have helped the adult learners in clarifying the concepts. Teaching materials may also have motivated the girls and women by arousing the curiosity of the learners. It might also be possible that the pace of learners might have increased with the help of teaching material used in the adult education programme - as a person can easily gain and recall the knowledge with the help of images, pictures, diagrams and different audio visual aids.

Hence, maximum number of teaching aids should be used by the instructors which should be attractive and able to catch attention appropriate to the content and should also have images, pictures of diagrams which would help the girls and women in sharpening their memory. However, in the case of demonstration method, adult learners were able to see and understand each step before proceeding to the next step. Hence, the clear view might have resulted in clear understanding on the part of girls and women. Shukla (1985) also found in her study that demonstration was found to be more effective than workshop method and significant difference in the opinion of girls and women regarding the adult education programme.

The finding of the study revealed that there were no significant difference in the opinions with respect to the age, educational level, personality dimension, and motivation to learn. Adult learners having age ranging from twenty years to fifty years or above were similar in their opinions regarding the adult education programme. Their age, educational qualification, personality and motivation in no way affected their opinion regarding the adult education programme. The reason may be that effectiveness of adult education programme was teaching. Instead of age, educational level, personality and motivation of the learners, if the instructors taught well with proper teaching aids, teaching methods, well-modulated voice, appropriate pitch, tone, they would be more appealing to the learners in spite of their different characteristics. Hence, this finding implies that for the adult education classes to be effective the content should be useful and instructors should be well trained so that the girls and women have high opinion in future also regarding the adult education programme.

However, significant difference was found in the opinion and regularity in attendance of the adult learners. Girls and women who were irregular had different opinion regarding the adult education programme in comparison to the adults who were regular in attending. The reason may be that irregular adults may not have found the programme meaningful. The adult learners who were regular in the programme might be very enthusiastic to know what next? May be they were acquainted with the presentation style of the programme, whereas, it might be possible that irregular adults had not got much ideas about the manner in which the programme is conducted. When the continuity of attending the programme breaks, they may be finding it boring and less interesting. Hence, they were indifferent in their opinion regarding the adult education programme.

Reasons for not Attending Adult Education Classes

It was found that majority of the girls and women had no reason for not attending the adult education programme as majority of them were regular. However, some of the adult learners stated that then were not aware about the place where the classes are conducted. The reason may be that the publicity for the programme may not have been done properly. Or they knew the Home Science Faculty, but they may not be knowing where the 'Pragati Centre' is located. It might also be possible that they asked the students of Home Science who did not know where exactly the adult education classes are conducted in the Department of Home Science extension and Communication as they may be from some other department. However, some of the girls and women were not attending the adult education classes because it was expensive for them to come to 'Pragati Centre'. The reason may be that because of the long distance they were either coming by auto rickshaw or by bus, which became expensive for them to pay for transportation daily as they were very poor.

Hence, this implies that transportation arrangement should be made by the Department of Home Science Extension and Communication for girls and women so that they can attend the classes regularly and they won't have any reason for not attending the adult education classes. It was also found that nearly twenty five per cent of the adult learners were not attending the classes because they had to look after sick family members at home, or take care of young children in the family. The reason may be that all family members were busy in their own work or may be girls and women could take care of them as well. Another reason reported for not attending the classes was lack of creativity amongst them. The reason may be that they feel inferior when they don't have the talent, which others have. As majority of the adult were found to be extrovert yet they felt out of place when they do not get the required attention.

Hence, while conducting the classes, the instructors should keep in mind that all girls and women should get proper attention, equal importance for their creativity and the hidden talents should be enhanced and polished so that they feel that they can also do the best. It was also found that girls and women were not attending the classes as they were tired of the household work. The reason may be that the other family members in spite of having a helping hand in the household work were not contributing enough. Hazarika (1971) also reported similar findings that on an average the women from the young, middle and old age groups had not attended the classes because of the burden of household work. They had to perform many responsibilities because of household work. Naik (1979) also found that adult learners left the adult education classes because of family circumstances.

Suggestions Given by Adult Learners

It was found that a high majority of the girls and women suggested that computer education should be provided which shows how enthusiastic the girls and women were to learn computers. The reason may be that they cannot afford to pay fee to learn computers and could get free computer education. Another reason could be that computer education is in demand in today's world. The adult learner might be feeling inferior and handicapped when they meet others who know computers.

Majority of the girls and women suggested that more opportunities should be provided for self-expression. The reason may be that they wanted to express their views in front of others so that others can understand them. The girls and women may also want others to listen to them. Opportunities for self-expression may also motivate them to share their experiences and discuss their problems freely so that they can also get the solution at the same time from different people and listen to different opinions.

It was suggested by a majority of girls and women that library facility should be provided. The reason may be that they wanted to enhance their knowledge and increase reading habit since because of low educational level, they may not have got the opportunity to continue their education but they may have a strong wish to learn more. It may also be possible that they wanted to engage themselves in reading so that family members may feel that they are free and they don't have any work to do. Hence, this finding implies that the library facility would help the adult learners to continue their education and develop reading habits.

Further, suggestions given by the girls and women included prior information before starting the adult education programme like place where the classes are to be conducted, timings of the instructors, what activities to be conducted in the programme, duration of the programme etc. This effectively means that advertisement or publicity should be done more effectively, neither too early nor too late and reminders should also be given to the adult learners about the programme so that girls and women can be motivated to attend the programme. It was also suggested that greater use of charts and posters through which instructors taught should be encouraged and the matter should be written and displayed along with them. The reason may be they could read on their own at their own pace and follow instructions easily. It may also help them to recall the content taught to them.

Table 11.11: Item-wise Distribution of the Respondents According to the Suggestions of the Adult Learners

(per cent)

S.N.	Items	Great Extent	Some Extent	Less Extent
1.	Computer education should be provided.	82.4	16.0	1.6
2.	More opportunities should be provided for self-expression.	75.2	19.2	5.6
3.	A library facility should be provided which would develop reading habits and increase knowledge.	74.4	21.6	4.0
4.	Further guidance to what should be done afterwards can make the programme more meaningful.	73.6	24.0	2.4
5.	A childcare centre facility should be provided so that women can attend the adult education programme free from the worry of their children.	70.0	24.8	4.8
6.	Exhibition can be put up for the products made in the adult education classes.	68.8	24.8	6.4
7.	Adequate transport arrangement should be made	64.8	28.0	7.2
8.	Awareness regarding marketing strategies shod be provided to see the products.	60.0	35.2	4.8
9.	Aspect of the programme you think needs renewal. a) Management of the programme	44.0	28.8	27.2

Girls and women further suggested that most topics should be taught through the drama. The reason may be that it is easy for them to comprehend through drama, may be because they can better concentrate on the content when it is presented through the drama rather than when it is presented in the form of lecture or talk. They also suggested that written information should be provided in the form of booklets. The reason may be that many things were going on in their mind because of which they may not be able to remember the content after the class. Or their memory may not be sharp enough or may be for further reference they wanted the content in written booklet form.

It was also suggested that adult education programme should be conducted in the community where they live. The reason may be that it will be convenient for them as they don't have to pay for the transportation and also nobody will have opposition for joining the adult educational programme when it is conducted in the community itself. As every thing has advantages and disadvantages, disadvantage for this suggestion is that instructors will not be able to use variety of media through which they convey the message effectively. Sometimes, facilities like electricity may not be available in the community hall. Hence, it may be difficult for the instructors to conduct the programme effectively in the community. Lastly, it was suggested that certificates should be provided to them so that they can have a proof that they had attended the literacy classes. It can act as an incentive and may also motivate the girls and women to attend the classes regularly.

Suggestions Given by the UBS/UCD Community Volunteers

Thoughtful attention about the needs of the learners, and openness which eases the expression of views and professional guidance, should be provided, was suggested by a majority of the UBS/UCD community volunteers. The reason for these suggestions may be that learners would take interest in the programme if it is based on their needs and interests. First their needs should be satisfied and this problem should be solved, then the instructors should proceed with the actual programme of delivery, which they feel is important. For that, instructors should identify the needs of the learners and plan programmes accordingly. If the programme is based on their interest, they will be motivated to participate in the programme and will naturally express their views. Sharma and Patel (1986) also reported that programme must be built on basic needs, expressed or unexpressed, immediate and felt problems and interests of the concerned people and their community.

To provide 'Professional guidance' was suggested by many. The reason could be that these girls and women may be having different abilities and hidden talents, which could be enhanced and utilized if proper guidance is provided to them. It was also suggested by Sharma and Patel (1986) that the emphasis should be laid on vocationalization related to the local environment. The aim of this programme should not only be to impart education to illiterate adults but also to improve the community life as well. The gap between the world of letter and world of work should be narrowed. Other suggestions given by the UBS/UCD community volunteers were that the programme should be conducted regularly i.e. for the whole year. The reason may be that large number of communities can be covered within a year where as the adult education programme is conducted for four months only. Hence, majority of the women who are from the weaker sections of the society can get the benefit of this programme.

Suggestions Given by the Teacher Supervisor

Teacher supervisors suggested that awareness regarding marketing strategies should be provided to sell the products. The reason may be that the adult learners had made so much of efforts to make the product but their efforts can be utilized if the knowledge regarding marketing is also provided. This can generate income, which may give them the feeling of satisfaction, motivation to learn further and they will also participate interestingly in the adult education programme. Suguna (2001) reported that participation has two dimensions - quantitative and qualitative. People's participation in terms of numbers has no meaning. Today there is a need for change from quantitative to qualitative. Hence, this finding implies that if the knowledge of marketing strategies will be provided to them, their quantitative participation can be changed to the qualitative participation in the programme.

Further, suggestions given by the teacher supervisors included ice-breaking sessions for the adult learners in the very beginning of the programme which would help the group to open up easily with the instructors and they can feel comfortable at the same time in the adult education programme. Further, it was suggested that product demonstration should be market-oriented, meaning it should have some value in the market or it should be demanded by the customers so that it can be sold in the market. More of "need felt" topics should be incorporated e.g. environment, energy and health etc. It was also suggested that message should be imparted through games. The reason may be that more number of games will make the programme interesting and also it will be easy for the adult learners to learn. Games like puzzles, quizzes, etc., should be included in the programme not only for recreation but also for imparting messages. The other reason may be that games can break the monotony and can encourage participation of adult learners.

Further, it was suggested that exhibition should be made a permanent feature of the programme. The reason may be that environment influences a person. A person will react according to the environment in which he/she is. Hence, through exhibitions, learning environment can be created in which girls and women can be encouraged and motivated to learn. This finding implies that a good learning environment should be created for the girls and women with the help of charts, posters, flashcards, flipcharts, mobiles, specimens, models and booklet etc. which can attract the attention of the girls and women so that they can concentrate in the adult educator programme without diverting their minds in the other matters of life.

Conclusion

The aim of this study was to evaluate the adult education programme by studying the opinion of girls and women and checking carefully the different aspects of the programme of 'Pragati Centre', which was essential for bringing about the improvement in the quality of the adult education programme of 'Pragati Centre' for future.

This study indicates that there are certain aspects, where adult learners seem to have gained from the adult programme but some aspects should be further strengthened like education, self-development, health and creativity. However, girls and women had an overall high opinion regarding the adult education programme. They found that the instructors were helping, friendly and confident while conducting the classes. They used appropriate methods and materials, which have helped them to gain and recall the knowledge more easily. The instructors were suggested to use more of drama and game methods for imparting education. Physical facilities were adequate and had made the adult learners feel comfortable in the 'Pragati Centre'. On the basis of above discussion, it can be concluded that the younger adult learners had low educational level but they were extrovert and in spite of having low motivation they were regular in the class. This shows that they were very enthusiastic and expressive which promoted active participation in the adult education programme. The results of present study depicts that overall the girls and women had high opinion regarding the adult education programme which shows their favorable attitude and willingness to learn as the programme was so well planned and executed by the instructors and teachers supervisors which resulted in an effective adult education programme.

Instructors gave good performance and put all their efforts to make the programme effective and meaningful. Physical facilities available at the 'Pragati Centre' had positive influence on the adult learners in attending the programme. Adult learners also had high opinion regarding the curriculum of the programme but still there is a scope to give more attention towards the curriculum. Teaching materials were every effective in catching attention, which have helped the adult learners in clarifying the concepts. However, significant difference was found in regularity of attendance of the adult learners. Those who were regular had high opinion in comparison to those who were irregular.

This study also gave emphasis that everyone in a learning society has to be literate. To justify any society, the adult learners should realize that how important the adult education programme is in removing the innumerable hurdles from a person's life as it is tool of learning and instrument of social change. Women oriented programmes, which are entertaining, economically beneficial and have immediate use is a boon for the society. Sincere involvement and deeper interest on the part of teacher supervisors and instructors will also help in the improvement and the success of the programme.

References

Nimbalkar M. R. Adult Education, Mittal Publications, Delhi, 1987.

Rastogi K. G. Evaluation of national adult education program. Indian Journal of Adult Education, Vol 39. No. 11-12 November December 1978.

Roy Ranjan Nikhil. Adult Education in India and Abroad, published by S. Chand & Co. New Delhi, 1967.

Saxena Radha Rani. Changing Roles of Indian Women in Society, Social Welfare, Vol, 48, No. 5, August 2001, 25-27.

Sharma Anuradha. Comparative study of attitudes rural and urban adult learners towards literacy campaign, Indian Journal of Adult Education, Vol. 61, No. 4. October - December 2000, 17-26.

Sharma Atul, Sharan G., Veena D. R, Parikh K. Bhanumati. Adult Education in India, Anmol Publication, New Delhi. 1989.

Shukla Mamta. Effectiveness of communication through demonstration and work shop in NFE centre-Pragati, Department of Home Science Extension and Communication.

Suguna B. Women's Empowerment: Concept and Framework. Social Welfare, Vol 48 No 9. 2001, 3-7.

12

Women Empowerment through Education

Y. Bhaskaracharyulu, D. Pulla Rao and Y. Nirmala

Education is the process that liberates mind. It is liberation from all forms of darkness and ignorance. Women's literacy is essential for economic viability and independence. Acquisition of knowledge is one of the prerequisites of human development. Today all development agencies agree on the importance of educating women in order to promote and maintain family education, health, nutrition and general well-being. The aim of education should be to train women in such a way that they apply their acquired knowledge to the pursuits of daily life and fit them for the position they have to fill. Education for women should always be directed towards their holistic development. Education enhances a women's sense of her own health needs and perspectives, and her power to make any health and family planning decisions. This, in turn, helps to reduce child and maternal mortality and morbidity rates. The increase in the education of women and girls contributes to greater empowerment of women, to a postponement of the age of marriage and to a reduction in the size of the families. Thus the educational level of women is particularly important because educational attainment can affect age of marriage, reproductive behavior, the use of contraceptives, the health and nutritional levels of the family, proper hygienic practices, migration trends and above all, their own status.

The University Education Commission (1948-49), just after Independence, felt the need of women's education and stated that, "there cannot be educated people without educated women. If general education has to be limited to men or women, that opportunity should be given to women, for then it would most surely be passed on to the next generation". On the other hand, female education has been found to have a more significant effect on poverty reduction and promotion of sustainable development, by influencing family size and female labour force participation.

Female Literacy Rates in India

In the field of education the disparities between male and female are still large. The gap between the literacy rates of males and females has been persisting since 1901 when the female literacy rate was 0.60 per cent as against 9.83 per cent among males. The disparity index (ratio of male literacy rate to female literacy rate) in 1901 was 16.38. On the eve of the initiation of planned economic development in 1951 the literacy rate of women was 7.93 per cent and it increased to 54.16 per cent by 2001. Table 12.1 shows the literacy rate among women has increased at a faster rate than among men. This is evident from the successively decreasing trend of disparity indices, which fell from 16.4 in 1901 to 3.1 in 1951 and to 1.4 in 2001.

Table 12.1: Gender-Wise Literacy Rates in India (1901 to 2001)

Year	Male literacy rates	Female literacy rates	Disparity index
1901	9.83	0.60	16.4
1911	10.56	1.05	10.1
1921	12.21	1.81	7.6
1931	15.59	2.93	5.3
1941	24.90	7.30	3.4
1951	24.95	7.93	3.1
1961	34.44	12.95	2.6
1971	39.45	18.69	2.1
1981	56.50	29.85	1.9
1991	64.13	39.29	1.6
2001	75.85	54.16	1.4

Source: Census Report, 2001.

Infant and Child Mortality

Infant and child mortality rates reflect a country's level of socio-economic development and quality of life and are used for monitoring and evaluating population and health programmes and policies. The objective of this paper is to analyze the trends and differentials in infant and child mortality rates by mother's education using National Family Health Survey (NFHS) (1998-99), Census 2001, and SRS data. In order to analyze the trends in IMR, growth rate for 20 years period data (1981-2001) have been calculated. Cross tabulations are made to ascertain differentials in IMR and child mortality rates by educational levels of the mother using NFHS data. Regression line has been estimated to measure exactly the impact of literacy rates of total, male and female population, using SRS and census data for the states.

Child survival is closely linked to the timings, spacing and number of births, and to the reproductive health of mothers. Early, late, numerous and closely spaced pregnancies are major contributors of high infant and child mortality and morbidity rates, especially where health care facilities are scarce. Where infant mortality remains high, couples often have more children than they otherwise would to ensure that a desired number survive. Thus, infant and child mortality directly affects women's childbearing responsibilities.

Five mortality indicators for analysis using NFHS data were:

- Neonatal mortality: The probability of dying in the first month of life.
- Post-neonatal mortality: The probability of dying after the first month of life but before the first birthday.
- Infant mortality: The probability of dying before the first birthday.
- Child mortality: The probability of dying between the first and fifth birthday.
- Under-five mortality: The probability of dying before the fifth birthday.

The infant mortality rate (IMR) for the world in 1990 was 73 per thousand, only 16 per thousand in the more developed nations, and as high as 81 per thousand in the developing nations. The IMR in Asia in 1990 was 74 per thousand.

As per the report from publication reference bureau, Washington, USA, 2001, the estimated infant mortality rate (IMR) for the world for the year 2001 was 56 per thousand, only 8 per thousand in the more developed nations, and as high as 61 per thousand in the developing nations. The estimated IMR in Asia for the year 2001 was 55 per thousand.

Trends in Infant Mortality Rate

Table 12.2 presents the trends in IMR in India and Andhra Pradesh during 1981-2001. It also gives rates of decline during the last 20 years. In India, infant mortality rate has declined from a high of 110 in 1981 to 66 in 2001, whereas in Andhra Pradesh it has declined from 86 to 66 in the corresponding period. The rate of decline is 2.65 per cent for India during 1981-2001 and it is 1.62 per cent in Andhra Pradesh in the corresponding period. It is quite interesting to note that the rate of decline is rather very slow for Andhra Pradesh and it should be examined in depth so as to find out the factors influencing these trends. Not only mean, but also CV is lower in Andhra Pradesh compared to all India trends.

Review of Literature

In a pioneering work Bourgeois-Pichat (1964) provided an analytical framework for child survival in developing countries. They identified two types of factors, viz., 'endogenous' and 'exogenous' that affect infant mortality. Biological factors constitute the first type and environmental factors constitute the second type. Later studies by Gandotra and Das (1988) classified the factors as underlying, viz., socio-economic, demographic, environmental and health care.

Pandy *et al.*, (1998) have analyzed NFHS-I data and conducted that mother's educational status is the most critical variable that influence IMR. Gandotra and Das (2001) have studied the determinants of IMR in Gujarat and Maharashtra and found that IMR takes the U-shape pattern by birth order. It is influenced more by socio-economic factors. In a study in Madhya Pradesh, Sarita, S (2001) concluded that IMR in MP is high and it can be reduced only through providing minimum dietary requirements for all as well as ensuring at least functional literacy for all especially for females.

Table 12.2: Trends in IMR in India and Andhra Pradesh

Year	India	Andhra Pradesh
1981	110	86
1982	105	79
1983	105	77
1984	104	78
1985	97	83
1986	96	82
1987	95	79
1988	94	83
1989	91	81
1990	80	70
1991	80	73
1992	79	71
1993	74	64
1994	74	65
1995	74	67
1996	72	66
1997	71	63
1998	71	62
1999	70	61
2000	68	65
2001	66	66
Mean	84.57	72.43
SD	14.40	8.19
CV	17.03	11.31
Growth rate (per cent)	-2.65*	-1.62*

*Statistically significant at 1 per cent level.

Source: SRS data are compiled from various reports of the sample registration system

In a study known as 'Khanna study' in Punjab during 1956-1959 the infant mortality rate was found to be 161.7 and the study underlined the importance of post-neonatal mortality in India. It is also observed that the infant mortality rate is 170 for male infants and 205.4 among females. The study has also found that infant mortality rate during the hot dry season was 156.2. The study suggested that the people to build their houses suitable to climatic conditions.

Satish B. Agnihotri (2001) made an attempt to study the declining infant and child mortality in India from the time series data starting from 1905 to 1997. The paper analyzed data for 16 major states in rural and urban areas for the period from 1982 to 1997. Less developed regions and states have a higher IMR than more developed ones.

The National Population Policy has set target of bringing down infant mortality to 30 per thousand by the year 2010. Satish (2001) made an attempt to analyze this aspect for West Bengal for 1981 and 1991 census data. The paper analyses the infant and child mortality data for the district level estimates. The study shows that mortality levels are high in certain regions and among certain groups. It was also observed from the study that the performance of the state in reducing mortality has been well above the all India average. The results were also compared with all India figures through the state level estimates. The paper suggested that mortality levels could be reduced through specific micro planning.

Sudha and Rajan (2003) examined levels and trends of estimated sex ratios at births and child mortality risk in India. They have used multivariate statistical analysis exploring social and economic covariates that affect the livelihood of gender bias in death, using 1981 and 1991 census data of each district in India. The female disadvantage is evident in birth and death spread over India in the decade 1981-1991. Though infant and child mortality levels fell for girls and boys, gender differences persisted, and penetrated the hitherto egalitarian south. Masculine SRB that were seen only in urban areas of the northwest in 1981 have spread to urban areas of many northern states in 1991. Multivariate analyses suggest that between 1981-1991, women's status variables become less associated with reduced gender bias. Modernization variables suggest less association with gender bias, or that a substitution of pre-natal for post-natal elimination of unwanted daughters may be occurring. These findings are situated in the literature on gender, education, paid work participation, and marriage system changes in India.

Mother's Education and Infant/Child Mortality

In this section cross-tabulated data of the infant and child mortality rates by mothers' education in urban, rural and total population is shown.

Tables 12.3, 12.4 and 12.5 present the differentials of infant and child mortality by mother's education in urban, rural and total population respectively.

Table 12.3: Mother's Education (Urban)

Background characteristic	Neonatal Mortality (NN)	Post neonatal mortality (PNN)	Infant Mortality ($_1q_0$)	Child Mortality ($_4q_1$)	Under-five Mortality ($_5q_0$)
Illiterate	44.1	23.8	67.8	28.8	94.7
Literate, < middle complete	30.8	11.8	42.6	14.7	56.7
Middle school complete	29.5	13.3	42.8	9.2	51.6
High school complete and above	22.2	8.2	30.4	3.7	34.0

Source: NFHS data are compiled from NFHS-2 India report.

Table 12.4: Mother's Education (Rural)

Background characteristic	Neonatal Mortality (NN)	Post neonatal mortality (PNN)	Infant Mortality ($_1q_0$)	Child Mortality ($_4q_1$)	Under-five Mortality ($_5q_0$)
Illiterate	57.0	32.4	89.4	41.5	127.2
Literate, < middle complete	44.0	20.3	64.3	20.0	82.9
Middle school complete	36.1	15.0	51.1	11.4	61.9
High school complete and above	26.9	8.8	35.7	5.6	41.1

Source: NFHS data are compiled from NFHS-2 India report.

Table 12.5: Mother's Education (Total)

Background characteristic	Neonatal Mortality (NN)	Post neonatal mortality (PNN)	Infant Mortality ($_1q_0$)	Child Mortality ($_4q_1$)	Under-five Mortality ($_5q_0$)
Illiterate	55.3	31.2	86.5	39.7	112.8
Literate, < middle complete	40.5	18.0	58.5	18.4	75.8
Middle school complete	33.7	14.4	48.1	10.5	58.1
High school complete and above	24.3	8.5	32.8	4.4	37.1

Source: NFHS data are compiled from NFHS-2 India report.

Data shown in the tables present the variations in neonatal mortality, Post neonatal mortality, Infant mortality, Child mortality and under-five mortality by mother's education levels viz., illiterate, Literate (< middle school complete), middle school complete, high school complete and above. It can be observed from the tables that the children of illiterate mothers are most likely to experience higher mortality than others. The rural children are at a higher risk than their counter parts in urban areas.

Regression Results

The following regression equation has been estimated for measuring the impact of literacy rate of male, female, and total population on infant mortality rate. The method of estimation is OLS, using SRS and census 2001 data, for the States and Union territories of the Indian Union.

$Y = b0 + b_1 X_1 + b_2 X_2 + b_3 X_3 + u$

Where,

X_1 = total literacy rate

X_2 = male literacy rate

X_3 = female literacy rate

Y = Infant Mortality Rate

b_1, b_2 and b_3 are the respective coefficients of X_1, X_2 and X_3

The estimated line is

$Y = 44.63 - 2.2009 X_1 - 2.6637 X_2^{*} - 2.8393 X_3^{**}$
(1.54) (2.89) (3.56)

* Significant at 5 per cent level, **significant at 1 per cent level

$\bar{R}^2 = 0.58$, F value = 9.3112

The regression results show that all the literacy rates have a negative impact on Infant mortality rate, which implies that if education levels increase, Infant mortality rate declines. However, female literacy is the most crucial, because the regression coefficient is the strongest (2.8393) and it is statistically significant at 1 per cent level.

The variables explain 58 per cent of the variation in Infant mortality rate and F value = 9.3112 and is significant at 1 per cent level.

Conclusion

The study shows that the expenditure on health programmes can yield good results only if the beneficiaries are in a better position in terms of education levels. Mere literacy may not be of any help. Females must be educated at least up to primary level if not secondary level. Such woman can appreciate the importance of reproductive and child health care facilities provided by the government and will be able to effectively use them. Infant and child mortality are directly related to health care facilities available in the nearest place. But this is only the necessary condition. The sufficient condition is that the woman/man must be capable enough by way of education to know the importance of such a health care provision.

References

Bourgeois-Pichat, J.: "Evolution reccente de la Mortalitec Infantile". Cited in United Nations, 1973. The determinants and consequences of population trends, Vol.1, Department of Economics and Social Affairs, United Nations, New York, p.126. 1964.

Chandra Sekhar, S.: Infant mortality in India 1901-1955, Allen and Unwin, London. 1959.

Chandra Sekhar, S.: Infant mortality, population growth and family planning in India, George Allen and Unwin, London. 1972.

Gandotra, M.M. and Das, N.P.: "Determinants and causes of infant mortality in Gujarat and Maharashtra", Demography India, Vol.30, No.2, pp.313-328. 2001.

Gandotra, M.M. and Das, Narayan: "Infant mortality: an analysis of recent births": *In:* Anrudh K. Jain and Pravin Visaria (eds.), *Infant Mortality in India – Differentials and Determinants*, Sage Publications, New Delhi. 1988.

Harriss, B.: "Differential child mortality and health care in South Asia", Journal of Social Studies, 44, pp.21-23. 1989.

Satish, B. Agnihotri: "Declining infant and child mortality in India: How do girl children fare", Economic and Political Weekly, Jan. 20-26, pp.228-233. 2001.

Satish, B. Agnihotri: Sex ratio patterns in the Indian population – a fresh exploration, Sage Publications, New Delhi. 2000.

Srinivas, K. and Mukherji, S.: Dynamics of population and family welfare, Himalaya Publishing House, Bombay. 1983.

13

Role of School in Gender Equality

Manisha Pathak–Shelat

Are Men and Women friends and co-travelers in search of harmony and happiness or are they two diametrically opposite species at loggerheads fighting for a bigger piece of the power cake?

Gender equations in any society reflect those in micro societies like the family, the school, and the peer group. In today's times mediated and virtual societies also cannot be ignored. "The basic value that sustains a democracy is the principle of individual dignity. Gender equality, therefore, is an important value for the Indian society, which ideologically supports basic democratic values like social justice, individual dignity, and freedom of speech and religion and equal protection under law. If this ideal is to be achieved, the existing patriarchal paradigm of the family and the resulting patriarchal constructions of masculinity and femininity have to change and values and attitudes in favour of equality have to be nurtured from the young age." (Pathak-Shelat, 2004) The National Policy on Education (GOI, 1992) recognised the importance of gender sensitisation at the school level and called for the education system to play a positive interventionist role in promoting the new values of equality in the division of roles, rights and responsibilities between men and women in every sphere. This however is a tall call for our schools because of the complex nature of value development and the complexities of gender construction itself.

Value Development: Complex Process

Value development is a very complex process. During the process of value development, several processes are at work simultaneously: learning from experiences, modeling, direct preaching and teaching, intellectualising and reasoning, understanding, appreciating and reacting emotionally. According to Dewey (1939), children learn moral values from the quality of their total social experience. As Gender is constituted biologically, socially, economically, culturally and above all politically (McLaren, 1988), formal and informal day-to-day interactions within the family, school and the community largely shape an individual's perspective on gender and his or her orientation towards gender equality as a value. Media are increasingly becoming a crucial component in an individual's total experience and thus have far-reaching influence in development of gender perspective.

Again, equality itself is a construct with enormous complexity. For a balanced holistic concept of gender equality one has to consider biological factors as well as the constantly changing dynamic nature of the society and critically examine the tendency to confuse the 'cultural' with 'natural'. Different groups have widely different perspectives on social change, the concept and nature of equality between men and women and also on approaches to social change. Thus there is no universal model for achieving the goal of gender equality. One can take the female superiority view and strive to transform the entire social system-values, institutions, relationship- according to women's vision of the world. Or one can ignore the inherent biases in the social system and try to get a better deal or more power for women without attempting to transform the society. One can take the male superiority view and try to improve women's situation so that it resembles men's situation; or one can hold on to the 'biology is destiny' theory and shun all attempts at social change. One can also follow the radical egalitarianism and practise what Hirst (1976) points out as 'applying an equal standard to qualitatively unequal classes' or subscribe to the concept of equity which allows for consideration of individual circumstances. Looking at the socio-cultural environment in which a large number of Indian schools are located, and the structural boundaries of the school system one can begin with a more pragmatic approach than the utopian one and concentrate on a few essentials of gender fair education.

The following guidelines (Pathak-Shelat, 2004) may help schools in shaping their program on gender sensitization.

- Both, woman and man are critical elements in gender issues.
- Men and Women are different in many ways but different does not always mean superior or inferior. Many of the differences perceived as natural are in fact, cultural.
- Role reversal or 'oppressed imitating the oppressor' can not be the alternative to role stereotype. Role sharing, which takes in to consideration individual differences among men and women, biological as well as socio-cultural-economic factors and balances individual and family needs, offers a better alternative.
- Equality is possible only through mutuality between sexes when in any given sphere no one sex is always a giver and no one sex always a receiver.

Gender Equality and School

School plays an important role in gender construction and perception because children spend a significant portion of their formative years in school environment. Cultures around the world have assigned important social, moral and educational functions to school. In rapidly changing Indian metros and large cities it is not uncommon to see children spending more waking hours at school then at home.

Reflecting on the ways and means by which the school can act as a counter-socialiser in sex-role learning, Krishnakumar (1986) emphasises that when cinema and television cast in conservative images of women and men, the school's media, that is, textbooks and other materials should offer images and symbols that motivates the reader to look at human beings in term of their own struggle for an identity rather than as reciting prefabricated conversations. He challenges the view that the school and community should be complementary to each other in socialising the young. "If one accepts this principle of complementarity, then there is no hope for changing the prevailing code for sex-typing through education, which means that there is no hope that education can intervene in the cultural reproduction of entrenched sex-roles".

The challenge is how to translate these utopian expectations in the actual discourses at the school level. Efforts in addressing gender issues through alternative media have been going on in India for several years now. These efforts include analysis of textbooks, development of self-learning modules and materials, publication of feminist or women-oriented literature, feminist journals, media advocacy groups working towards constructive intervention, and development of interactive media like songs, posters and street plays. Very few of these efforts, however, reach the adolescents at school. A well formed gender sensitization policy and its implementation through viable programs are the only ways in which schools can expect to be gender fair. It requires introspection, open debates and discussion, attention to total school environment and conscious planning to make necessary changes in building schools that are gender fair and strive to empower women as well as men.

In school formal teaching, text books and reference material constitute an important but only one aspect. Gender messages can use several other vehicles, visible and invisible.

- Teachers, administrators and other members of the staff
- School's structure and physical space planning
- Curricular material, textbooks and reference material
- Curricular options and activity choices
- Responsibilities and expectations vis-à-vis gender; Overt or covert preference for certain desirable traits in boys/girls

- Feedback-Praise, criticism, acceptance, non-acceptance, comments, taunts, punishment
- References to future and career guidance
- Sexual harassment of students or staff and reaction to it

Teachers, Administrators and other Members of the Staff

Teachers influence gender perceptions and construction of students through cognitive, affective and psycho motor experiences. They influence as mentors and models, directly and indirectly, within classroom and outside it. Teachers also play other social and educational roles as parents and grandparents, uncles and aunts, friends' parents, media persons, counselors, coordinators of events and competitors, managers and consultants.

Administrators, policy planners, curriculum planners and text book and reference material writers are other members associated with school whose perceptions about gender will shape the school's philosophy, value system and pedagogic and management practices.

Teacher-student interaction in the classroom is often influenced by gender, though a few teachers would admit or even know this. Paying attention to individual students based on their gender, asking questions, expecting a certain level and type of performance, giving praise and punishment, assigning tasks and responsibilities. If the teacher is not gender sensitive, each of this seemingly innocent classroom activities carry a gender related message.

Adults carry with them their own gender experiences, associations and emotional baggage. Critically looking at their own socialization and exposure to a range of different cultures, ideas and lifestyles broaden the perspective. School can provide its staff opportunities for reading, traveling and interaction that enhance exposure and result in clarity about gender and gender related issues.

Gender Sensitisation needs to be introduced as an important and mandatory component in teacher training programs. Sessions on gender sensitization has to be conducted only by qualified experts otherwise they do not achieve much. One interesting observation of my doctoral research was that girls can be as gender biased as boys and women teachers are not necessarily more gender fair than men teachers.

Oza (2006) has reported positive impact of gender sensitization program on teachers of primary schools of Gujarat and also observed improvement in participation of girls in curricular and co curricular activities. A majority of teachers were able to teach with gender concern in almost all subjects.

School's Structure and Physical Space Planning

The physical structure and space management in the school significantly dictate how people will behave and function. Gender based segregation in India is very common. While conducting experiment for my doctoral dissertation in urban middle class schools had ample opportunities to observe gender based segregation. Some schools had separate staircases for boys and girls, separate play areas and of course common rooms. The seating pattern in the class was always gender based and this continued to influence even out of classroom activities. If groups had to be made for discussion or competition it was without fail all-boys and all-girls groups competing against each other. Conversation between boys and girls was indirect, tinted with sarcasm and gender based ridicule and if any boy or girl tried to behave differently the others saw to it that they fell back in the common pattern. Of course there are times and situations when children need to be in the same gender groups and feel more comfortable but if gender based segregation is the norm of the school, it cannot impart the value of gender equality and camaraderie to students.

Curricular Material, Textbooks and Reference Material

"Each time a girl opens a book and reads a womanless history, she learns she is worth less" Myra and David Sadker, Failing at Fairness.

Sadker and Sadker (2005) have listed seven forms of bias in instructional materials. They are invisibility, stereotyping, imbalance and selectivity, unreality, fragmentation and isolation, linguistic bias and cosmetic bias. Women achievers in a range of different areas still do not find place in school material. Even today in India women who have entered conventionally male professions like police officer (eg Kiran Bedi) or space scientist (Kalpana Chawla) are highlighted much more, indirectly sending a message that the conventional male professions are superior. Mostly women are discussed in context of family and care giving where as men in context of professional role and success. History books eulogizing the high status of women scholars in vedic India gloss over the subjugation and oppression faced by ordinary women for centuries thereafter. "Many researchers have noted the tendency of instructional materials to gloss over unpleasant facts and events in our history. By ignoring prejudice, racism, discrimination, exploitation, oppression, sexism, and inter-group conflict, we deny students the information they need to recognize, understand, and perhaps some day conquer societal problems." (www.sadker.com).

In India the Delhi based NGO Nirantar has critiqued the National Curriculum framework from a gender perspective and conducted orientation sessions with principals of government schools and Egos. (www.nirantar.org). Oza (2004) has reported that gender sensitization efforts have shown some results in the textbooks of primary schools in Gujarat. Most of the textbooks maintained gender neutrality in terms of illustrations and names of boys and girls. There is however still the need to include and promote girls/women in non conventional roles in private and public fields. This is not reflected in the class either.

Curricular Options and Activity Choices

Indian schools can claim some progressive practices in the area of curriculum options and activity choices as many schools now allow boys and girls to choose from a common pool of options. This is however restricted to urban upper SES schools and is seldom seen in schools operating in more conventional communities. "Needlework for girls and carpentry for boys" may not be the dictate any more but one can still see clear gender based patterns in selection of subjects and activities. There is a worldwide concern about not enough number of girls opting for mathematics and science courses. Again, just providing equal options does not guarantee that boys and girls will get to choose what is closer to their heart. Peer group acceptance, treatment received by the minority gender in the chosen activity, attitude of instructors and gender fair work environment (including space, facilities, equipment) are all important factors. At times girls choose conventionally male options even though they are not genuinely interested because there is now a certain glamour and recognition attached to it. Thus a girl choosing aero modelling may be applauded but it may not be the same with a boy who chooses fashion designing or dance. A girl choosing culinary art may be labeled as a 'girlie girl' and may not get extra attention but a boy opting for cricket may have his share of fans. Schools, teachers and parents have to use discretion, allow the students to choose what they are genuinely comfortable with and not be overzealous in encouraging forced gender equality.

Responsibilities and Expectations vis-à-vis Gender

Gender roles concern rights, duties and expectations associated with being a man or a woman. Every society has its set of gender roles and in fact modeling young men and women to become the ideal 'gentleman' or 'lady' was considered a primary responsibility of schooling. Finishing schools are not the relics of the past yet. Under the guise of manners, socially desirable qualities and prized gender attribute boys and girls constantly undergo remolding, sometime gentle and covert; the other times aggressive and overt. Does the school reward pretty, petite and gentle girls by giving them prominent roles in school functions while the tomboyish and plain girls work unrecognized in the background? Does the school assign action oriented responsibilities to boys and decorative roles to girls? Do boys who are good at fine arts and girls who have financial acumen given opportunities to showcase their talents? Are cooperative boys ridiculed in favour of their competitive classmates? Schools have to understand individual differences among boys and girls and accept them.

Humans crave for acceptance and recognition. Feedback on physical traits, looks, behavior and performance from the significant others in life is an important factor in gender socialization. Being accepted and rewarded by teachers and peers affect self esteem of boys and girls.

Teachers are very important figures in younger children's life. Every positive or negative word and gesture by the teacher leaves an impact and can influence the way the child feel about herself or himself. It is amazing how the gender bias and gender myths permeates our most casual conversations and leave lasting impression on children. An incident during my doctoral experiment is a good example of this. In one of my discussion sessions at a school some of the boys (the usual mischief makers) started creating a lot of disturbance. They wanted to go and play volleyball. When their behavior started affecting other students the class teacher decided to intervene. At the end of the report he tried to motivate boys saying "You should be ashamed that girls are getting so much ahead of you in everything. Have you ever given it a thought that if this continues, it is not so far away in future that they will be occupying all the important posts and you boys will be handling tongs and ladles in the kitchen". In one sweep he created negative feelings of jealousy and resentment in boys towards girls and also indicated that work in kitchen is of a lower level and that boys should guard themselves against such work in future." Adolescents constantly hear remarks about their looks and behavior connecting lack of certain desirable gender specific traits to a deem future. "Who will ever marry you" is an overused reprimand in India hinting that all other achievements are secondary.

Schools where the child is treated as a person more than as a boy or a girl provide better environment for students to realize their potential without undue pressures to confirm.

It is often observed that boys receive stricter punishment for the same behavior than girls. A girl showing so called masculine behavior, wanting to dress like a boy and engage in boyish sports does not receive as much reprimand as a boy with more feminine traits.

References to Future and Career Guidance

Advocates of gender equality argue that both men and women should be given the opportunity any profession that they want and are qualified for and that reward should be equal for equal work. In reality however people label certain jobs as 'male jobs' and certain jobs as 'female jobs'. Most students already bring a heavy baggage of myths, attitude, fears and misinformation from home, especially when a certain profession is either missing from their immediate social circle or suffers from low respectability. Sometimes the gender stereotypes about career are based on social observations or lack of models. At times some jobs are seen as the 'natural' extension of traditional roles e.g. baby sitter. Rapid development in contraception and technology has however brought a tremendous change in work arena. Educated women now spend a miniscule part of their professional life in child bearing and support systems exist for child rearing. Technology has opened many new jobs for women which earlier were restricted to men because physical prowess was a key requirement. School's vocational counseling program and also staff's attitude should reflect the changing realities and School's vocational guidance program should be handled by a gender sensitive counselor.. As concept women centered counseling is yet not a norm in Indian schools. There is a tendency to help girls make choices which would help them fulfil all the conventional care giving roles and adjust well in the patriarchal family and work set up. Also when parents or teachers discuss future plans with students marriage, parenting and family take up predominant place for girls while rarely these important aspects are highlighted in discussing future with boys.

Counseling girls for professional choices is complex. Their natural aptitude and competencies are certainly to be considered but by the time girls are in their adolescence they have through observation and socialization got an indication of added responsibilities that marriage, home making and motherhood place on women. They have heard and read numerous stories about the 'male ego' and how a more successful wife may hurt the husband's ego and put her marriage in danger. Fear of success, apprehension about fulfilling the demands of multiple personal and professional roles, glamour and rewards attached to certain professions vis-à-vis the high personal price one has to pay for them etc are some of the factors that operate when girls make professional choices these days. The school has to play multiple roles here. One is to help each student develop his or her special potential and align it to the realities of professional world of today. There are a plethora of opportunities and possibilities today about which students are not aware due to limited exposure.

A profession demands certain skills, personality and qualifications but that is not all there is to a profession. With every professional choice a certain lifestyle and work circumstances are associated. For example any one aspiring to be a news reporter with news paper or a television channel cannot expect to be home in the evenings. Highly rewarding marketing jobs have travel as an essential component. Students need to be told all this so that they can make informed choices. Girls are very often discouraged in opting for demanding professions by citing all these lifestyle and family aspects. Instead the school should invite role models in such professions for girls to find out the pros and cons of choosing a particular career. These role models have experience in negotiating work-life balance and can offer useful guidance. An important contribution of the school and gender sensitization programs would be to prepare boys to share home and childcare responsibilities. School can impart the right attitude and skills and also support advocacy programs for gender fair work places.

Sexual Harassment of Students/Staff

Sexual harassment of students by peers or staff is a serious issue in school. It is barely addressed in open debates and policy discussions unless it takes a grave form and threaten to become a scandal. Sexual abuse of young boys by senior students or members of the staff have recently come to attention and most schools yet do not have any mechanism to deal with this serious problem. Sexual harassment of girls by peers or adults is comparatively a known phenomenon and the school's attitude toward the victim plays an important role in determining punishment, counseling and after effects on the victim as well as other students. If even informally it is suggested that it is the victim's behavior-dress, conversation or body language- that invites sexual harassment there is an enormous psychological impact not only on the victim but on other girls as well as boys. The victim is shame faced and is stigmatized for a long period and often would prefer to leave the school. Few schools have a formal committee to look into such matters and when they have one there is no guarantee that the members are gender fair and gender sensitive. It does not help to be over strict and punitive with boys because adolescence is an emotionally and sexually sensitive phase for them and there is little guidance available in how to handle it in a healthy manner. The popular cinema in India also has a contribution here as most films show eve teasing as something normal, macho, and worse, rewarding. The hero wins applause from his peers after the customary eve-teasing song and later also wins the girl. There is a hidden message that the girl's anger, denial or unwillingness to fall for the boy is only temporary or even fake. For the generation raised on the staple diet of Hindi popular films and film based television programs the reel life feels closer than the real life.

The school ideally has to have a sexual harassment committee that protects girls as well as boys and the members should be sensitized and trained in gender fair counseling. School's approach should go beyond punishment or victimization and it should encourage open discussion on such sensitive topics.

Co-education versus Single Sex Schools

It would be interesting to discuss the role of single sex schools in women's empowerment. Girls' schools, Women's colleges and SNDT, the well-known women's University have had significant contribution to women's education in India. Generations of women might have had no chance of literacy and higher education if these institutions were not there. However, in India single sex educational institutions mainly existed and still exist with the chief concern of sex based segregation having overtones of social and moral sanction. In the west too the beginning of single sex institutions was probably not much different. But for the last two decades single sex schools have been in discussion for their contribution to learning and personality development. Many theorists and educationists argue that single sex schools work better than co ed schools which were supposed to break gender stereotypes and that girls especially develop better in single sex environment.

The arguments in favor of single sex schools are many. Kennedy (www.privateschool.about.com) lists competition, academics and socialization as three key areas in which single sex education offers advantages. Girls and boys have different learning styles with each sex having its own strengths and limitations. Sexual and social pressures are minimized in single sex setting resulting in more concentration on academics and performance. Boys become less competitive and girls less shy. Both boys and girls get to play conventionally masculine and feminine roles and girls get more leadership opportunities. Thus it is argued that single sex institutions give opportunities to students to break away from gender stereotypes allowing them to be themselves.

There is also an emerging practice of blended or co institutional education where two single sex schools are run under the same roof. While routine schooling takes place in single sex environment boys and girls get together for certain activities and experiences. There are many research studies in the western countries showing that girls and boys both benefit from single sex education. The website of National Association for the Advancement of Single sex public Education (NASSPE) in the US quotes several such studies. My personal argument (not research based though), however, is that since in the larger society men and women have to coexist and work together it is better that they learn to do this well from the beginning. If we are sensitive to gender stereotyping and take necessary steps to make our schools gender fair, co ed schools give more opportunities to each gender to understand, know and support the other gender.

Conclusion

All gender related issues are dynamic, complex and multi dimensional. There is rarely one right approach towards the goal of gender equality or gender fairness and empowerment. The school, however good intentional, will have to constantly keep the debate alive and keep answering the two key questions. Under what situations boys and girls need to be treated in the same way and which are the situations that demand that girls and boys be treated differently considering the genuine demands of their bodies and brains? Which are the genuine gender differences and which are the myths? What is natural and what is culturally produced? And finally, since all girls and all boys are not the same how should the school optimally help each student achieve his or her highest potential irrespective of gender? The school will have to become a 'Dosti ki Pathshala' in the genuine sense where girls and boys learn the first lessons of being friends to each other and grow into women and men who together make this world a peaceful and bountiful place for all.

References

Dewey, J. Theory of Valuation. Chicago: University of Chicago Press. 1939.

GOI. Program of Action (National Policy on Education, 1986). New Delhi: Department of Education, Ministry of Human Resource Development, Government of India. 1992.

Hersh, R. Models of Moral Education. New York: Longman. 1982.

Krishakumar. 'Growing up Male'. Seminar. No.318, February. 1986.

McLaren, A.T. Gender and Society: Creating a Canadian Women's Sociology. Toronto: Copp Clark Pitman. 1988.

Oza Dipti. Gender Sensitization in Primary Schools of Gujarat on New Curriculum Structures. SSA Project report. Centre for Advanced Study in Education. Faculty of Education and Psychology. The M.S. University of Baroda, Vadodara. 2004.

Oza Dipti. A Study of Gender Concerns in School Activities and Classroom practices in Primary Schools. SSA Project report. Centre for Advanced Study in Education. Faculty of Education and Psychology. The M.S. University of Baroda, Vadodara. 2006.

Pathak-Shelat, Manisha Communication for Gender Sensitization: The Value Discussion Approach. Concept publishing Company: New Delhi. 2004.

Sadker Myra and David sadker. Teachers, Schools and Society. McGraw Hill Higher Education: Columbus. 2005.

14

Women and Education

Mumtas N.S.

The condition of a nation is reflected in the status of its women. The status of Indian women is evident in the census conducted by the Government of India in 2001. The literacy rates for Indian males and females are 75.85 per cent and 54.16 per cent respectively. Backwardness is not a new phenomenon. It is the history of humankind. A brief sketch of status of women during different periods throws light on this matter.

Ancient Period

Free and equal access to education for both sexes seems to have been available during the early Vedic period. Women then enjoyed equality with men in pursuing their interests freely and had the right to participate in academic discourses in fields such as astronomy, philosophy, logic, mathematics and geography. Love marriages (Gandharva vivaha) and remarriage of widows were permitted. In this period, both husband and wife were joint owners of the property. Both the girls and boys were permitted to vedic studies. An educated vedic woman had a voice in the selection of their husbands. The unmarried person was not eligible to participate in vedic sacrifices. This was not looked upon as compulsory for every girl. The matrimony was not compulsory for a woman and there was no limitation on the age of marriage.

In the upanishadic period, there were a large number of Brahmvadnis (Gargi, Maitrayee etc) who devoted their life in the study of philosophy. However, later (approximately in 500 BC), the status of women began to decline with the smritis. Social sanctions approving women's education equal to men's were erased by castes. Although reformatory movements like Jainism allowed women to be admitted to the religious order, by and large the women in India faced confinement and restrictions. Over the centuries, any formalised instruction to women became individualised and was provided at home, but this domestic instruction was mainly restricted to the upper classes.

Medieval Period

The Indian women's position in the society further deteriorated during the medieval period. Sati, child marriages and ban on widow remarriages became part of social life. The Muslim conquest in the Indian subcontinent brought the purdah practice in the Indian society. Polygamy was widely practised especially among Muslim and Hindu kshatriya rulers. In some parts of India, the Devadasis or the temple women were sexually exploited. Among the Rajputs of Rajasthan, the Jauhar (practice of the voluntary immolation of all the wives and daughters of defeated warriors) was practiced in order to avoid capture and consequent molestation by the enemy. The negligence of education and lowering of the marriage age brought disastrous consequences upon the position and status of women. Remarriage of women was stopped and they were asked to devote themselves to ascetic life at home. In South India many women administered villages, towns, divisions and heralded social and religious institutions. Guru Nanak, the first guru of Sikhs preached the message of equality between men and women. He advocated that women are allowed to lead religious assemblies, to perform and lead congregational hymn singing called kirtan (Bhajan), to become members of religious management committees, to lead armies on the battlefield, have equality in marriage and equality in Amrit (Baptism), etc.

Modern Period

During this period (19th and 20th centuries) the status of women was improved by the untiring efforts of different social reformers like Raja Ram Mohan Roy, Ishwar Chandra Vidyasagar, Maharishi Karve, Sister Nivedita etc. The basic reason of the change in the women status is the acceptance of the tenets of liberal philosophy from the western civilization. It emphasizes a rational outlook of life and its problems, freedom of speech, criticism of authority, authenticity of dogmas and insistence on the rights of man as opposed to his duties.

According to the Charter Act of 1813, the East India Company was entrusted with the responsibility of the education of the Indian people. But its efforts were restricted to the education of boys and no effort was made for the education of girls. The famous social reformer Raja Ram Mohan Roy argued for the abolition of Sati and in 1829 Sati was abolished and made it a crime. He established Brahma Samaj and advocated the principle of freedom of women and equality of sexes. Macaulay's minute (1835) did not contain any reference to the needs of women's education even though it contains the future policy of the East India Company towards education of Indians. The Woods Despatch (1854) set forth a scheme of education in which special girls schools were started by the newly created department of education.

The untiring effort of Ishwar Chandra Vidyasagar promulgated the Widow Remarriage Act (1856) and thus it became legal. In 1872 Civil Marriage Act was passed. This act made the registration compulsory and age of marriage of girls was raised to 14 years. It also permitted widow remarriage and its most remarkable feature is the enforcement of monogamy. Even though the Civil Marriage Act was passed in 1872, the Hindu society accepted the practice of monogamy and inter-caste marriage only in 1956.

The education of women became slow, but in steady progress during the period 1882-1902. In the last decade of the 18th century, Swami Vivekananda (1863-1902) gave a great impetus for the liberation of women from seclusion and bondage. A major landmark of this period was the establishment of the first women's university at Poona which was started as a college for young widows by Karve in 1896 and grew into a multi-faculty university. Later in 1916, it was renamed as Srimati Nathibai Damodar Thackersey (SNDP) University. By the end of the 19th century women entered in to the field of different professions. Mahatma Gandhi was also a strong advocate of equality of men and women.

Post-Independence Period

The University Education Commission (1948-49) made certain recommendations regarding women's education. But the most important development in the field of women's education after independence was the setting up of a National Committee for Women's Education in 1958 under the chairmanship of Smt. Durgabai Deshmukh. This committee recommended special measures to bridge the gap between girls' education and boys' education at the primary and secondary levels. It strongly recommended that special funds must be allotted in the various plan periods for furthering and developing the programme for girls' education.

The Union Ministry of Education set up the National Council for Women's Education in 1959. Most of the state governments have established state councils for women's education. Smt. Hansa Mehta Committee was appointed in 1961 by the National Council for Women's Education to examine the problem of curricula for girls at all stages of education. Another committee was appointed by the Council in 1965 with Shri. M. Bhaktavatsalan as the Chairman to look into the girls' education. The Education Commission (1964-66) also made valuable recommendations regarding women's education in India. The National Committee (1974) studied various aspects of the status of women and their education.

National Policy on Education (1986) added a new dimension to education for fostering equality between men and women. The National Education System will play a positive, interventionist role in the empowerment of women. Revised National Policy on Education and Programme of Action (1992) stressed that education for women's' equality is too important to be left to the individual proclivities of persons in charge of implementing programmes. It should be incumbent on all actors, agencies and institutions in the field of education at all levels to be gender sensitive and ensure that women have their rightful share in all educational programmes and activities.

The National Policy for the Empowerment of Women (2001) stressed the advancement, development and empowerment of women. Government has formulated several schemes and programmes such as mid-day meals, free uniforms, text books and attendance scholarships for promoting access, enrolment, retention and achievements of girls at the school stage. Scholarships have been instituted for making higher education free for girls in different states. Special efforts have been made to encourage participation of girls in scientific and technical courses.

Protection of Women from Domestic Violence Law 2006 demanded stopping of violence, custody of child, sheltering husband's house, monthly maintenance and stopping husband from selling his property.

Provisions in Five Year Plans

Education for women and their developments began mainly as a welfare oriented programme in the 1st Five year Plan (1951-56). The Central Social Welfare Board (CSWB) set up in 1953 undertook a number of welfare measures for women through the voluntary sector. This plan noticed the negligence of women's education and emphasized on the expansion of educational facilities.

The Second Five Year Plan (1956-61) organised women into mahila mandals to act as focal points at the grass root levels for development of women. It emphasised on the need to provide greater opportunities to girls and the efforts needed to educate parents on the importance of girls education. This plan recommended centrally sponsored schemes which include free accommodation for women teachers, appointment of school mothers, condensed course for adult women, stipends to women for teacher training, refresher courses, stipend for high school students to take up teaching, exemption from tuition fee, construction of hostels in secondary school for girls etc. for ensuring sufficient number of women teachers.

Third Five Year Plan (1961-66) emphasised the expansion of facilities for girls at various stages. This can be achieved through creating conditions for encouraging parents to send their daughters to school education, increasing number of women teachers from rural areas, encouraging urban women to go and teach in rural areas, select promising students and assist them with scholarships and stipends, scheme of condensed courses through Central Social Welfare

Board, etc.

In the Fourth Plan (1969-74), the role of education was focussed on enabling women to become better mothers and home managers. Decreasing infant and maternal mortality, improving nutritional status of children and regulating family size were seen as the major benefit of women's' education.

Constitutional directives received prominence in the Fifth Five Year Plan (1975-79). Provision of additional educational facilities was ensured by this Plan. Facilities through evening colleges, correspondence courses and private study was expanded. National Adult Education Programme (NAEP) and Integrated Child Development Services (ICDS) were launched.

Sixth Five Year Plan (1980-85) stressed on women's' role in development and emphasised economic upliftment through income generation and employment opportunities. Universal elementary education would be specially directed towards higher enrolment and retention of girls in schools through provision of balawadis attached to schools for sibling care, income generating programme for girls after school hours to supplement family income, expansion of incentives like free uniform, text books and mid-day meals, appointment of women teachers in rural areas and strengthening science teaching in girls schools and colleges to enable their participation.

During the Seventh Five Year Plan (1985-90), Department of Women and Child Development came under the newly created Ministry of Human Resource Development. This plan made the rural women visible by highlighting their economic contribution in agriculture, animal husbandry, etc.

The concept of literacy received attention in the Eighth Five Year Plan (1992-97). Since the plan recognised human development as the core of all development, literacy among the women is of much importance.

The focus of the Ninth Five Year Plan (1997-02) was growth with social justice and equality. Attention was given to the empowerment of women and socially disadvantaged groups. This plan ensured food and nutritional security for the vulnerable section of the society. This was be complemented by a strengthened and expanded system of primary health care and measures for women and child development.

The Tenth Five Year Plan (2002-07) demands the maternal mortality rate to be reduced from 4 per cent (1999-00) to 2 per cent in 2007 and reduce gender gaps in literacy and wage rates by 50 per cent by 2007.

Programmes and Policies to Improve Women's Status

Educational planners in India have tried a wide range of strategies to bridge the gap between men and women. Beginning with a welfare approach in the

1950s, the country gradually moved towards a 'development' approach in the mid 1970s and an 'empowerment' approach in the 1990s.

The Community Development Programme (1952) was initiated to promote agricultural development and social welfare in rural India. In 1954 there was a realisation that women workers would be needed to reach out to poor rural women and as a result, each development block in a district was provided with two Gram sevikas working under the overall supervision of one Mukhya Sevika. This scheme lead to the formation of Mahila mandals for creating greater awareness about health and nutrition among women. With the creation of the Central Social Welfare Board (CSWB) in 1954, welfare extension services were introduced to provide poor mothers with supplementary nutrition, health care etc. In 1970, the Government of India constituted a Committee on the Status of Women in India (CSWI) and they submitted their report 'Towards Equality' in 1974. This report provides valuable data and information about different dimensions of women's lives-women as agricultural workers, as daily wage earners, as primary providers in poor households etc.

The major aim of the Women's Development Project (WDP, 1984), introduced by Government of Rajasthan is to empower women through communication of information, education and training to enable them to recognise and improve their social and economic status. The National Commission for Self-Employed Women and Women in the Informal Sector (NCSW, 1988) highlighted the health hazards faced by women and advocated the importance of making women's work safe. It also argued for a more proactive role to promote women's education. During the period 1986-91 Women's Development Corporations (WDCs) were established in many states to promote women's economic advancement.

The Mahila Samakhya Programme was formulated in 1987-88 and this programme essentially revolved around the formation of women's groups with a focus on poor women, their training in order to build self-esteem and self confidence followed by concrete educational and other developmental inputs. The basic tenet of the programme was to respect women's existing knowledge and skill, build on their life experience and enable them to discover their strengths.

Inspired by the Gramin Bank of Bangladesh and Self Employed Women's Association in India (SEWA), Rastriya Mahila Kosh was launched in 1993 in order to enhance poor women's access to credit. NGOs are encouraged to manage and identify women's thrift and savings groups, enhance their managerial skills and give them a revolving fund to be used by group members for self employment. Though special commissions and committees were set up from time to time to access the progress of women's category, the task is not yet fruitful.

Why Empowerment?

India is the world's second most populous country with a population of 989 million. Women in India constitute approximately 50 per cent of the population, but have been historically less active in the mainstream of social development. Even though the Indian Constitution grants women equal rights with men, the strong patriarchal traditions made them in a suppressive mood. The origin of the Indian idea of an appropriate female behaviour can be traced to the rules laid down by Manu in 200 BC. Manu says: "by a young girl, by a young woman or even by an aged one, nothing must be done independently even in her own house".

While analysing the status of females, one can see their pathetic condition. This is because of many reasons such as women are uneducated, overworked, unskilled, mistreated, powerless, malnourished and in poor health.

India has the largest population of non-school going working girls. Women and girls receive far less education than men due to social norms and fear of violence. Women work longer hours and their work is more arduous than men's. Women's work is rarely recognised by the men and they consider most of the women's work as invisible. The impact of technology made a drastic negative change on women because the introduction of technological applications in the areas where women worked displaced them by men.

Unequal access to education restricts women's abilities to learn the skills which are necessary for different jobs. In the skill development, women are impeded by their lack of mobility, low literacy levels and prejudiced attitudes toward women. Higher officials have preconceived ideas of what women are capable of and stereotypes of what is considered as women's work. Violence against women and girls is the most pervasive human rights violation in the world today. Fear of violence is a cause of women's lack of participation in activities beyond the home as well as inside it. Today, the insecurity outside the household is the greatest obstacle in the path of women.

Women are subordinate in most marriages and they are kept as a servant and are even murdered by the practice of dowry. India's maternal mortality rates in rural areas are among the highest in the world due to many factors such as poor health conditions, malnourishment, reluctance to seek medical care for pregnancy etc. Women's nature to tolerate suffering and their reluctance to be examined by male personnel are the constraints in getting adequate health care. Women's health is also harmed by air, water pollution, lack of sanitation etc.

Even after 60 years of independence women continue to live in a state of negligence and exploitation. Even though our constitutional framework and policy initiatives have stressed on promoting gender equality in all walks of life, we often forget that women as human beings are also entitled to fundamental human rights. Our society have denied and continue to deny them the basic human rights. The low level of literacy not only has a negative impact on women's lives but also on their families' lives and on their country's economic development. Illiterate women have high levels of fertility and mortality, poor nutritional status, low earning potential and little autonomy within the household. Women's lack of education also has a negative impact on the health and well being of her children.

The concept of women empowerment was introduced at the International Women's Conference at Nairobai in 1985. The term empowerment was defined as 'a distribution of social power and control of resources in favour of women'. Empowerment is a process which includes the following components.

- Equal access to opportunities for using societies resources.
- Prohibition of gender discrimination in thought and practice.
- Freedom from violence.
- Economic independence.
- Participation in all decision-making bodies.
- Freedom of choice in matters relating to one's life.

Women empowerment came to be associated with social justice and equality. Equality in social systems is a necessary condition for empowerment of women, however it is not sufficient for their development, as development and empowerment are not synonymous. Empowerment of women help them to be politically active, economically productive and independent. It is an active process, enabling them to realise their full identity and power in all spheres of life. An empowered women has a positive self image and takes an active part in decision making related to herself, her family and the community.

Education and Empowerment

India is intended to becoming a super power, a developed country by 2020. This can become a reality only when the women of this nation become an empowered lot. In 1951, shortly after Independence, the Census recorded that only 8 per cent of women were literate. By 2001 Census, female literacy had risen to 54 per cent. The details of the literacy rates (approximately) in different years are given in Table 14.1.

Education is a milestone for women empowerment because it enables them to respond to opportunities, to challenge their traditional roles and to change their lives. Education is one of the most important means of empowering women with the knowledge, skills and self-confidence necessary to participate fully in the development process. The role of education is not only learning of three R's but includes raising awareness, critical analysis of various structures and acquiring knowledge for empowerment at all levels.

Table 14.1: Literacy Rates: Selected Years

S.N	Year	1951	1961	1971	1981	1991	2001
1.	Female literacy rate (in per cent)	8	13	19	30	39	54
2.	Male literacy rate (in per cent)	25	34	39	56	64	74

In order to empower women we need not only to give them more economic power but also bring changes in the entire social, political and legal systems of the country through education because these are responsible for women's lower status in society. Education empower the women by developing:

- Self esteem and self confidence.
- A positive image of women.
- Ability to think critically.
- Decision making abilities and action through collective process.
- Equal participation in development process.
- Knowledge and skill for economic independence.
- Legal literacy and information relating to their rights.

Hence the solution to the social, political and economic problems of women is to be sought through appropriate education.

Objectives of Women Education

Educating women is a high return investment in socio-economic development of the nation. The objectives of women education are as follows:

1. Elimination of illiteracy, universalisation of elementary education and, minimisation of the dropout rate and stagnation to negligible proportions.
2. Guarantee equal access to quality education and training in all subjects at all levels.
3. Guarantee equal employment opportunities.
4. Make every women as economically active.
5. Improve women's and girls' health by ensuring them access to adequate maternal health care, family planning and nutrition.
6. Reduce maternal mortality and increase the life expectancy.
7. Ensure that women with children have the right to work, to maternity leave and to other parental benefits.
8. Provide a wide scope for employment and economic independence through

vocationalisation.

9. Eliminate the existing sex bias in the system.
10. Inculcate positive and egalitarian attitudes.
11. Acquire knowledge and skills for social, cultural and economic advancement.
12. Secure women's right to vote, stand for election and hold public or political office.
13. Promote qualified women to positions of power at every level within political, legislative and judicial bodies with the goal of achieving parity with men.

In spite of the clearly set goals, the attainment of them are impeded by many a socio-economic factors, important among them are mentioned below.

Challenges Faced by Women Education

A number of challenges are responsible for poor female literacy and high dropout among girls. They are

- gender based inequality
- social discrimination such as parent's attitudes, customs, cultural constraints etc.
- inadequate school facilities
- fear of sexual harassment
- lack of sufficient number of qualified female teachers
- lack of transport facilities
- low retention rate and high dropout rate
- early marriage
- compulsion to work at home
- lack of hostel facilities for girls
- fixed schooling hours

Considering the different barriers for low levels of literacy among females in India, a number of measures can be taken to promote the existing condition and to achieve the needed target such as:

- Schooling facilities should be provided to the girls nearer to their place of residence within a walking distance,
- Provide alternative forms of schooling i.e., combine formal schooling with non-formal means for dropouts,
- Appoint more women teachers especially in rural areas and provide them with secure residential accommodation,
- Free education should be introduced for girls up to secondary stage by all stage (although the 93rd Constitution Amendment gives the legally

enforceable right to free elementary education to children between 6 and 14 years of age, the restriction of age between 6-14 years is a barrier, particularly in rural area),

- Separate institutions for girls should be established wherever it is needed,
- Adequate arrangements should be made for free transport of girls to school if it is situated more than the walking distance,
- Encourage women teachers by providing intensive training and regular educational support,
- Introduce facilities for bridge programmes to enable the dropouts to re-enter the school system,
- Awareness campaign should be conducted for the parents in rural areas where hesitation regarding girl's education prevails amongst the parents,
- Give emphasis to distance mode of education by opening more branches of NOS, IGNOU centers etc.,
- Provide incentives like uniforms, text books, exercise books, attendance scholarship etc.,
- Introduce flexible school timings and region specific school calendar,

Even though the culture, economy and polity may be barriers to women in certain parts of the society, still women are marching ahead with great conviction and confidence to keep themselves at par with their counterparts in every sphere. With the help of proper education, each and every women would be capable of discharging their social responsibility towards community and national development through active participation because an empowered society is imperative in the Indian democratic vision of a new social order.

References

Begum, M., Women Entrepreneurship in India: Challenges and Strategies. University News, 44 (15), 13-16. 2006.

Chand, D., General Studies Manual. Tata McGraw-Hill Publishing Company Ltd. New Delhi. 2006.

Dhamiya, N. and Panda, S.K., Women Empowerment through Education: Role of Universities. University News, 44 (27), 12-15. 2006

Forbes, G., Women in Modern India. Cambridge University Press, New York. 2000.

Govinda, R., India Education Report. University Press, Oxford. 2002.

Hari Chandan, D., Women's Education in India: A Historical Review. Education and Women's Empowerment. Association of Indian Universities, New Delhi. 1999.

Rao, D.B and Rao, D.P., Women Education and Empowerment. Discovery Publishing House, New Delhi. 2004.

Rao, D.B and Rao, D.P., Women's Education: Challenges and Advancement. Discovery Publishing House, New Delhi. 2005.

Srivastava, G., Women's Identity in the Indian Society: Educational Perspective. University

News, 44 (24), 4-8. 2005.

Vashistha, K.C. Metamorphosis in Women's Education at the Turn of Century. Education and Women's Empowerment. Association of Indian Universities, New Delhi. 1999.

15

Education for Women

K. Thangamani

Women constitute half of the humanity and they have to play a very important role in the national development of any country. They are equally important in the development of any family, community or a nation. They play a very crucial role in the family sustainability, stability and growth. Even though their role is accepted by all but still women are not empowered to the level as expected in the case of men. The education of girls and women has been recognized for several decades as a fundamental human right and a development necessity.

All over the world, education is regarded as the key factor in overcoming the barriers that women face and a basic tool in empowering women and bringing them into the main path of development. Education not only provides basic knowledge and skill to improve health and livelihoods, but it empowers women to take their rightful place in society and the development process. Education gives women the status and confidence to influence household decisions.

Hence education is the most important agent in the process of empowerment of women. Education is the strategic instrument that has its impact on social and economic status of women. Apart from providing facilities for education of women, it is also important to train the women so as enhance their skill, thinking ability, self-confidence and participation in decision-making process. Empowerment helps women to access to the new world of knowledge, leading to making new information choices in both their personal and public lives. Women's empowerment process must evolve a new undertaking of power and experiment with ways of power and experiment with ways of democratizing and sharing power building, new mechanisms for collective responsibility, decision making and accountability.

In India, education is the most important instrument for human resource development. Education of women, therefore occupies top priority amongst various measures taken to improve the status of women in India. In recent years, the focus of planning has shifted from equipping women from their traditional roles of housewives and mothers to recognizing their worth as procurers, making a major contribution to family and national income. Efforts have been made over the past three decades of planned development to enroll more girls in schools and encourage their stay in schools and contribute to their education as long as possible, and to provide non-formal education opportunities for women.

Women and Education in Various Periods: Rig Vedic Age (2500 to 1500)

The position of women was quite satisfactory. Girls were not as welcome as boys but they were well taken care of, educated and married at the age of sixteen or seventeen years. In practice though their status was subordinate to that of men, they could not inherit property.

During the Age of later samhitab, Brahmaus and Upanishads (1500 BC to 500 BC), women continued to have a satisfactory status. Girls were given education; but gradually there was a decline in female education. The marriage age continued to be sixteen years and girls, especially kshatriya girls, had a say in selection of partner. Women took part in religious activities and could perform sacrifices.

In the north, Swami Dayanand Saraswati (1827-1883) founded a religious order named Arya Samaj. The basic tenet of this order advocated equality of opportunity for all irrespective of caste, colour or sex. In a very active manner, this society worked for women's education. Dayanand broadened the scope of women's education by emphasizing education for self rather than linking it to their efficiency in familial roles. The curriculum for education devised by Dayanand was similar for both boys and girls. Hence, Dayanand emerged as the first reformer who advocated and evolved a comprehensive scheme of education for raising women's status not only at the level of family and society but for her own development as an individual.

Another prominent person of the nineteenth century, Ishwar Chandar Vidyasagar (1820-1891) helped the British Government to establish the first girls' school in Calcutta in 1849. He was further responsible for the establishment of forty girls' schools in Bengal between 1855-1858.

A brilliant national leader Gopal Krishna Gokhale (1866-1915) worked relentlessly towards raising the status of women in Indian society. He founded the "Servants of India Society" in 1905 and established as its main objective the education of women. Two religious leader who helped in bringing about the renaissance in the Hindu religion were Rama Krishna Paramahansa (1866) and Swami Vivekananda (1862-1902).

In the 19th and early 20th centuries there was also an improvement in the status of women in India. Two major movements that affected women's position during this period were the Social Reform Movement of the 19th Century and the

Nationalist Movement of the 20th Century. Spread of education was an important factor in bringing about social change and in improving status of the women.

Girls' Education since Independence

Equality between men and women with liberation from traditional constraints has been the cornerstone of Indian policy towards women since Independence in 1947. In 1958, the National Committee on Women's Education was established to address itself to problems of wastages and lapsing literacy. A review of women's education in 1959 recommended a bold and determined effort in the course of women's education (Report of Indian education Commission, 1982). Variety of factors have been found to be responsible for poor female literacy rate, viz; gender based inequality, social discrimination, economic exploitation, occupation of girl child in domestic chores, low enrolment of girls in schools, low retention rate and high dropout rate.

The National Policy on Education (NPE) sees education as an instrument to bring about basic change in the status of women and envisages a well-conceived edge in their favour. Building gender awareness into all the nuances of education has been a focal point for interventions across the system:

- Mahila Samakhya is one of the most successful efforts to link women's empowerment project with education, to create an environment for women, to acquire knowledge and information with a view to bring about change in their perception about themselves and that of the society.
- The Total Literacy Campaign (TLC) has been successful in raising the demand for education, especially among women. In most of the 428 districts, women make up over 60 per cent of the adults enrolled in the programme.
- The Non-Formal Education (NFE) system is being extended to meet particularly the needs of girls who are unable to attend formal school. NFE centers run exclusively for girls to get 90 per cent assistance from the central government.
- The University Grants Commission (UGC) has been encouraging institutions to take up research projects in the area of women's studies by providing necessary funds.

Programmes/Schemes

Various programmes have been launched and various agencies extended full support for the benefit of women's education. The recommendation of various committees have been taken into consideration and implemented during the last five decades for educating the women, viz, National Committee for Women's Education (1961), Sri Bhaktasavan Commission (1964-66) and The National policy on Education (1968 and 1986). Despite all the efforts put in by the Government, women organisations, NGOs, etc., women education and women's literacy programme are still not totally successful and these perilous problems are afflicting the nation. Hence, there is an urgent need not only to understand the importance of women's education but also effective measures towards addressing it, since it is a basic human right. New innovations however are inevitable accompanied by new threats and fresh challenges. Information and Communication Technology (ICT) brought tremendous change in the lives of the individuals, societies, and almost all fields of human life viz, political, economical scientific, communication, transportation, etc. The development of Information Technology Act, 2000 paved way for the new communication systems and digital technology and revolutionised the transactions in business. New challenges have risen in solving problems unique to storage and transmission of electronic data.

The Information and Communication Technology is now once again coming forward for rescue as an innovation in educating the girls' child. With new options available for instruction, evaluation, diversification of courses, virtual class rooms, online teaching, flexible scheduling of instruction, need based programme, self-learning and self-containing modules, the education process has taken a new shape.

It is a known fact that gender discrimination in education is quite a common phenomenon in traditional Indian context. This is ultimately resulting in girls being denied the opportunity of attending the public schools due to the socio-economic conditions. Indeed at this juncture, Information and Communication Technology comes into rescue to make the people aware and also to provide opportunities in educating the girl child. Due to the development of online access and the concept of virtual classrooms, now-a-days the traditional girl child can also have the accessibility towards education from her own residence. But this shift in phenomenon will not take place unless the economic factors are taken into consideration.

The role of Information Technology in educating the girl child is massive. This paper describes various measures to be taken up in integrating Information and Communication Technology into education, which provides the opportunity to increase the accessibility of education to girl child and also to meet the challenges in realising the objectives.

Information Technology is providing a greater opportunity for the girl child to educate herself without attending the formal classrooms. Due to the development of virtual classrooms, the girl child now can no longer be denied of formal schooling. Even in the context of prevailing social barriers, the girl child can now continue her education in her free time and without crossing the social and family barriers.

The provisions of distance learning, such as online teaching, TV and video lessons, video conferencing, radio teachings through programme like 'Gnana Vani' etc., are helping in providing the instruction to the girl child who is deprived of formal classroom instruction. The girl child is now equipped with all sorts of required knowledge on the web. The traditional schooling, which is giving irrelevant and outdated knowledge is replaced by relevant and useful Knowledge. There is a provision for the girl child to select the courses and content according to her interest, ability, attitude, aptitude and need. The course can be tailored according to the characteristics and time availability of the learners.

The learner can no longer depend on outdated text books and reading material but they can use electronic on screen reference books, updated day to day to day. Tele-conference networking and electronic mail is also being used in education. Especially in the communities where girl child is not allowed into the public for education, e-learning plays an important role by providing an alternative.

Because of the high visible and influential roles of computers and related technology in the post industrial economy and society, considerable attention is currently being paid to the concept of computer literacy in preparing students for work. The present Government and private sector are carrying their day-to-day activities in more electronic form rather than manual form. Many of the jobs in industries and offices are computer-based. This is resulting in IT enabled job opportunities and women are preferred for these jobs for their concentration, stability, hard work, carefulness, sensitivity and creativity. Computer-related skills and knowledge are being recommended for the work places in the present day information society.

There are greater opportunities for women in Information Technology sector today. Many of the jobs are well suited to the capabilities and creativities of women and they are extensively employed in the hardware industry of computers around the world. Co-operative industries like garment manufacturing, packaging industries, electronic equipment units, designing units for ornaments, home appliances, etc., are providing enormous opportunities for women to take the advantage of IT and earn their living at the same time for a quality life.

Women and Literacy Level

Everyone has a right to education, which shall be directed to the full development of human resources, and human dignity and potential, with particular attention to women and the girl child. Education should be designed to strengthen respect for human rights and fundamental freedom, including those related to population and development. The very fact that a Population Conference forced the international community to look into the inter-linkages between population, poverty, gender inequality and development, was a major departure from the past.

Table 15.1: State-wise Female Literacy Rate (2001)

Name of State /UT	Literacy rate		Rank
	Female	Male	
Bihar	33.57	60.32	35.
Jharkhand	39.38	67.94	34.
Jammu and Kashmir	41.82	65.85	33.
Uttar Pradesh	42.98	70.23	32.
Dadra and Nagar Haveli	42.99	73.32	31.
Rajasthan	44.34	76.49	30.
Arunachal Pradesh	44.24	64.07	29.
Madhya Pradesh	50.28	76.80	28.
Orissa	50.97	75.95	27.
Andhra Pradesh	51.17	70.85	26.
Chattishgarh	52.40	77.86	25.
Assam	56.03	71.93	24.
Haryana	56.31	79.25	23.
Karnataka	57.45	76.29	22.
Gujarat	58.60	80.50	21.
Manipur	59.70	77.87	20.
West Bengal	60.22	77.58	19.
Uttaranchal	60.26	84.01	18.
Meghalaya	60.41	66.14	17.
Sikkim	61.46	76.73	16.
Nagaland	61.92	71.77	15.
Punjab	63.55	75.63	14.
Tamil Nadu	64.55	82.33	13.
Tripura	65.41	81.47	12.
Maharashtra	67.51	86.27	11.
Himachal Pradesh	68.08	86.02	10.
Daman and Diu	70.37	88.40	09
Pondicherry	74.13	88.89	08
Delhi	75.00	87.37	07
Andaman & Nicobar Islands	75.29	86.07	06
Goa	75.51	88.88	05
Chandigarh	76.65	85.65	04
Lakshadweep	81.56	93.15	03
Mizoram	86.13	90.69	02
Kerala	87.86	94.20	01

Source: Census 2001

Women's and girls' education was placed at centre stage in the struggle for human development and social justice in the Copenhagen Declaration on Social Development in 1995. Both in economic and social terms, the most productive policies and investments are those that empower people to maximize their capacities, resources and opportunities. The Fourth World Conference on Women, Beijing 1995, reaffirmed the commitments made by governments and called upon the international community to intensify efforts. Four important World Conferences, one after another, bombarded our world with messages of equality, empowerment, human rights and universal access to the tools of knowledge i.e. education.

The Constitutional guarantee in Article 45, of endeavouring to provide compulsory education for all children under the age of 14 years has still not been achieved even after 60 years of Indian Independence. Even though the efforts were made by the Government to fulfill the task, the task has not been successfully achieved and is still a problem area. The girl child was not educated due to various reasons and it ultimately resulted in greater illiteracy, uneducatedness and unemployment which are the resultant causes for the slow growth of the economy.

Some of the major problems concerning women's education are constrained by socio-economic condition of the people, their attitude, values and culture. Social issues included *Purdha System*, hindrance of mobility of girl child after puberty, lack of relevance of school curriculum, lack of facilities in schools and hostels and low entry and retention in schools. These factors played a vital role in allowing the girl child to be illiterate and uneducated. In the urban areas and socially developed communities, it is a significant observation that they are allowing the girl child to take part in the educational process actively.

It is proved beyond doubt that women's education encouraged small family norms (by observing age for marriages, strengthening family planning and population control programmes). It reduced infant mortality rates, malnutrition and promoted better child care, leading to the child as an effective productive citizen of the future. Educated women are better organized in their rights and duties and were found to be effective participants in the national development programmes.

Empowerment of women is directly linked with education. In spite of considerable improvement in health, education and employment sectors, women still comprise the largest section of population living in absolute poverty and they represent the poorest of the poor. Women not only continue to be in marginal employment and low level of skills, their contribution continues to be 'invisible'.

Lack of education, training and low level of literacy not merely excluded women from social, economic and political power but knowledge power as well. During the last few decades, the female literacy rates improved from 29.8 per cent in 1981 to 39.3 per cent in 1991 and to 54.1 per cent in 2001. However, there are still wide variations regionally in literacy levels from Kerala to Rajasthan.

Table 15.2: Literacy Rates of Male, Female and Total Population of India: (1901 - 2001)

Year	Male	Female	Total
1901	9.30	0.60	5.30
1911	10.60	1.10	5.90
1921	12.20	1.80	7.20
1931	15.60	2.90	9.50
1941	24.90	7.30	16.10
1951	27.20	8.90	18.33
1961	40.40	15.40	28.30
1971	46.00	22.00	34.45
1981	56.38	29.76	43.57
1991	64.12	39.29	52.21
2001	75.85	54.16	63.38

Source: Literacy Facts at a Glance, NLM, 2001

Compulsory Education

Eradication of illiteracy is the first step towards empowerment of women. Knowledge is power. When a woman is educated, in effect the whole family is educated. Research shows that in families where the women are educated, social evils such as illiteracy of girl child, child labour, female infanticide and other superstitious practices are much less. It is the education that kindles the urge for independence, hard work, achievement and self- actualization. It may be mentioned that education that inculcates human and spiritual values is of great significance for the empowerment of women. These are needed not only in educational institutions but also in every walk of life. The entire population is to be involved to create a sense of awareness about values and the need to empower women through quality education. Education up to a minimum of 10th standard must be made available and compulsory for every child.

Elementary Education

High priority has been accorded to elementary education in the national development plans to fulfill the requirements under Article 45 of the Constitution for universal, free and compulsory elementary education for children up to age of

14 years.

Table 15.3: Gross Enrolment Ratios in Class I -V and VI-VIII: (1991-92 - 1992-93)

India/State	Class I - V			Class VI - VIII		
	Total	Boys	Girls	Total	Boys	Girls
All India - 1991 - 92	95.90	106.20	85.02	59.07	69.62	47.91
All India - 1992 - 93	102.74	116.61	88.90	61.15	74.19	47.40
All India - 1995 - 96	104.03	114.50	93.30	67.60	79.50	54.90

Source: Selected Educational Statistics (1991-92) and (1992-93)

According to the Fourth Education Survey (1978), in the plans 95 per cent of the population has access to a primary school within one kilometer of their habitation (having a population of 360 persons or more). Middle schools are available to 78.8 per cent of rural people within three kilometers from their habitation. But commuting to distant schools does pose a problem for girls. There are very few separate schools for girls. The parents, particularly in rural areas, are reluctant to send their daughters to co-education schools. Moreover, in most schools, the teachers are male. Despite considerable emphasis in the plans, the proportion of women teachers continues to be low provision for accommodation for women workers including teachers is far from satisfactory.

There is a progressive rise in the rate of enrolment in secondary education of girls during the various Plan periods as seen below:

The enrolment ratio of girls in the group 15-18 years for secondary classes is 14.3 per cent as against 29.3 per cent for boys. Secondary education continues to be more or less confined to urban areas, and is affordable and accessible largely to the higher castes and the upper and middle economic strata. Although a large number of secondary schools have come up in rural areas, their enrolment particularly, in respect of girls is low. The main constraints in improving secondary and higher level education among girls has been the lack of availability of trained lady teachers, dearth of separate institution for girls and lack of hostel facilities.

The 10+2+3 system of education was introduced with the aim of establishing a uniform pattern of education all over the country in terms of its structure, curriculum and mobility across the states. This system has laid a common foundation for higher education without differentiation between boys and girls.

In the light of women's role in digital revolution and digital economy, development in electronics, computer information and communication technology has brought tremendous changes in the lives of the people around the globe. Women are no exception to this global phenomenon. The changes in this sector have brought considerable changes in job opportunities and education opportunities for women. Information Technology has given a solution for educating the girl child in the context of many problem and hurdles faced in the Indian context. The opportunity, course facilities, need based and ability based course facilities, need based and ability based course virtual classrooms, etc., are paving way for a new hope in educating the girl child and ultimately resulting in empowering them to attain the gender equality.

Primary Education of Women

The Indian Constitution requires that primary education be provided for all children between the ages of 6 and 14. Education is compulsory in most states for children through age 11.

Most of the children who do not enter school, or drop out soon after entry, come from poor families where they are compelled to shoulder the burden of household chores or add to the income of the family. From age 7 onwards, these children begin to share the adult tasks. They do not have the leisure to attend school for 6 hours in the middle of the day.

Part-time primary education will have to be developed in a symbiotic relationship with the pattern of living and environment of the villages concerned, taking account of the work patterns of the children's families. Since working children can spare at the most about1½ hours to 2½ hours in the evenings, the curriculum and teaching - learning techniques must be adjusted to the available time. Finally, ways will have to be found to link up the part-time with the full-time system so they will jointly meet the needs of all the children of primary school age in the community. Along with experimental part-time education for children not attending school, the project proposes to develop programs to reorient the teachers of formal day schools and help them undertake improvement of schools and self-development.

Higher Education among Women

Regards higher education, in 1950-51, the total number of women enrolment was in the ratio of 100 men to 14 women. In 1994-95, total women enrolment was 2,065, which means the ratio of 100 men to 51 women. During the last fifty years we have made great progress in the field of higher education particularly in terms of quantity.

Reasons for Low Literacy

In India, education is the most important instrument for human resource development. Education of women, therefore occupies top priority amongst various measures taken to improve the status of women in India. In recent years, the focus of planning has shifted from equipping women from their traditional roles of housewives and mothers to recognizing their worth as producers making a major contribution to family and national income. Efforts have been made over the past three decades of planned development to enroll more girls in schools and encourage them to stay in schools, to contribute their education as long as possible, and to provide non-formal educational opportunities for women.

Table 15.4: Enrolment of Women in Higher Education

Year	Percentage of enrolment
1980 -81	27.2
1985 - 86	29.1
1987 - 88	31.0
1990 - 91	32.0
2000 - 01	43.0

Source: Selected Educational Statistics (2000-01)

Unfortunately the succeeding centuries saw slip-down in the field of women education. Opportunities for formal education got almost denied to women due to child marriage, purdah, enforced widowhood and Sati system. There was open criticism and opposition to girls' education. The society looked down upon the idea of girls stirring out of their homes.

Some other factors responsible for low enrolment are:

- The requirement for older girls to stay at home to take care of siblings when mothers are away at work;
- Need for girls to work in order to help in augmenting the family income;
- Early marriage of girls;
- Social customs that hinder female mobility after puberty;
- Lack of relevance of school curriculum; and
- Lack of facilities in the form of school buildings, hostels and women teachers, etc.

Women's Universities and Colleges

In many countries, especially in Asia, enrolment of girls in higher education is extremely low. Among conservative families and communities, parents, fearful of their daughters reputation and marriage prospects, are opposed to sending their daughters to a mixed gender institution. There is also a feeling that their performance will suffer in the face of the distractions provided by the presence of men students. In such circumstances, as a step towards enabling more female students to obtain the benefits of higher education, a number of countries have encouraged the establishment of all - women colleges and universities.

Women Development Programmes and Schemes

Everyone has a right to education, which shall be directed to the full development of human resources, and human dignity and potential, with particular attention to women and the girl child. Education should be designed to strengthen respect for human rights and fundamental freedoms, including those related to population and development. The very fact that a population conference forced the international community to look into the inter-linkages between population, poverty, gender inequality and development, was a major departure from the past.

Education policy has followed a slow path towards the realization that girls' schooling is fundamental to a country's success in achieving education for all. In the early years of the development movement, when many countries were newly independent, there was general enthusiasm for education as a vital factor in a nation's advancement.

National Policy on Education: Initiatives for Women

The National Policy on Education (NPE) 1986 is a landmark in the approach to women's education. It has attempted for the first time to address itself to the basic issues of women's equality. In the section titled "Education for Women's Equality", the policy states:

Education will be used as an agent of basic change in the status of women. In order to neutralize the accumulated distortions of the past, there will be well - conceived edge in favour of women. The National Education system will play positive, interventionist role in the empowerment of women. It will foster the development of new values through redesigned curricula, textbooks, training and orientation of teachers, decision makers and administrators.

Education Review Committee Report, 1990

On May 7, 1990 the government of India announced the appointment of a committee to a review the National Policy on Education, 1986. The Committee reviewed the NPE and its Programme of Action (POA) in the context of women's education and made various recommendations with regards to the following dimensions:

- Access to education and quality of learning.

- Content of education and gender bias.
- Vocational education.
- Training of teachers and other educational personnel.
- Research and development of Women's studies.
- Representation of women in the educational hierarchy.
- Empowerment of women.
- Adult education.
- Resources.
- Management.

National Perspective Plan for Women's Education (1998 - 2000)

This National Perspective Plan formulated some important specific objectives for women education so that women may actively participate in the areas of social, cultural, economic and political development. These important objectives in regard to women's education are:

- Elimination of illiteracy, universalisation of elementary education and minimization of the dropout rate in the age group 6-14 years and stagnation to negligible proportion.
- Ensuring opportunities to all women for access to appropriate level, nature and quality of education and also the wherewithal for success comparable with men.
- Substantial vocationalization and diversification of secondary education so as to provide a wide scope for employment and economic independence of women.
- Providing non-formal and part-time courses to women to enable them to acquire knowledge and skills for their social, cultural and economic advancement.
- Making education an effective means for women's equality by (a) addressing ourselves to the constraint that prevent women from participating in the educational process; (b) eliminating the existing bias in the system, (c) making necessary intervention in the content process of education to inculcate positive egalitarian attitudes, and (d) ensuring that teachers' perceive this as one of their essential roles.

Women's Education in Five Year Plans

First Five Year Plan (1951-56): First Five Year Plan provided due importance to women's education under its Chapter XXXIII - Education. It stated under point 8 'Women's Education', that the general purpose and objective of woman's education cannot of course be different from the purpose and objectives of men's education. There are, however, vital differences in the way in which this purpose has to be realized.

Second Five Year Plan (1956-61): This Five Year Plan described the importance of girl education in Chapter XXIII - Education under its head "Secondary Education (Girls Education)'. At the secondary stage, the education of girls seriously lags behind. At present, out of total population of 12 million girls in the age group 14-17 years, about 3 per cent are attending schools. Plans of states do not provide in sufficient measure for the education of girls, for the number of high schools for girls is expected to increase from 1500 to 1700 by the end of the Second Plan.

Third Five Year Plan (1961-66): This Five Year Plan describes importance of women education in Chapter XXIX. - Education under the head of 'Elementary Education (Girls education)'. It stated that a very large gap still exists between the proportion of boys and girls attending school. The National Council for Women's Education carefully considered the special measures needed for promoting the education of girls at the primary, middle and secondary stages and made a series of recommendations. These include the provision of quarters for women teachers, special allowances for women teachers working in rural areas, condensed education courses for adult women so as to enlarge the supply of women teachers, stipend for women teacher trainees, attendance prizes and scholarships, appointment of school mothers in co-educational institutions and provision of necessary amenities to some extent.

Fourth Five Year Plan (1969-74): This Five Year Plan describe the importance of education in its chapter XVI - Education and Manpower under the heading 'Girls Education'. It stated that sustained efforts to extend education among girls have been made from the First Plan period. Girl students, as a percentage of their population in the relevant age group, increased from 25 in 1950-51 to 1959 in 1968-69 in classes IX-XI. The gap between the enrollment of boys and girls is still considerable. During the Fourth Plan, the enrolment of girls will be further increased through the organization of special programmes the nature of which will vary from state to state.

Fifth Five Year Plan (1974 -1979): The central and state governments have taken a number of steps to stimulate the education of girls and women. These included creation of separate cells in the State Directorates of Education to look after the programmes of girls' education, establishment of polytechnics for girls, construction of staff quarters for women teachers in rural areas and girls' hostels, introduction of condensed educational courses, assistance to voluntary educational organizations working in the field of women's education and holding of seminars in different states to discuss problems and programmes of girls' education.

Sixth Five Year Plan (1980-1985): In the history of planning in India, the first time, the separate chapter on *"Women and Development"* was introduced in the Sixth Five Year Plan (1980-85). This chapter included three important sectors for women in India like: education, employment and health.

The Plan stated "in the field of education, under the programme for universalisation of elementary education, there has been a special drive for higher enrolment and retention of girls in schools. The enrolment of girls increased from 272.78 lakh (64.9 per cent) in 1979-80 to 281.18 lakh (66.2 per cent) in 1980-81, 291. 19 lakh (70.3 per cent) in 1981-82 and 301.58 lakh (72.4 per cent) in 1982-83 in classes I-V. The target for 1983-84 is 319.60 lakh (76.3 per cent). Similarly, for classes VI-VIII, the enrolment of girls improved from 61.53 lakh (26.0 per cent) in 1979-80 to 65.68 lakh (27.2 per cent) in 1980-81, 73.83 lakh (31.0 per cent) in 1982-83. The target for 1983-84 is 87.41 lakh (35.8 per cent)." There was also the provision of incentive for school-going girls, like uniform, free books, stationery and attendance scholarships. A centrally sponsored scheme on 50:50 basis with the State Governments was provided for the construction of hostel facilities for encouraging schedules caste and scheduled tribe girls.

Seventh Five Year Plan (1985-90): This Five Year Plan made the emphasis on women education under the following:

- Efforts will be made to provide 100 per cent coverage for education of girls up to the age of 14 years. Priority will be given to retain girls in school. Incentives like uniforms, text-books and attendance scholarships will be continued for the needy girls in all schools. Non-formal education will be expanded to benefit girls in 6-14 age group.
- It has been proposed to provide free education for girls up to the end of the higher secondary stage.
- The educational content of the adult-education programme is to be modified to incorporate new value systems in the community regarding the role of women in the family and community in addition to increasing the coverage of literacy. The number of non-formal education centres for girls will be increased. In the rural areas, Integrated Rural Development Programme (IRDP), National Rural Employment Programme (NREP), Training of Rural Youth for Self Employment (TRYSEM) and the other of such programmes will have a component of functional literacy for women.
- Talented girls all over the country will be encouraged to pursue higher education. For this, it is proposed to expand the 'Open Learning Systems'

including corresponding courses for women.

- For the promotion of technical and vocational education for girls, more and more polytechnics for women are to be set up during the Plan period. Programme for vocationalisation of education for girls is to be expanded.
- To boost education among the girls belonging to scheduled castes, scheduled tribes and other weaker sections additional facilities would continue to be provided under the 'Development of Backward Classes' sector.
- Priority will be given to women in teachers' training programmes to increase the availability of trained women teachers.

Eighth Five Year Plan (1992-97): The thrust areas of Eighth Five Year Plan in the field of education for both the sexes are as follows:

- Universalisation of elementary education, *eradication* of illiteracy in the age group of 15 to 35 and strengthening of vocational education so as to relate it to the emerging needs in the urban and rural settings.
- The need for according the highest priority to universalisation of elementary education is, therefore, well established. Within the overall school-age population, the focus would be on girls, who accounts for two- thirds of target and among adults the focus would be on women's literacy as well as other national objectives like population control and family welfare.

Ninth Five Year Plan (1997-2002): The Ninth Five Year Plan adopted the strategy of women's component plan, under which not less than 30 per cent of funds/ benefits were earmarked in all the women specific programmes: A review of the women's component plan during the Ninth Plan (1997-2002) has confirmed that nearly 42.9 per cent of the Gross Budgetary Support (GBS) in 15 Central Ministries / Departments aggregating a total amount of Rs.51,943 crore has been spent on women. In the departments such on family welfare, health, education, women and child and Indian systems of medicine and homeopathy as high as 50 per cent to 80 per cent of the plan expenditure was incurred on women.

Tenth Five Year Plan (2002-2007): The Tenth Five Year Plan has undertaken measures to strengthen women's component in plan programmes. In order to address the developmental issues relating to women, a Task Force on Women and Children was constituted by the government in August 2000 under the Chairmanship of Shri. K.C. Pant. This Task Force in its Report recommended the setting up of inter-ministerial standing Committee to review the various existing programmes and suggest strategies for the future.

Prevention of Atrocities

The programme of education work for prevention of Atrocities Against

Women, started in 1982, extends financial assistance to research and academic institutions like universities, colleges/ women's study centres and institutions of higher learning etc, and voluntary organizations for various items of education work, propaganda, publicity and research work such as production of publicity materials, research studies on particular aspects of violence/ atrocities against women; awards for best films, short stories, poems and other creative efforts, etc. Dissemination of information/publicity materials in regional languages is also envisaged under this Programme. The focus is on those women who are subjected to deprivation, brutality, extortion and exploitation.

Scheme for Adolescent Girls

For the first time in India, a special intervention has been devised for adolescent girls using the ICDS infrastructure. The scheme of adolescent girls focuses on school drop-out girls in the age group of 11-18 years and attempts to meet the special needs of nutrition, education, literacy, recreational and skill development of adolescent girls. It attempts to make the adolescent girls a better future mother and tap her potential as a social animator. The scheme for adolescent girls has been sanctioned in 507 Child Development Blocks and, when fully operationalised would benefit about 4.50 lakh girls.

National Commission for Women

In January 1991, the government constituted a statutory body called National Commission for Women (NCW) with a specific mandate to study and monitor all matters relating to the constitutional and legal safeguards provided for women; review the existing legislations to suggest amendments wherever necessary; and to look into complaints involving deprivation of the rights of women. Similar Commissions have also been set up in nine States. The NCW has taken up a number of activities which includes (a) setting up of 11 expert committees to tender advice on various women's issues; (b) conducting Pariwarik Lok Adalats, to which nearly 35,000 cases were referred; (c) complaints and pre-litigation cell; (d) legal awareness; (e) welfare of women prisoners under trails; and (f) action issues of women and children.

Empowerment of Women through Education

Women constitute 48 per cent of the total population of India as per Census and constituting about half of the world population, are the most important human resources central to development of any race, culture, nation or civilization. In Gandhi's view, one step for a woman ten steps for nation. As such the role and participation of women in society cannot be ignored. Like men, women are also found to be working in various fields.

Importance of Women's Education

Education for empowerment means women gaining an understanding and control over social, economic and political force in order to improve their standing in society. Education is a corner stone of women's empowerment because it enables them to respond to opportunities to challenge their traditional roles and to change their lives. This is true not only because education is an entry point to other opportunities, but also because it has ripple effects within the family and across generations. Investing in secondary school education for girls yields high dividends. Girls who have been educated are likely to marry later and have smaller and healthier families. Educated women can recognize the importance of health care and know how to seek it for themselves and their children. Education helps girls and women to know their rights and to gain confidence to claim them. The education of parents is linked to their children's educational attainments and the mother's education is usually more influential than the father's. An educated mother's greater influence in household negotiation may allow her to secure more resources for her children. India has also taken it as a challenge to develop its women by empowering them. This is not a matter of concern for only governments and social scientist and but also of the masses at large. Empowerment aims at giving the power to women to take her own decisions and to have control over her destiny. Above all, society should give due respect and regard to women. Educated women can get employment in all fields. They should no longer be dependents on their brothers, fathers or husband. They should be in position to manage their families with their own will. Education has far reaching benefits in the march of women towards empowerment. Education is the key to all ways and means of women's empowerment.

Empowerment is a process of awareness and capacity building leading to greater participation, to greater decision-making power and control, and to transformative action. Women's empowerment is a global issue and is being discussed all over the world. This concept has roots in the women's movement throughout the world and particularly for third world feminists. In the mid 1980's, the term empowerment became popular in the field of development especially with reference to women. The Ninth Five Year Plan gave special attention to the empowerment of women and the objective of the Plan was stated as 'empowering women as the agents of social change and development'.

Women empowerment is the most vital component for sustainable development. Empowerment equips women to be socially knowledgeable, economically independent, personally reliant and politically participatory. It is a process that involves intellectual enlightenment, economical enrichment and social emancipation on the part of women. Education is the most important tool for women empowerment.

Educational Experiences with Women at Grassroot Level

A study was conducted by Priyadharshini (2006) on "Literacy and Education of Tribal girls in Gudalur Taluk of Niligiri District, Tamil Nadu." The area selected for the study was Gudalur Taluk of Nilgiri district. There were four types of tribes - Kotas, Kurumbas, Irulas and Pariyas which existed in the selected taluk. Based on this preliminary information, twenty five girls from each tribal community, making the total size of the sample 100 were selected at random.

Tribal girls' education in Gudalur taluk of Nilgiri district - An observation.

- Majority 50 per cent of the respondents were found to be illiterate, 34 per cent of the respondents have undergone primary school education. The literacy and education of the tribal girls require much attention as the literacy level was found to be low here.
- Seventy one per cent of them belonged to nuclear families and the rest 29 per cent of them belonged to joint families.
- Majority 61 per cent of the tribal girl children were found to be illiterate, 22 per cent of the girls have undergone primary school education and only 2 per cent have undergone higher secondary school education.
- Two of them - one with higher secondary education and the other with a degree are working as teachers in a local private school at present. As the majority 61 per cent of the tribal girls were illiterates, the literacy and education of the tribal girls require much attention.
- About 47 per cent of the respondents stated that girls' education was not given importance in the past and they see that girls study more at present, girls were dependent throughout their life in the past and their life style has changed at present because of education as per 4.2 per cent of the respondents' observation.
- Twenty six per cent of the respondents opined that girls education is important for their security, following 24 per cent of the respondents stating that education brings out a bright future for the girls, 15 per cent of the respondents revealing that education of the girls improves their socio-economic status and the standard of living of their families.
- Regarding the type of education required for the tribal girls, 56 per cent of the respondents wanted vocational education to provide good job opportunities for tribal girls, 8 per cent of the respondents opined that education should

improve their life style to achieve better standard of living.

- Lack of access to educational institutions (32 per cent), domestic responsibilities (23 per cent), threat to security (18 per cent), least important and early marriage (16 per cent) and preference to male children and gender bias (11 per cent) were the constraints of the tribal girl children.
- Tribal girls as well as their parents should be motivated and given incentives (63 per cent), provision of scholarships and stipends for tribal girl students (22 per cent), preference in employment opportunities for tribal girls (10 per cent), and separate schools for tribal girl students (5 per cent) were the important suggestions given by these respondents for future improvement.

Rajalakshmi (1996) conducted a study on "Impact of education on conservation of household resources by rural families" in three villages namely Kovanur, Palanigoundamputhur and Mathampalayam belonging to Periyanaickenpalayam Panchayat Union in Coimbatore District, Tamil Nadu.

Three hundred homemakers at the rate of 100 from each of the three villages were included as the sample for the study. After education, there were time saving techniques adopted by the homemakers i.e., 82 per cent using labour saving devices like hay box, bio-gas, smokeless chulah and mud storage devices had conserved time, while 59 per cent had provided sufficient time to do all the tasks satisfactorily.

Roma Devi (1998) conducted a study on "Skill Development for the members of Urban Indira Mahila Kendras (IMKs)". The sample included 165 women from seven IMKs in Avarampalayam, Illango Nagar, Karuppaswami Nagar, Periyar Nagar, Shanmugagounder Nagar, Seeranaickenpalayam and Selvapuram areas of Coimbatore Corporation.

After the utilization of the skill there is significant difference at one per cent level, only fifty two per cent stresses the need for more training and 33 per cent of them demanded financial assistance and 15 per cent of them demanded marketing facilities.

Roopa (1996) organized a research study by "Imparting education on environmental protection to selected women Self Help Group members." at Kathirnaickenpalayam Village belonging to Periyanaickenpalayam block, Coimbatore District with 72 women members, included as the sample for the study.

The outcome of the Education on environmental protection in terms of gain in knowledge and extent of adoption was found out through knowledge test and checklist.

T.V. Rao in his study suggested that four important strategies could be used to empower women, namely educating girls and women, facilitating their involvement in economic activities through development of their entrepreneurial income earning capabilities and access to credit, involving women in policy formulation and decision making, encouraging social cultural change by exploring gender issues and promoting the effective implementation of equal rights legislation.

The education of girls and women brings particular benefits to society in a number of ways. Educated mothers tend to ensure that children in turn are educated and become effective members of society. They safeguard future generation's health and nutrition. No country can become developed without developing the capabilities of women and encouraging the empowerment of women.

Future Action on Women's Education

The programmes for women's education will have to be implemented as a priority so that women attain a comparable level of education by 2020. The strategy to be adopted for raising literacy levels and educating among women has to keep, in view the vast cultural, geographical and ecological variations as also the problems relating to poverty and ignorance. The cultural and geographical variations call for decentralization of educational planning. Within the national perspective planning, implementation and monitoring of educational programmes has to be done at district and block levels, keeping in view the socio-economic and geographic parameters of the area. The vocational and occupational components have to be designed in accordance with the availability of resources and job opportunities in the regions. Voluntary organizations and women's groups active in the area should be involved in the task. The objectives to be achieved by 2020 in regard to women's education are:

- Elimination of illiteracy, universalization of elementary education and minimization of the dropout and stagnation rate in the age group 6-14 years, to negligible proportions.
- Ensuring opportunities to all women for access to appropriate level nature and quality of education and also the wherewithal for success comparable with men.
- Substantial vocationalization and diversification of secondary education so as to provide a wide scope for employment and economic independence of women.
- Making education an effective means for women's equality.
- Providing non-formal and part-time courses to women to acquire knowledge

and skills for their social, cultural and economic advancement.

- Impetus to enrol in various professional degree courses so as to increase their number in medicine, teaching and engineering fields substantially.
- Creating a new system of accountability, particularly of the basic educational services, to the local community, inter alia, by active involvement of women.

Conclusion

India is rich in policies, thus almost every conceivable strategy to promote girl's education has been covered. The problem lies in implementation. It is therefore, necessary to concentrate on making the system work and deliver the services. The following areas need special attention and intensive advocacy to persuade political leader, policy makers and administrators to reform the system.

Shut the tap before mopping the floor. Unless every child - girl and boy - has an opportunity to go to school, and is retained and taught in school for at least five years there will be no significant change in the educational scenario in India. Adult and Non-formal education programmes will then make a qualitative difference. Non-formal and other forms of partial education programmes cannot be a substitute for universal access to elementary education. This is particularly important for girls' education. Ensuring every girl child experiences childhood and has access to schooling should be the priority of all educational interventions. Identify the most deprived sections of society and design and implement time-bound special programmes for girls.

References

Bhandari, Arvind, Women Deserve a Better Deal, The Tribune March 8, 2000.

Bhandari, Sarita, Problems of Women Education, Arise Publishers & Distributors, New Delhi, 2005.

Malhotra, Meenakshi, Empowerment of Women, Isha books, Delhi, Vol-1, 2004.

Malhotra, Meenakshi, Empowerment of Women, Isha books, Delhi, Vol-3, 2004.

Mishra, R.C., Women Education, A.P.H. Publishing Corporation, New Delhi, 2005.

Rao, R.K., Women and Education, Kalpaz Publications, Delhi, 2005

Sharma, Karta, Women Power in Twenty-first Century, Anmol Publications pvt. ltd., New Delhi, 2004.

Siddiqui, Hasan, Mujibul, Women Education: A Research Approach, Asish Publishing house, New Delhi, 2004.

Usha, Rao N.J. : Women in Developing Society, Asish Publishing House, Delhi, 2000.

16

Consumer Education for Women Empowerment

Rameshwari Pandya

Due to rapid industrialization and multifaceted development in India after Independence, there appeared a flood of consumer goods and services in the Indian market which almost changed the relationship between the consumer and the trader. Technological advancements in the field of media led to flooding of advertisements of goods and services, further worsening the otherwise grim situation. Lack of consumer awareness, illiteracy, poverty, etc. further led to the exploitation of consumers.

Every individual is a consumer and consumer is the determining factor in all market situations and changing socio cultural environment. The ups and downs of the market is determined by the consumers. The consumer is the final buyer and user of goods and services for the satisfaction of wants. The consumer especially the women which constitute about half of the population determines the changing environment of the fast changing world. The Indian consumers are generally victimized in the market place by misleading trade activities and in case of women it is more true as they do not raise their voice since they are unaware of their rights. The women who are heads of household find themselves in a particularly precarious position. The obstacles they face are directly related to their low education and low income as they live under extreme insecure conditions. Hence, women need to be informed of their basic rights. They need the information as well as motivation to improve the status of their families.

The buying practice of majority of women consumers is not very satisfactory. The women are uneducated and unaware as they lack basic knowledge regarding the market, price index and the role as consumers. The rural women consumers are landless labour, housewives and are unaware of the sources of reliable information and tend to do faulty buying. They get victimized by the malpractices of selling as they do not know which points to be considered while purchasing the goods and services.

Throughout the world, the incidence of female-headed households is on the increase (Youssef and Helter, 1984). It is unfortunate that because of centuries of inertia, ignorance and conservatism the actual and potential role of women in the society has been ignored, preventing them from making their rightful contribution to social progress. Since times immemorial, women have been working and making contribution towards the overall development of society.

In India, women in general and poor women in particular, are relatively powerless with no control over resources and little share in decision-making power. The status of women has been low due to their poverty and illiteracy. The global conference in USA in 1998, highlighted empowerment as the surest way of making women partners in development. Empowerment concept is equipping one to improve the living conditions.

Empowerment of women means becoming independent and self-reliant. There is continued inequality and vulnerability of women in all sectors. As women are oppressed they need to be empowered in all walks of life. Thus, women empowerment is a basic human right where she wants neither to beg for power nor search for power hierarchy to exercise power against others. Women and their problems have acquired growing importance in our social milieu over the last few decades.

The process of women's empowerment is in terms of ability to identify their own needs, problems and solutions, personnel assertions and confidence, growth of critical consciousness awareness about their roles and responsibilities and rights. Though women have many capabilities like high determination, sense of responsibility, better management etc. but they lack education and information.

Negligible number of women are educated on what, where, when and how much to buy in addition to how to pay. As they are uneducated so they are unable to compare prices. They must know the brand, expiry date and manufacturing date, place of buying, packaging and appearance. This information would help them in decision making and participation which would ultimately empower them.

It is needed to revamp the entire approach towards women, emphasizing the future challenges which the country has to face in the coming years. Consumer rights are like human rights which are recognized as the fundamental right of a human being. Women make tremendous contribution to society by their productive, reproductive and household work. The quality of life enjoyed by them is extremely important for the welfare of entire family.

Our women, who had a glorious past, lived a life of disgrace in post Vedic era. But they are regaining their lost respectful status in society now. Educational and economic empowerment of women is to develop their conscience and economic participation in family, community and national productivity. The choice the consumer makes will depend on the education and income level.

In India, there are a number of enactments for the protection of consumer. In fact each legislation in the country has some elements, which are directly, or indirectly aimed at consumer's welfare or protection. Some of the laws enacted to protect consumer interests directly are as under:

Year	**Legislation**
1930	Sale of Goods Act
1937	Agricultural Produce Act
1940	Drug and Cosmetic Act
1950	Emblems and Names Act
1952	Indian Standards Institution Act
1953	Prevention of Food Adulteration Act
1954	Drug and Magic Remedies Trade Practices Act
1955	Essential Commodities Act
1958	Trade and Merchandise Marks Act
1969	Monopolies and Restrictive Trade Practices Act
1972	Hire Purchase Act
1974	Water Act
1976	Standards of Weights and Measures Act
1980	Prevention of Black Marketing and Maintenance of Supplies of Essential Commodities Act
1981	Air Act
1985	Standards of Weights and Measures Act
1986	Environment Protection Act
1986	Consumer Act
1986	Bureau of Indian Standard Act
1987	Railway Claims Tribunal Act
1988	Electrical Appliances Order
1992	Securities and Exchange Board of India Act
2000	Electrical Wires, Cables, Appliances and Accessories Act

Consumer Awareness: Need of the Hour

Consumer being the center point of the plethora of economic activities is termed as 'Bhagwan' or the 'King', yet consumer has been and is being exploited across the globe in numerous ways and all of us being consumers come across and become victims of consumer exploitation in one form or the other. Consumers have been exploited since times immemorial since greed is a gateway to hell and it perverts the soul and often leads an individual on roads to crime. This era of materialism has sacrificed moral values at the alter of acquiring wealth by fraud, misappropriation, misrepresentation, corruption and adulteration which have merged as the new techniques of trade and commerce and profession more so in the era of industrialization, economic liberalization, globalization, wherein the consumer has, more often than not, fallen pray to ill practices being practiced by the manufacturers and sellers and has often been cheated in quality, quantity, potency and price of goods and services. Untrained consumer being no match to the businessman marketing goods and services on an organized basis and by trained professionals; a need for the protection of consumers was felt throughout the world. This led to enactment of consumer protection laws across the globe and India is no exception to this.

Consumer protection is part of social and economic justice which is one of the ideals enshrined in the Constitution of India. It, therefore, mandated the enactment of various laws dealing with social and economic justice including consumer protection. However, the various laws dealing, directly or indirectly, with the consumer protection failed to provide much needed relief to the consumers. The benefits of these laws did not reach the exploited consumers as the enforcing, controlling and supervisory machinery was found indifferent and ineffective due to inordinate delay, high cost and complex procedure. Therefore, a need was felt for the enactment of law dealing specifically and exhaustively on the subject and the Parliament obliged by enacting Consumer Protection Act, 1986, a legislation for the protection and promotion of consumer interests.

Consumer Protection Act, 1986

This law was enacted for better protection of consumers' interests. It provides effective safeguards to consumers against defective goods, unsatisfactory services, unfair trade practices and other forms of exploitation. The Act lays down a time frame for disposal of cases. It provides for quick and inexpensive redressal of grievances because no fee or other charge has to be made by a consumer. He can make a complaint on a simple paper without any legal or stamp paper. The Act provides for three-tier machinery consisting of District Forum, State Commissions and the National Commission. It also provides the formation of consumer protection councils in every state. These councils are expected to promote the cause of consumer protection through education. It covers six consumer rights: right to safety, to be informed, to choose, to be heard, to redress and to consumer education. After an amendment in 1993, the scope of the Act has been widened to include paid services like medical services.

1. **Right to Safety:** Certain goods may cause serious injuries. These goods are pressure cookers, gas cylinders, electrical goods etc. If there is any manufacturing defect in the goods, consumers have right to be protected against the fatal risk. The Consumer Protection Act safeguards such consumer interests.
2. **Right to be Informed:** A consumer has the right to be informed about the quality, quantity and price of the product. He should also be informed about the

ingredients of the product, date of manufacturing and expiry, method of use, side effects of the commodity and precautions to be undertaken. The information should be written on the package or on the separate piece of paper.

3. Right to Choose: The consumer has the right to choose the product of his choice out of the alternate products available. The seller should not adopt aggressive technique and force the consumer to buy certain product. The consumer must be given a chance to choose. The Act provides right to choose.

4. Right to be Heard: Every consumer must be granted right to be heard. He must be assured his complaints and grievances about the product and services will be heard and attention paid to it. There are certain organizations, which encourage consumers to communicate their opinion about the product. Newspapers have also stated inviting grievances from the consumers and publishing it in their newspapers and seeking redressal from producers.

5. Right to Seek Redressal: Consumers have the right to get their claims settled in their favour in case of being cheated and exploited by the producers. The Government has set up many consumer courts for this specific purpose.

6. Right to Consumer Education: The consumer must be educated about the rights to protect his interests, the law has granted him. He must know the law dealing with the malpractices of producers and manufacturers, so that he may not be cheated.

These rights are based on the basic rights of IOCU (International Organization of Consumers) viz., right to safety, to information, to choice, to be heard, to redressal, to consumer education, to healthy environment and to basic needs.

Role of Media in Creating Awareness

In the modern scenario, citizens come to know of events mainly through press, radio, television and cinema. This forms our opinion about the government policies for consumers. Media plays a vital role in providing information to the consumers thereby reducing the information gap. There is a growing demand for supply of consumers' information in the present area.

For this purpose, almost 30 consumer-oriented legislations, the impact of new professionals working in the media, the springing up of various active consumers associations etc., have contributed to the purpose. Consumer awareness through media is gaining momentum slowly. It is an important element for protection of consumer rights.

To provide awareness to the uneducated regarding quality and quantity of goods we have various programmes like 'Jago Grahak Jago' and advertisements through sound broadcasting by All India Radio and Doordarshan. In India, we have a large number of daily newspapers, which also shape the public powerfully but the main problem with it is that is read only by educated people. But the recent debut of mass media in the field of advertising consumer goods posed new dangers to the consumers.

The marketing experts and business stalwarts easily manipulate the media, which furnishes the information. This results in consumer exploitation extenuated by the increasing impersonalisation of communication structures, through the development of new technologies. Even in the information given by the media, which is owned by the state, there is no guarantee of the product, which is advertised through its agencies.

New technical products thrown in the market are of such nature regarding which the consumer is completely ignorant. The consumer has to face a number of product failures every day.

Since the problems are manifold and arise daily it is quite important to make them aware.

It is beyond doubt that only an aware consumer can protect his rights. Towards this the Government should make sincere efforts in the following gray areas:

- The government should release monthly updated bulletins, which contains the minimum prices of certain standard commodities available in the local market, since as per the existing laws the total price printed on the wrapper is excluding the local taxes.
- In India, the commercial tax system is so complicated that it is beyond anybody's capacity to remember the tax rates applicable to various items, which results in the trader charging abnormal rates. To counter this, regularly updated bulletins should be made available to the public.
- Paper pamphlets in the newspapers to inform and educate the consumer about the lowest prevailing price in the market may be distributed so that he could guard himself against excess charging by the traders.
- Government agencies and the local NGOs should strive to maintain a communication channel with the consumers and keep reminding them the protection available to them under the prevailing laws.
- In addition to the prevailing consumer protection mechanism through advertising in the newspaper, the government should ensure the publicity mechanism at play for highlighting the consumer friendly judgements delivered by various consumer courts throughout the country for redressal of consumer complaints.
- The most effective measure favouring the consumer is the historical

Consumer Protection Act (CPA) passed in 1986. International Conference on Consumer Protection held in Malaysia in 1997 hailed it as an unprecedented move in the field of protecting the rights of consumers.
- The government should consider amendments to the CPA to prevent manufacturers from selling goods that are detrimental to the consumers.

Role Home Scientists Can Play in the Promotion of Consumer Education

Home is the first school that any child goes to. The learning's acquired by the children about the science of home are therefore, the most fundamental in the entire education of the children. Home science in India is recognized as a fundamental education because of three major reasons:

- There is a cultural, philosophical and religious value placed on "home" in India, which makes all knowledge and services to home, worthy of teaching and research. Home science fulfills a role which is fundamental to Indian philosophy and culture, by its very virtue of specialized knowledge about improving the home and family living.
- The industrialization in India has affected the structure and function of homes. The aspirations of people about their standards of living, jobs, and education, have been so much elevated that the traditional home and family living have been rendered less contributory to the development of individuals. In the light of rising aspirations due to industrialization, a contemporary knowledge in home science has become necessary.
- The social consciousness of Indian people is the highest in the current decade. The people have felt the need to make their own efforts to improve their health, education, clothing and shelter. Home sgives knowledge to achieve better health; buy or make better garments and fabrics; and build or improve the house and its equipment and furnishings. The modern need of education is in addition, fulfilled by making home science a vocational education.

The broad objective of home science as stated by Thyagarajan (1977) is as follows: to impart general education in preparing pupils for a satisfying personal living, developing a wholesome personality, acquiring happy human relationships and enriching one's life. At the same time, it is also necessary to find the vocation for which one is most suited and getting prepared for it.

Home science is an interdisciplinary field of studies and has linkage with other subsystems in the family as well as in national perspective. It is important to interact with all these systems for pooling of the resources. Because of the tremendous change in the political, social and economic scenario, it is the need of the hour to educate the prospective consumer as well as prospective employees about it.

The home scientist can help in consumer-producer interactions and act as a catalyst. Home Scientists have very successfully contributed in various government programmes. On the same lines, it is high time that linkages should be established between the developed and developing worlds to ensure an exchange of better understanding of different value systems and culture and knowledge of technology which will ultimately help in a better quality of life.

Today the society is no longer only the immediate village, town or nation, but the world as a global village is bringing about vast political, economic, social and cultural changes and India is no special. No society remains static. A section of our society is already moving towards the so called "Western" culture as global changes are leading to a homogenized world society.

Home science has a unique problem to be tackled. There is a change in the urban section, which is very fast while another large section which co-exists in the rural society largely has tradition-bound culture of oppression and cxploitation. Both modern as well as traditional families need intervention to cope up with this change.

Today the environment in which the families are attempting to meet their need for food, clothing and shelter are constantly changing. So we need to constantly analyse the development opportunities and research possibilities relevant to the local situations.

In order to reflect the social and economic realities of current needs, we must consider the following points. Life style issues and emphasis on training, home based business for self employment and community based participation to develop skills to help poor households.

- Skills in formulation of public and family policy measures, which can help the policy makers.
- Consumer affairs, consumer advocacy and consumer protection issues.
- Economic development of families in this era of globalization.

With the world rapidly becoming a global village, the role of teacher becomes a more responsible one. They should reorganize and rearrange the curriculum to build the future generations more capable of utilizing the global network for the benefit of mankind.

Role of Students and Youth

A student is medium of mouth piece publicity of any system and they can organize different programme planning of companies for the awareness of the consumer. She can come to know about her rights as consumer by reading consumers education in her syllabus. She can introduce these rights to her family also. By identifying a good producer she can organize a big consumer organization group. At local level, she can make consumer organizations in villages and streets and with the help of these organizations she can demand to stop meaningless advertisement and file case related to consumer affairs in consumer court.

Younger generation is the power and vigour of the country or perhaps the younger generation is the most influential generation of the country. The youth can undergo to change the whole scenario. Before talking about the role of youth in consumer protection, we must know about the defects of our education system. The youth is the future of the nation. It can do a lot in awakening the people about their rights and duties. But the defective education system has created a vicious circle of unawareness.

Steps to be Undertaken by the Youth

- They can originate awareness among the people of backward areas by organizing camps, rallies etc.
- They can make associations in schools and colleges.
- They can also make posters, pamphlets, banners and can organize cultural programmes, group discussions, debates, extempore to aware the uneducated masses.
- They can also encourage the mass media to start the programmes related to consumer protection.
- Like other subjects, consumer awareness should be made a compulsory subject.
- Apart from this, seminars should be organized by the youth and for the youth.
- Last but not the least is that the practical part of "consumer awareness" subject should be highlighted instead of its theoretical aspect.

However, before implementing all the above steps, it is necessary that the teachers or the institutes through awards should motivate youth.

Recommendations

- Appropriate strategies should be evolved for improving interaction between journalists and consumer forum.
- Success stories of consumer forum need to be published through involving eminent personalities.
- Reports on consumer education, should be made news worthy by highlighting their relevance to society.

- Research on consumer needs to be strengthened.
- On Consumer Day, special supplements should be sponsored by advertisers in leading newspapers.
- Out reach of folk media needs to be expanded through the involvement of Panchayati Raj Institutions and NGOs in the development and utilization of media.
- Notwithstanding all the attractions of the media, nothing can substitute the vital inter-personal contact of the teacher and taught (here the volunteer and learners) who are close to each other.
- Objectives of consumer education have to be carried to the people in the shortest possible time. This is a public relations function.
- The massive training programme of consumer education personnel is to be reinforced by communication media.
- Create awareness about consumer's rights and educate the general public about consumer problems and remedies through seminars, workshops and training programmes.
- Dissemination and spreading consumer education.
- Some of the voluntary consumer organizations have successfully used public interest litigation to enforce consumer rights in several cases. They have filed cases in the court of law in the interest of the general public, not for any individual.
- Lobbying with the Central and State governments for a better deal for consumers.
- Pleading for the amendment of laws for better deal to the consumers.
- Publishing periodicals and journals to disseminate information among readers about consumer problems, legal reporting and other emerging matters of interest.
- Arrange comparative testing of consumer products through their own testing apparatus or accredited laboratories so as to evaluate the relative qualities of competing brands and the test results should be made public for the benefit of consumers.
- Make suggestions and recommend steps which government authorities should consider for policy making and administrative steps be adopted in the interest of consumer.
- Women themselves take initiative to organize action for their own development. Grassroot development workers for rural women seem to be more effective than top down workers.
- Social and economic empowerment can be ascertained through organizational

capacity building, formation of self help groups, providing consumer education and enriching their abilities with skill building strategies.

- Interaction between media and civil society is an ongoing dynamic process and the new wave of technology "especially digitalization and compression can be new binders on media and civil society".
- Students can play an important role in environment building like slogan writing, *nukkar nataks* etc. and can provide an important service in creating awareness about consumer rights and responsibilities.
- The centers should have a good network with other organizations working in the promotion of consumer education in country and abroad.
- The self-help groups, consumer associations and government officials should have good co-ordination for promotion of consumer education.

Suggested Curriculum Inputs

- Non-formal educational packages for all to develop work skills, social awareness and information about consumer education.
- Formation and management of credit and marketing cooperative.
- Communication technology especially to develop programmes on consumer education.
- Media skills related to focal areas of the curriculum for use in mass media for promotion of consumer education.

Conclusion

It is important to know how change takes when local and global interface takes place. It is very important to understand how people in Asia need not be marginalized but can live with the market and yet have property rights of indigenous knowledge and benefits of globalization.

Balanced development can only occur if we do not outright oppose the globalization yet find out ways to make people the stake holders in the change process and simultaneously gain from commercial exploitation of their resources. From the advent of globalization in 1991, it has affected the performance of all the major sectors of economy agrarian, industrial, banking and monetary, state, enterprises, trade and environment.

It is very important to understand globalization as a multi-dimensional process rather than as a project with a predetermined objective.

Thus, it can be safely concluded that the globalization which is in a way the result of new technology and communication, has tremendously shaken up the Indian psyche and has enlarged the horizon on one hand and on another it has diluted the concentration of quality. The globalization has given such a facelift that was not even dreamt of before.

However, a lot more still needs to be done in training and empowering the women to exercise their authority at all levels through training and capacity building with the help of NGOs, women organizations and research institutions. Government and some apex organizations have taken initiatives to empower women and bring them to main stream of development. Keeping in view the essentiality of streamlining the entire cycle of women's empowerment, specific measures have to be taken to exercise their rights towards life, health, education, dignity and information in proper manner. There is a need to organize awareness programmes for the women to orient them about their duties, powers, functions and making them an effective and empowered consumer. This will help them to develop positive attitude towards themselves and they can act as strong mobilizing force to motivate others of their own community to be a part of this noble mission.

References

R.K. Uppal, Consumer Protection Through Mass Awareness: New Challenges and Opportunities, Mahamaya Publishing House, New Delhi (India), 2007.

V. Sheshadri, Consumerism, Mittal Publications, New Delhi (India), 2006.

Veena Gandotra, Ami Divatia, Consumer Education, Dominant Publishers and Distributors, New Delhi, 2005.

Part III: Employment of Women

17

Institutional Management for Children

Rameshwari Pandya and Darshini Durkal

Women today are involved with men in sharing power, decision-making and implementation. Socio-economic changes, migration, and urbanization and need for more income have forced women to take up jobs outside home. Hence, they need to be educated suitably to meet the challenges of the changing society. In recent times the status of women or at least the role of women has changed particularly in the middle class. The status of family in the emerging Indian society is changing. The role and the status of women in family and society is also changing. Her role as a cook, parent and housewife has changed to earner worker, manager and an administrator. A look at women's earning over the past 20 years shows a mixed picture of progress.

Devi (1982) stated that women's working outside their homes as such is not altogether a new phenomenon, for women in rural India have always been working for a long time in factories as servants and construction labour but working out of home for employment reasons by educated middle and upper class women is a recent phenomenon. It was feared that emancipation of women from traditional household functions may lead them to neglect their obligations towards their home and children. Examining some statistics in relation to women's employment in middle class strata as well as regarding child care alternatives available, is of some value at this juncture. According to Desai and Patel (1985) due to the spread of education and expansion of the literacy sector, there has been an increase of women in white-collared jobs as well as professions like teaching, nursing, law, etc.

She became an earner not only because of the need of the family but also to improve the status of her family in the society. Since women earn about two-thirds of what men do, single mothers tend to have the maximum difficulty in meeting the child care services. Women believed that if they could not manage both these jobs, then they are failures. This has been referred to as the "superwomen syndrome". But as more and more men take on child-care responsibilities (either as part of two career families or as single parents) they are finding out how difficult is it to combine the two roles. In broader sense, the term "daycare" means institutional management of children or it simply means that some person other than member of a child's family takes care of a child during the part or a good part of a child's day.

Studies by NIPCCD (1978), Sharma (1986) and Kaur (1988) showed that the most prevalent child-care patterns are:

- Care by grandparents or family members.
- Part time or full time domestic servants or engaging full time *Ayaas*.
- The neighbours.
- Day care centres is the most common practice.

According to Consul (1989), the main objective of this study was to understand the existing situation of employed mothers in relation to child-care services. The major findings of the study were:

- Majority of children were cared at homes by relatives, the other common patterns being care of children by servants, family day care and care in institutions.
- Most of the mothers had support in child care and household activities with maximum help from fathers of the children.

Major changes in our society during the last 40 years has led to major changes in the ways children are being cared for today. More and more parents are working outside the home and need help in caring for their children. The demands of parenting affects working men and women in ways that we are only beginning to understand. Women can be successful entrepreneurs and self employed. Since the under-developed countries are capital-scarce economies with huge unemployment, the choice of technology problem assumes importance. Reduction of poverty and unemployment are the basic objectives of development planning in India. Entrepreneurship is an important ingredient of economic development and it is a must for the socio-economic upliftment of women. With increasing scarcity of jobs and rapid unemployment, entrepreneurship has assumed a big role and has become an important part of the economic policy of the country.

Entrepreneurship is today regarded as an important tool of development in all parts of the world. Therefore, an effort at involving women in the mainstream of development must include their training as entrepreneurs. An entrepreneur is a person who organizes, runs and is responsible for a business enterprise. She takes advantage of the market needs to earn profits. An ideal entrepreneur:

- Identifies the needs
- Takes calculated risk

- Seeks new opportunities to grow
- Invest money
- Makes important decisions, and
- Adapts business to changes in the market.

Day care centers offer many opportunities to women for self-employment, directly and indirectly.

The direct factors include - day care centres, *anganwadi*, nursery school, play centre, hobby centre, creative centre, toy library, library for children, centre preparing children for primary schools, toys, puppets, activity kit centre etc.

Indirectly, it would be taking care of young children whose mothers are at job. If care of young children is taken by such institutions, there is scope for many women to work outside. Compared to other areas of self-employment, childhood and care requires long-term planning. It is not a field of employment for quick input and output.

For successful self-employment, there are some basic requirements. These include:

- Basic Knowledge and Training - This could be obtained by attending short duration certificate courses from Continuing Education Centre, Open Universities, Distance Education Centres and correspondence courses. Attending relevant workshops, visiting and observing leading Nursery schools can be of great help.
- Personal qualities include resourcefulness, leadership for taking initiative, attitude towards the task, attitude and sensitivity towards the needs of the target group and readiness to learn new things, patience, cheerfulness and liking for children.
- Funds and physical facilities are needed for which bank loans are available for women. To start a day care centre one can have rented room. For equipments and materials one has to derive them from the community itself by tapping community resources.
- Management skills are very important as it is the crux of entrepreneurship. All the resources like human, material and financial resources are to be managed and utilized meaningfully keeping in mind the cost benefit ratio.

Entrepreneurial attributes can be improved to a great extent through training, as training further stimulates the development of the competencies in individuals. The entrepreneurship training thus helps the women to identify the weaknesses and the ways of improving them. To enrich the women with latest information, entrepreneurship training was organized under a project. The Project was undertaken in Baroda city in the year 2003 by Ms. Darshini Durkal and Dr. R.

Pandya under my guidance. The idea behind this Project was to train women in institutional management for children so that they could generate income.

Justification of the Project

Department of Home Science Extension and Communication has conducted several researches, action projects and community development programmes for helping women in income generation in order to uplift the status of women. This project will also contribute in this effort by changing women's status through training of self employment. While conducting the survey, project workers found that there were many day care centers in Baroda city, but their staff members were not trained, and many of them wanted to start their own day care centers. UBS/UCD workers of Baroda Municipal Corporation also had approached the project worker for training women for child care centers. The serious need for training and efforts to organize it at various levels had become imperative.

1. Need for Income Generating Activities: Income generating activities not only help in motivating, but also in sustaining their interest in continuing with the women's empowerment programme. This is one way by which women can contribute to the family income. These activities enable women to earn and add to the income of the family. These activities thereby:

- Improve women's social status.
- Make them economically independent.
- Can make them fight against the ill-treatment rendered towards them by the family and society.
- Help them utilize their leisure time more productively to avoid boredom.

2. Need for Self Development: A fruitful and purposeful utilization of leisure time is necessary for making life happier and fuller. There is the need to initiate the work of organizing people for self development through better utilization of their time. The society and family still does not expect women to be socially active in the community affairs or civic problems and prefer that women should remain confined to their homes.

Such training will enable women to work collectively in groups and make them socially active. It will bring them out from the confines of their homes and make them financially independent, giving them immense self confidence and also earn respect of their husband's and in-laws when they pool in additional income into the family income.

3. Recommendations of Symposia on 'Role of Banks in Empowering Women' (Sponsored by NABARD - Ahmedabad): Symposium on 'Role of Banks in Empowering Women' was organized by Centre for continuing Adult Education and Community Services, M.S. University of Baroda. Vadodara on 4th

and 5th January 2002, it being the year of women empowerment.

This Project was designed considering the above justification of promoting women and providing opportunities for vocational development. The main purpose of this project was not only to give training for starting day care centers but also to help women in establishing their own day care centers.

It was observed that majority of women faced economic problems, therefore the project titled, "An Action Project for Training Women to Start Day Care Centres in Baroda City in the year 2002-2003" was conducted.

Major Objectives of the Project

To help women in starting Day Care Centres.

Specific Objectives of the Project

1. To organize training programmes for starting day care centers.
2. To help women in developing project proposal for starting day care centers.
3. To help women in availing loans from banks for starting day care centers.
4. To collect reactions of the women regarding the training programme.

Methodology

The project was carefully planned so that it was completed on time and achieve the set objectives. The steps which were followed during the project are discussed under the following sections:

1. Feasibility Study: The project worker surveyed ten day care centers of Baroda city. The purpose of the feasibility study was to find out the functioning of day care centers and to understand the initial problems that one may face while starting a day care center. The project worker observed as well as interviewed people who were running the day care centers.

Major Findings of the Feasibility Survey

- Majority of the day care centers had female owner (90 per cent), only one day care center was owned by a male.
- Most of the owners of the day care centers were graduates.
- Main purpose behind setting up of the day care centers was to become economically independent and provide services to the working parents.
- Most of the persons in-charge of day care centers did not have any special training for starting day care centers. But they were interested in providing training to their staff members.
- Most of the day care centers used their own funds for starting their business.

2. Selection of the Content: As most of the owners of day care centers of

Baroda city did not have any special training for starting day care centers, it was decided to plan a training programme, in such a way that women could gain knowledge on how to start their own day care center and run it effectively.

The content of the training programme was decided by referring to different books, consulting experts and visiting various day care centers.

3. Contacting Resource Persons: The project worker contacted resource persons from different areas for conducting the training programme. The project worker invited the resource persons for their advice, suggestions and valuable tips.

Experts were invited from the different departments for conducting the following sessions:

Topics	Name of the Department
• Activities for children • Day care center and needs of children • Guiding young children and role of day care worker • Transition from home to pre-school • Develop skills for working with children • How to evaluate day care centers	Department of Human Development and Family Studies
Nutritious food safety for children	Department of Foods and Nutrition
Children's Health	Doctor, Health Center, MSU
Advertisements for day care centers	Department of Home Science Extension and Communication
Anganwadi Programme	Project Officer from ICDS
Role of Banks in starting day care centers	Planning Manager, BOB
Role of District Industrial Center in getting loans from banks	Planning Manager, DIC
Management of day care centers	Credit Manager, DIC
Experience shared by people running day care centers	Owners of the Day Care Centers

4. Preparation of Teaching Aids: The project worker visited different libraries for referring books on day care centers and for preparation of the teaching aids. To make any training programme successful, use of variety of teaching aids is very important. Teaching aids helps the learners to understand the concept easily. The project worker prepared different types of teaching aids given in the following table for the training programme.

5. Preparation of Booklet: The booklet on day care centers was prepared with the following purposes:

- To act as a manual for starting day care center.

- To act as reference material for future.

Different books were referred to make a complete and sound booklet. The booklet was prepared in Gujarati. The following topics were covered in the booklet:

- Planning for day care center - long term and short term goals.
- Setting up and running the day care center - Place, Materials, Workers, Registers.
- Reaching out to the parents - Parent's meeting, Newsletters, Celebrations.
- Role of day care worker.
- Preparation of indigenous materials for children.
- Nutrition for the children.
- Children songs.

Teaching Aids	Topics
Poster Charts	• For publicity of training programme • Planning for day care • Ideal points for a day care center
Flip Charts	• Things to be remembered while developing child's food habits • Bank schemes
Flash Cards	• Points that should be kept in mind while playing • Qualities of day care worker • Techniques of reaching out to parents
Handouts	• Children's songs • Bank Schemes • DIC Schemes

6. Selection of Target Group: The project worker wanted maximum number of women of Baroda city to take advantage of this training programme. For this purpose, she approached various institutions like - Vikas Jyot Trust, UBS/UCD Beneficiaries from Baroda Municipal Corporation, Integrated Child Development Schemes Worker (Anganwadi worker). The purpose behind visiting these institutions was to collect the names of women who were interested in getting training for starting their own day care center. The project worker also approached friends and relatives and informed them about the day care center training programme, so that these friends and relatives could further encourage other friends and relatives of theirs to take part in this training programme. In this way, the project worker did word of mouth publicity for the training programme.

7. Publicity through the Newspaper: The project worker gave press notes in local newspapers so that people could read it and take part in the day care center training programme. The project worker gave press notes in the 'Gujarat Samachar', 'Indian Express' and 'Sandesh' dailies.

8. Implementing the Training Programme: The project worker implemented the programme as per the plan for the training programme. The project worker collected the background information of all the participants.

9. Schedule of the Training Programme: The training programme was divided into fifteen sessions as the training programme was for fifteen days. The training programme on day care center was planned from 9th December, 2002 to 24th December 2002 from 10 to 5 p.m. Different experts were invited to conduct the training programme.

10. Place for Conducting the Training Programme: The project worker selected 'Pragati Center' of the Department of Home Science Extension and Communication, Faculty of Home Science, M. S. University, Baroda, for conducting the training programme on Day Care Centre. This center was selected as it had all facilities of space and physical arrangements like electricity, water and facilities of audio-visual aids.

11. Certificate and Booklet Distribution to the Participants: The project worker organized a valedictory function for the distribution of certificates at the 'Pragati Center' of the Department of Home Science Extension and Communication, on 24th December, 2002.

The criteria for getting the certificate and the booklet was announced in advance in the class to the participants, i.e. hundred percent attendance in the training programme.

12. Availing Loans from Banks for Starting Day Care Centres

- **Development of Project Proposal:** The project worker guided the women individually on the preparation of the project proposal for availing of loans. The project worker helped the women in collecting documents like quotations with registration numbers on it. The project worker also helped the women in calculating expenses for running the day care center, for example : the expenses required for toys and furniture for the day care center. The project worker helped the women to visualize the profitability of the enterprise.
- **Forms for Availing Loans:** The forms for loan application were collected from the District Industrial Centre, Narmada Bhavan, Baroda. The project worker guided women in collecting the required documents like light bills, school leaving certificates, quotation of toys and furniture and project proposal. The project worker also helped the women in filling up the forms and also checked the complete application forms.

Evaluation of the Project

Evaluation is an essential step in the extension process. It is through the process of evaluation that one arrives at judgements and conclusions that will aid in decision-making. It also helps in finding out the shortcomings of the programme, which in turn can be thought of for the next programme planning.

Suggestions Given by the Participants

1. Increase the duration of the training programme from 15 days to 1 month.
2. Include more practical experiences.
3. More visits to day care centers should be arranged.
4. During the day care visits, participants should be allowed to participate in the activities of the day care centers like managing the children.
5. Advertisement of the training programme should be given in advance.
6. Include more activities like

- Open group discussion
- Activities of children

7. The experts should evaluate the participants and give them some grading, whether they are eligible to run a day care center or not.

Problems during the Project Work

The project was undertaken with the objective of training women for starting their own day care centers. While working with these women and during the training programme, problems faced are listed below:

1. Problems Faced by the Project Worker

- It took a lot of time to locate women who were interested in starting their own day care center.
- Based on previous experience, banks were not ready to provide loans to some of these women. The project worker had to spend a lot of time in persuading the bank officer to sanction loans to these women.

2. Problems Faced by the Women Participants

- Though the women were keen and interested in starting their own day care center, due to family problems many of them were not in a position to start their own day care center.
- The attitude of the bank officers were not very encouraging.

Conclusions

The following conclusions can be made after the completion of the project:

- Such type of project gives opportunity of self development to the women.
- The project helped women to start their own day care centers.

- Women got an opportunity and experience to deal in government offices and banks in order to receive loans.
- Such type of training programme gave them an opportunity to interact within groups and thereby helped them in learning to cooperate with one another.

Recommendations

- Such training programmes can also be taken up for day care workers.
- Same project can be taken up in rural areas.
- A study can be undertaken on the following topics:
  a) Parent's opinion about their day care center
  b) Problems faced by the parents while choosing a day care center
- Comparisons of various kinds of child care facilities available to employed mothers.

Women can solve the problems of unemployment and poverty if entrepreneurship is developed among them. Women entrepreneurs are key players in any developing country particularly in terms of their contribution to economic development but, it is unfortunate that because of centuries of ignorance and conservatism, the actual and potential role of women in the society has been ignored, preventing them from making their rightful contribution to social progress. Entrepreneurship is an important ingredient of economic development and it is must for the socio-economic upliftment of the women.

If we want to give education to our students to undertake entrepreneurship, the curriculum would require the following inputs so that they can cope up with the changing environment:

- Focus of our curriculum should be on developing skills. This is required more than just a mere theory.
- The thrust should be on entrepreneurship development and course should deal with entrepreneurship planning, finance, bank loans, account keeping, advertising and marketing.
- Short term certificate or diploma courses can be started with the help of trained technical staff to impart skill training.

References

Ali Arshid, Entrepreneurship Growth and Development, Chirag Publication, Allahabad, 1980.

Arnold Gesell, M.D. Frances L. ILG MD, Child Development - An introduction to the study of human growth. Harper and Row Publishers. New York, 1985.

Carloni A.S. The impact of maternal employment and income on the nutritional status of children in rural area of developing countries, United Nations, 1984.

Chaturvedi, T.N. Administration for Child Welfare, Indian Institute of Public Administration,

New Delhi, 1979.

Chitnis S. Redistribution of familial functions in Devi, U. (1979) Status of working women, 1975.

Counsul, Mamta, Child care supports of employed mothers satisfaction and desire for alternatives. Dissertation, M.Sc. Department of Human Development and Family Studies, Faculty of Home Science M. S. U. Baroda 1989.

D. Paul Chaudhary, Child Welfare Development. Atmaram and Sons. Delhi 1980.

Franklin, A. and Benedict, E.A. Play centre for school children. A guide to their establishment and oppression. William Morrow and Co. New York, 1993.

Gopal A.K. Creches in plantations. National Institute of Public Cooperation and Child Development. New Delhi 1983.

Kanitkar Ajit, Grass roots entrepreneurship Entrepreneurs and Micro Enterprise in Rural India, Publishing for one world. New Age International Publishers Wiley Eastern Limited, 1989.

Kaur, H. Support availed for child-care and household tasks by nurses and its relationship to their perception of role performance. Unpublished Dissertation, M.Sc. Department of Human Development and Family Studies, Faculty of Home Science M. S. U. Baroda 1988.

Manila, Entrepreneurship Development, Tata McGraw Hill, Publishing Company Limited, 1998.

Moharana, Dash, C.R. Entrepreneurship Development. RBSA Publishers SHS Highway Jaipur, 1986.

Mutsuddi Nalinksha. "You too can be an Entrepreneur". Wheeler Publishing, New Delhi, 1986.

NIPCCD - Working Mothers and Early Childhood Education New Delhi, 1978.

Singh, K.P., Career and Family - Women's Two Roles, Indian Journal of Social Work. Vol. 16(2) 1972 pp 28-33.

18

Women Police: Public Perception

Om Raj Singh

Police image in a society depends on the degree of equanimity it has with public expectation. For police, the public is not a homogeneous entity. It is composed of many diverse and at times opposite interests. In the present study an attempt has been made to explore the emergence of women police, its impact on women police system and upon the society at large. The prime goal to undertake this venture was to analyse the role of women police in urban situation. Besides, the following objectives were also kept in view:

- To find out the social and economic background of the women police and to compare the socio-economic status of the different ranks of women police.
- To investigate the functions of women police and find out the difference between theory and practice
- To make an assessment of the status of women police in the society and in the department
- To examine the role of conflict in women working in the police
- To examine their own and public perception about women police
- To find out the future prospects of women police
- To evaluate their potentiality in ac ting as an agent of social change

Though only a few studies on the present theme have been undertaken, yet they provide a basic guideline. Some of the major assumptions generated by these studies in the past have been taken up for validations under local conditions.

In the light of the objectives stated earlier, the following hypothesis were formulated.

- Entry of women in police is a new phenomenon and still a less preferred avenue
- Male police officials do not realise their importance and competence
- Public perception about them is not healthy.
- Corruption, red tapism and delaying tactics are comparatively little them
- Their behaviour and dealing with the public is soft and humanitarian
- They are active and potent agent of social change
- Political pressure on them is comparatively less

Though the boundaries set by the traditional sex typing of jobs have lost their rigidity, allowing women in traditionally masculine occupations, yet the male domination in certain occupations continue. The sex typing of jobs has the consequences for the persons who are of weaker sex for role assuming and role performance. Policy, even today is considered a masculine domain. The strain for women in police is bound to be greater than in many other occupations. Not only the male counterparts of their own department but common people also have strong prejudices about them. It is important to study people's views and perception about the working, role performance and capabilities of women police. Before analysing this aspect let us first focus our attention at the specific aspects of her role performance.

Role of the Police

The police role connotes predominance of masculine attributes, like authority, assertion, physical strength, brutality and roughness which are quite contrary to be generally perceived feminine attributes of dependence, subjugation, delicate physique, softness, submissiveness, lack of confidence and accommodative spirit. It exposes women to work environment, which is not only male dominated, but also comprises of men who are generally considered to be rough, robust, and unrefined. Women police have to frequently interact with such groups of society that are socially condemned. Such exposures to criminals, deviants and the aggressive mobs are contradictory to the social norms that value female segregations.

The nature of tasks in police is such that necessitate women to greater contact with men at odd and late or early hours of the day. These are the timings when women are generally expected to be in their homes with their families. Their tasks involve field work, frequent physical mobility at different places, which is often inconvenient and contrary to the traditional norms of seclusion for women. There is 24 hours duty with no regular work timing and holidays. Such constraints interfere with the routine household chores.

Policing being considered a masculine role, the men are likely to resist women being accepted in police job for reasons: first, they may lack orientation to face this new situation of having women in police system; second, their deep rooted traditional values and social norms regarding women's role in society may pose barriers in accepting women in this traditionally male role. Such resistance from the male counterparts in the work set up may cause greater role strain for the police women. In the male dominated work set up, the police women may have to struggle hard to make a place for themselves by proving their worth at par with that of men. They may feel being watched very closely for all their actions.

As a result, their spontaneity of behaviour may get adversely affected, and their feeling of discomfort and strain may be enhanced. The police role also curtails social interaction with other occupational groups and segregates them to great extent from general civilian life (Mahajan, 1982; Lefkowitz, 1975) which may add to social and psychological pressures for the police women.

The existing contradictions may and do affect their role performance at job situation as well as in the family. Indeed they adversely affect their working efficiency. Their loyalties, interests and aspirations differ at the two situations. The role and functions of women police and how they perform their functions and discharge their tasks in two different situations. Now, the problem is what common people perceive about them. With this view, 500 people from different sections and groups were interviewed in Delhi.

Table 18.1: People Perception of Women Police: Respondents by Profession/Occupation

Category	Respondents	
	Number	Percentage
Political leaders	50	10
Journalists	23	4.6
Intellectuals	109	21.6
Social Workers	67	13.4
Business men	117	23.4
Aggrieved	15	3.0
Miscellaneous	119	23.8
Total	500	100

In order to explore public perception about women police, it was deemed necessary together views of public perception. Political leaders, Journalists, intellectuals, social workers, business men and the aggrieved were contacted. In all 500 persons from the different categories were selected on the basis of purposive sampling method.

In order to obtain the opinion of persons of different age groups the interviews were conducted with such groups. Nearby half (46 per cent) of them belong to the age group 21-40 years and a little more then one fourth (26 per cent) in the age groups 51 to 60 years. Respondents from different age groups were taken to elicit various shades of opinion

The role of women police will have to be assessed both by women as well as men hence an attempt was made to interview the members belonging to both the sexes. Nearly three fourths (70 per cent) of the respondents are male. It is because women are generally not ready to respond on issues connected to police.

Table 18.2: Age of the Respondents

S.N.	Particulars	Up to 20 years	21-30 years	31-40 years	41-50 years	51-60 years	Above 60 years
1	Number of Respondents	40	130	100	70	130	30
2	Percentage	8	26	20	14	26	6

Table 18.3: Sex of the Respondents

S.N.	Particulars	Male	Female
1.	Total number of respondent	350	150
2.	Percentage	70	30

Table 18.4: Knowledge about Existence of Women Police in Delhi

S.N.	Category	Responses	Percentage
1.	Yes	460	92
2.	No	40	8

Table 18.5: People's Perception of Delhi Police

S.N.	Category	Responses	
		Number	Percentage
1.	Very good	10	2
2.	Good	90	18
3.	Indifferent	230	46
4.	Poor/Bad	150	30
5.	No Response	20	4
	Total	500	100

It is heartening to state that the majority of people (92 per cent) are aware of the existence of women police in Delhi. It is so because most of the respondents are educated.

The image of police in Delhi does not seem to be very good. This is established by the responses of a cross section of society. Only 20 per cent people feel that the image is very good or good while 30 per cent are of the opinion that the image is poor or bad. Nearby half of them (46 per cent) are ambivalent. They might be fearful of police. It means that most of the people do not consider police as a friend, guide and philosopher in the metropolitan city of Delhi. Only few (4 per cent) did not respond.

Table 18.6: Does the Police Department Suffer From Social Stigma

S.N.	Category	Responses	
		Number	Percentage
1	Yes	410	82
2	No	50	10
3.	No Response	40	8
	Total	500	100

During the British period the police had to play a very difficult role. Though mostly natives, they were associated with the alien power. Corruption is considered a permanent feature of police department. Over and above abuse of power, high handedness, abusive language etc. are some of the features which have brought a bad name to the police. It is a sad commentary on the police that in spite of passing nearly six decades, the police could not improve its image. The association of voluntary organizations with the Delhi Police could not bring much change about the thinking of people regarding the image of police of Delhi. Eighty two per cent respondents still feel that police suffer from a social stigma. Perhaps this may be an important negative factor in preventing women from joining police service. Only 10 per cent respondents admitted that police does not suffer from social stigma. A majority of people indicated an urgent need to improve the image of police department. Unfortunately not much has been done in this regard.

Table 18.7: Image of Women Police in Delhi

S.N.	Category	Responses	
		Number	Percentage
1	Very good	-	-
2	Good	30	6
3.	O.K.	290	58
4.	Poor	140	28
5.	No Response	40	8
	Total	500	100

An analysis of the responses of different people reveals that the people's perception of police in general and women police in Delhi in particular is more or less the same. Twenty eight per cent of people have a poor image of women police, while 58 per cent are ambivalent on this issue. Only six per cent respondents have good image about women police, eight per cent gave no response. It is difficult to establish whether the responses of the people are based on their personal knowledge and experience or the borrowed general impressions.

Table 18.8: Attitude of Women Police towards Public

S.N.	Category	Responses	
		Number	Percentage
1	Helpful	90	18
2	Indifferent	20	4
3.	Rude	20	4
4.	Polite	60	12
5.	No Response	310	62
	Total	500	100

In order to get the opinion of a cross section of society about women police in Delhi, the researcher asked the respondent to react on the attitude of women police, as 62 per cent did not respond to this question. Obvious reason being, most of them have not come intó contact with women police in Delhi, hence unable to form any opinion. Of course 30 per cent said that they are helpful and polite; only eight per cent seem to be unhappy with the behaviour of women police. It reflects that attitude of women police is generally good

Table 18.9: Policing is only Man's Job

S.N.	Category	Responses	
		Number	Percentage
1	Yes	10	2
2	No	490	98
	Total	500	100

The general impression is that policing is a man's job. But it is surprising to know that practically all (98 per cent) have expressed their opinion against this traditional orthodox view. This opinion is held not only by women but by men also. This indicates a bright future for the women police in Delhi.

On the question whether women should join police service or not, the responses indicate that the people who pointed out that policing is not man's domain only are of the view that women should join police service. This indicates a subtle change that women can shoulder the hardest duty.

Table 18.10: Should Women Join the Police Force

S.N.	Category	Responses	
		Number	Percentage
1	Yes	490	98
2	No	10	2
	Total	500	100

Table 18.11: Should Educated Girls from Higher and Middle Classes Join the Police Service

S.N.	Category	Responses	
		Number	Percentage
1	Yes	470	94
2	No	20	4
3	No Response	10	2
	Total	500	100

While some respondents feel that the image of police in general and women police in particular in Delhi is not respectable one and the police suffer from social stigma, on the other hand 94 per cent viewed that educated girls from higher and middle class families should join police service. This seems to be contradictory. It might be interpreted that people want educated girls from good families to join police service so that the image of women police in Delhi is improved. Yet the facts present a different picture. Government must find out ways and means to attract educated girls from different strata of society.

Table 18.12: Should Women Police of Delhi be entrusted with Independent Powers of Investigation in Cases of Women Victimization

S.N.	Category	Responses	
		Number	Percentage
1	Yes	390	78
2	No	50	10
3	Not always	40	8
4	As per convenience	10	2
5	No Response	10	2
	Total	500	100

A great majority of the respondents (78 per cent) strongly felt that women police should be entrusted with independent powers of investigation in cases of victimisation of women. Only a few of them (10 per cent) are not in its favour. But on the general question whether women be always interrogated by women police only, the opinion is not the same. Only 46 per cent are in favour of women, others do not mind if it is done by male officers.

Table 18.13: Can Women Police Implement Laws Pertaining to Women More Sincerely and Effectively than Man Police

S.N.	Category	Responses	
		Number	Percentage
1	Yes	380	76
2	No	90	18
3	No Response	20	4
4	Not necessarily	10	2
	Total	500	100

All over the world it is agreed that women police should be used at least in matters where women and children are involved. Same opinion is established by majority of respondents (76 per cent). They held that women police can implement laws pertaining to women more effectively than men police. Only 18 per cent of the respondents did not agree to it. They feel that men police is more efficient.

Table 18.14: Women Police Can Interrogate Women and Children Better than Man Police

S.N.	Category	Responses	
		Number	Percentage
1	Yes	370	74
2	No	100	20
3	Not necessarily	20	4
4	No response	10	2
	Total	500	100

Nearly three fourth (74 per cent) respondents expressed their agreement to the question while one fifth (20 per cent) showed disagreement. It corroborates our presumption that women police should be given the function of interrogation of women and children.

Two third of the respondents (66 per cent) are of the view that women police should be given general functions of police as well as functions related to women and children while only about one third (30 per cent) view that they should be given only those functions which are related exclusively to women and children. None of the respondent opined that they should be given only those functions, which are dealt by men police. Respondents were enquired whether women should be interrogated only by women police.

Table 18.15: Functions of Women Police

S.N.	Category	Responses	
		Number	Percentage
1	Women Police should be given general functions of men police	Nil	Nil
2	Women police should be given functions pertaining to women and children	150	30
3	Should be given both the functions	330	66
4	Others	20	
	Total	500	100

Table 18.16: Women Should be Interrogated only by Women Police

S.N.	Category	Responses	
		Number	Percentage
1	Women police only	230	46
2	Male police in the presence of women police	150	30
3	Any police officer	120	24
	Total	500	100

Only 46 per cent respondents admitted that in cases related to women, the accused should be interrogated only by women police while 30 per cent respondents opined that men police may interrogate the women but women police should be present there. Nearly one fourth (24 per cent) expressed their indifference. In their opinion, there is no use to segregate the interrogating agency.

A little more than one fourth (26 per cent) respondents were of the view that dying declaration of women should be recorded only by women police while 18 per cent expressed that male police may record it but presence of women police should be necessary. More that half (56 per cent) respondents opined that there should not be any distinction in this regard.

Table 18.17: Who Should Record Dying Declaration of Women

S.N.	Category	Responses	
		Number	Percentage
1	Women police only	130	26
2	Male police in the presence of women police	90	18
3	Any police officer	280	56
	Total	500	100

Table 18.18: Presence of Women Police will Minimise the Use of Abusive Language

S.N.	Category	Responses	
		Number	Percentage
1	Yes	440	88
2	No	40	8
3	No response	20	4
	Total	500	100

Factors responsible for the poor image of police include abusive language and corruption. A great majority (88 per cent) respondents were of the view that presence of women police will be the main hindrance in the use of abusive language. Men police will hesitate to use vulgar language.

Table 18.19: Presence of Women Police will Minimize Corruption

S.N.	Category	Responses	
		Number	Percentage
1	Yes	230	46
2	No	230	46
3.	No Idea	10	2
4	No response	30	6
	Total	500	100

Two-third (68 per cent) of the respondents held that there is less corruption in women police and presence of women police will definitely minimise corruption in police. On the other hand more than one-fourth respondents did not agree to it.

At present political leaders give shelter to criminals and influence police actions. The women police easily succumb the political influence. Nearly half (46 per cent) of the respondents agree to it although similar number of respondents disagreed. In their opinion, politicians influence both alike.

Table 18.20: Do Women Succumb to Political/Other Influence Easily

S.N.	Category	Responses	
		Number	Percentage
1	Yes	230	46
2	No	230	46
3.	No Idea	10	2
4	No response	30	6
	Total	500	100

Table 18.21: Can Women Police act as an Instrument of Social Change

S.N.	Category	Responses	
		Number	Percentage
1	Yes	460	92
2	No	20	4
3.	No Idea	10	2
4	No response	10	2
	Total	500	100

In India as well as in Delhi, police still do not consider policeman as a friend. But people of Delhi seem to have a different perception regarding women police. Though people do not have a very high impression of women police in Delhi but they are confident that given an opportunity, women police can act as an instrument of social change. It is a pleasant feeling that a majority of the respondents (92 per cent) have corroborated the opinion that women police can act as an instrument of social change. This positive approach to the role of women police in Delhi is very heartening and promises a bright future for not only Delhi but for entire country.

The foregoing discussion shows that perception of people about women police is good and they feel that introduction of women police will be healthy for the trial of women and children.

References

Bhardwaj Aruna,: The Emergence of Women Police in Delhi, (PH.D Thesis), Department of Social Work, University of Delhi, Delhi. 1994.

Mahajan A. Indian Police Women, New Delhi: Deep and Deep Publications, P.71. 1982.

Lefkowitz J. Psychological Attributes of Policemen-A Review of Research and Opinion, Journal of Social Issues, Vol.31, No 1,P.13. 1975.

Singh, Om Raj (Role of Women Police in Urban Situation – With Special reference to Delhi). 1996.

19

Globalisation and Employment Status of Women in India

Tejpreet Kaur Kang

The concept of "Globalisation" indicates the 'aspiring' towards oneness by all countries, the desire to be part of one uniform world order. The distances both physical and mental are to be reduced to zero ways and means of communication to be advanced enough to enable people to live as a global *parivar*. In other words globalization is a network of interdependence at world wide distances. It is neither new nor just an economic phenomenon. Under this phenomenon markets have spread and tied people together resulting in an increased interdependence in environmental, military, social, and political spheres of activity.

Towards the end of the 20th century the world became unipolar and globalisation brought numerous benefits to the developing nations. The yawning disparities among the industrialised world and the third world countries were reduced to an extent. The triumph of democracy and open markets ushered in a new era of freedom and opportunity.

However, in the beginning of 21st century, observations were made that in the globalised world gap between the rich and the poor is growing at a fast rate. Globalisation is widening the gap between the haves and the have-nots. It benefits the rich and does little for the poor, perhaps even making their lot harder. Joseph Stiglitz, winner of the Nobel Prize for economics in 2001 has commented in his celebrated book "Globalisation and its Discontents" that the Western countries acting through the International Monetary Fund and the World Trade Organization have failed. They have mismanaged the process of privatization, liberalisation and stabilisation. Stiglitz also says "Globalisation today is not working, it is not working for many of the world's poor. It is not working for much of the environment. It is not working for the stability of the global economy".

Gender Dimensions of Globalisation

According to Ms. Kunzang Chungyalka, UNIFEM Asia Pacific Chief "Globalisation has intensified the existing inequalities and heightened the risky environment. Women have experienced globalization in a number of different ways. For the educated with professional skills, it has opened up new opportunities. But, for the unskilled, it has meant loss of livelihoods in the face of increasing competition. Women predominate in the informal sector where they work in exploitative conditions without labour rights or any form of social protection globalization has thus served to intensity existing inequalities and heighten the vulnerability of poor women. The search for efficiency in the whirlwind of international competition has also led to the dismantling of state structures. The assumption that the private sector would fill the critical gap in the provision of social services has not materialized. Much of the burden has, perhaps, shifted to the domestic sector where women bear the major burden. This transfer of cost from the state sector to the domestic sector is something that is not yet recognized in our economic models. As women's needs and contributions are generally not recognized, appropriate policy responses cannot be designed. The end result is the social dislocations which ultimately have impact on our well-being and productivity (Goel 2004).

Position of Women in India

Women of India have a background of history and tradition behind them, which is inspiring, but they have suffered much from various kinds of suppression and all these have to go, before they can play their full part in the life of the nation. Since the times immemorial, worth of the work done or services rendered by women has not been recognized. No serious efforts, except the occasional attempts clouded by bias and misconception, were ever made to evolve a reliable method to calculate women's contribution to the economic development of society. Adam Smith, the father of Economics, recognized the women's contribution to the economic development when he analyzed the concept of 'use value' and 'exchange value'. Unpaid household labour of a woman, who is treated as controller of the home, is generally ignored as what she creates is the 'use value'. A woman, who produces 'use value' through household work is considered to be unemployed and not contributing to the economic development when compared with a woman who produces 'exchange value' through her paid employment, ignoring the fact that hours of work put in by the house lady are much higher than the ones endured by the paid lady.

Women in India are leaving the four walls of their homes to venture out in search of work. The underlying reasons may vary with their socio-economic status. A majority of them belong to middle and lower socio-economic strata of society and they work due to sheer economic necessity, especially those belonging to the lower socio-economic class. Women from upper socio-economic strata of society may do so in pursuit of a career so as to be independent. The policies for globalization adopted in India definitely have significant implications for employment and the labour market in addition to their impact on overall economic growth of the country. But the results of unfettered operation of market force are not always equitable, especially in India, where some groups are likely to be subjected to disadvantage as a result of globalization. Women constitute one such vulnerable group and globalization has both positive and negative effects on their status.

Work and Employment

Over the past two decades we have witnessed a relative increase in the economic participation of women. Nothing hastens social and cultural change in women's social and cultural change in women's lives like economic opportunities. Gain over finances is the first big step towards improving the condition of women. This has already started to happen with globalisation having created greater employment opportunities in India. From jobs in unorganised sector to banking and information technology, women have entered domains that were hitherto considered to be male-dominated.

The female work participation rate increased from 19.7 per cent in 1981 to 25.7 per cent in 2001, but it is still much lower that of the male work participation rate in both urban and rural areas (Table 19.1).

Table 19.1: Work Participation Rates by Sex (1981-2001)

(per cent)

Census	Area	Females	Males	Persons
1981	Total	19.7	52.6	36.7
	Rural	23.1	53.8	38.8
	Urban	8.3	49.1	30.0
1991	Total	22.3	51.6	37.5
	Rural	26.8	52.6	40.1
	Urban	9.2	48.9	30.2
2001	Total	25.7	51.9	39.3
	Rural	31.0	52.4	42.0
	Urban	11.6	50.9	32.2

Source: Census of India, 1991, series 1 and census of India, 2001.

In state wise ranking of female work participation in India (Table 19.2) Mizoram is at top with 47.63 per cent participation followed by Manipur (40.51 per cent) and Chhatisgarh (40.04 per cent).

Table 19.2: State-wise Ranking According to Female Work Participation Rate in India (1991 and 2001)

	Female work participation rate and rank 2001	Female work participation rate and rank 1991
State		
Andhra Pradesh	34.93(10)	34.32(8)
Arunachal Pradesh	36.45(8)	37.49(6)
Assam	20.80(23)	21.61(17)
Bihar	18.84(24)	14.86(22)
Chhatisgarh	40.04(3)	-
Delhi	9.15(33)	7.36(30)
Goa	22.24(21)	20.52(19)
Gujarat	28.03(16)	25.96(15)
Haryana	27.31(17)	10.76(27)
Himachal Pradesh	453.69(4)	345.82(7)
Jharkhand	26.4(19)	-
Karnataka	31.88(14)	29.39(13)
Kerala	15.28(31)	15.85(20)
Madhya Pradesh	33.1(12)	32.68(20)
Maharashtra	32.59(13)	33.11(9)
Manipur	40.51(2)	38.96(3)
Meghalaya	35.02(9)	34.93(6)
Mizoram	47.63(1)	43.52(2)
Nagaland	38.25(7)	37.96(4)
Orissa	24.62(20)	20.79(18)
Punjab	18.68(25)	4.40(31)
Rajasthan	33.48(11)	27.40(14)
Sikkim	38.59(6)	30.41(11)
Tamil Nadu	31.32(15)	29.89(12)
Tripura	21.02(22)	13.76(23)
Uttaranchal	27.09(18)	-
Uttar Pradesh	16.28(30)	12.32(25)
West Bengal	18.08(27)	11.25(26)
Andaman & Nicobar Islands	16.45(29)	13.13(24)
Chandigarh	13.72(32)	10.39(28)
Dadra & Nagar Haveli	38.68(5)	48.79(1)
Daman & Diu	18.34(26)	23.17(16)
Lakshadweep	7.19(34)	7.60(29)
Pondicherry	17(28)	15.24(21)
India*	25.68	22.27

Figure in the bracket shows the rank.

Source: Statistical profile on women labour 2004, Ministry of Labour and Employment, GOI, New Delhi.

Women's share in organised sector has shown an increasing trend (Table 19.3), from 2.8 million (12.2 per cent) in 1981 to 4.8 million (17.2 per cent) in 1999. Between 1991 and 1999, rise in the percentage points of women was 3.1, in contrast the share of men has been declining. However, women's participation in the organised sector in still very low, as compared to men.

Table 19.3 Women in the Organised and Public Sector

Year	Organised Sector			Public Sector		
	Women	Men	Total	Women	Men	Total
1981	2.8 (12.2)	20.1	22.9	1.5(9.7)	14.0	15.5
1991	3.8 (14.1)	23.0	26.7	2.4(12.3)	16.7	19.1
2001	4.8 (17.2)	23.3	28.1	2.8(14.5)	16.6	19.4

Source: Director-General of Employment and Training, Ministry of Labour, GOI, New Delhi

Women's employment in the public sector has also shown an upward trend with an increase from 1.5 million (9.7 per cent) in 1981 to 2.8 million (14.5 per cent) in 2001 (Table 19.3) but, it is still much lower than that of men.

Indian women have outdone men in terms of employment growth in the public and private sector (Tables 19.4 and 19.5) with a 3.35 per cent rise in employment between 1998 and 2004 against a fall of about 8 per cent in case of men. According to findings of an industry body Assocham, the number of women employed in the public and private sectors has increased to 49.34 lakh in 2004 from 47.74 lakh in 1998, while the number of men employed has fallen to 215.09 lakh from 233.92 lakh during the same period. The public sector has been hiring women much more aggressively than the private sector. The number of women employed in the public sector has risen 4.6 per cent to 28.9 lakh in 2004 from 27.63 lakh in 198 while women staff in the private sector has grown 1.64 per cent to 20.44 lakh.

Table 19.4: Employment Growth Rate (per cent)

	Public sector		Private sector	
Year	Women	Men	Women	Men
1998	1.28	-1.05	5.34	-0.589
1999	1.74	-0.31	0.35	-0.85
2000	1.64	-0.89	2.38	-1.5
2001	0.07	-1.08	1.16	-0.27
2002	0.98	-2.41	1.96	-2.73
2003	0.62	-1.33	0.73	-0.41
2004	-0.52	-2.35	0.97	-2.44

Source: Study by Assocham

Table 19.5: Employment of Women Workers in Public and Private Sectors in India (in '000)

Years	Employment as on 31st March		
	Public sector	Private Sector	Total
1990	2250.1	1393.6	3643.7
1994	2564.6	1589.3	4153.9
1999	2810.7	2018.4	4829.2
2004	2890	2044.4	4934.4

Source: Ministry of Labour, Govt. of India.

During the year 2004 (Table 19.6), in public and private sector maximum number of women i.e. 2812.3 lakh were employed in community, social and personal services, followed by manufacturing (949.3 lakh) and agriculture, hunting, forestry and fishing (458.7 lakh).

Table 19.6: Major Industry Division-Wise Women Employment in Organized Public/Private Sector in India (As on 31.03.2003 and 31.03.2004)

Industry division	Employment (In '000)					
	As on 31.03.2003			As on 31.03. 2004		
	Public sector	Private sector	Total	Public sector	Private sector	Total
Agriculture, Hunting Forestry and Fishing	47.8	418.7	466.5	47.7	411	458.7
Mining & Quarrying	54.3	6.6	60.9	66	7.3	73.3
Manufacturing	86.6	923.2	1009.8	81.5	867.9	949.3
Electricity, Gas & Water	46.3	1.4	47.7	49.7	2.4	52.1
Construction	60.5	3.7	64.1	62.6	3.4	66
Hotels	14	30.5	44.5	14	32	46
Transport, Storage & Communications	180.3	8.7	189	179	10.4	189.4
Services	202	72.3	274.3	206	81.2	287.3
Community, Social & Personal Services	2212.9	598.7	2811.6	2183.6	628.8	2812.3
Total	2904.7	2063.7	4968.4	2890	2044.4	4934.4

Source: Ministry of Labour, Govt. of India.

Women's employment in central government has also shown (Table 19.7) an upward trend with an increase from 3.64 per cent in 1981 to 7.79 per cent in 2001.

Table 19.7: Women in Central Government (1981-2001)

Year	Women	Men	Total (in lakh)	per cent of female employees out of total
1981	124032	32.83	34.07	3.64
1991	288999	35.24	38.13	7.58
2001	2.6	30.00	32.6	7.79

Note: Figures in lakh
Source: Ministry of statistics and programme implementation, Govt. of India

Decision Making

1. Administrative: The representation of women in the decision-making levels through the premier services viz., the Indian Administrative Services (IAS) and Indian Police Services (IPS), which stood at 5.8 per cent in 1987, increased marginally to 7.6 per cent in 2000. However the figure is still very low, requiring not only affirmative action but also special interventions to help raise the number of women at various decision making lcvcls (Tablc 19.8).

Table 19.8: Representation of Women in Premier Services in India (1987, 1997 and 2000)

Service	1987			1997			2000		
	Total	Female	%	Total	Female	%	Total	Female	%
Indian Administrative service	4204	339	7.5	4991	512	10	5159	535	10.4
Indian Police Service	2418	21	0.9	3045	67	2.2	3301	110	3.33
Indian Foreign Service	480	53	10	575	71	12	-	-	-
Total	7102	413	5.8	8611	650	7.5	8460	645	7.62

Source: Department of Personnel and Training, GOI, New Delhi

2. Political: We are also witnessing an upsurge in the political empowerment of women close to a million women are part of panchayats and local bodies, thanks to thc 73rd and 74th amcndmcnts to thc constitution that madc onc-third reservation for women mandatory. These amendments have helped women not only in their effective participation but also decision making (Tables 19.9 and 19.10). Out of total 129871 elected members of Panchayat Samiti, 38582 are women. In the elections to Panchayati Raj Institutions held, women have achieved participation even beyond the mandatory requirement of 33½ per cent of the total seats in states like Karnataka (40.21 per cent), Kerala (36.4 per cent) and West Bengal (33.65 per cent) (National Commission for Women, 2001).

Table 19.9: Women in Panchayati Raj Institutions

(Figures in Thousand)

Year	Women	Men	Total
1995	318(33.5)	630	948
2001	725(26.6)	1997	27.22

Source: Ministry of Rural Development, GOI, New Delhi

Table 19.10: State-wise Women Chairpersons at Various Levels of Panchayati Raj in India: 2001

States/UTs	Gram Panchayat			Panchayat Samiti			Zilla Parishad		
	Women	Total	per cent	Women	Total	per cent	Women	Total	per cent
Andhra Pradesh	15065	-	-	366	1084	33.76	6	20	30
Arunachal Pradesh	-	-	-	-	-	-	-	-	-
Assam	645	2486	29.97	-	-	-	-	-	-
Bihar	-	-	-	-	-	-	-	-	-
Goa	-	-	-	-	-	-	-	-	-
Gujarat	4435	13316	-	60	184	32.61	6	19	31.58
Haryana	1986	5958	33.33	38	110	34.55	5	16	31.25
Himachal Pradesh	1070	2922	36.62	23	72	31.94	3	12	33.33
Karnataka	1880	5640	33.33	59	175	33.71	7	20	35
Kerala	331	-	-	51	-	-	5	14	35.71
Madhya Pradesh	11953	30922	38.66	123	459	26.8	17	45	37.78
Maharashtra	9203	27603	33.34	106	319	33.23	10	29	34.48
Manipur	55	166	33.13	-	-	-	2	4	50
Orissa	1862	5261	35.39	114	314	36.31	10	30	33.33
Punjab	158	11582	1.36	47	132	35.61	5	13	38.46
Rajasthan	3064	9185	33.36	80	237	33.76	10	31	32.26
Sikkim	1	148	0.68	-	-	-	-	-	-
Tamil Nadu	4323	12584	34.35	139	384	36.2	10	28	35.71
Tripura	175	525	33.33	5	16	31.25	1	3	33.33
Uttar Pradesh	19822	58620	33.81	372	901	41.29	23	76	30.26
West Bengal	153	3310	4.62	10	333	3	0	17	-
Islands	-	-	-	-	-	-	-	-	-
Chandigarh	-	-	-	-	-	-	-	-	-

Contd...

Dadra and Nagar Haveli	4	11	36.36	-	-	-	1	1	100
Daman and Diu	6	10	60	-	-	-	-	-	-
Lakshadweep	-	-	-	-	-	-	-	-	-
Pondichery	-	-	-	-	-	-	-	-	-
India	76291	2E+5	40.1	1593	4720	33.75	122	378	32.28

Source: National Commission for Women.

Although the number of women in Parliament has increased from 59 in 1998 to 70 in 2001, their share continues to be very low representing only 8.5 per cent (Table 19.11) of the total members in Parliament in 2001.

Table 19.11: Representation of Women in Parliament (1998-2001)

Year	Females	Males	Total
1998	59(7.2)	761	820
1999	67(8.5)	723	790
2001	70(8.5)	750	820

Note: Figures with in parentheses indicate percentage to total.
Source: Election Commission of India.

Representation of women in central council of ministers in India does not portray a rosy picture, showing only 7 women ministers against 68 male ministers in the year 2004 (Table 19.12).

Table 19.12: Representation of Women in Central Council of Ministers in India

Year	Number of Ministers			Number of Women Ministers		
	Cabinet Minister	Minister of State	Deputy Minister	Cabinet Minister	Minister of State	Deputy Minister
1995	12	17	3	1	4	1
1996	18	21	0	0	1	0
1997	20	24	0	0	5	0
1998	21	21	0	1	3	0
2000	29	45	0	1	7	0
2002	32	41	0	2	6	0
2004	29	39	0	1	6	0

Source: National Commission of Women, Govt. of India.

After globalisation women are able to get more jobs but work they get is more casual in nature or is the one that men do not prefer to do or is left by them to move to higher or better job. Globalisation has indeed raised hopes of women for a better and elevated status arising out increased chances to work but, at the same time, it has put them in highly contradictory situation where they have the label of economically independent paid workers but are not able to enjoy their economic liberty in real sense of the term. India is the first among countries to give women equal franchise and has a highly credible record with regard to the enactment of laws to protect and promote the interest of women, but women continue to be denied the economic, social and legal rights and privileges. Though they are considered to be equal partners in progress, yet they remain subjected to repression, marginalisation and exploitation. For increasing number of women, globalisation has meant migration.

More and more women are migrating on their own, as the primary earner in their household. The feminisation of migration presents significant challenges for human rights protection because of commitment and the difficulty in protecting the rights of migrant women. It is clear that if globalisation is to be pro-women and take the needs of the poor into account, it must be steered and shaped in accord with international human rights conventions and the development consensus reached at UN World Conferences (Goel 2004). Independent earning opportunities reduce the economic dependence of women on men and increase her bargaining power in the family. This bargaining power depends on the nature of work she is employed in (Amartya Sen 1990). But the income earning activities increase the workload of a woman unless the man accepts an increased share in domestic work. Much needs to be done to empower them across the fault lines of gender inequality. Thanks to changes in the constitutional apparatus, there has been a gradual improvement in several areas of women's lives, but more needs to be done. What remains to be seen is that how society reacts to the situation where women would have a major role to play in restructuring the society as well as the economy.

References

Dhillon R S, Globalisation and Its Impact on Society, Probable Latest Essay, Dhillon Group of Publications, New Delhi. 2005.

Goel A, Organisation and Structure of Women Development and Empowerment, Deep and Deep Publications Pvt. Ltd., New Delhi. 2004.

Kharole M, Status of Indian Women. *Social Welfare,* vol. 52 No. 4. 2005.

Kumar A, Women and Development (volume - 2), Anmol Publications Pvt. Ltd., New Delhi. 2005.

Labour Gains for Eves Across Sectors. The Economic Times, 8th March, 2007.

Mazur J, Labour's New Internationalism, Foreign Affairs, January-February. 2000.

Murty S and Gaur K D, Women Work Participation and Empowerment : Problems and Prospects. RBSA Publishers, Jaipur. 2002.

Philipose P, Figuring women, The Indian Express, March 8. 2007.

Price, Courtney and Monrol Stuart, Proceedings of Sixth ENDEC World Conference on Entrepreneurship in Transitional Economics, Nanyang Technological University, Singapore, held at Shanghai, People's Republic of China, 7-9 December, 1995.

Price, Courtney and Monrol, Stuart,. Proceedings of Seventh ENDEC World Conference on Globalisation and Entrepreneurship, Nanyang Technological University, Singapore, 5-7 December, 1996.

Quraishi S Y, Across The Fault Lines, The Indian Express, March 13. 2007.

Shanthi K, Empowerment of women, Anmol Publications Pvt. Ltd., New Delhi. 1998.

Singh D, Strategies for Empowering Women Workers. *Social Welfare* Vol. 53 No. 2. 2005.

Singh K, Globalisation and Employment Status of Women in India, http://www.goggle.com.

Women at Work, Hindustan Times, 8th March, 2007.

20

Women's Work and Empowerment

Trupti T. Shah

Women's work has remained a debatable area of research and policy. The early writings on women's work assume that working for income will necessarily mean improvement in the status of women and many of the recent policy documents talk about strategies of women's empowerment in terms of providing work or income generating 'activities' to them. It is necessary to unpack and analyze the concept of work as well as the concept of empowerment in the light of realties of women.

Women constitute nearly half the population of India but only 22.7 per cent of women were recorded as workers in the 1991 and 25.7 per cent in 2001 Census. However, this does not mean that women do not make significant contributions to the Indian economy. Several studies have proved that Census data do not provide a real picture of women at work. Women from the poor families were always working and they are working now also. The families below the poverty line depend heavily on the earnings of women for their survival.

The reality is that women are vital and productive workers in the Indian economy but they remain "INVISIBLE". The low participation rate in the Census data reflects the historical interplay of two major factors with the patriarchal structure of socio economic institutions like family, labour markets and policy making bodies. These factors are:

- The process of development of industrial capitalism in India and
- The concept of women's work in the data gathering system

If we look at the women's work participation in the historical context since the introduction of industrial capitalism in India, we can observe that the impact of reform movement, independence movement and consequent constitutional guaranty for women's equality has resulted in increasing women's education and work opportunity in certain areas of work. The entry of women in some of the areas, which are known as Men's work, is remarkable. "There have been more opportunities for middle class and upper class women to go in for remunerative work. More women are seen working in non- traditional jobs and are also holding decision making posts."

However, all these are positive impact on the women belongs to certain class and caste. As women are not a homogeneous category the factors affecting women's work participation are different for women from different class, caste, culture, religion and region. Thus on the other hand, colonisation of India and the development of capitalist economy has affected masses of women, who have always worked, adversely. This was brought to the light by the report of the Committee on the Status of Women – "Towards Equality" for the first time in 1974 with the help of evidences. Scholars working on the status of women realised that the status of women is declining since the beginning of the century. As the result of the introduction of market economy "not only has women's employment in the organised sector been reduced, but expansion of the informal sector has put women in the category of a reserve army. The increasing feminisation of poverty is a matter of grave concern."

This historical trend has been accentuated by the introduction of the structural adjustment programme. "In the 1990s, with the introduction of structural adjustment policies, there has been a tendency towards 'infromlisation' and 'casualisation' of the labour force."

Economic Reforms and Marginalisation of Women

The Indian government in 1991 officially adopted the new economic policy also known as Economic Reforms or Structural Adjustment. However as noted by several economic analysts, India had begun a process of 'adjustment' quietly since the beginning of the 1980's. As a result of the new Industrial Policy, investment from foreign governments and non-governmental institutions, multinational companies, non-resident Indians was welcomed in the name of capital formation and need for high-tech production process to compete in the world market. To make production and sales more efficient, bureaucratic processes are simplified and steps to abolish, 'license raj' was undertaken for the benefit of investors. On the other hand, workers in large companies, both in the public and private sector, have been pushed to accept voluntary retirement schemes. Labour laws are being changed to make hire and fire policies easier for the employers and also to restrict the rights of workers and trade unions.

According to the World Bank experts, "what the government can realistically achieve is lifting the labour regulations, which have been largely responsible for the lack of employment growth in organised manufacturing."

How does this policy tackle the problem of "Jobless Growth" since the production processes are capital intensive and do not generate new employment in significant ways, and labour policies do not protect even existing employment? What is the impact on the women's employment?

The opinion of economists, developmental practitioners and other people about the effects of the New Economic Policy on women, as well as other marginal sections in the economy, is divided. Some argue that like other countries of the developing world who have had implemented SAP, feminisation of labour force will take place in India also. More women will get opportunities to participate in the labour market. The other side argues that even if more women will get more jobs, this will be accompanied by feminisation of poverty. "The new policy will further marginalise the majority of women in many ways."

Both sides, i.e. supporters and opponents of SAP agree on one fact: that post-SAP, women's participation in the labour force will be mainly through the informal sector. Thus in the period of liberalisation, the informal sector is a very important segment of the economy. It is necessary to understand Women's role and status in the informal sector since they form significant proportion of this sector.

The foregoing discussion points to the fact that women in the Indian economy were always pushed into the unorganised or informal sector by dominant trends in the economy. Both the colonial rulers as well as planners in independent India have neglected the informal sector of the economy, and make the workers in this sector invisible from the economic data and policies of the government in spite of the fact that this sector provide employment to majority of the poor people and particularly women. About 90 per cent of the working women are concentrated in the informal sector. 'Shramshkti,' the report of the committee on self-employed women and women in informal sector, have provided wide range of documentation and data about how are the vital and productive women workers in the Indian economy remain 'Invisible', 'unrecognised' and most of the time under paid or unpaid.

The problem for women workers is accentuated by the patriarchal ideology operating behind the data gathering system in which the conceptual understanding of women's work is faulty. Since the system of census records was introduced by British rulers in India it is based on the premises that 'men are workers women are dependent'. The leaders and intellectuals connected with the planning process of the economy in independent India also had the same upper and middle-class world view which saw women as dependent on men. They simply ignored the reality of masses of working women in poor urban and rural families.

Some positive attempts are made to make the census data closer to the real estimate of women's work in the recent censuses but it is yet to become an inherent part of the data collection system as such.

But it is a long way to go since women are not recorded as workers, they remain invisible and their contribution unrecognised. The implication for women's empowerment are obvious.

The Concept of Empowerment

Some times the term empowerment is used very casually and statistics about employment, education, political representation, and share in the decision-making process etc. are used in an indiscriminate manner to indicate the empowerment of women. However, the empowerment of women has just not increased in a number of fields. "The term empowerment refers to a range of activities from individual self-assertion to collective resistance, to protest and mobilization that challenges basic power relations. For individuals and groups where class, caste, ethnicity and gender determine their access to resources and power, their empowerment begins when they not only recognise the systemic forces that oppress them, but act to change existing power relationships. Empowerment, there for, is a process aimed at changing the nature and direction of systemic forces which marginalise women and other disadvantaged sections in a given context."

It is a social process. "It is a process of redistribution of power within and between families/societies and a process aiming at social equality which can be achieved through disempowering some structures, systems, and institutions."

Work participation in the labour force is one of the indicators for the status of women and a necessary condition for women's empowerment but does not lead to empowerment in all the circumstances. It is necessary to analyse the nature of work women get in the labour market, its impact on the women access and control over resources, women's role in the decision making in their family and at their work place.

Present Study: Concerns and Methodology

Within the perspective described in the earlier sections, the present study is located in the slums of the Baroda city.

Baroda is one of the most important and industrialised cities of Gujarat State. But the nature of industrialisation in Baroda is very different from the other industrial cities like Ahmedabad or Surat. Unlike Ahmedabad or Surat, Baroda was not historically an industrial city. Baroda was an administrative headquarter and a city of cultural and educational institutions. In Ahmedabad and Surat, there are traditional industries as well as new industries, which specifically employ women labourers. In Baroda, industrialisation took off in sixties with the growth of public sector enterprises, having capital intensive technology. The private sector mainly consists of engineering units and chemical industries, which are not employers of women workers in a big way.

According to the Census data only 7.17 per cent of women in Baroda city were in the workforce in the year 1991. In 2001 Census the work participation rate was 9.55 per cent for women and 52.63 per cent for men. The Census does not give separate work participation data for slum population. However, several studies conducted in Baroda Slums gives some idea about the work participation of women.

The Operation Research Group (ORG) conducted a survey of slums, *chawls* and *khadkies* in 1982. In this study the WPR for males in Baroda slums was recorded as 56.6 per cent for male and 5.8 per cent women. In 1988 the National Institute of Urban Affairs (NIUA) did a sample survey of 213 households from Baroda slums. In the Institute of Social Science (ISS) study (1992) of 400 selected families the WPR for the slum population was recorded as 22.5 per cent for adult men and 5 per cent for adult women. In Baroda Citizen's Council's study in 1994 of all slums in Baroda the WPR for men was found to be 51.66 per cent and for women it was 4.7 per cent of total population of women.

Thus in all these studies the WPR for women in Baroda Slum is recorded around 5 per cent.

The strikingly low WPR for women was mentioned the ISS study in following words, " The percentage of working female adults in the work force in incredibly low at only 5 per cent which indicates that out of total adult female population of 435 only 22 or 5 per cent are engaged in any type of earning activities."

These observations raise several issues. Are women in Baroda slums not economically active or there is a problem of under-enumeration? Are women involved in such activities, which remain invisible and irregular? What is the relationship between low work participation rate and the nature of industrialisation in the city? What are the implications for these on the economic status of women and the process of empowerment for women? These are some of the issues that will be addressed in the following sections.

Methodology

The paper is based on secondary as well as primary data sources. Secondary data sources include Census data, NSSO data, and information collected from the Baroda Municipal Corporation.

Primary data are collected from the 12 slum pockets of the city of Baroda. Baroda city is divided into ten administrative wards. In the first stage five wards were selected considering various factors such as geographical location, number of slum pockets in the ward, number of families residing in the slums and nature of economic activities carried out in the ward.

In the first stage, slum pockets were selected on the bases of stratified random sampling method and in the second stage, 10 per cent of the households were selected from each selected pocket with the help of random sampling method. One woman was interviewed from each selected household with the help of a questionnaire in personal interview. In addition, if any woman from the household was found to be working for income she was further interviewed about her work and working condition. Total 357 women were interviewed. All of them were involved in housework. 138 were also involved in some work for income. Indepth interviews and observation methods were used for case studies.

Indicators of Economic Status and Empowerment

To analyse the economic status of women and it's implication on the empowerment of women following determinants were examined in the study : (1) Participation in the work force, (2) Type of work (3) Income (4) Working conditions and (5) Control over decision making in the family.

1. Participation in the Work Force: Participation in the work force is one of the most important indicators of economic status. We have examined the factors that enable women to participate in the work force and those that act as a hindrance for them.

We have used the term 'occupational status' for the analysis of women's work, which is divided into three categories. (a) Formal sector work (b) Informal sector work (c) Housework (H.W.). Housework undertaken by these women involves various kinds of work, that includes free collection of material for improving the house, processing and cleaning cheap food grains and vegetable, making mattresses from old clothes, etc. All these activities result in saving money and indirectly contribute to the family income. We recognise that it is necessary to include the value of all these unpaid works in the women's economic contribution. However, one of our objectives is to compare the work participation rate recorded in the census and other studies. To make this comparison possible we have used the same conventional definition adopted in the census and considered only those women as workers, who bring income to the family or contribute in family business for production or sale of marketable commodities and services. By analysing women's work in these three categories, we have examined the factors that influence women's entry in to the labour market as well as in the formal and informal sectors.

2. Type of Work: The other important indicator is the type of work women get in the labour market. The types of work within the informal sector are also not homogeneous. There are evidences of fragmentation within the informal sector as well. The work and working conditions in these various fragments are also different.

Hence we have further divided the type of work into following categories: (a) Factory work (b) Home based work (c) Casual work (d) Service (e) Self employment (f) Family business. From these category factory workers, home based workers, casual workers, and workers providing services are wage earners. We have further divided the self-employed into two categories i.e. self-employed women who are independent own account workers and women working in the family business as unpaid family workers.

3. Income: income of the worker is an important determinant of her economic status. The study is about women from the low-income group only but we have further differentiated the respondents into three categories. (a) Lowest income group having monthly income less than 500 rupees. (b) Lower income group having monthly income between 501 to 1000 rupees. (c) Income group having monthly income more than 1000 rupees, i.e. low income group.

4. Working Conditions: Conditions of work is an equally important indicator of the economic status. We have analysed working conditions in terms of the nature of work, benefits available as workers, effect on health and safety and presence of organisation at the work place. All these are indicators of women workers control over their working condition and affect the process of empowerment.

5. Control over Decision Making in the Family: It is important to analyse if the work or income provides more control to women over their lives in the family or not. We have examined (a) Women's self-perception about their status in the family and society because of their work. And (b) Relationship between their contribution to the family income and their role in the decision making within the family.

The Results

1. Participation in the Work Force: Occupational Status: The occupational status of women is a complicated area of inquiry because women's "productive" and "unproductive" works are very similar and many times carried out in the same place or environment, i.e. their home. The practice of considering most of the work performed by women as unproductive has affected women's perception as well. Many times women themselves tend to undervalue their occupational status. We observed during the fieldwork that many time women, who make significant contribution in the family income, consider their work as part of their duty to perform domestic work. This is particularly applicable for women involved in the family business because they do not get any monetary reward for the work they perform. Given this situation, we have tried to capture all the women who contribute in the family income through their monetary income or unpaid work in family business.

In our study of 357 randomly selected households from slums of Baroda the WPR for women is 22.91 per cent and for men 54.23 per cent in the entire population. The WPR recorded in our study is higher compared to the 1991 Census WPR for both men and women in the entire city and much higher in case of women. It is also very high compared to other studies conducted in Baroda slum, mentioned in the earlier section.

Table 20.1: Occupation of the Women

Occupation	Number	Percentage
Formal sector worker	10	(2.80)
Informal sector worker	128	(35.90)
Involved only in House work	219	(61.30)
Total	357	(100.00)

Source: field survey

Out of total 357 women respondents, 219 (61 per cent) women were engaged only in the housework and 138 (38.70 per cent) were involved in some kind of earning activities beside housework (Table 20.1).

Thus economic participation of urban women, belong to low income households is much higher than recorded by the census and other studies.

Based on comparison with the work participation recorded by these studies in Baroda slums we can conclude that the underestimation of women's work in all the available studies is as high as about 75 per cent. Thus the proportion of invisibility is very high for the women working in the urban informal sector. The implication of this is evident from the following quotation form M. Krishnaraj (1989).

"Why is visibility so important? First of all, it is important in the interest of veracity and accuracy. Economics stops where real life begins. More important however is the damage invisibility does to women's status. By a quirk of definition, women's work, which is crucial to survival, becomes marginal and women who support everyone appear dependent. This has serious implications for policy."

Why do they Work: The reason for participation in the labour market are interesting. 77 per cent of women work because it is necessary for them to work for survival. The usual response of the women was, "*Kamaiye nahi to khaiye* *shun?"* (What do we eat if we don't work?) *Badhane Kam to karvu j pade ne?* (Every one have to work). Thus for 77 per cent of women workers, taking up earning work was not a conscious decision or matter of choice but a matter of fact.

Some were indicating that because of rising prices it is not possible to survive on only male members' income. The economic condition of the family is such that if they stop earning it will be difficult for them to survive.

21 per cent of respondents reported that they work to support family income. The common responses were "*Kamaiye to chokara pacchal kharchi shakiye.*" (We can spend money for children if we earn.) Some other responses were, We feel good when we earn... Why to sit idle at home ... If we earn we need not ask for money from others. Thus 21 per cent of women feel that they have a supporting role in the family survival.

Reasons for not Working: The reasons for participation in the labour market were mainly economic but the reasons for not working can be divided in three categories **(1) social (2) economic and (3) lack of support services.**

Let us compare the relative importance of all the three. 81 (37 per cent) of women are not working because of restrictions from family, 47 (21.5 per cent) because work is not available and 45 (20.5 per cent) do not have time away from housework. Only 5 per cent women from poor families said that they do not need to work for income.

Thus, the patriarchal structure of family restricted 37 per cent of women from participating in the labour market. 21.5 per cent of these women do not get work because of the economic forces operating in the market. 20.5 per cent cannot work for two reasons, i.e. the prevailing ideology that housework and childcare are responsibilities of women and the non-availability of support services like childcare and cheap readymade food by the state or employer to fulfill these responsibilities.

Patriarchal norms or family norms are one of the most important factors that not only affect women's entry into the labour market but also the kind of work they can do in the labour market. Patriarchal norms, as shaped by caste, religion places of origin, etc. operate at both demand and supply side of the market.

Factors Affecting Women's Work: The structure of the labour market at first instance is determined by pre-entry factors like, gender, age, caste, religion, education, etc. We have examined the effect of these factors on women's work participation and nature of work they get in the labour market.

Caste was the mechanism for social division of labour before the introduction of market economy in India. Each caste had a specific occupation attached to them and it was obligatory on the part of the caste members to perform that particular task. Economic role of women was defined by the caste norms. Women from the so called lower castes were expected to participate in "productive" work but women from the so called upper castes were not allowed to work out side their homes. With the introduction of market economy this rigid association of caste with occupation did not remain same but it does have an impact on the labour market. Caste is one of the important factors in determining the form of labour market segmentation.

In our study, the percentage of women involved only in household work was highest in other castes (61.3 per cent) and lowest among the scheduled tribes (18.3 per cent). The reverse situation was found in case of informal sector work. Percentage of other caste women involved in informal sector was lowest and scheduled tribe women was highest. The higher number of scheduled caste women in formal sector employment was also due to their caste. Vadodara Municipal Corporation or large hospital employs these women in as scavengers. It seems that the only formal sector work easily available to the scheduled caste women was scavenging. It does give them stable and substantial income but not social status.

Marital status has a significant effect on the decision to take up work. 92 per cent of the women in our study were married but the proportion of married respondents among women involved only in the house work was 96.8 per cent. Looking at the total of formal as well as informal workers, 73.7 per cent of widows or separated respondents were working and 71.4 per cent of unmarried respondents were working. But in case of married women the proportion of working women was only 35.9 per cent.

It was assumed in the early writings on women's work that education gives more opportunity to women in the labour market. This is a partial truth. It is true for "upper" and middle-class-caste women. But "lower caste" women have always worked.

198(55.5 per cent) women in our study were illiterate, 104(29.1 per cent) had education up to primary level, 44(12.3 per cent) were educated up to secondary level and 10(2.8 per cent) had education up to H.S.C. or above. 50 per cent of the total formal sector workers were illiterate. 57 per cent of the informal sector workers were illiterate and 54 per cent of housewives were illiterate. So there is no significant difference in the occupation of the illiterate women. On the other hand only 10 women i.e. 2.8 per cent of the total sample were found to have education above H.S.C. From these 10 women 6 were housewives, three were working in the informal sector and only one was in the formal sector. Majority of the literate women has education up to primary level. The percentage of women in the labour force is not significantly different in each educational category.

The presence of a formal sector male worker in the respondent's family had significant effect on occupational status of the respondents. 143 families have at least one male member in the formal sector. 77.6 per cent of the respondents from such families were involved only in the housework and only 22.4 per cent were working. 214 families do not have any formal sector male worker. Proportion of working women is 50 per cent in such families, which is considerably higher from the families having male workers in formal sector.

Marginalisation: The other aspect of invisibility is concentration of the women in the lower segment of the urban economy. 94.21 per cent of the total women workers from Baroda slums were engaged in the informal sector work and only 5.78 per cent are in the formal sector employment. The corresponding figures for male were 35.48 per cent in the formal sector and 64.52 per cent in the informal sector. Out of total 138 women working for income majority of them, i.e. 128 were involved in the informal sector and only 10 were working in the formal sector of the economy.

Thus both men and women in the lower income groups rely more on the informal sector than the formal sector for their livelihood but women's access to the formal sector is far lower compared to men from their households.

We have considered all the women employed by the public sector as formal sector workers but it was not easy to separate formal sector workers from the informal sector in private sector units because of similarity of work and working conditions in both formal and informal sector units. For example, not all the ten factory workers could be considered as formal sector workers because of the casual or irregular nature of their work. Though they were working in the formal sector, they were not getting any benefit of formal sector workers.

The nature of work available to poor women in the formal sector needs further analysis. Four out of ten women who could enter the formal sector in our study were providing cleaning services to the public sector. The Municipal Corporation employed three workers as scavengers; and one was employed by the government hospital. The remaining six were working in the private sector. A school employed one woman. Two of them were basically working, as peon in the factory and one was a typist. Only two women were engaged in manufacturing process. One was working as helper in a factory making tin boxes and another was working in a drug factory for filling and checking injections and tablets.

Type of Work: As mentioned earlier, not only participation in the work force but the type of work is an equally important factor for determining the economic status of women.

Within the informal sector 39.9 per cent of women are in personal services,

16.7 per cent in homebased work, 15.2 per cent in self employment, 13 per cent in casual labour, 8 per cent in family business and 7.2 per cent in factory work. The corresponding figures for men were 2.8 per cent in the personal services, not a single man in home-based work, 29.4 per cent were self-employed, 11.8 per cent were casual labourers, 4.8 per cent were in family business and 46.5 per cent in factory work.

In the category of home based work, 16 women were engaged in the *papad* rolling. They were concentrated mainly in a few pockets in Kisanwadi ward. They used to get work from three nearby merchants. 3 women were engaged in various kinds of packaging work for factories. The rest were involved in work like brush making, sewing for the merchant and making food at home for shop keeper to sale.

Self employed women were vendors that include vegetable vendors, fruit vendors, fish vendors and cart puller. Some of them have started small shops in their residence or a place adjacent to the residence. Some of them sewed clothes and one of them was selling liquor.

Most of the women engaged in personal service were domestic servants. They are working in several houses for few hours in each to clean utensils, washing clothes cleaning house, etc. Some of them were involved only in cooking for a family or some establishment.

Casual labourers were working either as construction workers or agricultural workers. The proportion of construction workers and agricultural workers was equal among the casual labourers.

All the women engaged in the family business were involved in traditional family business like animal husbandry, buying and selling of old clothes, pottery making, blacksmith work, etc.

We can see from the Table 20.2 that women are mainly engaged in the categories of personal services, home based work, casual labour and family business. The entire workforce in the home based work consists of women. Men are more represented in factory work and even self-employment. In the category of personal services, men are engaged in marginal numbers.

The caste plays very significant role also in the type of work women are engaged. More than 50 per cent of the women from SC and ST were concentrated in personal services and none of them were in the family business. OBC women were involved in each type of work but they formed 72.2 per cent of casual labourers as well as 72.7 per cent of women involved in the family business.

The noticeable presence of OBC women in family business is not surprising since OBC represent artisan castes having caste-based family business. 52 per cent of the home based workers were women from other castes. The presence of other caste women in home based work indicates that the restriction on women for working outside is higher among other castes. Among self-employed women, the presence of OBC was highest followed by the other castes.

Table 20.2: Type of Work

Type of work	No. of women	Percentage	No. of Men	Percentage
Factory work	10	7.20	166	46.50
Home based work	23	16.70	0	0
Self Employed	21	15.20	105	29.40
Service	55	39.90	10	2.80
Casual labourer	18	13.00	42	11.80
Family business	11	8.00	17	4.80
Total	138	100.00	340	95.30*

* The total percentages of men do not add up to 100 because in 17 (4.7 per cent) families there was no male earner.

Like caste, religion also plays a significant role in deciding the type of work. All the women working as factory workers, self employed and casual labourers were Hindu. Muslim respondents were largely concentrated in home based work.

Income of the Women: In this section, we will examine the effect of various factors on the income of women workers. Some of the aspects examined in this section are, comparison between male and female income, income of the formal sector workers and informal sector workers. Some of the questioned examined, Are women engaged in various types of work concentrated in particular income groups or not? Caste, religion, etc. also have significant impact on women's income or not.

Comparison with Male Counterpart: Comparison of the income of the women and their male counterpart reveals that 84 (60.86 per cent) women are in the lowest income group and men in that income bracket are 39 (28.26 per cent). Proportion of women is decreasing as income increases whereas proportion of men is increases in each subsequent higher income group (Table 20.3).

In most of the families women earn less than men. Only three families in the income group Rs. 500 to Rs. 1000 and three families in the income group above Rs. 1000 are such that women earn more than their male counterparts.

Income in the Formal and Informal Sector: The income gap between formal sector workers and informal sector workers is remarkable. 9 (90 per cent) formal sector workers are represented in the income group above 500 rupees per month and only one was earning less than Rs. 500 per month. About 83 (64.8 per cent) women from the informal sector are concentrated in the income group less than Rs. 500 per month. Only 44 (35.2 per cent) women from the informal sector earn more than Rs. 500 rupees per month.

Table 20.3: Income of Women and Income of the Male Counterpart

Income M→ Income F↓	Less than 500	501 to 1000	Above 1000	Total
Less than 500	24	28	32	84 (60.86)
500 to 1000	9	15	15	39 (28.26)
Above 1000	6	3	5	14 (10.14)
NR/DK	0	1	0	1 (0.7)
Total	39 (28.26)	47 (34.05)	52 (37.68)	138 (100)

Source: field survey

Income and Type of Work: 84 women, i.e. 60.9 per cent of all working respondents belong to lowest income group. They are concentrated mainly in home based group. 91.3 per cent of home based workers, 72.2 per cent of casual workers and 70.9 per cent of respondents in personal services belong to the lowest income group. In case of male workers, 33, i.e. only 9.7 per cent belong to the lowest income group. Majority of them are casual workers and self employed. Proportion of factory workers and women in family business is negligible in lowest income group. Factory workers, self-employed and women in family business are concentrated in the income group Rs. 501-Rs.1000. In case of men, factory workers were the lowest among the low-income group.

14 women, i.e. 10 per cent of the total working respondents were earning more than Rs. 1000 per month. 42 per cent of them provide personal services. This implies that the range of income in the various types of personal service is very wide since the latter include the majority of the lowest income group as well as majority of the higher income group. In case of men, 214 (63.1 per cent) of them earn more than Rs. 1000 per month. 129 (60.3 per cent) of them are factory workers. The second group is self-employed.

Time spent in the earning activity and number of years in the labour force has a positive impact on the income. But exemptions are also important in this regard. There were 31.1 per cent of women who spend more than 8 hours in the earning activity who earn less than Rs. 500 per month. **Thus, low income is not necessarily the result of less work but lower valuation of the type of work women perform.** 50.5 per cent of women who work for more than 8 hours a day earn between Rs. 501 and Rs. 1,000. This is much below the minimum wages of even unskilled labourer.

Education had a positive effect on men's income but not very clear effect

on women's income. Most of the women in our study were only educated up to the primary level. Several studies show that returns of elementary education to women is lower than that of men.

Working Condition: 52.7 per cent of women are engaged in such type of work which is treated as women's work. There are no men involved in the type of work they do.

94 (68.1 per cent) of women reported that they have health problems due to their work but only five (2.9 per cent) of the women get benefit of ESI. 87 per cent of home-based workers, 83 per cent of casual workers, 72 per cent of women in personal services reported health problems due to work but none of them get any benefit from the health system created for workers. Only six women from 138 total working women had an identity card to prove that they are workers of particular employer. Five women had benefit of provident fund and pension. All of them were scavengers in Municipal Corporation. Five women get E.S.I. card, 21 get advances from their employers.

65 (47.1 per cent) women reported that they get bonus. This statistics about bonus needs further probing. The bonus received by these workers during Diwali festival is in no way comparable to the right of bonus under The Payment of Bonus Act. For most of the domestic workers and bonus means Rs 50 or Rs 100 and some used clothes or steel utensils. Similarly 38 (27.5 per cent) of the women responded that their work is permanent. It is critical to note that the term 'permanent' used by the respondents does not mean that they get the benefits, to which a permanent worker is entitled. This is a reflection of the subjective feeling on the part of women that they can continue to do this work permanently. This finding suggests that there is a need to go beyond statistics to understand the realities of women in the labour force.

Contribution in the Family and Share in Decision-making: 295 (82.6 per cent) of women spend about 5 to 8 hours in household work. 35.3 per cent of them are working for income as well. Thus most of them perform double day work. On the one hand women work under precarious work conditions and on the other hand working outside does not reduce their responsibility of domestic work.

12 women were sole earners in their families and 36 (25 per cent) contributed more than 50 per cent in the family income. 121 (34 per cent) women do not have any say in decision making to family. 28.8 per cent were working women from them.

Thus both in the labour market and in the family their contribution is ignored and under valued. They do not have control or say neither in choosing their working conditions nor in decision-making within the family. Given this reality it was not surprising that only 21 (15.2 per cent) of the working women felt that because of their work their status in the family has increased.

51 (14.3 per cent) women were decision-makers in their families. 35 per cent from them were housewives and 65 per cent were working women.

Savita is working in a factory. She never loses the opportunity to work overtime because she wants to educate her son and daughter. Her husband is an auto rickshaw driver. He hardly gives any income to her. Most of his income is spent in liquor and gambling. Sometimes he gives a meagre amount to her to get back more than what he gave her for some excuse like repairing his auto. She is the decision-maker in her family. However, this kind of decision making is not a privilege and indication of real empowerment.

Once again in this case also statistics are deceiving. We conclude that statistics are important to understand the magnitude or quantity of any fact or problem but it is equally important to go beyond statistics to understand the qualitative aspects of reality.

Some Concerns /Conclusion

Work Participation and Visibility of Women Workers: The underestimation of women workers up to 75 per cent have very serious implications for the empowerment of women. In the present study, we have adopted the same definition of work as adopted by census to maintain comparability among the data, the source of the gap between various estimates is not definitional but operational. The probable reasons for low WPR for women in these studies can be the result of the lack of clarity in the way the question was formulated and personal biases of the enumerators and respondents. Since the ISS and BCC studies were conducted in the context of poverty alleviation programmes, underestimation of women workers in these studies disclose the type of problems women face in getting benefits from various poverty eradication schemes of the government.

Thus we need to work towards better definition for women's work as well as better operational mechanisms to enumerate women's work in order to breaking the circuit of low visibility. It is this low visibility which not only indicates low status but also operates as a cause to perpetuate low status.

This leads to an important conclusion of our study that the efforts for changing or expanding definition of work in the data gathering systems at the macro level is an important task but not sufficient. It is equally and perhaps more important to train enumerators not only for national level data gathering surveys but even for city level or micro surveys because that will affect the actual/ immediate living and working conditions of women workers. At the same time spreading wider awareness in the society (among men and women) about the value of women's work to avoid biases on the part of respondents is also needed.

Nature of Work

Majority of women in lower income households work in the urban informal sector. We conclude that both men and women in the lower income groups relay more on the informal sector than the formal sector for their livelihood but women's access to the formal sector is far lower compared to men from their households. The high concentration of women in personal services, mainly as domestic servants, and homebased work shows that women are concentrated in the lowest segments within the informal sector as well.

We can conclude from the various activities in which women were involved in the informal sector that the urban informal sector is much more diverse compared to the rural informal sector. Lack of information and understanding about the complex nature of the urban informal sector is one of the reasons for their invisibility in the formal data gathering surveys.

The strategy of capital intensive industrial growth has left women with fewer choices for work in the urban economy at the national level. Our study observed the same trend is Baroda as well.

The pressure to remain in the home forced women to take up homebased work. The other reason for preferring homebased work was that women could combine their domestic work, look after the children and also do their work for earning. The presence of other caste women and Muslim women in homebased work can be explained by the working of two factors. One is the necessity to work for survival that is pushing them in to the labour market and another is castes and religious norms that force them to take up particular type of work. The control over women's sexuality and labour power operates simultaneously in this case.

Though the castes based social division of labour is not the principle of economic organisation of present capitalist system, caste is an effective variable for market segmentation.

The comparison of the effect of these factors on the nature of work participation shows that in case of women these factors interact with gender and the combined effect of gender, caste, religion, culture create different processes and results for women in the labour market.

Income and Working Conditions

There is a gap between income earned by women in the formal sector and informal sector. But this was not uniformly the case. There were women from the formal sector whose incomes were comparable to the informal sector workers.

There is also a gap between women's income in different types of work available within informal sector. Home-based workers and casual workers earn much less compared to other workers. The income gap between men and women is considerable. The lack of significant impact on income due to hour of work, duration of years in the labour market and educational level shows that there is no economic logic behind the lower income earned by women but the reasons are located in the patriarchal values operating in the family and labour market which consider women as less productive compared to men. The precarious working conditions are also result of the same attitude that women can adjust any how and any way. The desperate need to meet the ends of family budget push them in the labour market but the double burden of work prevents them from spending some time to participate in workers organisation.

This type of work does not give them status and recognition as a productive worker in the economy nor any decision making power in the family.

Market forces have resulted in the marginalisation of women as well as the informal sector in economy. The intensity of these forces has been increasing after the introduction of the New Economic Policy in the early 90s. The process of casualisation of labour force has become intensive.

The number of registered large and medium scale industries have stagnated during last few years in Baroda. The number of registered shops and establishments have also stagnated. Several large and small-scale industries have been closed and many more are in process of closure. Several large-scale industries have shifted their production to small and ancillary units by giving them sub-contracts. Privatisation (disinvestment) of large public sector enterprises like IPCL and GCEL and announcement of voluntary retirement schemes by many enterprises have pushed many people or women from their family in the informal sector.

All these developments in the city are bound to have significant impact on the nature and magnitude of the informal sector in the city. The availability of work and working conditions are also affected by these developments. Further study on the effect of NEP on the informal sector and particularly women in the informal sector of Baroda is necessary.

In spite of precarious working condition we did not find any well-organised efforts on the part of women workers. There were some spontaneous instances of protests to get their demands but lack of organised and sustained efforts was noticeable. As we have seen, the nature of work available in the informal sector is very diverse. Although there are similarities in living and working conditions for women across the segments in the informal sector, development of a collective consciousness about their rights as workers is perhaps hampered by the diversity of work available to them.

Based on the present study, we can conclude that given the situation of women workers, in the informal sector and the increasing pace of economic reforms we feel that their rights cannot be protected without a strong and innovative organisation of workers which can voice the specific nature of women's exploitation as workers as well as women.

References

Acharya, S.: Employment of women and women in India: A Historical Review, 1901-1951 in Sharma A. N. and Singh S. ed. Women and Work, Indian Society of Labour Economics, Patana. 1993.

Archna Gosh et al.: Basic Services to Urban Poor – A study of Baroda, Bhilwara, Sambalpur and Siliguri, Concept Publishing Company, New Delhi. P. 35.

Banerjee N. ed. (1991); Indian Women in a changing Industrial Scenario, Sage publications, Delhi. 1995.

Banerjee, N.: How Real is the Bogy of Feminisation? , Indian Journal Of Labour Economics, Vol. 40, No. 3. 1997.

Bennett L.: Women, Poverty and Productivity in India; Economic Development Institute of World Bank, Washington, D.C. 1988.

Breman, Jan: Wage Hunters and Gatherers, Oxford University Press; New Delhi. 1994.

Dandekar V. M.,"Integration of women in Economic Development, Paper presented at the Conference on Development Perspectives for 1980s, Asian and Pacific Development Centre, Kuala Lumpur. 1981.

Datar, C.: "Women's Work: perspective on Status Production under Patriarchal Relation." Paper presented at the Seminar on Women and Work, Centre for Social Studies Surat. Jan. 1990.

Desai, N. and Krishnaraj M.: Women and society in India, Ajanta Publications, Delhi, (Second ed.) P. 46. 1990.

Deshpande S.: Feminisation through Flexible Labour in India: Evidence and Future Prospects, in The New Economic Policy and women by Indian Association of Women's Studies. 1993.

Deshpande S. and Deshpande L.: Impact of Liberalisation on Labour Market in India- What Do Facts From NSSO's 50th Round Show? Economic and Political Weekly May 30, 1998.p. L-31. 1998.

District Census Hand Book, District Vadodara, Census of India, series- 7 Gujarat, part XII- A&B. 1991.

Duvvury N. and Isaac T. M.: Women in Labour Force: Biases in Recent Indian Estimates in Krishnaraj M. edited Women in Indian Data System, Research Centre for Women's Studies, Bombay. 1989.

Everett, Jana and Savara, Mira: Women and Organisations in the Informal Sector, Himalaya Publishing house; Bombay. 1994.

Gandhi N. and Shah N.: Issues at Stake: Theory and Practice in the Contemporary Women's Movement in India, Kali for Women, New Delhi. 1991.

Gandhi N. and Shah N.: Shadow Workers, Bombay. 1992.

Gandhi, G. K.; Labour force participation, return to education and sex-discrimination in India, The Indian Journal of Labour economics, Vol. 40, No. 3, 1997.

Geraldie, F. (1998): Women in Modern India, Cambridge University Press, South Asian ed.

Ghosh Archna et al; 'Basic Services for Urban poor, A study of Baroda, Bhilwara, Sambalpur and Siliguri, Concept publishing company, New Delhi, 1995, p 19.

Ghosh, J.: Gender Concern in Macro Economic Policy; Economic and Political Weekly April 30. 1994.

Government of India: Towards Equality, Report of the Committee on the Status of Women in India, p.148. 1974.

Government of India. National Perspective Plan for Women. 1988.

Government of India: Shramshakti, Report of the committee on self-employed women and women in informal sector, New Delhi, p.26. 1988.

Institute of Social Science Studies Trust, New Delhi. The major points of the discussion are covered in the report, Technical Seminar on Women's Work and Employment, 1982.

Jabwala R.: Women workers Under Structural Adjustment: Some Issues and Strategies for India in Rajput P. and Swarup H.L. ed. op cit. 1994.

Jain Devaki et al: Can we Convert The Crisis Into An Opportunity? in The New Economic policy and Women, Indian Association of Women's Studies.pp11-35. 1993.

Jhabvala R.: Minimum Wages Based on Worker's Needs, Economic and Political Weekly March 7. 1998.

Kalpgum, U. ; "Labour and Gender" ; Sage Publication, New Delhi, 1994.

Krishnaraj M.: Measuring and Valuing Women's Work: some Improved Methodologies, in Women in Indian data System, Research Centre for Women's Studies, SNDT University, Bombay. 1989.

Krishnaraj M.: Feminist Approaches to Economic Theory, Indian Association of Women Studies. 1995.

21

Women and Self-employment

Saraswati Raju Iyer

Indian society is a developing society passing through transitional changes. Their attitude towards women working outside the house is not so rigid, unfavouable as it was earlier. Now we find women coming out of their homes in a large way breaking all barriers of the family and society and start their own enterprises. The social constraints imposed on them, the attitudes that inhibit the development of women enterpreneurs, the atmosphere in which they have to work and their general society are some of the forces responsible for helping the number of women, working outside their homes small and insignificant.

The phenomenon of self-employment among women is of recent origin as they have been employed at home without wage and outside at very small wage coupled with discrimination and exploitation. Women are engaged in several occupations, such as agriculture, forestry, cattle rearing, dairying, fishery, poultry, sericulture, mining, tobacco and bidi work, construction work, khadi and handloom, handicrafts, peddling, food processing, head load carrying, domestic work, factory work, trade and business.

Women employment is considered not only as an important indicator of their status but also an instrument of their integration in development. Some of the women, however enter employment/labour market by force of circumstances. Women are seen working in informal and formal sectors, as also organised and unorganised sector. Women are also seen as entrepreneurs which is a recent phenomena. Self-employment among women is considered vital to tackle the problem of poverty on one hand and enhance the self esteem of women on the other hand.

Self-employment among women is a challenging field. A self employed woman is seen as an investor, promoter, organiser, manager, co-ordinator and also as a capitalist. These roles were played by her at home and she would have to extend it outside her home. Her duties as a wife, mother, a daughter keeps her busy and engaged. She takes decision with regard to work inside the house and the same would be extended in the work place.

A Self employed can be understood as an individual

- "Who organises and manages the business undertaken and assumes the risk for the sake of profit"
- "An organiser who combine various factors of production to produce a socially viable product"

Characteristics of Women in Self-employment

Studies have established the existence of some common personal characteristics of enterpreneurs, some of these are:

- A high level of energy.
- Desire to pursue innovative goals.
- A deep involvement in work.
- Optimistic belief in future.
- Predictive mentality about the market.
- Self confidence.

Qualities of Women in Self-employment

There are certain essential qualities that enable women enterpreneurs efficient. Some of the qualities that are considered significant are :

- Mental ability.
- Human relation.
- Communication skills.
- Technical knowledge.
- Decision making ability.
- Conceptual ability.

Types of Self Employed Person

The different types of self employed persons which makes them distinct are given below:

- **Innovative Person:** An innovative person is one who introduces something new into the economy or employ a new technique of introduction, opens a new market, exploit a new source of raw material and reorganises the whole enterprises.
- **Immitating Person:** They are suited to developing countries which is constrained to take up expensive research. Benefits enjoyed by them are however the same as those by original innovators.
- **Fabian Person:** They are cautious in adopting and implementing any change. They are very scared and lack the will to adopt new methods. Their dealings are determined by customs, religion, tradition and past practices.

- **Drone Person:** They are inert and traditional and are hurdles in economic development. They struggle to resist, not to grow.

Functions of Women in Self-employment

There are certain important functions to be performed by the women enterpreneurs. They are:

- Determination of the objectives of the enterprises.
- Development of the organisation.
- Securing adequate financial resources.
- Requisition of efficient technological equipment and its revision consonant with technical change.
- Development of market and devising new products and to meet anticipated consumer demand.
- Maintenance of good relation with public authorities and society at large.
- Management of human relation.
- Financial management.
- Production management.

Nature of Women's Self-employment

Although the number of women enterpreneurs is small in our country, they have adventured in different type of enterprises. It is not true that only conventional fields are open to them but women are engaged in manufacturing like tailoring, garments, furnishing and garment exports, marketing drugs and pharmaceuticals, chemicals, fabrication and rural house hold industries producer like basket-making, agarbathi making, bidi making etc.

When we compare self-employment between rural and urban, variant features will exist according to its geographical location, availability of resources and condition of self-employment in terms of manufacturing process and quality of products.

Credit Facilities for Self-employment

With a view of facilitating self-employment among women credit is one of the important inputs. At present various development schemes of rural development and social welfare have element of loans and subsidies because it is not only difficult but far too expensive for women to arrange credit. However, they still find it difficult not only to have access to credit but also to repay loans because of illiteracy and cumbersome procedures of banks and IRDP authorities. SEWA of Ahmedabad had some innovative approaches to this problem. The

Commission on self-employed women have also made some recommendations on credit facilities for Self-Employed Women. The State Women Development Corporations fulfil the credit needs of self-employed women to some extent.

Following governmental agencies are helping the women to start and maintain their business.

- Directorate of Industries-Delhi.
- Small Industries Development Organisation.
- Development Commissioner of Small Scale Industries.
- Small Industries Service Institute.
- National Small Industries Corporation (NSIC).
- Small Industries Governmental Corporation.
- Industrial Development Bank of India (IDBI).
- Tamil Nadu Industrial Investment Corporation (TIIC).
- District Industrial Centre (DIC).
- Small Industries Development Bank of India (SIDBI).
- State Finance Corporation.
- Industrial Credit and Investment Corporation.
- National Research Development Corporation of India.
- Khadi and Village Industries Corporation.
- Central Social welfare Board (CSWB).
- Lead Banks.
- National Institute for Enterpreneurship and Small Business Development.
- Indian Finance Corporation of India (IFCI).

Rural Women Self-employment

With a view of tackling the problem of rural poverty, schemes and projects have been undertaken under the Integrated Rural Development Programme for the rural families below the poverty line who are identified on the basis of a family income criteria. The beneficiaries under the scheme are small and marginal farmers, artisans, agricultural labourers, scheduled castes, scheduled tribes and women, who have not been able to get benefits from normal development programmes. The programme covers schemes like Development of Women and Children in Rural Areas (DWACRA) and Training of Rural Youth in Self-Employment, (TRYSEM) and Agricultural Labourers Employment Guarantee Scheme, Food for work, as part of National Rural Employment Programmes, etc. with a view of providing employment opportunities wherein around 30 per cent of beneficiaries have to be women. Whereas women participation in these programmes was around 10 per cent in 1985-86, it was 23 per cent in 1988-89 and 25 per cent during 1989-90 and 24.36 per cent during 1990-91 (Ministry of Rural Development, 1990-91).

Under these programmes, group of 15-20 women in the age group of 18-25 years are given training in different vocations under DWACRA and TRYSEM. They are also given training in agriculture and related activities, cottage industries etc. Dairy, masala making, agarbatti making etc. are also included in the vocational training programmes for women. Every group of women is given funds for purchasing raw materials. The subsidy and loans are being given to individual women during training or apprenticeship period. Whereas under DWACRA all beneficiaries are women, under TRYSEM at least one-third beneficiaries should be women.

Women are unable to take full advantage of these schemes, because of lack of literacy, training facilities like training centres, master craftsmen, purchase of raw material, sale of articles etc. The cumbersome procedure of getting loans and subsidies also create problems for women. Under this Programme around 4,00,000 women have been brought above poverty line. There is a need for opening training centres and establishing more women's organizations. There is also a need for giving information and creating awareness about the employment schemes to the rural women.

Problems of Women in Self-employment

- Lack of viable concept and lack of market knowledge among women due to traditional system of society.
- Lack of technical skill and business know how, because women are not prepared to learn a foresaid aspect.
- Lack of motivation among the women towards a set of language.
- Social ceremonies of the society pertaining to the women affects the women's self-employment
- Lack of managerial skills for procurement, utilisation and controlling of manpower of the enterprises.

Measures to Develop Women's Self-Employment

- The areas and sectors where women's employment is low or on the decline are to be identified and corrective measures to be initiated to promote additional avenues for employment.
- Determined efforts are to be made to promote self-employment for ensuring progressive reduction in the incidence of poverty and unemployment, to

achieve this objective, assistance need to be intensified in the areas of training and managerial skills, making available easy credit facilities, exploring marketing outlets apart from developing the necessary infrastructure. This will enable the women to start their ventures and to pursue vocations and activities to which they are trained or have aptitude and capability.

- A major step in the direction of promotion of women's employment and self-employment has to be in expanding and diversifying the education facilities and training opportunities available to them.
- There is an urgent need to implement the banking policy in favour of women. It would be beneficial if loans are advanced to women through agencies like Mahila Mandals, Women's Groups, State Advisory Boards and Women's Development Corporations.
- There is a need for setting up an exclusive credit body for poor and self-employed women in view of their socio-economic realities and the inability of the existing institutionalised credit system to cater to the needs of women workers.
- Self-employment programmes for women should be strengthened and designed on the basis of their needs at the micro level. Planning should incorporate measures like child care and child development, use of technology to reduce drudgery, organisation of women and their over all development.
- Women should be treated as independent entities in the labour market and joint titles should be given to improve their access to the credit market.
- DWACRA and such related organisations could be improved by detailing guide-lines for programmes; strengthening training, entrepreneurship and management, streamlining the supply of raw-materials, improving marketing facilities and introducing continuous sympathetic evaluation of programmes. Agencies like Mahila Mandals, voluntary agencies and cooperatives should be utilised for assisting women in completing formalities for getting credit.
- There is a need for providing more support and financial facilities to grass-root organisations which have proved more effective in reaching out and mobilising the poor women. Women who have education, knowledge, and leadership qualities

References

Chowdhry Paul. D., Women in Rural Development, Women Welfare and Development-A Source Book. Women in South Asia Series W013 Inter-India Publications, New Delhi, 1992.

Andersen L. Margaret, Thinking About Women, Macmillan Publishers, USA, 1983.

M. Haralambos with R.M. Heald, Sociology: Themes and Perspectives, OUP, Delhi, 1980.

22

Emotional Intelligence at Work Place

Om Raj Singh

The women being better half of men, make up 45 per cent of the world work force and provide nearly 60 per cent household income worldwide. Emotional make up and women's work interface is a crucial question. Women in India are very closely associated with family and its various responsibilities. At the same time when more and more women are joining, the labour force and coming out of home to earn without much support at home and even at the work place it becomes very difficult for women to cope up both physically as well as emotionally persistent poverty, unequal pays, lack of education, training, access to productive funds, dismal participation in socio economic activity and decision making emotional weakness has hit women very hard. This has devalued their own lives and inclines them to look towards men as the protector and someone superior. This results in loss of self-esteem and self confidence because of being emotional, the adverse impact is felt everywhere. The social attitudes and prejudices inherent in our milieu, which are unfavourable towards girls and women, need to be changed. It is important to understand the Emotional Intelligence.

Emotional Intelligence (E.I.) increases with age, it can be learnt, cultivated and increased in adulthood and that the place to learn it is not workplace but the school. For instance, children, who have trouble being accepted by there to drop out. Aggressiveness has been linked to inability to handle in pleasant scenes at home. At present, emotional education of children is being left to change. Academic intelligence has little to do with emotional life. Based on rationality, school pays little or no attention to emotions lest they disrupt the class. Intelligence Quotient is a measure of one's emotional Quotient. It describes the qualities of a person. Those who are insensitive to emotions in others will not see the need to care for others.

The nature of human intellect has fascinated scholars for centuries. Over the last few decades the study of intelligence has proved as one of the strongest claims of practical and applied psychology. The vicissitudes to intelligence have intrigued the learners of this phenomenon, particularly psychologists and educationalists, and the most basic question, which abound and proliferate in theoretical and empirical literature is; what intelligence? The consensus arrived over the years to describe the phenomenon expresses itself as a function of consequences that helps the individuals to adapt to the complex environment around it, it acts as a selecting agency, an efficacious instrument of survival. Such a philosophical stand reflected itself in the form of attempts at understanding the process of intelligence as a cognition and intellection. The initial years of conceptualization of intelligence led to an over emphasis on genetic or developmental approach to a psychological ontogenesis of the phenomenon. In other words, the psychometric approach to intelligence has become increasingly less popular during the second half of the 20th century primarily because it has little, if anything, to say about mental processes and also due to the realization that factor structures of intelligence are complex and tend to vary considerable across culture. Apart from this, researchers become increasingly dissatisfied with the fact that general intelligence as understood today correlated very poorly in predicting the life success and adaptation of the individual to his or her environment. The attention of the researchers in the field is now gathering around the concepts like wisdom, prudence, practical intelligence, social intelligence, emotional intelligence and spiritual intelligence.

To meet the varietal present day needs of contemporary society, education of youth should be changed from the world of school to the world of work and life. Now-a-days, education system, perse, does not give guarantee success in life. Our experiences and experiments highlight that even the persons with high intellect cannot be always successful in life. A lot of people have been trying to fill the gap between the success and failure either of which is caused by interaction of mind and heart. Studies on this issue are still ongoing not only in developing countries like India but all over the world. Recently, psychologists Joshn D. Mayer, Peter Salovey and Daniel Goleman have came with an answer by introducing the concept of Emotional Intelligence (EI).

Emotional Intelligence refers to the ability of the individual to set a goal in life, work towards achieving it, negotiate it and feel empathetic towards a fellow being. It involves the ability to deal with feelings and the ability to communicate. In fact, the lack of these skills has far reaching impact, and resulting to unhappiness and inability to form positive relationships. It guarantees a well balanced personality. While intelligence is basically determined at birth, emotional intelligence is essentially learned. Recent findings have identified emotional intelligence as the single most important factor predicting success and happiness in life.

Until 1980s there was no talk of emotional intelligence. In 1989, John Mayer and Peter Salovey first coined the term Emotional Intelligence to describe a person's ability to understand one's own emotions, the emotions of others and act appropriately. The term EI became popular in 1995 with the best selling book, Emotional Intelligence: Why it can matter more than intelligence Quotient by Daniel Goleman, Doctorate in psychology from Harvard University and science writer with New York Times. He followed it up with another title Emotional Intelligence in a work place. The emergence of the EI gave the explanation that people with high IQ might not necessarily be successful and a theory that true intelligence is actually a combination of both EI and IQ. Emotional Intelligence refers to the capacity of recognizing our own feelings and those of others for motivating ourselves and managing emotions well in ourselves and in our relationships (Daniel Goleman, 1998).

Does IQ Differ from EI?

According to Goleman, an individual's success at work to the tune of 80 per cent is dependent on EI and 20 per cent on the more commonly known intelligence Quotient (IQ). IQ is a measure of one's emotional level. It describes the qualities of a person e.g. self motivation, self awareness, impulse control and empathy. It means being smart about one's emotions. It is different from IQ in that it can teach the children EI skills to give them a better chance to use their genetically given intellectual potential i.e. IQ. Those who are insensitive to emotions in others will not see the need to care for others. While intelligence is basically determined at birth, EI is an acquired trait. Emotional skill such as empathy can be taught and developed as children grow, and live out their lives. Emotions therefore may be the true measure of human being. Emotional intelligence has its roots in the concept of social intelligence first coined EI. Thorndike in 1920 defined social intelligence as the ability to understand and manage men and women, boys and girls to act wisely in human relations. According to Mayer and Salovey, Emotional Intelligence is a type of social intelligence that involves the ability to monitor one's own and others emotions, to discriminate among them, and to use the information to guide one's thinking and actions. The difference between Intelligence Quotient and emotional intelligence can be described in the following way.

A high IQ is all about how quickly you can do puzzles, and how many words you know, but emotional intelligence is about feelings, and understanding the feelings of other people. For example, a high IQ might get a person a high marks or grades in academics but it will be more their emotional intelligence which determines how happy he or she is and thereafter how well he or she can get along with others on work and in life.

Emotional Intelligence can change unlike IQ, which generally stabilizes when a person is around 18 years of age. A person with a low EI score on empathy today can have a higher empathy score in the future – if that person recognizes his limitations, changes his attitude, adopts a learning strategy and practices key listening and empathy skills. EI is in a way, pre-requisite of leadership. An analysis has shown that it plays an increasing important role at the highest levels in a corporate structure, where differences in technical skills are of negligible importance. In other words, the higher the rank of a person considered to be a star performer, the more EI capabilities show up as the reason for his effectiveness.

Peter Salovey offers a framework for EI through the life, personal intelligence characteristics of self awareness or knowing one's own emotions, the ability to manage one's emotions and impulses, self motivation skills, empathy or the ability to sense how others are feeling and lastly, social skills or the ability to handle the emotions of other people.

Self awareness is the cornerstone of emotional intelligence. It reflects the ability of a person to be able to know the reason for his emotional response, thus improving his chances of handing it in an appropriate manner. People incapable of soothing themselves have to constantly fight against feelings of distress, while those who excel, can bounce back more quickly from life setbacks. This is not easy skill as emotions often appear in disguise as with a present yelling at a child for running on the road, anger borne out of anxiety. Yet, for all its complexity, self awareness is the most crucial skill, says Goleman, as it allows us to exercise self control. It also allows people to develop coping mechanisms during period of intense emotional upsurge. For instance, going out for a brisk jog when one is feeling tense may be a trigger response in the body mind that is incompatible with the earlier feelings. Self awareness can also be identified during performance reviews. Persons with this quality know about their limitations and strengths and they often demonstrate a thirst for constructive criticism. However, people with a low degree of self awareness interpret the message that they need to improve as a threat or a sign of failure. Self aware people have more degree of self confidence and have a firm grasp of their capabilities. They know when to ask for help. The risks they take on the job are calculated. They will never ask for a challenge that they know they cannot handle.

Managing emotions or self regulations is that component of EI which frees us from being prisoners of our own feelings. People engaged in such conversation feel emotional impulses just as everyone else does but they find ways to control them and even to channel them in useful ways. Self regulation is very important for leadership qualities. People who are in control of their feelings and impulses are reasonable and are able to create an environment of trust and fairness, in such an environment, politics and infighting are sharply reduced.

Motivating oneself or marshalling emotions is essential for self motivation and creativity. A singularly important factor for all effective leaders is motivation. Many people are motivated by external factors e.g. big compensation packages or the status that comes from the position one enjoys in an organization. On the other hand, those with leadership potential are motivated by a deeply extended desire to achieve for the sake of achievement. People with high motivation remain optimistic even under unfavourable circumstances. In all such cases, it is said that self regulation combines with achievement motivation to overcome the frustration and depression that comes after a setback or a failure.

Empathy is another important factor that recognizes emotions in others. People, who are empathic, are more attuned to the subtle social signals that indicate what others want. Empathy is defined as thoughtfully considering other's feelings along with related factors in the process making intelligent decisions. It is particularly important today as a component of leadership for various reasons. The reasons include increasing use of teams, the rapid pace of globalization and the every growing need to retain talent. Teamwork is possible only in the environment of mutual understanding and trust for which empathy is the basic ingredient. In globalization, cross cultural dialogue can easily lead to misunderstandings and in such cases, empathy is an antidote. People, who have empathy, have a deep understanding of the importance of cultural and ethnic differences. Retention of talent has become very important, particularly in our age and times. Leaders have always needed empathy to develop and keep good people.

Social skill is another important component of emotional intelligence. The art of relationship is basically a skill in managing emotions of others. It involves social competence and specific skills, which help in this direction. People, who excel in these skills, do well in anything that depends on interaction with others. Socially skilled people tend to have a wide circle of acquaintances and they have knack of finding common ground with people of all kinds, such people have a network in place when the time for action comes.

Emotional Intelligence increases with age, says Goleman. It can be learned, cultivated and increased in adulthood and the place to learn it is not the workplace but in school. For instance, children, who have trouble being accepted by their classmates, are five times more likely to drop out. Aggressiveness has been linked to inability to handle unpleasant scenes at home. At present, emotional education of children is being left to chance. Academic intelligence has little to do with emotional life. Based on rationality, school pays little or no attention to emotions lest they disrupt the class. Many of the natural abilities of children are not in handling complex mathematical calculations or memorizing ancient history, but rather in perceiving and understanding inherent emotional situation.

Emotional intelligence probably overlaps to some extent, the general intelligence. The emotionally intelligent person is skilled in four areas i.e. identifying emotions, using emotions, understanding and regularly emotions.

According to Goleman (1995), emotional intelligence consists of five factors namely: Knowing one's emotions, Managing emotions, Motivating oneself, Recognizing emotions in others and Handling relationships.

Importance of Emotional Intelligence

Emotional Intelligence allows us to think more creatively and use our emotions to solve problems. Daniel Goleman believes that emotional intelligence appears to be an important set of psychological abilities that relates to life success. It is empathy and communication skills as well as social and leadership skills that will be central to your success in life and personal relationships.

Goleman further argues that men particularly need to develop emotional skills, and he gives many examples of men with high intelligence who were not successful because they had problems with their people skills. He found from his research that people with high emotional intelligence generally have successful relationships with family, friends and fellow workers.

Emotional Competencies and Emotional Intelligence Inventory

For the first time, Daniel Goleman in 1998, a framework of emotional competencies which determines the extent of emotional intelligence acquired by an individual. An emotional competence, according to him is a learned capacity based on emotional intelligence that results in understanding performance at work (1998). This earlier framework consisted of five domains or dimensions such as self-awareness, self-regulation, self motivation, empathy social awareness and social skills. Based on Extensive Research, Goleman (1995, 1998) proposed five dimensions of emotional intelligences

- Self awareness
- Self Regulation / Management
- Self Motivation
- Social Awareness (Empathy)
- Social Skills

Self Awareness

1. Emotional Self Awareness : Recognizing one's emotions and their effects.

2. Accurate self assessment and: Knowing one's strengths and limits.
3. Self Confidence: A strong sense of one's self worth and capability.

- I am able to identify my feelings.
- I have learned a lot about my self through feeling and emotions.
- I understand the reasons for my moods.
- I am clearly able to see how my feelings impact my performance.
- I am aware of my strength and weaknesses
- I frequently seek feedback on my behavior/performance.
- I have full confidence in myself and in my decisions.
- I take initiative to meet people in social situation.
- When I contribute to group discussions I believe my contributions are as valuable as those of others.
- If I am convinced that my position, even if it means becoming unpopular.
- I am clear what I want from life.

Self Regulation/Management

1. Self Control: Keeping disruptive emotions and impulses in check
2. Trust worthiness: Maintaining standards of honesty and integrity
3. Conscientiousness: Taking responsibility for personal performance
4. Innovation: Flexible in accepting new ideas
5. Adaptability: Comfortable and Flexible in handling novel ideas and appropriateness

- I can achieve what I want through determination.
- I do not easily give up even if I received setbacks.
- When I have a problem that creates undue tension, I try to relax and gain a feeling of tranquility so that I can re-evaluate things.
- When I face a problem I focus on what I can do to solve it.
- I can adjust very quickly to new challenges, problem and information.
- I am sensitive to the development in the environment and capture the opportunity there.
- I am able to anticipate changes and I plan in advance to encash the opportunities.
- I am able to handle multiple demands and rapid changes.
- I am quite flexible in my approach to life and problems.
- I can frequently anticipate solution to my problems.
- When I certain approach to a problem does not work, I can quickly reorient my thinking.

- I seek out fresh ideas from a wide variety of sources.

Self Motivation

1. Achievement drive: Striving to improve or meet a standard of excellence.
2. Initiative and: Readiness to act on opportunities
3. Optimism: Persistence in pursuing goals despite obstacles and setbacks.

- I constantly try to improve my performance.
- I set challenging goals for myself and strive to achieve them.
- I work hard for "better" future reward rather than accept a lesser reward now.
- I constantly scan the environment to seize any new opportunity.
- I prefer to pro act.
- I mobilize others through unusual enterprising effort.
- I take initiative to start dialogue for a new adventure.
- I prefer to be idea leader.
- I believe in performance rather than just following the rules.
- I believe where there is a will there is a way.
- I start any activity with the firm determination to complete it.
- Under pressure, I am confident I will find the way.

Social Awareness (Empathy)

1. Understanding of others: Sensing other's feeling and perspectives and taking as active interest in their concerns.
2. Developing others: Sensing other's development needs and bolstering their abilities.
3. Service orientation: Anticipating recognizing and meeting persons need.
4. Organizational Awareness: Inspiring guiding and making individual and group to work.

- People do not have to sell me that they feel; I can sense it.
- I can sense the pulse of others and state unspoken feelings.
- I listen to the feelings of people while they are talking.
- I can sense the feelings of people when I walk into a room.
- I anticipate people's need and try to satisfy them.
- I try to understand meet the expectations of people.
- I seek information about people's need and then provide service accordingly.
- I take initiative in talking to people in order to serve them better.
- I am very comfortable in working with people of different background.
- I am able to identify who has real power in the group/organization.

- I am able to relate well with people who matter in the organizational dynamics.
- I am able to influence the opinion of import people.

Social Skills

1. Communication: Listening openly and sending convincing messages.
2. Conflict management: Negotiation and resolving disagreements.
3. Building bond: Initiating and nurturing instrumental relationship.
4. Collaboration and cooperation: Working with others towards shared goals.
5. Team Capabilities: Creating group synergy in pursuing collective goals.

- I am able to convince people
- I present myself in such a way that people get impressed.
- I keep my knowledge base updated and influence people through that.
- I am able to read the needs to the hour and influence people through my initiative.
- I am a good communicator.
- I am able to put across my messages effectively.
- I use a variety of medium of communication to get the desired response.
- I am able to arouse enthusiasm in people.
- I emerge as a natural leader during unstructured situation.
- I recognize the need for change and work for removing the barriers.
- I create such an atmosphere where people enthusiastically interact and participate in the team work.
- I build team identity and promote commitment among team members.

According to Mayer and Salovey, to measure EI, there are four branches i.e.

- Identifying emotions – the ability to recognize how you and those around you are feeling.
- Using Emotions – the ability to generate emotions, and then to reason with these emotions.
- Understanding emotions – the ability to understand complex emotions and emotional chains - how emotions transit from one stage to another.
- Managing emotions – the ability which allows you to manage emotions in yourself and in others.

In conclusion, we can say that IQ gets you hired but it is E.I. that gets you promoted. Those organizations, that grow their people with outstanding EI, will be successful in future. The future will belong to those who have excellent relationship skills. Human capital will then truly leverage performance through people, pride and profits. No doubt, the emotional intelligence will contribute much to a happy living of an individual and the community.

Check your Emotional Intelligence Level

Psychologists hold that the success of the people in most walks of life, depends much on the level of Emotional Intelligence, to the tune of 80 per cent as observed by analysis. The level of emotional intelligence can be assessed in sufficient measure by analysis of actual perceptions. Here are some statements which will help you measure your emotional intelligence quickly. You have to mark (A) if you agree and (D) if you disagree.

1. I work hard but since there is no planning, I am unable to complete the task in time. Therefore, I suffer from tension/become stressful.
2. I always have full faith in whatever I do.
3. When in anger, my language become indecent.
4. When I compare myself with other I feel gratitude towards God that I am intelligent and able person.
5. When I face someone is angry mood I talk to them with cool mind.
6. I take the practical rather than theoretical decisions and get it done confidently.
7. I have been a successful person in my life therefore, I always observe restraint.
8. Occasionally, I feel that I am the happiest person in the world.
9. I do not have any difficulty in developing relationship with the emotional persons.
10. I always have the feeling that the world is so beautiful and enjoyable.
11. I have full confidence in me. I can do any work in the world.
12. Whenever I have not met with success, it was due to lack of preparation as per the planning. I learn the lessons from my mistakes.
13. I am not worried about the reward. I do my work with least expectation.
14. Without any wish for return, I help needy persons.
15. Before developing intimacy with somebody, I study the person minutely.
16. I trust other because I feel that everybody is a good person at the core.
17. I do not take others for granted.
18. I have full control on my emotions, and do not allow my emotions and sensitivity to interfere with relationship.
19. I am a giver rather than a taker.
20. I understand my emotions and sensitivity and do not face any difficulty to solve the problems.
21. I develop friendship with others too soon.

22. I am action-oriented person irrespective of success or defeat.
23. I make it a point to congratulate other for their success.
24. I always feel that I do not achieve as much as I deserve. Therefore, I go on making efforts to forge ahead.
25. I am always confident that I can do it well.

If women are equipped and understand the whole dynamics of their E.I. and the world of work, it will help them to adjust well. But the truth remains that most women's jobs are clustered in 'Female' occupations that pay poorly. She has to work as mother, wife, manager, administrator and facilitator, overseer, counselor and earner too. There is need of assistance mentally and physically too. The women empowerment is very basic to the basics of human rights where she wants neither to beg for power or search for power hierarchy to exercise power against others. On the contrary she demands to be accepted as human first of all.

In order to achieve the balance between work and family life in India, underlying issues need to be understood, researched and steps should be taken for richer, healthier and peaceful women and family. It is important to have proper emotional status of working women, understood issues problems and pressures on working women. We must offer directions for alleviating the difficulties and foresee a future, which would include improved quality life of women through balanced interface between women's work and emotions. Models, strategies developed or created can be certainly taken for replication by other economically poor countries.

References

Bedi Singh Dalijit: Emotional Intelligence: The Management Tool, Employment News, 25th September – 10th October, 1909.

Bedi Singh Dalijit: Emotional Intelligence: The Management Tool, Employment News, 25th September – 10th October, 1999.

Geleman, Daniel, Working with Emotional Intelligence, Bantam Books, New York, 1998.

Goleman, Daniel, Emotional Intelligence, Pantam Boks, New York, 1998.

Goleman, Daniel, Emotional Intelligence, Pantam Boks, New York, 1995.

Goleman, Daniel, Working with Emotional Intelligence, Bantam Books, New York, 1998.

Mayer, J.D. and Salovery, P. The Intelligence of Emotional Intelligence, Intelligence 17(4), 433-442d, 1993.

Mayer, J.D. and Salovery, P. The Intelligence of Emotional Intelligence, Intelligence 17(4), 433-442, 1993.

Sampson, E.E. The debate on individualism: Indigenous psychologies of the individual and their role in personal and societal functioning. American Psychologist 43, 15-22, 1998.

Shanwal, V. K. Emotional Intelligence - The Indian Scenario. Delhi: Indian Publishers and Distributors, 2004.

Shweder, R.A. Aourne, E.J. Does the concept of the person vary cross culturally? In R.A. Shweder and R.A. Levine, (eds) Culture theory: Essays on mind, self and emotions (pp. 158-

199) Cambridge University Press, 1984.

Sibia, A, Srivastava, A.K. and Misra, Emotional Intelligence: Western and Indian, perspectives. Indian psychological abstracts and reviews, 10, 3-42, 2003.

Solvey P., and Mayer J.D. Emotional Intelligence, Imagination, Cognition and Personality, 9, 185-211, 1990.

Srivastava, A.K. and Misra G. Social representational of intelligence in the Indian folk traditional. Journal of Indian Psychology 17, 23-38. 1989.

Srivastava, Anjali, Naidu, R.K. and Misra G. Impulse control stress and performance. Upanishad manuscript, Department of Psychology, University of Allahabad, Allahabad, 1986.

Sternberg R.J. Wisdom: Its nature, origins and development Cambridge: Cambridge University Press, 1990.

Sternberg R.J., Wagner R.K., Williams, W.M. and Hovath, J. Testing common sense. American Psychologist, 50, 912-927, 1995.

Sudarsan S. and Sasi Kumar: Traditional Intelligence and Emotional Intelligence, University News, March 25-31, 2002.

Sudarsan S. and Sasi Kumar: Traditional Intelligence and Emotional Intelligence, University News, March 25-31, 2002.

Thorndike, EI, Intelligence and its uses, Harper's Magazine, 40, 227-235, 1920.

Thorndike, EI, Intelligence and its uses, Harper's Magazine, 40, 227-235, 1920.

Weisz, J. Rothbarm, F.M. and Blackrun, T.C.L. Standing out and standing in: The psychology of control in America and Japan. American Psychologist 39, 955-969.

Part IV: Self-help Groups (SHGs) and Empowerment of Women

23

Empowerment of Women in Kerala: A Case Study

V. Girija Devi

The status of women in India is intertwined with socio-economic and political hierarchies since the vedic times and women have received different status depending on class and caste hierarchies.[Majumdar et al,1994] There are varying accounts about the status of women in the early and late vedic period, most studies indicate that there was a gradual decline in the socio-political and economic status of women. Since the UN Declaration of the International decade for women[1980-1990], greater interest has been paved to look at women and development not as a separate development, but as part of the main stream development process. The development of women is an integrated and unified concept stretching across economic, political and cultural field. Health education and employment are generally deemed to be very crucial for women's development, since poverty is the single biggest cause for backwardness. Various socio-economic factors, history, geography and cultural pattern of the region play a significant role in the development of women anywhere in the world.

Women are vital and productive workforce of our national economy, constituting 48 percent of the total population. In the early decades of planning problems of women were looked upon as problems of social welfare rather than of development. The drawback of the welfare approach was that it did nothing to eliminate the social discrimination against the subordination of women. In almost all plans for poverty alleviation and social change, disadvantaged women became a 'target' in developmental activity rather than a group to be opted as active participants.[Beijing conference 1996]. Through out the third world particularly in the past 15 years, there has been proliferation of policies, programmes and projects designed to assist low income women. Women development' has assumed greater significance in the context of globalization.

The Government of India and various State Governments have been implementing a number of alternative approaches based on equity, poverty alleviation, efficiency and empowerment programmes. These approaches are not entirely mutually exclusive and have been categorized in general as the Women in Development [WID] approach. In spite of the tremendous development Kerala could achieve in several areas, like literacy and health care, poverty refuses to leave the state. More than fifteen lakh Kerala families of the state, alias 'gods own country' are still in the clutches of poverty.

Poverty cannot be reduced or removed simply by giving doles or by charity. Most of the anti-poverty programmes implemented in the state during the last decades, though seemingly well conceived, have failed due to various reasons. Almost all the programmes adopted income criteria for identifying the poor, which lacked people's involvement and was also susceptible to under reporting and manipulations. The programmes of the past presumed that the poor are totally resourceless and therefore did not envisage any involvement and commitment from the poor themselves. The poor were never involved in their own identification and assessment of their problems and needs. The programmes, therefore, tend to supply the outsiders perception rather than meeting the felt needs of the poor. The poor remained mere 'beneficiaries' of others decision, as they were not involved in the implementation of the programmes. The programmes were also generally individual oriented and did not harness community's group dynamics.

Every programme of the past tried to meet only one of the disadvantages in the lives of the poor and the programmes were implemented by a host of agencies with no co-ordination with one another. The programmes therefore lost focus and the resources got scattered. Being implemented by different agencies also meant many parallel structures for delivering, resulting high delivery costs. The programmes were also centrally planned with little flexibility to suit local needs. The target-oriented programmes did not take into account the resource handling capacities of the poor. Manifestations of poverty like ill health, malnutrition, un-employment, non-existence and non-availability of basic needs and facilities are seen through out the state in varying intensity. The situation is worse in tribal belts, coastal belts and urban slums. Especially women and children are the prime victims of the curse.

What is Empowerment of Women?

According to Narayana [1998] 'Empowerment of women is a process whereby the powerless or disempowerment gain a greater share of control of resources and decision- making'. So the process of gaining control over self, over ideology and over resources which determine power may also be termed as empowerment. The first and foremost reason attributed to the disempowerment of women is the 'unjust differentiation and inhuman discrimination against women' persisting in the Indian Society and which is highly inegalitarian and male chauvinistic. They are not allowed to enjoy equality in opportunities in various fields like social, economical, political and skill development due to set pattern and cultural beliefs, superstitions, behavioral training etc.

Why Should Women be Empowered?

It is optimistically believed that women's empowerment will lead to a world where women and men ensure that resources are utilised not just equitably but sanely and safely. Gita Mukherjee, M.P rightly said in the House that 'empowering would not merely benefit women, but the country as a whole'. Previous studies have proved that empowerment of women in turn give greater voice and leverage in family decisions ad enhances their social standing

IFAD[International Fund for Agricultural Development] evaluation done in India in late 1999 suggested certain measures for empowerment of women. [The Republic of India, 2000] Four of the main processes that could lead to women's empowerment, as defined by the IFAD were:

- changes in women's mobility and social interaction;
- changes in women's labour patterns;
- changes in women's access to and control over resources; and
- changes in women's control over decision-making.

A. Changes in Women's Mobility and Social Interaction. An evaluation study revealed that women had become more mobile and begun to have new interactions with a range of officials. There was even a growing willingness on the part of group members to approach the Panchayats and Collectors with petitions or grievances. The study observes that this type of change was most likely to occur among women group members when:

- the women involved were heads of households or were older;
- the women involved had participated in training;
- their group members had accessed a bank loan;
- their group had undertaken community action initiatives; or
- their group had been organized into a federation and encouraged to participate in special events (such as Women's Day, Rural Women's Day)

B. Changes in Women's Labour Patterns. The evaluation did not find any major changes in gender division of labour. However, there were indications of such changes beginning. For instance, the group meetings themselves forced some of the husbands to look after children and feed themselves while their wives attended the meetings. The evaluation found that the extent to which men helped in reproductive tasks was related to the health of the woman (men helped more if women were sick), the type of household (men helped more in a nuclear household), and the gender and age of the children (men helped less if girl children were present to help).

There was comparatively greater change reported in non-domestic productive tasks. Not all the changes in such labour patterns can be viewed as beneficial to women. Therefore, the changes in women's labour patterns were mixed, and not as positive as along other dimensions. There was little indication that women's control over their labour had undergone a marked change, and the evaluation noted that many women may simply have gone from undertaking paid work outside the home to becoming unpaid family labourers (in male-managed enterprises). At least self-employment allows women the possibility to have better working conditions, save on travel time, and be able to more effectively combine reproductive and productive roles.

C. Changes in Access to and Control over Resources. The evaluation also looked into women group members' access to non-loan-related resources and benefits, and particularly to common resources. It seems that a number of the groups undertook activities that would give their communities better infrastructure or services, for instance in water supply, child-care facilities, health care services and improved roads. In this sense, they played a key role in promoting changes in collective access to resources.

D. Changes in Intra-household Decision-making. The evaluation concluded that there seemed to be a slight improvement in women's involvement in household decision-making in male-headed households, on such issues as credit, the disposal of household assets, children's education, and family health care. However, the traditional gender-based divisions persist in intra-household decision-making. Women basically decide on food preparation, and men make the financial decisions. But group members had become more aware of their property and political rights (which was part of group training). As in the case of mobility and social interaction, the evaluation again found greater improvements among women heads of households, older women, and more educated women.

Status of Women in Kerala

The status of women in Kerala is far better than their counterparts elsewhere in the country. It is the only state where female literacy and education levels are much better than the national average. But in the employment scenario the picture is totally different.

- Kerala is a State with an impressive array of achievements in the field of women development. It has a high female literacy rate of 86.2 per cent, a low IMR of 13 (against the national average of 80) a favourable sex ratio of 1032 female/1000 male, low MMR 0.8/1000, High Life Expectancy ratio 74 female/70 male etc., just to mention a few. But in spite of all these achievements the conspicuous absence of women in the public domain remains as a paradox of the Kerala model of development.

- The economic marginalisation of women in the development process has drawn considerable attention during recent years. While the female work participation rate in India increased from 19.7 per cent to 22.7 per cent between 1981 and 1991, in Kerala the ratio declined from 16.6 per cent to 15.9 per cent during the same period. The incidence of unemployment among females in the State is higher than that among males by 5 times in rural areas and 3 times in urban areas. (The unemployment in Kerala is severe and is 3 times larger than that in India.)
- The sexual division of labour has resulted in the concentration of women in low paying unorganized sectors such as agricultural labour, cottage and traditional industries and selected service sectors. Despite the powerful trade union movements, equal wages for equal work still remains a mirage and gender discrimination at the work place is widely prevalent.
- The marginalisation of women in the economic process and lack of control over resources have been major impediments in improving the status of women.
- The violence against women and incidence of sexual harassment continue to increase (number of registered crimes increased from 1862 in 1991 to 4937 in 1996).
- Despite the general progressive political environment in the State, active involvement of women in various leadership levels are virtually lacking.

Experiences in many countries demonstrate that poor women make investments wisely and earn returns [Human Resource Development, 1995]. The need to create a grassroots organizational base to enable women to come together to analyse issues and problems themselves and to fulfil their needs was strongly advocated. New organizations which have emerged mostly during the last ten to fifteen years are particularly autonomous women's group which have been fighting for women's rights in a militant manner

One of the pre-requisites to promote empowerment of women is promotion of organizations among women. Women can be organized through a variety of means namely through formation of cooperatives, Mahila Mandals, Self-help Groups and the like. Through collective action women can be empowered socially, economically, and politically. (Selvi, 2005)

The Concept of Self-help Groups [SHG]

The concept of Self Help Groups gained significance especially after 1976 when Prof. Mohammed Yunus of Bangladesh began experimenting with micro-credit and women SHGs. The strategy made a quiet revolution in Bangladesh in poverty eradication by empowering the poor women. SHG are small informal associations created for the purpose of enabling members to reap economic benefit out of mutual help solidarity and join responsibility. The benefits include mobilization of savings and credit facilities and pursuit of group enterprise activities .The group based approach not only enables the poor to accumulate capital by way of small savings but also helps them to get formal credit facilities.

Self-help has been the philosophy of the projects of voluntary organizations since the beginning. The projects proceed with the assumption that any neighbourhood, no matter how poor, can do something to improve itself by its own efforts and that any approach for that matter has not exhausted its own resources fully. To give women visibility, they must get organized into self help groups. Group approach is a viable set up to empower women economically, socially, and technologically for improved life. Grouping together is the beginning, Standing together is the strength, Thinking together is the success and Working together is the development. Role of Self-help Groups (SHGs) is emerging as a promising tool in this context. SHGs are voluntary associations of women /men residing in a given area, formed democratically and without any political association. According to NABARD, SHG is a homogenous group of rural poor which is formed voluntarily to save whatever amount they can conveniently save out of their earnings and who mutually agree to contribute to a common fund of the group to be lent to the members for meeting their productive and emergent credit needs .

The basic principles on which SHGs function are group approach, mutual trust, organization of poor, manageable small groups, group cohesiveness, spirit of thrift, demand based lending, collateral free, women friendly loan, peer group pressure in repayment, skill training, capacity building and empowerment. In promoting alternative credit delivery system SHGs can be broadly termed group organization among women labour force, those promoting savings by inculcating spirit of thrift and enabling provision of credit for the members. Organisation of groups among rural women focuses on mobilization, collectivisation, group cohesiveness and empowerment of women.

Many NGOs in India especially in the south have promoted village sangams/SHGs to encourage periodic group based savings and credit among group members is used as an entry point programme for group members towards group organization and empowerment. This kind of thrift and credit groups are expected to lead to new assets and responsibilities on community basis. Periodic cash savings and credit by the group provides very simple but powerful mechanism to enable groups to initiate, manage, control and finally own their institutions nurtured around local savings and credit. The group based lending ,though initially available for a shorter period nearly exceeding 6 to 9 months in smaller amounts, provides greater flexibility, especially to the rural women as cash is made available untied to any particular scheme. SHGs are emerging as one of the promising and prime sources of informal banking in Indian villages.

Evolution of Kudumbashrees in Kerala

The success of SEWA of Ahmedabad ,Myrada of Mysore and several other experiments in different other parts of the country has attracted many states for replicating this strategy has been widely accepted that the programme ,if taken and implemented at the right sense ,would be very effective in poverty eradication and women empowerment. SHG's in Kerala had made significant strides in this field.

In 1992, a three tier Community Based Organisation [CBO] of poor women was formed in Alappuzha town, Kerala to implement Urban Basic Services [UBS] and Urban Basic Services [UBSP] for the poor. This women oriented and participatory and convergent approach to fight poverty was a phenomenal success. This same three tier CBO structure was used in the implementation of Community Based Nutrition Programme and Poverty Alleviation Project in Mallapuram in Kerala. All these experiences emphasized the necessity to adopt a holistic approach to fight poverty, with the active participation of the community. The phenomenal success of the CDS systems of Alappuzha Municipality and Malappuram district were also encouraged the planners to formulate a participatory, community-based programme for fighting poverty. The concept of Kudumbashree thus took definite shape.

Kudumbashree, the State Poverty Eradication Mission was launched by the Government of Kerala with the active support of Government of India and NABARD for wiping out absolute poverty from the State within a period of ten years. This project is implemented through Local Self Governments formed by the 73rd and 74th Constitutional Amendments.

This poverty eradication project was officially launched in Kerala State by the Honourable Prime Minister Shri Atal Behari Vajpayee on 17th May 1998. Formal activities of Kudumbasree started on 1st April 1999. Dismal experiences of the past shaped the objectives of the project.

Mission Statement

In the 'mission statement', the objective of Kudumbashree is unequivocally declared as follows:

To eradicate absolute poverty in ten years through concerted community action under the leadership of local governments, by facilitating organization of the poor for combining self-help with demand-led convergence of available services and resources to tackle the multiple dimensions and manifestations of poverty, holistically .'

Apart from stating the objective, the mission statement also proclaims the means, method and approach, which will be adopted for the crusade against poverty. 'Reach out the families through women and reach out the community through families' is the guiding slogan of the Mission

Structure of Community-based Organisations in Kudumbashree

The Kudumbashree project envisages a three tier social system, which is an exclusive women managed programme. Frequent group meetings, sharing of experiences and training would broaden their outlook. Improved economic status of women gained through CDS thrift and self-employment will boost their status in their own families and community .The enlightened income generating women will refuse to accept poverty as their destiny .Once they realize their collective strength ,they will fight poverty and atrocities against them most valiantly

The Three-tier System of Kudumbashree

A. Neighourhood Group [NHG]: For effective convergence of the programme, a three tier community based group organization [CBO] is in action. The lower most tier constitute the Neighbourhood Group consisting of 20-40 women members selected from the poor families. Meetings are convened on a weekly basis in the house of NHG members. In the meeting various problems faced by the Group members are discussed along with suggestion for improving the situation. Government officials are also invited for the meeting for explaining the schemes implemented by them In the weekly meeting all members bring their credit, which will be collected and recycled by way of sanctioning loans. In each NHG, 5 volunteers are selected for undertaking various functional activities. They are:

- Community Health Volunteer- She will look after various health related aspects of the group members including children, women and aged. Convergence of various programme undertaken by Health and Social Welfare Departments are also carried out under the leadership of community Health Volunteer.
- Income generation Activities Volunteer; The collection, consolidation and maintenance of books of accounts and registers in connection with thrift

mobilization is looked after by this volunteer. Necessary training is imparted by NABARD for increasing their capability.

- Infrastructure Volunteer-Infrastructural backwardness of the group is tackled with the help of various on going governmental programmes under the leadership of this volunteer. It is proposed to take micro-contracting as an income generating activity by this group after sharpening their functional skills through a series of training programmes. She will liaison with the local bodies and acts as a catalyst for local Government.
- Secretary;-The proceedings of the meeting are recorded by the Secretary and necessary follow up including motivation and team building are the responsibilities of the Secretary.
- President;-She will preside over the weekly meetings and will impart necessary leadership and guidelines to the group members.

B. Area Development Society [ADS]: The second tier is ADS, which is formed at Ward level by federating 8-10 NHGS. The activities of ADS are decided by the representatives of the poor elected from various federating neighbourhood groups. Area development society function through three distinct bodies viz.,

- General body-consists of all presidents and secretaries of federation NHGs along with representatives of resource Persons selected from that area.
- Governing Body-constituted by electing a President, Secretary and five member committee from among the General Body.
- Monitoring and Advisory Committee.

To streamline their activity with the activities of Local Self Governments, a ward level monitoring and advisory committee is formed under the chairmanship of ward member of the Local body.

Chairperson: Ward Councilor/Ward Member

Members: Community Organiser [UPA], All RCVs of the Ward, 2 Co-opted NHG presidents, Anganvadi workers of the Ward, Junior Health inspector , JPHN in charge of the ward, Not more than 3 members co-opted from among retired persons, Specialists, Social workers, Literacy Instructors and TOC members.

The salient feature of this arrangement is the fixation of priorities by the poor, in tune with the policy framework of Local Self Governments.

C. Community Development Society [CDS]: At the panchayat level, CDs is a registered body under the Charitable Societies Act and is formed by federating various ADSs. The CDs has three distinct bodies viz.,

- General Body- It consists of all ADS Chairperson and ADS governing Body members along with representatives of Resource Persons. Officers of the Local Body who are involved in implementing various poverty alleviation and women empowerment programmes.

- Governing Body –The Governing Body consists of President, Member Secretary and five selected Committee Members. The president will be elected whereas the Member secretary is the project officer of UPA programmes. Other Government Officials and representatives of resource persons will be nominated to the Governing Body.
- Monitoring and advisory Committee-Municipal Chairperson/President of the Panchayat will be the chairman of the monitoring and advisory committee which is convened by Municipal Secretary /Panchayat Secretary as Convenor. In Urban areas the Urban Poverty Alleviation project officer will be the Joint Convener.
- Chairman- Mayor, Chairperson/ President
- Convener –Secretary of the LSGIs

Members-Chairman of the statutory committee under the Municipalities Act, 5 Women nominated councilors /All women members of LSGIs, District medical officer or his nominee and District Immunisation Officer, Superintendent of the Taluk Hospital, District Hospital, Assistant education officer/District education Officer, Municipal Health Officer or Health supervisor or health inspector, Corporation , Health officer, Engineer.

The advantage of the system is that, the representatives of the poor manage it wholly. The aspirations of the poor along with their genuine demands voiced out in the neighbourhood group meetings form the micro plan and these will be scrutinized and prioritized to form a mini plan at the level of ADS.

The Facets of Kudumbashree are:

- Empowerment of women through community based organization
- Formation of informal banks
- Formation of micro-enterprises
- Convergent community action
- Human resource development
- Establishment of rural marketing network through out the State.

Kudumbashree aims at the empowerment of women, giving them the central place in the programmes meant for their benefit. They will no longer be passive recipients but active leaders. The action plan charted out is:

- Formation of women collectives. The poor women from families identified will be organised into Neighbourhood Groups (NHG) representing 15 to 40 families. A five-member team elected from the NHGs will be the cutting edge of the programme. NHGs will be federated democratically into Area Development Societies (ADS) at the Panchayat/Municipality Ward level and then into Community Development Societies (CDS) at the Panchayat/Municipal level. Their organizational structures will provide opportunities for collective public action.

- More information/Training. Weekly meetings of NHGs, sharing of experiences, discussions, organised/unorganized trainings etc., will broaden their outlook on better health, better education, better social and economic status
- Skill upgradation Trainings. To facilitate economic development, suitable skill upgradation trainings will be given to women.
- Thrift - credit operations and 24 hour banking system. Enabling women to realize their latent potential, strengthening them through self-help are the main objectives of Kudumbashree. Small savings generated at the families are pooled at various levels as thrift and used to attract credit from banks, which will operate as 24-hour bank for the poor, acting as a sub-system of the formal banks.
- Better living conditions - Infrastructural facilities. The needs identified at NHG level are shaped as micro plans which are integrated into mini plans at ADS level and action plan at CDS level. This will be the anti-poverty sub plan of the local body and this will facilitate convergent delivery of Government programmes meant for the poor. Rather than the traditional system of heavily subsidized approach, Kudumbashree promote self-help approach for building houses, latrines, access to drinking water, sanitary facilities etc., availing the minimum support from Government. Common infrastructural facilities in the community strengthen them further.
- Micro-enterprises for sustainable economic development. Providing skill upgradation trainings, self-employment opportunities and infrastructural development through wage employment schemes are the preparing grounds for further development of successful micro enterprises. Kudumbashree is bent on giving necessary resource support and facilitate forward/backward linkages etc, to promote micro-entrepreneurship among poor women.
- Power to the people especially the poor women. The skill for identification of needs, fixing priorities, availing resources, bridging gap between needs and resources in a cost effective manner etc., are taught to the poor women groups in various phases. In the decentralization of power to the local bodies and common man, Kudumbashree can act as a healthy sub-system facilitating participation of poor women in the planning, implementation and monitoring

of the programme .

- Leadership - Decision making power. Interaction in women collectives will help them to have a better understanding, which will lead to the emergence of leadership. This will help to ensure efficient women leadership to elected bodies in future.
- The Ultimate Goal. Reaching out family through women, and community through family, is the ultimate target of Kudumbashree.

Ground Rules for Group Working

- A group should have about 20 members.
- Members should be below poverty line as described by the group.
- Group should conduct regular meetings in respective villages.
- Attendance to the group members is compulsory
- The group should frame its own rules and regulations. The office bearers should be changed once in 6 or 12 months
- The group should have regular savings and raise capital on their own
- Loans should be given on priority basis
- The group should decide about the interest rate, repayment schedules etc.
- All the members should undergo training.
- Remittance of money should be done by office bearers and challenge should be produced at the next meeting.
- Members should participate actively in group proceedings and decision makings process.
- Repayment should be made only in the group meetings.

Kudumbashree in Kerala: Achievements at a Glance

- The Kudumbashree Programme, which covered the entire area in three phases created 147989 NHGs for the women from risk families, covering urban, rural and tribal areas of the State - 13262 ADSs at the ward level. and 991 CDSs at LSG level. The community based organization, which had a coverage of 2923425 families, mobilised a sum of Rs. 537.01 crore as thrift and disbursed credit to the tune of Rs. 1259.91 crore to its members.
- Formation of 7863 thrift and Credit Societies are operating in the 58 urban areas covering the major 58 towns, 110122 in rural areas, in 991 Panchayats.
- Formation of 14,125 vibrant micro-enterprises in Urban and 47,000 in Rural areas.
- Delivery cost of antipoverty programmes has come down.

- Poor women have become active participants in the planning and implementation process of various antipoverty programmes.
- The morale and confidence of the women are now very high.
- Status of women in families and community has also improved.
- Capability of poor women has gone up considerably.
- Kudumbashree has already gained national and international acclaim as an ideal and workable developmental model.
- The economic activities of the women groups of the Mission have even rejuvenated the economy of the state to some extent.

Advantages of Kudumbashree as identified from several studies are stated below:

- Thrift habit among women is developed.
- Members have developed skills relating to efficient management of funds.
- Groups initiate learning and serve as forums for sharing of ideas and skills.
- Exploitation by the non institutional source is averted.
- Repayment through peer- group pressure is assured.
- Both consumption and production requirements of the women are fulfilled.
- Micro credit to rural women.
- Interest earnings are shared collectively.
- Women become articulate and self expressive through interaction.
- Attitude change towards progressive outlook and development planning.
- Women act as leaders of the group , account keepers and decision makers.
- Women's mobility increased due to participation training and study tours.
- Kudumbashree function as platforms for raising social issues.
- Grass root level planning with active involvement of the people.

Women Empowerment-The Ultimate Goal of Kudumbashree

In spite of the commendable achievements Kerala could make in Social sector, the women in the state have only secondary status in the Society. However in the inception of Kudumbashree, the scenario has been changing drastically. Women empowerment is a major concern and prime priority activity for the Mission. Every activity of the project is geared to take the beneficiary class towards this ultimate goal. Weekly meetings, discussions, thrift and credit operations, participation in planning and implementation process of developmental activities conducted by Kudumbashree CBOs enhance the confidence and capacity of poor women. Moreover micro-enterprises and thrift and credit operations have enhanced the economic status of the poor women in families and society. It is an unarguable fact that the Kudumbashree Mission and its activities, including capacity building exercise of the beneficiaries, have really improved the status of poor women in the urban and rural areas of the State.

Conclusion

In traditional societies, even more than elsewhere, women's empowerment does not occur easily or overnight. In India, there was evidence of such change beginning, to which the project had apparently contributed. It was most noticeable among certain types of women. Perhaps one of the most important emerging lessons is that women's groups themselves, in their social aspects, play a role in such empowerment.

The core objectivity of Kudumbashree Mission in Kerala, is yet again the old 'development cliché of the planners-'eradication of poverty'. But this time the style is different, the approach is new, the strategies are positive and determination is staunch.

The poor people of Kerala, especially women have already accepted Kudumbashree as their own movement. Within a short span of less than three years, the Mission could surpass many a major milestones. Developmental specialists and social activists from several Indian states and foreign countries visit the project to enlighten themselves in areas, pertaining to participatory poverty reduction approach

Kudumbahree in Kerala is envisaged as a process and delivery mechanism for the poor which gives importance to health, nutrition, education, employment and improvement of economic status and the social improvement of a family. It is significantly observed that Kudumbashree have set a baseline for the formation of social capital at grass root level, especially empowering the poor, socially, politically and economically.

References

Aboobacker.M.A. ed. Small steps- great leap-Success Stories of Kudumbashree micro enterprises, Kudumbashree. Ernakulam. 2001.

Bai, Meera. M. ed. Women and economic reforms -Kerala Experience: Serials Publication. New Delhi. 2006.

Datta Rekha and Judith Kornberg eds .Women in Developing countries –assessing strategies for empowerment:. Viva book private Ltd. New Delhi. 2005.

Government of Kerala. Economic Review: State Planning Board. Thiruvananthapuram. 2005.

Jaya S. Anand. Self –Help Groups In Empowering Women –Case study of selected SHGs and NHGs KRPLLD, Centre for Development Studies, Thiruvananthapuram. 2002.

Ministry of Human Resource Development. Rashtriya Mahila Kosh, A Publication of the development of Women and Child Development, New Delhi. 1996.

Majumdar R.C, H.C Raychaudhuri ,and Kalilinkar Datta, An Advanced History of India:.Macmillan Co . Madras. 1994.

Narayana S Shashi. Empowerment of women through social mobilization Women's Link, Jan-March. 1998.

Pillai, Vijayachandran.B. and V.Harikmar. Self-hHelp Groups in Kerala, July, 54(9). 2006.

The Republic of India, Tamil Nadu Women's Development Project Completion Evaluation Report 340-IN, April. Rome. 2000.

24

Economic Reforms and Women Empowerment

Harnek Singh, Muninder Sidhu and Gaganpreet Kaur

Economic reforms are the most over-whelming feature of the contemporary scene, in the sense that great nations are now-a-days caught in its web. Basic process in these reforms is the application of modern science and described as 'social change involving the elements of science and technology'. The scientific and technological inventions have brought about remarkable changes in the whole system of social relationship and installed new ideologies in the place of traditional ones. This process has its economic, political, educational, technological, military, administrative, cultural and other faces. These reforms involve a change from simple and traditional techniques towards the use of scientific knowledge and technology. Hence, industrialization indicating mass production and liberalization means spread of each and everything to every place. The whole process of manufacture of goods has received a tremendous shift. In the present society, a growing number of women and young people purchasing cars have promoted many motor manufacturers to introduce vehicles with 'option packages'. There emerged environment-friendly product lines - from cleaners and shampoos and cosmetics - along with their standard range of goods.

There is a great role of knowledge and innovation in the organization of production rise of industries based upon breakthroughs in micro-electronic and information technologies. The present society is powered by electricity and is based on micro-circuit machinery. Knowledge of technology has led to a fall in the number of manual manufacturing jobs. There emerged service sector which is characterized by non-manual work. It is also known for its creativity. So, the structure of professional occupations has undergone a number of changes. There is much emphasis on information processing and sometimes this industrial society is called information society. Even, some people say to it, a confused society and others a dynamic society.

In the present society, there is an emergence of knowledge, division of society, new characters of modern economy and empowerment of women. These aspects have been taken into account for further appraisal.

Today, more and more emphasis is given on knowledge as the source of societal change. The knowledge i.e. information processing, comes from the new technical persons in the universities, government institutions and economic enterprises. Side by side there is always some element of conflict in the society. On the one side, there are technocrats and bureaucrats and on the other, a range of social groupings including workers, consumers as well as students (Doshi;2003). The focus of the coming society is on knowledge and information as the driving forces bring multinational cooperation together for economic growth. In addition to this, there is a growth of service sector, where a little amount of manual labour is performed. The labourers who were required to put its physical dexterity, have now entered into service sector where creativity phenomena is also prevalent

Technology has altered the structure of employment within the society. There appeared a vast change in the kinds of work, i.e. the occupational structure witnessed professional change and manual labour gave way to service class sector. This has led to division between aristocracy, well paid workers, on the other a growing mass of unemployed people. This labour force generally consisted of males who worked manually. But, with the recent developments, there appeared gender inequality in the professional class. Now, women outnumber the male technocrats in some sectors. These women are disproportionately concentrated in work indicating sharp gender division. (Shiva, 2005)

New Character of Modern Economy

The primary institutions of western modernity acquired a new significance in the era of micro-electronic information technology. Globalization involves a profound recording of time and space in social life. Now, it appears that the world can develop a cosmopolitan order based upon liberty, justice and equality for all humanity. So, globalization is a new character of present society.

Commercialization, modernization, export-oriented development, growth of private sectors have opened new channels for employment (Singh;1996). Many urban and rural youth are getting opportunities of entering the portals of higher education. There have been more opportunities for middle class and upper class people especially the women to go in for remunerative work. More women are seen working in non-traditional jobs and are also holding decision making posts. One very hopeful development which has occurred during the last ten years is the emergence of women's movement where in they have started raising their voice against inequality, patriarchal values and in egalitarian social structure.

There is a great change in the position of women with the recent developments with the help of liberal economy in the society. Today, status of women is measured by the means of different indicators. The situation analysis of impact on women was measured in terms of literacy rate, enrolment of boys and girls, women employment, and population on the basis of selected indicators.

Education: The level of literacy has increased in case of males and females over the years (Table 24.1). In 1981, it was 43.57 which rose to 52.21 in 1991 and 64.84 in 2001. About 13 percent more persons had got education in the last 10 years. In addition to this, the gap between the literacy level of male and female has decreased to a large extent. There is a great increase in case of females than their counterparts since 1991 onwards. It all reflects that women are also trying to come at par with men in case of literacy.

Table: 24.1 Literacy Rates of Males and Females

Year	Persons	Males	Females	Male-Female literacy gap in literacy rate
1981	43.57	56.38	29.76	26.62
1991	52.21	64.13	39.29	24.84
2001	64.84	75.85	54.16	21.69

With different incentives for education, the enrolment at the elementary level has increased from 78.4 percent in 1994-95 to 82.50 percent in 2002-03 (Table 24.2). It shows that the inclination of parents towards giving education to their wards has increased in the primary as well as upper primary levels. The rate of increase in the number of girls is more than that of boys from 2001 onwards. So, the participation of girls at all the levels of school education has improved appreciably over the years (Economic Survey; 2004-05)

Table 24.2: Enrolment of Boys and Girls over the Years

Year	Primary (I-V)			Upper Primary (VI-VIII)			Elementary (I-VIII)		
	Boys	Girls	Total	Boys	Girls	Total	Boys	Girls	Total
1994-95	96.9	78.2	87.7	68.9	50.0	60.0	87.2	68.8	78.4
95-96	97.1	79.4	88.6	67.8	49.8	59.3	86.9	69.4	78.5
96-97	97.0	80.1	88.8	65.8	49.2	58.0	85.9	69.4	78.0
97-98	99.3	82.2	91.1	66.3	49.7	58.5	87.4	70.7	79.4
98-99	100.9	82.9	92.1	65.3	49.1	57.6	87.6	70.6	79.4
99-2000	104.1	85.2	94.9	67.2	49.7	58.8	90.1	72.0	81.3
2000-01	104.9	85.9	95.7	66.7	49.9	58.6	90.3	72.4	81.6
01-02	105.3	86.9	96.3	67.8	52.1	60.2	90.7	73.6	82.4

Employment: The impact of economic reforms can be judged from the fact that the employment in each and every sector has increased over the years for both males and females. The highest increase is in the sector of services, trade, hotel and restaurants followed by construction, manufacturing and agriculture. It has gone down a little bit in industry, mining, quarrying, electricity, gas water supply, community, social and personal services. On the whole, there is an increase of 21 million personnel in all the sectors. Similarly, the employment of women has also gone up in all the sectors of employment .The number of women working in industry, construction and manufacturing has decreased (Table 24.3) but it has increased in financial, insurance, real estate, transport, electricity and agriculture sectors. It indicates that number of women are coming out from the four walls of the houses to do work with higher level of education and employment opportunities in different sectors.

Table 24.3: Women Employment in Major Sectors (Employment in'000)

Sectors	2000	2001	Per cent change
Agriculture	510	512	0.5
Industry, Mining Quarrying	66.4	64.0	-3.7
Manufacturing	1033	1031	-0.3
Electricity, gas, water supply	44.6	46.0	3.2
Construction	68.1	67.3	-1.1
Services Trade, hotels, Rest.	46.0	46.8	1.7
Transport, Storage	176.9	182.9	3.4
Financial, insurance, real estate	235.0	245.0	4.3
Community, Social & Personal Services	2742.8	2754.5	0.4
All Sectors	4922.8	4949.3	0.5

Health: As per Census of India, the birth rate and death rate and infant mortality rate has gone down to a considerable extent (Table 24.4). It shows that there is great development in the health of people in India. In addition to this, life expectancy shows a great increase in case of males and females but this increase is much more in case of females. Though, they have to play two roles i.e. at home and at the office, but they try to keep themselves fit from health point of view. It is more visible from infant mortality rate of both the sexes in Punjab State. It is much low (52.3 per 100 live births) in both (males and females) than the average (67.8 per live birth) of our country. It all indicates that women are rising in their own status in all the spheres

An Empirical View

An empirical study was conducted to know the impact of recent developments/ economic reforms on decision-making process of working women. A self-structured questionnaire was used to collect information from120 women teaching in Home Science and Agriculture College at Punjab Agricultural University, Ludhiana. Out of the total sample 63.33 percent had age up to 35 years and others (36.76 percent) were of 36 years and above (Table 24.5).

Table 24.4: Selected Health Indicators

S.N.	Parameters	1951	1981	1991	2001
1.	Crude Birth Rate (Per 1000 pop.)	40.8	33.9	29.5	25.4
2	Crude Death Rate (Per 1000 pop.)	25.1	12.5	9.8	8.4
3.	Infant Mortality rate (Per 100 live births)	146	110	80	66
4.	Life Expectancy Ratio				
	Male	37.2	54.1	59.7	63.9
	Female	36.2	54.7	60.9	66.9

Table 24.5: Background of the Respondents

Characteristics	Home Science N=60	Agriculture N=60	Total
Age:			
Up to 35 years	60.00	66.67	63.33
36& Above	40.00	33.33	36.67
Education:			
Msc/M.A	13.33	20.00	16.67
Ph.D	86.67	80.00	83.33
Occupation:			
Assistant Prof.	56.67	50.00	53.34
Associate Prof	23.33	23.33	23.33
Professor	20.00	26.67	23.33
Family Income (Per month)			
Rs.20,00-30,000	3.33	6.67	5.00
Rs.30,000-40,000	26.67	30.00	28.33
Rs.40,000-50,000	33.33	40.00	36.67
Rs.50,000& Above	36.67	23.33	30.00
Other sources of income:			
Agriculture	10.00	26.67	18.33
Business	-	6.67	3.33
Transport	-	3.33	1.67
Remittances from Abroad	13.33	23.33	18.33
No other source of income	76.67	40.00	58.33

Education level of 16.76 percent respondents was post graduation and 83.33 percent had post doctorate degrees. More than half of them were assistant professors and about one fourth each were associate professors and professors. Maximum number of (36.67 per cent) respondents had monthly income between 40,000-50,000 and 30 percent of them above Rs. 50,000 per month. Job was the only source of income for 58.33 percent whereas 18.33 percent were also getting additional income from agriculture and same number were receiving remittances from abroad.

Decision and its Execution

The decision making and execution power of the women regarding children, social ceremonies and household matters was studied. According to Table 24.6, out of the total sample 76.67 per cent women agreed that they are responsible for taking decision regarding children's education followed by decision regarding children's marriage and dowry.

Table 24.6: Decision and Execution Regarding Children, Ceremonies and Household Matters

Matters	Home Science		Agriculture		Total	
	Self	Spouse	Self	Spouse	Self	Spouse
Children						
Education	80.00	20.00	73.33	26.67	76.67	23.34
Marriage	46.67	53.33	66.67	33.33	56.67	43.33
Dowry	46.67	53.33	60.00	40.00	53.33	46.66
Employment	30.00	70.00	50.00	50.00	40.00	60.00
Ceremonies						
Day	33.33	66.67	60.00	40.00	46.67	53.33
Date	66.67	33.33	66.67	33.33	66.67	33.33
Place	50.00	50.00	33.33	66.67	41.66	58.34
Material goods	40.00	60.00	40.00	60.00	40.00	60.00
Purchases						
Household Articles	100.00	-	86.67	13.33	93.33	6.67
Kitchen Articles	100.00	-	100.00	-	100.00	-
Clothing	76.67	23.33	86.67	13.33	81.67	18.33
Large Articles	33.33	66.67	46.67	53.33	40.00	60.00
Jewellery	66.67	33.33	63.33	36.67	65.00	35.00
Plot	40.00	60.00	33.33	66.67	36.66	63.34
Plot size	43.33	56.67	33.33	66.67	38.33	61.67
Vehicle	23.33	76.67	26.67	73.33	25.00	75.00
Vehicle colour	26.67	73.33	33.33	66.67	30.00	70.00

Multiple responses

In case of decision regarding employment of children, spouse's opinion was considered more important. Regarding family functions and ceremonies, two third of the women played important role in deciding the date of the event whereas spouses were given the responsibility of fixing the day, place and material goods (articles) to be purchased or gifted. It indicated that almost all the women were overall in-charge of household and kitchen purchases. Clothing for the family was also decided by a large number of women followed by the purchase of jewellery whereas purchases regarding vehicle, its colour, plot, its size and large articles were generally taken into account by male members.

Social Interaction and Day-to-day Activities

Mostly day to day activities and relations are taken into care by the women folk. According to Table 24.7, different functions to be attended were jointly decided by both of them whereas amount of the *shagun* to be given was decided mostly by the women themselves. Similarly, decision regarding visiting friends and dropping children to school were mostly taken mutually by them. In the total sample, the routine activity of making bed tea, and other kitchen activities were decided and preformed by most of the women. Out of total sample about 44 percent of husbands also helped them in chores related to dinner.

Table 24.7: Decision and Execution Regarding Interaction and Day-to-day Activities

Matters	Home Science		Agriculture		Total	
	Self	Spouse	Self	Spouse	Self	Spouse
Relations						
To attend function	50.00	50.00	50.00	50.00	50.00	50.00
Sagan	56.67	43.33	60.00	40.00	58.33	41.66
Visiting friends	60.00	40.00	50.00	50.00	55.00	45.00
Day-to-day activities						
Bed Tea	86.67	13.33	90.00	10.00	88.33	11.67
Dropping Children	66.67	33.33	33.33	66.67	50.00	50.00
Help in Kitchen	93.33	6.67	76.67	23.33	85.00	15.00
Evening Tea	83.33	16.67	83.33	16.67	83.33	16.67
Dinner	53.33	46.67	60.00	40.00	56.66	43.33
Recreation						
To go to tourist places	50.00	50.00	33.33	66.67	41.66	58.34
Watch movie	66.67	66.67	40.00	60.00	36.66	63.34
To Attend cultural prog.	66.67	66.67	60.00	40.00	46.66	53.34

Multiple responses

Decisions regarding recreation were dominated by males. But 46.66 per cent women decided about the cultural programmes to be attended and the tourist places to be visited followed by movie to be watched. Out of the total respondents 93.25 percent believed that they are getting due recognition in their jobs, 82.50 per cent were satisfied with their respect and status in the family.. In addition to this they perceived that everything is going well for them. Almost all of them perceived that they are getting freedom and equality in the society and their educational and cultural rights are being fulfilled (Table 24.8). Respondents perceived that they will own property in their names in future and exploitation against them will go away over a period of time. The latest reforms has indeed empowered women with decision making power. Almost all the category of professors have similar opinion in both the colleges. So, the women may be working in different sectors of economy but they share their opinions and feelings. As it is clear from the above results women are responsible for taking major decision in the families specially in the case of children, their education and marriage. They also decide about social relations and visits in the family They are satisfied with the respect, recognition and their status and perceived to have full equality and freedom in the society. But women still accepted that major decisions like children's employment, purchase of vehicle or property, vacations or outings are made by their husbands.

Table 24.8: Perceptions Regarding Different Rights in the Society

Perceptions	Home Science	Agriculture	Total
Equality	88.00	100.00	94.00
Freedom	92.00	100.00	96.00
Possession of property	87.00	87.00	87.00
Constitutional remedies	91.50	91.50	91.50
Educational and cultural rights	86.50	97.00	91.75
Against exploitation	68.00	100.00	84.00

Multiple responses

Conclusion

The findings of the present study suggested that women who are joining the paid work force in large numbers are changing the way people have defined work, home and hierarchy of wages. Families and the employers are making the profound discovery that house work is not what a women must do alone, nor is it unproductive labour. Also that each child has two persons (parents) both of whom must be responsible for raising him/her. Now a days across the board from the professions to politics and from arts to business, the feminine paragons of our times are taking charge of their lives, competing with men in the public sphere, succeeding in their jobs, rescripting their family lives, nurturing their children, running elegant homes and may be doing a little social service on the side. So, the transformation/ reforms of the society has made our future flexible. Where shall we move beyond this is only a matter of guess. It is hoped that better society may emerge from all these developments.

References

Census of India, Office of Registrar General of India, Government of India, New Delhi. 2001.

Doshi, S.L,2003, Modernity, Post Modernity and Neo-Sociological Theories, Rawat Publications, Jaipur and New Delhi. 2003.

Economic Survey, Ministry of Finance, Government of India, New Delhi. 2004-05.

Singh, Jaspal., Society, Culture and Socio-cultural change, National Book Organization, New Delhi. 1996.

Shiva, Vandana, The effects of WTO on women's rights
http:www.navdanya.org/artcles/seeds.htm. 2005.
http:/www.southcentre.org/info/southbulletin/bulletin 42

Sharma, Devinder, The Indian Experience of Liberalization of Agriculture, Talk Delivered at Roundtable Conference on Agricultural Trade and Development at Canberra, Austrialia.17th August. 2005.

25

Empowerment of Women through Micro Finance

D. Padmavathi

The principle of gender equality is enshrined in the Indian Constitution in its Preamble, Fundamental Rights, Fundamental Duties and Directive Principles. The Constitution not only grants equality to women, but also empowers the State to adopt measures of positive discrimination in favour of women.

Within the framework of a democratic polity, our laws, development policies, Plans and programmes have aimed at women's advancement in different spheres. From the Fifth Five Year Plan (1974-78) onwards has been a marked shift in the approach to women's issues from welfare to development to empowerment from the ninth five year plan in recent years, the empowerment of women has been recognized as the central issue in determining the status of women. Steps taken by India for the empowerment of Indian woman were like setting up, the National Commission of Women in addition to the 73rd and 74th Amendments (1993) to the Constitution of India have provided for reservation of seats in the local bodies of Panchayats and Municipalities for women.

India has also ratified various international conventions and human rights instruments committing to secure equal rights of women like Convention on Elimination of All Forms of Discrimination Against Women (CEDAW) in 1993. The Mexico Plan of Action (1975), the Nairobi Forward Looking Strategies (1985), the Beijing Declaration as well as the Platform for Action (1995) and the Outcome Document adopted by the UNGA Session on Gender Equality and Development & Peace for the 21st century, titled 'Further actions and initiatives to implement the Beijing Declaration and the Platform for Action" have been unreservedly endorsed by India for appropriate follow up.

For empowerment of women, initiatives have been made by the women's movement and a wide-spread network of non-Government Organisations which have strong grass-root presence and deep insight into women's concerns.

However, there still exists a wide gap between the goals enunciated in the Constitution, legislation, policies, plans, programmes, and related mechanisms on the one hand and the situational reality of the status of women in India, on the other. This has been analyzed extensively in the Report of the Committee on the Status of Women in India, "Towards Equality", 1974 and highlighted in the

National Perspective Plan for Women, 1988-2000; The Shramshakti Report, 1988 and the Platform for Action: Five Years After - An Assessment'.

What is Empowerment?

According to M.C. Whirter (1991), "empowerment is the process by which people, organisations or groups who are powerless (a) become aware of the power dynamics at work in their life context, (b) develop the skills and capacity for gaining some reasonable control over their lives, (c) exercise this control without infringing upon the rights of others and (d) support the empowerment of others in their community".

Empowerment of Women is possible by:

- Creating an environment through positive economic and social policies for full development of women to enable them to realize their full potential.
- The de-jure and de-facto enjoyment of all human rights and fundamental freedom by women on equal basis with men in all spheres-political, economic, social, cultural and civil.
- Equal access to participation and decision making of women in social, political and economic life of the nation.
- Equal access to women to health care, quality education at all levels, career and vocational guidance, employment, equal remuneration, occupational health and safety, social security and public office etc.

Women comprise the majority of the population below the poverty line. The reality of Indian women is they are subjected to social discrimination, and denied of their rights and they cannot participate in decision making. Most of the Government policies and programmes are oriented towards economic development of women. Unless we address these Programmes and make them aware of the activities, it is not possible to develop and move them towards empowerment. Steps have been taken for mobilization of poor woman and convergence of services, by offering them a range of economic and social options, along with the necessary support measures to enhance their capabilities.

In order to enhance women's access to credit for consumption and production, steps were taken for the establishment of new and strengthening of existing micro credit mechanisms and micro finance institutions. Other supportive measures are strictly implemented to ensure adequate flow of credit through financial institutions and banks so as to enable all women below poverty line to have an easy access to credit.

In this background, the paper tries to analyze modalities of the micro-finance institutions and the empowerment of women to guide the self help groups (micro savings) of women and to empower them.

Many different relations can be offered for placing a priority on increasing women's access to micro finance services.

- Assetless – Poor does not have any assets and if any few assets are there, women do not have any assets for them as well they do not have any practical right over the assets.
- Unskilled – As women are not better taken care of, the skill development opportunities either at parental or procreation families are meager and the skill levels among the women are very low which results in low earning potency.
- Powerlessness – women lack power either in the family or in the society. The decision-making patterns in the patrilineal and patriarchal families are not pro-women and considering the female opinion even in women related activities is negligible.
- Income less or unpaid works – women work for the family which does not yield any cash income. As life in urban areas is more related to the cash, transactions and yields generate lesser privilege and status for women.
- Low nutritional food or malnutrition – the fact that India has exceptionally high rates of child malnutrition is because of the tradition that women eat last and least throughout their lives and poor does not have more / enough food for women too.
- Neo literacy or lack of Education – families are far less likely to educate girls than boys and far more likely to pull them out of school either to help at home or for wage earning.
- Less social capital – (non physical) – as the social capital in form of the social networks is less in urban areas and the women does not have any.social groupings which can cater the needs of women unlike to their rural counterparts.

Gender and Development

Research done by UNDP, UNIFEM, and the World Bank, among others, indicate that gender inequalities in developing societies inhibit economic growth and development. For example, a recent World Bank Report confirms that societies that discriminate on the basis of gender, pay the cost of greater poverty, slower economic growth, weaker governance, and a lower living standard of their people. The UNDP found a very strong correlation between its gender empowerment measure and gender-related development indices and its Human Development Index. Overall, evidence is mounting that improved gender equality is a critical component of any development strategy.

Table 25.1: Human Development Index for India

States / Uts	1981 Value	1981 Rank	1991 Value	1991 Rank	2001 Value	2001 Rank
Andhra Pradesh	0.298	9	0.377	9	0416	10
Assam	0.272	10	0.348	10	0.386	14
Bihar	0.237	15	0.308	15	0.367	15
Gujarat	0.360	4	0.431	6	0.479	6
Haryana	0.360	5	0.443	5	0.509	5
Karnataka	0.346	6	0.412	7	0.478	7
Kerala	0.500	1	0.591	1	0.638	1
Madhya Pradesh	0.245	14	0.328	13	0.394	12
Maharashtra	0.363	3	0.452	4	0.523	4
Orissa	0.267	11	0.345	12	0.404	11
Punjab	0.411	2	0.475	2	0.537	2
Rajasthan	0.256	12	0.347	11	0.424	9
Tamil Nadu	0.343	7	0.466	3	0.531	3
Uttar Pradesh	0.255	13	0.314	14	0.388	13
West Bengal	0.305	8	0.404	8	0.472	8
All India	0.302		0.381		0.472	

Micro finance has come to play a major role in many of these donors' gender and development strategies because of its direct relationship with both poverty alleviation and women. These have been recognized in the gender policy. Attention to gender equality is essential for a sound development practice at the heart of economic and social progress.

Development results cannot be maximized and sustained without explicit attention to the different needs and interests of women and men. As part of its poverty reduction priority, programs have been providing increased access to productive assets (especially land, capital, and credit), processing, and marketing for women. By giving women access to working capital and training, micro finance helps mobilize women's productive capacity to alleviate poverty and maximize economic output. In this case, women's entitlement to financial services, development aid, and equal rights rests primarily on their potential contribution to society rather than on their intrinsic rights as human beings and members of that society.

Women are the Poorest of the Poor

It is generally accepted that women are disproportionately represented among the world's poorest people. In its 1995 Human Development Report, the UNDP reported that 70 percent of the 1.3 billion people living on less than $1 per day are women. According to the World Bank's gender statistics database, women have a higher unemployment rate than men in virtually every country. In general, women also make up the majority of the lower paid, unorganized informal sector of most economies. These statistics are used to justify giving priority to increasing women's access to financial services on the grounds that women are relatively more disadvantaged than men.

Although many scholars and development agencies have noted an apparent trend toward the "feminization of poverty," measuring the extent to which this is occurring presents many challenges. Because most methods of measuring poverty assess the level of poverty of the household as a whole, it is likely that poverty experienced by women as a result of discrimination against them *within* their households is underreported to a great extent. In addition, Baden and Milward note, "Although women are not always poorer than men, because of the weaker basis of their entitlements, they are generally more vulnerable and, once poor, may have less options in terms of escape." By providing access to financing for income-generating activities, micro finance institutions can significantly reduce women's vulnerability to poverty. A reduction in women's vulnerability can sometimes also translate into empowerment if greater financial security allows the women to become more assertive in household and community affairs.

Women Spend More of Their Income on Their Families

Women have been shown to spend more of their income on their households; therefore, *when women are helped to increase their incomes, the welfare of the whole family is improved.* In its report on its survey findings the Special Unit on Micro finance of the UNCDF explains, "Women's success benefits more than one person. Several institutions confirmed the well-documented fact that women are more likely than men to spend their profits on household and family needs. Assisting women therefore generates a multiplier effect that enlarges the impact of the institutions' activities." Women's Entrepreneurship Development Trust Fund (WEDTF) in Zanzibar, Tanzania, also reports that "women's increased income benefits their children, particularly in education, diet, health care, and clothing." Women who are empowered will have the power to make the life choices that are best for them, and although many empowered women will choose to invest in their families, development organizations must be prepared for the possibility that some will not.

Efficiency and Sustainability: Arguments have been made for and against targeting women on the grounds of efficiency and sustainability. Proponents of targeting women on the grounds of sustainability cite women's repayment records and cooperativeness. A collective wisdom has emerged that women's repayment rates are typically far superior to those of men. Lower arrears and loan loss rates have an important effect on the efficiency and sustainability of the institution. Many programs have also found women to be more cooperative and prefer to work with them for that reason as well.

Women's equal access to financial resources is a human rights issue. Because access to credit is an important mechanism for reducing women's poverty it has been an explicit focus of a variety of human rights instruments.

Women and Micro Credit: Present Scenario

According to Micro Credit Summit Campaign 2001 Report, 14.2 million of the world's poorest women now have access to financial services through specialized micro finance institutions (MFIs), banks, NGOs, and other non-bank financial institutions. These women account for nearly 74 percent of the 19.3 million of the world's poorest people now being served by micro finance institutions. Most of these women have access to credit to invest in businesses that they own and operate themselves. The vast majority of them have excellent repayment records, in spite of the daily hardships they face. Contrary to conventional wisdom, they have shown that it is a very good idea to lend to the poor and to women.

Although women's access to financial services has increased substantially in the past 10 years, their ability to benefit from this access is often still limited by the disadvantages they experience because of their gender. Some MFIs are providing a decreasing percentage of loans to women, even as these institutions grow and offer new loan products. Others have found that on average women's loan sizes are smaller than those of men, even when they are in the same credit program, the same community and the same lending group. Some differences in loan sizes may be a result of women's greater poverty or the limited capacity of women's businesses to absorb capital. But they can also indicate broader social discrimination against women which limits the opportunities open to them, raising the question of whether micro enterprise development programs should do more address these issues. And looking at the leadership of many MFIs, we see very few women. Their contributions- whether setting the vision on a board of directors, designing products and services, or implementing programs- are missing. Thus, as the industry becomes more sophisticated in developing targeted products and services, it makes sense to look at both targeting women and empowering women.

Micro finance programs have the potential to transform power relations and empower the poor-both men and women. In well-run micro finance programs, there is a relationship of respect between the provider and the client that is inherently empowering. This is true regardless of the methodology or approach (whether the institution takes a minimalist approach of delivering financial services only or amore holistic or integrated approach). As a consequence, micro finance has become a central component of many donor agencies' and national governments' gender, poverty alleviation, and community development strategies. Several studies and the experiences of a number of MFIs have shown, however, that simply putting financial resources in the hands of poor women is not enough to bring about empowerment and improved welfare.

Last, but not least and most important, one of the often articulated rationales for supporting micro finance and the targeting of women by micro finance programs is that micro finance is an effective means or entry point for empowering women. By putting financial resources in the hands of women, micro finance institutions help level the playing field and promote gender equality.

Does Access to Credit Automatically Lead to Empowerment?

The basic theory is that micro finance empowers by putting capital in their hands and allowing them to earn an independent income and contribute financially to their households and communities. This economic empowerment is expected to generate increased self-esteem, respect, and other forms of empowerment for women beneficiaries. Involvement in successful income-generating activities should translate into greater control and empowerment. Closer examination shows us, however, that this equation may not always hold true and that complacency in these assumptions can lead MFIs to overlook both opportunities to empower women more profoundly and failures in empowerment. The ability of a woman to transform her life through access to financial services depends on many factors- some of them linked to her individual situation and abilities, and others dependent upon her environment and the status of women as a group. Control of capital is only one dimension of the complex and ever-changing process by which the cycles of poverty and powerlessness replicate them. Women also face disadvantages in accessing information, social networks, and other resources they need to succeed in business and in life. Only by evaluating the needs of women will an MFI be able to maximize its empowerment potential.

At the center of the framework are women and girls themselves- it is their opinions and observations that lie at the heart of this study. The central box reminds us that woman and girls do not share a single identity. Their ability to take advantage of new opportunities and the impact of change on them is strongly influenced by factors such as the stage they are at in their life cycle and their social position. This is a critical determinant of their authority and autonomy, their preferences, their household status and the livelihood options open to them.

The changes that women and girls spoke about fall broadly into the following three categories:

- Change on the economic front (mainly in the form of new income earning and livelihood options);
- Change on the socio-cultural front; and
- Change in human capital.

These three categories are by no means inclusive of all the changes that are important to women and girls in Bangladesh, but they are reflective of their most prominent interests and concerns. Change in one dimension obviously has an impact on and implications for other elements of women's and girls' livelihoods. These relationships (sometime positive and sometimes not) are represented by the arrows in the framework. An example of this dynamic is the emergence of garment and other factory work for women and girls- it is , at first look, an economic phenomenon relating to wages and spending power. However, a second look shows that the ascendancy of garment work also has profound social effects (more women in public places, women exerting more influence in the household) and human capital effects (some increased health risks, possible implications for quality of children's care).

Finally, while these are the general characteristics of micro credit, a great deal of discussion of the "micro credit alternative" has been on the institutional mechanisms for the delivery of micro credit. A very important component of the argument in favour of a large scale micro credit effort is that commercial banks cannot and should not directly be responsible for disbursing micro credit loans (because of transactions costs that are allegedly very high and poor recovery). The Micro-credit Cell of the RBI, for instance, states clearly that "NGOs has widespread appeal as micro-finance delivery vehicles" (RBI 1999a). In the plank of Action of the Micro credit Summit, the responsibility for achieving the goals of the Summit was placed clearly on "the thousands of existing micro credit NGOs, cooperatives, credit unions, grassroots groups, and poverty banks that at present comprise the micro credit movement" (Micro-Credit Summit, 1997). Thus "micro credit" as commonly used means credit provided mainly by the private sector, including NGOs, where the private sector not only controls disbursement but also determines the terms and conditions attached to each loan.

Micro credit is usually associated with:

- very small loans,
- no collateral,

- borrowers from among the rural and urban poor,
- loans for income-generation through market-based self-employment,
- the formation of borrower groups, and
- privatization, generally through the mechanism of NGO control over disbursement and the determination of the terms and conditions attached to each loan.

In India, as we have noted, micro-finance has been described as the way to go with respect to rural banking for the poor. However, NGO-controlled micro credit is not yet as widespread and does not represent in general a policy towards rural credit in India as in Bangladesh, for instance.

Table 25.2: SHG-Bank Linkage Programme Status as on March 31, 2005

S.N.	Particulars		Cumulative as on 31 March 2005
1.	No. of SHGs linked		1,618,476
2.	% of women groups		90
3.	No. of participating banks:		560
	ii. Regional Rural Banks		48
	iii. Co-operative Banks		196
4.	Bank Branches participating		35,294
5.	No. of States/Uts		31
6.	No. of districts covered		563
7.	No. of Partners		3024
8.	Bank Loan (Rs. in billion)		68.98
9.	NABARD refinance (Rs. in billion)		30.92
10.	No. of poor households assisted (in million)		24.25
11.	Average Loan/SHG Rs.		42.620
12.	Average Loan/Family Rs.		3,044
13.	Model Wise Linkage (cumulative) (%)		
	i	SHGs formed and financed by Banks	21
	Ii	SHGs formed by other agencies but directly financed by banks	72
	Iii	SHGs financed by banks using financial intermediaries	7

References

Bachrach, P & Baratz, M.S., Power and Poverty: Theory and Practice. New York: Oxford University Press. 1971

Barnes,,B., The Nature of Power. Cambridge: Polity Press. 1988

Batiwals, S., Empowerment of Women in south Asia: Concepts and Practices. New Delhi: Asian-South Bureau of Adult Education & freedom from Hunger Campaign. 1983

Boulding, K,. Three Faces of Power, London: Sage. 1988

Canadian international Development Agency (CIDA)., CIDA's Policy on Gender Equity. Hull, Canada. 1999

Dah;. R.A., Who Governs? Democracy and Power in an American City New Javen & London: Yale University Press. 1961

Davis, L., Leijenaar, M. Oldersma, J. (eds), The Gender of Power London: Sage. 1991

Giddens, The Constitution of Society. Cambridge: London. 1984

MC Whirter E.H., 'Empowerment in Counselling', Journal of Counselling and Development. 69: 222-227. 1991

Naila Kabeer., Money can't buy me love? Re-evaluating gender, credit. Empowerment in Rural Bangladesh, IDS Discussion Paper 363 (Brighten, England: Institute of Development Studies , University of Sussex). 1998

Ngau, P.M., Tensions in empowerment: the experience of Harambee (Self-help) movement, Kenya, Economic Development and cultural Change 35/3:523-538. 1987

Parsons, R.J., 'Empowerment: Purpose and Practice Principle Social Work' *Social Work with groups* 14/2:7-21. 1991

UNIFEM., Women's Empowerment and Micro finance: A Participatory Learning, Management, and Action Approach. Resource Manual for Practitioners and Trainers, draft. UNIFEM, 2001

UNFEM., Empowering women through micro finance Draft UNIFEM. 2002

UNDP., Human Development Report. New York, UNDP. 1995

World Bank., Engendering Development: Through Gender in Rights, Resource and Voice Summary. Washington, D.C: World Bank. 2001

26

Empowerment of Women in India

Ravi Prakash Yadav, Raginideep and Puja Roy

"Empowering women is a prerequisite for creating a good nation, when women are empowered, society with stability is assured. Empowerment of women is essential as their thoughts and their value systems lead to the development of a good family, good society and ultimately a good nation."

— former President A.P.J. Abdul Kalam

Women have a distinct role to play in the development of the nation. In the role of mother, a woman shapes the personality and character of children and hence the 'character of nation'. As a house wife, she maintains the productivity of the human capital of making a contribution to the economy of the nation. Apart from this a woman herself represents a unit of human capital, and is therefore capable of making a contribution to the economy of the nation. Sexual equality is very much essential from the point of view of development of an economy. Women constitute about 50 percent of nation's population (Census, 2001).

Empowerment is a process which generates changes in our ideas and perceptions and creates awareness about one's rights and opportunities for self-development in all important spheres of life (D. Das and S.N. Mishra, 2001). Dimensions of Empowerment may broadly be categorized as Economic, Social, Political and Legal. The situation of women in India is worse still. Women in the country suffer rape and sexual assault on a daily basis. In spite of progress for women, choices, awareness and confidence are still lacking. In this context, Empowerment of Women becomes a very important issue for the policy makers, Intellectuals, social activists etc.

A glance at some important data below reflects the worldwide situation of women.

1. Of world's one billion illiterate, 67 per cent are women.
2. Out of the world's 1.3 billion poor, nearly 70 percent are women.
3. Women hold only 11 percent of the seats in world's Parliament.
4. Only 24 women have been elected as heads of government in the last century.
5. Women work approximately twice the unpaid time men do.
6. The value of women's unpaid house work and community work is estimated

at 35 percent of GDP worldwide.
7. Out of 130 million children worldwide 2/3 are girls who are not in school.
8. Out of world's 27 million refugees 75-80 per cent are women and children.
9. Rural women produce more than 55 per cent of all food grown in developing countries.

Need of Empowerment of Women

Women were considered as a weaker section of the society. According to Manu Smirti "She is protected by the father in her childhood, by the husband in adulthood and by the son in her old age".

Women in India are less endowed than men with education, health, employment, politics, administration, medical, skill and productive assets. In fact the socialization process in India has rendered women faceless and invisible. Gender discrimination is visible against adolescent girls, adult women and girl child in 'intra-household' food allocation. Most rural health surveys have recorded a much higher incidence of illness among women and girls than men and boys. The 'state of health' of women is poorer than male. Women in poor households often contributes substantially to family income and at time more than their husbands. Inequalities in food intake relative to men are particularly exacerbated for women and children. Women workers are always treated as 'supplementary earners'.

Poor women are not a 'homogenous mass'. They belong to all castes, tribes and communities, but suffer in common, deprivation and discrimination of the worst kind. The vast majority of poor Indian women are 'assetless' and illiterate, with little access to resources, education, training in modern skills, tools, even to space unequal social and economic status and compulsions that drive them to take up any kind of work have pushed them into their invisibility, undervaluation and vulnerability.

Women have, through the centuries, remained confined within the four walls of the home, and dismissed as the 'second sex'. Related to the background, they have faced social, economic and political discrimination in many countries. In the western countries, due to factors like education, urbanization and changing social norms, women are marginally better off than their counterpart in the underdeveloped and developing nation, where poverty and illiteracy combine to hold them down and prevent them from emerging as a 'potent force' in society.

1. Educational Status of Women: Various development indicators reinforce the fact that women are way behind men according to the yardsticks of development. The imbalanced sex ratio was 933 women per 1000 men in 2001. The educational status of females compared to males is quite discouraging.

Table 26.1: Female Literacy Rate (1951-2001)

S.N	Year	1951	1961	1971	1981	1991	2001
1.	Literacy per cent	8.86	15.35	22	30	39	54
2.	Gap (M-F)	18	25	24	26	24	22
3.	Sex-Ratio	946	941	930	934	927	933

Source: Census 2001

Differences in female and male literacy rates is one aspect of this broader phenomenon of gender based inequality in India. This is reflected not only in such matters as education and opportunity to develop talents, but also in the more elementary fields of nutrition, health and survival. The recognition of 'female education' as a social issue is very recent in India. (Amratya Sen, 1996). But widespread female literacy is a twentieth century phenomenon.

2. Status of Employment: It was observed by National Commission on labour that the pattern of employment of women had been employed either on 'unskilled jobs' or jobs requiring traditional skill. National perspective plan for women 1988-2000 also observed that the women have been found to be concentrated in occupations which are usually the lowest rung.

Table 26.2: Work Force Participation Rates of Males and Females

(per cent)

S.N	Year	Rural		Urban		Total	
		M	F	M	F	M	F
1	1977-78	55.2	33.1	50.8	15.6	54.3	29.7
2	1987-88	53.9	32.3	50.6	15.2	53.1	28.5
3	1995-96	55.1	29.5	52.5	12.4	54.4	25.4

Source: S.R. Hashim's Paper, 31st Dec. 1998, ISLE, Hyderabad.

The political position of women and the numbers of women parliamentarians is not satisfactory. Fifty per cent women hold only 7 percent seats in Parliament.

3. Empowerment of Women: Conceptual Framework: Women's empowerment is a term widely used now-a-day. In recent years, empowerment of women has been recognized as a 'Central Issue' in determining the status of women. First we see the meaning of power. Power means control over material, social, physical as well as intellectual assets and resources. Similarly, Empowerment covers aspects such as women's control over material and intellectual resources. Empowerment is a multidimensional process, which should enable the individuals or a group of individuals to realize their full identity and powers in all spheres of life.

Table 26.3: Category-wise Employment of Male and Female

S.N	Name of categories	Total	Male	Female
1	Agriculture	64.7	58.3	78.0
2	Mines	0.7	0.9	0.4
3	Manufacturing	10.5	11.0	9.3
4	Electricity, Gas and Water	0.4	0.5	–
5	Building Construction	3.2	4.1	1.2
6	Trade	7.4	9.5	3.2
7	Transportation	2.8	4.0	0.3
8	Service	10.3	11.7	7.6
	Total	100	100	100

Source: India Development Report, 1999-2000

Table 26.4: Number of Women Members (MPs) in Lok Sabha

S.N	Name of Lok Sabha	I	V	IX	X
1	Year	1952	1971	1989	1996
2	Women MP (Nos.)	22	22	28	39
3	Percentage	4.4	4.2	5.1	7.1

Source: Dutta Mishra, Anil (1999), Gender Perspective, Radha Pub., New Delhi.

Empowerment of Women (EOW) involves many things: economic opportunity, property rights, political representation, social equality, personal rights and so on (Sheetal Sharma, 2006). The increasing use of term 'Women Empowerment' by various departments has resulted on its multiple meaning and interpretation and its association with a diversity of strategies. Virtually Empowerment is a process that enables a 'powerless women' to develop autonomy self control and confidence and with a group of women and men, a sense of collective influence over oppressive social conditions (Rotter, 1966).

It may also mean equal status to the women, opportunity and freedom to develop her. EOW would mean equipping women to be 'economically independent' and personally self-reliant, with a positive self-esteem to enable them to face any difficult situation (Valsamma Antony, 2006). The empowerment of women should be able to participate in the process of 'decision-making'. So the process of EOW is not merely a means of bringing about improvement in the physical and social conditions of women but also the one that ensures equal participation in the decision-making process.

Empowerment is a process, not an event, which challenges 'traditional power' equations and relations. Virtually it is a 'growth process' that involves intellectual enlightenment, economic enrichment and social emancipation on the part of women.

Hence, Empowerment of Women means many things, including:

1. Helping women fight their own fears and feeling of inadequacy and inferiority.
2. Women becoming economically independent and self-reliant.
3. Creating and strengthening women's group and organization.
4. Establishing equality of opportunities and equality between different gender and social classes.
5. Promoting qualities of nurturing, caring, gentleness.
6. Women having access to control over and benefit of resources like capital, land, property and technology.
7. Women having control over their own bodies.
8. Reducing women's burden of work especially within home.
9. Lastly Empowerment is both the process and the product of the process.

4. Empowerment of Women and Government Efforts: The principle of gender equality and gender justice has been basic to Indian thinking for over a century. It was fully realized that the progress of the nation was integrally linked with the status of women and for that the advancement of women was placed at the centre stage of Indian planning and policy.

A. Indian Constitution: The Constitution of India itself has provided women a significant position in the socio-economic life of the nation. The Constitution of India not only grants equality to women but also was the stage to adopt measures of 'positive discrimination' in favour of women for neutralizing the cumulative 'socio-economic, educational and political disadvantage' faced by them. The Preamble to the Constitution resolves to secure for all its citizens, justice, socio-economic and political, liberty of thought, expression, belief, faith and worship and equality of status. The Constitution also promotes them all, fraternity assuring the dignity of the individual and the unity and integrity of the nation.

Article 14 confesses equal right and opportunities for men and women in the political, economic and social spheres. While Article 14 prohibits discrimination on the ground of religion, race, caste, sex etc,. Article 15 prohibits discrimination on ground of sex. Article 15(3) enables the state to allow 'affirmative discrimination' in favour of women. Article 16(1) and 16(2) guarantees equality of opportunity in public employment. Article 30 provides equal means of livelihood and equal pay for equal work. Humane and just conditions of work and maternity benefit are assured to women under Article 42. According to Article 51-(e), the State also imposes a fundamental duty on every citizen to renounce practices derogatory to the 'dignity of women'.

B. Legislative Measures: To uphold the Constitutional mandate, the state has enacted various legislative measures intended to ensure equal right. Government, through legislations, counter social discrimination and various forms of violence as well as atrocities. The basic objective of such type of acts is to provide support service especially to 'working women', so as to ensure that the constitutional guarantees provided to women do not remain 'paper guarantees' and are translated into reality. There has been a support of legislation in favour of women. Changing perceptions among legislators, policy makers and public pressure have resulted in amendment to the existing laws to ensure that exploitation of women ceases. Although all laws are not gender specific, the major provisions affect women significantly. There are mainly three type of legislations – social, economic (for working women) and political. Some of the significant efforts in this regard are as follows:

Social Legislation for General Women:

- **Hindu Marriage Act, 1955:** Under the HMA, a Hindu follower can not contract a 'second marriage' with another till the first marriage is dissolved by divorce or decree. The Act permits marriages of people from different religion without changing their religion. The Act was amended in 1976 to provide for the right of the girl to repudiate before attaining maturity marriage as a child whether the marriage had been consummated or not. If this law is violated, the person can be prosecuted by law.
- **Hindu Succession Act, 1956:** Under this, daughter has also right in the property of her father. This Act confers the right of absolute ownership over property. The woman can make a will leaving her share of property to the heirs.
- **The Child Marriage Restraint (Amd.) Act, 1976:** Under this Act, the age of marriage for girls has been raised from 15 to 18 and for boys from 18 to 21 years. Offences under this Act have been made cognizable.
- **The Medical Termination of Pregnancy Act, 1971:** It regularizes abortion by qualified doctors on 'humanitarian' and medical grounds.
- **The Dowry Prohibition Act, 1961:** Under this Act taking or abetting dowry is a social crime. The minimum punishment for taking or abetting dowry has been raised to five years and a fine of Rs. 15,000. A new offence of dowry death has been included in the IPC, consequent to the amendment in the Act.
- **Immoral Traffic (Prevention) Act, 1956:** The new Act has made the penal provision most stringent regarding trafficking in women and girls for the purpose of 'Prostitution', as an organized means of living.
- **The Indian Evidence Act, 1983 (Amd.):** The IPC and the Criminal

Procedure Code have been amended in 1983 to make the offence of 'rape' and other crimes against women most stringent and to make a new provision in the IPC for making cruelty against married woman by the husband or other relative punishable.

- **The Indecent Representation of Women (Prohibition) Act, 1986:** It has been enacted with the objective of having a separate legislation to effectively prohibit the indecent representation of women through advertisements, books pamphlets etc.

Labour Legislation for Working Women:

- **The Factories Act, 1948, the Mines Act, 1952 and the Plantation Act, 1951:** Under this Act, every factory should provide and maintain adequately lighted and ventilated latrines and urinal, in sufficient numbers for male and female workers separately (s-19 b,c,d). Secondly, no women is to be employed in any part of a factory for 'pressing cotton' in which a cotton opener is at work (s-27). Thirdly, adequate and suitable washing facilities for the use of men and women workers separately have to be provided in every factory (s-42 b). Fourthly, the Act also required the provision and maintenance of 'crèches' in every factory where more than 30 women workers are ordinarily employed (s-48). This Act prohibits employment of women between 7 p.m. to 6 a.m. in factories, mines and plantations and also regulates the working hours and connected provision for their safety and health.
- **The Employee State Insurance Act, 1948:** Under this Act, a new scheme has been introduced giving maternity benefit (84 days/12 weeks leave with wages), disablement benefit (injured women workers), and dependent benefit (benefit in the form of pension to dependent). In addition to this, medical benefit (in the form of treatment and attendance at an E.S.I. Hospital, dispensary or clinic Rs. 345 per family P.A.) and funeral benefit is also provided for women workers (s-46(1), 50(1)).
- **The Maternity Benefit Act, 1961:** This Act makes a provision for maternity benefit so that the women can play her productive and reproductive role efficiently. The Act extends to the whole of India and is applicable to every factory, mine, plantation and to every establishment for payment of maternity benefit. The maximum period for which any woman is entitled to M.B. is 12 weeks i.e. 6 weeks up to and including the day of her delivery and 6 weeks immediately following the day of delivery. Every woman entitled to maternity benefit, shall also be allowed a medical bonus of Rs. 250/-. Every women who returns to duty after delivery of child; shall in addition to the

interval of rest allowed to her, be allowed in the course of her daily work, two breaks of 15 minutes duration each for nursing the child until the child attains the age of 15 months. This Act is based on ILO Maternity Protection Convention, 1919 and the purpose was to support and protect the women in pre and post pregnancy period. There are so many experiences in which it was found that so many organizations refuse to employ married women because of maternity benefits burden which will be paid by them to women workers. But in many cases Supreme Court termed it unconstitutional. Maternity Protection in India is provided by some other schemes too such as Beedi and Cigar Workers Act, Beedi Cigar Workers Welfare Fund, Newspaper Employee Act, 1955 etc. In spite of this, a National Maternity Benefit Scheme (1995) was also introduced under National Social Assistance Programmes to provide financial assistance to women who are BPL.

- **The Equal Remuneration Act, 1976:** The Act provides for payment of equal remuneration to men and women workers, for same work or work as a similar nature. The Act also prevents discrimination on ground of sex against women in the matter of employment (recruitment, promotion, training and training). With a view to honour I.L.O. "Equal Remuneration Convention No. 100", Government of India had rectified it and introduced the above mentioned Act. The provision relating to 'equal pay for equal work' is issued as a directive to the State in Part IV of the Constitution.
- **The Contract Labour Regulation Act, 1978:** It regulates the working condition of contract labour including women as regards payment of wages and provides for welfare activities and crèches for the children of working women engaged in construction work.

C. National Commission for Women, 1990: The National Commission for Women (NCW) was set up as a national apex statutory body in 1992 in accordance with the NCW Act, 1990. The function of Commission is to investigate and examine the legal safeguards provided for women under the constitution and other laws and to recommend measures to government for their effective implementation.

The National Commission for Women is assisted by various committees. These committees work on the issue of social security, prostitution, employment, custodial justice for women, problem of S.C. women. The NCW has also collaborated with national level NGOs by making arrangements. A National Commission on Self-Employed Women has been also set-up by the government to make a comprehensive study of the working and living conditions of poor women in the unorganized sector. Not only this, a Department of Women &

Child Development has been created by the government for the holistic development of women in India.

D. Five Year Plans and Empowerment of Women: The Five Year Plans have space for the problems of women. At first, the Central Social Welfare Board (CSWB) was set up in 1953 which symbolized the 'welfare approach' to the women's problem. Secondly, the Second FYP ((1956-61) recognised the need for 'organisation of women as workers' and the need to perceive the social prejudices from which they suffer. The Third FYP (1961-66) centered mainly on female education, maternity benefit, child care, wealth, nutrition and family planning. The Fourth FYP (1969-74) recommended a programme of 'functional literacy' to equip women with skills and knowledge to perform the functions of a house-wife. Including child care, nutrition, health care, home economy etc. The Sixth FYP recognised that women's lack of access to resources is a critical factor impeding their development. The Seventh FYP emphasized the 'qualitative aspect' of the development of women. The Plan emphasized the need to open new avenues of work for women, since women were perceived as a 'crucial human resource' for development of the country. The Ninth FYP (1997-2002) emphasized on the 'empowerment' for development of women. The Ninth FYP stated that the objective of Plan is the focus on the growth with 'social justice' and equity. In this Plan the planners adopted the strategy of 'women's component plan', under which not less than '30 percent of funds/benefits' were earmarked for all women-related sectors and women specific programmes. The Tenth FYP (2002-2007) has also focus on WCP.

So from the Fifth FYP (1974-78) onwards, there has been a marked shift in the approach to women's issue from 'Welfare' to 'Development'. In recent years, the empowerment of women has been recognised as the central issue in determining the status of women. The National Commission for Women was set up by an act of Parliament in 1990 to safeguard the right and legal entitlements of women. The 73rd and 74th Amendment (1993) to the Constitution of India have provided for reservation of seats in the local bodies of Panchayats and Municipalities for women, laying a strong foundation for participation in decision making (Political Empowerment) at the local levels. India has also ratified various conventions and human rights instruments committing to secure equal rights for women. Key among them is the ratification of the convention on the elimination of all form of discrimination against women in 1993. The Mexico Plan of Action 1975, the Nairobi Forward Looking Strategies (1985), the Beijing Declaration as well as the Platform for Action (1995), have been unreservedly endorsed by India for appropriate follow up.

E. Beijing Declaration, 1995 and National Policy of Empowerment of Women: The 'IV World Conference' at Beijing in September 1995, organized on the occasion of the 50 anniversary of the Foundation of the United Nations was based on the following principles:

- Acknowledging the voices of all women every where and taking note of the diversity of women and their roles and circumstances, honouring the women who paved the way and inspired by the hope present in the world's youth.
- Enhancing the advancement and empowerment of women all over the world, including the right to freedom of thought, conscience, religion and belief, thus contributing men, individually or in community with other and thereby guaranteeing them the possibility of realizing their full potential in society and shaping their lives in accordance with own aspirations.

In the Conference, India had made a commitment to the formulation of a National Policy for Women. The policy would among other things lay down strategies and action points to bridge the gap between the constitutional and legal equality enjoyed by women and de-facto and de-jure situation of women in the country. It would continuously guide and inform action at every level and in every sector by mainstreaming a gender perspective in all laws, regulations, plans, policies, programmes and budgetary allocations. The National Policy for EOW, 2001 envisaged introduction of a gender perspective in the budgeting process as its 'operational strategy'. As a follow up action, a discussion paper on the policy prepared by the Department of Women and Child Development Ministry of HRD, Government of India was considered by a core group of experts on 08-11-1995.

F. Important Programme for EOW

- **Vocational Training Programme for Women (VTPW), 1977:** This Programme has launched with ILO/SIDA assistance just to provide equitable opportunities for women's employment in the industry and service sectors and in self employment. In this Programme, diverse types of training are arranged by the organizer like secretarial practice, electronics, hair and skin care, dress making, instrument mechanic, data programme, computer software, architecture (basic skills), embroidery, business services (advanced skills) and instructional skills etc.
- **Support to Training and Employment (STEP):** Under this Programme, women are provided training in new technologies in agriculture, dairying, horticulture, fisheries, handicrafts, handlooms etc.
- **Rashtriya Mahila Kosh (RMK):** The RMK was set up in 1993 as a national instrument for extending credit to poor and needy women in the

informal/unorganized sector and has sanctioned worth 113.50 crore (up to Oct. 31, 2002). More than 4.28 crore women have been benefited through 1046 NGOs. The objective of RMK is to create an environment for accessing women to sources of credit and to increase the outflow of RMK's funds to the needy women through the intervention of Women Self-help Groups (SHGs). The SHGs promote saving, build up a thrift fund and builds leaders who manage the activity. Handling money is a process of empowerment of women. It is even a greater empowerment, when they learn to apply the funds for income generation and for improvement of their economic status.

- **Family Counselling Centres:** It is a 'preventive and rehabilitative' service centre for such women and children who are victims of atrocities and family maladjustment. Since its inception in 1984, about 27,749 women has been benefited by 417 FCCs during the year 2001-02.
- **Short Stay Homes:** It is a national plan of action for the rescue, rehabilitation and reintegration of women and girls trapped in commercial sex. Under this Scheme, about ten thousand beneficiaries during 2001-02 had been benefited through 328 home services. In addition to this, a new scheme has been introduced last year in the name of 'Swadhar'. This Scheme provides food, shelter, health, counselling and training to women and girls who are in difficult situations.
- **Gender Budgeting in Union Budget:** The Ministries of Central Government of India have 41 'Gender Budgeting Cells' like Ministry of Power, Rural Development, Small Scale Industries, Tribal affairs, Water Resources, Youth Affairs & Sports, Tourism, Panchayati Raj Institution, Agriculture, Culture, Heavy Industries, Home Affairs, Information and Broadcasting, Labour and Employment, Law and Justice etc. The Expenditure Budget (volume-I 2005-06), included for the first time a statement on gender-budgeting.

Table 26.5: Women and Union Budget 2005-2006 (in crore)

S.N.	Programmes	2001-02		2003-04		2004-05	
		BE	RE	BE	RE	BE	RE
1.	Women specific Schemes	3260	3035	3675	2897	3556	3225
2.	Pro-women allocation in pro- women schemes	10596	11205	13297	14956	15001	16935

Source: *Yojana*, 2006, October, p. 12.

In order to empower the women and children, Government of India constituted a Task Force on Women and Children in August, 2000 under the chairmanship of Shri K.C. Pant. The Task Force recommended amendment of '22 Laws' to make them more effective. It is a good sign that related ministries and their departments have initiated necessary action for amending these laws.

Conclusion

However, there still exists a wide gap between the goals enunciated in the Constitution, legislation, policy, plans, programmes and related mechanisms on the one hand and the 'situational reality' of the status of women in India, on the other. This has been analysed extensively in the Report of the Committee on the Status of Women in India, "Towards Equality" (1974), and highlighted in the National Perspective plan for Women (1988-2000) and the Shram Shakti Report (1988). Gender disparity is manifest itself in various forms, the most obvious being the trend of continuously declining female ratio in the population in the last few decades. Social stereotyping and violence at the domestic and societal levels are some of the manifestations. Discrimination against girl children, adolescent girls and women still persists.

Despite government efforts to plug the existing 'loopholes' in the law and to bring about reforms, it is obvious that such measures are deemed to fail, unless there is a growing 'awareness' among the women about their needs for better educational and health facilities, about their rights: social, economic and political conferred upon them by law and about their duty to contribute to the gains of development. Without this awareness and consciousness women cannot emerge as a force to reckon with.

It is a fact that only legislation has not been able to bring about the socio-economic transformation in the country. One reason is that women are not aware of the availability of law. The 'mass media' should therefore, be involved in publishing the facilities available. Parents should not be allowed to make a will disinheriting them from their rightful share of property. All matrimonial property should be registered in the joint name of husband and wife and the right of the wife to the matrimonial home must be guaranteed. Lastly, we can say – "when women move forward, the family moves, the village moves and the nation moves".

References

Amartya Sen & Jean Dreze, The Economic Development and Social Opportunity, Oxford Pub. 1996

Bina Agrawal, Women, Poverty and Agriculture Growth in India. 1996

Madhubala Nath, Women Issues : From the periphery to the Centre, Journal of Rural Development, Vol. II, No. 5, Sep. 1992

Sheetal Sharma, "Educated Women, Empowered Women", Yojana, Oct., New Delhi, P. 52. 2006

Sayed Afzal Peerzada and Prema Parande "Empowerment of Women : A Study", Kurukshetra, Nov., P.7. 2005

Valsamma Antony, "Education and Employment – The Key to Women Employment", Kurukshetra, Feb., pp. 27-28. 2006

L.N. Mittal, "The State of womanhood in Indian Society", BGMS, Indore, March, PP. 6-7. 2005

Jyoto Sthapak and Mahima Singh, "Empowerment of High Risk Learner Women through Vocational Education", BGMS, Indore, March, PP. 9-10.

Rotter, Generalized expectancies for Internal versus External control of Reinforcement, Psychological monographs, 80, 609. 1996

27

Role of Banks in Women Empowerment

Habilslade O. Ogale

Within the last two decades, global cognizance of the significance of women's role in the development process and women's participation in nation building task has brought women's issues to the forefront of government, academic and activist concern in third world countries. However, despite commendable attempts such as allocation of funds for women's development, legislative measures to improve and protect the rights of women, institutional attempts to boost national machineries and credit information cells, international efforts through multilateral and bilateral agencies to keep the aid flowing, expected outcome has not been brought forth.

Women comprise about 50 per cent of India's population. They play a predominant role in India and there is an imperative need to bring them into the main stream of economic, social and cultural development of the economy. There is also a need to facilitate and sustain the growth and progress of women and nurture their talents and skills in every field of economic activity and even in the area of industry.

Most of the Asian countries have of late adopted a deliberate policy of promoting and encouraging small enterprises as a strategy for the overall development of their countries. During the past six decades, India has been engaged in the task of promoting and developing entrepreneurship. Priority has been accorded to small–scale industries and stimulating and funding entrepreneurs. The agencies promoting entrepreneurial development try to cater to the needs of two types of clientele: the spontaneously emerging entrepreneurs, and those who have been included to take up entrepreneurial activity by the promotional agencies.

The Government of India initiated several welfare-oriented programmes for the women development right from the first five-year plan. The socio-economic parameters of the Human Development Index including health and education are not in favor of women.

Against this background, the government introduced for the first time a statement on gender budgeting in the Union Budget of 2005-2006. This was because of the realization that women are facing gender specific barriers to access the public services.

The 11th Plan strategy of gender balancing takes care of the special needs of women for their economic and social independence. As women's low status stemmed from their powerlessness, it is the duty of the government, through banks and society to empower women folk.

Definition of Empowerment

"Empower" means making one powerful or equipping one with the power to face the challenges of life to overcome disabilities, handicaps and inequalities. So, empowerment is an active multidimensional process, which should enable women to realize their identity and powers in all spheres of life. Further empowerment would consist in providing greater access to knowledge and resources, more autonomy in decision-making, greater ability to plan their lives, more control over the circumstance, which influence their lives and freedom from custom, belief and practice.

In many instances whether it is men or women motivated to take to some entrepreneurial activity by themselves may not be in a position to finance their enterprise. Financial institutions especially the banks by their assistance to the neo or ongoing entrepreneurs really create a positive impetus for accelerating and successfully running the enterprises small or large. When we say banks, the concept stands for all kinds of financial institutions helping the entrepreneurs in general, thus women included, in their ventures.

Hence it is paramount to look into the role banks play, as they constitute a significant factor as vital partners in the task and the approach to including entrepreneurial ventures on the part of a large number of people in the country in general and women in particular.

Banks as Partners in Entrepreneurial Development Programmes (EDP)

Though organizations such as the District Industries Centers, Small Industry Service Institutes and other state corporations are engaged in the primary task of stimulating and supporting entrepreneurial activity, it is the banks and other financial institutions that have a major role in developing entrepreneurship. Until recently, the activity of EDP has been rather confined to the promotional agencies but today the banks are more involved not only in the financing the enterprises of the entrepreneurs, but they do associate themselves in stimulating, and motivating entrepreneurial activity.

The volume of activity on the part of the banks in entrepreneurial development is not only quantitative but also qualitative. There is a change in the orientation of the banks' role in this field. Today, the need and the emphasis is to go beyond the financing of the enterprise. It is to motivate and develop entrepreneurial climate in the otherwise excluded community, specifically of women. In the context of developing women entrepreneurship, we are dealing with induced entrepreneurs, and the banks have to take into account the limitations on the part of the new entrepreneurs, and appreciate their problems and their unfamiliarity with banking institutions.

The banks alone are not in the field; several agencies as mentioned earlier are engaged in the task of EDP and unless there is an inter-institutional coordination, the effectiveness of the whole activity will be lost. There is a need for teamwork in the case of agencies engaged in the task. The banker as a major promoter of EDP has to work in unison with other promotional agencies.

In the interaction between the banker and the customer, the communication on the part of the banker may be emphasized. Whether this interpersonal communication is oral or written the banker has to see that he speaks and writes to the customer in the wave length of the latter, so that the customer understands and appreciates the role of the bank, and the bank in turn, builds up confidence in the customer and contributes to the credibility of the bank. The personnel of the bank who meet and interact with the customer need a special kind of orientation especially in the case of women entrepreneurs.

It is presumed that banking institutions are facing some institutional and procedural problems. Since the banks are playing and need to play a significant role in EDP, the banking system has to attend to these problems and streamline the entire working system, internal as well as inter-institutional to help and facilitate rapid and sustained growth in the specific field of women entrepreneurial development.

Specific Role of Banks

The Reserve Bank of India has continued to lay stress on the need for financial inclusion of the under-privileged sections, which have hitherto remained outside the periphery of the banking system. Through a series of new measures announced in its Credit Policy for 2006-2007, it has once again shown concern for this segment of population that has been unable to draw benefits from the banking system despite the extensive network of banks in general and the public sector banks in particular. India is the oldest example of a developing country that set out as a matter of policy to employ the institutional credit for the purpose of development. This policy was adopted in the 50s and expanded further in the 60s and 70s culminating in the establishment of an apex institution at the national level in 1982 under the name of National Bank for Agriculture and Rural Development (NABARD).

Within the priority sector lending besides agricultural loans, loans for small scale industries, retail trade, small business, professional and self employment, consumption loan, loan for education and housing, there are numerous government schemes like IRDP (Integrated Rural Development Programme), DWCRA (Development of Women and Children in Rural Areas), PRY (Prime Minister Rozgar Yojana) and DRI (Differential Interest Rate Scheme). Besides, there are several specific schemes for providing better opportunities to women in rural India through priority in loans.

With the nationalization of major commercial banks in 1969, banks have been playing a pivotal role in development financing, the small sector in particular, as also contributing to the development of backward regions of the country with the abetment of other development institutions. In the context of the continuing paucity of entrepreneurial talent and scarcity of invest able resources, commercial banks in India are playing a dynamic and positive role in igniting the forces of innovation and helping to foster and broad- based new entrepreneurship.

The functions of development banking include providing loans and working capital, formulating of project ideas, identification of specific projects suitable to local conditions, location and induction of new entrepreneurs into entrepreneurial activity and offering of technical and managerial guidance.

The public sector banks have been experimenting with wide range of special schemes to finance engineers, doctors, technically qualified entrepreneurs apart from promoting several schemes for funding self-employment endeavors and self help groups of in which women are dominant among the weaker sections of society and the educated unemployed. Wherever possible, banks are collaborating with other development institutions representing industry, trade or commerce. Various schemes have been in the preparation of area optional studies, bankable projects and collection of information useful to potential entrepreneurs. For enterprises that are export-oriented, apart from financing, banks offer a wide range of services.

Specific to entrepreneurial activity, Nationalized banks are guided in their endeavor to provide the following services:

- Assisting entrepreneurs in selection of industry, preparation and evaluation of project reports and conducting market survey.
- Providing short-term and long-term finance.
- Assisting in obtaining clearance, machinery and equipment.
- Assisting in setting up production and control processes, offer management and technical guidance.

The banks and other financial institutions as instruments of economic development and welfare of people have basically two things to work with, the material resources and the human resources. Wherever finance is a factor to harness and boost these two basic resources, it will be the bank that would play a prime and sustaining role. The banks as they are doing today, will extend their support and guidance of technical and managerial, to the ongoing and potential entrepreneurs and establish themselves as pervasive and enduring institutions.

It may be the individual who meets the bankers and who establishes an enterprise, but as the individual is placed in the social-cultural network, there is a need on the part of the bank to go beyond the individual, developing rapport with the group and the community of the individual. The banks are to motivate the individual, and to do so; they have a role to educate the community in which they operate, to make the bank a partner in the development of community resources and in raising the standards of living in the community. The banks through their activities and involvement over a period of time should become an integral system of the individual and community development.

Statistically speaking, the banks today may be touching only a small segment of the economic community in the country. The vision that one envisages is that banks play a major and specific role to extend their supportive limbs of financial inclusion to include the, otherwise excluded and potential individuals and families in empowering and developing them so that they develop the resources towards attaining a meaningful quality of life. As financial inclusion to include the otherwise excluded section of the society becomes top in the agenda of 11th five year plan, the RBI has moved to enforce multiple policy and industry changes:

- Banks have been asked to voluntarily make available a 'no-frills' account, and all printed bank material has to be made available in regional languages.
- KYC procedures have been simplified for low-income groups.
- Significantly, since January 2006 banks can provide a full range of banking services through 'business facilitator and correspondent'.
- The Credit Information Bureau Act, 2006, will eventually establish a credit bureau that makes available credit histories of individuals and small businesses. This should lower risk for banks, in extending credit further.

In order to accelerate industrial development in backward areas, banks are now involved in identifying industrial potential and motivating entrepreneurs to take up activities to exploit it. Banks are identifying and training entrepreneurs by conducting EDPs for them. Each of these programmes is followed by a support phase, which provides counseling and consultancy services on a continuing basis. Banks are nominating project leaders to assist entrepreneurs in product selection and see them through various phases of the project until the unit is established.

Another contribution that banks are making towards EDP is by deputing their officers for posting to District Industries Centers as Credit Managers. These officers facilitate entrepreneurial activity by speeding up completion of formalities relating to sanctions, approvals, quotas, etc. These personnel are also actively involved in designing and organizing training programmes and coordinating such programmes in various parts of the country by preparing training manuals.

Conflicting Situations

While the polices and priorities of the Govt. are directed towards development banking and while the focus is on weaker sections and inducing entrepreneurship or industrial activity among the people who are new to these, and who have never approached the banks for any developmental purpose, the managers of branches who are the ultimate people in assessing, appraising and advancing loans to new entrepreneurs, meet with certain dilemmas; on one hand the directives from above are to lend money to a variety of customers, who may not, in terms of security meet the requirements, but at the same time, such customers are to be helped. And in such a context, the branch manager meets with a conflicting situation; Whether he should discharge his functions as per the policies and directives of the government or not and at the same time save his position.

Moreover many of the branch managers of banks today are experiencing among others two major obstacles to greater financial inclusion. The first is simply commercial. Transaction costs for both banks and clients remain high, particularly in disbursing credit, which is essentially a high cost, distributed business. Further interest rates remain high in the absence of structured credit assessments. The second obstacle is policy requirements such as know your customer (KYC) procedures that limit the geographical reach of financial services beyond physical bank branches.

Consequences of Financial Exclusion

Consequences of financial exclusion will vary depending on the nature and extent of services denied. It may lead to increased travel requirements, higher incidence of crime, general decline in investment, difficulties in gaining access to credit or getting credit from informal sources at exorbitant rates, and increased unemployment, etc.

The small business may suffer due to loss of access to middle class and higher-income consumers, higher cash handling costs, delays in remittances of money. According to certain researches, financial exclusion, of which majority of women have fallen victims can lead to social exclusion. Therefore banks need to redesign their business strategies to incorporate specific plans to promote financial inclusion of low-income group treating it both as a business opportunity as well as a corporate social responsibility to augur well with women empowerment.

28

Welfare, Development and Empowerment of Women: The Indian Experience

Praveen Devgan

Status of Indian Women: Past, Present and Future

In the Indian society the status of women has changed from time to time; position of women in society is the index to the standard of social organization. We can divide the past (history) in three phases to analyze the status of women. They are: Ancient Period, Medieval Period and Modern period.

In ancient period women enjoyed equal status with men in all fields of life. She received the same education like men. In fact, many Hindu religious books like Vedas, Upanishads, Ramayana and Mahabharata have mentioned the names of several women who were great scholars, poets, philosophers during that time. The wife was 'Ardhangini' which means she is half of her husband. An unmarried man was considered to be an incomplete man. All religious ceremonies were performed by the husband along with the wife. This shows the importance given to the women in ancient period.

The worth of a civilization can be judged from the position that it gives to women. Of the several factors that justify the greatness of India's ancient culture, one of the greatest is the honoured place ascribed to women. Manu, the great law-giver, said long ago, "Where women are honoured there reside the Gods." According to ancient Hindu scriptures no religious rite can be performed with perfection by a man without the participation of his wife. Wife's participation is essential to any religious rite. Married men along with their wives are allowed to perform sacred rite on the occasion of various important festivals. Wives are thus befittingly called *Ardhangani* (better half). They are given not only important but equal position with men.

In Medieval Period, the status of women went down considerably. She was considered to be inferior to man. Many historians have called this age as the 'dark age'. Her position became very miserable. Decline in the status of women in Indian society begins with the advent of Muslims rule.

During the Muslim period of history they were deprived of their rights of equality with men. They were compelled to keep themselves within the four walls of their houses with a long veil on their faces. This was definitely due to Islamic influence. Even today, in some Islamic countries women are not allowed to go out freely. The conservative regimes of Iran and Pakistan, for example, have withdrawn the liberties given to women folk by the previous liberal governments. Even in India the Muslim women are far more backward than their Hindu, Christian and Sikh counterparts. The sight of Muslim women walking with long *Burkas* (Veils) on their person is not very rare. The women are, as a matter of fact, regarded as captive and saleable commodities in Muslim families. One man is allowed to have many wives with the easiest provision of divorce. The husband can divorce a wife just by saying 'I divorce you' under the provision of Muslim laws.

However, in the Modern period, in the wake of Raja Ram Mohan Roy's movement against women's subjugation to men and British influence on Indian culture and civilization, the position of women has once again undergone a change. However, it was only under the enlightened leadership of Mahatama Gandhi that they re-asserted their equality with men. In response to the call of Gandhi they discarded their veil and came out of the four walls of their houses to fight the battle of freedom shoulder to shoulder with their brothers.

The position of women in modern India has changed considerably. Her position in modern Indian society is equal to that of men, socially, economically, educationally, politically and legally. Her sufferings from sati, child marriage, institution of temple prostitution do no longer exist. Now, she has the right to receive education, inherit and own property, participate in public life and political life of the nation. She has become economically independent. She can seek employment anywhere and remains not a domestic slave. So, she is certainly enjoying the equal status with men in all respects. For this change in the status of women, several factors like women's education, reform movements by many social reformers, women participation in politics and numerous social legislations are held responsible.

The result is that the Indian Constitution today has given to women equal status with men. There is no discrimination between men and women. All professions are open to both of them with merit as the only criterion of selection and through their newly gained freedom, Indian woman have distinguished themselves in various spheres of life as politicians, orators, lawyers, doctors, administrators and diplomats. They are not only entrusted with work of responsibility but they also perform their duties very honestly and sincerely. There is hardly any sphere of life in which Indian women have not taken part and shown their worth.

Women contributions in politics and social services have also been quite significant, for example, Indira Gandhi, who shone so brilliantly and radiantly in the firmament of India's politics. In the field of social service, Indian women have also done some excellent jobs. They have not only served the cause of the suffering humanity but have also brought highest laurels for the country. The name of Mother Teressa cannot but be mentioned. She brought the Nobel Prize for India for her selfless services to the poor, destitute and suffering people of our country in particular and the needy and handicapped people of the world in general. Today, we need services of educated women who can tour throughout the country and help in removing human sufferings. They can train them in sewing, knitting, embroidery and nursing in which women by nature excel. They can also train them in the art of music and dancing.

But all this should not lead us to conclude that the women should look down upon domestic life. The main sphere of action for them who have not taken up jobs outside should be essentially a happy home which is their real kingdom and where their sweet manners and mature advices as wife, mother, sister and daughter make tremendous effects on the male members of the family.

They should also discourage their husbands and sons from indulging in bribery and other corrupt practices. This they can do only when they learn the art of simple living by discarding their natural desires for ornaments and a living of pomp and show. In many cases families have been running in deficit due to the extravagance of the housewives in maintaining a high standard of living. There is no denying the fact that women in India have made a considerable progress in the last sixty years but yet they have to struggle against many handicaps and social evils in the male dominated society.

In contemporary India, women occupy a paradoxical status. On the one hand, there are goddesses featuring in the Hindu pantheon and revered by men. On the other, some wives are burnt because they did not bring enough dowry (the horrible institutionalized and illegal practice of expecting the woman's parent to provide a large purse to the groom); women are victimized by powerful local and their family.

In the country's development and progress the women and her awareness plays an important role. Women constitute nearly half of our population, so they cannot be left out of any endeavor for building up the nation. On the one hand, there has been some awareness about the need for gender equality. Women's organizations have led powerful movement and struggles for their rights. Many laws to protect them are on the statute book. On the other hand, oppression and atrocities against women have been on the increase for some years now. Cases of wife beating, dowry deaths, kidnapping, molestation, rape and amniocentesis (killing of female foetus in womb) are common. Everyone knows that a number of cases are not registered with the police due to the social stigma attached to rape cases.

One woman dies every 102 minutes in India due to dowry related violence. In many parts of India she would lose any right to dignity and happiness. She might be forced to immolate herself. One of the women is molested every 26 minutes in India, or raped every 54 minutes, or kidnapped every 43 minutes (National Crime Bureau). Moreover, there has been increasing cases of "dowry deaths" with increasing reports of death of young brides in kitchen accidents. Dowry deaths are heinous and barbarous crimes committed by the cruel and inhumane persons and when the whole bunch of clichés comes to mind – rape dowry, crime, violence, sexual harassment, incest, wife beating, discrimination, rights, quotas, gender, sexism, feminism, the list of problems and issues seems endless.

The above scenario is evidently a reckless violation of human rights.

Fortunately, many things are being done to address these problems. After Independence considerable efforts have been made to uplift the status of women in general and of the women labour in particular.

There is a National Human Rights Commission for Women, which handles all human rights violations against women. There is a National Council for Women which advocate policies for women. There is an entire ministry for women that manage policies for women. There is a very large body of educated women professionals, many publications that were created by women, run by women, and are for women, several vocal women journalists and pundits, special courts for dowry deaths, and countless women-specific NGOs. The present Government also sponsored and passed a Law that required all political parties to maintain a count of at least one third of the total candidates in elections to be women. Hence, despite media sensationalism, especially in the west, the outlook for women's status in Indian society looks promising. A number of committees legal rules, departments, incentive schemes etc. such as – Swablamban (1982), Women & Child Development Department (1985), Step (1986), Mahila Samakhya (1989), Mahila Aayog (1990), Mahila Action Plan (1992), Rastriya Mahila Kosh (1993), Swayamshakti (1998), Istri Shakti Purskar (1999), Rastriya Mahila Shakti Sampannta Niti (2001), Swadhaar (2001), Swayamsiddha (2001), Mahila Sashaktikaran (2001), Mahila Sambidhan, Kanoon Evam Vidhan (2002), Mahila Samvedi Budget Evam Mukhyadhara (2004), Hindu Succession (2005), Divorce Gets Easier (2006), Protection from Domestic Violence (2006), Marriages to be Registered (2006), have been formed to study, investigate, and analyze and recommended the measures to improve women's condition, since the status of women is one of the most important aspects of any society. It is with this perspective that several campaigns towards women's movement in India have focused on amendment in Laws.

Women empowerment is an important issue addressed by all nations who prepare themselves for national development. One of the main concerns of our freedom fighters was how we would sustain our Independence. The national leaders made several plans for industrialization, boosting technical education, empowering military and the farmers, and above all women's education. Rightly so, women comprise almost half of any country's population. Every country would works towards women empowerment in order to improve its manpower resources.

What is Empowerment?

- Positive attitude towards self and others
- Improved self-image through formal education
- Independent decision-making on economic matters
- Role in decision making on policy matters
- Power to participate in economic decisions
- Access to better health care and health facilities

Once women start enjoying freedom in all these areas, we can say that they are empowered. It would contribute to better self-image, which will encourage her to perform better not only for the sake of herself but for the family and the society as a whole.

During the International Conference on Population and Development Program of Action, women's empowerment was defined as "the process by which women gain inner power to express and defend their rights and gain greater self-confidence, self-esteem and control over their own lives and personal and social relationships. Women empowerment is the process by which the unequal power relations are transformed in women's favour."

The known advantages of women empowerment are:

1. If women are empowered with education and life skills then they can discharge their duties very well.
2. If woman is educated she educates her children and the whole family stands to gain.
3. The woman can take up employment if she so desires, which would contribute to her family income and her own economic empowerment.
4. She is more equipped to handle life crisis situations.
5. She is aware of her rights, duties and privileges. She is a vigilant citizen and understands consumer rights, legal rights, social disparities and reckon health services.

Objectives of Women Empowerment

- Creating an environment through positive economic policies for full development of women to enable them to realize their full potential
- The *de-jure* and *de-fecto* enjoyment of all human rights and fundamental freedom by women on equal basis with men in all spheres – political, economic, social, cultural and civil
- Equal access to participation and decision making of women in social, political and economic life of the nation
- Equal access to women in health care, quality of education at all levels, career and vocational guidance, employment, equal remuneration, occupational health and safety, social security and public office etc.
- Strengthening legal systems aimed at elimination of all forms of discrimination against women
- Changing societal attitudes and community practices by active participation and involvement of both men and women
- Mainstreaming a gender perspective in the development process
- Elimination of discrimination and all forms of violence against women and the girl child, and
- Building and strengthening partnerships with civil society, particularly women's organization.

Dimensions of Women Empowerment

Main dimensions of women empowerment are as follows:

- Judicial Legal Systems
- Gender Equality
- Decision Making
- Political Empowerment
- Constitutional Provisions and Policies
- Economic Empowerment of Women
- Empowering Women in Poverty
- Social Empowerment of Women
- Globalization
- Women and Agriculture
- Women and Industries
- Health and Well Being
- Science and Technology
- Women in Difficult Circumstances

- Violence against Women
- Promotion of Women's Right as Human Rights

Empowering Women: International and National Strategies and Initiatives

International Efforts in the Process of Empowerment: The 20th century has witnessed the upsurge of women empowerment movement universally. The Universal Declaration of Human Rights (1948) reaffirming faith in the fundamental Human Rights, in the dignity and worth of the human person, and in the equal right of men and women, contemplated the entitlement of all cherished freedoms to all human beings with out any distinction of any kind, including discrimination based on sex. The World Conference on Human Right at Vienna in 1993 had declared the human right of women and the girl child to be "inalienable, integral and indivisible part of universal human rights" and eradication of any form of discrimination on the basis of sex, is the priority objective of the international community. The Convocation on the Elimination of All forms of Discrimination against Women (CEDAW), 1979 is United Nations landmark treaty marking the struggle for women's right. Described as the Bill of Rights for Women, it spells out what constitutes discrimination against women.

ASEAN ministers share best practices in advancing women's rights in national development planning.

United Nations, Bangkok, 15 November 2006 - Ministers and senior officials in charge of women empowerment and development from ASEAN countries shared experience and best practices at the "ASEAN High-Level Meeting on Gender Mainstreaming in the Context of CEDAW, BPFA and MDGs" on 15-16 November. Opened in Jakarta by Indonesia's Minister for Women Empowerment, Prof. Dr. Meutia Hatta, the meeting was jointly organized by the United Nations Development Fund for Women (UNIFEM) and ASEAN with the Ministry of Women Empowerment, Indonesia acting as host. The meeting was one of the regional activities to operationalise the Declaration on the Elimination of Violence against Women in ASEAN under the aegis of the ASEAN Committee on Women.

CEDAW is the Convention on the Elimination of all Forms of Discrimination against Women. All ten ASEAN Members Countries are among 184 States to have ratified this "women's bill of rights" which is a cornerstone of all UNIFEM programmes. The Beijing Declaration and Platform for Action (BPFA) is a document adopted by governments at the Fourth World Conference on Women that sets forth governments' commitments to enhance women's rights. The Millennium Declaration and Millennium Development Goals (MDGs) outline a set of time-bound and measurable goals and targets to promote gender equality and to combat poverty, hunger, disease, illiteracy and environmental degradation by 2015.

These three agreements form a set of mutually-supporting instruments that enable planners to link international conventions to national development planning when it comes to ensuring women's rights in plans, policies, legislation and programmes in all areas and at all levels. This ASEAN forum on this theme was co-hosted by the Ministry of Women Empowerment, Government of Indonesia where the women's Ministry has played a vital role in placing gender and women development on the national agenda, and this encouraging start can be reinforced by these three instruments," says Dr. Jean D' Cunha, Regional Program Director, UNIFEM East and Southeast Asia Regional Office.

Within ASEAN Indonesia, Cambodia and Thailand are the countries that have made efforts to address women's rights within the framework of these three international agreements. Minister of Women Empowerment Prof. Dr. Meutia Hatta said: "Indonesia's national policy formulation and planning that takes into account women's rights are reflected in various laws, regulations and development programmes, including economic empowerment of women through income generation activities, micro-credit facilities, less discriminatory labour regulations. We hope to learn how we can through the exchange of views and experience at this forum among our colleagues from ASEAN and experts from UNIFEM."

ASEAN Member Countries are committed to addressing and mainstreaming gender issues in the two ASEAN Declarations on the Elimination of Violence against Women in ASEAN. The implementation of these two declarations took place under two operational documents - the work plan on women's advancement and gender equality (2005-2010) and the work plan to operationalise the Declaration on Violence against Women (2006-2010).

The convening of the ASEAN High level Meeting on Gender Mainstreaming within the context of CEDAW, BFPA and MDGs offers a space for regional discussion where good practices or successes of Member Countries can be shared. It opened a forum for sharing challenges faced and finding solutions together in mainstreaming the gender concerns Furthermore, the coming together can regionally assist Member Countries to better coordinate (nationally and with each other) to meet respective commitments under the UN processes.

The majority of women in developing countries are in informal employment. In developed countries, part-time work and self-employment are a more important source of income for women then for men. Moreover, women generally earn less then men, have less access to quality jobs, and fewer opportunities for the education that could help.

The Palestinian women have used small loans to jump-start their food business and turn it into a profit-making venture. They find better, safer means of income. These are some of the finding of Progress of the World's Women 2005: Women, Work and Poverty, published by the UN Development Fund for Women (UNIFEM). The Report makes the case for an increased focus on women's economic security and argues that more should be done to achieve appropriate legal and social protection for women in the informal economy and ensure that their work is valued and supported in policy-making.

United Nations Development Fund for Women (UNIFEM) provides financial and technical assistance to innovative programmes and strategies that promote women's human rights, political participation and economic security. Within the UN system, UNIFEM promotes gender equality and links women's issues and concerns to national, regional, and global agendas by fostering collaboration and providing technical expertise on gender mainstreaming and women's empowerment strategies.

The ASEAN Committee on Women coordinates and monitors ASEAN cooperation in women's issues and concerns. The ACW meets regularly every year, and each Member Countries assume responsibilities of the ACW Chair on a rotational basis. The ACW monitors the progress made by ASEAN Member Countries in implementing or addressing key regional priorities identified in the 1998 Declaration on the Advancement of Women and the 2004 Declaration on the Elimination of Violence against Women in ASEAN.

National Efforts for Empowerment

1. **Judicial Legal Systems:** Legal-judicial system should be made more responsive and gender sensitive to women's needs, especially in cases of domestic violence and personal assault. New laws should be enacted and existing laws be reviewed to ensure that justice is quick and the punishments meted out to the culprits is commensurate with the severity of the offence.

The evolution of property rights in a patriarchal system has contributed to the subordinate status of women. The Policy would aim to encourage changes in laws relating to ownership of property and inheritance by evolving consensus in order to make them gender just.

2. **Gender Equality:** The concept of gender equality is a common concern all over the world. The same has now acquired new dimensions with the advent of Information and Communication Technology (ICT). The ICT has a potential to bring development for a nation. It can reduce trade distortions, poverty, empower weaker segments including women etc. The same is, however, possible only if a

nation follows sound ICT strategies and policies. We have to set our priorities to those areas where we are lagging far behind. One such area is the unequal access of ICT to women.

To orient ICT projects so that they address these areas, ICT project planning and implementation for social developments and gender equality must take place in a context which consists of five main components:

- Creating an enabling environment which supports and encourages strategies to promote women's equal access to and opportunity to benefit form ICT projects, as well as creating a regulation and policy environment which supports women's use of ICTs;
- Developing content which speaks to women's concerns and reflects their local knowledge, and which is of value for their daily lives, business enterprises, and family responsibilities;
- Supporting increased representation of women and girls in scientific and technical education, and using ICTs to promote their increased participation in education at all levels;
- Promoting increased employment in the IT sector for women and the use of ICTs for women SMEs.
- Implementing e-governance strategies which are accessible to women and promoting women's lobbying and advocacy activities.

Taking women's empowerment seriously means gender equality at the centre of the human development equation. Policies, programs and systems will be established to ensure mainstreaming of women's perspectives in all developmental processes, as catalysts, participants and recipients. Wherever there are gaps in policies and programmes, women's specific interventions would be undertaken to bridge these.

Coordinating and monitoring mechanisms will also be devised to assess from time to time the progress of such mainstreaming mechanisms. Women's issues and concerns as a result will specially be addressed and reflected in all concerned laws, sectoral policies, plans and programmes of action.

The past three decades have witnessed a steadily increasing awareness of the need to empower women through measures to increase social, economic and political equity, and broader access to fundamental human rights, improvements in nutrition, basic health and education. Along with awareness of the subordinate status of women has come the concept of gender as an overarching socio-cultural variable, seen in relation to other factors, such as race, class, age and ethnicity. Gender is not synonymous with women, nor is it a zero-sum game implying loss for men; rather, it refers to both women and men, and to their status, relative to each other. Gender equality refers to that stage of human social development at which "the rights, responsibilities and opportunities of individuals will not be determined by the fact of being born male of female," in other words, a stage when both men and women realize their full potential.

3. Decision-Making: Women's equality in power sharing and active participation in decision-making, including decision-making in political process at all levels will be ensured for the achievement of the goals of empowerment. All measures will be taken to guarantee women, equal access to and full participation in decision-making bodies at every level, including the legislative, executive, judicial, corporate, statutory bodies and also the advisory Commissions, Committees, Boards, Trusts etc. Affirmative action such as reservations/quotas in higher legislative bodies, will be considered whenever necessary on a time bound basis. Women-friendly personnel policies will also be drawn up to encourage women to participate effectively in the developmental process.

The Secretary-General's Report on equal participation of women and men in decision-making processes at all levels (document E/CN.6/2006/13) analyses the current situation of women in decision-making processes and the conditions required for achieving their successful political participation and leadership. The incremental changes over the past decades, according to the report, have been too slow. The concept of building a "critical mass" of women's leaders has proven to be an effective mobilization tool, and quotas have also been used very successfully in the political arena. However, even where women's numerical representation has increased, much more needs to be done to ensure effective participation and potential to influence decision-making processes. The Report also takes into account the linkages between the political and economic empowerment of women, which must also be recognized when considering the participation of women in decision-making.

Promoting greater participation of women in the decision-making process remains another major objective in several countries of the region towards the goal of empowering women. Awareness of the need for promoting the greater participation of women in the decision-making process is on the rise. In several countries of the region, women have reached the highest positions of political authority. Parliamentary representation is also on the rise in several countries. Yet, women by and large still find themselves excluded from the state or governments apparatus in many countries of the region. Regional experience suggests that women tend to do better in terms of participation in the decision making process when proactive policies are in place, backed up by a social consensus on the need for empowering women.

4. Political Empowerment: Political empowerment refers to the equitable representation of women in decision-making structures, both formal and informal, and their voice in the formulation of policies affecting their societies. The Inter-Parliament Union reports a world average of only 15.6 per cent in combined houses of parliament.

For centuries, women in this country have been socially and economically handicapped. They have been deprived of equal participation in the socio-economic activities of the nation. The Constitution of any country is supreme law of the land and is followed absolutely, subject to the limits provided in the solemn document itself. So much is the importance of the Constitution that if a statutory law is in conflict with it the same would be "unconstitutional" and void in nature. The Constitution is organic and living in nature. It is also well settled that the interpretation of the Constitution of India or statutes would change from time to time. Being a living organ, it is ongoing and with passage of time, law must change. New rights may have to be found out within the constitutional scheme.

The Constitution of India recognizes women as a class by itself and permits enactment of laws and reservations favouring them. Several articles in our Constitution make express provision for affirmative action in favour of women. It prohibits all types of discrimination against women and lays a carpet for securing equal opportunity to women discrimination against women and lays a carpet for securing equal opportunity to women in all walks of life, including education, employment and participation. Article 51 of the Constitution obligates the State to honour international law and treaty obligations. Our natural obligation to renounce practices derogatory to dignity of women has been elevated to the status of fundamental duty by Article 51-A. The Constitution of India recognizes equality of the sexes and in fact provides for certain provisions under the Chapter on Fundamental Rights more favourable to women but in actual practice they are observed more in breach than in compliance. In our society the freedom of women to seek employment outside the family is a major issue. This freedom is denied in many cultures and this attitude in itself is a serious violation of women's liberty and gender equality. The absence of this freedom militates against the economic empowerment of women, with many other deleterious consequences.

The position is worst when it comes to women and that too, rural women. In our society, whether they belong to the majority or the minority group, what is apparent is that there exists a great disparity in the matter of economic resourcefulness between a man and a woman. Our society is male dominated both economically and socially and women are assigned, invariably, a dependant role, irrespective of the class of society to which she belongs. It must be appreciated that a nation that does not respect the class of society to which she belongs cannot be described as a civilized nation at all. Such a nation cannot grow and develop and will ultimately perish due to its own rudimentary and tyrannical dogma. Thus, the national consensus should concentrate on betterment of women by suitably empowering them. The plight of the women, however, cannot be improved till they are duly represented in the "Power structure" of the nation. In a democratic country the voice of women can be heard only to the extent they are sharing the power structure in the supreme governance of the country. Thus, ICT can play a major role in women empowerment if they are provided employment opportunities at the village level after providing them suitable training. We have to open more village kiosks so that greater women participation can be there. This cannot happen till we first make the e-governance and ICT strategies and policies transparent and accountable. Mere computerization is not e-governance.

5. Constitutional Provisions and Policies: The principal of gender equality is enshrined in the Constitution of India (in the Preamble and fundamental rights) where by the Constitution upholds and grants equality to women. The National Commission for Women, which was set up in 1990 through an Act of Parliament to safeguard the rights and legal entitlements of women, is considered to be the apex body to ensure rights and legal work towards women empowerment. In terms of Five-Year Plans, the Fifth Five Year Plan (1974-78) is considered to be very crucial from the point of view of women development with 1975 being declared as International Year of Women. The 73rd and 74th Amendments of Constitution of India in 1993 are landmarks to ensure political empowerment of women. The 9th Plan also recommends the adoption of National Policy for the empowerment of women along with a well-defined Gender Development Index for the monitoring and evaluation of women's rights and empowerment. The ratification by the Government of India of various International Conventions like Convention on Elimination of All Forms of Discrimination Against Women (CEDAW) in 1993, speaks of the political will. The endorsement by the Government of various declarations consolidates the administrative willingness. The description of such provisions incorporates the perception of absolute women empowerment.

These provisions surely ensure of legal protection of women's rights, but socio-economic rights of freedom and decision-making is still not realized to the extent of social empowerment. One of the reasons is the rigid patriarchal structure of the Indian Society. The rate of illiteracy among women hampers the awareness and the claims of such provisions. The distinct socialization of girls from the beginning also contributes to the easy acceptance of suppression by women. The changing trends of education and employment among women have relatively transformed the situation towards the positive direction. However, the nature of problem has also changed its direction in the sense that crime against women at work place are on steep rise. The workable and pragmatic commitments of the Government of India at various forums and National Policy for the empowerment of women can prove to be a milestone in ensuring women's rights and facilitate women empowerment. Universalization of mother and child care program has to reach out to every corner of the country.

National Policy for the Empowerment of Women (2001): The goal of the National Policy for the Empowerment of Women is to bring about the advancement, development and empowerment of women. Some of the specific objectives of this policy are: a) creating an environment through positive economic and social policies for full development of women to enable them to realize their full potential, b) equal access to health care, quality education at all levels, career and vocational guidance etc. and c) elimination of discrimination and all forms of violence against women and girl child.

The Policy also provides for economic empowerment through poverty eradication, micro-credit programmes and training of women to facilitate them in playing efficient role in agriculture and industry. The social empowerment of women is facilitated through effective provisions of education, health, nutrition, drinking water and sanitation, gender sensitization, and elimination of all forms of violence against women - physical and mental, whether at domestic or societal levels, including those arising from customs, traditions and accepted practices. A National Resource Center for Women (NRCW) is being set up which will provide relevant technical back up for the successful implementation of the Policy. The Government has also committed for the following provisions to ensure women's rights and women empowerment. Some of the commitments are: To increase investment in education to 6 per cent of the GDP with major focus on women and the girl child.

6. Economic Empowerment of Women: India envisions a future in which Indian women are independent and self-reliant. Their participation in remunerative work in the formal and non-formal labour market has increased significantly in the past decade. Women's income is becoming very necessary to households of all types in the wake of globalization and changing economic structures.

It is estimated that India is home to 92 million working women, though 90 per cent of them are working in the unorganized sector. The female Work Participation Rate (WPR) increased from 14.2 per cent in 1971 to 22.3 per cent in 1991. Women's share in the organized sector meanwhile, increased from 11 per cent in 1971 to 15.9 per cent in 1997. Requisite steps have to be taken to recognize this and take cognizance while framing economic policies and programs.

The need of the hour is economic independence of women. To translate this hope into reality, the Department of Women and Child Development (DWCD) has taken up various projects directed towards advancement of women. Besides coordinating various programs, the Department monitors 27 beneficiary-oriented schemes. The concept of a 'Women Component Plan' was mooted in the Ninth, Plan document. This is an important strategy to ensure that not less than 30 per cent of funds/benefits from other development sectors flow to women.

The schemes include the Support for Training and Employment Program (STEP), which aims to raise the incomes of rural women by updating their skills in the traditional sectors, such as dairy development, animal husbandry sericulture, handloom and social forestry. Since its inception in 1987, this program has benefited 4,48,000 women.

Assistance has also been extended by the Norwegian Agency for Development Cooperation (NORAD) for training and skill development, and also for promotion of self-reliance through the generation of income for women in non-traditional trades. Till date, 1745 projects have been sanctioned to benefit 2,49,000 women.

Balika Samriddhi Yojana (BSY), the prosperity of the Girl Child was launched in 1997 and revamped in 1999, with the specific objective of changing attitudes towards the girl child, and improving their enrolment and retention in school.

The Department of Rural Employment and Poverty Alleviation of the Ministry of Rural Development has initiated several schemes in which 30 to 40 per cent of the benefits are reserved for women below the poverty line. The underlying philosophy of these schemes is to encourage entrepreneurship and self-help among women.

Swarna Jayanthi Gram Swarozgar Yojana Scheme (SGSY), the amended and merged version of the erstwhile Development of Women and Children in Rural Areas (DWCRA), Integrated Rural Development program (IRDP) and Training of Rural Youth for Self Employment (TRYSEM), was launched in April 1999. It is a holistic credit-cum-subsidy program, covering all aspects of self-employment. Under this Scheme, the stipulated 40 per cent reservation for women will be implemented through the panchayat samitis (local self-government).

Jawahar Rozgar Yojana (JRY) provides facilities for women through training and employment. The Indira Awas Yojana, an arm of the JRY, aims at providing houses free of cost to poor people. The houses are allotted to female members, or in the joint names of the husband and wife to enable women to own assets.

A new scheme, called the Trade-Related Entrepreneurship Assistance and Development (TREAD), was launched by the Government in 1998. It was designed to generate self-employment for 45,000 women in rural and urban areas. The package involves financial assistance and services through NGOs in the non-farm sector.

The National Bank for Agriculture and Rural Development (NABARD) links banks with self-help groups with the objective of meeting the credit needs of the poor. As many as 85 per cent of the groups linked with the banks are women's groups.

Women's development corporations set up in 19 States since 1986-87, have play a catalytic role in identifying women entrepreneurs as well as providing consultancy and other assistance. Support systems have been set up in the form of 841 working women's hostels for 59,591 working women with 301 creches/day centers for 7,878 children of working mothers.

In a landmark judgment in the Vishaka Case, the Supreme Court passed an order on 13 August 1997, laying down certain norms and guidelines to be followed by employees while tackling incidents of sexual harassment at workplace. The Supreme Court has, in March 2000, also ruled that Maternity Benefit Act, 1961, be extended to those women (muster roll) employees of municipal corporations and bodies who have been working on daily wages.

In 1998, the Central Government Service Rules made provision for paternity leave of 15 days - an important beginning in creating an environment conducive to the equal sharing of family responsibility. Employment exchanges take special care to cater to the employment needs of the women registered with them. Women's cell under the Directorate General of Employment and Training (DGE&T) coordinates with States for the vocational training of women.

Indira Mahila Yojana (IMY) was launched in 1995 in over 200 blocks of India, for the holistic empowerment of women. IMY is being implemented in 238 blocks and till now, 40,000 women's groups have been formed under the Scheme. Of these, 3,000 groups were formed in 1999-2000.

Rural Women's Development and Empowerment Project (Swa Shakti Project), was launched in 1998, for strengthening the process of empowerment of women in six States through the establishment of self-help groups.

Rashtriya Mahila Kosh (RMK), a national credit fund extends credit facilities to poor and needy women. The RMK has extended loans to 20,000 self help groups of women and has a membership of over 3,00,000. It is instrumental in encouraging women to take control of their own development, and helped build confidence and political awareness. Till today, the RMK has been able to sanction credit limits of more than Rs. 773.6 million, with the help of about 688 NGOs which it works through, and has reached out to more than 3,49,752 women.

At the initiative of the DWCD, the process of monitoring the implementation of 27 beneficiary-oriented schemes for women was reviewed by the Prime Minister's Office. The existing Review Committee has been renamed the Committee for Monitoring of Gender Mainstreaming in the Governments to reflect the changed focus.

A task force has been constituted in 1999 to review all existing legislations and government schemes with a view to enhancing the access of women to national resources and ensuring that they task force will also chalk out specific programs for observing the year 2001.as "Women's Empowerment Year". This is one of the most crucial areas of work that has been taken up by the Government. The primary aim is to make women economically independent and help them gain full confidence in themselves.

7. Empowering Women in Poverty: Significant progress has been achieved in alleviating the worst forms of poverty in many countries of the region through sustained economic growth supported by active and well targeted public policy. Progress in poverty alleviation also seems to be uneven, with many countries falling far behind. Of the poor, women constitute the majority, with the number of rural women in poverty rising over the last 20 years by about 50 per cent compared with an increase of about 25 per cent for rural men. Recent studies also indicate that the proportion of female-headed household has been increasing and a disproportionate number of those household are among the very poor. In the context of this, the importance of poverty reduction as a tool to empower women in poverty has been widely recognized.

The importance of poverty reduction as a goal to empower women has been widely recognized. However, in spite of the preponderance of the poor being female and the increasing feminization of poverty, anti-poverty interventions have tended to be gender blind, or at best gender neutral. Most countries lack a coherent, balanced agenda for combating female poverty.

It is therefore important that poverty reduction strategies be approached from a gender perspective and that the underlying causes of female poverty be addressed and measures to empower women to combat poverty be undertaken.

i) **Poverty Eradication:** Since women comprise the majority of the population below the poverty line and are very often in situations of extreme poverty, given the harsh realities of intra-household and social discrimination, macro economic policies and poverty eradication programmes will specifically address the needs and problems of such women. There will be improved implementation of programmes which are already women oriented with special targets for women. Steps will be taken for mobilization of poor women and convergence of services by offering them a range of economic and social options, along with necessary support measures to enhance their capabilities.

ii) **Micro-Credit:** In order to enhance women's access to credit for consumption and production, the establishment of new and strengthening of existing micro-credit mechanisms and micro-finance institution should be undertaken so that the outreach of credit is enhanced. Other supportive measures would be taken to ensure adequate flow of credit through extent financial institutions and banks, so that all women below poverty line have easy access to credit.

iii) **Women and Economy:** Women's perspectives should be included in designing and implementing macro-economic and social policies by institutionalizing their participation in such processes. Their contribution to socio-economic development as producers and workers should be recognized in the formal and informal sectors (including home based workers) and appropriate policies relating to employment and to her working conditions should be drawn up. Such measures could include :

- Reinterpretation and redefining of conventional concepts of work wherever necessary e.g. in the Census records, to reflect women's contribution as producers and workers.
- Preparation of satellite and national accounts.
- Developments of appropriate methodologies for undertaking (i) and (ii) above.

iv) **The Economic Participation of Women:** Their presence in the workforce in quantitative terms – is important not only for lowering the disproportionate levels of poverty among women, but also as an important step towards raising household income and encouraging economic development in countries as a whole.

Amartya Sen makes a compelling case for the notion that societies need to see women less as passive recipients of help, and more as dynamic promoters of social transformation, a view strongly stressed by a body of evidence suggesting that education, employment and ownership rights of women have a power influence on their ability to control their environment and contribute to economic development. Economic participation concerns should not only be actual number of women participating in the labour force, but also their remuneration on an equal basis. Worldwide, outside of the agricultural sector, in both developed and developing countries, women are still averaging slightly less than 78 per cent of the wages given to men for the same work, a gap which refuses to close in even the most developed countries.

Economic opportunity concerns the quality of women's economic involvement, beyond their mere presence as workers. This is a particularly serious problem in developed countries, where women may gain employment with relative ease, but where their employment is either concentrated in poorly paid or unskilled job "ghettos," characterized by the absence of upward mobility and opportunity. This is most commonly the result of negative or obstructive attitudes, and of legal and social systems which use maternity laws and benefits to penalize women economically for childbirth and child care responsibilities and discourage – or actively prevent – men from sharing family responsibilities.

The ghettoization of female lobour is a phenomenon which crosses all cultural boundaries, and professions, affecting women in virtually all countries. Internationally, women arc most often concentrated in "feminized" professions, such as nursing and teaching, office work, care of the elderly and disabled – termed "horizontal occupational segregation" – where they tend to remain in lower job categories than men. Typically, because these functions are carried out by women, they are the lowest paid, in addition to offering limited or no opportunity for advancement. The term "feminization of poverty" is often used to illustrate the fact that the majority of the 1.5 billion people living on US$1 a day or less are women and that the gap between women and men caught in the cycle of poverty has not lessened, but may well have widened in the past decade.

At the other end of the spectrum, advancement within professions, such as law, medicine and engineering, in which women are increasingly well represented in developed countries, is of great concern.

8. Social Empowerment of Women

- **Social Safety Net:** In addition, where many women have been forced in such circumstances to seek additional income outside the home, this has put pressure on girl children, who have to take up some of the activities of the household and child care otherwise performed by their mothers. It is widely acknowledged that in many Asian societies, especially South Asia, social and cultural norms are such that women and girl children face disproportionately excessive cuts in their food consumption when house hold per capita access to food declines. Where adjustment programmes have also tended to include effective cuts in public distribution system for food and essential items, these place a special burden on females with in family.

  There are also specific problem facing migrant women workers in the wake of the present economic crisis. In some instances, migrant workers could become the focus of local hostility with growing job losses. Returning workers face the added burden of re-establishing themselves economically and socially in their home countries. Measures such as forcible repatriation can become a problem if urgent measures are not adopted to safeguard the interests of the migrant workers.

- **Empowering Women to Transform Society:** Empowering women is critical to advancing human development and achieving progress towards the MDGs. Gender equality is and will always remain an end in itself. But we must also recognize that when women suffer abuse and discrimination, when they do not play an active role in shaping the world around them, everyone in society loses out. Making headway in alleviating poverty and promoting equitable growth is inextricably linked to improving women's lives and increasing their participation in decision-making. Women's empowerment has raised economic productivity and reduced infant mortality. It contributes to improved health and nutrition and increases the chances of education for the next generation.
- **Education:** Equal access to education for women and girls should be ensured. Special measures should be taken to eliminate discrimination, universalize education, eradicate illiteracy, create a gender-sensitive educational system, increase enrolment and retention rates of girls and improve the quality of education to facilitate life-long learning as well as developments of occupation/vocation/technical skills by women. Reducing the gender gap in existing policies should be achieved with a special focus on girls and women, particularly those belonging to weaker sections including the Scheduled Castes/Scheduled Tribes/Other Backward Classes/Minorities. Gender sensitive curricula should be developed at all levels of educational system in order to address sex stereotyping as one of the causes of gender discrimination.
- **Education and Training of Women:** A project on technology exchange for food processing and establishment of a database on grass-roots organizations to strengthen women entrepreneurs was completed in 1998. It has provided hands-on, practical training and exposure in the area of low-cost and appropriate technologies in the food processing sector to over 130 NGO-associated women and men. ESCAP is currently implementing two projects to promote literacy for women in 3 sub regions and 10 countries in the region. The projects in South Asia, involving Bangladesh, India, Nepal and Pakistan, focus on post-literacy programme development.
- **Educational Attainment:** Educational attainment is, without doubt, the most

fundamental prerequisite for empowering women in all spheres of society, for without education of comparable quality and content to that given to boys and men, and relevant to existing knowledge and real needs, women are unable to access well-paid, formal sector jobs, advance within them, participate in, and be represented in government and gain political influence. Moreover, the risk increases for society as a whole that the next generation of children will be similarly ill-prepared. If, as a broad body of empirical work has shown, education and literacy reduces mortality rates of children – including the bias toward female child mortality – and helps reduce fertility rates, the importance of literacy for women is all the more greater, considering that women still constitute two-thirds of the world's illiterate population.

Information and communication technologies, which have become a potent driving force in the development process, represents yet another dimension in which a knowledge gap has emerged between women and men: a gender based digital divide. Countless women in the developing world are further removed from the information age because of their lower levels of education and deeply ingrained negative attitudes towards other forms of achievement. "Without access to information technology, an understanding of its significance and the ability to use it for social and economic gain, women in the developing world will be further marginalized from the mainstream of their communities, countries and the world."

9. Globalization: Globalization has presented new challenges for the realization of the goal of women's equality, the gender impact of which has not been systematically evaluated fully. However, from the micro-level studies that were commissioned by the Department of Women & Child Developments, it is evident that there is a need for re-framing policies for access to employment and quality of employment. Benefits of the growing global economy have been unevenly distributed leading to wider economic disparities, the feminization of poverty, increased gender inequality through often deteriorating working conditions and unsafe working environment especially in the informal economy and rural areas. Strategies should be designed to enhance the capacity of women and empower them to meet the negative social and economic impacts, which may flow from the globalization process.

10. Women and Agriculture: In view of the critical role of women in the agriculture and allied sectors, as producers, concentrated efforts should be made to ensure that benefits of training, extension and various programmes reach them in proportion to their numbers. The programmes for training women in soil conservation, social forestry, dairy developments and other occupations allied to agriculture like horticulture, livestock including small animal husbandry, poultry, fisheries etc. should be expanded to benefit women workers in the agriculture sector.

11. Women and Industry: The important role played by women in electronics, information technology and food processing, agro industry and textiles has been crucial to the development of these sectors. They would be given comprehensive support in terms of labour legislation, social security and other support services to participate in various industrial sectors. Women at present cannot work in night shift in factories even if they wish to. Suitable measures should be taken to enable women to work on the night shift in factories. This should be accompanied with support services like security, transportation etc.

- **Support Services for Women in Industries:** The provision of support services for women, like child care facilities, including creches at work places and educational institutions, homes for the aged and the disabled should be expanded and improved to create an enabling environment and to ensure their full cooperation in social, political and economic life. Women friendly personnel policies should also be drawn up to encourage women to participate effectively in the developmental process.

12. Health and Well Being

- **Health:** A holistic approach to women's health which includes both nutrition and health services should be adopted and special attention be given to the needs of women and the girls at all stages of the life cycle. The reduction of infant mortality and maternal mortality which are sensitive indicators of human development is a priority concern. This policy reiterates the national demographic goals for Infant Mortality Rate (IMR), Maternal Mortality Rate (MMR) set out in the National Population Policy 2000.

  Women should have access to comprehensive, affordable and quality health care. Measures should be adopted that take into account the reproductive rights of women to enable them to exercise informed choices. Their vulnerability to sexual and health problems together with endemic, infectious and communicable diseases such as malaria, TB and water borne diseases as well as hypertension and cardio-pulmonary diseases should be taken care of. The social developmental and health consequences of HIV/AIDS and other sexually transmitted diseases should be tackled from a gender perspective. To effectively meet problems of infant and maternal mortality and early marriage, the availability of good and accurate data at micro level on deaths, birth and marriages is required. Strict implementation of registration of births and deaths should be ensured and registration of marriages would be made compulsory.

In accordance with the commitment of the National Population Policy (2000), to population stabilization, the Policy recognizes the critical need of men and women to have access to safe, effective and affordable methods of family planning of their choice and the need to suitably address the issues of early marriages and spacing of children. Interventions such as spread of education, compulsory registration of marriage and special programmes like BSY should impact on delaying the age of marriages so that by 2010 child marriages are eliminated.

Women's traditional knowledge about health care and nutrition should be recognized through proper documentation and its use should be encouraged. The use of Indian and alternative systems of medicine should be enhanced within the framework of overall health infrastructure available for women.

- **Nutrition :** In view of the high risk of malnutrition and disease that women face at all the three critical stages viz. infancy and childhood, adolescence and reproductive phase, focused attention should be paid to meeting the nutritional needs of women at all stages of the life cycle. This is also important in view of the critical link between the health of adolescent girls, pregnant and lactating women with the health of infant and young children. Special efforts should be made to tackle the problems of macro and micro nutrient deficiencies especially amongst pregnant and lactating women as it leads to various diseases and disabilities.

  Intra-household discrimination in nutritional matters vis-à-vis girls and women should be ended through appropriate strategies. Widespread use of nutrition education should be made to address the issues of intra-household imbalances in nutrition and the special needs of pregnant and lactating women. Women's participation should also be ensured in the planning, superintendence and delivery of the system.
- **Drinking water and Sanitation :** Special attention should be given to the needs of women in the provision of safe drinking water, sewage disposal, toilet facilities and sanitation with in accessible reach of household, especially in the planning delivery and maintenance of such services.
- **Housing and Shelter:** Women's perspectives should be included in housing policies, planning of housing colonies and provision of shelter both in rural and urban areas. Special attention should be given for providing adequate and safe housing and accommodation for women including single women, heads of households, working women, students, apprentices and trainees.
- **Environment:** Women should be involved and their perspectives reflected in

the policies and programmes for environment, conservation and restoration. Considering the impact of environmental factors on their live hoods, women's participation should be ensured in the conservation of the environment and control of environmental degradation. A vast majority of rural women still depend on locally available non-commercial sources of energy such as animal dung, crop waste and fuel wood.

13. Science and Technology: Programmes should be strengthened to bring about a greater involvement of women in science and technology. These shall include measures to motivate girls to take up science and technology for higher education and also ensure that development projects with scientific and technical inputs involve women fully. Efforts to develop a scientific temper and awareness should also be stepped up. Special measures should be taken for their training in areas where they have special skills like communication and information technology. Efforts to develop drudgery should be given a special focus too.

14. Mass Media: Media will be used to portray images consistent with human dignity of girls and women. The policy shall specifically strive to remove de-meaning, de-grading and negative conventional stereotypical images of women and violence against women. Private sector partners and media networks should be involved at all levels to ensure equal access for women particularly in the areas of information and communication technologies. The media should be encouraged to develop codes of conduct, professional guidelines and other self regulatory mechanisms to remove gender stereotypes and promote balanced portrayals of women and men.

15. Women in Difficult Circumstances: In recognition of the diversity of women's situations and in acknowledgement of the needs of specially disadvantaged groups, measures and programmes shall be undertaken to provide them with special assistance. These groups include women in extreme poverty, destitute women in less developed regions, the disabled widows, elderly women, single women in difficult circumstances, women heading households, those displaced from employment migrants, women who are victims of marital violence, deserted women and prostitutes etc.

16. Violence against Women: All forms of violence against women, physical and mental, whether at domestic or societal levels, including those arising from customs, traditions, its accepted practices shall be dealt with effectively with a view to eliminate its incidence. Institutions and mechanisms/schemes for assistance should be created and strengthened for prevention of such violence, including sexual harassment at work place and customs like dowry; for the rehabilitation of the victims of violence and for taking effective action against the perpetrators of such violence a special emphasis should also be laid on programmes to deal with trafficking of women and girls.

Violence against women constitutes another form of gross violation of women's right as human rights. It has become a grave social problem, requiring urgent attention. Although the problem in the region is not new, it has so far attracted limited social recognition and legal redress owing to the complexities of patriarchal values, traditions, norms and standards. Even laws often discriminate against women and offenders go unpunished. Violence against women takes a variety of forms, including physical, mental and sexual abuse. While many countries in the region are engaged in combating violence against women in cooperation with NGOs and women's organizations, there is a need for more cooperation at the regional and sub regional levels, particularly in those areas which affect women from several countries.

17. Promotion of Women's Right as Human Rights: The promotion of women's right was one of the main objectives of the Beijing Platform for Action. In that context, ratification and implementation of the Convention on the Elimination of All Forms of Discrimination against Women has become as important instrument in empowering women in the region. As of January 1999, the Convention had been ratified by over two thirds of ESCAP members and associate members. Of those, nearly one third have entered reservations for reasons of religion, culture and conflict of law. Such reservations and/or declarations effectively dilute the human rights standards set by the Convention for women in those countries and also for the region. Even where ratification has been without reservation, implementation has been slow in a number of countries, there by allowing existing discriminatory practices against women to continue under the sanction of religious principal or cultural and customary values. Given the differences and the degree of sensitivities posed by the cultural and religious particularities of individual countries of sub-regions, a rights-based approach to gender equality may provide some common ground which can yield positive results.

In recent years, trafficking in women has attracted a great deal of attention. It is now widely seen as one of the worst forms of the violation of women's right. It has become a serious problem with out border, affecting countries within Asia as well as other parts of the world. Women have been trafficked for prostitution and other forms of sexual exploitation such as sex tourism and pornography, domestic workers, labourers in sweat shops and on construction sites and as beggars and brides. The increasing use of new information technologies, in particular, the Internet, presents a new dimension to the problem faced. Poverty and economic deprivation have also subjected women to trafficking. In many instances, trafficked women are becoming victims of highly organized networks. Women victims in these situations lack legal protection and legal rights. Although reporting on the problem has increased, it is unclear whether this is a reflection of a growing problem or whether it is the result of increased attention to the problem at the national, regional and international levels. Quantitative estimates of the dimensions of the problem are not available as there are almost no reliable estimates, although many countries are beginning to compile information on the problem. The General Assembly, in its resolution 52/98 of 12 December 1997, emphasized the need for more concerted and sustained national, regional and international action over the alarming levels of trafficking in women and girls.

- **Ageing Women:** As ageing in general becomes a major issue with serious social and economic consequences, the emerging challenge of a growing number of ageing women needs to be recognized. Several countries would find it difficult to cope with increase in life expectancy that has created conditions in which the region's population can be expected to age rapidly. Sex differentials in mortality imply that the number of older women will be higher than that of older men. Ageing women are increasingly finding themselves having to depend on their children and other relatives for economic survival and social safety nets, an increasing number of older women will find themselves without any economic and social support. Appropriately designed policies and systems are needed to cope with this important emerging challenge.
- **Rights of Girl Child:** All forms of discrimination against the girl child and violation of her rights shall be eliminated by undertaking strong measures both preventive and punitive with in and outside the family. These would relate specifically to strict enforcement of laws against prenatal sex selection and the practices of female foeticide, female infanticide, child marriage, child abuse and child prostitution etc. Removal of discrimination in the treatments of the girl child with in family and outside, and projection of a positive image of the girl child shall be actively fostered. There should be a special emphasis on the needs of the girl child and earmarking of substantial investments in the areas relating to food and nutrition, health and education and in vocational education. In implementing programmes for eliminating child labour, there should be a special focus on girl child.

Challenges

1. **Challenges: Filling the Half-empty Glass:** A recent analysis of national reports on progress toward meeting the Millennium Development Goal 3

(Promote, Gender Equality & Empower Women) (MDGs) found that "Despite the rights-based perspective reflected by most reports in discussions on Goal, the approach to women in discussions under other goals continues to be instrumental rather than rights-based. Examples are the discussions on child mortality in several reports, where women's lack of knowledge of care and feeding practices is most commonly identified as a barrier to achieving the goal. Such a formulation ignores the gendered variables that mediate child survival, while accepting without comment the invisibility of fathers in parenting and care."

Even 10 years after Cairo, the report found that "women are still being seen in terms of their vulnerabilities" and cast most often within their traditional roles of mothers or as victims - not as actors in the development process.

Other impediments to progress include the continued lack of good quality data disaggregated by sex, the paucity of financial and technical resources for women's programmes at both international and national levels, and confusion about the relative merits of gender mainstreaming versus women focused programmes.

Data without sex-disaggregated data, it becomes impossible to put benchmarks on or monitor policy or programme effectiveness. In most countries, serious gaps still exist in available data on women's economic activity and decision-making ability and on the differential impacts of anti-poverty or other programmes. Data that allows cross-country comparisons is hardly available. Efforts currently under way to fill these gaps need to be prioritized and strengthened.

2. Limited Resources: A second ongoing problem is the paucity of resources. Many commitments made by governments and agencies cannot be met because of the lack of funds. National programmes promoting women's advancement are particularly susceptible to arbitrary budget cuts in times of fiscal stringency.

A particularly unfortunate trend is the tendency to cut funding to women-focused programmes or agencies based on the argument that gender is now being mainstreamed throughout the institution.

3. Gender Inequality: Gender inequality is a major obstacle to ending poverty and meeting the MDG targets. An effective way of tackling this gender gap is by helping governments develop budgets that reflect the specific needs and interests of women. Analyzing national budgets from the perspective of their impact on women and men, boys and girls, promoting equity across the development spectrum by identifying who is allocated what in diverse development fields, including education, health and employment, are areas that are crucial to empowering people and reducing poverty. Through a partnership with the Japan Women in Development Fund, UNDP sponsored the training of development practitioners, economists and representatives from ministries of finance from more than 50 countries in gender budgeting. Today, an international pool of over 90 specialists are engaged with their own countries in spreading the knowledge they have gained and providing technical supports to carry out gender budget audits.

Governments and non-governments representatives from 14 countries of the region adopted the Bangkok Accord and Plan of Action to Combat Trafficking in women at two-day Regional Conference on Trafficking in women, held at Bangkok in November 1998. The Bangkok Accord and Plan of Action represents regional consensus on joint action needed at the national, sub-regional and regional levels to tackle trafficking in women. The adopted Plan of Action is divided into two parts, action at the national level and those at the sub-regional and multilateral levels. At the national level, comprehensive humanitarian treatment of victims, repatriation and reintegration, sanctions against traffickers, medical and psychological intervention, information and monitoring mechanisms and participation of concerned parties is important. At the other levels, provisions includes creation of sub-regional, coordination and cooperation among international agencies to maximize existing resources by avoiding duplication of activities and approaching the issue from new dimensions and perspectives, such as promotion of human security and combating and preventing organized crime.

A sub-regional workshop on eliminating violence against women was held at Dhaka in December 1997 as part of phase two of the project on promotion of women's right as human rights focused on violence against women (phase II). NGOs from six countries is South Asia participated in reviewing gender discriminatory laws as they relate to women in the context of violence against women and trafficking in women and girls. The Project aimed at assisting policy makers and NGOs in their consciousness-raising activities on violation of women's human rights, with special emphasis on physical and psychological violence against women. Activities included documentation of successful practices in the prevention and elimination of violence against women in the sub-region and proposed recommendations to governments, NGOs and international organizations in increasing awareness about many forms of violence against women, acceleration of the formulation of laws on the elimination of violence against women, revision of gender discriminatory laws and strengthening of networking among governments and NGOs working in this area.

A project on the promotion of the Convention of the Elimination of All Forms of Discrimination against Women through women in development NGO-networks in the Pacific is being implemented to facilitate the promotion of the

Convention in the four Pacific island countries which have ratified it: Fiji, Papua New Guinea, Samoa and Vanuatu. At this stage, national workshops are being conducted following the identification of national NGOs in the four countries. Efforts will be made to integrate the promotion of the Convention into existing regular programmes of NGOs and government agencies. The activities of the project were reviewed at a sub-regional meeting of Pacific NGOs in 1999.

ESCAP also participated in consultative meeting on the implementation of Convention mechanisms in the Pacific, held at Nadi' Fiji in July 1998. This activity was organized jointly by SPC, the United Nations Development Programme and ESCAP. The meeting provided an opportunity for exchange of information on the implementation of the Convention between the countries that have ratified the instrument, those countries planning ratification in the near future, and those contemplating ratification.

4. Inequality in Health Programmes: Many programmes to reduce unintended pregnancy work in settings where women have little autonomy and tend not to be assertive about their relationship with husbands or health care providers.

Interventions such as the Better Life Options Programme for young women in India, the Programme for Adolescent Mothers in Jamaica and the Training of Trainers in Health and Empowerment in Mexico aim to strengthen women's practical skills in long-term thinking, problem-solving and decision-making, and to persuade them that they are capable of making important decisions about their lives and health.

Some successful programmes educate women about reproductive and human rights; others training in literacy, employment skills, legal rights, parenting child health, and social mobilization.

Road Ahead

Old theories, stereo typed ideas and conventional methods of action are being challenged to new laws. For recognizing the status of women & empowering them, following actions are required:

- **Advent of ICT:** The global scenario and many unexplored areas are now open for encashment. It is for us to utilize the benefits to the maximum possible extent. The best art about Information & Communication Technology (ICT) is that it is capable of various adjustments as per needs and requirement of women. So much so that it can be operated from every home irrespective of its location. This means that even the traditional and orthodox families can allow the women to participate and use ICT from their respective homes. In India there is an abundance of "women entrepreneurs" who are capable to making their mark at the global level. However, the awareness and facilities are missing drastically. The national policies and strategies have not yet considered this unexplored potential pool of intellectual inputs. With simple training and awareness programmes we can make a big difference. Further, we can also encourage the establishment of "Small and Medium Enterprises" (SMEs), Small Scale Industries (SSIs), etc. The need of the hour is to show a positive will to achieve this much needed purpose.

- **Mainstreaming Efforts:** Gender mainstreaming became the approach of choice in the 1990s in response to the recognition that women-focused programmes or agencies are easy to isolate or marginalize. However, gender mainstreaming is a difficult process and one in which good practices are still evolving.

  The UNFPA Global Survey found considerable shortcomings in understanding of what a gender equity approach means and how to operationalize it within programmes and policies as called for by the ICPD. Mainstreaming efforts, undertaken without a women's agency to back it up, can be unfocused and even easier to ignore than women-focused initiatives. What is required is a combination of mainstreaming efforts (with a clear operations research approach to determine what works and what doesn't and why within key institutions (13) and a well-funded and resourced women's machinery (including ministries for women's affairs or gender equality and focal points for gender issues within ministries, commissions and departments) that has the technical capacity and political placement to spearhead policies and programmes.
- **Political Will:** Behind these factors lie the questions of political clout and commitment. In situations where a vocal national women's movement is able to advocate for needed policies, programmes and resources, forward movement can be quick. In other situations, NGOs or other civil society organizations are running interesting programmes for gender equality, but most are not scaled up into government supported programmes. However, even in situations where the women's movement is not strong, political leadership can play an important role in advocating for gender equality and women's empowerment at the policy level.
- **Educating a Woman Means Educating a Family:** We know very well that a society cannot develop without the development of its womenfolk. The Constitution of India enjoins upon every citizen the duty to "renounce any practice derogatory to the dignity of the women." Our religious scriptures also accord due respect to women and assert that God lives where women are

worship.

In the true spirit, the principle of basic equality of sexes has never been put into practice. This is not possible without the development of women. For this, education of women is a must. Educate a man, and you educate one person. Educate a woman and you educate the whole family. This is a well said dictum.

- **Awaken Her Socially and See the Difference:** Gender discrimination has been a universal phenomenon in human history since times immemorial. On account of her biological constitution, social taboos and scriptural sanction, the social position of woman has always been considered inferior and subordinate to man in society. With the existence and advent of old values organization, industrialization, urbanization, disintegration of joint families, economic and technical developments, pressures of consumer society, more opportunities for work, development of means of communication and transportation and social mobility, a great change has occurred in the attitude towards women. Subsequently, the position of women has certainly been enhanced.

  We need more opportunities for the development of women entrepreneurship in the socio-economic, industrial and commercial spheres so that women can play a definite role in the economic development of the country and contribute significantly. The women should not be taken as an object of liability, property or a sex symbol but as an equal human being. Although she has awakened to her potentialities, she still needs more awareness and alertness about her rights and duties.

- **Man's Psyche Must Change:** 21st century must become synonymous with the time the woman finally got her rightful place in the society and her status at home will largely determine her standing in the world. Respect for a women, her needs and aspirations are essential because only then can she give her best to the society. A happy woman will make a loving home and bring up sons and daughters who have a healthy outlook towards life and are not scared to denounce the evils afflicting every little step of our walk towards a peaceful existence.

- **Change the Patriarchal System:** Whether out of convenience, or conviction, the traditional Indian society over the centuries has been "Unfair" to the fair sex and "discrimination against women has its roots in the tradition in which parents watch with tears in their eyes the birth of a female child and are thrilled if a male child is born". If we expect a fair deal from society, we will have to change the patriarchal system.

- **Administrative Will:** One of the biggest obstacles in the way of emancipation of women in this materialistic world is the evil of dowry. Worse is when at times even women play a role, whether active or passive, in the perpetration of this practice. To save the women from this malpractice, strong administrative actions are required to be implemented.
- **A Comprehensive Legislation is Required:** "Equality to all" as promised in our Constitution, still evades, Indian women. Strong legislation is required to protect their rights. Women do not lag behind their male counterparts. The Indian woman has not only to liberate herself from this suffocation, but also has to fight the forces of rural and urban violence. The Central Social Welfare Ministry and the National Commission for Women are putting in creditable efforts, but a lot remains to be achieved.
  India is a vast country and we have plenty of intelligent, talented and socially-committed women, who should come forward and try to improve the lot of Indian women. The topic of reservation for Indian women is still a talk and needs to be given a definite shape. A comprehensive legislation, if brought forward, can go a long way in improving the condition of Indian women. It has taken years for the Indian women to speak up for their cause, and the only way this confidence can be further kept is by making them self-reliant.
- **No Social Oppression:** Despite the Constitutional provisions, we continue to have inequality and women are treated as inferior and subservient beings. Men in our society do not consider women their equals, and when a woman tries to assert this equality in family there is a tremendous backlash. This is a basic factor behind all crimes against women. Perhaps, people should be more humane, compassionate and honest in all their dealings, and they should be more pleasant to each other. The society needs to move from consumerism to self limitation. Society has become more operative to women because of materialism.
- **Give Equality and Respect:** The plight of women in India is a sad reflection on our society. By overlooking the injustices meted out to them at the social, political and economic levels, the state becomes party to the discrimination being faced by women in this "man's world". Despite the laws enacted to give equality to women in all spheres of life they are denied the basic right to live with dignity. Society has not recognized the contribution of women. It is time that the invisibility and marginalization that has been her lot till now gives way to the woman getting their dues. The contradictions inherent in our society wherein goddesses and cows are worshipped but living girls and women are bereft of a respectable existence must end. People are quick to

point a finger at the woman but nobody extends the hand of support. What is expected is support and help, not protection. Before the situation goes worse, all agents of socialization viz., schools, religion, home, politics, etc. must be activated to ensure fair deal for this section of society which has been battered for ages.

- **Recognize the Dual Role of Women:** The perception of society should be one which is free of class consciousness, gender bias, communal prejudices and exploitation of all kinds. The society should represent a truly adroit humanity which promotes social harmony in thought and deed by offering equal opportunities to its members, irrespective of the gender, cast and creed. In keeping with our tradition and cultural heritage, a genuine community feeling of mutual respect, trust and understanding is expected from the society.
- **Accept Her as *Shakti*:** To demand peace from others, we don't need to display our capacity to destroy. India is to remember that for us, power is *shakti*, power in female form, a creative power in peaceful form. We cannot create nuclear disarmament through nuclear explosions. A feminist has said "You cannot break the master's house using the master's tools" Such movements need to be launched on a war-footing for granting economic and social justice to women. The educated Indian women today is full of power and vision and none can match her prowess when challenged. Basically, what is required today is to bring an awakening among them by providing ample opportunities for education and awareness of their rights.

References

Armin Rahul, Becker Stan and Byes Abdul, "NGO-Promoted Micro credit programs and women's empowerment in Rural Bangladesh: The Journal of Developing Areas, Winter 1998 : 221-236.

Batiwala, Sri Latha "The meaning of women's empowerment New concepts from action" Pp 127-138 in population policies reconsidered : Health, empowerment and right. G. Sen, A Germain, & L.C. Chen, eds. Cambridge MA : Harvard University Press. 1997

Empowerment of Women & Human Rights . The Indian Journal of Home Science an official Publication of the Home Science Association of India, Vol. 27, No. 1 & 2, Dec. 2001 Published by the Home Science Association of India.

Empowerment of women in Asia and the Pacific http:/www.unescap.org/55/e 1133e.htm, 01/23/2007.

FAD/OE-, The Republic of India - Tamil Nadu Women's Development Project:- Completion Evaluation, Report 340- in Rome, April. 2000

George Abraham, "empowerment of women in Rural India." Paper presented at the conference of empowerment of women in Developing countries, Action Alliance on women's Health, Santa Fe. New Mexico, USA-26-27.

Ghosh J. "Economic empowerment of women" Paper Presented at UN Economic and Social Cfor Asia and the Pacific Conference. 1999

Hashemi Syed, Sydney Ruth Schuler and Ann Riley "Rural Credit Programs & Women's empowerment in Bangladesh" World Development, Volume 2n. 4: 635-653. 1996

Jaya Prakash Deverinda : Status of Indian women and the role of legislation-from Internet. Goggle Search.

Malhotra, Anju & Mark Mathur, "Do Schooling and work empower women in developing countries? Gender and Domestic Decisions in Sri Lanka." Sociological forum,: 12(4) 599-630, 1997

National organization for women 2005. "10 for change" on line at http:/www.10 for change. org/issue/violence brief pdf.

National Policy for the empowerment of women, 2001

National Policy of Education 1986.

Page Manette and Ezuba Chery. "Empowerment : What is it? Journal of extension, October, Volume 37,5. 1999

Praveen Dalal all rights reserved with the author managing partner Perry 4 Law, Law Firm, New Delhi India.

Tamil Nadu women's Development Project: IFAD/OE, The Republic of India: Completion Evaluation, Report 340- in Rome, April. 2000

The women's place in society - The Global Gender Gap Report 2006.

Towards the empowerment of Indian women send E-mail to BSS with questions or comments about this website. Publish on March 13, 2001.

Uniform Progress of the World's women 2000. Biennial Report. on line at http:/www.unpacca/wagegaph/html, 2000

Vimla Dang, Sharmila Joshi, M.L. Kak & Sheila didi 50 years of Indian Independence. This issue which focuses on women & Society was published on June 19, 1998.

Wage Equality between women & men for similar work. Executive opinion suelley 2004

Women Empowerment: A Challenge for the Home Scientist, National Seminar 7 to 9 Jan 2007, Souvenir, Dayalbagh Educational Institute Deemed University, Dayal Bagh, Agra.

Women's Economic Empowerment Through Co-Operative Farming Vocational Training & Business Development, Document 28974 Expires Sunday, December 31, 2006.

Women's Empowerment year 2001, Chapter-17 Page 201-215, Women & Child development department, Minister of Human Resource Development India- Annual Report 2001-2002

World Bank, Engendering Development : Through Gender Equality in Rights, Resources & Voice, New York - Oxford University Press, 2001.

World health organization/UNICEF. 1996 Revised 1990 estimates of maternal mortality. A new approach by WHO and UNICEF. Geneva WHO/UNICEF April. 1996

29

Towards Women Empowerment

Manjari Acharya and Rupal N. Thakkar

The issue of women empowerment has received perhaps most attention in today's development debate that is fairly reflected in the contemporary development literature. Women empowerment is not too old a phenomenon. In oriental belt of globe, it has got currency only in the recent past. Even the western thinkers looked at woman empowerment in the second half of the last century. Group of western development experts in research notice that women's participation in the development process was lacking. Real development happens only when women become integrated. Women in Development (WID) has set a specific trend in including women in the theories of development. In 1980s women empowerment has acquired a strong ground. It is usually assumed that gender discrimination will evaporate itself if women perform their duties and activities in development along with their male counterparts. A woman in development does not only speak of socio-economic and political development but also of domestic uplifts. Since its inception, women development has often been used along with welfare, poverty alleviation, participation, development and many more, until now it has assumed various facets. It has to be perceived and realized as a whole that includes social, psychological, economic and political facets.

The concept of women empowerment originates from the idea of the Brazilian educationist Paulo Freire. Empowerment as a form of development change is brought about by local problem solving efforts and techniques. The term "Empowerment" is frequently used to describe a process where in the power-less gain greater share of control over resources and decision making, and since women are generally accepted as being the most powerless members of the opposed classes. Empowerment has been described as nurturing, liberating, energizing the un-affluent and the un-powerful people. (Barkat et.al.1994) In a common sense, empowerment can be defined as a process of achieving more controlling power to face the question on existing power and over the source of power. Empowerment is a process and, at the same time, the result of the process. It is the process of challenging existing power relation and of gaining graters control over the source of power. (Batliwala, 1994)

Women empowerment is commonly associated with women's struggle for social justice and equality. It is a process aimed at changing the nature and direction of systematic process that marginalize women and other disadvantaged section of the society. Empowerment is one type of perseverance to achieve strength through which a woman can establish her control on various assets; the concept empowerment in this sense is to confer power on controlling the wealth and taking decision (Rahman, 1997)

Empowerment means emancipation of women and harmonious co-existence with men in the society. Power provides social recognition, dignity, prosperity, property, value and security; hence empowerment has acquired a considerable aura of responsibility and social status in the development vocabulary. (Tondon, 1995)

Empowerment is a way of acquiring the ability and opportunity to participation in decision-making and implementation; and influencing the decision with proper knowledge self-dignity and self-confidence. From women's perspective if we look at power, it is being able to contribute to society at all levels. UNDP (1994) claims that empowerment enables individual or group to change balance of power in the society and redistributes power from the powerful to powerless.

Johnson (1992) stated that the prime aim of empowerment is to have self-reliance. This self-reliance mainly refers to individual's economic independence.

Shetty (1991) expressed that empowerment refers to a complete change of social and economic attitude towards women. Empowerment guides women to know and have clear view of formal and informal choices, which let them have insightful withstand against any form of oppression.

Moser (1993) has classified demands of women into parts; one is strategic- a complete emancipation from male domination and other is practical that is made out in the context of present problems. To Moser, strategic demands are not considered in the formation of development plans because development planners do not consider the fact such as women's unpaid service to men, living with them and suffering under male dominations.

Women Empowerment Approach

Thoughts on women empowerment have generally been flourished more in the hands of the Third World feminist writers and grassroots development organizations than in the hands of western feminists. (Moser 1991)

In the context of this, the empowerment approach comes from women's groups who seek to empower themselves through greater self-reliance. They also seek women to gain control of and access to resources. This approach differs from the Equity approach in origin and strategy. The Empowerment approach recognizes the triple role of women and seeks to meet strategic practical needs. (Unnayan Padokkhep, 1995)

The Empowerment approach stresses on the liberation and strength for women independently without having assistance from males. This empowerment approach, the case as such, needs to provide emphasis both on the short term and long term plans of action.

Aims of Women Empowerment

Women empowerment aims at achieving a number of objectives. In broad head women empowerment proceeds to: overcome patriarchal values and causes of women subordination and then to establish women's rights; to bring about changes in the family, society, class, religion, caste, manner, politics and economy, and to amend education, media and law; attain control over knowledge resources and mental resources; ensure women to join the mainstream; economical duties with men to share equal contribution to the growth of the society while doing household works like processing food and baby care. (Parvin, 1998)

Assumption of Women Empowerment

The empowerment of a person or a group of people is the mechanism of giving them power and status in a particular situation. In this respect the term empowerment is in some sense passive with a sense of subordination to somebody else. (Islam, 2000) Power from the powerful is redistributed to the powerless. (UNDP, 1994) But empowerment is more than participation in decision-making; it must also include the process that leads people to perceive themselves as able and entitled to make decisions. (Prasad and Sahay, 2000)

Through empowerment a community takes control and acts to eliminate obstructions. By empowerment, women are mobilized to understand, identify and overcome gender discrimination so as to achieve equality, welfare and access to resources. (Bangladesh Jati Sangha Samiti, 1988) The UN traces five important issues that have become basics to the assumptions of empowerment. These are welfare, access to poverty, control and rights, women consciousness and participation. (Islam, 2002)

Features of Women Empowerment

Every part of human being concerns with empowerment ranging from security to getting access to resources to meeting demands, political decision-making process - everywhere there is an influence of empowerment.

Nevertheless, women empowerment manifests some special features:

Equality in Every Sphere: This feature was nicely pointed out in a seminar on women empowerment. It entails that women empowerment does not mean that women will be the supreme power of the society; rather in every sector, especially in decision-making process, women should participate equally. This equal participation has to be maintained in all cases starting from a day laborer to the highest official. It does not mean - no gender discrimination in jobs; no gender discrimination in the choice of profession; and no gender discrimination in salary and job conditions.

Securing Public Voice: The famous theorist Johnson (1992) pointed out this feature, as a tool of gaining voice, having mobility and establishing a public presence.

Acquiring Uniqueness: Women empowerment is an active multi-dimensional process that enables women to realize their full identity and power in all spheres of life. (Pillai 1995)

Realisation of Rights: Empowerment requires gaining all rights that are due. It is the complete achievement of rights on material things like land, forest, humanitarian goods like human physique, financial property such as money, into that property like knowledge, information and concepts. (Rahman 1997) Women empowerment mostly hinges on political empowerment. Providing them with political power to decide independently will lead them to attain autonomy in socio-economic perspectives.

Indicators of Women Empowerment

The indexes of empowerment is the ability to take decisions, participation in household and financial activities, right of access to property, dexterity to take shelter in laws and own power to decide regarding birth and ability to expand own area. (Khanum 1999) Two of the indexes are usually applied for assessment. These are the quantitative and qualitative indicators (The Draft Country Paper-India 1995).

The qualitative indicators of women empowerment are: increase in self-esteem and individual and collective confidence; increase in articulation, knowledge and awareness levels on issues affecting the community at large, and women in particular, such as women's health, nutrition, reproductive rights, legal rights, literacy etc., participation in other events related to their lives; increase in bargaining power of the women as an individual in the home and community as well as in the collectives of women, women's decision making power over the kind of work she is doing, her control on own income and expenditure and whether she is still subservient to male members in the family or not (The Draft

Country Paper- India 1995).

The quantitative indicators of women empowerment are; demographic trends such as mortality rates, fertility rates, sex ratio, life expectancy at birth and average age of marriage; number of women participating in different development programs; and participation of women in political processes at the local levels (The Draft Country Paper- India 1995)

The main indicators of women empowerment identified in general are: mobility of women life; women's socio-economic security; women's poor purchase competence; and involvement in political practices (Islam 2002) - the above yardsticks of measurement as such can assess women empowerment.

Dimensions of Women Empowerment

The process of empowerment runs through three dimensions; resource, agency and achievement. The existing choice set is defined by access to resource both material and non-material. The process of women's agency consists of being able to choose effectively from the choice set. These dimensions are interrelated and interdependent.

Since empowerment is a process of change in different dimensions, the degree to which women is empowered will vary. A triadic scheme is developed by Rowlands (1997) to indicate the dimensions of women empowerment which is as given below.

Personal Empowerment: the core of empowerment process involves fundamental psychological process of change to which individual women are tied.

Collective Empowerment: the dimension of collective empowerment is very closely related to the personal dimension; since without empowerment at a personal level it is very hard for the individual to be active collectively.

Empowerment within Close Relationship: to have sense of empowerment in relation to other people is associated with and, to a large extent, dependent upon self-confidence, self-esteem and sense of agency. Such skills themselves also represent changes demonstrating personal empowerment (Prasad and Shay 2000).

Empowerment process is dynamic and the three dimensions of empowerment suggested are closely linked. Change in one dimension can encourage change in another dimension.

Personal Development is a sense of individuality and self-confidence and capacity for undoing the effects of internalized oppression.

Collective Development is where individuals work together to achieve a more extensive impact than each could have had alone. This individual involvement in political structures might also cover collective action-based co-operation rather than competition. Collective action may be locally focused. Relational development is the ability to negotiate and influence the nature of a relationship and decisions made within it. (Prasad and Shay 2000)

In practice, empowerment involves forms of group work. The role of outside professional in this context becomes one of helper and facilitator; anything more direct is seen as interfering with the empowerment of the people concerned.

Five Tiers of Women Empowerment

- Control
- Participation
- Conscientisation
- Access
- Welfare

Welfare: Provision of some basic facilities is very important for women, as they need to have education, health, sanitation, income and economic liberty where women are completely discriminated. At the same time they will have to be organized and make attempts to eliminate obstacles to the provision of these facilities.

Access: Women indeed do not have due control over resources neither as owner nor as user.

Conscientisation: One must consider that women are not totally responsible for subordination and distressing condition. This subordination is neither natural nor biological. It is the outcome of social conditions. Society has structured this subordination of women to men.

In such a case it is said that consciousness in women is a must to address gender issues and to devise policies to put the plans into action.

Participation: It is the heart of all programs for women development. Women empowerment requires that women must participate in all socio-economic and political activities and in the process in which decisions are made and implemented. Women should influence decisions and contribute to national growth.

Control: Woman must attain control by which they will achieve power to decide and to assess their strategic benefits in the long run. Women will not be a separate entity but will be co-workers in the community.

It is worth quoting Bhasin (1992) to bring out the assumptions of women empowerment: recognizing women contribution, women's knowledge, women becoming economically independent and self reliant; reducing women's burden of work and promoting qualities of nurturing gentleness.

An often-quoted framework of women empowerment is a quadruple composed of resource, perception, relationship and power (Chen 1990). Power increases ability on the part of women to change and control their external environment. All these will gradually lead to women empowerment.

Six Stages of Women Empowerment

- Awareness Building Stages
- Skills and Capacity Assessment Stage
- Capacity Building and Skills Development
- Participation and Greater Control in Decision-Making Stage
- Action for Change Stage
- Evaluation Stage

Awareness Building: Ideology is the absolute platform for those who want to challenge others to establish their own rights. They must figure out that they are humans and not such submissive social beings as they are taught and made by patriarchal values. It is to be understood by women that men will not eradicate women's problems unless men are questioned and challenged.

Skills and Capacity Assessment Stage: The powerless and sufferers have to be informed about their rights and causes of their distress. They may not demand their dues spontaneously since they have been under male domination for years that has imprinted lots of dogmas in their mind.

Capacity Building and Skill Development: Movement has to be launched as an integrated one where all classes of women will take part in achieving the target. What one woman can change is micro factor. Women from all walks of life have to be brought into one stream to augment social movement in order to change the present discriminating society; because collective movement is the most powerful and effective way.

Participation and Greater Control on Decision-Making: Women empowerment is not confined to any particular point. The process of women empowerment takes a lot of turns to reach the target. It also deserves recognition nationally and internationally; since a good number of global factors are associated with women empowerment.

Action for Change: Disagreement is there as to the process of women empowerment. Development agencies and representatives want immediate solution to the problems of women; others want to obliterate those traces that cause women problems. In this regard, some feminist sociologists have differentiated between women state and women condition. State is material.

Patriarchal social system always keeps women under domination which is perpetual that simultaneously causes sufferings for women. The process of women empowerment thus combines in itself treating with both state and conditions.

Evaluation: Women empowerment is not a one–way traffic; rather it is a never-ending process. The whole process of women empowerment, therefore, has to be evaluated to continue through feedback mechanism maintaining a dynamic homeostasis.

The IFAD supported the Tamil Nadu Women's Development Project, India in late 1999. The Project aimed to bring about the social and economic betterment of women. At the time of evaluation, the Project acted not as just "a credit-cum-subsidy project, but as a genuine process of empowerment." The evaluation concluded that such empowerment lay in the interaction between the social and economic aspects.

Four of the main processes that could lead to women's empowerment are:

- Changes in women's mobility and social interaction;
- Changes in women's labor patterns;
- Changes in women's access to and control over resources; and
- Changes in women's control over decision-making.

Changes in Women's Mobility and Interaction: The evaluation found that women had become more mobile and begun to have new interactions with a range of officials. There was even a growing willingness on the part of group members to approach the Panchayats and Collectors with petitions or grievances.

- 50 per cent of women group members had visited new places and traveled longer distances; and
- 94 per cent had experienced new interactions with staff of institutions such as banks, district and block development organizations, NGOs and the project itself.

The study observed that this type of change was most likely to occur among women group members when:

- The women involved were heads of households or were older
- The women involved had participated in training
- The group members had accessed a bank loan
- The group had undertaken community action initiatives, or
- The group had been organized into a federation and encouraged to participate in special events (such as Women's Day, Rural Women's day etc.).

Changes in Women's Labor Patterns: The evaluation did not find any major changes in gender division of labor. However, there were indications of such changes beginning. For instance, the group meetings themselves forced some of the husbands to look after children and feed themselves while their wives attended the meetings. The evaluation found that the extent to which men helped in reproductive tasks was related to the health of the women (men helped more if women were sick), the type of household (men helped more in a nuclear household), and the gender and age of the children (men helped less if girl children were present to help).

There was comparatively greater change reported in non-domestic productive tasks. Not all the changes in such labor patterns can be viewed as beneficial to women.

- Fully 30 per cent of women who had taken bank loans reported a marked change in gender roles, and 70 per cent reported a small change. (Greater change was reported by women heads of households, which implies that changes in the division of labour were not always involved, but that the women themselves adopted new productive roles).
- However, the income-generating activities of the majority of women in male-headed households (for which loans had been taken) continued to be managed by men (presumably, the women's husbands).
- The workload of 94 per cent of the women who had taken loans increased compared with their previous workload (many had been wage laborers).

Therefore, the changes in women's labor patterns were mixed, and not as positive as along other dimensions. There was little indication that women's control over their labor had undergone a marked change, and the evaluation noted that many women may simply have gone from undertaking paid work outside the home to becoming unpaid family laborers (in male-managed enterprises). At least self-employment allows women the possibility to have better working conditions, save on travel time, and be able to combine reproductive and productive roles more effectively.

Changes in Access to and Control over Resources. The evaluation also looked into women group members' access to non-loan-related resources and benefits, and particularly to common resources. It seems that a number of the groups undertook activities that would give their communities better infrastructure or services, for instance in water supply, child-care facilities, health care services and improved roads. In this sense, they played a key role in promoting changes in collective access to resources.

Changes in Intra-household Decision-making. The evaluation concluded that there seemed to be a slight improvement in women's involvement in household decision-making in male-headed households, on such issues as credit, the disposal of household assets, children's education, and family health care. However, the traditional gender-based divisions persist in intra-household decision-making. Women basically decide on food preparation, and men make the financial decisions. But group members had become more aware of their property and political rights (which was part of group training). As in the case of mobility and social interaction, the evaluation again found greater improvements among women heads of households, older women, and more educated women.

In traditional societies, even more than elsewhere, women's empowerment does not occur easily or overnight. In the Indian case described, there was evidence of such change beginning, to which the project had apparently contributed. It was most noticeable among certain types of women. Perhaps one of the most important emerging lessons is the women's group themselves which in their social aspects, play a role in such empowerment. This argues for placing emphasis on sustaining groups beyond the life of the project, which indeed was done in this instance. The project evaluation also recommended that communication support (films, radio broadcasts and so on, with sensitization and training content) be used to speed up the empowerment process.

In the end, here are a few need and strategies to develop women empowerment. Today's education is geared to meet the emerging needs and challenges of contemporary society through proficiency and training in sciences, arts and humanities blended together to improve the quality of life, participation in structuring one's life and fulfilling own aspiration – is the first step towards empowerment. Although the Universal Deceleration of Human Rights affirms that all human beings are equal in dignity and right without any distinction of any kind based on sex, it has taken considerable time and effort for the world community to accept the fact that women's right are an integral part of human rights. Discrimination against women as regards access to food, healthcare, education, training, and employment opportunities still exists in a substantial way. For women who earn a living by working outside their homes, sexual harassment is a major factor at workplace and women are denied even the right to choose their reproductive rights which is a very vital area for empowerment.

What is urgently required is a significant change in thinking. It is essential to promote an alternative image for women so that she knows that she CAN and SHOULD make informed choices. Any movement for empowerment must fight these enfeebling socio-economic practices and must create an enabling environment in which women can participate as equals in social, economic, political and cultural life of the nation and discharge their responsibilities to the family, the society and the nation.

To bring empowerment among the women **Commandments** of women empowerment should be practiced seriously by politicians, educationists, feminists, and society people together to give justice to women and enhance empowerment amongst them. The priorities are:

- Education and training should provide SWOT and introspection to females so that they realize their strengths and weaknesses.
- Self-defense training - the physiological limitation emphasis that she be trained to be self for self protection and capable of protecting her and be self-reliant.
- Increase in skills of decision-making ability and boosting her ability to judge.
- Training them to say "No" instead of always giving in to the suggestions/ proposals of male counterparts.
- Training to taking responsibilities for bearing the consequences of the decision.
- Let women come up and fill the gap of jobs/seats reserved for them and prove their worth.
- Develop self-respect, dignity of labor, understanding amongst women and imparting wisdom to counterparts to give respect, dignity and patient listening to women, training male members to enhance the female empowerment.
- Societal psyche change, attitude change and opportunity change towards females.
- Legal protection and laws against rape, punishment to culprits of dowry and other social evils should be implemented effectively.

These commandments of women empowerment should be practiced seriously in society by guatea female - children-older people, politicians, educationists and feminists to give justice to women.

References

Bangladesh Jati Shangha Samiti (1998): Narir Marjada O Khamatayone Jati Shongher Bhumika (The role of the UN in Enhancing the status and Empowerment of Women). Dhaka.

Barkat and Rhaman, Azizur (1994): "Women's Empowerment in Nasir Nagar Thana- A large Scale Sample Survey". Prepared for save the Children, USA.

Batliwala, S. (1994): Empowerment of Women in South Asia: Concepts and Practices, New Delhi, South Pacific Bureau of Adult Education and FAO freedom from Hunger Campaign.

Bhasin, Kamla (1992): "education for Women Empowerment: Some Reflection", Educational Development.

Chen,M.(1990): " Conceptual Model for women's Empowerment". Paper presented in a seminar organized by saves the children, USA.

Islam, M.(2002):Naribadi chinta O Narijiban (feminist Thought and Life of Women),Dhaka.

Islam, Sadequl (2000): "Political Empowerment of women in Bangladesh in world perspective: An Analysis," Rajshashi University Studies, Part-c, Vol.8.

Johnson, H.(1992): "Women's Empowerment and public Action: Experience From Latin

American Wuyts et al, Development policy and Public Action, Oxford, Oxford Uni. Press.

Khanum, Sultana Mustafa (1999): "Get way to hell; The Impact of Migration on Bangladeshi women's Territory: P Position and Power in England:, Empowerment.

Moser, Caroline O.N. 919930: Gender Planning and Development: theory, London:

Mosir, O.N. (1991): " Gender planning in the Third World: meeting Practical and Strategic needs in R. Grant and K. Newland, Gender and International Relations, OUP.

Parvin, S. (1998): "Narir Khamatayon" (Women Empowerment) Unnayon Padakkep, Dhaka.

Pillai, J.K (1995): "Women and Empowerment", New Delhi,Gyan Publishing House.

Prasad, R.R. and Sahay, S. (2000): "Models for Empowering Women", in Sinha, K., Empowerment of Women in South Asia, AMDISA, Hyderabad.

Rahman Shaheen (1997): "Gender Paribhasa Shabdakosh" (A Dictionary of Gender Terminology, Unnoyon Padakkhep.

Rowlands, J. (1997): Questioning Empowerment: Working with women in Hondurs, Oxford, cited in Empowerment of Women in south Asia.

Shetty, S. (1991): " Development Projects in Assessing Empowerment", Occasional paper Series No.3, New Delhi, SPR.

Tondon, Y. (1995): "Poverty, processes of impoverishment and empowerment: a review of current thinking and action, in empowerment: Towards Sustainable Development, London.

UNDP (1994): Human Development Report 1994, Delhi: Oxford University Press.

Unnayon Padokkhep (1995) " More About gender", Steps towards Development, 2, Ap-June, 77.

Part V: Problems of Rural Women

30

Rural Women Work Force

Tinku Paul

The present paper is an attempt to highlight the fact that gender neutral economic theorizing over the past two centuries has serious consequences in the evolution of concepts, theories and framing of policies. This gender insensitivity makes women's work invisible, unaccounted and therefore remains of no value. It cautions the limitations of data (Census and NSSO) in capturing the changing and varied dimensions of women's work. It also tries to bring about the realities behind the much celebrated increases in the Female Work Participation Rates in the Census 2001. The paper tries to focus on increasing marginalization and casualization of feminized work force. Three important issues which have been associated with women and the world of work are:

- **Invisibility or Undervaluation of Women's Work**: Most of the women's work is unacknowledged and conceptually falls out of the purview of monetized production activities.
- **Concentration in Subsistence Sector:** Rural women's work is excessively concentrated in the traditional or conventional activities and occupations which mostly get intermingled with the non-economic or extended SNA (system of national accounts) activities which leave them out of enumeration.
- **Feminization of workforce:** The process of feminization of workforce operates in the two ways. Firstly female workers are said to replace male workers in jobs, which were traditionally reserved for male workers. Feminization could also happen when additional jobs are created and women become the source for these jobs. Mostly women are employed in the sectors in the unorganized sector which are low paid and low skill manual and monotonous jobs. The sex role based stereotyping and gender division of labour that is prevalent in all categories of employment, irrespective of educational and skill development, exhibits resilience.

Emergence of the Concept of Work

Work as a category traversed through three broad stages of transition before acquiring the present meaning. In the eighteenth century 'work' appears both as a means of increasing wealth and as a mechanism for the emancipation of the individual. The two dimensions were that: (a) work is an individual service which can be the subject of exchange and of contractual arrangement, and that (b) it is a sum of individual efforts whereby the individual is integrated into society as a whole and social relationships are organized. This process was termed '*Bildung*' by contemporary German culture and eventually came to be known simply work. Work evolved in its true sense in this period with proliferation of inhuman working conditions and with the debate on pauperism. Work, thus, became a synonym for creation and self-expression and at the same time the activity proper to humankind. Despite Karl Marx's conception of work, he was aware that work had yet to become a liberating creative activity that could occur only in conditions of absolute freedom and when wage labour is abolished and a world of abundance created.

The third stage (theorized in German social democracy) tries to recover the basic inherent idea of work-the fulfilling nature of work and the necessity of the pursuit of abundance. Instead of abolishing wage labour the German social democracy made wages the vehicle whereby wealth was to be distributed and a new social order-more just based on labour and on capacities gradually came into being. From then the State was entrusted with the related tasks of guaranteeing continued economic growth and full employment. Departing from the original version of Marx's social democracy wherein fulfillment was to come from work itself, the new version fulfillment was to be attained from increasing wages and consumption. Thus, the present social democracy is an amalgam of two contradictory conceptions. Dominique summarizes work as a construct that has definitely not always been associated with the creation of value, with transformation of natural world, or with self-fulfillment; that it is multi-faceted because of its multiple meanings (as a factor of production, as creative freedom, as a mechanism for the distribution of income, status and security), but also because it is a mixture of elements, some objective and some made up of largely Utopia, fantasy and dream.

For the purpose of the present paper we study the conceptual framework of the two main data sets on employment and unemployment and the changes in the concepts over the years. These two data sets are Census and NSSO.

Defining Work Participation

These two main data sources for employment and unemployment in India, the Census and NSSO, suffer from different concepts and definitions in the different rounds which makes the comparison of data among these sources quite difficult.

However, efforts have been made by various sources to standardize the definitions, particularly NSS, to ensure comparability of data over time. Brief description of changes in the concepts and definitions in two main sources, namely Census and NSSO, are discussed below.

Population Census

The information on economic activity of the individual was collected since 1872 Census. In the Censuses of 1872 and 1881, only one question relating to **occupation** used to be asked and classified according to various occupations. In 1891, the concept of **means of subsistence** was introduced. From 1901 to 1921, the information on principal and subsidiary occupation or means of subsistence of actual workers was recorded. The term **actual worker** also included persons who were in receipt of income without doing work such as rentiers and pensioners etc. In 1931 Census, the term 'actual worker' was replaced by the **earner**. The population was classified into earners, working dependents and non-working dependents.

In 1941 Census, **Means of Livelihood in Order of Importance** was recorded for each worker. Owing to World War II, the tabulation of 1941 Census was greatly curtailed and a 2 percent random sample of the original individual Census slips was retained for each state.

The 1951 Census ascertained the two economic characteristics of every individual- his economic status and his means of livelihood. According to economic status, every person was classified as **a self supporting person** or **an earning dependent** or **a non-earning dependent.** Thus, in 1961 it was decided that economic data for 1961 Census should be collected on the basis of work; i.e. the population should be divided into two classes- Workers and non-workers. The workers category was further sub-divided according to four broad industrial categories- (1) Cultivators (2) Agricultural Labourers (3) Household Industry Workers (4) Other workers.

At the 1971 Census, considerable departure was made in respect of the economic questions. The main activity of a person was ascertained according to time spent as a worker producing goods and services or as a non-worker. For regular work, the reference period was the week prior to the enumeration and for seasonal work, the last one year work involved not only the actual work but also effective supervision and direction work.

In the 1981 Census, instead of a dichotomy of workers and non-workers, a trichotomy of main workers, marginal workers and non-workers was adopted. In the 1981 census, for the main workers, a time criterion of engagement in work for major part of preceding year, i.e., at least 6 months or 183 days, was adopted. For all the economic questions canvassed at the 1981 Census, the reference period was the year preceding the date of enumeration.

In the 1991 Census instead of four broad industrial categories followed in 1981, the main and marginal workers were divided into 10 industrial categories. In 1991 Census, in instructions to enumerators it has been clearly laid down to take sufficient care in recording responses of women as *"Women are often classified as non-workers because of non-reporting of their work. It also happens that women who work for the major part of the year are reported as working for less than six months"*. A uniform reference period of one-year preceding the enumeration was adopted for recording activity status in the 1981 Census irrespective of whether the activity was seasonal or regular.

With a view to net persons engaged in unpaid work on farm or in family enterprise, the word "Including unpaid work on farm or in family enterprise" was inserted in the schedule itself.

Definition of work as adopted during the 1991 Census has been retained as such in 2001 Census. In Census a person is categorized as **worker** when he/she participated in any economically productive activity anytime during the reference period. Unlike the 1991 Census, workers were classified into one of the four broad categories of economic activity, viz., cultivators, agricultural labourers, workers engaged in household industry and other workers. The Provisional Population Census 2001 Report in its introductory note has a column on Approach to Gender Issues. *Milk production for home consumption only also has been treated as work with a view that in previous Censuses, those who were engaged in milk production for self consumption only were left out and treated as workers.* This definitional change has resulted in increase in work participation rate of women in general and rural females in particular.

National Sample Survey Organization

The NSSO adopts and provides four different measures of employment and unemployment capturing different facets of the employment-unemployment situation following the recommendations of the Expert Committee (Dantwala Committee) on Unemployment Estimates (1970) set up by the Planning Commission of India. The NSSO has defined 'work' or 'gainful activity' as the activity pursued for pay, profit or family gain or in other words, the activity which adds value to the national product. Normally, it is an activity, which results in production of goods and services for exchange. However, all activities in 'agricultural sector' in which a part or whole of the agricultural production is used for own consumption and does not go for sale are also considered as gainful. The survey has adopted three different approaches to measure employment and unemployment.

The NSS classifications of economic activity are generated separately for four quarters of year. These quarters are almost co-terminus with four 'seasons'. This helps to study the seasonal pattern of employment and unemployment.

Female Work Participation Rate

The level of employment, its composition and the growth in employment opportunities are not only critical indicators of the process of development in any economy but also indicators that, in most cases, directly capture the economic attainments and hence the level of well-being of individuals.

During the period of six years ending June 2000, for males, the usual LFPRs decreased by about 2 percentage points in rural areas but remained stable in urban areas whereas for females it remained stable for both rural and urban areas. However, when 'all workers' viz. 'workers' considering both principal and subsidiary statuses are considered, usual status LFPRs for females show a decrease during the period- by about 3 percentage points in rural areas and 2 percentage points in urban areas.

Compared to LFPRs of the current statuses, the usual status ('all') LFPRs were higher in both the sectors and more so for rural females. This *reflects that some employed usually withdraw from labour force due to irregular availability of work, rather than reporting themselves as unemployed in the current status.* The difference is more for females in the rural areas where the seasonality in work is believed to be substantial. Yet as is reflected the gender gap in labour market participation exists. This is more marked for urban areas as compared to the rural areas.

Table 30.1: Number of Persons in the Labour Force per 100 persons (LFPR) According to Usual, Current Weekly and Current Daily Statuses (all India)

Status	Number of persons/ person-days in Labour Force									
	Rural					Urban				
	Male		Female		SRLF	Male		Female		SRLF
	1993-94	1999-00	1993-94	1999-00		1993-94	1999-00	1993-94	1999-00	
Usual-ps	549	533	237	235	422	538	539	132	126	214
Usual-all	561	540	330	302	536	543	542	165	147	249
CWS	547	531	276	263	474	538	539	152	138	234
CDS	534	515	232	220	410	532	528	132	123	234

SRLF = Sex Ratio of the Labour Force.

Source: NSS Report No. 458: Employment and Unemployment Situation in India, 1999-

00, pp. 60.

Distribution of Main and Marginal Workers

Out of the total population of the country, as per the 2001 Census, 313 million or 30.5 per cent are main workers and 89 million or 8.7 per cent are marginal workers. Among males, 45.3 per cent are main workers and only 6.6 per cent are marginal workers. The corresponding percentages of main and marginal workers among females are 14.7 and 11.0 respectively. The main workers in the country decreased from 34.1 per cent in 1991 to 30.5 per cent in 2001 giving a decline of 3.6 percentage points.

Table 30.2: Distribution of Total Workers, Main Workers, Marginal Workers and Non-Workers

India	Area	Sex	Proportion to Total Population			
			Total Workers	Main workers	Marginal Workers	Non-workers
2001 Census (Provisional)	Total	Persons	39.3	30.5	8.7	60.7
		Males	51.9	45.3	6.6	48.1
		Females	25.7	14.7	11	74.3
	Rural	Persons	42	31	10.9	58
		Males	52.4	44.5	7.9	47.6
		Females	31	16.8	14.2	69
	Urban	Persons	32.2	29.3	2.9	67.8
		Males	50.9	47.5	3.4	49.2
		Females	11.6	9.1	2.4	88.5
1991 Census (Excluding J&K)	Total	Persons	37.5	34.1	3.4	62.5
		Males	51.6	50.9	0.6	48.4
		Females	22.3	15.9	6.3	77.7
	Rural	Persons	40	35.7	4.3	60
		Males	52.5	51.8	0.7	47.5
		Females	26.7	18.6	8.1	73.3
	Urban	Persons	30.2	29.5	0.7	69.8
		Males	48.9	48.6	0.4	51.1
		Females	9.2	8.1	1	90.8

Source: Provisional Results of Census 2001.

As regards male main workers, their proportion has also gone down from 50.9 percent in 1991 to 45.3 percent in 2001. There is a decrease in percentage of female main workers as well but of lower order, i.e., it has gone down from 15.9 to 14.7 percent in 2001 i.e., a net decrease of 1.2 percentage points.

Thus, what can be deduced from the above table is that the increases in the work participation rates both for males and females has been on account of the increase in marginal workers. This is a matter for worry contrary to the celebrations being made for increases in FWPR.

Trends of Male-Female Work Participation Workers

Table 30.3 reflects that the workforce participation rate (WPR) of rural men has been nearly constant since 1971 except for the fall in 1991. But the rural female work participation rate has been fluctuating from as low as 15.5 per cent in 1971 to 31 percent in the 2001 Census. The FWPRs for all the Census figures have been low as compared to the NSS figures except for the 2001 Census which displays a higher female work participation rate as compared to the NSS 55th Round figures. Female Work Participation Rate (FWPR) exhibited a moderate rise in the 2001 census reaching 25.6 per cent, up from 22.3 percent in 1991. But, the NSSO, 55th round 1999-2000, shows that the female work participation (FWR) has actually fallen from 33.1 per cent in 50th round to 30.2 percent in the rural areas and from 16.4 per cent to 14.7 per cent in urban areas.

Table 30.3: Trends of Rural Male-Female Work Participation Rates

Years	Data Source	Male	Female
1951	Census	53.5	25.0
1955	NSS (9)	59.2	26.6
1961	Census	58.2	31.4
1971	Census	53.6	15.5
1972-73	NSS (27)	54.5	31.8
1977-78	NSS (32)	55.2	33.1
1981	Census	53.8	23.2
1983	NSS (38)	54.7	34.0
1987-88	NSS (43)	53.9	32.3
1989-90	NSS (45)	54.8	31.9
1990-91	Census	55.3	29.2
1991	Census	52.5	26.7
1992	NSS (48)	55.6	31.3
1993-94	NSS (50)	55.3	32.8
1999-00	NSS (55)	53.1	29.9
2001	Census	52.4	31.0
2004	NSS (60)	54.2	31.5

Source: Indira Hirway, (2000), Estimating Work Force Using Time Use Statistics in India and its Implications for Employment Policies. NSSO, 60th Round, Report No. 506: Employment and Unemployment Situation in India: January-June, 2004

It may be noted that certain procedural changes were made in course of the earlier rounds. Prior to NSS 50th round survey (1993-94), a tricotomous classification. According to the tricotomous classification, persons were directly classified into any of the three categories viz. 'employed' or 'unemployed' or 'out of labour force' based on major time criterion. In the later rounds of surveys, a two-stage dichotomous classification was adopted.

As compared to the fall registered in the FWPR in the 55th round NSSO survey, the 60th round shows an increase in the work participation rate of females by at least 1.6 percentage points.

Category-wise Distribution of Workers

Table 30.4 reveals that one out of four women in the rural areas is an agricultural labourer. As compared to this only 27.5 percent of the males engage as agricultural labourers and 42 percent are cultivators. This category of female agricultural labourers is vulnerable to the worst forms of poverty. There are larger proportion female workers engaged in household industries than males in both rural and urban areas. The distribution of women across nature of employment has shown that women account for the flexible labour category with a high proportion of contract and casual women workers. The employment of women and young girls are always a strategy to reduce cost when there exists a comparable difference in the wages between male and female workers.

However, with the swelling rates of unemployment among males, combined with the high insecurity in employment, the reservation prices of male workers seems to have gone down, making them as cheap as that of women counterparts. The distribution of women across nature of employment has shown that women account for the flexible labour category with a high proportion of contract and casual women workers.

The employment of women and young girls are always a strategy to reduce cost when there exists a comparable difference in the wages between male and female workers.

The important trend that needs to be highlighted is the considerable increase in the number of women engaged in trade, hotels and restaurants of which retail trade accounts for majority of the workers. Considerable change is visible in the community, social and personal services of which, excepting personal services all other categories have registered growth.

A majority of women workers in India are employed in the rural areas, primarily as cultivators and contract labourers. In the urban areas a majority of women workers are employed in the unorganized sector, in the household industries, petty trades and services, building and construction, etc.

Table 30.4: Total Workers (Main +Marginal) and Their Categories: India, 2001

Category of Workers	Total/ Rural/Urban	Persons/ Males/Females	Total workers (Main + Marginal)	per cent to Total Workers
1	2	3	4	5
Cultivators	Total	Persons	127,628,287	31.7
		Males	86,328,447	31.3
		Females	41,299,840	32.5
	Rural	Persons	124,682,055	40.1
		Males	84,046,644	42.2
		Females	40,635,411	36.5
	Urban	Persons	2,946,232	3.2
		Males	2,281,803	3
		Females	664,429	4.3
Agricultural Labourers	Total	Persons	107,447,725	26.7
		Males	57,354,281	20.8
		Females	50,093,444	39.4
	Rural	Persons	103,122,189	33.2
		Males	54,749,291	27.5
		Females	48,372,898	43.4
	Urban	Persons	4,325,536	4.7
		Males	2,604,990	3.4
		Females	1,720,546	11
Household Industry workers	Total	Persons	16,395,870	4.1
		Males	8,312,191	3
		Females	8,083,679	6.4
	Rural	Persons	11,709,533	3.8
		Males	5,642,112	2.8
		Females	6,067,421	5.4
	Urban	Persons	4,686,337	5.1
		Males	2,670,079	3.5
		Females	2,016,258	12.9
Other Workers	Total	Persons	151,040,308	37.5
		Male	123,468,817	44.8
		Female	27,571,491	21.7
	Rural	Persons	71,141,562	22.9
		Male	54,761,555	27.5
		Female	16,380,007	14.7
	Urban	Persons	79,898,746	87
		Male	68,707,262	90.1
		Female	11,191,484	71.8

Category of Workers	Total/ Rural/Urban	Persons/ Males/Females	Total workers (Main + Marginal)	per cent to Total Workers

Source: Provisional Results of Census 2001.

Based on the above table the Index of Casualisation (IOC) calculated show that female casualisation is very high. This is more marked for the rural areas (three times higher than males) as compared to urban areas.

In the process of casualisation or marginalization it is the female workers who suffer comparatively more due to lower access to productive resources and lack of skill. Thus, greater in security and discrimination in wages occur. Ghosh (1995) in his study of "Employment and labour under Structural Adjustment: India since 1991" has pointed out that this is evident not only in the growth causal labour but also in the growth of self-employment. One more significant fact to be noticed is that 40 per cent of the female workforce in the rural areas is casual. Thus, the fact that women are facing the worst forms of discrimination and are more vulnerable to insecure conditions and terms of work is established.

Table 30.5: Sex-wise Degree of Casualisation in Rural and Urban Areas

			Rural			
Males			IOC	Females		IOC
Rounds	Regular	Casual		Regular	Casual	
38th	10.3	29.2	283.5	2.8	35.3	1261
43rd	10.0	31.4	314	3.7	35.5	959
50th	8.3	33.8	407	2.8	38.7	1382
55th	8.8	36.2	411	3.1	39.6	1277
			Urban			
Males			IOC	Females		IOC
Rounds	Regular	Casual		Regular	Casual	
38th	43.7	15.4	35	25.8	28.4	110.9
43rd	43.7	14.6	33	27.5	25.4	92
50th	42.1	16.2	38	28.6	25.8	90
55th	41.7	16.8	40	33.3	21.4	64

Source: Various Rounds of NSSO

Need for Redefining Work Participation of Women

A major index of neglect is that many of women's economic contributions are grossly undervalued or not valued at all-on the order of $11 trillion a year.

Analyzing the trends of female work participation rates over the years Hirway hypothesizes that the decline in the NSS-based WPRs in the nineties could be a result of the increased share of the unpaid component of the SNA, and hence, in a way is not really a decline but a shift, indicating deterioration in the quality of employment. Attacking on the concepts and methods adopted by the NSS 55th Round, she argues, "It seems to us that the concepts and methods used by NSSO to net work and workers, are not able to capture the work of the poor, particularly of women, satisfactorily. It is possible that the decline in the WPRs in the nineties is due to the expansion of non-reported (by the NSSO) part of the workforce that is employed in what is known as *'difficult to measure' sectors* (such as, subsistence work, home based work or informal work) of the economy".

Invisibility of Women's Work

The argument that women bear disproportionate share of burden of adjustment was made on two grounds. Firstly, structural adjustment policies resulted in worsening income distribution and the re-orientation of the economy towards exports, women increased their participation in the labour force, in order to maintain themselves and their families. They were often incorporated into informal employment under insecure and worsening conditions of work. (ii) They tended to increase their unpaid domestic labour in the face of falling incomes.

The famous statement of Alfred Marshall about the housemaid and the housewife is pertinent here. Many tasks of the housewife have alternate market prices and hence every housewife is performing work in the economic sense of the term irrespective of the fact of direct payment.

Instead, real income is generated in the household by several tasks and this could not find its way into the national income estimates due to its operational limitations. Most part of the women's work at home is economic in nature as many studies on time use pattern reveal.

Identification of the Hidden Contribution of Work

Women play a critical role in the family. In different cultural, political and social systems, various forms of the family exist. The rights, capabilities and responsibilities of family members must be respected. Women make a great contribution to the welfare of the family and to the development of society, which is still not recognized or considered in its full importance. The social significance of maternity, motherhood and the role of parents in the family and in the upbringing of children should be acknowledged. The upbringing of children requires shared responsibility of parents, women and men and society as a whole. Maternity, motherhood, parenting and the role of women in procreation must not be a basis for discrimination nor restrict the full participation of women in society. Recognition should also be given to the important role often played by women in many countries in caring for other members of their family.

The under valuation of women is reflected in the undervaluation of their work and in the absence of recognition of the contribution that they make. The debate therefore, must cover equality of rewards as well as equality of opportunity. Data on time use by women and men for a sample of 31 countries tell a dramatic story:

- Women work longer hours than men in nearly every country. Of the total burden of work, women carry on average 53 percent in developing countries and 51 percent in industrial countries.
- Of men's total work time in industrial; countries, roughly two-thirds is spent in paid activities and one-third is spent in paid activities. For, women the situation is reverse.

Men's work in the market is often the result of *"joint-production*", not a solo effort, since much of it might not be possible if women did not stay at home looking after the children and household. *If more human activities were seen as market transactions at the prevailing wages, they would yield gigantically large monetary valuations. A rough order of magnitude comes to a staggering $16 trillion- or about 70 per cent more than officially estimated $23 trillion of global output.*

Such revaluation of work will thoroughly challenge the present conventions. The time use survey results of the Government of India indicates that, "If…SNA and Extended SNA activities are taken together…women are found to be working of longer hours than men...the average of women's work to the total work of male and female, …works out to 55 per cent, which compares quite well with the figure of 53 per cent quoted in the UNDP Human Development Report for 1995. Therefore, if extended SNA activities are included in economic activities, the contribution of women will be higher when compared to men".

On an average, males spent about 42 hours in SNA activities as compared to only about 19 hours by females. However, situation reverses for extended SNA activities. In these household and care related activities males spent about 3.6 hours as compared to 34.6 hours by females. Therefore, female spend about ten times more time in extended SNA activities as compared to male. In Non-SNA activities, which pertain to learning, leisure and personal care, male spent about 8 hours more as compared to females. On an average an urban female spends only 5 per cent of her time in SNA activities as compared to 13 per cent of rural female. But comparatively spends more time in Non-SNA activities which pertains to learning, leisure and personal care.

The gender differences are sharper in rural areas. Lack of education, joint family system and stringent patriarchal ideologies in the rural areas can be collectively held responsible for this situation.

Thus, when huge amounts of money is being pumped in by the government to bring about empowerment of women and when women's employment is viewed a policy prescription for poverty alleviation it becomes all the more important to explore the hidden contribution of women to the economic development of a country like India wherein most of the female work is concentrated in the subsistence sector.

Table 30.6 (a): Weekly Average Time (In Hours) Spent on SNA, Extended SNA and Non-SNA Activities by Sex and by Sector (Combined States)

Activities	Rural			Urban			Total		
	Female	Male	Total	Female	Male	Total	Female	Male	Total
1	2	3	4	5	6	7	8	9	10
SNA	22.53	42.31	32.72	9.16	41.06	25.77	18.72	41.96	30.75
Extended SNA	33.95	3.74	18.40	36.44	3.44	19.26	34.63	3.65	18.69
Non-SNA	111.50	121.98	116.89	122.44	123.47	123.03	114.58	122.42	118.62
Total	167.98	168.03	168.01	168.04	167.97	168.06	167.93	168.03	168.06

Table 30.6 (b): Percentage of Weekly Average Time Spent on SNA, Extended SNA and Non-SNA Activities by Sex and by Sector (Combined States)

Activities	Rural			Urban			Total		
	Female	Male	Total	Female	Male	Total	Female	Male	Total
1	2	3	4	5	6	7	8	9	10
SNA	13.41	25.18	19.48	5.45	24.44	15.34	11.14	24.98	18.30
Extended SNA	20.21	2.23	10.95	21.69	2.05	11.46	20.61	2.17	11.13
Non-SNA	66.37	72.61	69.58	72.88	73.49	72.23	68.20	72.87	70.61
Total	100.0	100.0	100.0	100.0	100.0	100.0	100.0	100.0	100.0

Source: Report of the Time Use survey, conducted by the Central Statistical Organization during 1998-99, in the six selected states of Haryana, Gujarat, Madhya Pradesh, Orissa, Tamil Nadu and Meghalaya.

Note: Total may not tally due to round-off.

Some glaring data released by the CSO, 2000 reveal that nearly 45099 female suicide deaths were registered during the year 1999. It is interesting to find that 52 per cent of these were housewives (not working). Also suicide rates tended to decline with level of education. Nearly 25,728 female suicide victims were either illiterate or with very low educational standard (primary). This impinges on the need for providing education and gainful employment opportunities as well. It is evidently clear that no doubt employment of women results to overall empowerment of women but at the same time quality of employment becomes inherently important. Unfortunately, because of the invisibility and non-recognition of women's work and its contribution to the economy, women continue to be disempowered. The vast majority of women work from dawn to dusk: ironically, women work long hours, but their work is not recognized as work at all. They are the primary caregivers in the home; often they are major contributors to the market as well. But all this fails to get encapsulated within the realm of *Economic Activity*.

References

Asia Pacific Centre for Transfer of Technology. Entrepreneurship Development for Rural Women, Vol. I. 1995.

Beneria, L. and M. Roldan, "Crossroads of Class and Gender", Chicago, IL, University of Chicago Press. 1987.

Census of India, Series-10, Provisional Population Totals, Paper 3 of 2001, Distribution of Workers and Non-Workers, Directorate of Census Operations, Uttar Pradesh. 2001.

Dominique MÉDA, "New Perspectives on Work as Value", in 'Women, Gender and Work' eds. by Martha Fetherolf Loutfi, Jaipur & New Delhi, Rawat Publications. 2001.

Dutta, Sujit Kumar and Ghosh, Dilip Kumar, "Empowering Rural Women" NSS Report No. 458: Employment and Unemployment Situation in India, 1999-00. 2001.

Government of India, *Report of the Time Use Survey*, Central Statistical Organization, Ministry of Statistics and Programme Implementation, New Delhi, April. 2000.

Hirway, I. "Employment and Unemployment Situation in the 1990s: How Good are NSS data?" Economic and Political Weekly, Vol. 37, No. 21, May 25-31, pp. 2027-2036. 2000.

Kumar, Prahlad and Paul, Tinku, "Informalization and Need for Gender Sensitive Statistics", paper presented in a National Conference by Indian Political Economy Association on 'Globalization, State and the Weaker Sections' held at G.B Pant Social Science Institute on 11-12 June, 2004.

Marx, Karl, "Excerpts: Notes of 1844", in G. Hillman (eds): Texte zu Methode und *Praxis*, Hamburg, pp. 180; translated by David McLellan: *Marx before Marxism*, London, Macmillan, 1970, p. 179.

Murid Gilardone, Isabelle Guerin and Jane Palier, "The Weight of Institutions in Women's' capabilities: How Far can Micro-finance Help!", Conference Proceedings-Promoting Women's Capabilities: Examining Nussabaum's Capabilities Approach, 9-10 Sept., 2002, von Hugel Institute, St. Edmund's College, Cambridge. 2002.

Tinku Paul, "*Gender Dimensions of Development*", Chapter published in an edited book entitled Human Development: Concept and Issues in the Context of Globalization" edited by Dr. S. K. Pant, published by Rawat Publications. 2006.

UNDP, Human Development Report. 1995.

Women and Men, CSO, Government of India, pp. 120,121, 1999-2000.

Yasodha Shanmugasundaram, "Rethinking in Economic Sciences", lecture delivered at R. Balkrishna Memorial Lecture on Dec. 28, at the 82nd Annual Conference on the Indian Economic Association, held at Guru Nanak Dev University, Amritsar. 2003.

31

Women in Agriculture in Punjab

D.S. Dhillon and Harnek Singh

Agriculture is the main occupation of the Indian economy since more than 76 per cent of population is dependent on it. Women have all along been active partner in farming and undertake management along with men. There are certain unit operations in production agriculture in which women dominate both in production agriculture and post-harvest management and agro processing. But, due to lack of training to women and social *taboos*, many such jobs after mechanization and modernization have scaled up to industrial enterprise and tend to become male domain where women nudged out. Feudalistic traditions and *taboos* also prevent women of certain middle and upper sections from engaging in economic activities, especially farming and live stock related activities, trade, marketing etc. Such social factors do not come in the way of women who are contributing to family kitty and feel economically secured in developed and socialistic developing countries. As a result in such societies, women can be seen as workers, supervisors and managers in every economic activity including farming, agro-processing, marketing of farm produce and processed products. All this indicates that women have an equal contribution to make in every sphere of human development activity whether it is in agriculture, industry, services or small business, their role cannot be minimized.

Women represent one of the crucial development forces in the world. As per the world economic profile, they form about 50 percent of the world population, contribute 60 per cent working force, making up to 30 per cent of the official labour force and contribute 50 per cent in the food production. At the home front, about 84 per cent of all economic active women in India are engaged in agriculture and allied activities.

Women in Farming

Women play a significant and crucial role not only in agricultural development and allied fields including crop production, livestock production, horticulture, post-harvest operations, agro-social forestry and fisheries but also in non-farm operations and household activities.

The participation of women in agricultural operations varies from region to region, crop to crop, operation to operation depending on the agro-climatic and socio-cultural variations. More explicitly, it varies greatly between hilly areas and plains, irrigated and dry-land, template and tropical, tribal and non-tribal regions. There are number of factors which are responsible for these variations. Some of the major ones are diversity of crops, cropping patterns, cropping intensity, irrigation facilities, work load in the household, socio-economic status, castes/tribes, social customs and cultural norms.

According to the Census (2001), the female work participation rate in the rural areas (the proportion of worker to total population) increased from 23 per cent in 1981 to 27 per cent in 1991, albeit with wide regional variations. As reported by Hansra and Dhillon (1995) 34.55 per cent of the female workers were cultivators, 43.56 per cent were agricultural labourers and 4.65 per cent were engaged in livestock, fisheries and forestry. Of the female marginal workers, 47.91 per cent were cultivators. 41.43 per cent were agricultural labourers and 1.64 per cent were engaged in livestock, fisheries and forestry. Remaining 17.26 per cent female main workers and 0.02 per cent female marginal workers were in non-agricultural sector. Families in the upper castes and the middle class are traditionally not inclined to employ their women in different farm operations.

On the whole, women are an integral part of the agricultural activity. They are less paid, do more work and much of their work is invisible. Farm women constitute so significant part of the working population, that it necessitates a full understanding of their present status and role and also the prospects and problems of their development in future. Such understanding will show the magnitude of their contribution to agricultural development.

Activities Performed

The agricultural production is the highest in Punjab State than all other States of India. The fertile soil, irrigation facilities through canal and tube wells, farm mechanization on large and medium land holdings, rational thinking of farming community to use the farm inputs contribute to increasing productivity. This State contributes the highest share of wheat and rice in the central pool and accordingly is recognized as 'Food Bowl of India'. The State is bounded by Jammu and Kashmir in north, Himachal Pradesh in north-west, Haryana and Rajasthan in south and Pakistan in west. According to agro-climatic conditions, the State is divided into five agro-climatic zones. The major crops grown are wheat and paddy. The other cash crops like sugarcane, cotton, vegetables, oil seed crops etc. are also grown in some of the areas of State.

The activities of Green Revolution in the State demanded a full support of women to act as catalyst for increasing food production. This was followed by

White Revolution where the women had to make a balanced contribution between farming and dairy farming thereby, adding work load along with household responsibilities. Agriculture being a family enterprise, the women have to adjust to changing roles and responsibilities. Today, the production of major crops has reached its peak and there is a gradual shift for diversification in agriculture. The role of women is accordingly getting modified to new farming system. The women have assumed the role of caretakers by extensively participating in seed selection and seed treatment of high yielding varieties of oilseed and vegetable crops. Besides this, the women of farming households are shifting their managerial and supervisory roles as per demand of the situation.

Working of Women in Different Climatic Zones

Across the agro-climatic zones with the exception of sub-mountainous undulated zone that is in close proximity to hills of Himachal Pradesh, the participation of women in agriculture remains almost to be the same. Landholding wise also except for landless families, women's participation in other categories remains to be uniform. By and large, the women are in advantageous position because farming is combined with subsidiary occupations that generate income and thereby, improve the socio-economic status of the family. Moreover, farming is mechanized, the farm size is large and use of farm inputs like spraying of weedicides, pesticides and application of fertilizers are carried out by men or hired labour. Harvesting, threshing, winnowing and filling of bags are also mechanized which does not require women to perform these farming operations. However, the wage earners do find ample avenues to put their share in these activities.

The scenario of women from sub mountainous undulating zone is different where men have undertaken jobs in the cities or have migrated abroad leaving the responsibilities of farming on the shoulders of women. This scenario also prevails on account of small landholdings, scanty irrigation facilities, and less employment opportunities for men in the villages. Men folk generally visit the village for preparing land for sowing, harvesting and marketing of produce. Therefore, women become the caretakers of their farm and perform different farming occupations.

Working in Different Agricultural Operations

The women of landless households are the wage earners across the State. They work as labourers on the field, undertake paid jobs in village households as domestic helper or in urban households that are in the vicinity of the village and also as skilled labourer in the nearby factories. As field labourers they perform the task of transplanting, weeding & hoeing, harvesting and post-harvest activities. However, the present trend in Punjab is to hire migratory labour during peak seasons of farming and therefore, the proportion of women farm labour is very small. Moreover, the seasonality factor in agriculture disallows women to have a constant flow of income due to which they prefer to be engaged in other wage earning occupations.

In spite of direct or indirect contributions of women in agriculture, their decision making role remains to be largely over shadowed by men. The women are generally consulted more for selected agricultural decisions like amount of grains to be sold, used and stored, getting credit and its repayment, employment of family and casual labour for operations like sowing, weeding and harvesting, buying new cattle, buying new equipment and selling and buying land and property. Farm women in higher socio-economic status did not enjoy as much involvement in decision-making process regarding farm operations, as those of middle or low socio-economic status families.

Harvesting and Post-harvesting Operations

Harvesting and post-harvesting operations are mainly done mechanically and therefore, the women play a restricted role in these activities. Harvesting of fodder, unscaling of maize cobs, digging of groundnut, potatoes, picking of cotton pods, shelling the pods and vegetable picking are some of the harvesting operations performed by women. Only after the grain reaches home, the women either independently or jointly with other female members or with the help of hired labour attend to care of storage structure, cleaning, drying and storage of grains for household consumption and seed purpose. All decisions pertaining to domestic storage of grains fall within the purview of women. They do cleaning, threshing and grinding of pulses and also participate in drying fish, drying fruits, vegetables and root crops, thereby reducing the losses resulting from seasonal gluts.

The women of medium to small sized land holdings and landless families play a prominent role in vegetable growing belts of the State. They work in the fields throughout the year for digging of potatoes, weeding & hoeing, picking of vegetables, scaring of birds, seed selection, seed treatment, etc. In flower cultivation which has been taken up by well-to-do farmers, the contribution of women for nurturing and care of crops is highly significant. They perform the task of seed processing and production, controlled pollination and harvesting. These operations being delicate, the women tend to perform these tasks with efficiency and hence they are getting inclined to accepting work in this diversified area of agriculture.

Supervision of Farm Operations

As compared to southern states, women's participation in supervision of agricultural operations is less in Punjab. The possible reasons for this are that they themselves participate in these operations. Women supervise such activities as arranging for the sales of the products, picking the pods and vegetables, picking of cotton, unscaling of maize cobs, cutting and carrying fodder, hoeing and weeding, transplanting seedlings, sowing etc.

Working in Animal Husbandry Operations

Rearing of livestock in the past was associated with milk production for consumption by family members. Today, the scenario has changed and the rural families rear livestock primarily for sale of milk. The consumption of milk and milk products at home has been drastically reduced and milk is sold for cash earning. Women however, continue to play physically taxing role in care and management of livestock. It is only in large land holding households that hired help is used for animal care, fodder management, milking and cattle shed management.

Women of other land holding categories across the State are extensively involved in livestock management. For them the chain of activities begin with fodder management and extends to feeding, care of animals and cattle shed, collection of dung for preparing dung cakes and manure. The women of landless category who own small herd size for selling milk, perform all livestock management activities. They shoulder the additional burden of fodder collection due to their economic background. The rural women in Punjab shoulder the burden of livestock management but when it comes to selling of milk, it is the men who take charge and keep the cash under their control.

Role in Different Activities

Women play a significant role in different dairying activities like:

- Milking cattle
- Fodder cutting collection, bringing fodder from field and chaffing of fodder
- Preparing feed for calves, pregnant and milch cattle
- Preparing and giving concentrates to pregnant and milch cattle
- Bathing and cleaning cattle
- Cleaning cattle shed
- Providing drinking water to animals
- Care of new born calves
- Isolating and attending to sick calves and adult animals

- Collection of dung, preparation and storage of dung-cakes, storing hay
- Grazing of animals and
- Preparation and storage of dairying products.

In addition to these roles, they also play an equally important role in decision-making regarding number of milch cattle to be kept, feeding of milch cattle, purchase of cattle feed, place of keeping animals in summer and cold seasons and selling and buying new cattle. Besides dairying, women also actively participate and play an important role in running successfully other enterprises like poultry, piggery, goatry, duckery, quail rearing, sheep rearing, rabbit rearing, fisheries, sericulture, silviculture, apiculture and mushroom cultivation. In poultry, they play an important role in daily feeding and watering of poultry birds, giving feed additives, collection of eggs and marketing plus some other management practices. Mushroom cultivation is mostly home bound and requires very little space and is easily done by women. However, its cultivation is undertaken only after obtaining proper training. Training facilities are available in State Agricultural Universities, State Departments of Horticulture and other research centres.

Other Activities

The rural women keep themselves occupied during slack periods by undertaking weaving with agro-based products. They weave cotton *Daries, Khes, Nala* and towel by spinning and dying cotton thread at home. These are the traditional handloom articles that are being kept alive by women across the State. These articles are primarily made for use at home but a large majority of women from small land holding and landless category take up these activities for income generation. According to ICAR (2003) Coordinated Research Project in Punjab State, most of women have participated in farming activities especially in harvesting, weeding and seed selection. In case of post harvest activities, about 90 per cent of women did operations of drying and storage. In case of livestock - management activities, 92.83 per cent of women did the work of cattle shed management. Almost the same number of women did this work in almost all type of land holdings. When we have a glance on the decision making profile of women, more than half of them reported that they are involved for seeking employment. These women were not much involved in decision making in respect of obtaining bank loans and insurance of animals.

Problems Faced by Women in Agriculture

Women's involvement in agricultural tasks by and large is a source of drudgery to them. The drudgery ridden agricultural tasks are assigned to women only because of male dominated social order. They have to do hard physical work in number of farm activities like transplantation especially in paddy crop, house holding and threshing of wheat, bending for a long time in rain and scorching heat, dehusking, winnowing and grinding of cereals by traditional methods. They have to perform these activities in addition to home activities such as child bearing and child rearing simultaneously. As women are physically weak, the tasks assigned to them are those which are considered demanding less physical power, lower skills and more time. These tasks are monotonous in nature, low paid and the major force influencing the sex assignment of task is the social value.

Suggestions to Improve Role of Women Participation in Agriculture

There are certain constraints that restrict women in their participation in the use of modern scientific technology. The following suggestions will help in improving the role of women participation in agriculture:

- The participation of women in agriculture should be promoted and recognized by the society.
- They cannot benefit from the new technological developments because of their low literacy level. Most of the technology transfer and training programmes are held in the Institutions far away from rural areas and it is inconvenient for them to attend such training courses due to heavy family responsibilities. So, training should be given to them at their native place and at a time when most of them are free from household work. Moreover, training should not be conducted during peak labour seasons.
- The existing channels of communication in the development programmes do not have necessary provision to reach farm women. There is a strong need to strengthen them by revitalizing the earlier group discussions exclusively for farm women.
- In order to reach farm women, it is suggested that women should be employed as village extension workers so that rural women can be easily contacted.
- For relieving women from household drudgeries, it is utmost important that the household work related to child care should be supported by giving them incentives.
- The training for women should be on the skills needed for motivation, employment, leadership and participation.
- The constraints which hamper the productivity of women farmers should be

identified and appropriate institutional supportive measures should be suggested to overcome them.

- Efforts should be made to modify the technology/machinery/ equipments which are already available for use to make them more convenient to be operated by women farmers.
- The rate of wastage of time and energy in most of the operations performed by women must be reduced to the least possible extent by developing appropriate technology which is small and handy in order to raise the work efficiency of women.

Conclusion

Women play different roles in agriculture as participants in different farm operations either as cultivators or as agricultural labourers, in management and decision-making. With consequent growth of industry, men are abandoning agriculture in favour of careers offering better conditions and remuneration in other sectors, while women are left to live on marginal lands. Disadvantaged by her inferior level of formal education, her double (or triple) role-burden of farm, chores of household activities as well as her physically and emotionally demanding biological role ill equipped with necessary scientific knowledge and technical know-how with marginal access to assets and extension services, women are facing the challenge of agricultural productivity and food security. These handicaps stand in the way of full utilization of their potential. So, there is a strong need to make women aware of recent technologies, their rights, and opportunities, to bring desirable changes in knowledge, skill and attitude to increase their capabilities. In this way, their contribution to agriculture will significantly be realized. It all indicates that

- Participation of women in different areas of farming should be recognized, appreciated and rewarded.
- Access to literature and extension should be improved considerably by providing education to all girl children and non-formal education for adults.
- Training areas for women should be identified. These must include decision-making, managerial skills, field crops production, post-harvest technology, storage of grains, management of dairy cattle and poultry birds, horticultural crops, social forestry, sericulture etc.
- Women should be educated regarding finance management to maintain a balance between declining trend of form income and increasing trend of expenditure on personal and social aspects.
- Non-traditional as well as home based income potential enterprises like fish

culture, agriculture tissue culture, rabbit farming, mushroom cultivation, floriculture should also be given special attention.

- Agro-processing units at micro and macro level should be established to provide income generation avenues to women.
- To promote value added processing like processing of milk, milk products simple technology and hygienic handling through simple equipments and appliances, requirements of women coupled with opportunities for remunerative marketing of the resultant products should also be given due consideration.

References

Ahuja, Ram, *Indian Social System*, Rawat Publications, Jaipur and New Delhi. 1984

Gill, M.S. (ed.), *Punjab Society–Perspectives and Challenges*, Concept Publishing Company, New Delhi. 2003

Gill, T.K. and Gill S.S., Women's Role in Agricultural Development in Tripathi, R.S. & Tiwari, R.P. (ed.) *Perspectives on Indian Women: Policies & Strategies* Classical Publishing Company, New Delhi. 1999

Government of India, *Census of India*, New Delhi. 2001

Hansra, B.S. and Dhillon, D.S. Role of Women in Agriculture and Other Allied Areas in : R.K. Samanta (Ed.) *Women in Agriculture, Perspective, Issues & Experiences*, M.D. Publications Pvt. Ltd., New Delhi. 1985

Indian Council of Agricultural Research, All India Coordinated Research Project on Home Science, *Qualitative Data Base on Rural Women–Ecological Friendly Empowerment*, ICAR Publications, New Delhi. 2003

Indian Council of Agricultural Research, New Delhi, All India Coordinated Research Project on Home Science, *Data Book on Women in Agriculture*, Foil Printers, Gobind Nagar, Ludhiana. 2003

Murty S. & Gaur K.D. (eds.), *Women Work Participation and Empowerment: Problems and Projects*. RBSA Publishers, SMS Highway, Jaipur. 2002

Murty, S., *Feel Good and Bad Factors in Different Sectors*, RBSA Publishers, Jaipur. 2005

Sharma, Promila, Women and Organic Agriculture: Issues and Initiatives, *Journal of Agricultural Development and Policy*, 2 (XI), 83-93. 1999

32

Women in Agriculture

Minaxi Pathak

The economy of India is predominantly agriculture oriented. The majority of the Indian workers are agricultural labourers who constitute the major segments of rural work force. With the rural population of 741 million (73.3 per cent of the total) India continues to live in villages (6,07,491 villages in 592 districts). Indian women population stands at 496 million out of the total population of 1027 million, thus accounting for 933 women for every 1000 men. 2001 Census reveals that there were 72 million female workers as compared to 240 million male workers, indicating a smaller work force of women in the economy. Female economic activity rate was 42.2 per cent and it is only 50 per cent of male economic activity rate of the country. There is no disagreement of opinion that rural women have been contributing largely to the nation's economy, which is mainly based on agriculture and allied sectors. The labour force participation rate of women is 31.56 per cent as compared to men's rate of 68.44 per cent. Agriculture is found to be the highest employer of women's labour to the extent of 84 to 97 per cent in India. Farmwomen carry out 75 to 80 per cent farm work with 50 to 66 per cent of them contributing to agricultural labour. In the case of livestock, more than 90 per cent of the work is done by women. Their economic activities are usually under paid, unskilled, semi skilled and drudgery filled jobs. Some of the problems faced by them are scarcity of resources, economic deprivation gender bias in wages, deprival in decision-making, denial in using income generated by farm activities.

Farmwomen have tremendous workloads with dual responsibilities for many of the farm activities with management of home. Farmwomen have played and continued to play key roles in conservation of basic life support systems such as land, water, flora and fauna. They tend to look at problem in their totality. i.e. from sowing of the crops to its ultimate utilization of food, feed, raw materials of industry and waste for recycling and reuse. Farmwomen irrespective of their socioeconomic status perform almost all the activities related to farm. However their role differs according to their socio-economic status.

1. Women belonging to large cultivating households generally do not work in field, such household engage wage labourers for manual work both farm and

homestead activities. They perform some supervisory functions.

2. Women who have adequate land for subsistence do not seek wage employment. They generally work as unpaid family labours in own field or exchange labourers in other's farm.
3. Women belonging to landless household or insufficient land had to hire themselves out as wage labourers to fulfill the minimum requirement of family need. Pearson (1979) classified the role of farmwomen into the following categories:

- Independent producers, who manage farm largely by themselves.
- Agricultural partners, who share most aspects of work, responsibilities, and decision making with their husbands.
- Agricultural helpers who only participate in the farm work at busy time when extra time is needed and
- Farm homemakers, who contribute to the farm production indirectly by preparing meals and attending those working in the field.

Economic Role of Women: Global Experience

The economic development involves a natural process of utilization of resources both nature and human. The stages of economic development, through which the society has been passing determines the extent of women employed outside the house. Thus involvement of women in economic activities is closely related with stage of development of the society, socio economic attitude towards women role and socio economic status. In a developed economy many activities of women are monetised and considered as employment. Whereas, in India such activities are not recognized and as such, they remained invisible. Due to inconsistencies and poor method in data collection and reporting and because of narrow definition of work and employment in national statistics, data often fails to capture the real contribution of women's work in developing countries like India. The employment profile of women in India as per the 1991 Census indicates that 81.23 per cent of all economically active women are engaged in agriculture and agro enterprise.

As a result, there has been a widespread erroneous notion that women in developing countries have marginal role in all sectors of the economy including agriculture. Economic role of women in terms of female work participation rate is above 40 per cent, in countries like Romania (48 per cent), Bulgaria (46 per cent), former USSR (44 per cent), between 25-40 per cent in Germany (40 per cent), Denmark (37.8 per cent), Japan (37.6 per cent), U.K. (32.25 per cent), Australia (25 per cent) and below 20 per cent in countries like India (14 per cent), Pakistan

(8 per cent), Egypt (4 per cent) and Iraq (2.15 per cent). Participation of women in economic activities is very high in Eastern and Western North America. In USA, Canada, UK, Australia, New Zealand, Norway, Sweden and Switzerland, the female participation rate is concentrated in non-agricultural sectors. In some other countries such as USSR, Australia, Finland, Hungary, Japan, Poland, Denmark, Federal Republic of Germany, a sizable proportion of women are engaged in agricultural occupation, through their participation is relatively more in non-agricultural sectors. In developing countries, female work participation rate is higher in agricultural sectors. Such countries where agriculture is dominant sector are grouped into three categories:

1. The first group of countries where participation is very high but confined to agriculture includes Haiti, Nepal, Nigeria, Thailand and Turkey.
2. In the second group the Female participation is medium high level includes country like India, Malaysia, Morocco, Tunisia.
3. The third group of countries where participation of women in farm operation is less includes countries like Latin America, Iraq and Pakistan.

The average female participation rate in Muslim countries is low as because women of these countries are virtually absent from clerical occupation, factory work and fieldwork outside the home. In India, agriculture sector employs 80 per cent of all economically active women in the country as compared to 63 per cent of men about 50 per cent of these are agricultural labourers and over one third are cultivators. It is estimated that there are 75 million women in dairying as against 15 million men and 20 million women in other live stock activities as compared to 1.5 million men (Anonymous 2002 b).

The role of women in agriculture vary from region to region. For example in Tamil Nadu men uproot rice seedlings and women transplant while in Kerala and Upper Assam, both the operations are exclusively performed by women. Threshing is primarily men's responsibility in Tamil Nadu, Assam and Punjab, while it is women's responsibility in Kerala. In Tribal societies of Arunachal, Tripura, Mizoram, Nagaland, KarbiAnglong, Manipur where Jhum cultivation (shifting cultivation) is generally practiced, women in work areas play a major role. In Karnataka, Tamil Nadu and Andhra Pradesh, Assam, the entire work of sericulture from feeding of silk worms to reeling is done by farmwomen.

Through out the country women belonging to high caste do not engage in fieldwork. On the other hand most of the field works are assigned to female labour from scheduled/low cast or scheduled tribes. Level of participation of women in various enterprises in the rice based farming system is greater than that of men in hills and at per with men in plains. In hilly regions where ploughing cannot be done, women are expected to dig small plots of land with spade.

Majority of the farm operations are performed by women in hilly areas, while their husbands migrate to plains in search of work (Plate 1-6). As such their workloads become double. In Bangladesh women are not generally engaged in fieldwork. They are responsible for all operations related to post harvest processing and for food preparation for hired labour (Abdullah and Zeidenstein, 1982). In Phillippines, women supervise hired labour and in Indonesia, women from larger farm households are responsible for contracting, hiring and paying of farm labour. In south Asia, women generally market the rice crop as well.

Due to the rigid necessity of carrying out agricultural operations during specific time span, the employment of agriculture is characterized by peak and slack seasons. The nature of demand for female labour in rural labour market is different from that of male labour. Female labour demand is subjected to sharp fluctuations while demand for male labour exist throughout the agricultural season. Farm activities of female spread during a span of 9 months i.e. May to January. Demand for female labourers increases sharply during transplanting, harvesting, post harvest operation as these were done mainly by female. The average man days worked by females were 35.38 days for transplanting, 28.30 days for harvesting, 9.56 days for post harvest activities with increase in total man days along with increase in farm size. It was also observed that in paddy cultivation of Assam, female workers directly contributed 31.42 per cent of the total man days required for cultivation (Saikia,1997).

Participation of women also vary depending on cropping system. Women's participation was much greater in rice based cropping system than in dryland farming. Women contributed only 9 per cent of agricultural labour in Northern China's wheat production region but 29 per cent labour in double cropping rice areas of Southern China. Throughout Asia women play an important role in rice seed selection. They are often responsible for selecting plants to provide seeds, for storing seeds and for testing and germinating seeds.

Despite the vital role performed by women in agriculture their economic role is not recognized, they are the meager recipients of the world income. The world economic profile of women shows that women represent 50 per cent of population, make up 30 per cent of the official labour force, perform 60 per cent of all working hour, receive 10 per cent of the world income and own even less than one per cent of the property (FAO, 1980).

Participation of Farm Women in Agriculture

The whole range of agricultural operations except those involving animal and machine power is performed by women jointly or independently. Except ploughing cart driving, arranging farm inputs, and selling products, women were found to have been engaged in all other farm operation, like compost making. Sowing, weeding, application of fertilizer and manure, protection of crops from birds, harvesting, winnowing and storing. Farmwomen are also engaged in looking after milch animal, poultry, kitchen gardening etc. In a document on "most farmers in India are women" published by FAO (1991), it is mentioned that the rate of rural women better called the farm women in the third world countries has been labeled as farmer as they play a major role in cultivation, post harvest processing, and marketing. In most parts of the country the job traditionally done by women are generally transplanting, sowing, weeding, harvesting winnowing and threshing (National Committee on Status of Women, 1974). Details of sex-wise distribution of work as presented by Sigh and Punia (1988) in the International Conference on Appropriate Agricultural Technologies for Women (Appendix 1) clearly indicates that in India, women force is overwhelmingly engaged in agriculture either as main workers or marginal workers. Kaur (1982) studied participation of farmwomen in Agriculture in Haryana which revealed that 72.6 per cent of female were participating in work force and this participation was the highest in backward region. Farm work consumed maximum time of women, as average time devoted was 2.6 hours, followed by food preparation, cleanliness, care of animals, clothing, childcare, grain processing and flour grinding. Average working hour for women worked out to be 13.2 hours.

Devi and Reddy (1984) studied role expectation and role performance of farmwomen in Andhra Pradesh. It was observed that farmwomen belonging to low economic categories performed all agricultural activities. Where as, women of high and medium categories performed allied agricultural activities. It was also reported that women belonging to small farm holdings lower caste with low socio economic status with less education with less material possessions and with having less urban contact were participating more in agricultural activities. Another study conducted by Kaur (1987) in Haryana District shows that, on an average a farm women spent 8.70 hours daily in home activities, 1.73 hours in farm activities and 1.72 hour in live stock activities. On an average 12.21 hours were being spent by women in household chores, agriculture and animal husbandry. Further, Munjal *et.al.* (1988) worked out the time allocation pattern among rural women. The study reveals that farm women spent 12.19 and 13.13 hours on home, dairy, and farm activities during slack and peak period respectively (Table 32.1).

AICRP on Home Science (1996-2000) revealed that farm women kept themselves occupied for 15-16 hours a day with variety of chores of farm and home related activities. Marginal difference of time expenditure existed between slack and peak periods of farming, where time used during peak periods increased for farming activities and decreased for household activities. It is also reported by Kaur (1987) that of all the agricultural activities, maximum time was spent in harvesting in both the seasons (141.15 hours) in Kharif and (100.18 hours) in rabi season, followed by weeding (109.07 hours), threshing (37.64 hours), post harvest activities (936.22 hours), pre-sowing activities (21.58 hours) in kharif season and threshing (54.61 hours), weeding (44.62 hours), post harvest activities (38.17 hours), pre-sowing activities (17.47 hours) in rabi season. The study also revealed that age of the respondents, caste, size of landholding per capita income, socio economic status and level of farm mechanization were found to be related negatively and significantly with time devoted in activities related to agriculture. From various studies conducted in different states, it was observed that most of the physically exhaustive fieldworks were performed by low or scheduled caste women. But in some activities like threshing, winnowing, dehusking and parboiling etc., participation of schedule cast women was not preferred.

Table 32.1: Average Time Spent by Women in Home, Farm and Dairy Sectors during Slack and Peak Period

Sector of Activity	Slack Season		Peak Season	
	Average Time (hours)	Day C.V* (per cent)	Average Time Hours	Day C.V* (per cent)
Home	7.50	32.28	6.38	38.92
Farm	0.72	229.07	3.98	90.11
Dairy	3.97	48.63	3.57	53.67
Total Time spent	12.19		13.93	

C.V* =Co-efficient of variation

Source: Kaur, S. (1987), Women in Rural Development, Mittal Publication, Delhi.

Devi (1987) identified eight major roles with eighty sub roles to find out the actual performance of role. The study revealed that harvest and post harvest role has ranked first, followed by pre sowing and sowing, food preparation, Child and family care, allied agriculture, inter-cultivation, housekeeping and social cum leisure time activities. It was also observed that the performance of their roles in farm and home management was either low or average but none recorded high performance.

The AICRP in Home Science (1996-2001) studied activity-wise participation pattern of farm women in home, farm and allied activities. The study reveals that in the case of field operation a larger majority of women (54 per cent) reported to be joint partner with men, one third of the respondents (35 per cent) were joint partners with female and one tenth of the respondents (11 per cent) work independently in field operation. In the case of the post harvest operation joint participation of farm women with female members was relatively more i.e. 49 per cent, followed by joint participation with male (37 per cent), and 14 per cent performed these activities independently. In the case of life stock management 44 per cent were joint partners with male, 34 per cent were joint partners with female and 22 per cent emerged to be independent workers. Further, joint participation with men to a higher extent was observed in the activities like seed selection, seed treatment land preparation, Nursery raising, sowing, fertilizer application irrigation management, plant protection threshing and marketing. Health care of animals pre and post delivery care joint participation with female was noticeably high in transplanting, weeding, processing of rains, drying, grading, shelling cleaning and storing animal care and cattle shed management. Equal proportion of joint participation with men or women was observed in harvesting, dehusking and winnowing, feed, water and fodder management.

As regards to homestead activities 5 per cent performed homestead activities independently, where as, 44 per cent reported to be joint partners with female. A meager percentile were joint partner with male (5 per cent) The study confirmed the fact that farmwomen play distinct participatory role in farm and live stock activities in addition to their home role which she mostly played independently without getting any assistance from male members of the family. Among the farm activities involvement of farmwomen in post harvest activities was relatively higher than that of pre-sowing & sowing activities. Roy & Pathak (2000) conducted a study in Orissa to find out the role of women in post harvest activities which revealed that major percentage of farm women participated always in the activities like mopping of threshing floor (86 per cent), sweeping of threshing floor (84 per cent) removing of hay from grains after threshing (53.38 per cent), sun drying of grains (52 per cent). The farmwomen rarely participated in activities such as, carrying of grains heaping of grains bagging of grains, treating with chemical and pesticides and account keeping. Kalita & Pathak (1996) studied the extent of participation of farm women in post harvest operation, in Assam which reveals that 60 per cent of the total farm women participated partially, where as 18 per cent fully and 16 per cent rarely participated in post harvest activities.

Majority of the respondents who rarely participated in storing grains belonged to large farmers where paid help for some of the activities were engaged. Kaur & Punia (1998) studied participation of farmwomen in farm, home, and allied activities in Haryana. It was revealed that 60 per cent of the respondents were involved in activities related to farm. Few activities such as paddy transplanting, weeding, harvesting and winnowing were entirely performed by women either independently or jointly with women. Women were equal partners in harvesting and threshing. Arunachalam (2005) conducted a study on involvement of farmwomen in farm management in Tamil Nadu. The study revealed that self-doing was more in drying and cleaning, storing and wage distribution. Jointly doing was noticed in collection of seed for future use, seed treatment, preparation of compost, application of weedicide & pesticide, transplanting to market and marketing of produce. In the case of land preparation such as, stubble collection, land leveling, application of manures, cleaning the field boundaries and forming ridges and furrows, most of the farmwomen (65 per cent to 86 per cent) play supervisory role. Beohar et. al. (1999) reported that use of female labour was more than male labour in transplanting, interculture operation and transplanting harvesting of paddy crop.

It was also observed that with the increase of family size, the involvement of family women labourer decreased, but it was reverse for female hired labourer. Mishra etal (1999) also reported that participation of family women decreased as farm size increased, however, total employment hours increased with farm size. Saikia (1997) studied nature and extent of participation of women in agriculture in Assam and found that the proportion of mandays worked by female was the highest in transplanting (89.91 per cent), harvesting (89.51 per cent) followed by post harvest activities (28.25 per cent). Human labour comprised of 64 per cent of total cost of production, out of the total labour requirement family labour comprised of 25.45 per cent of it. Hazarika (1998) studied involvement of Karbi women in *jhum* cultivation and revealed that cent per cent of the labour employed for selection of seeds for sowing and cleaning of seeds for storing. A higher percentage of total labour utilized in hoeing of land (66 per cent), land leveling (66.02 per cent) and cleaning of boundaries (70 per cent). Highest percentage of total labour used in inter-cultivation activities were found to be contributed by female labour i.e. weeding (94 per cent) and watching of standing crops (88 per cent).

Farm Women in Decision-making

Decision-making is considered as the smallest unit of management. It is inescapable and indispensable in any phase of management. The capacity to decide in a unique attribute of a human being. Although, no physical work is involved in making decisions it is not an easy job. A decision refers to a course of action chosen from a number of possible alternatives. Decision-making is the process of consciously choosing course of action from available alternatives and integrating them for achieving desired goal. It involves decisions related to goals. The wise decision making in the families is crucial to create a friendly home environment, that will help each person to develop his or her potential. As such, family member must interact in some manner, because neither harmony nor conflict can occur without interaction. In the farm households though the women are active partners of male counterpart in all aspects of farm activities, yet their participation in decision-making is not visible.

Outwardly decision-making is the prerogative of the male head of the farm family. Since in Indian economy, farm business is a family enterprise participation of farmwomen in farm decision is of utmost important. Because cumulative effect of everyday decisions made and implemented both by the husband and wife in the areas of farm enables smooth functioning of farm business and thereby strengthen the rural economy. The success of farm business depends upon how meticulously family members follow the farm decisions and to what extent the family members, particularly the farmwomen is consulted and how often her views are considered seriously. But it is observed that, due to many factors participation of farmwomen in farm management is relatively less than that of home management. Sometimes, it is observed that based on the long-standing experiences farmwomen do take part in farm decisions. But they are very few in numbers. Such role in decision-making is generally complementary in nature. The involvement of farm women in decision making process is influenced by the level of knowledge, age, experiences, marital status, socio-economic status, exposure to outside world and knowledge gained through training as well. Several studies have been conducted on role of women in decision-making.

Kadlag (1999) observed that there is a positive impact of participation of farmwomen in decision-making on productive crops. She also reported that participation of farm women in decision making is prominent among the respondents who belong to middle age group (35 and above), small family size, low economic status and low annual gross income. She also confirms the fact that dominance of men in the family, illiteracy of farm women, less exposure to outside world, lack of confidence, shyness, lack of knowledge regarding improved agricultural technologies are the common reasons for low participation in farm decisions. The study conducted by Rajkishor *et.al.* (1999) also indicated that respondents belonging to middle age group (36-45 years and above 45 years) had participated more in decision making as compared to younger age group. Participation of farmwomen in decision-making is also affected by one's level of experience with the activity. That may be the reason why participation of farmwomen is comparatively more in post harvest activities than that of other farm activities.

Further it is observed from several studies that women are usually consulted in decisions related to transplanting, harvesting, storing, retention of seeds for future consumption and amount to be marketed etc. Sharma and Singh (1970) reported that larger proportion of women participated in decision-making in the areas of seed storage and harvesting Kakati (1996) studied the involvement of Assamese women in farm decision-making. Study reveals that participation of respondent's in decision making was the highest in buying and selling of live stock (91 per cent). In decisions regarding plant protection measures, use of fertilizers, purchase of family machinery more than half of the respondents were never and ever consulted.

Choudhury and Singh (2006) conducted a study in Jaipur district of Rajasthan to find out the participation of farmwomen in agricultural task. It was found out that crop selection, type and quantity of food grained to be stored are the major areas where participation was maximum with rank 1, 2 and 3 respectively and whereas participation is negligible in the areas like amount to be spent on farm power, implements and selling of food grains and farm products with the rank 28 and 27 respectively (Table 32.2).

AICRP on Home Science (1996-2001) reveals that most of the farm women were joint decision makers either with male or female members. In the case of farm operation one third of the farmwomen took joint decision with male members whereas equal portion of respondents either did not take farm decisions or took joint decision with female members. The study further reveals that joint decision with male was highest for purchase of agricultural land, input and implements, marketing of farm produce and to a considerable extent for sowing related matters crop care and nurturing, retention of seed for storage and marketing of farm produce. The decision area which exhibited fairly high profile of joint decisions with female members included decisions regarding harvesting and storage, quantitative retention of farm produce for consumption. Further, the decision areas in which highest percentage of farm women did not take decision included seeking employment as farm labour, employment and management farm labour, repayment of loan, obtaining loan and credit for farming. Their role as independent decision maker was negligible. The study further confirmed that farm women play an extensive participatory role in various areas, but their decision making roles remains to be weak.

Kaur (1987) observed that women of middle and upper middle age group were more involved in decision making process. Usually elderly women were consulted before taking any final decision. It was also reported that extent of participation in decision making was higher in the case of women belonging to nuclear family, medium farm size group, middle and upper caste, medium socio-economic status.

Table 32.2: Participation of Farm Women in Decision-making about Agricultural Activities

S.N	Activities	MS	Rank
1.	Decision making in economic tasks.		
	a) Amount to be spent on land.	1.64	23
	b) Amount to be spent on seed.	1.71	20
	c) Amount to be spent on fertilizer	1.68	21
	d) Amount to be spent on farm power and implements.	1.24	28
	e) Amount to be spent on farm labour.	2.53	13
	f) Decision of taking loans.	1.79	19
	g) Decision of repaying loans.	1.83	18
2.	Decision making in purchasing farm materials.		
	a) Buying farm power and implements.	1.58	25
	b) Purchasing of land.	1.89	17
	c) Purchasing of seed.	1.92	16
	d) Purchasing of fertilizers.	2.01	15
3.	Decision making in marketing of farm product.		
	a) Selling of food grains and farm product.	1.44	27
	b) Selling animals.	1.63	24
	c) Time to disposal of farm products.	1.67	22
	d) Quantity of disposal of farm products.	2.81	04
	e) Place of disposing.	1.52	26
	f) Rate at which product should be dispose.	2.51	14
4.	Decision making in agricultural aspects.		
	a) Field selection (area allocation to crops on farm).	2.69	09
	b) Crop selection.	2.90	01
	c) Varietals selection.	2.59	12
	d) Use of chemical fertilizer and manure.	2.62	11
	e) Use of insecticide and pesticides.	2.65	10
5.	Decision making in allied agricultural activities.		
	a) Type of food grains to be stored.	2.88	02
	b) Quantity of food grains to be stored.	2.83	03
	c) Size of subsidiary enterprise.	2.76	08
	d) Type and amount of feed for animals.	2.78	06
	e) Type of animals to be kept.	2.77	07
	f) No. of animal to be kept.	2.80	05

Source: Choudhury, H. and Singh, Sangram "Participation of Farm Women in Decision-making about Agricultural Task" Rural India, June-July 2006.

The study also confirmed that change agent link innovation proneness with high level of exposure to mass media were associated with high level of participation of women in decision-making. Talukdar and Karmakar (1997) conducted a study in Assam to find out the problems face by farmwomen in decision-making in agriculture. The major problems faced by the farmwomen in decision-making were lack of economic resources under their control (90 per cent), lack of contact with information sources (87 per cent), lack of pertinent knowledge about agriculture (81 per cent). Further, some other constraints like lack of support from extension agencies, lack of command in implementation of decisions, low educational status and low mobility were also reported by farmwomen as problems in decision-making.

Farm Women and Drudgery Involved in Work

Drudgery is usually conceived as physical and mental strain, agony, monotony and hardship experienced by human being that ultimately lead to reduction of her efficiency, productivity and over all dissatisfaction. Women in general, farm women in particular are subjected to physical and mental fatigues exploitation, pain, economic stress, malnutrition etc. In addition to it they are exposed to biological, chemical, physical and mechanical hazards while working in the field. Improved work, worker and workplace interaction is the emerging issue which need to be considered seriously while formulating policies and implementing them in action.

AICRP on Home Science (1996-2001) conducted a study to find out the drudgery prone activities performed by women in the areas of farm, allied and home. It was observed that transplanting, cutting/uprooting and weeding activities were performed by maximum numbers of women. The time spent and difficulty scene were also found high in these activities and thus indicating maximum drudgery under farm activities. Peak heart rate value and peak energy expenditure for transplanting, collecting and bringing fodder and fetching water were found more than the acceptable limit. Angle of bend during transplanting was maximum for long duration resulting severe pain in the back, calf muscles, ankles, and feet. The classification of work load on the basis heart rate and energy expenditure is presented in Table 32.3.

Impact of Drudgery Prone Activities on Farmwomen

It is observed that most of the farm women perform farm activities with traditionally designed tools, which leads to low efficiency and output, coupled with dissatisfaction and drudgery. Since all the farm activities are performed under scorching sun and rainy season with a awkward posture they have to suffer from health problems such as – sun burn, skin diseases, abortion, miscarriage and severe muscular skeleton problems. Acute pains in the body parts, especially in the neck, shoulder joints, elbows, lower back, wrist, knees etc. are common health problems, which the farm women, continued to bear and ready to bear as agricultural workers. The *feminization of agriculture* warrants that women should adopt technologies to increase their production and work efficiency, over come strain and stress, improve time use pattern and enhance quality products.

Table 32.3: Average and Peak Heart Rate and Energy Expenditure of Women Performing the Farm Activities and Classification of Workload

Activity	Working HR (b/min.)		Energy Expenditure (KJ/min.)		Classification of workload.	
Farm activities	Avg. HR	Peak HR	Avg. EE	Peak EE	Average	Peak
Cotton picking.	94	104	6.25	7.81	L	MH
Dibbling.	102	107	7.42	8.19	L	MH
Harvesting.	114	155	9.45	15.93	MH	VH
Sun drying of grains.	109	123	8.64	10.84	MH	H
Tea plucking.	95	103	6.4	7.65	L	L
Top dressing of fertilizer.	101	121	7.26	10.56	L	MH
Transplanting.	113	139	9.2	13.38	MH	VH
Weeding.	101	112	7.56	9.18	L	MH
Wheat harvesting.	115	135	10.24	12.74	MH	VH
Bundling.	133	143	12.4	14.01	H	VH
Uprooting of seedlings.	122	144	10.74	14.1	H	VH

L=Light; MH=Moderately Heavy; H=Heavy; VH=Very Heavy.
Source: All India Coordinated Project in Home Science (1996-2001), Education Division, ICAR, New Delhi.

Relevance of Technology for Farm Women in Developing Countries

Basic aim of application of farm technology includes increasing productivity, reducing drudgery, improving quality of products and produce, diversification of output and enriching quality of life of rural households. Several research institutes and State Agricultural Universities are involved in generating new technologies for farm households. Now the question is whether the technologies, which are developed, are in a position to reinforce the traditional role of farmwomen? How women are benefited from emerging technologies? Available evidences reveal that improved farm technologies due to green revolution tend to improve productivity and expansion of livestock. As a result, conventional animal husbandry and milk production is revolutionized by cross breeding imported breed with the local one. The position of women is also revolutionized in the process. Traditionally women cared for an undemanding cow, which ate hay and harvest waste and whose milk were either sold in near by areas or processed for their own consumption. Today women must feed, milk, and care several high yielding cows, which are more time consuming and energy demanding. Further, milking is done by women but milk is delivered to a collection point by the male counter part.

Thus, marketing and processing of milk products are either attended by the male member or engage male labour instead of female one. As a result male members of the family directly enjoy the benefit of white revolution as it increases regular flow of cash income to the hands of men. On the other hand work load for women increases for most of the cases. It was also reported that, technological advancement had displaced women from their traditional role. The mill technology is diffusing rapidly into rural areas, it reduces processing cost and at the same time brings a larger profit to its owners. Consequently, availability of rice mills displaces a larger number of female wage labourers. It was estimated that household labour for husking fell from 63 per cent to 55 per cent and hired labour from 32 per cent to 16 per cent. It was also found that 73 per cent of the household presently using rice mills had formerly employed female labour for this task in Bangladesh (Ahmed 1993 and Begum (1983) quoted in Duff & Paris 1988).

Moreover, decreasing the availability of female works in the field, decreased the demand for female workers. Proportion of women labour once engaged in weeding in paddy cultivation was relatively higher than any other activities. With the application of weedicide and harbicide demand of women labour decreases especially in large farm size group. As a result of introduction of direct seedling of rice, the participation female labour in uprooting of seedlings declined to a great extent. As a consequence of modern technology in agriculture, demand for female labour in women dominated activities decreased. In contrast due to double cropping, farm mechanization etc. demand for male labourers in male activities such as land preparation, fertilizer application, threshing etc. increased. Sinha (1980) reported that technological advancement has displaced women from their traditional activities and they have been marginally replaced in nonagricultural activities such as grass cutting, vegetable selling, cow dung collection, domestic servants etc. Farm mechanization (especially in transplanting and harvesting of rice) relieved Japanese women from heavy drudgery tasks and women's work pattern has gradually shifted from mainly agriculture to both in agriculture and in off- farm employment. Reduction of farm labour input did never result in increased (free) time for rest and/or leisure. Rather rural women selected an alternative path of diversifying work activities (Kada & Kada, 1983).

Full mechanization successfully relieved the women of high socio economic status but it had negative effect on women from lower caste and lowest income group by reducing demand for employment in peak season. Due to advancement of technology in many areas women have been displaced from the traditional jobs, because, technology necessitates training, up-gradation of knowledge and skill, which are out of their reach. Outwardly, it is observed that improved agricultural technology accompanied by partial mechanization had affected women from all socio economic background positively, either by relieving the women cultivators who were from higher socio-economic status or by increasing employment of women who were from lower socio economic status.

With view to reduce drudgery and to save time some of the Institutes like Indian Council of Agricultural Research (ICAR), CRRI Cuttack, CIAE Bhopal and Home Science Colleges of State Agricultural Universities have designed some improved ergonomically sound farm implements. However, the level of adoption of those tools are not that satisfactory because of the following reasons.

- Lack of awareness of women regarding physiological cost of work and its importance.
- Lack of financial resources among farmers to possess
- Lack of appropriateness to the agro climatic conditions
- Manufactures/entrepreneurs are skeptical about the demand for improved tools.
- Lack of technical backup to support local commercial production of improved tools.
- Lack of coordination between anthropomatric measurements of women and implement especially designed for them.
- Lack of training on use of improved tools.
- Lack of subsidy and rural credit for financial assistance to procure improved technologies

An attempt was made by AICRP on Home Science (1996-2001) to assess the impact of technology in reducing physiological and muscular stress while performing various activities related to farm, home and allied activities. It was observed that back pain and grip fatigue of the farmer women were reduced to a significant level with the use of improved 'dibbler'. Further, 'finger blade' and '*kilta*' increased work efficiency along with reducing drudgery including finger injury. Improved spreading tool encouraged the farmwomen to adopt right posture and to reduce drudgeries in sundrying of grains. (Wasnik 2006) stated that the impact of new farm technologies on farm women would be different than that of men, as women occupy different position in the social system. The farm women have multidimensional roles as mother, housewives, producers and entrepreneurs. Therefore, it is essential to adopt a multidimensional technology approach for women, covering essentially four space namely psycho-space, related to mental makeup, & attitudes, socio space related to her home and society, techno-space related to her productive aspects and eco-space related to credit aspect. Women in farm households will get benefits from new agricultural technologies when they have control over the income from household land and labour. Emerging technologies will have an impact on demands for women labour when they are socially appropriate, women friendly, economically accessible. The design of such farm technologies should be such which can be maintained in local environment.

Conclusion

Agriculture is the largest predominant private sector in which majority of the rural women are engaged. In Indian agriculture, women perform four different types of role as worker (a source of power) as operator (a controller) as manager (a farmer) and as an entrepreneur (a business person). Their role ranges from manager to landless labourer, depending on their land owning status. In order to empower women economically, there is a need to design some specific programmes like vocational orientation with capacity building strategies, marketing and banking awareness, financial management etc. Further, farmwomen need to be empowered with technical knowledge. The failure of adoption of new technology among farmwomen specifically is due to the fact that women are not aware of new technological inventions and its importance in relation to physiological cost of work.

As such, provision of demonstration on new technology may help in disseminating technical know how to farmwomen. With a view to empower farmwomen socially and psychologically, there is a need to conduct training in agriculture for the women, by the women and of the women. Training module should be made by keeping in view farmwomen as farmer and producer of crop. The Indian National Policy for Empowerment of Women (2001) has stressed the need to mainstream *gender perspective* in the process of development and envisages women specific interventions where there are currently gaps in policies and programmes. As such promoting gender equality and empowering women is an important agenda of the Millennium Development Goals, since it is considered as the third important goal. Women have to be targeted for development. Their multidimensional role in agriculture must be empowered. Because when women are empowered, the benefits are enjoyed by entire family. As often quoted **"educating a women is as good as opening a school and enterprising a**

woman is as good as opening an industry in rural areas." As such timely information, and adequate education with appropriate communication system and resource support will empower farmwomen in agriculture, which in turn will enhance the quality of life of women in particular and confirm rural development in general.

Appendix 1: Sex-wise Distribution of Work

S.N	Nature of work	Male/Female participation in percentage	
		When hired	When self-employed
1.	Ploughing	100M	100M
2.	Hoeing	100M	100M
3.	Sweeping up dry leaves etc. carrying and burning it in the fields as pre-monsoon soil treatment.	SN	SN
4.	Filling baskets with kitchen ash or cowdung for manuring.	60-70M, 30F	SN
5.	Carrying the manure basket – loads to the fields.	100F	SN
6.	Carrying baskets of seeds to fields.	100M-80F	SN
7.	Sowing the paddy seed by broadcasting.	100M	100M
8.	Cutting out green leaf for manure:		
	a) If from house compounds and easily accessible bushes.	30M-70F	SN
	b) If cut from slopes and ridges less easily accessible or from trees.	100M	100M
	c) Collecting leaves cut down, bundling and carrying head- loads to the field	30M-70F	SN
9.	Spreading the green leaf by broadcasting it in the fields (swinging and throwing twigs of it far out).	90M-10F	90M-10F
10.	Submerging the leaf manure by tramping over in muddy rice-transplanting bed of the field.	90M-10F	90M-10F
11.	Covering the narrow boundary ridges (about 2-4 feet broad) with sticky soil to stand the monsoon flooding.	100M	100M
12.	Leveling the ploughed slushy field with draft animals.	100M	100M
13.	Transplanting:		
	a) Picking the paddy seedlings and banding them.	10M-90F	20M-80F
	b) Carry bundled seedling to the transplant.	20M-80F	30M-70F
	c) Planting the seedlings.	10M-90F	30M-70F
14.	Weeding.	100F	100F
15.	Harvesting:		
	a) Budding the harvested stalk.	30M-70F	SN
	b) Carrying it to threshing yard.	SN	SN
	c) Threshing.	20M-80F	40M-60F

S.N	Nature of work	Male/Female participation in percentage	
		When hired	When self-employed
16.	Cowdung washing and preparing threshing yard.	100M	100F
17.	Winnowing:		
	a) Standing over four feet high level and dropping grain.	90M-10F	70M-30F
	b) Fanning against the dropping grains to waft out chaff.	10M-90F	30M-70F
18.	Preparing huge haystacks shaped conically to resist wind and rain.		
19.	a) Cutting huge legs and splitting.	100M	100M
	b) Hoeing pieces into handy sizes for storage.	70M-30F	SN
20.	Tree, climbing, plucking, fruits such as coconut, arecanut, jack fruit, or climbing tree for any purpose.	100M	100M
21.	Husking of coconuts for sale except when in small number of less than 20-30.	100M	100M
22.	Cleaning homestead yards and coating cowdung lotion for drying and processing of any crop yield (grains, straw).	100F	100F&C
23.	Watering the vegetation with shoulder loaded earthen containers.	100M-90F	SN&C
24.	Cutting grass for fodder from the hill slope areas.	10M-90F&FC	10M-90F&FC
25.	General caretaking of draft animals.	100M	100M
26.	Cattle grazing and guarding crops against stray cattle menace.	100F&C	100F&C
27.	Cleaning cattle sheds daily and dumping the dung in storage pits.	100F	100F&C

Note: M: Males; F: Females; C: Children male or female of 8 to 15 years; SN denotes sex-neutrality which means that a male or a female can be employed.

Source: Har Swarup Singh & R/L/ Punia, "Role and Status of Women in Agriculture Retrospect and Prospect" – Paper presented in the International Conference on Appropriate Agricultural Technologies for farm Women 30 Nov. – 6 Dec., 1988, ICAR New Delhi.

References

Abdullah, Tahrunnesa, A., and Zeidenstein, Sondra. Village Women of Bangladesh: Prospects for change, Pergamon Press Ltd., Oxford, England. 1982

All India Coordinated Research Project in Home Science. Education Division, ICAR, New Delhi. 1996-2001

Anonymous. Proceedings of National Workshop on Women in Agriculture: Farmers to Farmers Extension, 5-6 March, 2002, organized by Ministry of Agriculture, Govt. of India, New Delhi. 2002b

Arunachalam, R. Involvement of Women in Farm Management Activities, Indian Farming, 56(4).

2005

Beohar, B.B., A.K. Sarawgi and Choudhuri, A.K. Women's Contribution in Paddy Cultivation – A case study of a village of Chattisgarh Region of Madhya Pradesh, Indian Journal of Agricultural Economics. 1999

Chayyadevi, L. A study on the Participation of Farm Women in Decision Making on Farm and Home Aspects in Dharwad District of Karnataka State. Thesis Abstracts. 1980

Choudhury, H. and Singh, S. Participation of Farm Women in Decision Making about Agricultural Tasks, Rural India, June-July. 2006

Devi, A.L. and Reddy, S.V. Role Expectation and Role Performance of Rural Women in Farm Activities. Indian Journal of Extension Education. 1984

Devi, L.. Rural Women – Management in Farm and Home Northern Book Centre, New Delhi. 1987

Duff, B. and Paris, T. Women in Rice System: Synthesizing Research and Development, Paper presented at ICAR/IRRI sponsored conference on appropriate technology of farm women: Linkage and strategies, Nov.20 – Dec.4, New Delhi. 1988

FAO (1980). Report of the Workshop on Integration of Women in Agricultural & Rural Development at NIRD, Hyderabad, India, Nov. 17-22. 1988

Hazarika, R. A study on involvement of Karbi Women in Jhum Cultivation and their perceived Drudgery in performance of Farm Operations. M.Sc.(H.Sc.) Thesis, Assam Agricultural University, Jorhat. 1998

Kada, R. and Kada Y. "The changing role of women in Japanese agriculture: the impact of new rice technology on women's employment", Women Rice Farming, Gower Publishing Company, U.S.A. 1983

Kadlog, Sangita. Role of Women in Decision Making in Farming in Sangamner Tahsil of Ahmednagar District, Unpublished Thesis of M.Sc. Agril. Economics submitted to MPKV Rahuri, Dist. Ahmednagar. 1994

Kalita, M. and Pathak, M. Participation of Farm Women in Storing Grains and their knowledge towards it. Indian Journal of Hill Farming, 9(1&2):64-67. 1996

Kaur, M. Emerging Status, Role of Rural Women in the Context of Changing Technology in Haryana, Unpublished Ph.D. Thesis, HAU, Hissar. 1982

Kaur, S. Women in Rural Development. Mittal Publications, Delhi. 1987

Kaur, S. and R.K. Punia. Work Participation of Women in Rural Households – An empirical Study, Guru Nanak Journal of Sociology. 1998

Mishra, P.K., R.M. Sahu and Agrawal G.P. Extent and Proportion of Women's Participation in Paddy Cultivation – A case study of Kymore Platean and Satpura Hills of Madhya Pradesh, Indian Journal of Agricultural Economics, 54(3) Seminar Issue. 1999

Munjal, S.; Sangwam, V. and Grover, S. "Work Participation and Time Allocation Pattern Among Rural Women". Women and work in Indian Society (ed). Discovery Publishing House, Delhi. 1988

33

Rural Female Agricultural Workers in West Bengal

Jabir Hasan Khan and Md. Mustaquim

Women in the world as well as in India constitute about half of the total human population. Women's participation in economic activities is very common in all the countries of the world and their role in the process of economic, social, cultural and political development has been recognized all over the globe. Women are prominently engaged in all activities of the economy, in agriculture and industry, in trade and commerce, in transport and communication, in banking and insurance, in education and health, in all organized and unorganized sectors of the economy and also as housewives, performing all types of jobs so-called non-productive household duties. But the participation of females is absolutely as well as proportionately lower than the males in various types of economic activities in both rural and urban sectors. There are certain factors which determine the participation of females in labour force (Sabhanayakam, S., 1988). It has been explained by Correa (1963) that relative scarcity of labour, per capita income and economic structure also influence the participation of women in the labour force. In India there is no scarcity of labour and the per capita income is also very low. The limited participation of females in economic activities is caused by a number of socio-economic and cultural factors such as customs, traditions, religion, caste, taboos, size of the family, level of education, level of industrialization, nature of work, structure of employment, family income, fertility level etc. Only in the recent times, the outlook of females has been changing towards engaging themselves in employments and that is due to economic compulsions only. Improved standard of living and investment in human capital can result in the increased participation of females in the workforce (Sabhanayakam, S., 1988).

The development is an outcome of the efforts made for the eradication of poverty and unemployment and removal of inequalities of regions (Seer, D., 1969). It may also be expressed that development is the state of change from a given situation of a region to become better one within a given period of time (Sharma, R.C., 1989). The development of a region can be identified with increase in the employment opportunities, availability of infrastructural facilities and services, proper distribution of resources, increased production, investment and consumption and so on (Verma, S.S., 1993). As a whole it may be said that development is a progressive change in norms, values, belief and standard of living of the people in between two points of time to get better one (Sharma, R.C. and Kumar, N., 1993).

The prosperity and growth of a country or region depends on its females as they not only constitute nearly half of the population but also exert a great influence on growth of the remaining half of the human population. The importance of the rural female agricultural workers in socio-economic development has emerged out of need to maximize output in growth, to reduce population growth and to control factors that interfere with productivity and growth. There is a direct relationship between rural female agricultural workers and factors of socio-economic development. In this direction, the role of rural female agricultural workers cannot be ignored from the process of socio-economic development in India in general and in the state of West Bengal in particular.

Therefore, a detailed study needs to better understand the relationship between rural female agricultural workers and levels of socio-economic development in West Bengal.

Objectives of the Study

The present study outlines the following objectives:

- to examine the existing spatial distribution of rural female agricultural workers (cultivators and agricultural labourers),
- to identify the levels of socio-economic development,
- to find out the relationship between rural female agricultural workers and levels of socio-economic development,
- to explains the linear relationship and test them to find out the significant levels of selected variables of socio-economic development influencing rural female agricultural workers and
- to suggest a blue print to minimize the gap in the levels of socio-economic development and share of rural female agricultural workers.

Data and Methodology

The present paper is completely based on secondary sources of data obtained from Census of India publications, New Delhi and district-wise indicators of socio-economic development collected from Bureau of Applied Economics and Statistics, Government of West Bengal, Kolkata for the year 2001. In the present study, a set of forty five (45) socio-economic indicators of various sectors have been taken into account to measure the levels of socio-economic development in seventeen districts of West Bengal. These indicators fall into ten categories such as population characteristics, education, literacy, agriculture, industry, health, power, transport and communication, per capita income and finance. In the first step, the raw data for each variable which influences the variations of socio-economic development have been computed into standard score. It is generally known as Zi value or 'Z' score. The score measure the departure of individual observations, expressed in a comparable form. This means it becomes a linear transformation of the original data. It may be expressed as:

$$Z_i = \frac{X_i - \overline{X}}{SD}$$

Where, Zi is the standard score, Xi is the original or individual value for observation, $\overline{X}$ is the mean value for the variable and SD denotes standard deviation.

In the second step, the Z-scores of all variables have been added district wise and the average has taken out for these variables which may be called as composite score (CS) for each district and may be algebraically expressed as:

$$CS = \frac{\sum Z_{ij}}{N}$$

Where, N refers to the number of indicators (variables), ΣZij indicate Z-score of an indication j in district i. The positive values relating to the districts Z-score show high level of socio-economic development and negative values the low level of socio-economic development. T-test technique has been applied to find out the determinant which is significant at 1 per cent and 5 per cent level.

Study Area

West Bengal has been selected as a study area which is located between 21o25' to 26o50' north latitudes and 86o30' to 89o58' east longitudes with three international frontiers, Bangladesh, Nepal and Bhutan. It covers an area of about 88,752 sq. km. (2.70 per cent of the India's total geographical area) and stretching from the Himalayas in the north to the Bay of Bengal in the south. It is surrounded by Sikkim and Bhutan in the north, Assam and Bangladesh in the east, the Bay of Bengal in the south and Orissa, Jharkhand, Bihar and Nepal in the west. According to 2001 Census its total population is 80,176,197 (7 79 per cent of India's total population), density is 904 persons per sq. km. (In terms of population density West Bengal is on the top among the Indian states). Females literacy rate is 60.22 per cent (while in India as whole it is 54.70 per cent). Total female working population is 70,93,646 (18.32 per cent of West Bengal's total female population and 1.43 per cent of India's total female population).There are eighteen districts in the state. But in the present analysis, the Kolkata district has not been taken into account because it is fully urbanized, therefore, the study covers only seventeen districts of the state.

Discussion

Regional Distribution of Rural Female Cultivators: For the analysis of rural female cultivators in West Bengal Z-score technique has been applied. Among the districts of the state it varies from –1.10 scores in Haora districts to 2.57 scores in Puruliya district. The entire range of variations of scores may be arranged into three categories like high (above 0.50 scores), medium (-0.50 to 0.50 scores) and low (below –0.50 scores).

The general pattern of rural female cultivators reveals that four districts of the state namely, Koch Behar, Uttar Dinajpur, Dakshin Dinajpur and Puruliya have high grade (above 0.50 scores) of rural female cultivators and fifty per cent of them constitute a linear region in the northern plain of the state.

Six districts with Z-scores of –0.50 to 0.50 belong to medium category of rural female cultivators and five of them make two distinct regions in the state. One which is comparatively large in size locates in the south-western part of the state including the districts of Bankura, Medinipur and Twenty Four Parganas (South). The second region occurs in the northern part of the state comprising the districts of Darjeeling and Jalpaiguri. The low grade (below –0.50 scores) of rural female cultivators is found in seven districts of the state namely, Maldah, Murshidabad, Barddhaman, Nadia, Twenty Four Parganas (North), Hugli and Haora. All these districts combined form a prominent region which stretches from Maldah districts in the north to Twenty Four Parganas (North) and Haora districts in the south.

Geographical Distribution of Rural Female Agricultural Workers

In the present analysis rural female cultivators and agricultural labourers are combined together in terms of scores, and average is worked out to represent the performance of rural female agricultural workers. In the State, the scores of rural female agricultural workers vary from –1.24 in Haora district to 1.36 in Puruliya district (Table 33.1). These range of variations may be graded into three groups i.e. High (above +0.50 scores), Medium (-0.50 to 0.50 scores) and Low (below –0.50 scores).

Table 33.1: District-wise Distribution of Rural Female Agricultural Workers and Levels of Socio-Economic Development in West Bengal, 2001

District	Z- score of		Composite Mean Z-score of Rural Female Agricultural Workers	Composite Mean Z-score of Socio-economic Development
	Rural Female Cultivators	Rural Female Agricultural Labourers		
Darjeeling	0.49	-1.32	-0.42	0.14
Jalpaiguri	-0.15	-0.76	-0.46	-0.09
Koch Behar	1.56	0.67	1.11	0.12
Uttar Dinajpur	0.77	1.16	0.96	-0.25
Dakshin Dinajpur	0.54	1.18	0.86	0.07
Maldah	-0.63	-0.50	-0.56	-0.15
Murshidabad	-1.06	-1.28	-1.17	-0.22
Birbhum	-0.25	0.62	0.19	0.02
Barddhaman	-0.76	1.31	0.28	-0.05
Nadia	-0.87	-0.84	-0.85	0.03
Twenty Four Parganas (N)	-0.85	-0.65	-0.75	-0.05
Hugli	-0.76	0.98	0.11	0.15
Bankura	0.50	1.20	0.85	0.20
Puruliya	2.57	0.15	1.36	0.20
Medinipur	0.28	0.41	0.34	0.15
Haora	-1.10	-1.38	-1.24	-0.05
Kolkata	No Rural Area	No Rural Area	No Rural Area	No Rural Area
Twenty Four Parganas (S)	-0.29	-0.94	-0.61	-0.21

Source: Calculation is based on district level published data, Census of India, 2001 and Statistical Abstract, Govt. of West Bengal, 2002-2003.

The high level of rural female agricultural workers is found in five districts of the state. They are Koch Behar, Uttar Dinajpur, Dakshin Dinajpur, Bankura and Puruliya. Four of them make two distinct regions, one occurs in the northern plain and other region lies in the western part (Rehar region) of the state. Nearly thirty three per cent districts of the state laying under the medium grade (-0.50 to 0.50 scores) of rural female agricultural workers and constitute two separate belts in the state. The largest one is located is the southern part of the state including the districts of Birbhum, Barddhaman, Hugli and Medinipur. The second region composed of Darjeeling and Jalpaiguri districts, lies in the northern part of the state.

The low category districts (below –0.50 scores) of rural female agricultural workers form a continuous belt in south-eastern margin of the state comprising the districts of Maldah, Murshidabad, Nadia, Twenty Four Parganas (North), Twenty Four Parganas (South) and Haora.

Levels of Socio-economic Development

The levels of socio-economic development, in fact as an average picture of the attainment of the districts with respect to various selected socio-economic variables recorded uneven spatial patterns of socio-economic development. The composite mean Z-scores of socio-economic development by districts is given in Table 33.1.

It will be seen from the Table 33.1 that there are wide range of variations in the levels of socio-economic development among the districts of the state. It varies from -0.25 scores (Uttar Dinajpur district) to 0.20 scores (Bankura and Puruliya districts). The entire range of variation may be grouped into three grades i.e. High (above 0.16 scores), Medium (-0.16 to 0.16 scores) and Low (below -0.16 scores).

Table 33.1 depict that the high level (above 0.16 scores) of socio-economic development is found only in two districts of the state. These districts are Bankura (0.20) and Puruliya (0.20) and constitute a region in the south-western part of the state. Nearly 67 per cent districts of the state fall under the moderate grade (-0.16 to 0.16 scores) of socio-economic development and they make three distinct regions in the state. The first region which is relatively large in size locates in the southern part of the state including the districts of Birbhum, Barddhaman, Nadia, Hugli, Haora, Twenty Four Parganas (North) and Medinipur. The second region lies in the northern part of the state comprising the districts of Darjeeling, Jalpaiguri and Koch Behar, and the third region of this slab occurs in the southern part of the north Bengal plain, which is composed of Dakshin Dinajpur and Maldah districts.

The low level (below -0.16 scores) of socio-economic development is concentrated in three districts of the state and they are scattered all over the state. So, they fail to make any identifiable region in the state. The overall picture that emerges from the spatial distribution of composite scores of socio-economic variables is that the level of socio-economic development is high in the southern districts as compared to the northern districts of the state.

Rural Female Agricultural Workers vis-a-vis Socio-economic Development

The regional dimensions of rural female agricultural workers vis-a-vis levels of socio-economic development among the districts of the state of West Bengal. In the index of map, abscissa refers rural female agricultural workers and ordinate represents the level of socio-economic development. The districts with reference to composite mean Z-scores of socio-economic development may be arranged into three grades such as high (above 0.16 scores), medium (-0.16 to 0.16 scores) and low (below –0.16 scores), whereas in terms of composite mean Z-scores of rural female agricultural workers, these categories may be grouped as above 0.50 scores (High), -0.50 scores to 0.50 scores (Medium) and below–0.50 score (Low).

About 28 per cent districts of the state come under the high category of rural female agricultural workers, of which two districts have high, two medium and remaining one low levels of socio-economic development. A dominant region of high grade of rural female agricultural workers vis-a-vis high level of socio-economic development is observed in the south-western part of the state comprising the districts of Bankura and Puruliya. One-third districts (six districts) of the study area lie under the medium level of rural female agricultural workers and all these districts are also associated with medium category of socio-economic development. Nearly eighty three percent of these districts constitute two distinct regions in the state. The first region which is relatively big in area is located in the southern part of the state including the districts of Birbhum, Barddhaman, Hugli and Medinipur. The second region occurs in the northern part of the state which is composed of Darjeeling and Jalpaiguri districts. There are six districts in the low grade of rural female agricultural workers; four of them show medium level of socio-economic development and remaining two districts low grade of socio-economic development. Out of four, three districts of low grade of rural female agricultural workers versus medium level of socio-economic development make a linear region in the south-eastern margin of the state comprising the districts of Nadia, Twenty Four Parganas (North) and Haora.

The foregoing discussion reveals that only two districts of the state have high level of rural female agricultural workers versus high grade of socio-economic development whereas only one district of the study area is under the high level of rural female agriculture workers with low level of socio-economic development. Not a single district come under the low grade of rural female agricultural workers vis-à-vis high level of socio-economic development. It means that there is more or less positive relationship between rural female agricultural workers and level of socio-economic development.

Correlation (r) Between Rural Female Agricultural Workers and Other Selected Variables of Socio-economic Development

The testing of simple association among rural female cultivators (Y_1), rural female agricultural labourers (Y_2), rural female agricultural workers (Y_3) and selected socio-economic variables was attempted. Among the forty five variables, only five variables are significant at 99 per cent level of confidence in their relationship with the rural female cultivators (Y_1), namely, X_{26} (employment rate), X_{29} (rural employment rate), X_{30} (urban employment rate), X_{31} (percentage of workers in cultivation) and X_{37} (number of hospitals and primary health centers per lakh of population). Only one variable i.e. X_{30} has indirect relationship, whereas the remaining four have direct relationship with rural female cultivators (Y_1).

There are seven variables, out of forty five selected variables of socio-economic development, which have high significant degree of positive relationship with rural female agricultural labourers (Y_2). They are: X_{12} (percentage of ST and SC population to total population), X_{26} (employment rate), X_{28} (female employment rate), X_{29} (rural employment rate), X_{31} (percentage of workers in cultivation), X_{37} (number of hospital and primary health centers per lakh of population) and X_{42} (number of post and telegraph offices per lakh of population). Among all the 45 variables, X_2, x_4, X_5, X_6, X_9, X_{17}, X_{19}, X_{20}, X_{23}, X_{30}, X_{36}, X_{39} and X_{40} are significant at 95 per cent level of confidence in their relationship with rural female agricultural labourers (Y_2) in the state. The variables X_4 and X_6 are positively correlated whereas remaining eleven variables are negatively correlated with rural female agricultural labourers (Y_2).

It is also found that only two variables X_{29} and X_{32} are significant at 99 per cent level of confidence and both are positively correlated with rural female agricultural workers (Y_3). Moreover, four variables such as X_{27} (employment rate), X_{27} (male employment rate), X_{31} (percentage of workers in cultivation) and X_{37} (number of hospitals and primary health centers per lakh of population) are significant at 95 per cent level of confidence and all have positive relationship with rural female agricultural workers (Y_3).

It may be concluded that the spatial variations in the distribution of rural female agricultural workers in the study area have been mainly caused by population density, percentage of ST and SC population, level of urbanization, female literacy rate, educational facilities, intensity of cropping, industrialization, infrastructural facilities like, electricity, surface road, hospitals, primary health centers, etc.

Conclusion

The foregoing analysis for rural female cultivators, agricultural labourers, agricultural workers and socio-economic development separately and rural female agricultural workers vis-à-vis socio-economic development clearly shows that there is a wide regional variation among the districts of the state of West Bengal. The rural female agricultural workers increased from south to north and east to west in the study area. The level of socio-economic development is comparatively high in the western and south-western districts as compared to the northern districts of the state. The high level of rural female agricultural workers with high level of socio-economic development is mainly found in the south-western districts of the state, whereas, the districts of low grade of rural female agricultural workers verses low as well as medium categories of socio-economic development are mainly located in the eastern and south-eastern parts of the state. Moreover, it has been also noted in the study that some districts have high level of rural female agricultural workers with high level of socio-economic development, some have high grade of rural female agricultural workers verses low level of socio-economic development and some others have low levels of both rural female agricultural workers and level of socio-economic development. Therefore, the priority in the developmental planning should be given to those districts which have low grade of rural female agricultural workers and low level of socio-economic development for minimizing the inter-district variations in the levels of development.

References

Bagchi, K.K. and Sarkar, S., Development of Social Sector in West Bengal: A Study in Inter-District Disparity, *Indian Journal of Regional Science*, Vol. 35, No. 2, pp. 115-130. 2003.

Banerjee, S. (1973), The Labour Force and Economic Development, *Indian Labour Journal*, Vol. 14, No. 1, pp. 1-20. 1973.

Beohar, Prabha, Women's Participation in Agriculture, in Murty, S. and Gaur, K.D. (ed.) *Women Work Participation and Empowerment: Problems and Prospects,* RBSA Publishers, Jaipur, pp. 124-125. 2002.

Bhattacharya, J., Present Socio-Economic Features and Related Problems of Puruliya District, West Bengal, *Geographical Review*, Vol. 66, No. 1-4, June, pp. 131-142. 2004.

Boserup, E., *Women's Role in Economic Development,* Allen and Unwin, London. 1970.

Census of India, *Primary Census Abstract, Total Population*, Series 1, Table A-5. 2001.

Chandna, R.C., Female Working Force in Rural Punjab-1961, *Manpower Journal*, Vol. 2, No. 4, pp. 47-62. 1967.

Chandrasekhar, C.P., Agrarian Change and Occupational Diversification, Non-agricultural employment and Rural Development in West Bengal, *The Journal of Peasant Studies*, Vol. 20, No. 2. 1993.

Correa, H., *The Economics of Human Resources,* North Holland Publishing Company, Amsterdam. 1963.

Dewan, R., Rural Female Labour and Development, *Economic and Political Weekly*, Vol. 14, p. 26. 1979.

Dixon, R.B., Women in Agriculture: Counting the Labour Force in Developing Countries, *Population and Development Review*, Vol. 8, No. 3, p. 35-42. 1982.

Durand, J.D., *The Labour Force in Economic Development,* Princeton University Press, Princeton, New Jersey. 1975.

Gadgil, D.R., Employment in Rural Areas, *The Indian Workers*, part 1, Vol. 19, No. 43,

July 26, pp. 5-8. 1971.

Gosal, G.S., Occupational Structure of India's population, *National Geographical Journal of India*, Vol. 4, pp. 137-148. 1958.

Gosal, G.S. and Krishan, G., Regional Disparities in Levels of Socio-economic Development in Punjab, *Kurukshetra.* 1984.

Government of West Bengal, Statistical Abstract, 2002-03, *Bureau of Applied Economic and Statistics,* Kolkata. 2003.

Gulati, L., Female Work Participation: A Study of Inter-State Differences, *Economic and Political Weekly*, Vol. X, No. 1 & 2, pp. 35-42. 1975.

Harold, W., Women's Work, Economic Growth, Ideology and Social Structure, *Industrial Relations*, Vol. 7, No. 3, p. 2. 1968.

Khan, J.H. and Shafiqullah, Female Work Participation in Primary Activities in Uttar Pradesh, in Rai, R.K., Singh, S., Nayak, D.K. and Mipur, B.S. (ed.), *Environment Resources and Development*, The Geographical Society of North-Eastern Hill Region, Shillong, pp. 354-358. 2001.

Kumar, N.P., Regional Disparity in the Status of Women Across Indian States, *Indian Journal of Regional Science*, Vol. XXXVIII, No. 2, pp. 1-14. 2006.

Kundu, A., Trends and Pattern of Female Employment in India: A Case of Organised Information, *The Indian Journal of Labour Economics*, Vol. 40, No.3. 1997.

Mondal, S.K., *Agricltural Wages and Employment in West Bengal,* Fastern Publishers, Kolkata. 1992.

34

Gender Issues in Agriculture

Rekha Bhagat and Surya S.

Agriculture has been and will continue to be the life-line of Indian economy, and the agrarian character of the economy is likely to be unchanged at least in the near future. In Indian agriculture, rural women play a vital role and participate in all stages of crop production, as they constitute 50 per cent of rural labour force. Most of the women perform various works for their livelihood and agriculture is considered as the biggest unorganized sector where a large number of Indian rural women takes part actively. These rural women who work in the farm participate in a wide range of farm activities by slogging alongside with men in the field as well as taking care of the home and children, thereby performing a dual role that of a homemaker and of a partner in the farming activities outside the home. The 2001 Census data indicates that 43.6 percent of women are working as agricultural labourers and 34.5 percent as cúltivators (Census of India 2001). Despite their important contributions in crop production, post harvest processing, livestock management and food security, Indian women have always been discriminated against men in the development process.

Table 34.1: Working Population Ratio (WPR) 1955-1999/00

Year	Rural		Urban	
	Male	Female	Male	Female
1955	59.2	26.6	51.4	11.6
1972-73	53.6	31.4	49.4	13.2
1977-78	54.4	32.6	50.0	15.3
1983	54.3	33.7	50.9	14.9
1987-88	53.9	32.3	50.6	15.2
1993-94	55.3	32.8	52.0	15.4
1999-00	53.1	29.9	51.9	13.9

Source: NSS Survey

While looking into the international scenario, UNDP has reported that 67 per cent of the works are done by women in the world, while only 10 per cent of the global income is earned by them and a mere 1 per cent of global property is earned by them. Still women in many countries lack right to property inheritance, right to own land, access to education and credit, to work outside home and also face food insecurity and severe malnutrition.

Indian Women in Agriculture: Environment and Rural Production

Female-headed Households: The number of female-headed households is increasing significantly in rural areas in many developing countries as rural men migrate due to the lack of employment and other income-generating opportunities. In sub-Saharan Africa, 31 per cent of rural households are headed by women, while in Latin America and the Caribbean and Asia, women head 17 percent and 14 percent, respectively. While there are different types of female-headed households, in almost all countries female-headed households are concentrated among the poorer strata of society and often have lower incomes than male-headed households. The problems of female-headed households in rural areas vary according to their degree of access to productive resources. FAO has identified, for example, the potential consequences of the absence of male labour both in terms of declining yields and outputs or shifts in production toward less nutritious crops requiring less labour and in terms of increased reliance on child labour which, in turn, has further implications for the family and for the human capital of the country This gives rise to feminization of agriculture leading to feminization of poverty. Therefore, in these cases women's access to labour-saving technology is of particular importance.

Table 34.2: Status of Women in India

Particulars	
Total population (million)	1,025.25
Total women (million)	494.82 (48.26 per cent of total population)
Work participation rate (per cent)	25.67
Total cultivators(million)	127.62
Female cultivators (per cent)	32.35
Total agricultural laborer (million)	107.44
Women agricultural laborer (per cent)	44.62

Source: Census 2001

Table 34.3 presents the estimates of population and work force as on 1st January 2000 by rural-urban location and by gender along with corresponding estimates for 1st January 1994 drawn from Visaria (1998) with WPRs drawn from the NSS 50th Round Employment-Unemployment Survey (July 1993-June

1994). Also presented in this table are the underlying (crude) worker-population ratios drawn from the two quinquennial surveys.

Table 34.3: Population, Work Force and Crude Worker Population Ratios (WPRs) by Rural-Urban Residence and Gender in India

Segment	Population		Work Force		WPRs	
	1993-94	1999-2000	1993-94	1999-2000	1993-94	1999-2000
Rural Males	339.360	367.24	0187.660	195.000	553	531
Rural Females	317.950	344.640	104.290	103.050	328	299
Rural Persons	657.310	711.880	291.950	298.050	444	419
Urban Males	125.200	147.440	65.100	76.370	520	518
Urban Females	112.590	135.010	17.340	18.770	154	139
Urban Person	237.790	282.440	82.440	95.140	347	337
Males	464.560	514.680	252.760	271.370	545	527
Females	430.540	479.650	121.630	121.820	286	254
Persons	895.100	994.330	374.390	393.190	420	395

Source: Census 2001

A striking result is the near-stagnation in the number of female workers in the country as a whole and an absolute reduction in the number of women workers in rural India. This reduction in the number of women workers in rural India, by a little ovel.3 million is just about offset by a rise in the number of urban women workers (1.4million).

Working Participation Rate of females in India (Table 34.4) across states vary significantly. Notwithstanding the stability in WPR at macro level, there has been a significant variation in WPR across states for both men and women. Some states like AP, Gujarat, Rajasthan, Maharashtra, MP, Karnataka, and TN shows a consistently higher WPR than all India average. These states are predominantly dryland regions. In the dryland regions there is a greater importance of livestock economics. In livestock management women are more engaged. In drylands the predominance of crops like rice or cotton where women have been traditionally engaged. Apart from these reasons, higher WRP among females in dryland regions might also be due to the migration of male members of the households and a higher incidence of commercialization. When crop production takes place under a highly risky environment employing hired labour and female labour, if not enough males are available, may give significant pay off. This is probably why the percentage of female workers engaged in agriculture is relatively higher in these regions except for Rajasthan.

Table 34.4: Women's WPR in Rural Areas (All ages)

States	1961	1971	1981	1993-94	1999-00
AP	64.3	60.2	60.2	52.1	47.8
Bihar	56.0	52.7	51.1	17.2	17.3
Gujarat	55.3	52.8	54.2	39.6	41.3
Haryana	52.9	47.5	49.8	27.1	20.2
Karnataka	60.4	56.4	57.2	43.0	38.0
Kerala	47.4	45.3	45.2	23.8	23.8
MP	61.6	55.3	56.4	42.0	38.2
Maharashtra	58.1	52.6	55.4	47.7	43.4
Punjab	53.5	53.8	54.5	22.0	28.0
Rajasthan	60.1	53.6	52.2	45.7	38.8
TN	62.2	58.6	59.2	47.8	43.0
UP	59.2	53.0	51.5	21.9	20.1
WB	53.5	48.5	50.6	18.5	16.0
All India	58.2	53.5	53.8	32.8	29.9

Source: NSSO 1999-2000

Changing Composition of Rural Households - Impact on Women's Work

A rapid increase in population has exerted pressure on land, shrinking the size of landholdings especially among marginal farmers. For instance, between mid 1970s and 1990s the proportion of households having marginal holdings (i.e. between 0.002 to 1.01 ha) increased from 62.6 per cent to 71.9 per cent. Along with this the proportion of landless households increased from 9.6 per cent to 11.3 per cent and semi landless households increased from 37.4 per cent to 42.4 per cent. By mid 90's about 34 per cent of the rural households were landless or semi landless, where, among those having land, 72 per cent had holdings which were much smaller than what is considered as economically.

Table 34.5 indicates that there is a moderate progress in terms of level of wages and gender differentials in wage earnings. This is because there was an increase in agricultural wages when wages in non agricultural sector were also showed an upward movement. Now that the growth of employment in the rural non farm sector has declined, the positive features observed on agricultural scene might also cease to continue. The gender gaps in wage earnings persist in specific operation where women tend to have greater presence like transplanting, weeding etc. Women's job, because they are women's job, are paid less regardless of other considerations like productivity. In India, food security as a national objective was placed on the policy agenda much earlier than in other developed and developing countries. With the Green Revolution technology, India has achieved self-sufficiency in food grains. Approximately 35 per cent of the households below the poverty line are headed by women. Women have a share of only 25.7 per cent in earned income. The proportion of pregnant women (age 15-49 aged) with anemia is as high as 88 per cent. Women's key role in the production of major grains and minor millets illustrates their invaluable contribution to the food security. In addition, women play a crucial role in ensuring supply of food as food vendors and post-harvest processors of livestock and fishery products. As major buyers of family food and meal-makers, women ensure adequate food security. As primary providers of nutrition to the young children, women are the major decision-makers in ensuring nutrition to the next generation.

Table 34.5: Real Agricultural Wage Earnings in Rural Labour Households at 1960-90 prices

States	1964-65		1974-75		1983		1993-94	
	Male	Female	Male	Female	Male	Female	Male	Female
AP	0.9	0.4	0.8	0.6	1.1	0.8	2.0	1.4
Bihar	0.9	0.8	0.8	0.7	0.9	0.7	1.4	1.2
Gujarat	1.1	0.9	1.0	0.8	1.2	1.0	1.9	1.8
Haryana	-	-	1.4	1.1	1.2	0.9	2.3	1.8
Karnataka	0.8	0.5	0.8	0.5	0.8	0.7	1.7	1.3
Kerala	1.6	0.9	1.6	1.1	2.0	0.6	3.3	2.3
MP	0.8	0.6	0.6	0.4	0.7	0.6	1.4	1.2
Maharashtra	1.0	0.5	0.7	0.4	0.9	0.6	1.8	1.1
Orissa	0.9	0.6	0.7	0.5	0.6	0.5	1.4	1.1
Punjab	1.5	1.0	1.9	1.0	1.8	0.9	3.2	2.8
Rajasthan	1.2	0.8	1.0	0.7	1.1	0.6	2.2	1.8
TN	1.0	0.6	0.9	0.6	1.0	0.7	2.4	1.4
UP	0.7	0.6	0.8	0.6	0.8	0.5	1.6	1.3
WB	1.3	1.0	1.0	0.8	0.9	0.9	2.2	1.7
All India	1.0	0.6	0.9	0.6	1.0	0.7	1.9	1.6

Source: NSSO 1999-2000

Agriculture: Rural Indian women are extensively involved in agricultural activities. However, the nature and extent of their involvement differs with the variations in agro-production systems. The mode of female participation in agricultural production varies with the landowning status of farm households. Their roles range from managers to landless labourers. In overall farm production, women's average contribution is estimated at 55 per cent to 66 per cent of the total labour with percentages much higher in certain regions. In the Indian Himalayas a pair of bullocks works 1064 hours, a man 1212 hours and a woman 3485 hours in a year on a one-hectare farm, a figure that illustrates women's significant contribution to agricultural production. Women provide one half of the labour in rice cultivation in India). In the plantation sector women are the crucial labourers. Depending on the region and crops, women's contributions vary but they provide pivotal labour from planting to harvesting and post-harvest operations. Traditionally, women had usufruct rights to the community land. But after the land reforms, land titles were given to men, denying women, access to land. In general, women in tribal households enjoy more decision making power than women in many other Indian households because of their greater contribution to household income.

Crop production: India has a variety of crops grown in irrigated and rain fed areas. Rice, wheat, jowar, maize and bajra are the major food grains. Oilseed, sugarcane, cotton and jute are the important cash crops. Likewise, tea and coffee are important plantation crops. India's agricultural production systems also include a wide range of horticultural crops. Rice is widely grown in Southern, Eastern and Northeastern states. Wheat is mainly grown in Punjab and Haryana. Jowar and Bajra are important food grains in dry land areas. Assam and West Bengal are famous for tea, whereas Karnataka, Tamil Nadu and Kerala are coffee and coconut producing states. In the highly diversified Indian context, no simple gender division of labour exists with regard to crop production. In certain areas in India women play a key role as seed selectors and in seedling production. Their knowledge on seeds and seed storage contribute to the viability of the agricultural diversity and production. As weeders, women contribute to crop management. Women prepare and apply green and farmyard manure. As integrated pest management practices are introduced, it could be expected that women's work will increase due to more labour-intensive activities.

Livestock: In India, livestock plays a multi-faceted role in providing draught power for the farm, manure for crops, energy for cooking and food for household consumption as well as the market. In animal husbandry women have a multiple role. With regional difference, women take care of animal production. Their activities vary widely ranging from care of animals, fodder collection, cleaning of animal sheds to processing milk and livestock products. In livestock management, indoor jobs like milking, feeding, cleaning, etc. are done by women in 90 per cent of families while management of male animals and fodder production are effected by men. Women accounted for 93 per cent of total employment in dairy production. Depending upon the economic status, women perform the tasks of collecting fodder, collecting and processing dung. Dung composting and carrying to the fields is undertaken by women. Women also prepare cooking fuel by mixing dung with twigs and crop residues. Though women play a significant role in livestock management and production, women's control over livestock and its products is negligible. The vast majority of the dairy cooperative membership is assumed by men, leaving only 14 per cent to women.

Forestry: The Indian population, particularly the rural, is highly dependent upon forests. Fuel wood contributes 84 per cent of the total household energy consumption. There are 66.5 million tribals in India and with few exceptions; the majority of them are forest dwellers. Unfortunately, forests are deteriorating massively due to encroachment of agricultural production, mining, construction of dams, industrial and railway demand. Gender roles in using forest resources vary widely depending upon the region as well as socioeconomic class and tribal affiliation. Rural Indian women's interface with the forests is varying -gathering, wage employment, production in farm forestry and management of afforested areas in the community plantation. In India, women are the major gatherers and users of a much more diverse range of forest products than men. Depending upon the socio-cultural variations among different communities, primarily Non-timber Forest Products (NTFP) is collected by women and timber by men. In several parts of India, large proportions of the population depend on NTFP as their main source of livelihood. Apart from fodder and fuel, women collect food, medicinal plants, building materials, material for household items and farm implements. Women primarily collect sal and Tendu leaves. As women are the ones who have traditionally been collecting forest products, they possess the knowledge of properties and potential uses of these products.

Fisheries: India is among the top ten fish producing countries in the world. In India, nature and extent of women's participation in fishery varies across the states. Fish drying/curing, marketing, and hand braiding and net mending are the main areas of women's involvement in Tamil Nadu, Andhra Pradesh and Orissa. Women are also involved in shrimp processing in these states. In addition, in Andhra Pradesh, women are engaged in mollusc and shell collection on a seasonal basis in a few places along the coastline. However, marine fish capture is a men's domain. Among the mangroves of Bhitarkanika on the Orissa coast, both women and men fish in the fresh water estuarine areas. Men cast nets while women and children catch fish with hands. But men exclusively perform fishing by boat in the flood tides. In contrast, women's participation in small-scale fisheries is very limited in West Bengal. Men dominate even ancillary industry, which in the other Indian east coast states is a women's domain, as a relatively low number of days in a year is spent on actual fishing. In the fishing villages, both women and men who do not belong to the fishing community perform fish drying/curing. In coastal aquaculture, women are involved in prawn and seed collection to a very limited extent.

Environment: Sharp decline in common/real estate property land on one hand and the deterioration of the remaining land have jointly contributed to hardship for the rural community, particularly for women of the poor households. Deforestation has increased time and distance involved in grazing and collection of fuel and food. Distance to forests or other sources of fuel, type of farming system, etc. have explained increases ranging from 45 minutes to 5hours in women's work time. Moreover, it has also threatened income-generating opportunities for women by affecting livestock rearing and collection of NTFP. Reduced or non-availability of NTFP has shifted women from self-employment to wage employment. In areas where traditionally men also collected fuel wood, deforestation resulted in decrease in men's participation, as it was no longer possible to collect fuel wood in bulk. Women play a key role in both land use and management. They supply inputs from the forests as fertilizer to the soil as well as fodder for the cattle, which produce fertilizer for the soil. Women have also been the source of knowledge relating to conserving and maintaining the quality of water. Depleting water resources have also impacted women severely in terms of longer walk and more work, as they are principal collectors of water. Nonetheless women in different states have varying degree of involvement in water collection. In Mizoram in the north-eastern hills women have the knowledge of animal ecology that male hunters acquire. In the island ecosystem of Lakshadweep, off the coast of Kerala in the Arabian sea, women are more conversant with the resources around their homes and along the reef and shore, while men who go further to fish and collect coconuts are more knowledgeable about land, lagoon and sea. Rural production

Women in rural India generate income in various ways. Women are highly involved in processing of the NTFP, particularly in small-scale enterprises. This includes basket, broom, rope making, tasar silk cocoon rearing, lac cultivation, oil extraction, and bamboo works, etc. Women constitute 51 per cent of the total employed in forest-based small-scale enterprises. However, this does not mean that men do not have any role in these activities. Among the schedules-caste weavers in Orissa, men collect grass for basket making while women cure it and make the basket.

Women and Food Security: Women produce between 60 and 80 percent of the food in most developing countries and are responsible for half of the world's food production, yet their key role as food producers and providers and their critical contribution to household food security is only now becoming recognized. FAO studies confirm that while women are the mainstay of small-scale agriculture, farm labour force and day-to-day family subsistence, they have more difficulties than men in gaining access to resources such as land and credit and productivity enhancing inputs and services. Food security, in fact, has been defined by FAO not only in terms of access to and availability of food, but also in terms of resource distribution to produce food and purchasing power to buy food where it is not produced. Given women's crucial role in food production and provision, any set of strategies for sustainable food security must address their limited access to productive resources. Women's limited access to resources and their insufficient purchasing power are products of a series of interrelated social, economic and cultural factors that force them into a subordinate role, to the detriment of their own development and that of society as a whole. The international initiatives and efforts developed, especially since the 1975 World Conference on Women in Mexico, have contributed to a greater recognition of women's key participation in rural and other domains of development. However, much remains to be done.

Issues of Women in Agricultural and Allied Activities

Even though women play a very significant role in agricultural production, they are always being under valued, unrecognized and have been discriminated against men in various developmental activities with utter disregard to their actual and potential contribution to the sector. In reality rural women are invisible in statistics, they remain unreached and unattended in the planned developmental efforts and with no access and control over resources. The following are some of the areas where women face discrimination against men.

Access to Resources: Despite their role as the backbone of food production and provision for family consumption in developing countries, women remain limited in their access to critical resources and services. While in most developing countries, both men and women farmers do not have access to adequate resources, women's access is even more limited due to cultural, traditional and sociological factors. Accurate information about men's and women's relative access to, and control over, resources is crucial in the development of food security strategies.

Access to Land: Not even 2 percent of land is owned by women, while the proportion of female heads of household continue to grow. Land reform programmes together with the break-up of communal landholdings have led to the transfer of exclusive land rights to males as leads of households which ignores both the existence of female-headed households and the rights of married women to a joint share.

Access to Credit: For the countries where information is available, only 10 percent of credit allowances are extended to women, mainly because national legislation and customary law do not allow them to share land property rights along with their husbands or because female heads of household are excluded from land entitlement schemes and consequently cannot provide the collateral required by lending institutions.

Access to Agricultural Inputs: Women's access to technological inputs such as improved seeds, fertilizers and pesticides is limited as they are frequently not reached by extension services and are rarely members of cooperatives, which often distribute government-subsidized inputs to small farmers. In addition, they often lack the cash income needed to purchase inputs even when they are subsidized.

Access to Education, Training and Extension Services: Two-thirds of the one billion illiterate in the world are women and girls. Available figures show that only 5 percent of extension services have been addressed to rural women, while no more than 15 percent of the world's extension agents are women. In addition, most of the extension services are focused on cash crops rather than food and subsistence crops, which are the primary concern of women farmers and the key to food security.

Access to Decision-making: Given the traditionally limited role of women in decision-making processes at the household, village and national levels in most cultures, their needs, interests and constraints are often not reflected in policy-making processes and laws which are important for poverty reduction, food security and environmental sustainability. The causes of women's exclusion from decision-making processes are closely linked to their additional reproductive roles and their household workload, which account for an important share of their time.

Access to Research and Appropriate Technology: Women have little access to the benefits of research and innovation, especially in the domain of food crops, which in spite of ensuring food security at the household and community levels, have a low priority in crop improvement research. In addition, women farmers' roles and needs are often ignored when devising technology that may cause labour displacement or increased workload.

Access to Market Infrastructure, Information and Facilities: Low-income women have tended to be marginalized by distant and poor market facilities. Insufficient emphasis has been put on market facilities that attract the participation of women in marketing. Moreover market information remains restricted to the literate as well as more urban-based farmers. Because of persistent low levels of literacy among low-income women, information regarding farming and particularly food security does not readily reach women farmers. Besides, most of the information packaging and dissemination channels are unsuitable for them.

Other problems faced by them includes:

- Women labour are underpaid and undervalued
- Women's work contributions are unaccounted
- Face workload of house, farm and community works
- Lack participation and access to skills, trainings and information
- Women face food insecurity and malnutrition

Empowerment of Women

Empowerment is an active process which enables women to realize their identity and power in all aspects of life. It enables women to have more access to knowledge and resources, greater autonomy in decision making, greater ability to plan their times, free from the clutches of irrelevant customs, builds and practices.

The National Policy of Education (1996) enumerated parameters of empowerment as follows:

- to build a positive self image and self confidence
- developing ability to think critically
- building up group cohesion and fostering decision making and action
- ensuring equal participation in the process of bringing about social change, and
- providing the wherewithal for economic independence

The approaches for empowerment of rural women can be divided into four broad heads:

1. Educational Empowerment.
2. Social Empowerment
3. Economic Empowerment
4. Technological Empowerment

1. Educational Empowerment: Education is the key which opens the door to life, develops humanity and promotes national development. Education can be an effective tool for women's empowerment. It enables rural women to acquire new knowledge and technology required for improving and developing their tasks in all fields. Therefore, at least one Functional Literacy Centre should be opened in each Gram Panchayat area with a view to make all and rural farm women functionally literate and adult education necessary.

2. Social Empowerment: Empowering women contribute to social development. Economic progress in any country whether developed or underdeveloped could be achieved through social development. Hence, women's empowerment cannot be ignored, while devising various policies for rural and socio-economic development.

- **Status of Women:** Even though the country has made progress in developing women's capabilities, inequalities continue to exist between women and men. The low status of women is the outcome of a variety of causes in which patriarchal values reinforced by tradition, media and other socio-political institution playa major role. Thus, the institutional bases of women's oppression have to be sensitized to accept the gender equality and moreover, women's perception of themselves would also need to be changed.
- **Gender Bias:** Cultural traditions and economic necessity have always mean a significant role for women in agriculture. In India it is not uncommon that women do not have control over the land. Even, where women constitute a larger share of a agricultural producers, there are cultural constraints as regards easy communication between men and women, because almost all extension workers are men.
- **Health and Nutrition:** Health and nutrition are two very important basic needs for empowerment of rural women. To achieve real and quicker development in health sector, an extensive as well as intensive "Health Education and Awareness Campaign" (HEAC) needs to be given topmost priority and it should mainly stress on nutritional education, benefits of immunization, family planning etc.

3. Economic Empowerment: Empowering women with economically productive work will enhance their contribution to agricultural development.

- **Access to Resources:** The farm women need to have control over limited resources like land and livestock, so that they could take away decisions and implement them in anyway that is required. Ownership and control over productive assets will create a sense of belonging and owning. It will thus help to take responsibility in family and local group activities. Other impact of control is to enhance their decision-making ability to meet some physiological needs like self-esteem and confidence.
- **Micro-Credit Programmes:** Micro-credit Programmes extend small loans to poor people for self-employment projects that generate income allowing them to care for themselves and their families. In most cases, micro-credit Programmes offer a combination of services and resources to their clients in addition to credit for self-employment. Access to productive resources is critical for enhancing women's economic choices. Since, formal credit institutions rarely lend the poor, special institutional arrangements may become necessary to extend credit to those who have no collateral to officer their enterprises. In order to have access to credit,, setting up self-help group,

local banking system by women, Non-Governmental Organizations and provision of facilities by Government need to be established. The policy challenge is to support effective grass-roots credit schemes and intermediaries and ensure that low-income have assured credit from the formal financial system.

- **Access to Cooperatives and Local Women's Organizations:** Collectivization has been recognized as a tenet of women's empowerment. It has been defined as a process of bringing a group of women together at a base to become an integral part of an economic activity. Organizational efforts should be made for integrating farm women into development. Organization of Mahila Mandals, Cooperatives. Societies and Discussion Groups will serve this purpose. The control of these organizations should be in the hands of womenfolk themselves. Also, the present beneficiary approach to women's development should be replaced by participatory approach.

4. Technological Empowerment: Though women are involved in almost all agricultural operations, in rural areas yet, they have inadequate technical competency due to their limited exposure to the outside world. This has compelled them to follow the age old practices which in turn result in poor work efficiency and drudgery.

- **Capacity Building:** Capacity building and empowerment are important for which there should be decentralized capacity building among the rural women particularly farm women. Empowerment projects should go beyond the provision of basic social services for all. They should include components vital for enabling the poor to participate in economic activities. It is important to develop the skills among farm women in order to increase their productivity and to keep them abreast of modernization and technological changes for being competitive in the market.
- **Exposure to Mass Media:** The transfer of technology approach, which mainly includes mass media are also not paying due attention towards dissemination, of adequate and timely agricultural & marketing information to the farm rural women. Therefore, there is utmost need to provide adequate coverage to the Programmes related to women and they must get exposure to mass media for improving their communication and meditation skills to strengthen their capacity to contact and mediate with external world.
- **Appropriate Training Programme:** Training is an important component of HRD which enhances knowledge, skill and attitude. For building technical competency among farm women, need based skill-oriented training programmes to reinforce their role in farm activities need special attention.

The training Programmes should initially be organized on their felt-needs and then be switched over to unfelt but essential needs. To achieve this sacred task, infrastructural facilities in terms of more numbers of KVKs, FTCs and BRLP should be established in the district on priority basis.

- **Appropriate Technology for Women:** In order to cater the technological needs of farm rural women, women specific technologies should be developed. While evolving agricultural technologies, indigenous practices used by women should be paid due attention for blending with the frontier ones for greater adoption. Also there is need to strengthen linkage between various research and extension organizations engaged in transfer of technology.

Measures to Strengthen Women's Empowerment and Rural Development

Empowerment of women is the prime objective of all development programmes and policies. These programmes could be planned properly and implemented effectively in order to attain self sufficiency and self-reliance. U.N. Commission on Status of Women says: Women constitute half of the world's population, accomplish about two thirds of its work hours, receive one tenth of the world's income. The following measures can strengthen self employment in rural area in the service sector, which will generate additional income leading to economic independence of women:

- Identification and organization of innovative and high income generating activities suitable for women.
- Development of entrepreneurial abilities of women by organizing special types of training.
- Encouraging women to take up part-time jobs while being in the house itself, to earn additional income to support the family.
- Effective planning at the micro-level.
- Adequate representation of women experts in the case of women related development planning.
- Central and state governments to place more emphasis on untouched areas in the service sector to involve women.
- Government can establish a separate mechanism at the Center, state and district levels to look after women's employment and their problems.
- Development of infrastructure facilities and supportive services like land, building, transport and also to look after the children.
- Encouraging women through formal and non-formal education to involve themselves in. the service sector.

- Organizing women labour in the service through women's associations, cooperative societies or mahila mandals, self-help groups etc.
- Establishment of supervisory bodies to monitor the implementation of Constitutional provisions related to women.
- Steps to make women aware of technical and financial assistance available to women entrepreneurs, and to encourage them through concessions and incentives to enter into the service sector related to women.
- Government should encourage research and development in the service sector to find out high income generating activities suitable for women.
- Wide publicity to training programmes in the service sector.
- Creating awareness among educated and uneducated women about the availability of facilities and concessions for entrepreneurs

Institutional Interventions for Women

The Report of the National Commission on Self- Employed Women observed that women on being given institutional support, demonstrated high productivity, a better record of payment of loans and the assets are sustained. However, in doing so, it's important to recognize women as a major earner, not as a supplementary worker. The major institutional support is provided to the women by the government, financial institutional and voluntary agencies.

1. Interventions of Government: The recognition of the need for tackling women's problems through organized institutional mechanism was first, evident in the Community Development Programme. Economic component -in the women's programme was missing. They were primarily seen as house wives, with major focus on their physical welfare with a slant on social education. The programme for rural women followed this course till the sixth plan, when there was a major shift in the government policies and programmes for women in India by recognizing them as important economic agents. The Sixth Plan introduced some major changes in the programmes for women's empowerment, primarily through economic independence. It stipulated that women were to form at least one third of the beneficiaries under the scheme of Training of Rural Youth for Self-Employment (TRYSEM). Credit from banks and subsidies to the beneficiaries below poverty line was provided for self-employment and income generating activities in a variety of sectors like animal husbandry, other land based activities, weaving, handicrafts etc. But the Seventh Plan acknowledged that during the first three years of Sixth Plan, benefits were not flowing to women in adequate measures. A new scheme of Development of Women and Children in Rural Areas (DWCRA) was launched on a pilot basis. This programme aimed at enabling women to take up income generating activities. Simultaneously, the National Rural Employment Programme (NREP) and Rural Landless Employment Guarantee Programme (RLEGP) were introduced during the Sixth Plan. Even though directives were issued to include at least 30 per cent women beneficiaries in these programmes, the actual involvement was far below the target across the years.

Constraints:

- Understanding and concern for women's issues at the policy and programme formulation level is considerably attenuated by the time the programmes are implemented on the ground.
- The women focused programmes like any other government programme, suffered from the problems of mis-identification of beneficiaries, inadequate coverage of remote areas, absence of forward and backward linkages, leakages due to corruption, favoritism etc.
- Use of 'household' approach in allotting the schemes prevented women quite often from receiving the benefits.
- Inadequate recognition of the special needs and constraints of women for participation in economic activities as the women's programmes were being implemented through the traditional male-oriented delivery system with insignificant support of women extension staff.
- Lack of attempts in promoting non-traditional economic activities for women either at the training stage or at the stage of giving loans.

2. Interventions of Financial Institutions

Commercial Banks: The National data on allocation of credit based poverty alleviation scheme shows that less than 15 per cent of the beneficiaries were women, which was barely half the target of 30 per cent. An in depth study of credit low by gender in a RRB branch and a commercial bank branch in one district in Andhra Pradesh, suggested that disbursement to women ranged between 6 to 12 per cent all, but dropped to zero for agricultural loans.

Constraints: Since land has been the major source of collateral, women's lack of ownership has barred them from the access to the formal credit system, thus limiting their ability to acquire other productive resources such as cattle, poultry, looms or working capital for trade in farm forestry produce, food processing etc.

Persistent low recovery with very poor repayment not only for IRDP loan extended to clients below the poverty line, but for all types of rural lending have made the credit institutions shy of extending credit. Arrears to commercial banks according to a study were 46 per cent.

Cooperative Credit: If one assesses the percentage of women members in about 6.5 crore membership covering 9000 Multipurpose Cooperative Societies in India, it is baffling to find that it is not even 10 per cent.

Constraints:

- Women do not own land in their own right. Even though tenant cultivation without any land rights are eligible for membership, women's cases have never been raised.
- Difficult to promote the integration of women in male dominated cooperatives. Domination of rural elites in the management of cooperative societies, who are averse to providing credit to weaker sections including women.
- It is rather easier to establish exclusive Women's Cooperative Societies, than attempting to carve out benefits for the women from general societies. The successful experience of All Women Dairy Cooperative Societies in Andhra Pradesh strengthens such view point.

3. Interventions of NGOs: In additional to their over all small number, the geographical distribution is such that the power region and rural areas have fewer than proportionate number of NGOs. However, their participation in the process has contributed in a variety of ways like providing programme implementation support at grassroots, training support to women cadres of Mahila Mandals and DWCRA groups and in some cases even to the government staff; assistance to the state, central government or financial institutions in pilot projects and feedback through field research and critiquing policy.

There have been several successful NGOs' involvement in watershed development, livestock development and development of non-conventional energy sources etc., which if simulated in bringing about development of women in agriculture, can successfully contribute to organizing women in such activities.

Strengths:

- Flexibility in approaches make them mould programmes suitable to the localized needs.
- Free from bureaucratic procedures.
- They can deliver services at a lower cost, with a higher degree of effectiveness than their government counterparts.
- Also perform critical functions, such as organizing poor around common problems, challenging vested interests, exposing inefficiency and corruption in public life.

Constraints:

- Lack of highly committed people at all levels, particularly at grass roots.

- Has to hire people at the field level from the residual job market.
- Remuneration paid to staff lower than the private and public sector. As a result, have to depend upon poorly trained, generalist staff, with a limited degree of motivation to perform critical tasks of interfacing with the community.
- Strong dependence on source of funding external to the communities they serve
- An effective linkage should be established between the Government and NGOs. It may be useful on the part of the Government agencies to design development programmes with NGO participation in mind.

4. Self-help Groups and Micro Credit: Organizing women into groups has been proved to be a good intervention. Membership in a group can initially substitute for the individual women's lack of "bureaucratic know-how" and her unfamiliarity with public discourse. More importantly, it can transform women from the status of "beneficiaries", into "clients", who are in a long-term reciprocal relationship with the institutions those are meant to serve them. The Self-help Groups or the thrift and credit groups are mostly informal groups whose 'members pool their savings and lend within the group on rotational or need basis. The SHGs provide a group approach to the micro credit programmes. Along with implementing the micro finance programmes, SHGs take up many other important social issues like health care, sanitation, family planning, literacy, management of common resources etc. It will in the long run, make the delivery system more responsive to local priorities and replace centrally determined prescriptions and top-down approaches with more flexible planning of both contents and mechanism of service provisions.

SHGs take loans from banks/voluntary agencies/self-help promoting institutions to meet the needs of the farmwomen. The SHG itself with the help of NGO makes assessment of individual credit needs of its members and submits to the bank for sanction of collective loans in its name. The NGO helps the SHG in procuring raw materials and also marketing of the produce. The entire loan amount disbursed to the SHG is refinanced by NABARD to the financing bank. Emphasis therefore shifted from the rapid disbursement of subsidized loans to target populations, towards the building of local sustainable institutions to serve the poor.

Mainstreaming Women in Agriculture: Strategies

Gender concerns need to be mainstreamed in the agricultural extension process. Public extension systems, which must disseminate new technology and information, are still largely male dominated. Hence, the necessity to target women is to ensure work.

1. Emancipation of women is not an act of charity; the liberation of women is a fundamental necessity. In order to ameliorate the status of women, it is imperative that specially designed research, training, extension and economic programmes are organized at various levels using various approaches on systematic and scientific lines leading to an improved standard of living and quality of life; catering to the special needs and roles of women both within and outside the home.
2. Education is the key which opens the door to life, develops humanity and promotes national development. Education can be an effective tool for required for improving and developing their tasks in all fields. Hence, no amount of effort will solve the problem, unless and until women themselves are initiated into a thinking-reflecting- questioning acting process. This cannot be achieved until women can be hauled out of their acceptance of the anachronism of tradition to demand a better deal from family and society. Only and only education has this power. Therefore, at least one Functional Literacy Centre should be opened in each Gram Panchayat area with a view to make all farm women functionally literate.
3. Empowering women contributes to social development. Economic progress in any country whether developed or underdeveloped could be achieved through social development. Hence, women's empowerment cannot be ignored, while devising various policies for rural and socioeconomic development. Cultural traditions and economic necessity have always meant a significant role for women in agriculture. In India it is not uncommon that women do not have control over the land. Even, where women constitute a larger share of agricultural producers but, there are cultural constraints to easy communication between men and women, because almost all extension workers are men. Therefore, the role of agricultural extension workers is very significant. Besides, cultural norms have to be addressed before we tackle other dimensions.
4. Access to productive resources is critical for enhancing women's economic choices. Since, formal credit institutions rarely lend to the poor, special institutional arrangements may become necessary to extend credit to those who have no collateral to offer their enterprise. In order to have access to credit, setting up self-help group, local banking system by women, Non-Governmental Organizations and provision of facilities by Government need to be established. The policy challenge is to support effective grassroots credit schemes and intermediaries and ensure that low income women have

assured credit from the formal financial system.

5. Collectivization has been recognized as a tenet of women's empowerment. It has been defined as a process of bringing a group of women together at a base to become an integral part of an economic activity. Organizational efforts should be made for integrating farm women into development. Organization of Mahila Mandals, Cooperatives Societies and Discussion Groups will serve this purpose. The control of these organizations should be in the hands of women folk themselves. Also, the present beneficiary approach to women's development should be replaced by participatory approach.
6. Training is an important component of HRD which enhances knowledge, skill and attitude. For building technical competency among farm women, need-based, skill-oriented training programmes to reinforce their role in farm activities need special attention. The training programmes should initially be organized on their felt-needs and then be switched over to unfelt but essential needs. To achieve this sacred task, infrastructural facilities should be augmented on priority basis.
7. In order to cater to the technologies needs of farm women, women specific technologies should be developed. While evolving agricultural technologies, indigenous practices used by women should be paid due attention for blending with the frontier ones for greater adoption. Also there is need to strengthen linkage between various research and extension organizations engaged in transfer of technology.
8. Technological upgradation is necessary for increasing the work efficiency of women in various income generating activities. Various issues which needs attention while deciding on the technological options are formulation of an inventory of technological options in the traditionally women dominated areas of operation, macro and micro level assessment of the impact of the modern farming technologies on the employment potential of women in agriculture, front line technological options with a promise to fit into the environment of women in agriculture etc.
9. For transfer of technology, understanding of the cultural norms of the community is vital. The importance of training for transferring information and technology and training programmes for rural women should be well planned and should be given in small groups in an interactive and participatory mode for greater effectiveness while creating awareness among the rural women.
10. Appropriate extension mechanisms are needed to be devised for equipping the women on the technological options with increased knowledge, skill and orientation.

11. An individual is empowered when he/she participate in his/her own decision making process. When we talk about empowerment of women it is the first step that we give them chance to develop themselves to be able to decide what is good and appropriate for them and what is not and try to achieve it.

Thrust Areas for Future

Creating a Repository of Gender Disaggregated Data and Documentation: Gender disaggregated information in the field of agriculture and allied areas are scanty and scattered .Such information need to be collected, collated, synthesized and published in order to make them easily available to the users, The research information from various units of the Indian agricultural research system and also from neighboring countries shall be collected, classified, synthesized and published, This will be achieved by launching a short-term ad-hoc research project under A.P. Cess Fund of the ICAR with a multidisciplinary team of scientists, All these information will be utilized to develop comprehensive database and inventory for case analysis for its further use in advisory and consultancy services.

Technology Testing and Refinement: Research efforts rarely take into account the gender perspectives. Perspectives differ between men and women farmers in adoption of technologies. For example, in selecting a nee variety, men and women will differ in plant type, cooking quality and taste. There are numerous technologies in(agriculture system But their performance and suitability for women are not established. The NRCWA shall take lip programmes to identify the relevant technologies, test in women perspective and refine to make them women friendly. Technologies especially in the field of horticulture, agro-processing and value addition, animal husbandry and fishery should be tested though on-farm trials.

System Development and Management: In the wake of emerging problems related to sustainability, the focus has shifted to studies on performance of systems as a whole and their components. Situation warrants that studies related to women's livelihood and development should be taken up in system approach as women meet their diverse needs from different sources that are inter-related In a varying way and related to larger system. It is also felt that studies on systems such as farming systems would help find solutions to some of the immediate problems faced by women. Due attention should be given to socio-cultural parameters while developing systems in agriculture and allied sectors.

Drudgery Assessment and Reduction: Drudgery of farm women is an important aspect that has attracted wide attention of researchers. It is needless to emphasize that farm women are involved in numerous activities. If measured by the extensiveness and intensiveness of their involvement, farm women shoulder much more burden than men. Importantly, women are involved in more strenuous activities as compared to men. Many of such activities are drudgery, prone to varying degree. Even women suffer from different health problems which adversely affects their working efficiency ad family welfare. Unfortunately data on the extent to which women are affected in the working environment and the effect on their work output are not available. Hence, it is required that studies should be commissioned on drudgery assessment, and drudgery reducing interventions should be identified; and there NRCWA is to play vital role Further, NRCWA will work on evolving suitable mechanisms to intervene the household drudgery faced by rural women.

Innovating Extension Approach: Considering the fact that in India farm women are largely illiterate with very little or almost no exposure to scientific knowledge and technological know-how due to reasons largely of socio-cultural nature and these women differ with their male counter part on several accounts, a separate extension strategy need to be developed for Implementing development programmes intended to benefit farm women The NRCWA shall formulate different extension modules in the various subject matter areas like integrated farming system, post-harvest technology, integrated pest and nutrient management, poultry and fish farming, tribal development, rural development, employment guarantee programme etc, and test those modules in the neighboring areas of the centre in order to make them appropriate. The methodologies followed and results obtained will be shared with implementing agencies and institutions operating at different levels. Action researches will be conducted

- to identify, mobilize and develop women-specific technologies for promoting effectiveness and sustainability through on-farm trials and on-campus demonstrations;
- to identify gender issues and test appropriateness of available farm-technological programmes/policies with women perspective for empowerment of farmwomen and capacity building of scientists, planners and policy makers to respond to the needs of the farm women; and
- to identify areas and mechanisms on establishment of institutional linkages between various departments, agencies and institutions at the grass root level for facilitating effective resource management in rural and tribal development
- to work out modus operandi for registration of women workers at the panchayat level;
- to find out and standardize ways, means and methods for effective use of participatory mode in planning, implementing, monitoring and evaluating

development actions by partnership of women in agriculture with implementing agencies.

Capacity Building of Scientists and Functionaries: Scientists, both in research and extension systems, need orientation to appreciate the vital role of women in agriculture and the areas in which their efficiency of work could be enhanced either by technological intervention in agriculture and allied sectors on Important problems or by improving their knowledge and skills for better job performance. In the first instance the scientists of NRCWA need to be given required training in certain identified areas so that the centre can address researchable issues on priority. Based on the research outcomes, suitable training capsules can be developed according to the need of various stakeholders like policy makers, directors, scientists, KVK, development functionaries and women activists.

Conclusion

On a sociological level, mother is the basic element of the household. At the cultural level, she is obviously the one who transmits the cultural and social values to future generations. The contribution that a woman gives to agriculture is an unsung saga like that of a housewife toiling for her family. She is the 'invisible producer' who is never credited with any achievement. Indian agriculture cannot improve without making the women equal partners in its development efforts. An overall change in perception of treating farmer as a man should be changed. It is high time that the role of women in agriculture is acknowledged and interventions should be made on all fronts of the farming system in which each of them are involved. Any initiative to develop agriculture sector should target this large work force too.

If women can be the backbone of a family, she can be trendsetter in the field of agriculture also, but it needs encouragement from the society and policy backing. There is a need of change in the present situations. To improve the position of women workforce it is necessary to improve their production potential by treating them as important economic actors, not as dependent members of the family. Men and women must have equal access to the benefits of development interventions, as equality is an indispensable precondition for sustainable development. Rural development can be brought out only by envisaging programmes to enhance capacities and responsibilities of women farmers in production.

In the context of mainstreaming of women in agriculture, the basic issues revolving around appropriate income generating activities for these technological options, extension and institutional support have to be sorted out to decide on a strategy which will enable the women to become equal partners in the process of national development. Thus it is high time to bringing up policy changes which gives equal opportunities and equal status to both men and women, and these policy decisions need to be implemented and monitored properly, to give due recognition to women for her contributions in agriculture. Agricultural extension has to play a very crucial role in this regard.

References

Economic Survey. Ministry of Finance and Company Affairs, Government of India, 2002-2003.

Geetha Kutty. M, Training Module for Gender Sensitization in Agriculture, NRCWA, 2006.

Patil, A and Mathu, A., Women Entrepreneurship: Issues and Challenges, Kalpaz publications. 2007

Singh, Indrabhushan and Usha Kumari., Rural Development and Women Empowerment, Kurukshetra, pp. 3-8. 2007

Singh, Jhamtani, P Singh, and Wason, M, Training Manual on Sensitization for Empowerment of Women in Agriculture. 2002

35

Role of Women in Agricultural Sector

Varsha H. Patil and Vidya R. Khapli

Women and men, both play important role in agriculture throughout the world; producing, processing and providing the food for every human being. 60 to 80 per cent of the world's food production is by women. Rural women in particular are responsible for half of this production. In global development strategies women farmers are frequently underestimated and overlooked in spite of this huge contribution.

We have observed that while women in most developing countries are playing important role in agriculture sectors, the farm labour force and food systems and day to day family activities, they are the last to benefit from. Also in some cases women have been negatively affected by prevailing economic growth and development processes.

Because of gender bias and gender blindness, farmers are generally perceived as "male" by policy makers, development planners and agricultural service deliverers. Due to this reason, women find it more difficult than men to gain access to valuable resources such as land, credit and agricultural inputs, technology, training and services that would enhance their production capacity.

Women's contribution in production is underestimated and also their role in global development strategies is overlooked because much of their labour consists of unpaid labour in fields that is produced for household rather than for the market. As a consequence it goes unrecorded in national statistics. This unrecognized economic resource represents an efficiency loss for household, society and economy as a whole.

Statistics on Women's Labour and Employment in World

Women and men play critical roles in all fields. But statistics on labour and employment about women in the world as per FAO Report is as follows,

- Women do 2/3rd of the world's work and earn 1/3rd of the world's income.
- In Southeast Asia, women provide up to 90 per cent of labour for rice cultivation.
- In India, women's participation in agricultural labour is huge.

- More than 25 per cent of women's labour is unpaid.
- Statistics are difficult to estimate the amount of women's work towards production and help in self-sustenance of household than the marketed products.
- Only 15 per cent of the world's agricultural extension agents are women.
- Fewer than 10 per cent of women farmers in India, Nepal and Thailand own land.
- ILO recommends that a woman be counted as employed if she works at least l/3rd of the working hours. It is important to take into account the secondary employment statistics and self-sustenance statistics. Lack of this information affects the amount of development that is visualized.

Rural women make a tremendous contribution to food and agricultural production. They also play a crucial role in determining and guaranteeing food security and well being for the entire household. Equitable, effective and sustainable agriculture and rural development cannot be pursued without an explicit recognition of these realities. In a global atmosphere of increasing poverty, food insecurity, rural out-migration and environmental degradation, all potential actors in development must be given the support and access to resources they need to pursue sustainable livelihoods and strategies for a better life.

Role of Women in Agriculture and Food Production

Agriculture is the main source of livelihood for the people of countries like India. Women play critical roles in agriculture throughout the world, producing, processing and providing the food we eat. Women make up over 50 per cent of the agricultural labour force worldwide; in Southeast Asia, women provide up to 90 per cent of the labour for rice cultivation. Rural women in particular are responsible for half of the world's food production and produce between 60 and 80 per cent of the food in most developing countries.

Rural women are the main producers of the world's staple crops - rice, wheat, maize - which provide up to 90 per cent of the rural poor's food intake. Women sow, weed, apply fertilizer and pesticides, harvest and thresh the crops. Their contribution to secondary crop production, such as legumes and vegetables, is even greater. Grown mainly in home gardens, these crops provide essential nutrients and are often the only food available during the lean seasons or if the main harvest fails.

Yet, despite their contribution to global food security, women farmers are frequently underestimated and overlooked in development strategies.

Women's specialized knowledge about genetic resources for food and agriculture makes them essential custodians of agro-bio-diversity. In the livestock sector, women feed and milk the larger animals, while raising poultry and small animals such as sheep, goats, rabbits and guinea pigs. Also, once the harvest is in, rural women provide most of the labour for post-harvest activities, taking responsibility for storage, handling, stocking, processing and marketing.

Visible Role, Invisible Women

Despite the fact that women are the world's principal food producers and providers, they remain 'invisible' partners in development. A lack of available gender disaggregated data means that women's contribution to agriculture in particular is poorly understood and their specific needs ignored in development planning. This extends to matters as basic as the design of farm tools. But women's full potential in agriculture must be realized if the goal of the 1996 World Food Summit - to halve the number of hungry people in the world by 2015 - is to be achieved.

However, women's status in the agricultural activity is quite contradictory. Their contribution towards agricultural activities is mainly limited to the production of the agricultural crops marketing. Despite their contribution to global food security, women farmers are frequently underestimated and overlooked in development strategies.

Although rural women are assuming an increasingly prominent role in agriculture, they remain among the most disadvantaged of population. War, rural-to-urban migration of men in search of paid employment and rising mortalities attributed to HIV/AIDS has led to a rise in the numbers of female-headed households in the developing world.

However, women's contribution to and role in food security is often underestimated and overlooked because much of their labour consists of unpaid labour in fields that produce for the household rather than the market. As a result, it goes unrecorded in national statistics. This unrecognized economic resource represents an efficiency loss for the household, society and the economy.

Gender Bias and Gender Blindness

In most developing countries, both men and women farmers do not have access to adequate resources, but women's access is even more constrained as a result of cultural, traditional and sociological factors. Accurate information about men's and women's relative access to, and control over, resources are crucial in the development of food security strategies.

FAO studies demonstrate that while women in most developing countries are the mainstay of agricultural sectors, the farm labour force and food systems (and day-to-day family subsistence), they have been the last to benefit from - or in some cases have been negatively affected by prevailing economic growth and development processes.

Gender bias and gender blindness persist: farmers are still generally perceived as 'male' by policy-makers, development planners and agricultural service deliverers. For this reason, women find it more difficult than men to gain access to valuable resources such as land, credit and agricultural inputs, technology, extension, training and services that would enhance their production capacity.

Studies have shown that men and women have different access to resources, and tend to benefit differently from the output and income from their labour and has a negative impact on women's livelihood.

Decisions related to produce, provide, and prepare food in the face of already of crop grown, the sale and the marketing of the crops and utilization of the agricultural income are taken mainly by the male counterpart of the family.

Suggested Action Plan

Poverty, food insecurity and environmental degradation are recognized as critical development problems and have been given highest priority in the international development agenda. These problems have a disproportionate negative impact on rural women, due to their inferior socioeconomic, legal and political status as well as their critical roles as producers and household managers. The causes and effects of these impacts are systemic, with far-reaching implications for agricultural and rural development as a whole and for all initiatives aimed at raising levels of nutrition, improving production and distribution of food and agricultural products, and enhancing the living conditions of rural populations.

Therefore, we must think of an action plan, that will be an effort to bring about positive changes by promoting women to start agro based business of their own and to make them economic self reliance. We have following areas to be considered, analyzed and acted upon.

Areas of action

- **Access to Land:** Ownership of land encourages farmers to invest time and resources in long-term improvements and facilitates access to agricultural support services. Inheritance and land tenure laws limit women's ownership and use of land.
- **Access to Credit**: Short- and long-term credit is needed to pay for inputs and hired labour. In the developing world, banks and credit associations are less inclined to lend to women because, without property and land rights, they

lack collateral.

- **Access to Agricultural Inputs:** Improved seeds, fertilizers and pesticides are a vital means of enhancing production. Extension services and cooperatives distributing inputs rarely reach women who also lack the necessary cash to purchase even government-subsidized inputs.
- **Access to Extension and Training:** Agricultural extension programmes inform farmers about new technologies and plant varieties. Few extension services are targeted at rural women, few of the world's extension agents are women and most of the extension services focus on commercial rather than subsistence crops -the primary concern of women.
- **Access to Education:** Investing in human capital reduces poverty and encourages sustainable economic growth. But prevailing attitudes about women's social, political and cultural rights severely limit girls' access to education throughout the developing world.
- **Access to Technology:** Labour-saving technologies are an important means of increasing production and improving people's quality of life. But the needs and priorities of women are rarely considered in the research and development of agricultural technology.
- **Access to Rural Organizations:** Agricultural cooperatives and farmers' organizations help members obtain resources and represent members' interests before government. But a common prerequisite for membership of these rural organizations is, very often, 'head of household status' or land ownership, which applies solely to men.
- **Access to Services:** Services such as transport and market facilities help farmers expand their income-generating activities. Although women have a role in the trading of goods and the food they produce, illiteracy and lack of legal rights prevent them from joining formal service institutions.

Within this context, women's empowerment will be central to raising levels of nutrition, improving production and distribution of food and agricultural products, and enhancing the living conditions of rural populations.

FAO Plan of Action for Women in Development (1996-2001)

The FAO Plan of Action for Women in Development (1996-2001) defines the role the Organization will play in stimulating and facilitating efforts to increase the involvement of rural women as contributors and beneficiaries of economic, social and political development. In order to address the root causes of persistent poverty and food insecurity among rural women and the families they support as well as the factors contributing to degradation of the environment, the Plan pursues three strategic objectives.

Plan Pursues Three Strategic Objectives

- to promote gender-based equity in the access to productive resources;
- to enhance women's participation in decision and policy-making processes at all levels;
- to promote actions to reduce rural women's workload and enhance their opportunities for remunerated employment and income.

Conclusion

It is extremely important that women should be appreciated for their contribution in all roles played in the society while pursing agriculture as a career. They should also nurture and cherish their qualities of culture, compassion, courage and creativity. And above all, the cooperative spirit. The five C's are personified in women personality. Through this let us once again prepare ourselves to contribute immensely in all spheres of cultural and other roles. The contribution of women in agriculture in national development is abundantly clear.

Let us conclude by presenting to you a complete personality profile of a woman. It is from the poem "Stray Birds" from Guru Ravindra Nath Tagore:

"Women, when we move about in your household service your limbs sing like a hill stream among its pebbles.

Women thou hast encircled the worlds heart with the depth of the tears as the sea has the earth.

Women in your laughter you have the music of the fountain of the life."

Therefore, we must work on above mentioned action plan, that will be an effort to bring about positive changes by promoting women to start agro based business of their own and to make them economic self reliance.

References

FAO Documentation: Women in agriculture and rural development 1980-1989, FAO, Rome (Italy). Library and Documentation Systems Div., JobNum: T8250, 1989

Lambert, J.C.; Soukehal, A., Amelioration de la technologie du fromage tchoukou au Niger, JobNum: T3080, 1994

Morogo, R.J., Activities and experiences in the field of gender and agricultural engineering in Kenya, ISBN "92-5-103706-X", 1996

Muylwijk, J., Bibliography on gender and agricultural engineering for small farms in developing countries, 1996

Nabasirye, M.; Kolijn, S., Gender in agricultural engineering activities of the Post-Harvest Programme of Uganda. 1996

Rangnekar, S., (Development Research Foundation, Ahmedabad (India)); Vasiani, P.; Rangnekar, D.V., A study on women in dairy production, JobNum: T3080, 1994.

Part VI: Women, Media, Politics and Human Rights

36

Women Prisoners

Smriti Bhosle

Crime and criminal both have become the focus of attention in the present society. Crime is increasing at rapid rate. In India, crime has been considered a male behaviour. But today the former notion is proved wrong. Women, like men, suffer from tensions, frustration, jealousy enmity and hatred, which motivate them to criminality. They indulge in all sorts of crimes. The changing social norms and values as well as the impact of other cultural patterns culminating in the complexity of life are largely responsible for this change.

Female criminality is indeed a serious social problem, it may be considered a crucial problem because of its impact on family, upbringing of children and the overall fabric of society. As women's roles change and become more open to opportunities and tensions associated with the male-role, their criminal activities will be transformed in kind and degrees.

The predominant factors which are found to determine criminal tendencies in Indian women are economic insecurity, social deprivation and emotional disturbances. Besides, family and domestic quarrels and destitution may also significantly affect the criminality of women. Social environment and deviance are highly relevant to the subject of criminality. Migration from rural areas to urban areas and the imbalance in their adjustment to city life may also result in an increase of crime in cities. It is obvious now that female criminals do not form an isolated group from the normal population.

We have seen the image of women in various media as the preservers of social norms, traditions, customs, morality and family cohesiveness. But in recent years, the increasing crime rate among females has drawn the attention of researchers. An earlier Indian study on criminals has concentrated on male criminality. Within the past few decades, professional interest in female criminality has increased along with interest in the general topic of women.

"Any woman who violates the law, is reported to the police, gets arrested and prosecuted, shall be included in the category of criminals". The term 'undertrial criminal' is being used in my study of female criminals – to refer to unconvicted persons in prison custody. The term 'undertrial criminal' is applied to a person whose trial has begun.

The above definition has been adopted in order to analyze female crime phenomenon in Mumbai. No doubt there is a loophole in the above definition. For example, all undertrials may not be convicted and it is not correct to consider them as offenders. Morally too, it is incorrect to consider 'undertrials' as 'offenders'. But there is no choice other than to keep in mind the margin of error and analyze the situation.

The Bombay Jail Manual (1935) describes that, undertrial and awaiting trial are synonymous terms and refers to persons committed to prison whilst the charges against them are under judicial investigation. The long detainment of undertrials in the prisons is due to the slack procedures of the police in investigation of the cases and filling the charge-sheets, and later of the courts in delaying the trials of the undertrial prisoners.

Right from the introduction of modern prison system, undertrial prisoners are kept in the prison. We thus see considerable increase in undertrial prisoners. The undertrial prisoners are in the Judicial custody of the Magistrates but are under the control of the executive organization i.e., prison.

The undertrials are detained in the prison and are subjected to general prison discipline. Undertrial prisoners are generally confined in separate yards/wards in district/central prisons. Section 27 of the Prison Act, 1894 provides that criminal prisoners who are not convicted are to be kept apart from convicted criminal prisoners. They are given more concessions than convicted criminal prisoners. They are allowed to supplement their diet from outside, permitted to use their own clothes and not required to do labour. The rules in the 'Maharashtra Prison Manual' make generous provisions to ensure that detention does not hamper the undertrial prisoner in preparing his/her defence.

Duration of Trials for IPC Crimes by Various Courts during 2000

It is observed that out of 9,32,774 completed trials at various levels of courts from all the States/UTs, only 3.4 per cent were completed after 10 years of trial, 12.4 per cent between 5 to 10 years, 24.2 per cent between 3 to 5 years, 30.7 per cent within 1 to 3 years, 18.1 per cent between 6 months to a year and 11.2 per cent within 6 months (excluding information for Sikkim state).

Arrests during 2000: A total of 26,75,923 persons were arrested by the Police under various IPC crimes during 2000 against 26,00,876 persons in 1999. Thus, the number of total arrestees increased by 2.9 per cent during 2000 over 1999.

The female criminality in the total IPC crimes amounted to 5.2 per cent, which was 3.4 per cent in 1991. Of the total number of persons arrested during the year 2000 under IPC crimes, the significant involvement of women was under the head of Dowry Deaths (21.3 per cent) followed by Cruelty by husband and relatives (20.6 per cent) and Kidnapping and abduction of women and girls (8.8 per cent). On the other hand very negligible number of females were involved in the crimes of preparation and assembly for Dacoity (0.1 per cent), Sexual harassment (0.6 per cent) and Robbery (0.9 per cent). Not a single woman is found involved in the crime of 'Importation of Girls' (0.0 per cent).

The percentage of females arrested under SLL crimes at All-India level was 4.6 per cent against 5.2 per cent of IPC crimes. Percentage of female criminals arrested under SLL crimes in 1991 was 4.2 per cent. The percentage of female criminals under the Immoral Traffic (Prevention) Act (87.2 per cent) and Indecent representation of women (Prevention) act (82.3 per cent) is found to be a significant involvement. As against this merely 0.1 per cent females were arrested under Arms Act and also under Gambling Act. The above table shows zero per cent involvement of women in Terrorist and Disruptive Activities Act (TADA) and Antiquity and Art Treasurers Act.

Tenth United Nations Congress on the Prevention of Crime and the Treatment of Offenders Vienna, 10-17 April 2000

The Fourth World Conference on Women, held in Beijing from 4 to 15 September 1995, called upon Governments, the international community and civil society to take strategic action in a number of critical areas of concern, one of which was violence against women. The term "violence against women" means any act of gender-based violence that results in, or is likely to result in, physical, sexual or psychological harm or suffering to women, including threats of such acts, coercion or arbitrary deprivation of liberty, whether occurring in public or private life.

Within the framework of criminal justice administration, the continued marginal status and position of women in society and vis-à-vis legal systems have also resulted in their special needs also being regarded as marginal. Criminal justice systems are male-oriented and male-dominated and typically do not regard gender issues as relevant. The status of women is such that women are in a problematic situation as offenders, detainees, victims and even practitioners. It underlines the need to guarantee women their legal rights and fundamental freedoms, equal protection under the law and fair treatment in the justice system.

The issue of women committing offences has to be understood in the context of the status and quality of life of women and opportunity structures with respect to women. The consideration of the criminal nature of the activity in which women are engaged typically overrides that of the victimization itself. Women constitute a minority of the detainees in prison systems. Prison systems are designed, organized and administered predominantly by males and with a predominantly male population in mind. Many women are held for extensive periods in pre-trial detention centres. Reviews and evaluations concerning the terms of imprisonment of women identify problems of inadequate or inappropriate health services (especially in relation to maternity), classification and segregation, family visitation, programmes geared towards males and limited access to other programmes. Post-incarceration difficulties relate to the preparedness for and support upon release and reintegration into society.

In general, the stigma associated with criminality is far greater for women than for men; communities are often far less forgiving of a female criminal. Women may be rejected not only by their community but also by their families. This situation has to be acknowledged and addressed in the development of post-release options and programmes and community-based rehabilitation or alternatives to imprisonment. There is a need for immediate review and monitoring of criminal justice policies and practices. Separation from their families and anxiety about the well-being of their children are major issues for women in detention.

Research has demonstrated that women and girls who commit crime often have a history of prior victimization. Familial abuse may force women to try to survive on the streets. Women who are illegal migrants might be pressured to further violate the law in order to avoid deportation. Trafficked women might have been physically and psychologically coerced, or false pretences or duplicity might have been used to get them to enter into the sex trade. Attempts by such victims to resist rape and exploitation or to defend themselves against violence perpetrated by family members, intimates, associates, sponsors or employers commonly result in the victims committing additional criminal acts.

Committee on Empowerment of Women (2001-2002)

The Committee on Empowerment of Women took up the subject 'Women in Detention' for detailed examination and report. This Report is based on the inputs including material received from the Ministry of Home Affairs, Ministry of Human Resource Development (Department of Women and Child Development) National Commission for Women and impressions gained during on-the-spot visits to jails in some of the States where women are confined.

The conditions in an average Indian prison present a very depressing picture. Overcrowded, unhygienic and hopeless, these prisons far from being any kind of correctional centres, often produce hardened criminals who truly become a menace to society.

Although women in detention constitute only around 3 per cent of the total prisoners in various jails in the country, their condition is pathetic in terms of the prison's environment, the treatment meted out to them in the jail and the social ostracism they suffer. Women prisoners suffer from greater disabilities than men. The psychological stress caused by separation from children, the unhelpful attitude of close relations, uncertainty about the future are all factors which make their life miserable in jail.

Over 80 per cent of the women prisoners are undertrials who have been there for years together. No one knows when the trial will take place or when they will be able to come out of the prison walls. The slow moving judicial machinery, apathy on the part of the State and insensitivity of the jail authorities have made prison reforms almost impossible. There are, of course, some individual initiatives at reform, like in Tihar Jail. But firm initiatives on the part of the State are missing. A landmark report made by the Justice Krishna Iyer Commission on Women in Detention in 1987 is yet to receive serious attention of the Government. Committee strongly feel that immediate steps need to be taken by the Union Government as well as the State Governments to reform the conditions in jails. It further stated that, as Parliamentarians we have a duty to highlight the problems of these unfortunate women who, in most cases, are victims of circumstances.

Committee's Findings and Recommendations: The Committee observed that, women in prison suffer from unhealthy living conditions, exploitation, unnecessary prolonged severance from their families and lack of gainful and purposeful employment. The Committee laid emphasis on training of custodial staff in prisons to handle women prisoners with a reformative attitude. Finally, the Expert Committee on 'Women Prisoners' constituted by the Government in 1986-87 under the Chairmanship of Mr. Justice V.R. Krishna Iyer made a number of very useful recommendations for women prisoners and suggested a National Policy for Custodial Justice for Women. It laid particular emphasis on the need for adoption of a specialised approach towards handling, treatment and rehabilitation of women prisoners.

The Committee has noted that the legal issues on custodial justice are covered by the Prisons Act of 1894 which is also a Central Act providing for the regulation of prisons almost throughout India. This Act defines the duties of prison officers including medical officers, admission, removal and discharge of prisoners, food, clothing and bedding and different categories of prisoners as well as issues relating to their health and employment while in prison. Above all, there are also provisions defining prison offences and arrangements. Therefore, the

Prison Act is an important piece of legislation that regulates situations in custody as well as treatment of jail inmates. Being a Colonial Act, it demands a fresh look to reflect the special needs of women.

The Ministry of Human Resource Development (Department of Women and Child Development) had set up an Expert Committee at the national level to identify the gaps and drawbacks of the existing facilities and services and suggest a more humane policy towards the women offenders. The Committee under the Chairmanship of Justice V.R. Krishna Iyer submitted its report in the year 1987. In his report, Justice Krishna Iyer had observed that the "existing malpractice and the delinquencies in the various forms of custody tend to effect women more adversely than men. This is on account of the fact that the women are still a marginal group in the custodial population and tend to be less vocal, demanding and violent in demonstrating against custodial or other injustice.

The Ministry of Home Affairs have added that in view of the status of women in family and society, their special needs/problems and their vulnerability while in prisons, special provisions have been made in the Prison Manual of States for the segregation, protection, care, treatment, training and rehabilitation of women prisoners which in prisons. Immediately after admission to prison, every women prisoner has to undergo a thorough medical examination so as to ascertain whether she is pregnant or not. The result of such examination has to be recorded in the relevant records and such women prisoners are given special medical care either in the prison hospital or in outside hospitals to ensure better medical health both physically as well as mentally to them. They are taken to the local maternity hospital for the purpose of delivery. While registering the birth of a child of women prisoners the place of birth indicated is the name of the hospital only instead of indicating the name of the prison/institution in which they are confined. The pregnant and nursing women prisoners are being provided a prescribed special diet and exempted from unsuitable type of work in addition to their regular medical check-up as advised by a competent medical officer.

The Prison Manual of States also provide for special diet for the children accompanying women prisoners, as prescribed by the medical officers from time to time and suitable clothing. Prisons have a system of classification for the segregation of various category of women prisoners like convicts, under-trials, habitual offenders, prostitutes, procuresses, etc. Women prisoners are provided the facilities of maintaining contacts with their families through letters, visits from relatives and leave. Suitable clothing including sanitary pads are being provided to the women prisoners along with the adequate quantity of washing and toilet soaps in order to maintain proper cleanliness and hygiene while in prisons.

Some of the important impressions gathered by the Committee during their visits to these jails are as under:

- Most of the jails do not have exclusive women's prisons but only separate enclosures for women.
- Special Courts/Lok Adalats were not being held in the jails for expeditious disposal of cases for under-trials and for petty offences.
- In Arthur Road Jail, Mumbai, the women prisoners were far more than the authorized capacity leading to acute shortage of space and discomfort .
- General conditions relating to food, lodging, clothing, recreation etc. were far below standard and needed considerable improvement.
- In most of the jails, there was one common kitchen and no separate kitchen for Women prisoners, who desired that they should be allowed to cook food or alternatively a separate kitchen should be allotted to them.
- Most of the jails do not have counselling cells for women. There was urgent need for counselling centres especially for psychiatrist counselling in each prison.
- There was an urgent need for simplification of bail procedures for women prisoners.
- A need was felt to strengthen the free legal aid cell for women prisoners. It was felt that students from Law Colleges should be involved to render legal assistance to women prisoners.
- Facilities for vocational training, elementary education, legal literacy, free legal aid, etc. were lacking at most of the places.
- Women prisoners were finding it difficult to sustain their relation/contact with family members.
- Counselling, support and rehabilitation facilities for women after their release from jails, were almost negligible.
- In some jails convicts and under-trials were lodged together.
- Seriously ill patients and women with infectious diseases were not segregated.
- There was no bailer to bail out some of the women inmates who had received bail.
- The jail authorities were not taking the initiative for premature release of women prisoners.
- The female jails/enclosures were not managed by women personnel but were staffed by male members.
- In some jails foreign prisoners were given special facilities in regard to food, clothing, etc.

- It was difficult to conduct surprise visits to jails to see the conditions prevailing there as prior permission from jail authorities was required.
- Vacancies in the prison cadre especially of female staff were not filled-up.
- At times the women prisoners were not aware of the grounds of their arrest.
- Mentally ill patient were languishing in jails and many have breakdowns after coming to jail. They were locked up without any proper care/treatment/help.
- There were also some cases of exploitation of young women prisoners by the jail staff for immoral purposes.

Dr. (Smt.) Kiran Bedi, Joint Commissioner of Police who had joined Tihar Jail, Delhi as I.G. (Prison) was instrumental in initiating several reforms affecting the women prisoners. These reforms were widely appreciated. The Committee, therefore, decided to hear the views of Dr. Bedi on her experience in bringing about reforms in one of the biggest jails in Asia. Accordingly, the Committee interacted with Dr. (Smt.) Kiran Bedi, Joint Commissioner of Police and the following suggestions emerged there from:

- There was an urgent need to start educational, literacy para-legal and vocational training programmes. for women in jails.
- There should be separate schools for children of women prisoners.
- Reliable NGOs and other voluntary organizations should be associated by jail administration in the rehabilitation and counselling of women inmates. Community entry would give prisoners an environment of social acceptance and understanding.
- Counselling and legal aid centres should be opened .
- There was need to set up exclusively jails for women.
- There was urgent need for expeditious trials of cases of under-trials.
- Convicted and under-trial women in jails should be segregated.
- Custodial staff is the key element in bringing about custodial reforms. To achieve the objectives of prison reform, there is need for motivation and better promotional avenues for prison staff.
- There was need for a separate prison cadre headed by an I.G.
- Legal panchayats inside the prison should be held.
- There was need for more Rehabilitation Centres/Half-Way Homes for women.
- The Indian Prisons Acts, 1894 and the Police Act, 1861 should be thoroughly reviewed and amended.
- There was lack of coordination between Central and the State Governments, and amongst State Governments themselves on matters affecting prison

reforms.

- Computers should be widely used in compilation of data and other details of prisoners including women inmates in the country so that there could be better networking in this regard.

Observations/Recommendations by the Committee

The inequality between the socio-economic status of men and women reinforces the vulnerability of the latter, which makes them more susceptible to social maladjustment, abuse and exploitation. It is this process of victimization of women and their induction into criminality that makes them the subject of custodial and correctional welfare. More than 8000 women are lodged in prisons. The steady increase in the number of women prisoners requires greater effort on the part of the authorities to ensure custodial justice.

The National Expert Committee on 'Women Prisoners' (1987) had made a thorough study of the subject and outlined a number of recommendations of far reaching consequences in their Report. This Report considered as a landmark on the subject had *inter alia* mentioned that "womenhood and childhood even in criminal wrappings and behavioral aberrations deserve to be nursed in dignity and restored to working normally using all the material, moral and spiritual resources at the society's command".

The Committee had visited a number of jails in the country viz. Arthur Road Jail, Mumbai, Tihar Jail, Delhi, Model Jail, Chandigarh, Central Prison, Orissa, Presidency Jail, Kolkata, Nari Bandi Niketan and District Jail, Lucknow. The Committee have come to the conclusion that there is total neglect on the part of the concerned authorities in providing basic needs to women prisoners. There is overcrowding, mal-nutrition, lack of medical care, educational, vocational and legal facilities in almost all the jails. The general condition relating to food, clothing, recreation, hygiene is not proper and needed considerable improvement. Further, very few counsellors visit jails to give much needed advice to the inmates. The status of women even in custody requires attention, recognition and protection which have not been forthcoming in an adequate manner. The majority of the female population in jails consist of undertrials and they languish in jails for offences for which sentences would have been far less if they had been convicted. What is more pathetic is the fact that the women inmates who obtained bail were still languishing in jails for want of surety. The Committee, therefore, strongly feels that the remedial measures must be taken expeditiously by the Centre and State Governments, to bring about perceptible improvement in the conditions of women in custody.

The Committee understands that the status of women in custody is not uniform throughout the country. There is a wide difference in the facilities provided to women inmates in different jails. This is mainly because of the fact that the matters relating to prisons, reformatories, borstal institutions, etc., and persons detained therein are a State subject. But the recommended measures for upgradation of custodial justice involve functions to be performed by the Centre also. The Central Government, therefore, cannot absolve themselves from the responsibility of ensuring proper custodial justice for the women detained in the various jails of the country.

The Committee found that the Ministry of Home Affairs had released Rs. 124 crore to the States from 1987 to March, 2001 for strengthening security, communication and transport, repair and renovation of old prison buildings, facilities to women offenders, vocational training, modernisation of prison industries and training to prison personnel. However, this does not appear to have brought about the desired results. Not only is the Ministry of Home Affairs responsible to ensure proper and optimum utilisation of the funds sanctioned in this regard, but there should be frequent visits by the officials of the Ministry of Home Affairs to various jails and there ought to be consultations and coordination at the appropriate level with the concerned State Government officials to ensure that basic needs of the women prisoners are properly met by the jail officials.

The Committee felt that prisons should have a remedial, rehabilitative and reformative approach where avenues should be built for advancement of basic skills, activities, wages, scope for moral and intellectual growth, leisure and recreation. In this connection, a vital role is to be played by the custodial staff which is the key element in bringing about custodial reforms. The prison officers should act in a way that upholds the rights and dignity of women in prisons, in police stations and other custodial institutions. An attitudinal change is required on the part of prison officials to keep pace with theoretical laws. The jail officials should look upon their duty as a developmental function and jail as a place of reforms and persuasive deterrence rather than intimidation and conformity. Motivation and ensuring sustained level of involvement of the prison staff in the process of correctional reform in the institutional settings are of prime importance. The Jail Superintendents must appreciate the problems of women prisoners and deal with a variety of issues keeping in view their background and differing needs. It is, therefore, of paramount importance that Prison staff are specially selected given training on these lines and they are sensitised to women's issues and their needs.

As per the information furnished by the Ministry of Home Affairs, there are only 16 women prisons against the total number of 1133 prisons in the country.

Most of the States do not have exclusive women prisons but only have separate enclosures for women. There is need for more separate women's jails managed by female staff in every State in accordance with the size, population and number of women convicts in each State. They should have every facility to serve as correctional and rehabilitative institutions and all women convicts in the State should be transferred there. It has come to the notice of the Committee that when women prisoners are shifted to a women's prison, out of their district, their families stop visiting them because it becomes expensive for them. The Committee hope that with the opening of more separate women's jails, it would be possible to shift the women prisoners to a women prison nearest to their district.

The Committee found that at times the undertrials get bail but they still languish in jails for want of persons who can bail them out. The Committee strongly recommend that the undertrials who are unable to furnish surety should be released on personal bonds and where this is not possible jail authorities should explore alternative measures through NGOs.

Facilities Available for the Undertrial Prisoners

In general the accused should be produced before a magistrate by the police within 24 hours from the time of her arrest excluding the traveling time. At this time, the accused is said to be in/under police custody. If the police require the accused for further investigation, the magistrate can pass orders accordingly. If the police have completed their investigation then the magistrate can remand the accused to judicial or prison custody and is given a court date. If the accused is able to get out on bail then she must appear in court for her trial on the given date. But if the accused is not able to get out on bail she is detained in prison.

As an undertrial there are certain facilities available in prison. According to the Maharashtra Prison Manual, the facilities are as follows:

- In every prison, in which women are confined there shall be one or more women jailors and/or matrons, who shall maintain discipline in the women's section of the prison. No woman undertrial shall be removed from the women's section except with the special permission of the superintendent and for the purpose of being taken to court, interviews, release or transfer.
- No male officers, including Superintendent and Deputy Superintendent shall on any pretext enter the women's section without the women Jailor or Matron, and the two shall not separate whilst in the section.
- A register shall be maintained at the gate of the women's prison or women's section of a prison. Whenever any woman undertrial is taken out, an entry

shall be made in the register. Whenever any visitor enters the section, an entry indicating name of the visitor, day and time of such visit shall also be made in the register.

- Undertrial prisoners should be admitted during usual working hours of the prison. On admission they shall be examined by the medical officer for marks of violence, birthmarks, etc. And a printed card should be sent to the undertrial's family giving information about the inmate's institutional number and address, brief summary of rules regarding interviews, letters, etc.
- It is the duty of every prison officer to find out whether an undertrial prisoner has been previously convicted and such information should be immediately forwarded to the concerned Superintendent of Police for necessary action.
- When an undertrial prisoner has been notified by the trying magistrate or the police as an approver or a confessing accused, she should be kept separate from others concerned in the same case.
- Children of women undertrials may be admitted if suitable arrangements for their care cannot be easily made outside.
- Private clothing to meet reasonable requirements should be allowed to undertrial prisoners. An undertrial prisoner who has no sufficient clothing of her own may be provided with the same at government cost.
- Food from outside may be allowed. Prisoners allowed to receive outside food, shall not be given prison food. Undertrial prisoners should not be allowed to cook their food separately in the institution.
- Four letters per calendar month, two at her cost, and two at government cost, shall be allowed to be written by an undertrial prisoner. There shall be no limit on the number of incoming letters to prisoners.
- One interview per calendar week with family members or relatives or close friends or lawyers may be allowed.
- No newspapers shall be supplied to undertrials at government cost.
- Unless she so desires, no undertrial prisoner shall be allotted any work except that it shall be her duty to keep her bedding, clothing and yard clean.
- An undertrial prisoner may make purchases from the canteen as per canteen rules.
- Women undertrial prisoners should normally be escorted by women police. Separate conveyance should be provided for the transport of women undertrial prisoners.
- Every Superintendent of a Prison shall, on the first day of each month, submit to the sessions Judge or the Chief Presidency Magistrate a statement of cases of all undertrial prisoners pending for more than three months in the court of

the Judicial Magistrate.

- Undertrial women prisoners accused of the offence of traveling ticketless released on bail should be paid traveling allowance if the Superintendent considers that it is necessary to do so in the interest of the released woman prisoner.

As far as possible women undertrial prisoners should be handed over to their relatives after release. If this is not possible a woman police or woman prison guard should escort the released woman undertrial prisoners to the nearest station or bus stand.

Women undertrials having children below 4 years of the age can keep the children along with them in the prison, while children above 4 years of age for whom no arrangements can be made outside, are placed in Children's Homes.

For the children, milk, banana and rice is provided. Medical facilities are also extended to them. But there are no educational or recreational facilities for these children.

Criminal Justice Process

The criminal Justice Process is the entire system of criminal prevention, detection, apprehension, adjudication and punishment. It includes all those agencies such as the police, correctional institutes, courts and legislatures that are responsible for enforcing criminal laws. The right to life and liberty guaranteed in the constitution is the primary source of criminal law. This right is then translated into 'Indian Penal Code', 'Criminal Procedure Code and Evidence Act' and also in Local and Special Laws (non-code legislation). The Directive principles of state policy set down the responsibility of the state to provide for free legal aid where required (for reasons of economic or other disabilities). This is to ensure equal justice for all citizens and to further the guarantee of equality before the law, as provided in Article 14 of the Constitution. There are also departmental rules, special manuals and standing orders to guide the functioning of the courts, as well as the police, prisons and social welfare departments. Relevant court decisions, too, are integrated into these regulations, as they identify gaps in the system – situations not specifically defined, for whatever reason.

The criminal court is the core of the criminal justice process. It has the duty to supervise the work of the police, prosecutor and defence counsel and implement the laws. A trial is a court proceeding during, which the judge listens to the evidence as presented by the defence and the prosecution, and determines whether the defendant or accused is guilty beyond a reasonable doubt or not. On completion of investigation, the police must file charges in court. The charge sheet becomes the basis of the trial.

A fair trial implies a speedy trial. Speedy trial is the essence of the criminal justice. However, there is no specific criterion of promptness. The Indian Constitution does not specifically guarantee to the accused the right to a speedy trial. But Article 21 along with Articles 14, 38, 39 and 39-A make it a necessary concomitant of social justice promised in the preamble. Right to speedy trial is also recognized in Article 3(i) of the Universal Declaration of Human Rights. It says that arrest and detention constitute restrictions on the right of personal freedom.

Legal Aid: Legal aid is crucial for a suspect and each individual has the right to obtain it. The Supreme Court has even held that free legal services are the "constitutional right of every accused person who is unable to engage a lawyer and secure legal services on account of reasons such as poverty, indigence or incommunicable situation and the state is under a mandate to provide a lawyer to an accused person if the circumstances of the case and the needs of justice so require." It is also important to note here that legal aid is urgent for the suspect from the moment of detention, and not only during the trial.

Specific legal and administrative provisions exist with respect to women suspects and prisoners. These provisions are intended to provide directions to the police, courts and prison authorities in the handling of this group of women prisoners.

Prison Act, 1894: 1. Section 24(3) provides that in the case of female prisoners, the search and examination (on admission) shall be carried out by the matron under the general or special orders of the Medical Officer.

2. Section 27(1) provides that in a prison containing female as well as male prisoners, the females shall be imprisoned in separate buildings, or separate parts of the same building, in such manner as to prevent their seeing, or conversing or holding any intercourse with male prisoners.

3. Section 46 states that no female shall be liable to the imposition of any form of handcuffs or letters, or to whipping, as punishment for prison offences.

Criminal Manual Issued by the High Court of Bombay, 1960: Women accused of any offence if arrested soon after childbirth, cannot be at once taken before the magistrate as this may cause personal suffering and risk to health. They should not ordinarily, be removed until they are in a proper condition to travel. In such cases, sanction must be obtained by the police from the nearest magistrate for their detention at their homes, or in the dispensary beyond a period of 24 hours allowed by Section 61 of the Criminal Procedure Code.

Criminal Procedure Code, 1973:

1. Sections 51(2) and 100(3) make it obligatory that a woman should be searched by woman, and with strict regard to decency.

2. Section 160(1) Criminal Procedure Code prohibits the police from requiring any woman to appear at any place other than the place of her residence for the purpose of examination by police.

3. Section 53(2) states that the medical examination of a female accused should be conducted only by or under the supervision of a woman medical practitioner.

4. Section 437 provides that in the case of a non-bailable offence, a court (not being the sessions or high court) may direct a woman accused to be released on bail.

5. Section 360(1) provides that a woman of any age, if convicted of an offence (not punishable with death or imprisonment for life), and with no previous conviction, may be released on probation for good conduct instead of serving the sentence (in contrast, a man would have to be below 21 years of age to obtain this benefit; or, if over 21 years, to be convicted of an offence punishable with fine only or with imprisonment for seven years or less).

6. Section 416 enacts that if a woman sentenced to death is found to be pregnant, the High Court shall order the execution of the sentence to be postponed and may, if it thinks fit, commute the sentence to imprisonment for life.

Lacuna between the Laws and Everyday Reality

The arrested person must be informed of the ground of his arrest, his right to bail and to engage a lawyer. But some officers are not conscious of their duty and they do not inform the accused of the grounds of his/her arrest.

When the police no longer require the individual for the purposes of investigation and if a prisoner is not released on bail, she is transferred to prison custody. In prison, the under-trial continues to be remanded and produced in court on the next date given. This process of giving remands may go on for weeks or months before the hearing actually starts. Most of women under-trials were uneducated and unaware of their legal rights. They were unable to defend themselves and were totally ignorant about the ways and means of securing legal help. They were unaware of the rules of remission-or premature release and are at mercy of the officials. Legal aid is the right of the suspect and free legal services are the constitutional right of every accused person who is unable to engage a lawyer and secure legal services on account of reasons such as poverty or some other reason. State has to provide a lawyer to an accused person if the circumstances of the case and the needs of justice so require. But it is totally at the mercy of the jail officers. Right to speedy trial is recognized in Article 3(i) of the Universal Declaration of Human Rights. It says that arrest and detention constitute restrictions on the right of personal freedom. Speedy trial is the essence of the criminal justice. However, there is no specific criterion of promptness.

Liberty is a most valuable right and when the accused applies for bail, he/she seeks this right from the court. In offences which are specified in the code as bailable, bail is a matter of right. But most of the women under-trials are unaware of their legal rights. The Indian Jail Committee (1919-20) stressed the need for proper classification of prisoners. Unfortunately, state governments have paid scant attention to this recommendation.

The arrested person has a right to be treated with human dignity and it is an offence for the police to inflict bodily pain on the individual. Custodial violence is a matter of concern. It is aggravated by the fact that it is committed by persons who are supposed to be the protectors of the citizens. Over the years, police commission at national and state levels have been emphasizing the need to reform and humanize the police force. But no concrete efforts have been made to implement them. Our jail manuals are outdated, our policeman are not trained in methods of interrogation, they have no access to scientific methods which would automatically curtail the use of force. Suspects are picked up and detained for days and weeks, third degree methods are employed.

An Overview

The subject of female crime was generally neglected in Western and Indian criminology until the 1950s. In India, interest in women offenders was manifested by very few scholars and only recently. Most of such work focuses on female offenders at the micro level with generally modest-sized samples drawn from a single prison. The only study entailing a reasonable sample-size, and more than one prison and region, is sponsored by the Bureau of Police Research and Development, Government of India. Female criminality is socially viewed as more serious and it is reportedly on the increase. It may be seen that the main causes of crime in female offenders are family maladjustment, emotionalism, frustration and emotional insecurity.

It is found that, in committing crimes like sale of illicit liquor, gambling, prostitution and dacoity, the women were helped actively by their men folk. Regarding the place for committing crimes, it is observed that most of the homicides committed by women took place within home and kitchen. The analysis reveals that while committing murders women concentrate mostly on persons who live closer to them.

Most of the crimes committed by women are due to stressful family situations, marital maladjustment, disharmonious and often conflict-prone relationship with husband. It is clear that maladjustment in interpersonal relationship within the family is one of the most important causes of criminality amongst women.

All types of crimes are the result of human nature (adjustment), needs (biological, economic and social condition), and situation (environment) which turn into unnatural behaviour (role). It may be explained that poor women have real economic needs which are not being met, and in many cases engage in illegal activities as a viable economic alternative. In recent times, women have been participating in various aspects of social life, and this growing participation could be one of the contributing factors for the increase of crime among them. It has been argued that, "the socio-economic vulnerability of women is the dominating factor which explains the rising trend of crime among women".

The study of female criminality was more or less neglected up to 1950s. It was only in the late 1960s and early 1970s that the need for a new perspective for understanding female deviant behaviour was realized, and professional interest in female criminality has greatly increased along with general interest in women's studies.

Theoretical Explanations of Female Criminality

The theories on female criminality, are generally contaminated by popular stereotypes and myths regarding women. Both classical and contemporary criminologists have failed to dismantle the sexist notions and common sense perceptions about women in general and female offenders in particular. The shared proposition of all these scholars is that female crime is the result of physiological or psychological characteristics of individuals. They have not given any importance to socio-cultural factors but have viewed the biological characteristics as pathological distortions or departures from the normal inherent nature of women. Obviously, the assumptions in all these explanations about biological and psychological traits of 'normal' and criminal women are questionable.

Thus it is clear that the theoretical basis of female criminality still depends on biological determination and foundation. We can now turn to the major important theories which explain the causes of female criminality which are as follows:

Theory of Anomie: Durkheim defines crime as acts which "offend strong and definite states of the collective conscience". Crime for him is a social fact. It is normal and universal in its varying forms, in all cultures and societies, at all stages of their development. A certain amount of crime is inevitable, normal and healthy in any society. Durkheim further argues that crime is not only inevitable, it can also be functional. Social change begins with some form of deviance and society itself generates deviance for its own well-being. Repressing criminal behaviour completely is not desirable, for that would create a situation that is inimical to innovation and social change.

Robert Merton borrowed ideas from Emile Durkheim. According to Merton, criminality is caused by pressure or tension. The source of this tension is stimulated aspirations to achieve certain goals coupled with obstacles to their achievement. Frustrated individuals turn to crime either to release this tension or to achieve their goals via illegitimate avenues. Merton used the word 'Anomie'. To Merton, anomie was not a state of normlessness which precipitated anti-social behaviour, but the condition experienced by individuals taught to want the goals of their culture but denied access to them. Deviant behaviour occurs when social structure restricts or completely closes a person's access to the approved models of reaching these goals. Some social structures exert a definite pressure on some persons to engage in non-conformist rather than conformist conduct.

Strain Theory: American Social Scientist Albert Cohen, in his work, "Delinquent Boys", took up Merton's idea of 'strain' explicitly to explain the different patterns of male and female crime, in particular the crimes of youth. He interpreted strain as the main catalyst in the formation of delinquent gangs by male working-class American youth. Cohen unintentionally extends this theory by proposing that when their aspirations for status are frustrated in the middle-class milieu, lower class boys tend to set up a delinquent structure. This theory has been praised for replacing the psychological approach with the sociological approach to deviance and for offering a valid premise concerning the aspiration opportunity gap.

Theory of Differential Opportunity: Instead of discussing pressures and motivations leading to criminal acts, this theory gives importance to adoption of particular kind of criminal act. This theory is presented by Richard Cloward and Lloyd Ohlin. The theory attempts to answer the question why different criminals adopt different forms of crime to express or fulfill their wishes or resistance. They consider that all individuals live in two kinds of opportunity structures. One is the legitimate opportunity structure and other is the illegitimate opportunity structure. As some people in society have limited access to achieve goals by legitimate ways or means, they may turn to illegitimate opportunities. A person may even directly turn to illegitimate opportunities. But the nature or pattern of illegitimate behaviour depends upon the access to a learning environment of such behaviour.

Thus the theories of status frustration and opportunity draw our attention to structured inequalities, which lead to variations in crime rates. These theories also explain why a particular class of society turns to a particular kind of crime pattern. In short these theories analyze societal and structural roots of crime and criminal behaviour.

Labeling Theory: The most notable contribution about this theory is made by Franklin Tahnenbaum in his book 'Crime and the Criminality'. Criminologist Howard Becker has stated his theory in his volume 'The Outsiders'. According to the labeling theory, super-ordinate parties apply the deviant label to subordinate parties; being labeled deviant produces unfavourable consequences for the individual so labeled; and labeling others as deviant generates favourable consequences for the individuals, groups or communities that do the labeling. Becker observed that society itself creates 'outsiders' by generating the rules that define crime and other kinds of deviance. He noted the importance of the process of stigmatization and labeling.

Differential Association Theory/Learning Theory

Edwin Sutherland introduced the theory of 'Differential Association'. He gave two explanations for criminal behaviour. Situational and genetic or historical. Situational crime is crime on the basis of the situation that persists at the time of crime and genetic crime on the basis of a criminal's life experiences. He himself used the second approach in developing the theory of criminal behaviour. Sutherland's main thesis is that individuals encounter many inharmonious and inconsistent social influences in their life-time and many individuals become involved in contact with carriers of criminalistic norms, and as a consequence become criminals. He called this process 'differential association'.

The theory states that criminal behaviour is learnt in a process of communication with other persons, principally in small intimate groups. This learning includes the techniques of committing the crime. The specific direction of motives, drives, rationalizations and attitudes is learned from definitions of the legal codes as favourable or unfavourable. This theory states that a person will become a criminal if he or she associates more with criminal than with anti-criminal people and ideas.

Control Theory: The control theory perspective suggests that, every person has bad and good qualities only because of the social environment, social values and norms around him. This theory states that what causes conformity is control and therefore the lack of control causes deviance. The group of control theorists consists of three sociologists – Walter Reckless, Ivan Nye, and Travish Hirschi. Reckless refers to the casual factor of conformity as containment, Nye as 'social control' and Hirschi as 'bond to society'. Control theory would predict that, "girls who are most like boys ('masculine' girls) would offend as much as boys because of a similarity of strength of social bonds – which should be weaker than those of more feminine, more confirming girls".

Masculinity Theory: This theory comprises of two ideas: Crime is symbolically masculine and masculinity supplies the motive for a good deal of crime. The qualities demanded of the criminal-daring, toughness, aggression all exemplify maleness. As an explanation of female behaviour, masculinity theory expounds the unsuitability of crime for women, thereby explaining their conformity. The masculinity theory of offending was first expounded by Talcott Parsons. Parsons offered an account of the greater delinquency of boys as compared to girls based on nuclear family. He stated that "The tendency of girls seems to be more law-abiding than boys". Criminologists assume that crime for females is a form of expression of gender role. Modern theorists speak in terms of the pernicious effects of the gender roles imposed on women and rather than regarding them as appropriate and functional, they advanced nevertheless a view of women at least as controlled, as conformist and as ineffectual as Parsons conceived.

Role Theory: Recently, criminologists have used role theory to explain women's crimes. While advocating this theory, it is pointed out by scholars like Frances Heidensohn and Marie-Andree Bertrand that owing to close supervision and social restrictions on women, socialization, development of consciousness, and self-perception vary considerably between boys and girls. Girls are usually trained to be passive, domesticated and non-violent and are not allowed to learn how to fight or use weapons. Contrary to this, boys are aggressive, ambitious and out-going. Girls thus shrink from violence and do not possess the necessary technical ability or strength to engage in crimes of violence, armed robberies, gang fights, etc. At worst, they engage in petty or domestic offences. Different expectations of standards of behaviour appear to be important in the genesis of women's crime. Normally girls are expected to adhere strictly to moral standards whereas boys are considered as normal violators of moral standards. So it is seen that women are less involved in immoral behaviour.

The Role theorists highlight the way in which opportunity structures predispose males rather than females to delinquency. Woman's criminality can be theorized in terms of 'contradictory or ill-defined roles in the family'. However, there are some inbuilt limitations to the role theory. Carol Smart observes that, role theory fails to discuss motivation or intention as an integral part of female criminality. For example role theory does not explain why even though women are socialized into primarily conforming patterns of behaviour a considerable number of them still engage in crime.

Social Bond Theory: Ram Ahuja has put forth an explanation from an Indian perspective for women's crime. His work attracted the attention of a number of sociologists and criminologists to the area of female criminality in India. This perspective is primarily concerned with the pattern of family relationships. Through analyzing the structural problems of family organization and the types of functional problems in women's families of procreation, crimes committed by women are examined in terms of maladjustment in interpersonal relationships within the family.

The factors endogenous or exogenous to family create provocation, temptation, strains and stresses in a woman's life. These provocations or stresses produce a desire or a need to deviate from social and/or legal norms. The personality structure or the biological and psychological characteristics like temperament, attitudes, frustrations, deprivations or dominant underlying need prevent this deviation in some women, but fail to do so in other cases. Thus, both personality system and pressures of environment in which woman functions, contribute to woman's criminality.

Thus, the woman's "crime" (e.g., husband's murder) will be the outcome of interaction between her personality system and totality of situations in her family. The crime will develop in interaction process over time through a series of stages. In this process of spread in time, the "criminal behaviour" will emerge not by the 'past' alone but by the 'current' situation and by triggering or precipitating circumstances too. In simplified form, conjunctive theoretical model in women's criminality accounts for differences in women's families and other institutional structures as well as in their personalities. Ahuja has analyzed intra-family problems of relationships that is the structural problems of family organizations. He presented his theory on the basis of interaction of women with their family members. He tried to explain etiology of female crime in terms of 'maladjustment' in interpersonal relationships within the family.

Women's Liberation Thesis

The impact of the women's liberation movement on female crime has become the basis of a heated debate in the criminological literature on women. The catalyst was Freda Adler's 'Sisters in Crime: The rise of the New Female Criminal'. To Adler, "the liberation of women in western society is a 'fait accompli'. Women have fought and won their battle for equality. They have 'come of age' and the phenomenon of female criminality is but one wave in this rising tide of female assertiveness". Adler's analysis of the nature of the new female criminal seems to rest on two points. One is that women's liberation has brought out women's competitive instincts. Women are now more assertive, more aggressive, and, indeed, more 'masculine'. Her other argument is that women's liberation has opened up structural opportunities for women to offend.

For example, women now have more opportunities to engage in crime in the workplace. Thus, liberation is causing women to engage in more crime.

Different theories and explanations for the causes of crime have been suggested by writers at different times. However, no single theory can explain all crimes and delinquency. Different patterns of crime require different explanations. Therefore, understanding criminal behaviour requires examining the individual and the situation because basically criminal behaviour depends upon how the individual perceives and interprets a situation.

Naffine examines in his review various theories of criminality and explores the idea of 'female voice' for the construction of women in criminology. However, theories discussed above, have given the proper perspectives in understanding the nature of crime and criminals. These theoretical frameworks have been taken as guidelines for my study of 'Undertrial Female Criminals in Mumbai City - A Sociological Study'. In this study of undertrial female criminals, the target group was undertrial females of Arthur Road Central Prison, Mumbai. Therefore, the universe of the study is the women's section of Arthur Road Central Prison.

Summary of the Findings

Demographic Profile: The demographic profile of 90 undertrial female criminals from a women's prison in Mumbai was examined. It was noted that undertrial female criminals were found in all age groups, majority of them were illiterate residents of Mumbai and its suburbs, slum/chawl dwellers, Hindus, Marathi speaking population, belonged to upper, S.C./S.T. and O.B.C. castes in descending order, married and widowed/deserted, married before 18 years of age.

Socio-Economic Background: It was found that majority of respondents were from nuclear families, illiterate family background, belonged to the families of which the monthly income was less than Rs. 3,000 per month.

Economic condition of the family does not necessarily indicate the role of poverty in female crime, yet, it is significant, in the sense that low income is an important contributory factor to family tensions; and a combination of unsatisfactory social relationships and poverty is conducive to criminal behaviour. It was also noticed that these women were preponderantly breadwinners of their families. Most of the respondents have less than three children. A majority of respondents did not have friends before their arrest and have had friendly/good relations with their neighbours. Majority were unable to decide on any matter without their husband's consent and did not have decision making powers. Most of the respondents did not live in criminal surroundings.

Nature and Causes of Female Crimes: It revealed that majority of respondents had been arrested for thefts and murders. In most of the murder cases, the victim was a member of the respondent's family. Majority had committed offence with the help of others, indulged in offence for the first time, did not think about the results of their action before committing crime, claimed innocence about their crime and committed crime predominantly for financial causes. Majority of the women in the age group of 18 to 29 and 30 to 39 years were more involved in property offences. Illiterate and graduate undertrials were also more involved in property offences. Majority of Hindus were found participating in property offences while, Muslims were more involved in 'other offences' i.e., NDPS Act, Passport Act and Immoral Traffic Act offences. Upper caste women were more involved in offences against the person. Majority of S.C./S.T. and N.T./D.T. caste women were involved in property offences while, O.B.C. caste women were more involved in 'other offences'. Married and widowed/deserted women category showed their involvement in property offences, while, unmarried women were equally involved in property offences and 'other offences'. Majority of housewives had been arrested for offences against the person. Those who were engaged in some occupation were involved in property offences predominantly. Majority of the respondents in the income group of below Rs. 3000 per month were seen to be involved in property offences.

Respondents belonging to nuclear families were more involved in property offences, while respondents belonged to joint families were more involved in offences against the person. Respondents who themselves were breadwinners in the family were involved mostly in property offences. In most of the cases, those who belonged to nuclear families, had their spouses as companions in criminal act, while respondents from joint families mostly received help from family members other than spouse.

Attitudes and Feelings of Respondents

It was noted that majority of the respondents felt that decisions about their arrest and custody were unjustified. They showed perception of themselves as innocent, found prison custody as forced separation from family, showed favourable attitudes towards co-inmates, did not find any difference in treatment by prison authorities. It was also observed that majority of the respondents have the belief that after their release they would be treated by their family members as before. However, most of them neither received support from their families not did their family members come to visit them. Most of them did not receive or send letters to family members.

Undertrial female criminals possess positive attitudes towards people in the society outside the prison and have expressed negative responses about the query as to whether they feel like taking revenge on the people responsible for getting them arrested. Majority of respondents spoke in favour of their children and expressed that the happiness of their children is the main factor which makes them feel happy. They have a desire to go out. On the other hand, they have acute feelings of insecurity and anxiety.

Observations

This study of 90 undertrial female criminals shows the changing forms of female criminality. The findings of this study indicate that, today women of all age groups are equally involved in crime. Illiteracy and low level of education dominate the crime scenario. Higher percentages of criminals are seen to be emanating from urban areas. In urban areas, checks imposed on women both by the community and the authorities operate less effectively. This relative freedom lies behind the exposure to the evil effects of city life. In the city, the influence of relatives and community has weakened. Moreover, urbanization has led to the breaking up of the joint family.

The findings of the study also show that dwelling in slums produces more criminals in the city. Slums and unauthorized structures are an outcome of irresistible inflow of population into the city and subsequent pressures on land and resources. It reflects inhuman living conditions coupled with hardships in life and have a far reaching impact on the quality of life. The earlier studies highlighted the involvement of married women as prominent in crime, while this study shows an almost equal proportion of married and widowed/deserted women involved in crime. Most of the empirical studies in India showed that offences against the person were dominant offences. However, the present study shows that property offences are higher than offences against the person. The majority of female criminals were found to belong to poor sections of society, with either very low or no stable source of monthly income. Economic deprivation is the main cause for criminal activities. Fluctuation in crimes seemed to be clearly tied to economic conditions and to two factors in particular: prices of consumer goods, especially food and availability of work.

Although, women still represent only a small fraction of those arrested for NDPS Act offences, their involvement may be increasing. It is also found that women committed passport act offences. The motivation behind it was the chance of getting a job in a city like Mumbai.

The general point made in almost all the studies is that the impact of socio-economic status on trends in crime is revealed most strongly. Most of the respondents came from nuclear families and in many cases respondents were playing the role of breadwinner of the family. Hence, the respondents must have experienced strain and pressures as a result of economic conditions.

Majority of the married women were unable to decide on any matter without their husband's consent. In a male dominated society, decision making power also indicates family culture and understanding in the family. The processes of modernization and industrialization transformed socio-economic environment. More and more women started working outside and supplementing the income of their families. The increasing rate of family breakdown, widowhood and desertion, home responsibilities, rearing children and financial difficulties all contribute to the incidents of female criminality.

In the present study, poverty was found to be a significant factor in provoking a woman to crime and it may be the root of marital or other frustrations. Poverty creates severe economic strain on women; search for alternative sources of livelihood and it may be a stimulus to crime. In a city like Mumbai, there are great opportunities for theft. The findings indicated that, these females are mostly from lower income backgrounds. The rising prices have forced women to seek jobs in cities. As urbanization increases, property offences in cities also increase.

However, low socio-economic status of the family and family circumstances or stressful situations within the family may be at the root of female criminality.

The socio-economic analysis emphasizes poverty and financial crisis as the primary causes of crime. Female crime rates have increased mainly in economic crimes. Today, women are more involved in property offences because they have more opportunities to commit such crimes.

On the basis of review findings, it may be viewed that the main causes of female criminality are economic insecurity and family circumstances. The people of lower socio-economic status face more deprivations throughout their life. It is difficult for them to satisfy their economic needs, therefore, they are tempted to commit crimes.

Very often women are themselves responsible for becoming criminals. Since, a large number of crimes committed by women are due to their adjustment problems or circumstances and are not due to their criminal tendencies, and also, most of them are first offenders. There is a great need for a flexible policy for female criminals.

Conclusion

The present study covers a variety of aspects related to female criminality. Certain conclusions can be drawn based on the findings of the present study about the nature and trends of female criminality. The analysis of the variables helps in hypothesizing the role of low socio-economic status and stressful situation within the family caused by illiteracy, early marriage and poverty, in female crime.

The analysis detects low socio-economic level to be more influential. As far as women are concerned, their inferior status, both within the family and society can put unusual stress on them leading them to deviance in reaction to such stress. In the case of females in India this stress is enormous because of cultural norms. A woman is not supposed to leave her husband's house no matter how many hardships she may suffer. If the Indian woman seeks freedom at home and asserts her rights, it creates further stresses and strains in the marital relationship.

The present study reveals that the female criminality was more prevalent among illiterate women and poverty was predominantly at the root of marital or other frustrations. Majority of the female criminals were found to have an income below Rs. 3,000 per month. This is significant in the sense that low income is an important contributory factor to family tensions and a combination of unsatisfactory social relationships and poverty leads to criminal behaviour. For example, most of the thefts committed by women are not the result of social deviation but are due to family and economic compulsions.

The findings of the present study reveal that majority of the respondents were married at a young age (below 18 years) and therefore were open to stress and strain of an early marriage. Economic instability and lack of adjustment in family also explains crime among women. There is no doubt that family is an influential institution. The influence of family on women is complex and cannot adequately be explained in simple causal terms. So, family's role appeared as one of the most significant factor pushing most of the women towards criminal behaviour. In fact, financial cause is the chief factor which gives rise to different situations of stress and strain compelling the individual to think of and take to different types of deviant behaviour. Frustration is associated more closely with lower socio-economic status. This status creates additional problems and resulting to frustrations.

The present study reveals that in most murder cases, the victim was a member of the respondent's family. This shows that the respondent had primary relationship with the victim. Not only in murders but also in other crimes, family was found to be an important factor in criminality. This supports that stressful situation within the family plays an important role in the life of female criminals. B.R. Sharma also observed that strained interpersonal relations with husband and other family members, husband's extra-marital relations, deprivation and denial of basic needs of life, like – affection, security, etc., were the main causes of frustrations and ultimately of crime. It is observed that insecurity, anxiety and frustrations are highly significant in the undertrials. They were also anxious about the care and happiness of their children. On the other hand, they were worried about their future due to the stigma of imprisonment.

Drawbacks of Existing Judicial Process: Criminal processes beginning with arrests and ending in release and readjustment with society involves a lot of deprivation including the deprivation of contacts with family members and the inevitable disruption of management and care of children. On the other hand, it is also true that the imprisonment of a woman is dysfunctional to her family and particularly to her children. When women are imprisoned, the ramifications of their confinement are twofold. Not only are they affected, but their children are consequenced as well. Women tend to be the fabric which binds many families; when they are imprisoned their families collapse.

As such, it is important to consider the implications of children growing up motherless. This perpetuates a cycle of criminality in which victimized children habitually become adult criminals. So they should be released on probation and allowed to live in their homes, because arrest and custody affects the under-trial prisoner as well as their families and their children in particular. It will prevent the both, viz. under-trial prisoner and her family to suffer from social and psychological deprivation and also from the social stigma attached to imprisonment.

Imprisonment cannot be pleasing to anyone. There is no doubt about the fact that removal of the offender from the family has a very serious and disabling impact on her family. One of the prison system's greatest failings may be treating all insiders similarly, because not every one in prison is a criminal. A major problem which under-trial female prisoners face is delayed trial period. It is not only criminal justice system which is partial and silent about women but even outside its circle; society, family, religion are equally responsible for the present miserable conditions of women prisoners, e.g. if family members are arrested for the same offence, the family spends money and also provide more legal support to defend male relatives rather than female. In that case, female members stay in prison for long periods.

The National Expert Committee on Women Prisoners (1986-87) headed by Justice Krishna Iyer was constituted in order to identify the gaps in or drawbacks of existing facilities and services and to evolve a more humane policy towards women offenders. The Committee noted that existing malpractices in the various terms of custody affect women more adversely than men. Specific and specialized interventions are necessary to dispense custodial justice to women and to protect her dignity and her person in custody. The Committee has proposed interventions addressed to policy making, reviewing enforcement and organizational and infrastructural level.

Suggestions: A criminal is not a born criminal, efforts can and should be made to correct and re-socialize the individual. Those who commit crime as a matter of choice or as a means of livelihood are few indeed. A large number of criminals are victims of situations or criminals by accident.

One of the prison system's greatest failings may be treating all insiders similarly, because not everyone in prison is a criminal. A woman going in for one or two weeks out of her whole life, who may never offend again, is not a criminal although a jail sentence usually means that to the community. As soon as such a woman is released, friends and neighbours shy away from her as though she was contaminated. At this point, chances are high that such a woman might offend again because of community attitudes.

There is no doubt about the fact that removal of the criminal from the family has a very serious and disabling impact on her family. In fact, her family may be as much affected as that of the victim, or even more so because of the stigma involved in it. Further, the prevalent conditions may force the children of the criminal to take to anti-social modes of behaviour. When the criminal has committed a crime, she has to be punished. Whether her children or other family members who have not been involved in the crime should also suffer for it, is an important issue that needs to be looked into. The most important reason for this is that, efforts have not been made to evaluate or even to understand the impact of policies and practices in the criminal justice system on family life. A family is very greatly affected by the sentence passed on its members. It has to be understood and dealt with. This is by no means an easy task. But, it is an important task which has to be performed.

Women prisoners are hardly a bunch of dangerous criminals. Less than a handful might need to be locked up for public safety. There is also the possibility of female criminals being psychologically disturbed rather than criminal.

Keeping all this in view, the following steps are found necessary at different levels to improve conditions of female criminals:

Legal Aid:

- All women in custody must be informed of their rights in custody including their right to demand legal aid if needed. Efforts should be made to provide legal aid.
- If the family of the prisoner has problems and is not able to arrange legal assistance, then legal assistance may be made available to prisoners in jails.

Voluntary Organizations/NGO's: There is a need to involve more voluntary organizations while dealing with female criminals. NGO's and activists should be allowed to study their situations.

Criminal Justice Procedure:

- More family courts should be established for the smooth and flexible administration of justice and for speedy disposal of the cases.
- Justice needs to be less expensive. As early as possible, undertrials should be brought into the judicial procedure and cases should be settled.
- There should be female judges to deal with the cases of female offenders, which might ensure better understanding of the situation which led these women to crime.
- Imprisonment stigmatizes persons. Most female criminals can easily be released on probation. This will also reduce over-crowding in prisons.
- During the training period police should be properly sensitized over issues related to women.
- The whole judicial system needs to be sensitized towards women's issues. The judges, magistrates and advocates require a thorough sensitization and orientation for a more sensitive handling of judicial and legal procedures affecting women.

It can be concluded that more adequate programs are necessary to meet the needs of female offenders. Offering programs conducive to the needs of women offenders not only benefits them, but also their families and society in general.

Effective Alternatives: Following services should be provided to female offenders after their release. It includes:

- more information regarding release planning;
- less conditions imposed for women released on full parole;
- the option to decline treatment programs or counselling;
- greater availability of low-cost housing; programs for employment,
- financial advice and support .

It was found that the women required programs which heightened self-esteem and allowed the women to become empowered in order to enable them to challenge conventional norms. "Empowerment is the process through which women gain insight into their situation, identify their strengths, and are supported and challenged to take positive action to gain control of their lives". The inequities and lack of opportunity traditionally endured by women have left many with feelings of inadequacy and the subsequent low levels of self-esteem.

Women prisoners require pertinent information which will allow them to make meaningful and responsible choices about their lives. Women need to be advised as to the availability of resources and the implications of their decisions so they may select the most appropriate options. Allowing women to make informed decisions provides them with a sense of control over their lives and, in turn, builds their self-esteem and self-worth.

The principle, 'respect and dignity' reflects the idea that respect is essential between and among prisoners and staff of correctional services. This precept is based upon the belief that a person treated with respect and dignity is likely to gain self-respect and to respond to others in a similar fashion. A positive and supportive environment can foster personal development and promote physical and psychological health. It is the responsibility of all levels of government, correctional services, businesses, voluntary and private sector groups, and the community to aid in the development, implementation, monitoring and evaluation of programming services for women prisoners. This approach allows women to gain control of their lives and become productive, contributing members of society.

Programs must take into account the social, political and economic contexts of women's lives and reflect individual needs in relation to the world in which women live. Women are regarded as experts on their individual life experiences and treated with respect. The survival strengths within each woman are focused upon in order to promote empowerment and effect change.

References

Adler Freda, "Sisters in Crime: A Rise of the New Female Criminal", McGraw Hill, New York, 1977.

Ahuja Ram, Becker Howard, "Female Offenders in India", Meenakshi Prakashan, Meerut, 1969.

Caldwell Robert, Cloward Richard and Ohlin L.E., "Criminology", University of Pennsylvania Press, New York, 1956.

Cohen Albert K., Durkheim Emile, "Delinquency and Opportunity", Routledge and Kegan Paul, London, 1961.

Crime Problem, Appleton, New York, 1967.

Criminality of Women, University of Pennsylvania Press, Philadelphia, 1950.

Deviance and Control, Prentice Hall of India Pvt. Ltd., New Delhi, 1970. "Suicide", translated by J.A. Spaulding, Free Press, New York, 1951. Merton Robert K.

Extracts from the Maharashtra Prison Manual, published by Vidhayak Sanvad, Maharashtra and Human Rights Law Network, Mumbai, 1996.

Family Structure and the Socialization of the Child" in 'Family, Socialization and Interaction Process' ed. T. Parsons & R.P. Bales, Free Press, New York, 1954.

Female Crime: The construction of Women in Criminology", Allen & Unwin, London, 1987.

Model Prison Manual, 1976

Naffine N., Parsons Talcott, Pollak Otto, Reckless Walter "Social Theory and Social Structure", Free Press, New York, 1949.

Report of National Expert Committee on Women Prisoners, Vol. I & II, 1986-87, Ministry of Human Resource Development, Department of Women and Child Development, New Delhi.

Report of the Committee on Empowerment of women, Ministry of Home Affairs and Ministry of Human Resource Development, (Department of Women and Child Development). 2001-

2002.

Report of the National Workshop on Custodial Justice to Women, National Institute of Public Co-operation and Child Development (NIPCCD), New Delhi, 1989. The Bombay Jail Manual, 1935.

Reports: Crime in India – National Crime Record Bureau (N.C.R.B.), Bureau of Police Research and Development, Ministry of Home Affairs, Government of India, New Delhi, Reports from 1991-2000.

Smart Carol, "Women, Crime and Criminology: A Feminist Critique", Routledge & Kegan Paul, London, 1976.

Sutherland Edwin H. and Cressy Donald R., "Principles of Criminology". Routledge & Kegan Paul, London, 1965.

37

Women Employment and Quality of Life

Madhur Bala and O.P. Monga

The quality of life of people, as an area of research has gradually become the focus of attention of the researchers from various disciplines including sociologists from the decades of 1960's. Since then, there is a growing world-wide concern with the quality of life of people. It is becoming more oriented towards women, which constitute a distinct half of the humanity, both in the context of family and outside. Although, it appears that study of the quality of life in India is a recent phenomenon, yet scant attention has been given to this. The reasons attributed to this are: first, there are few research studies in India on the quality of life of people in general and of the women in particular; second, the developmentalists have focused on analysis of the Gross National Product to measure the economic development and they have done a little to analyze the quality of life, and predominantly, researchers in India devoted themselves in finding out the impact of development programme in terms of economic indicators; and third, family researchers in India have also concentrated on the study of break down of traditional patterns and social problems facing the women in India. The paucity of literature on this area of sociological research can be attributed to the lesser importance of the women themselves, who have been given superficial attention in the process of national development. Above all, most important reason is an apathetic attitude of the society towards women, which prefers to adopt and nurture traditional image of women, Therefore, the quality of life studies have not emerged as research problem. It is only recently, that in India researchers have become alive for taking up the quality of life issue of women.

Implicitly or explicitly social development focuses upon the improvement of the quality of life of all the citizens. And it is now recognized that any aberrations like a poor quality of life of people in general and women in particular can not only spoil their benefits to the human organisms, but can also spoil their benefits to the family systems which is recognized as the basic unit of society. The quality of life as a phenomenon is the outcome of both positive and negative experiences of human being. It brings together, the wants, the needs, the aspirations, the expectations and the subjective feelings, which implies greater social interactions both quantitatively and qualitatively. The spectrum of the quality of life does not remain constant but it revolves between relative harmony and disharmony in the wants, the needs, the aspirations, the expectations and the subjective feelings or the perceptions.

American sociologist Andrews and Withey (1988), pointed out that assessment of human well-being involves the standard of living as well as the degree of excellence of an individual's life style. Psychologists understand that quality of life of an individual or group of individuals have objective and subjective components. The former relates to standard of living or level of living, where as the later includes own judgment about his life. World Health Organization (WHO) has explained the quality of life as composite measure comprising of physical, mental and social well-being as perceived by each individual or by group of individuals, that is to say happiness, satisfaction and gratification as health, marriage, family work, financial situations, educational opportunities, self-esteem, creativity, belongingness and trust in others.

It is generally held that economic growth brings about changes in the quality of life as well as in the interpersonal relationships. The employment of women, which is an important aspect of economic developments, is also believed to serve this purpose to a great extent. If it is true, that economic growth and employment should also help women to get the injustice, perpetuated through sex discrimination and other social practices vindicated. They should have an equal access to health, education and occupations. With in the family they should have an equal say in the decision making and control over their lives. In short, employment should help in improving the quality of life of women. It also adds to individual's social position in the society. In traditional Indian society, employment of women beyond her domestic engagement was considered a taboo. In modern society, especially in India employment has been considered as one of the major tool for empowerment of women. It brings change in position of women from purely domestic individual to a co bread winner in the family.

It is not out of context to point out that in modern world women are increasingly entering in almost all occupation, such as, health, education, engineering, management, defense forces etc which were earlier dominated by men. In this context a pertinent question emerges, whether employment improves status or the quality of life of women? Theoretically speaking, within the philosophy of empowerment, major assumption in providing employment to women has been that employment would give some share to women in the decision-making process within the family. It can also be assumed that employment leads to reduction in household responsibilities of the working women and places them at a higher level of status. Employment makes women more conscious about their individual rights and they seem to be positively associated with the reading and enjoyment programmes.

Employed women are more conscious in the matter of interaction with other people through participation in the social organization. Enhanced family income, reduced disparity between earning and purchasing power improve quality of life in term of food and nutrition, their illness behavior, living condition education, recreation, health, social aspect of well being and economic autonomy in the form of equality between men and women in the decision making (Bergman,1986). With regards to the relationship between work and women, Engel in his famous account origin of the women's subordination appreciated the significance of marriage and specific family form in its reproduction, but he also argues that emancipation of women would follow from their full entry into social production.

Marks and Engel held that in capitalist society, the demand for wage labour will raise the status and power of the proletarian women within the family and their relation between the sexes will improve. They believed that the economic independence of women would free them from male dominance within the family (Harlambos1980; Engel 1902). By providing exposure to women in outside world, especially at work place, it influences her outlook towards life.

In India number of females entering into the labour force has increased over the last two-three decades. The state of Himachal Pradesh ranks seventh in female work participation rate, first being Sikkim and last being Punjab (Census of India, 2001). This indicates change in traditional social attitude towards female employment. In this backdrop of theoretical explanations that employment improves the quality of life of women and the steady increase in number of women in labour force in the nation as a whole and in the state of Himachal Pradesh during the past two or three decades, the basic concern of this paper is to empirically investigate the impact of employment on the quality of life of the women. This issue is not only of vital sociological significance but is also very crucial for the purpose of planning, evolving and modifying strategies in future, for betterment of the quality of life of women, who constitute almost half of the mankind on this planet` The Earth'.

Methodology

The present study was undertaken in Nahan town, the headquarters of district Sirmour, which lies in the Southern part of the state of Himachal Pradesh. The data was collected by interviewing 200 married women (100 employed and 100 un-employed) purposively selected for this study. The employed women belonged to public sector.

Since employment is considered a major factor in bringing a change in the attitude of women by exposing them to outside world and new work situations, therefore, the question, what is perception of women towards their own overall life, is very crucial. It is represented in terms of life satisfaction or happiness according to Warr and Parry (1982), while giving reference of Compbell, Convense and Rodger (1976) points out that it is often assessed through a single question, for example, taking all things together, how would you say things are these days; would you say are you very happy, pretty happy, or not too happy.' Life satisfaction may tapped through separate question about specific domain (marriage, income and community etc.) responses to which are summed e.g. Nye (1963), or by a single report of how satisfied people are with the way they are spending their lives (e.g. Ferree,1976). There are number of scales available to measure the quality of life e.g Life Satisfaction Scale by O. G. Alam and Ram ji Srivastva 1960; and Life Satisfaction Index - A by Neugarten and Havigharst (1961). These scales have inherent difficulties due to their inadequacy in application for varied populations, methods and techniques of evaluations. As per method adopted by Warr and Parry (1982), in this study life satisfaction was assessed by asking a single question, how do you perceive your overall life? The major assumption was that employed women will be more satisfied from the life situation as compared to their unemployed counterparts.

Findings arrived at on the basis of statistical treatment of data are explained in the proceeding paragraphs. However for the sake of convenience two categories of life satisfaction, that is, satisfied and dissatisfied have been used for analysis. The former category i.e. satisfied here indicates very high level of satisfaction, whereas the latter i.e. dissatisfied conveys very low level of satisfaction from overall life.

Observations and Conclusions

From the analysis of information with regard to the impact of employment on the quality of life of women very interesting findings have emerged. On the whole it was found that majority of women are satisfied from their overall life. It is evident from the fact that about three fourth (76.5 per cent) of the subjects included in this study expressed their satisfaction and the remaining a little less than one fourth (23.5 per cent) said that they were dissatisfied with their over all quality of life. On comparing life satisfaction between employed and un-employed groups, it was observed, that overwhelming majority of employed women were satisfied. In the selected population their proportion was 97.00 per cent as against 56 per cent in the unemployed category (Table 37.1).

Table 37.1: Employment and Quality of Life

S.N	Level of Satisfaction	Employment Status		Total
		Employed	Unemployed	
1	Satisfied	97	56	153 (76.5 per cent)
2	Dissatisfied	03	44	47 (23.5 per cent)
	Total	100	100	200 (100 per cent)

df 2 $X^2 = 46.75$, $p > 0.01$, Highly Significant

The quality of life of working and non-working women was further analyzed across the variables, such as, age, education, caste, marriage and income to see the influence of these on the level of satisfaction. Observations in this context are outlined below.

Age of Women and Quality of Life

Age is a biological and demographic variable. It not only determines individual's physical and mental maturity but also affects one's attitude and perception towards life. Age also shows an individual's capacity and level of adjustments in different situations. Thus it is assumed that with the increase in age there is increase in level of satisfaction about life. In the present study, the quality of life has been analyzed in relation to the age of respondents and their spouses.

It was observed that middle aged women are more satisfied from their life. Intra-group comparison showed that percentage of women who expressed pretty good level of satisfaction from their life was significantly greater (98.41 per cent) among employed, whereas it was lower (70.58 per cent) among the unemployed (Table 37.2). Further as we see the quality of life through various age categories the level of satisfaction increases from younger age towards the late middle age in employed group whereas it decreases in the late middle age group among unemployed women. Dissatisfaction in late middle age may be due to the fact their values are not in consonance with present day life situations and they have not experienced the kind of exposure in which younger generation is placed. Statistical results show that age is positively associated with the quality of life of irrespective of employment as the value of X^2 is greater at 0.01 level of probability. Contrary to the statistical results that satisfaction decreases in old age further research is needed on a larger scale to supplement or to refute this finding.

Duration of Married Life and Quality of Life

Institution of marriage exposes men and women to new positions, which have different rights and obligations. It gives an opportunity to the actor to adjust to variety of situations and establish their position in the context of intra and inter familial network. Duration of married life indicates one's happiness or unhappiness, success or failure in social life. Duration of married life, therefore, was thought to be an important sociological variable, which influences the level of satisfaction.

Table 37.2: Age of Women and Quality of Life

Level of satisfaction	Employed Group				Unemployed Group			
	21-30	31-40	41-50	Total	21-30	31-40	41-50	Total
Satisfied	18 90.00	62 98.41	17 100	97	22 45.83	24 70.58	10 50.55	56
Dissatisfied	02 10.00	01 01.59	00 ----	03	26 54.17	10 29.42	08 49.45	44
Total	20	63	17	100	48	34	18	100

Employed group, df2, $X^2 = 4.307$, $P>0.01$, significant
Unemployed group, df2, $X^2 = 5.13$, $P>0.01$, significant

It was very significant to note that on the whole women are satisfied with their life. On comparative analysis between employed and unemployed respondents with regard to level of satisfaction and duration of married life it is discernible that more than 93 per cent women in all groups mentioned satisfaction with their life as against 44 to 70 per cent among the unemployed women (Table 37.3). This may be due to the feeling of economic security and adequacy in fulfilling of various social obligations towards their family members and children. Statistical findings show that the duration of married life is not associated with the quality of life as the value of Chi-square $X^2 = 2.34$ and $X^2 = 6.54$ is less than the table value at 0.05 level of probability.

Table 37.3: Duration of Married Life and Quality of Life

Level of satisfaction	Employed Group				Unemployed Group			
	01-10	11-20	21-30	Total	01-10	11-20	21-30	Total
Satisfied	45 93.75	32 100	20 100	97	22 44.89	22 62.85	12 75.00	56
Dissatisfied	03 02.25	00 ----	00 ----	03	27 45.11	13 37.15	04 25.00	44
Total	48	32	20	100	49	35	16	100

Employed group, df3, $X^2 = 2.34$, $P<0.05$ Insignificant
Unemployed group, df3 $X^2 = 6.38$, $P< 0.05$, Insignificant

Caste and Quality of Life of Women

Caste is one of the major bases of the organization of the Indian society. Rural as well urban societies are divided in to two hierarchal strata. Traditionally caste divisions in Indian society are associated with different customs, traditions and cultural practices. They also differ in their social status and prestige- the Brahmins occupies superior most and the Shudras inferior most position. It can not be denied that this institution has undergone marked transformation in all its aspects, but people are still graded on their caste position and this is truer of the hilly study area of Himachal Pradesh. Being members of different caste groups, people are exposed to different cultural and social life and therefore it is assumed that level of satisfaction will be more among respondents of higher caste than that of the respondents of lower caste.

Findings with regard to caste and the quality of life are very interesting. The comparative analysis between employed and unemployed women shows that overwhelming majority in the former group is satisfied irrespective of whether they belong to higher caste or scheduled caste. From comparative view point 96.36 per cent of higher caste women in employed group conveyed satisfaction from life as against 72.72 per cent from the unemployed group (Table 37.4).

Table 37.4: Caste and Quality of Life

Level of Satisfaction	Employed Group			Unemployed Group		
	Higher Caste	SC	Total	Higher Caste	SC	Total
Satisfied	53 96.36	44 97.77	97	32 72.72	24 42.25	56
Dissatisfied	02 03.64	01 02.33	03	12 27.28	32 57.20	44
Total	55	45	100	44	56	100

Employed group, df3, $X^2 = 2.45$ $P < 0.05$ Insignificant
Unemployed group, df3 $X^2 = 9.77$ $P > 0.05$, Significant

Similar findings are also clear in case of women belonging to scheduled caste in employed and unemployed category. Interestingly proportion of dissatisfied unemployed scheduled caste women is significantly lower (42.85 per cent) than those in the employed group (97.97 per cent). In case of employed group statistically it was found that caste is not associated with the quality of life as the value of X^2 =2.45 at the degree of freedom 3 is less than the table value at 0.05 level of probability, whereas in case of unemployed group the caste is associated with the quality of life as the value of X^2 is 9.77 at degree of freedom 3 is greater than the table value at 0.05 level of probability. It further shows that the influence of caste still persists in case of unemployed respondents, whereas in case of employed group it is negligible. It may be attributed to the fact that employed Scheduled Caste women are economically secure and have better status than their unemployed counterparts.

Women Education and Quality of Life

Education is considered as one of the major factors in the process of human resource development and empowerment of women in modern society. It helps a person to acquire to rational and scientific outlook towards different aspects of social life. It also helps an individual to know about different dimensions of social issues and social problems and the ways to solve them. It equips individual with the knowledge ant training of methods to adjust with diverse conditions of life. In traditional Indian society the education of girls was very much restricted, as it was believed that their duties are confined to the four walls of the house but with modernization this attitude has undergone change we find that female literacy over the years has increased but it continues to be lower in comparison to male. It was thought that education is an important variable for the study of quality of life of women. It is therefore assumed that the level of satisfaction will be higher among respondents with higher education.

Women having acquired education matriculation and beyond seems to cherish satisfaction from their quality of life. However on comparing the two groups with education up to matriculation it can be seen that more employed (94.88 per cent) indicated satisfaction from their life as against 73.90 per cent of the unemployed women (Table 37.5).

Table 37.5: Women Education and Quality of Life

Level of satisfaction	Employed Group				Unemployed Group			
	Illiterate	Matric	Graduate	Total	Illiterate	Matric	Graduate	Total
Satisfied	00 00.00	62 96.87	35 97.22	97	10 41.66	38 73.99	08 100	56
Dissatisfied	00 00.00	02 02..33	01 02.88	03	14 58.34	30 26.61	00 ---	44
Total	00	64	36	100	24	68	08	100

Employed group, df 5, X^2 =0.514, P< 0.05 Insignificant
Unemployed group, df 5, X^2 = 21.22, P > 0.05, Significant

Similar observations are evident in case of women having education up to graduation and above. Significantly all graduate and above women in unemployed group pointed out their full satisfaction To be more explicit the number of dissatisfied low educated respondents in unemployed group was more whereas in among employed low educated respondents no one expressed of dissatisfaction. Higher proportion of satisfied subjects in employed educated respondents may be due to the fact that education along with employment contributes to the satisfaction of the respondents by providing psychological and economic security. Statistical analysis shows that in case of employed respondents education is not associated with the quality of life as the value of X^2= 0.514 at degree of freedom 5, which is less than the table value at 0.05 level of probability, whereas in case of unemployed respondents education was found to be significantly associated with quality of life as the value of X^2 =21.22 at degree of freedom of 5, is greater than the table value at 0.05 level of probability.

Socio-economic Status and Quality of Life of Women

Socio-economic status is very important as it indicates one's standing or position in society with respect to class. Socio-economic status is a composite index of a number of sociological variables. Socio-economic status affects individual's standard of living and interaction with other groups in the community. It also affects people's attitude towards individual and social goals. Though it is very difficult to collect accurate information about different sociological variables, which covers socio-economic status, but it was thought worthwhile to analyze level of satisfaction of respondents in relation to their socioeconomic status. It is assumed that higher socio-economic status increases one's satisfaction towards social life. In the present study socio-economic status has been assessed by using socio-economic status scale urban (1977) of Kuppuswamy. This scale uses three important variables - education, occupation and income. Based on the score, five socio-economic categories (upper, upper middle, lower middle, upper lower and lower) were formed. But for the sake of convenience of analysis these five categories accommodated into three categories i.e. upper, middle and lower.

Women belonging to upper socio-economic status were more satisfied from their life, however, it was not the case with the unemployed respondents. More unemployed respondents from middle and lower socio-economic categories put forward that they were satisfied with their life. Employed and unemployed respondents were compared with respect to socio-economic status and quality of life. Employed group did not show association between socio-economic status and quality of life, because the value of X^2 =1.07 at degree of freedom 2 is less than the standard value at 0.05 level of probability. In contrast to this, among unemployed respondents there emerged a significant association between socio-economic status and level of satisfaction about the quality of life among the respondents. The value of X^2 =12.3 at degree of freedom 2 is greater than the standard value at 0.05 level of probability. The sizeable proportion of satisfied respondents in upper and lower socio-economic groups in unemployed segment may be attributed to that they have lower level of economic aspirations and are therefore satisfied (Table 37.6).

Table 37.6: Socio-economic Status and Quality Of Life

Level of satisfaction	Employed Group				Unemployed Group			
	Upper	Middle	Lower	Total	Upper	Middle	Lower	Total
Satisfied	82 97.61	13 92.85	02 100.00	97	03 100.00	15 88.23	38 90.47	56
Dissatisfied	02 02.39	01 07,15	00 00.00	03	00 00.00	02 11.77	42 09.53	44
Total	84	14	02	100	03	17	80	100

Employed group, df 2 X^2= 1.07, P< 0.05 Insignificant
Unemployed group, df 2 X^2= 12.3, P > 0.05, Significant

In sum it can be concluded that employment significantly affects satisfaction level of woman. It is also evident from the statistical data that overwhelming majority (97.00 per cent) employed women expressed satisfaction from their present overall life conditions as against only 3.00 per cent who indicated dissatisfaction from their life. It may be due to the fact that on one hand employment adds to economic gains and on the other hand, enhances one's position in the society and exposure to outside world which brings change in the attitude and outlook towards life. The observations on the quality of life across various sociological variables such as age, education, caste, duration of married life etc. needs to supplemented by more research studies on a larger and controlled sample.

These findings correspond to the views held by Sethi (1988); Kumar(1993); Das (1993); UNICEF(1998); Suswagata and Khan(1999); Chritopher (2001) and Vijaypara (2001) who on the bases of their research studies indicated that employment improves personal and social life of women. Contrary to this, on the other hand , Sharma (1973); Aggarwal (1985); Kalia (1999); Verma and Larson (2001) argued that employment dose not improve the quality of life of women These scholars point out that employment increases the burden of women as they have to shoulder the responsibilities of work place in addition to their domestic activities. However, our informal discussions with employed women attest to this fact of increased burden but our respondents were very categorical in saying that employment has added to their life satisfaction. There can not be any denial that in spite of these contradictory views it is now widely recognized and accepted that employment improves the quality of life of women. That is why modern development planning is laying increased emphasis on empowerment of women in public and private sectors of economy and also on self-employment, on short and long term basis. Hence employment seems to be most important tool in the empowerment of women in contemporary Indian society.

References

Aggarwal, Kuntal. Status and role of middle class educated earning women in the Indian family. In Women and Work in Indian society. 1985

Andrews, F.M. and Withey, S.B. *Social Indicators of Well-being: Americans' perception of life quality*. New York: Plenum Press. 1988

Bergman, R.B. *The Economic Emergence of Women*. New York: Inc. Publishers. 1986

Census of India. Series. 1. Delhi. Directorate of Census Operations. 2001

Das, M.S., Lenna. Decision making practices of employed and non employed home makers. Journal *of North-East India Council for Social Science Research*. Vol.(17). 1993

Haralambos, M. *Sociology themes and perspectives*. New Delhi, Oxford Uni. Press. Pp. 371-390. 1980

Kalia, H.L. Occupation health survey of women in industry. *Social Welfare*. Vol. (46). 1999

Kumar, N. Regional Dimensions of the status of women in India. *Social Change*, Vol. (23). 1993

Kuppuswamy ,B. *Mannul of Socio-economic Status Scale (urban)*, Manasayan, 32, Netaji Subash Marg, Delhi- 6. 1977

Sethi, R.M. Status and Power of working women with in the family: A test of Marxian perspective . *Journal of Sociological Studies*. Vol.(8), 1988

Sharma, K.D. *Socio-economic study of women employees*. Ujjain, Vikram University. 1973

Suswagata, Dey Paul and Gorachand Khan. Working Wives in Malda. Bearing a dual burden. *Social welfare*, Vol. (46). 1999

UNICEF (United Nations Children's Fund). *The state of the world's children*. Oxford University Press. 1998

Verma, S and Larson, R.W. Indian women's experience of household labour: oppression or personal fulfillment. *The Indian Journal of Social Work*. Vol.(62).Issue1.pp. 47-61. 2001

Vijayapriya S. Attitude of youth towards status of women. Social Welfare, Vol. (48) No. 3.pp 8-18.15. 2001

Warr, J and Parry. Paid employment and women's psychological well-being. *Psychological Bulletin*, 91:pp.498-516. 1982

World Health Organization (W.H.O.). Techn.Rep.Ser., No.600. 1976

38

Women in Urban Slums

Rameshwari Pandya and Anuradha Mathu

The process of urbanization is understood as higher rate of increase of urban areas than general population. Urbanization has led to various changes in the social and physical state of an area. People from rural areas migrate to cities in search of better housing and employment. They are new to the place and less skillful; hence they cannot match with the urban people initially. This leads to development of suburbs and slums.

On the other hand people living in urban areas face a change in lifestyle affected by the emergence of slums. Urbanization is a part of the larger process of economic and social change which is affecting not only the existing urban centres but the countryside as well. Urbanization implies that the growth of urban population is at a faster rate than the average rate of the growth of the nation. Peculiar characteristics of urbanization include increase in number of persons per household and development of non-agricultural sector more than the agricultural sector.

Urbanization is due to industrialization, improved transport facilities, irregularity in agricultural yield, better job facilities in the cities and access to education, recreation and science and technology. Problems of urbanization are many, to mention a few like, growing slums, energy crisis, environmental degradation, problems of housing, disposal of solid and liquid waste. Hence, scientific and technological advancements are for the benefit of the human beings but they can also pose health hazards for to him. Pollution of air we breathe, water we drink and food we eat, has been a very serious problems in the industrialized countries.

In the successive Five Year Plans, the Government of India has launched several social housing schemes for different income groups under which, loan/subsidy is given to the low income and economically weaker section families. The implementation of these schemes on a country-wide basis has created great awareness of the desirability of improving their housing and environmental conditions among all sections of the population including women.

Several other measures which have been taken include providing housing building advance, housing finance at low rates of interest through financial institutions, fiscal incentives, bulk acquisition and development of land, land use regulations, promotion of housing through cooperatives, setting up of "Housing Boards" and "City Development Authorities" and "Slum Clearance Boards" to augment the housing stock.

A Central Scheme of assistance for construction of hostel buildings for working women was initiated in the year 1972. The scope of the Scheme was widened in the year 1980 by including a provision for day-care centres for children. Financial assistance is given to voluntary organisations for construction or expansion of hostel buildings for working women. Local bodies are also eligible for taking up these programmes. The total number of hostels sanctioned so far is 429 with a total capacity of 27,292 working women with day-care centre facilities for 2,920 children, since the inception of the Scheme in the year 1972. It has been decided to reserve 5 per cent seats in the hostels for widows and other women in distress who are otherwise, eligible for hostel accommodation.

Under the "Minimum Needs Programme" to ameliorate housing and environmental conditions, the Government of India has been implementing various schemes viz., "Slum Clearance Improvement Scheme", "Scheme for Environmental Improvement" in slum areas and the Scheme for Provision of House Sites to landless workers in rural areas and other social housing schemes for improving the living conditions of the urban and the rural poor. The benefits of the schemes accrue to women also.

In the "Twenty Point Programme" in the year 1986, high priority was accorded to provision of drinking water supply (Point No. 7), improvement of housing conditions for 14.6 million rural landless families (Point No. 14) and those living in slums and squatter settlements (Point No. 15).

Large scale housing programmes have been taken up in different states under the "National Rural Employment Programme" (NREP) and "Rural Landless Employment Guarantee Programme" (RLEGP). Housing schemes with employment as the main feature have also been taken up in many States. For implementing the "Indira Gandhi Greh Nirman Awas Yojna", an allocation of Rs. 125 crore annually has been provided in the Seventh Five Year Plan to build one million houses for scheduled castes and tribal families.

Improvement in the quality of life of people depends to a great extent on the quality of housing and related facilities which determine the physical environment. It is in recognition of this fact that the world conference of the "International Women's Year" adopted a "World Plan of Action" in the year 1975 which included aspects related to housing amongst its recommendations. The Plan suggested that settlement planning and policies should be formulated keeping in view the trend to recognize women's role in the development process and should prioritize investments in infrastructure therein according to the needs of women. Subsequently, following the declaration of the year 1987 by the United Nations as the International year of Shelter for the Homeless, the Ministry of Urban Development of the Government of India formulated a Draft National Housing Policy (March, 1987) with a view to ensuring every family shelter by the end of this century. Nowhere in its text, however, had the draft acknowledged that housing and women's needs required to be closely linked. Passing references to women was made only at page 12 para 13.4 of the Draft wherein it stated that special efforts would be made to improve women's skills and working conditions in the housing sector.

For women, housing has a wider meaning. It implies their working and living environment to which they are confined for a greater portion of their lives, performing their multiple roles - that of production which is often home based and therefore implies the use of the shelter and its environs as the working space; that of reproduction which is traditionally viewed as their primary role and includes child rearing activities linked to domestic chores; and that of management of resources and assets within the family unit which includes activities such as storage, managing domestic provisions, processing, etc.

Slums are a corollary of urbanization in nearly all societies going through transition from an agrarian civilization to an industrial one. All slums share certain common characteristics such as poor housing, shortage of basic amenities, like water, electricity, drainage, health, etc. which ultimately leads to unhealthy environment and filth.

To solve the slum and squatter problems, the Government of NCT of Delhi initiated various schemes, such as:

- Slum clearance and Improvement scheme (1956).
- *Jhuggi-Jhompri* Removal Scheme (1960-67).
- Major Resettlement Programs (1975-76).
- Urban Basic Services Programmes (1985-90).
- Sites and Services Scheme.

The Urban Basic Services Programmes recognised social development and behavioural changes as an the important criteria for the physical improvement of the settlements. Emphasis on child care, education, women's welfare, change of attitude and peoples participation was were established.

Commission on Urbanization (1988) gave impetus to the reconstruction of urban local government. This is reflected in Constitution - the 'Nagar Palika Bill' introduced in Parliament on 7th August, 1989. Many of the suggestions of these committees and councils have been implemented by the government and shows a collectively progressive trend. This covers:

- Unification and rationalization of municipal laws of state government, and
- Establishment of urban development authorities.

Role of cooperation can be better understood by understanding the two types of functions it plays.

A. Obligatory Functions

- Supply of wholesome water and construction and maintenance of water works.
- Supply of electricity.
- Scavenging, removal and disposal of filth and rubbish.
- Measures for prevention and checking of dangerous diseases.

B. Discretionary Functions

- Construction of parks.
- Public housing.
- Detention of animals causing nuisance.

Most of the urban bodies follow the first course of option. Traditionally, the local government statutes provide bifurcation of functions in obligatory and discretionary categories.

It will have to identify "core" services to ensure a minimal balanced urban development. In this option, some of the traditional functions may not be attended by the local body as it apparently operates on a restrictive scale. Also, the development functions may not be co-terminus with pressure groups demand, but it will definitely provide the essential services in the context of developmental needs.

The issue which an urban local body may face if it opts for the second course of action is what constitutes the core services to ensure minimal balanced urban development of the city. The task force on Financing Urban Development (1983) provides a model of such kind of priority based classification of various function/services to be provided by the local government.

It has classified functions of local government into core categories. The core services are:

- Water supply
- Sewage/sanitation
- Solid waste disposal
- Water drainage
- Roads
- Street lighting

Health Needs of Urban Slum Dwellers

Health Needs: Health needs have been defined as "deficiencies in health that calls for preventive, curative control or eradication measures".

The need for medical care, safe water supply, adequate nutrition, immunization, family planning are all community health needs.

The main health problems, especially in urban slum populace are as follows:

1. **Infective and Parasitic Diseases:** These are pulmonary tuberculosis, cholera, diarrhea, dysenteries, enteric fevers, infectious hepatitis, malaria, etc.
2. **Nutritional Disorder:** These are chiefly protein - calorie malnutrition. Person have deficiency of iron, other vitamins and any other due to which diseases occur.
3. **Poor Sanitation:** Lack of safe drinking water, inadequate and inefficient disposal of excreta and other human wastes, abundance of houseflies, mosquitoes and other vectors of disease. Poor sanitation forms part of the vicious cycle linking poverty, disease and ignorance. It also puts a brake on social and economic development.
4. **Shortage of Health Personnel:** The doctor-population ratio in India, in comparison with other countries is far less. There is also a wide disparity in the doctor-population ratio between the rural and urban areas. The doctor population shortage is almost certainly accompanied by shortage of in almost other categories of health personnel.
5. **Population Explosion:** This is currently the most important problem in the developing countries. Due to population explosion people cannot get proper health facilities, housing water supply, sanitation and such facilities.
6. **Emergent Health Problems:** Some of these are cancer, cardiovascular disease, mental illness, allergic disorder; environmental pollution could be mentioned as emergent problems due to changing pattern of diseases and causes of mortality in the community.

Prevalent Environment in Urban Slums

The "Environment" is defined as an aggregate of all external conditions and influence affecting the life and development of an organism, human behaviour and society.

The internal and external comprises the total environment according to ecological approach. Disease represents maladjustment of human organism to this environment. The external environment consists of three main components outlined below:

- Physical environment

- Biological environment
- Social environment

Physical Environment: Physical environment is applied on non-living things and physical forces e.g. water, soil, air, climate, water, geography, food, housing, heat, light, radiation with which a human being is in constant interaction. Physical environment has been responsible for most of the improvement in health during the past century.

Biological Environment: Biological environment is the universe of living things, which surrounds man including man in himself. The living things are the viruses and other microbial agents, insects, rodents, animal and plants, which have their influence.

Social Environment: The third area of our environment, i.e. the social environment, includes complex interplay of factors and conditions, such as cultural values, customs, habits, beliefs, attitudes, morals, religion, education, occupation, standard of living, community life, availability of health services, social and political organization.

Meaning and Role of Environmental Health Administration

Environmental Sanitation Administration is an activity of diagnosing and controlling the environmental factors which exercise or may exercise a deterious and unhealthy effects on the physical, social and mental life of the people.

The objective of the Environmental Sanitation Administration is to plan thoroughly to change favourably the environment itself and modify the interaction of human-beings with the environment so that people can enjoy a good quality of life.

The administrator responsible for such programmes must plan to attack the unfavourable factors in concern with one another. Here are some important areas which need immediate attention of the planners, policy makers and the administrators to solve these impending problems, such as:

- Potable safe water supply and controlled water pollution
- Solid waste management
- Air pollution control
- Occupational health
- Food sanitation
- Urban planning and housing slum clearance
- Soil erosion
- Noise pollution

Needs and Problems Related to Environment

Air Pollution: The substances causing pollution are said to be pollutants. These pollutants in air cause air pollution. In slum houses, because of poor ventilation the air is polluted which causes disorders in to people living inside these houses. The disorders could be nausea, headache, and sometimes genetic disorder.

Disease agents may be conveyed by air.

- Man has polluted the atmosphere so heavily that much of the population now breathes a mixture of highly toxic gases with every lungful of air.
- A sudden increase in air pollution has often been associated with immediate increase in mortality and morbidity.
- The disease currently suspected being casually related to air pollution includes chronics, bronchitis and primary lung cancer.
- In slums, people use traditional sources and energy like wood and coal, which increases their risk further.

Solutions of Problems Related to Air Pollution

- Forests help in maintaining the oxygen content and preventing air pollution and also help in the formation of underground water.
- Forest cover provides us vegetables and fruits also.
- Use of unconventional energy.
- Providing energy education.
- Better ventilation through windows and checking the designs of housing?

Water in Urban Areas

- The International Institute for Environment and Development rightly observes that, water is everywhere the key to human health - clean water is the key to human comfort, health and even survival.
- The provision of ample supplies of safe water and the sanitary disposal of excreta has a direct and far-reaching effect upon the health and well-being of population.
- Provision of safe and convenient water supply is the single most important activity that could be undertaken to improve the health of people living in rural areas of the developing world.

Water Pollution in Urban Areas - Pollutants in the water can be from industrial wastes, city sewerage and such sources. It leads to diseases like cholera, hepatitis, malaria, etc.

Problems of Water

WHO estimates that as much as 80 per cent of all diseases in world is associated with water. Briefly, these include:

- Water borne diseases are those in which infectious agent remains alive in drinking water e.g. typhoid, paratyphoid, gastro enteritis, etc. The incidence of these diseases can be reduced by the purification of water.
- Water washed disease include the outer body surface e.g. trachoma, skin ulcer, scabies and typhus, etc. The incidence can be reduced by augmenting water quantity.
- Water based infections e.g. schistosomiasis, guinea worms. The infections occur when the skin is in contact with water or through drinking water.
- Water breeding or water proximity diseases are caused by mosquitoes or flies living near aquatic conditions.

Solutions

- Good modes of disposal and sewage.
- Construction of soak pits.
- Recycling of waste through acquifier system.

Housing

The WHO prefers to use the term "residential environment" which is defined as the "physical structure that man uses and the environs of that structure including all necessary services, facilities, equipment and devices needed or desired for the physical and mental health and the social well-being of the family and the individual".

A healthful residential environment is one in which the "family can develop and flourish physically, mentally and socially".

Housing Shortage: The increase in housing stock has, however, failed to keep pace with the alarming demand of population. Though the actual demand for housing is placed at about 50,000 dwelling units per year, the actual rate of construction has only been between 40 to 50 percent of the annual requirement and this has only tended to widen the overall backlog in housing deficit in the city. The extent of housing shortage can be gauged from overcrowding conditions of slums.

Criteria for Healthy Housing: An Expert Committee of the WHO (1974) recommended the following criteria for healthful housing.

- Healthful housing provides physical protection and shelter.
- Provides adequately for cooking, eating, washing and excretory functions.
- It should be designed, constructed maintained and used in a manner such as to prevent the spread of communicable diseases.
- Provides for protection from hazards of exposure to noise and pollution.

- Is free from unsafe physical arrangements due to construction or maintenance and from toxic or harmful materials.
- Encourages personal and community development, promotes social relationships reflects, a regard for ecological principles, and by these means promotes mental health.

Problems of Poor Housing

Respiratory Infections such as common cold, tuberculosis, influenza, bronchitis, measles etc. occur due to poor housing.

Skin infections such as scabies, ring worm, impetigo, etc.

Rat Infestations cause diseases like plague and such skin problems.

Arthropods: Houseflies, mosquitoes, flies and bugs, also cause and spread many diseases.

Accidents: Accidents occur when the houses are not properly constructed in slums and the majority of them go to the open grounds and such places for defecation and thereby pollute the environment with human excreta.

Over Crowding

Under conditions of continous contact in crowded families, an increased secondary attack rate for respiratory infections has been established. There is empirical evidence that the high mortality in acute infections, including those affecting the respiratory system, is mainly attributed to delay in reporting by inhabitants living in over-crowded houses.

Women exposed to smoke pollution suffer from chronic bronchitis and heart diseases. The biomass extensively used for cooking produces carbon monoxide and for moldehyde when burnt Co is a toxic gas, which reduces the Hb, in blood and continuous inhalation leads to heart diseases and impair fetal development. Poor housing facilities lead to reduced sanitation, which also acts as a major environmental factor for premature diseases and infection in human beings leading to poor health status of the women.

Bases of Extension Education

Extension education in community health needs to be based on the health requirements and problems of a community, as well as on the knowledge, skills, and resources of the extension workers. The health problems are to be solved in the context of social milieu that a community has developed and hence, the socio-psychological factors also need to be borne in mind while educating a community regarding health problems.

Three categories of bases thus needs to be considered for extension education in community health. These are (i) rational, (ii) administrative, and (iii) socio-psychological bases.

Rationale Bases: Rational bases include:

- Evidence of illnesses, predispositions for diseases, epidemics and accidents which requires health education for restoration of community health.
- Evidence of malnutrition due to ignorance, poverty, or adherence to social customs and taboos regarding food and food preparation.
- Population of unmarried persons and couples in the child-bearing age group who would benefit from family planning education.
- Squalid and dirty localities with polluted water supply, faulty garbage and sewage disposal and unkempt ponds, pits, walls and drains, could be some factors.

Administrative Bases: Administrative bases are:

- Material and financial resources of the community or of the extension agency.
- Availability of extension workers who have the necessary knowledge of extension methods, health problems, human behaviour and cultural determinants of social change.
- Selection and skills in use of teaching equipment, aids and materials.
- Availability of medical care and consultation.
- Possibility of collaboration of medical personnel and extension personnel on community surveys and health projects.

Socio-psychological Bases: The socio-psychological bases of extension education in community are the following:

- Knowledge of prevalent social norms and sanctions, goals and facilities, and power and ranks of community members.
- Knowledge of communication patterns and problems within communities.
- Knowledge of the ways of motivating people to change their beliefs and values to facilitate acceptance of health education.
- Knowledge of various factors affecting community health, such as extent of industrialization, urbanization, and cultural factors.

The concept of extension education in community health is acceptable on the basic rational premise that health is a necessity. But not all that is rational is acted upon. It was Herbert Spencer who said, "the preservation of health is a duty. Few seem conscious that there is such a thing as physical morality". And extension education based on such a rational ground, as well as on the stronger but not so obvious sociological and psychological considerations, may motivate communities to preserve the standards of Spencer's 'physical morality'.

Women's housing needs, arising from their multiple roles, have been listed as follows; as child bearers, they need access to sanitary facilities and a healthy living environment; as child rearers, they need space for child care and recreation within or outside the house; as managers of households, they need water, fuel, waste and garbage disposal, proper light and ventilation and space to perform domestic chores; and as producers, they need a working space as well as space for storage of raw materials and finished products, besides space for processing of materials. In addition, women also need privacy and security as well as facilities for education, recreation, production and training within the housing space. Housing thus, implies space beyond the confines of the immediate shelter.

An effective public distribution system for essential commodities like rations and cloth is a necessary support for women, especially women workers in the unorganized sector. Poor women are denied ration cards which forces them to purchase basic necessities from the open market at exorbitant prices. Even women with ration cards are often denied rations due to understocking or diversion of stocks.

Each of the above roles indicates that women's efficiency and effectiveness in performing the productive and reproductive tasks are linked to the quality of housing. Since they are in effect the primary users of housing, women must have a role to play in decisions regarding housing as well as ensure that they have assessed to ownership of the same.

In planning for women's development, priority needs to be given to creating access to assets for single women and female headed households. An estimated 30-35 per cent of households in rural India are headed by women according to available micro studies. Women have hitherto had no rights to ownership or inheritance of property within the framework of customary law. Recent legislative provisions have tried to remedy this situation but ancestral property still remains inaccessible to women. By and large, the patriarchal patterns of land ownership and transfer have implied that land is transferred to males. This pattern has been adopted by the planners in formulation of housing programmes so that men are recognized as heads of households and land is distributed in their names. Although, distribution of land deeds or *pattas* has been legally sanctioned for men and women jointly, in effect, women are able to gain access to land or assets, they are often required to have a man stand surety for the same, as also for loans and credit

Within the patriarchal norm, women may not customarily claim ownership of the matrimonial home. This has often denied women access to shelter in times of crisis. In cases where women have been deserted and are destitute, they have not had any legal right to claim access to shelter, housing or any such assets. Only recently have policy makers and legislators realized that, and thus it is imperative to accord priority to the provision of housing for single and women headed households.

Various strategies have been evolved to augment the housing stock in the country by urban planners and specialists especially for economically weaker sections. The target groups have however seldom been involved in planning for such housing. The norms applied to make such houses affordable for the identified target groups have ignored women's needs for space in the dwelling unit. It is necessary to scrutinize established standards and develop norms in housing especially for economically weaker sections, and to determine their adequacy for women. There must also be visible participation of women in the planning and execution of housing programmes in order to ensure that women's needs are adequately considered in the housing designs.

Women have had no traditional access to capital assets or to institutional finance and credit for housing. They have had to resort to borrowing from traditional credit sources at exorbitant rates of interest. Institutional sources of credit such as banks have not recognized women as credit worthy individuals in their own right so that they may borrow through existing schemes at differential rates of interest. Various agencies have tried to play an intermediary role in creating access for women to institutional credit but their outreach has been limited. It is essential, therefore, that institutions such as HDFC and HUDCO recognize women in their individual capacities as beneficiaries for housing credit and finance.

Ignorance, illiteracy, poverty, lack of communication and transport add to the problems of inadequate availability of health care at desired places. Women need to be educated about their own health and men need much greater awareness about the health problems women face.

The messages should be so effective that women are empowered to build a positive self image and self confidence and encourage group action in order to bring about change in the society.

Information dissemination to achieve goals of better health and development can be drawn up on the following lines:

- Personal hygiene and environmental education.
- Campaigns about immunization, diarrhea oral dehydration, simple foods for common aliments.
- Media activities should be organized as a regular feature.

More T.V. and radio jingles/documentaries on public health should be screened to educate and motivate people in the slums.

Co-operation between various departments such as education, information and public relation should be sought on a wider scale for organizing more effective and co-ordinated publicity campaigns.

There is lack of proper information about programmes and availability of services provided by the public sector and NGOs. Information, education and communication (IEC) activities are poorly planned and managed. The poor implementation of programs and special schemes in various sectors can be attributed to a lack of identification of clearly defined objectives, a lack of clearly outlined action plans, a lack of coordination and a lack of project monitoring processes.

Information, education and dissemination of health education are critical for creating awareness which in turn improves the health status of women in India.

Only practical expediency determined such considerations in the past, and these were relatively simple. Community health today is concerned with various protective, curative and contributory measures, such as:

- Control of communicable and other diseases through protective measures, like vaccination, DDT and BHC spraying, free treatment for certain diseases such as tuberculosis, malaria by the government.
- Provision of food from infection and contamination and of drinking water through purification.
- Provision of recreational facilities like playgrounds and parks.
- Relief from natural and man made catastrophies like famines, fires, floods.

Several other measures of community health can be added to this list.

Role of Higher Education in Improving the Conditions of Slums

The role of the university and college system in implementing programmes for upliftment of health status of women, housing and environment needs to be worked out within the broad parameters indicated by the National Policy on Education and its Programme of Action.

Mass Motivation and Mobilization

The following steps will help in mobilizing mass action:-

- Creating mass awareness.
- Motivational campaigns.
- Spreading messages through students.
- Involvement of people's participation.
- Sharing success stories.

Techno-Pedagogic Inputs

- Demonstration, technical support, improved learning material.
- Linking technology transfer.

- Preparing database information will help in technology transfer.

Need for Action

The need for educating the people regarding cleanliness is evident. Lack of basic facilities like latrines, trash-barrels, sweeper services contribute to unclean surroundings.

- The knowledge of how to keep clean with limited facilities and to improve certain simple facilities is an urgent need.
- Different educational activities can be carried out like organizing exhibition on "cleanliness as a precaution against diseases".
- Mass cleaning programme of surroundings. Sweeping and disposing filth in pits.
- Film shows on cleanliness, clean wells, ponds, streets and houses.

The concept of community health becomes more complex with the complexity of life. The modern ways of living have been affected by science and technology which has both solved and created problems for protecting community health. The contrast between modernity in cities and backwardness in slums remains till date.

Traditionally, women have had a significant role in resource management including housing management. It is important to recognize this role and provide for women's participation in development programmes, and for incorporating their needs in schemes for improvement of housing and environmental conditions in the following manner:

1. Identify the needs of women in relation to housing and community facilities and build them in an integrated manner into housing development programmes.
2. Integrate environmental factors into development planning for women as well their requirements in settlement planning.
3. Involve women at all levels of decision making and bring about their participation in programme implementation so as to ensure that the benefits of housing, essential services, and community facilities are directed to women in general and to the poor and vulnerable among them in particular.
4. The special needs of women should be identified and adequately catered to while formulating minimum housing standards.
5. Necessary facilities in homes should be provided to lessen the burden and drudgery of women in performing productive and reproductive roles.
6. Priority investment in infrastructure such as water supply, sanitation, energy, transportation, working women's hostels, public distribution of basic needs etc., should take into consideration the needs of women.

7. Provision of housing for working and / or single women is recommended on priority basis. In addition, women in difficult circumstances such as widows, refugees, destitutes, victims of social oppression, seasonal migrant workers, victims of natural disasters etc. must be provided shelter as part of an integrated rehabilitation programme.
8. The National Housing Policy which has been formulated, must pay adequate attention to the special needs and roles of women in the implementation of housing programme.
9. The social and economic constraints which comes in the way of women's participation should be removed and their active involvement in housing should be promoted by:

- Allotting house-sites in the joint name of wife and husband;
- Mobilizing savings of women for housing;
- Organizing self-help in undertaking house construction work;
- Imparting training so that women could become skilled labour (including masons and other skilled labour); and
- Ensuring access for women to institutional credit at low rates of interest without collateral.

Suggestions and Recommendations

There are many constraints or barriers which impede the delivery of health and environment related services to the low SES Community dwellers. These are:

1. It is usually found that the young dwellers of SES and women in particular have very low level of awareness about their health in particular and surroundings i.e. environment in general.
2. The married couples of such communities are at more and serious risk due to

- Early marriage
- Early sexual activity
- Early child bearing

3. Further, there is lack of information about various health and environment related programmes provided by the government, public sector and NGO's. So, there is scope and thus the role of Communication and Extension personnel to plan IEC -information, Education and Communication strategies which are focused or tailor made for this group of people - low SES Communities.
4. The role of Home Science Extension and Communication personnel should mainly focus on the following dimensions of the health, housing and environment of their target group i.e.

Awareness: Are the concerned people aware about these services and programmes?

Accessibility: Are these services, programmes and policies accessible - where and how? Are they within the physical reach?

Availability: Are these services available, if yes, then where and whom should these people approach?

Affordability: Are the people able to afford these services? Are these programmes within the economic limit of the community?

- The Extension and Communication Experts can help in improving in implementation of the programme by way of identifying the "felt - needs" and thus clearly formulating the objectives of the programme.
- The major role of Home Scientists could be in making the programmes of the NGOs and Government, more sustainable. These programmes are short - lived due to shortage of funds from the state governments. Lessons learnt are rarely shared and efforts to sustain programming are rarely given a serious thought.

In India, a large population of urban populace lives in slums-shanty towns - "Jhoppad Pattis". So, far the government initiation seems to have failed in giving some reasonable and decent solutions for brining this vulnerable section of population into the mainstream.

It is here that our role as Home Science Extension and Communication experts needs to be understood and deliberated upon. Several programmes and policies have been formulated and initiated in the public and NGO's sector. No programmes or policies, however, so far have addressed this problem of "urban slums" in totality.

So, the important recommendations are briefly outlined below:

1. Strengthen Public Health and Environment Care System at All Levels - with clearly specified and formulated policies, strategies and activities focusing on this section of population. This would require the Municipal Corporations to develop additional infrastructural facilities for providing the required services for this group of population in:

- Housing
- Water
- Sanitation
- Municipal Drainage System

2. Promote and Strengthen Intersectional Coordination at the Policy and Programme Levels: There are many policies and various programmes which could work as complimentary and supplementary to each other and thus focus on the felt needs and objectives that we need to address to. This will further help in avoiding wasting of time, energy and other such resources and duplication of efforts and will bring synergy in both action and outcome.

3. Develop a Systematic and In-Depth Assessment Of Health, Environment And Housing Needs: This effort of assessment should involve participation of the community members and reflect their perspective of "felt - needs".

This would require the Home Science Faculty to research their needs in the areas of:

- Biomedical concerns
- Social
- Psychological needs
- Environmental needs
- Community Behaviour and problems
- Myths and Misconceptions regarding Health and Nutrition amongst this population
- Practices in the areas of Nutrition, Health, Diseases, Sanitation
- Sexual and Reproductive Behaviour.

4. Networking with GO's and NGO's: The Home Scientists can liaison with government offices and agencies and also with Non-Governmental agencies working in the areas of:

- Health and Sanitation
- Housing for Urban low SES
- Environmental needs

This will help in strengthening the hands of government and non-government agencies in reaching to these beneficiaries i.e. "urban slum-population".

5. Help in Resource Mobilization: The Home Science students and teachers can help in resource mobilization by way of making their "felt-needs" more visible through propaganda and campaigns.

6. Organising Exhibitions: Film shows:

- Seminars, workshops
- Training programmes
- Group discussions, focused discussions, panel discussions and symposia.
- Developing information, education and communication materials.

7. Collaboration with Agencies and Organisations

- Collaborating with funding agencies, corporate houses, banks and the like.
- Collaborating and working with builders, developers, landscapers and architects.

References

Ahmed Manzoor, Community participation. The Heart of Primary Health International Council for Education Studies, Essx, Connecticut, U.S.A. 1980

Arole, M and Arole, R, a Community Rural Health Project in January. In Health by the people, edited by C. W. Newell, W.H.O., Geneva. 1975

Baroda Municipal Corporation, Baroda, - "A Basic Plan for Baroda City". 1975

Bijdani S. - Urban Problems, Indian Institute of Public Administration, New Delhi. 1990

Deodhar, N.S., Primary Health Care. India Journal of Public Health Policy. 1982

Ghanshyam shah, - Public Health and Urban Development. Published by: Sage Publications, New Delhi. 1997

Government of India, Health for all by 2000 A.D. Report of the Working committee (1981). Ministry of Health and Family Welfare, New Delhi. 1983

H.D. Kopardekar, - Managing Urban Development All India Institute of Local Self Government Bombay. 1987

J.E. Park and K. Park, - Textbook of Preventive and Social Medicine. Published by: Banarsidas Bhanot Publishers, Jabalpur. 1977

Mohit Bhattacharya - Municipal Government Problems and Prospects.

Monica Das Gupta, Lincoln. C. Chen, T. N. Krishnan, -Women's Health in India Risk and Vulnerability. Published by: Bombay, Oxford University Press, Delhi, Madras, Calcutta. 1995

Operation Research Group Baroda, - Report on the Chawls and Khadkis of Baroda. 1977

P.K. Shukla, - Nutritional Problems of India. Published by: Prentice Hall of India Private Limited, New Delhi. 1982

World Health Organisation, Primary Health Care. Report of the International Conference held at Alma Ata in September, 1978. Health for all Series, W.H.O., Geneva. 1978

39

Women and Media

H.R. Sudhindra

As woman emerges successful in the professional arena, she breaks new domain and dawns new role, the social acceptance and ample opportunities come her way on its own in the modern world. Indira Gandhi, Medha Patkar, Bachendri Pal, Arundhati Roy, Kiran Bedi, Kiran Mazumdar Shah, Sudha Murthy, Kalpana Chawla, P.T. Usha, Sania Mirza and Barkha Datt among many others have created a niche for themselves in their respective fields. They were and are women of substance who had the conviction to overcome social barriers and successfully pursue their life mission.

Today women have made their presence felt in areas that was earlier considered as men's bastion. This is basically because our leaders of the freedom movement emphasized on female literacy. Since independence the governments have also stressed on the welfare of the girl child. Though gender inequality persists in the country, the traditional bias against education of girls is waning. Broadly speaking Indian society is no longer intolerant towards education of girls. Going by the admission statistics in schools and colleges one can conclude that parents are today inclined towards educating their daughters if the circumstances around them are favourable. Educated parents have realized that educated daughter is better than illiterate one. A comparison of number of girls learning in institutions of higher education during 60s and now will clearly prove that female education in the country has improved.

Educated women can compete with men on equal footing. Today in certain professions women are considered more suitable than men. In some they have challenged the domination of men. One such profession is journalism. The women are topping in journalism courses of the country and their writing skills are exemplary. During 2006-07, Mangalore University MA journalism discipline had nine boys and seven girls. In the Institute of Journalism and New Media, 32 girls had opted for journalism and there were only 10 boys. In Bharatiya Vidya Bhavan, 5 boys and 4 girls for English and 20 boys and 13 girls in Kannada took diploma in Journalism. The English national newspaper offices are teeming with young women journalists. Though in the regional and vernacular press women are yet to make inroads. Increasing opportunities in the electronic media are beckoning more number of women to journalism.

Before independence there were not many women who entered journalism. Illiteracy, lack of opportunities and social restrictions were reasons for these. In Karnataka the first newspaper came into existence in 1843. But it was only in 1922 that 'Saraswathi', the first women oriented newspaper was started by Smt. Kalyanamma. Till 60s women were denied employment in newspapers in India particularly in the vernacular press. When the late Prabha Dutt graduated from the Chandigarh school of Journalism with honours and did her in house training with Hindustan Times in 1964, the editor of the newspaper told her that the paper did not employ women. Senior journalist Mrs. Mrinal Pande was once quoted as saying that when she joined Times of India in early 1980, women did not figure in any organizational concerns. There were no rest rooms and the general attitude was –why is she here and not in Femina? The Delhi Statesman was one of the first newspapers to employ a fulltime female sub-editor in the fifties. But those were only exceptions. In the reporting side no woman was employed. Veteran journalist Mrs. Coomi Kapoor was the only woman in the editorial section of Times of India for close to eight years since 1964.

During 1970s women were visible only on the deskwork or in the Sunday sections of the newspapers. They wrote about social gossip, party circuits, films and celebrities. A senior journalist once told me that since there were only a few women in service, they received undue attention from the male colleagues. This sometimes hampered their growth professionally. Senior women scribes say that prime beats such as political parties, crime etc were kept out of their purview. Instead they were asked to cover flower shows, fashion shows, health and education, considered as soft beats.

From the 80s the scene began to change in the English language newspapers. Women started occupying senior positions. Ms. Usha Mahadevan, Gauri Chatterji, Dr. Poonima and a few others rose in position in the newspaper offices. They were eligible for maternity leave and received better pay parity as men. Newspaper offices made arrangements for separate toilets for them. Women's point of view was respected and women's issues received better reception. However in the language press the preference for women remained low. In Karnataka there are only a few women who have put a long service in the newspaper. Arrival of electronic media has altered the media scene altogether. Sometimes one tends to think that beauty has taken over brains in the recruitment of media persons in news channels. When news show host Ms. Grata Van Susteran moved from CNN to Fox TV in 2002, she surgically altered her face to appear younger and more 'beautiful'. Many analysts interpreted it to mean that the way a woman looks is far more important than what she has to say. One of the analyst, Mr. Robin Gerber noted that Ms. Van Susteran's facial transformation with the objective of looking beautiful, "has become a painful reminder of women's inequality. By trying to become just another pretty face, Van Susteran instead became another cultural casualty." In India the sports channels tend to commit this folly. During 2003 world cup Mandira Bedi was signed in to be the anchorperson who revealed a lot of skin during the programme. She was not an expert in cricket but helped improve the viewer ship of the programme.

General Perception about Women Journalists

In India both men and women carry conventional characteristics. We all nurture such notions and perceptions about men and women due to our past experiences. We are moulded and groomed to bear such notions by our elders. Girls are taught to be good sisters, wife or mothers. Emphasis is on caring, rearing and bearing. Girls are told to nurture certain feelings and ostracise others. We are cast in Father or Mother's mould. We are so as to say programmed to react to situations in a certain way. Hence men and women cultivate different interests and habits. Generally speaking, men maintain closer proximity to politics, sports and science and technology and women to social and family matters. Women convey emotions and feelings in a better way and hence become good columnists, they gel well in parties and social gatherings. Men on the other hand react to situations with pragmatism and are analytical in their approach. Women are good conservationists and hence conduct good talk shows. Oprah Winfrey show in America is one such example. They give aesthetic sense to the programme. They add glamour and charm. Hence they can be successful anchorpersons, compere and newsreaders. It is more convenient for men to report on action stories. They can be more mobile and agile, take risks, run with the camera in hand and push themselves into a gathering crowd. They can do night shifts. Women can be better in maintaining and sustaining the source of the news and show consistency in follow up stories.

A study shows that a lot of women journalists are putting off marriage or postpone having a child as it may impede their career growth. The general perception is that employers are reluctant to employ young women in the reproductive age groups in the language press. It is said that the employers fear that women journalists will show greater priority to their homes, especially if they have children.

Countering the Perceptions

General perceptions emerge from our experiences. They may be true or false or they may be partially true or false. I leave it to the individuals. However, I would like to counter these perceptions with factual information. I am going to list those incidents now, which are evident of women daring to report without fear, taking good care of any subject under the sun. Take the case of Ms. Ogulsapar Muradova, Radio Free Europe's Correspondent in Russia who was killed in Turkmenistan in 2006. Another journalist from Russia Ms. Anna Politkovskaya played with her life for her opposition to Russian Government policies in Chechenya. Out of 82 journalists killed worldwide in 2006, nine (11 per cent) were women. Nearly 13 per cent of journalists killed in the course of their work in 2005 were women. Atwar Bahjat of Al Arabiya TV in Iraq was abducted with her crew and killed. Ms. Raeda Wazzan, news presenter in Iraq was executed by her captors. A total of seven women journalists are in prison in 2006 in Sri Lanka, Eritrea, Ethiopia, Iraq, Uzbekistan and Rwanda (2 people).

In India Ms. Shikha Das of Jansatta was attacked by a knife in Pithora, Chattisgarh for writing on trafficking in women. Unlike in India, where freedom of the press is sacrosanct, in some countries women have joined pressure groups to defend press freedom. Sihem Bensedrine in Tunisia, Tadjigul Begmedova in Turkmenistan, Rozlana Tankina in Kazakhistan, Zanna Litvina in Belarus, Sayda Kilani in Jordan are a few who have fought with their brethrens for freedom of the press. They run NGO movement with grit, determination and courage in spite of threat to their lives in defense of freedom of the press. In countries like Iran and Afghanistan where fundamentalists rule the roost, women lead a life behind veil. It is a wild wild world for women journalists in here. It is also a rare honour to become a journalist in Afghanistan where 80 per cent women are illiterate. Sharifa Akhlas was born and educated in Afghanistan, but during the Taliban rule worked in exile as a radio and television producer and reporter for the Afghan Media Resource Center based in Peshawar, Pakistan. In 1998 she was arrested and beaten for carrying out her role of a reporter. Risking her life, she pays clandestine visit to Afghanistan and interviews women there and brought news to the international community. In April 2000, she was arrested and beaten after being caught by the Taliban once again.

In Iran Shahla Sherkat founded the monthly magazine Zanan(women) in Tehran. She was dismissed from the government owned weekly magazine Zan-e-Rouz (Today's women) for opposition to the magazines coverage of women's issues that appealed only to conservative, religious ethos, an image set forth by the Iranian Government. A forum named Reporters without Borders mentions in its website that "Increase in violence against female scribes is due to the fact that more women are working as journalists, holding riskier jobs in the media and doing investigative reporting likely to upset someone."

A young female reporter working for Prajavani in Bangalore was rhetoric when asked whether female scribes are reluctant in taking risks in their job. She retorted that it is male chauvinism that prevents women journalists from taking risks. She felt that they are not given free hand in handling daring stories. The management and senior journalists are scared that for any untoward incident concerning women journalists they will be blamed. Hence they play safe in assigning softer beats to them, she explained. Her burning desire to achieve something by going away from the beaten track is chocking without an outlet. It is the daring that brings recognition and gives the satisfaction of success, she rued. This young journalist with an experience of just 3 to 4 years expressed a desire to remain anonymous. I could feel the pain when she was citing me the example of Barkha Datt standing in front of the camera with Bofors guns blazing at the backdrop.

This sight of women journalists working on daring assignments has inspired innumerable young girls to opt for journalism. One visit to institutes offering journalism courses will make this obvious. The young girls here with twinkle in their eyes carry such mammoth aspirations that it drives down deep in you the sense of pride and remove all prejudices that one cultivates against women journalists.

An organization named International Women's Media Foundation has instituted the Courage in Journalism Award for woman journalists. This is given in recognition of the pursuit of integrity in journalism, despite assaults, death threats and risks to their livelihood and lives. Since its inception several women journalists have been honoured by this award. I will just mention two of them here. Gao Yu, a freelance journalist who lives in Beijing, has twice been jailed for her reporting. She continues to fight against censorship, expressing her belief in human rights and the value of democracy. Gao initially received the Courage in Journalism Award in 1995 but was unable to accept it due to her imprisonment. On 21 March 1997, the UNESCO/Guillermo Cano World Press Freedom Prize was awarded by an independent international jury to Gao Yu. Another recipient of the Award Sumi Khan worked as crime reporter for the Daily Jugantor in Dhaka, Bangladesh during 1999. She received a death threat from the student wing of the Jamaat-e-Islami fundamentalist party after she reported on the group's ties to criminal and terrorist activities. Khan has challenged the odds by successfully working as a woman journalist in a male-dominated society.

The general perception is that men are good at political reporting. But to show that women too can excel in this discipline here is an example. A versatile television personality Sukanya Krishnan from India won the Indian American political Awareness Committee's "Creating a voice award". Recently she received the New York Emmy Award in the on-camera: programme host/moderator category. Awards have come seeking the women journalists. M Suchitra from Kerala has won the Developing Asia Journalism Award for the year 2006. Barkha Dutt of NDTV was awarded the 2006 Kostas Kyriais, Greece's most prestigious Journalism Award. Such awards have helped remove cobwebs from the minds of skeptics and demolished those general perceptions that were on air without basis.

In Russia 80 per cent of total journalists are women, in Sweden they are 48 per cent, Norway 41 per cent and Germany 35 per cent. But in India women remain a minority among the journalistic fraternity. According to a survey by the Media Study Group Men: women ratio in Hindi newspaper is 86:14 and in Hindi electronic media it is 89:11 and in English print media it is 84:16 and 68:32 in the English Electronic media. This glaring disparity is perturbing. The National Commission for Women had commissioned a study on status of women journalists in India. This study conducted by the Press Institute of India has given a very gloomy picture of working women Journalists. It found out that only 17 per cent of the key decision makers in media are women. It further found by social profile of more than 300 senior journalists in 37 Hindi and English newspapers and television channels in the capital that women are grossly underrepresented in relation to their share in the population. According to the Indian Newspaper Society report in 2006 women's magazines Femina, Women's Era, Cosmopolitan, New Women, Elle and Savvy have seen a dip in readership.

Such a situation warrants a need for setting up an institutional support, an incentive base and pressure groups for women journalists in India. Luckily such organizational set up exists in India. These groups are putting their efforts to improve the working conditions of women journalists and enhance their role in the media. I am just listing some of them here.

Network of Women in Media

The Network of Women in Media (NWM) in India was born on January 30, 2002. The Network of Women in Media, India, is an association which aims to provide a forum for women in media professions to share information and resources, exchange ideas, promote media awareness and ethics, and work for gender equality and justice within the media and society. Local groups linked to the NWMI are currently functioning in 16 centres across the country.

International Association of Women in Radio and Television: IAWRT was founded in 1951. It is a forum for personal contact and professional development among women broadcasters worldwide. It has a consultative status with the United Nations Economic and Social Council. They arrange Conferences with workshops, screenings, lectures, training sessions and professional networking.

International Women's Media Foundation: The International Women's Media Foundation is a network of thousands of women journalists working internationally to elevate the status of women in the media. They have created groundbreaking programs to help women in the media develop practical solutions to the obstacles they face in their careers and lives. It has also constituted the Courage in Journalism Awards. The Foundation's mission is to strengthen the role of women in the news media around the world, based on the belief that no press is truly free unless women share an equal voice.

Press Institute of India: The Institute has a focus on human development. It was started in 1963 by a group of leading newspapers. It looks closely at population, development and gender issues. It manages a website called reportingpeople.org. It brings out a 16 page quarterly newsletter called People in English and Hum Log in Hindi. PII encourages journalists to report on grassroots issues. It conducts training workshops for journalists, which is held in-house, or in the cities and rural areas of India. Over the years the PII has trained over 4000 professionals-editorial and management - from India, Pakistan, Sri Lanka, Bangladesh and other parts of Asia.

Opinion of Women Journalists on Core Issues

Name: Monideepa Choudhuri
Age: 39 Yrs.
Location: Assam
Media: Print

1. General perception on women journalists during 1970s and now:

- The general perception towards women journalists in the 1970s was one of awe. They were regarded as a 'different breed', to be admired from afar. These days, with women invading all work spheres, including unconventional careers, women journalists are no longer held in awe. The admiration has been diluted, and in many pockets of the country, they are brushed aside as irritants.

2. Do you notice any difference while executing your professional duties between women and men? Is there any gender bias in media?

- Yes. Men tend to stick together and often insinuate that a woman stands a better chance of getting good bytes or a scoop because she has the advantage of fluttering her eyelashes and acting coy.

3. Who is your role model and which book on journalism has left indelible

effect on you?

- I have no role models, nor have I read any book on journalism. But yes, I wholeheartedly admire journalists who do developmental and human-interest stories.

4. Your opinion about women magazines and newspaper supplements

- Most women's magazines are glamorous and slick rehashes. Newspaper supplements are good enough time pass.

5. Do you think that women in the newspapers preferably work on soft news? If yes, why so, if no, kindly explain.

- Largely yes, because it gives them the leeway to juggle the demands of a home.

Name: R Chitra
Age: 47 Yrs.
Location: Chennai
Media (Print, Electronic, Online) Print

1. General perception on women journalists during '70s and now:

- There are more women in the media now than before and doing more daring stories.

2. Do you notice any difference while executing your professional duties between women and men. Is there any gender bias in media?

- There is no gender bias. I was the first woman news editor of The New Indian Express and so didn't feel any difference on account of gender.

3. Who is your role model and which book on journalism has left indelible effect on you.

- No role models and no books.

4. Your opinion about women magazines and newspaper supplements

- They have their uses. I am not the type that reads women's magazines because I am interested in the general news carried by magazines and papers. Newspaper supplements are useful in generating revenue and for giving news/stories that cannot be accommodated in a regular paper.

5. Do you think that women in the newspapers preferably work on soft news? If yes, why so, if no, kindly explain.

- I have known women who have worked on very newsy, hard news. It depends on the attitude of the chief reporter and that of the management. And to a large extent on the individual, the woman reporter.

Name: Leena Misra
Age: 38 Yrs.
Location: Ahmedabad

Media: (Print, Electronic, Online) Print

1. General perception on women journalists during 1970s and now

- Most women journalists then used to be analysts or column writers, or news readers if they were in the electronic media. Today they are into investigations, and their roles on television has become that of news anchors, which goes much beyond news reading.

2. Do you notice any difference while executing your professional duties between women and men? Is there any gender bias in media.

- There is not much difference between the genders anymore and neither are there biases. The focus is mainly on performance - who delivers what and how fast.

3. Who is your role model and which book on journalism has left indelible effect on you.

- No particular role model yet, and there has been no book on journalism that left a mark, or maybe i just missed them!

4. Your opinion about women magazines and newspaper supplements

- I think most women's magazines are still stuck in a time warp, they should provide more on what today's women want. Newspaper supplements used to make good reading, but today, most of them only talk about glamour and gossip. Maybe that's what majority of the readers are looking for.

5. Do you think that women in the newspapers preferably work on soft news? If yes, why so, if no, kindly explain.

   Firstly, what is soft news- one has to define what one means by it. Women do all kinds of stories, even news stories. They are at an advantage because they have a better perspective to things, and hence can even do better features.

Leena Patel
Media Consultant
SEWA

1. Do you notice any difference while executing your professional duties between women and men? Is there any gender bias in media?

- as my understanding its not only gender bias, but as a Dalit media woman, I have found out cast bias also.

2. Who is your role model and which book on journalism has left indelible effect on you.

- As a Dalit and also as a woman Dr. Baba Saheb Ambedkar is my Idol. Because he has done work not only for Dalit but also for Indian women, weather they are labour women, household or any, Hindu code bill is a witness of it.

3. Your opinion about women magazines and newspaper supplements

- As a Gujarati if I will talk about vernacular magazine and supplements still cooking, fashion, beauty is main object for women. The real women issues can't be found in it.

4. Do you think that women in the newspapers preferably work on soft news? If yes, why so, if no, kindly explain.

- yes, I feel. Till women journalist working on fashion, beauty... Few women are there who are working on Mainstream issues. As my understanding Now News paper run like business... More profit, More Advt. and related not for Mass but for "KHAS" people of city.

Name: Jaskiran Kaur
Age: 27 Yrs.
Location: Chandigarh
Media (Print, Electronic, Online) Print, Indian Express, Chandigarh

1. General perception on women journalists during 70s and now:

- I feel the women journalists in 70s were far more courageous for they broke norms and joined a profession completely alien to the woman kind. Everything is open and accessible today and it's there's no exclusivity today.

2. Do you notice any difference while executing your professional duties between women and men? Is there any gender bias in media?

- Till there is man and woman, there will always be gender bias. It's the law of nature.

3. Who is your role model and which book on journalism has left indelible effect on you.

- None.

4. Your opinion about women magazines and newspaper supplements.

- Women magazines are destructive literature that looks good on coffee tables and beauty parlours. they are a good time pass when it comes to the gloss, gossip and pictures. As for newspaper supplements, they are good for the future lies in features.

5. Do you think that women in the newspapers preferably work on soft news? If yes, why so, if no, kindly explain.

- No, it's a myth that women prefer soft news. This is where the gender bias comes in. It's a personal choice and the ones I have worked with and are part of my organisation are pretty much jhansi ki ranis!

Name: Teresa Rehman
Age: 31 Yrs.

Location: Guwahati, Assam
Media: (Print, Electronic, Online) Print

1. General perception on women journalists during 70s and now.
- Well, in Assam or the Northeast India, Journalism is still in a nascent stage. I don't think there were that many hardcore women journalists in the 70s. Its a new breed now.
2. Do you notice any difference while executing your professional duties between women and men. Is there any gender bias in media.
- I think the bias is positively inclined rather. Being a lady its easy rather to gain access to many places.
3. Who is your role model and which book on journalism has left indelible effect on you.
- Sorry none
4. Your opinion about women magazines and newspaper supplements
- Women magazines are a different brand of journalism which should be encouraged. I think newspaper supplements are for light reading should be made more readable with emphasis on local problems (for local dailies).
5. Do you think that women in the newspapers preferably work on soft news? If yes, why so, if no, kindly explain.
- Well sometimes its alloted to them and sometimes its by choice. I feel women can deal with a soft issue in a more sensible and sensitive manner. But they are equally capable of dealing with hard stories. Actually its also a matter of personal calibre, being a man or a woman hardly matters in this profession.

The study shows that a lot of women journalists are putting off marriage or postpone having a child as it may impede their career growth. The general perception is that employers are reluctant to employ young women in the reproductive age groups especially in the language press. It is said that the employers fear that women journalists will show greater priority to their homes, especially if they have children. I could feel the pain when she was citing me the example of Barkha Datt standing in front of the camera with Bofors guns blazing at the backdrop.

This sight of women journalists working on daring assignments has inspired innumerable young girls to opt for journalism. One visit to institutes offering journalism courses will make this obvious. The young girls here with twinkle in their eyes carry such mammoth aspirations that it drives down deep in you the sense of pride and remove all prejudices that one cultivates against women journalists.

40

Women in Politics

Rameshwari Pandya and Babita Shukla

The Constitution of India provides for universal adult suffrage (Article 326) and Indian women have been active participants on every Indian election. Yet towards equality charges, women have had only limited impact on the political process. To be sure, women have been highly visible participants, they have served in both houses of Parliaments, and in the State legislatures, been governors and chief ministers of states, and served at the national level. Despite the achievements of an elite few, women as a whole have been under represented throughout India in both appointed and elected positions; they have minimal power within the parties and they participate in elections as candidates and as voters with less frequency than men.

The history of women's large scale participation in the nationalist movement is well known and in fact, one can go back to 1905 when women freedom fighters showed immense courage in fighting the British Rulers. More strikingly, mass participation of women was recognized during the Civil Disobedience Movement in 1930 and also during the Quit India Movement of 1942, when thousands of women courted arrest. Some women participated in the revolutionary movement as couriers distributing literature, risking police repression, imprisonment and even capital punishment. There was a Nari Bahini (Women's Volunteer Force) which would help guard villages at night. Studies have recorded many stories of women's courage, militant spirit and innovation during these struggles.

Policy documents concerning Indian women have been guided by the Constitution. The Preamble of the Constitution of India assures "to secure to all its citizens: Justice, social economic and political; Liberty of thought, expression, belief, faith and worship; Equality of status and opportunity; and to promote among them all Fraternity assuring the dignity of the individual and the unity of the Nation". To attain these national objectives, the Constitution guarantees certain fundamental rights and freedoms such as freedom of speech, protection of life, personal liberty and the prohibition of discrimination or denial of equal protection.

Indian women are the beneficiaries of these rights in the same manner as

Indian men. For instance, Article 14 ensures 'equality before law' and Article 15 'prohibits any discrimination'. There is only one specific provision in Article 15(3) which empowers the state to make 'any special provision for women and children'. This is in violation of the fundamental obligation of non-discrimination among citizens, inter alia of sex. Consequently, this provision has enabled the State to make special provision for women, particularly in the field of labour legislation like the Factories Act, the Mines Act and so forth.

Article 16(1) guarantees "equality of opportunity for all citizens in matters relating to employment or appointment to any office under the State". Article 16 (2) forbids discrimination "in respect of any employment of office under the State" on the grounds only of "religion, race, caste, sex, descent, place of birth residence or any one of them".

Enunciated in Part IV of the Constitution, the Directive Principles of State Policy embodies the major policy goals of a welfare State. Together with the chapter on Fundamental Rights they concretize, the Constitutional vision of a new Indian socio-political order. Even though the state is charged with "a duty... to apply these principles in making laws" and are "... fundamental in the governance of the country" (Article 37) these Principles are declared as non-justiciable. They were made non-enforceable in courts because it was felt that their fulfillment would require a time-dimension of a few decades. Whereas the constitutional values embodied in the Fundamental Rights chapter needed immediate implementation. In the case of the Directive Principles this was not possible to save at the cost of the viability of the state.

Juridically, the Directive Principles are a vital part of Indian Constitutional Law. Like the Preamble, they reflect high ideals of a liberal democratic polity. They are meant to be used by all agencies of the State as guidelines to action as major goals of policy. Courts can use them as a body of values and standards relevant to the act of judicial choice-making. But the Directive Principles confer no power or legislative competence, rise to a cause of action for which remedy is available in a court of law, bestow rights, or create remedies. At the same time, they cannot be amended, through the prescribed procedure.

Some of the Directive Principles are "women-specific". Others concern women indirectly or by necessary implication. Amongst those which concern women directly and have a special bearing on their status include: Article 39 (a) - the right to an adequate means of livelihood for men and women equally; Article 39 (d) - equal pay for equal work for both men and women; Article 39 (c) - protection of the health and strength of workers - men, women and children from abuse and entry into avocations unsuited to their age and strength; and Article 42 - just and humane conditions of work and maternity relief.

In the second category, falls the omnibus provision of Article 38 which in brief directs the state to secure just social, political and economic order, geared to promote the welfare of the people. Article 39(b)(c) and (f) - for the distribution of ownership and control of material resources of the community for the common good, prevention of concentration of wealth and means of production to the common detriment and probation of childhood and youth against exploitation and moral and material abandonment. Article 40 - organization of village panchayats to promote self government. Article 41 - right to work, education and public assistance in cases of unemployment.

In 1971 following a resolution of the Ministry of Education and Social Welfare, the Committee and the Status of Women in India (CSWI) was constituted at the instance of the U.N. General Assembly. The presentation of the Report of the CSWI, "Towards Equality" coincided with the celebration of 1975 as International Women's Year. To operationalize the recommendations of the CSWI, a Blueprint of Action Points and National Plan of Action for Women, 1976 was formulated by the then Department of Social Welfare, Government of India. This in turn led to the presentation of the Report of the Working Group on Employment for Women, 1978 as well as the Report of the Working Group on Development of Village Level Organizations of Rural Women, 1978. It also formed a part of the Sixth Five Year Plan exercise. The impact of these reports resulted in a separate chapter on Women and Development 1980-85 in the Sixth Five Year Plan. It also resulted in women being perceived as productive contributors to the nation's economy.

Following an agreement signed between the then Ministry of Agriculture and Irrigation, Government of India and the Food and Agriculture Organization (UN), a Report of the National Committee on Role and Participation of Women in Agriculture and Rural Development 1980 was submitted. The Report of the Working Group on Personal Policies for Bringing Greater Involvement of Women in Science and Technology - 1981 reviewed the extent of participation of women in scientific establishments and suggested measures for promoting greater involvement of women in science and technology.

In the Seventh Five Year Plan, the Chapter on Socio-Economic Programmes for Women - 1985-90 moved further away from a "welfare" approach to a more positive "developmental" approach to women's concerns. More recently, the Indian Parliament adopted a National Policy on Education - 1986 which included a chapter on Education for Women's Equality.

The Government of India launched the Twenty Point Programme in 1975 in terms of importance of areas requiring special thrust which would show immediate tangible results. The Programme was subsequently recast and redefined in 1982 and then in 1986.

The Report of the National Expert Committee on Women Prisoners (1987) identifies the gaps and drawbacks in existing facilities and services for women offenders and recommends a more humane policy for them. The National Commission on Self Employed Women and Women in the Informal Sector was appointed in January 1987 to look into the ways and means to ameliorate the sufferings of the unprotected laboring women. In its report Shramshakti submitted in June, 1988 the Commission has outlined many comprehensive policy recommendations towards this end. Also in 1987, a Core Group was set up by the Department of Women and Child Development to formulate a National Perspective Plan for Women 1988-2000 A.D. The Report was released in October, 1988.

The year 1975 was declared as International Women's Year by the United Nations. As a result of the World Conference held during June-July 1975, the Declaration of Mexico Plans of Action, 1975 was adopted. The purpose was to promulgate 30 principles for the equality of women and their contribution to national development and international peace. Also, the Action Plan stipulated 14 minimum objectives to be met before the midterm appraisal in 1980. In December 1979 the U.N. General Assembly adopted the Convention on the Elimination of All Forms of Discrimination Against Women.

The United Nations Economic and Social Commission of Asia and the Pacific held a preparatory meeting for the World Conference on Women, at the Ministerial level in March 1984. The deliberations of the meeting resulted in the Report of the Regional Intergovernmental Preparatory meeting for the World Conference to Review and Appraise the Achievements of the United Nations Decade for Women: Equality, Development and Peace - 1984.

At the Ministerial level, another conference took place in April 1985 of the Non-Aligned and other developing countries. The intention was to approach the World Conference on Women with full knowledge of their achievements and failures as well as to evolve a strategy to tackle the problems confronting the world. The recommendations were compiled into New Delhi Document on Women in Development, 1985.

Finally, at the end of the United Nations Decade for Women, the World Conference was held in Kenya in 1985. The World Conference adopted Forward Looking Strategies for the Advancement of Women, 1985 to serve as guidelines for creating a new world order based on equality, development and peace. For the closing conference of the Women's Decade, the Ministry of Social and Women's Welfare prepared Women in India: Country Paper, 1985. This status paper assessed the impact of the Decade on the development of women, the constraints that exist and strategies for the advancement of women.

One significant step has, however, been the formation of the Department of Women and Child Development which is part of the Ministry of Human Resource Development. The Constitution of a separate Department of women has helped in focusing programmes for women's development. Efforts are also being made to reach out to the women in the poverty sector through various welfare schemes and programmes.

Political participation is broader than the one covering women's participation only in the electoral and administrative processes, including voting, supporting the political groups and other related activities. Political participation can be considered to include an involvement in any form of organized activity that affects, or seeks to affect, these power relationships.

Women's participation has covered a range of activities including movements, protests and support meetings on all issues connected with labour, dowry, rape, domestic violence, price rise and deforestation, as also movements for the promotion of peace. The Women's Reservation Bill is pending in the Parliament for the last 10 years because of lack of consensus between the political parties. This is indicative of the general attitude towards women's issues and their lives. Even where women's representation in politics is visible, they are marginalized from the actual decision making process.

Gender equality is a pre-requisite for effective participation of women in strengthening the institutional structure of democracy. Women have been marginalized because of several socio-economic constraints. The number of women in leadership position at the local, village, district and national level is still not commensurate with their numbers in society. Women's entry presupposes and also introduces change in the electoral system in order to remove the current trend the entry of women into politics will transform the total scenario.

The "top down" approach began with the framers of the constitution, and consists of establishment of constitutional and other legal rights. This approach rests on the assumption that formal recognition of women's rights will ensure women's equality and thus their integration into the political mainstream that the mere existence of a right at the top necessarily means that it will be invoked at the bottom. The "grassroots" approach is exactly opposite in nature, attempting to mobilize women from the bottom up. Grassroots efforts pinpoint a group need and exert political pressure to correct the problem, assuming that such acts will ensure women's political equality and integration. Both conceive of politics as a hierarchy beginning with local informal problem-solving and building through progressively more formal levels to the most formal mechanisms of central government. They wrongly conceive that a change at one end of the pyramid will automatically filter upward or downward, affecting the whole in a uniform manner.

The question of women's participation in political process and decision making bodies forms a key concern of the women's empowerment in India. An analysis of the democratic system and representation of various sections of the population therein reveals that women are far behind than their male counterparts. Their under-representation become critical especially in the context of declining sex ratio, increasing violence and crimes against women and their marginalized status in the employment, education, health and over all development.

One of the major and most common areas of research on women and politics and contemporary India is the political participation of women. Political participation is, by and large, interpreted as the voting behavior of women voters. This is true partly to the dominant role electoral politics plays in parliamentary democracy in India. There is a need to make women more aware of their rights, be it social, political or economic. By gaining political rights, they can put across their views among the people and this could lead to deeper understanding of the problems women face in society. This can be achieved only when more and more women come forward and expose their own cause. Political participation would make a significant difference if it came from those who are at the helm of affairs, and if women are there wielding power, the situation can improve to a great extent political participation would give women a sense of dignity as an individual.

Specifically, political empowerment may be perceived as a cycle, beginning and ending with the individual, and continuing indefinitely. A women becomes aware of her rights, perceived an injustice in her own life, relates her experience to that of others, acts with them to define the need and exert pressure for reform, and ultimately through this collective process gains a fuller sense of her own identity and power. Any social, economic or political problem, may serve as a catalyst for this cycle. The following diagram illustrates clearly, group empowerment and individual empowerment exist in symbiotic relation to each other. One cannot exist without the other, and herein lies the key to understanding past failure at political reform.

A deeper analysis of the socio-economic and cultural factors, more particularly the family position and power relations within the family, and of factors that prevent women from gaining access to political information and education is mostly lacking. Equally conspicuous by its absence is the analysis of any mobilization and organization of women, their participation in activities.

Many studies have shown that the women politicians face peculiar problems in their political life. Which are totally unknown to their male counterparts. These problems inhibit their performance in the parliament. The reasons for women's diminished role in political arena include traditions, physiology, lack of vertical mobility, concern for home and family, psychology and lack of patronage, particularly from women politicians.

Their social, family responsibilities are the barrier to take part in politics. There may be many more reasons, which hinder women's active involvement in politics. In fact, studies on such issues have been very rare and no systematic and comprehensive study appears to have been done on these issues.

Today, one of the issues of concern is the level of women's participation in political life. This is because achievement of equality in all areas is seen as inseparable from active political participation. Here, political participation includes the right to vote, right to contest, right to candidacy, women as campaigners, women as members, women's involvement in the decision-making process and appointment of women at all levels of government. But the major obstacles to women's full participation in politics are a nearly universal societal attitude that has valued women principally as mothers and wives. Because of this, women have been restricted from equal opportunity.

Women make up almost half of the adult population in the world. Their work is imminent individually in family, in society, in nation and in politics on the whole but they are evaluated not at par with the men. Women are still vastly under-represented in political and administrative posts that make important policy decisions affecting them. Reserving seats for women in the political institutions will provide them an opportunity to raise their grievances and other related personal and social problems in a formal manner.

Women as Voters and Candidates

Voting has a tremendous strength and weakness and has impact for equalizing and mobilizing women. Yet, it has to be noted that voting requires the least initiative and interval motivation. Many time woman treats the day of voting as a welcome break from her dull and tiring routine and does not appear to have a notion of why she should vote for a particular candidate. Though women's participation in the political process has increased both in the elections and in their readiness to express their view on issues directly concerning their life, but their ability to produce an impact on the political process has been negligible because of the inadequate attention paid to their political education and mobilization by both political parties and women's organizations, as political parties see women voters as appendages of the males.

The number of women contestants in parliamentary elections has not increased significantly over the years. Political parties seem uniformly reluctant to field women candidates. The high cost of electioneering is another deterrent to most women candidates. Because of these factors there is an increasing tendency among women to contest elections as independent candidates.

Women in Panchayati Raj Institutions

Participation of women in Panchayati Raj institutions has been recognized as a step towards equality. The Committee on Panchayati Raj Institutions, 1978 recommended the reservation of two seats for women in panchayats and to co-opt women in case they did not come through elections. The co-option of two women members in panchayats, has not brought any perceptible impact on women's participation in the Panchayati Raj bodies. Co-option is done only in letter and not in the spirit of getting the women involved in panchayat activities. The participation and it is today hardly gives one great difficulty with the Indian political scene is that it is impossible to generalize about the inter-relationship between any single factor and political behaviour. Patterns of political behavior from different regions show different relationships, influenced as they are by inter-related factors like the social status of women, their economic position, the cultural norms, and above all, the regional outlook towards women's participation in the wider society.

Thus, the record of women's participation in political processes other than the formal has been quite creditable. Of course, while women have been visible in mass movements, group upsurges and protest struggles, their presence is not felt in structured decision making institutional settings. Even in the structures where women's participation is substantial, they have not been given positions of power. However, it can be stated that protests made by women activists and scholars have resulted in their role in the grass roots level movements being recognized.

None of these facts is unique to India. The percentage of women in the Lok Sabha compares favourably with that in many western democracies. While in 1984, for example, the U.S. Congress and the British House of Commons each had fewer than five per cent female members, female Membership in the Lok Sabha has ranged from a low of 2.8 per cent in the first election in 1952, to a high of 8.5 per cent in the 1984 elections.

The participation of women in the electoral process is an indicator of their political consciousness as well as their aspiration for status enhancement. A quick glance at women's participation in elections over the past decades and Twelfth and Thirteenth general elections confirms the initial hopes placed in them. The figures concerning women's formal participation in the electoral process, both as actors and objects of attention bring out a few facts. This participation has been more or less steadily expanding over the years through various elections as voters and as candidates and in terms of participation in campaigning. The number of women getting elected to representative bodies has been steadily increasing.

Table 40.1 shows that the representation has reached a high point of 8.83 per cent only in 1999 General Elections. However, it falls short of 33 per cent, the critical mass of women required for decision-making strength. Numbers reveal a story of bias that just keeps getting worse with each passing year (Tables 40.2 and 40.3).

Table 40.1: Representation of Women Members from First to Thirteenth Lok Sabha

Lok Sabha	Total Seats	No. of Women Contestants	No. of Women Elected	Percentage
First (1952-57)	499	51	22	4.4
Second (1957-62)	500	45	27	5.4
Third (1962-67)	503	70	34	6.7
Fourth (1967-70)	523	67	31	5.9
Fifth (1971-77)	521	86	22	4.2
Sixth (1977-79)	544	70	19	3.4
Seventh (1980-84	544	142	28	5.1
Eighth (1984-89)	544	164	44	8.1
Ninth (1989-91)	517	198	27	5.2
Tenth (1991-96)	544	325	39	7.16
Eleventh (1996-97)	544	599	40	7.35
Twelfth (1998)	544	271	44	8.10
Thirteenth (1999)	543	277	48	8.83

Table 40.2: Representation of Women Members in Rajya Sabha

Year	Total Seats	No. of Women	Percentage of Women
1952	219	16	7.3
1957	237	18	7.6
1962	238	18	7.6
1967	240	20	8.3
1971	243	17	7.0
1977	244	25	10.2
1980	244	24	9.8
1985	244	28	11.4
1990	245	38	15.5
1996	223	20	9.0
1998	223	19	8.6

Source: Election Commission of India

Table 40.3: Sex Ratio

Census	Child Sex Ratio	Overall sex ratio
1951	NA	946
1961	976	941
1971	964	930
1981	962	934
1991	945	927
2001	927	933

Source: Census of India, 2001

There could not be more telling of the state of India's women than the sex ratio. In five decades between the 1951 and 2001 Censuses, the picture has worsened significantly so that for every 1,000 males there are only 933 females today. What's worse the child sex ratio - the number of girls for every 1,000 boys in the 0-6 age group - is now even lower at 927. The discrimination that begins from the foetus continues in the form of the neglect of the girl child whether it is nutrition or education.

Given such a situation, it is hardly surprising that few women are able to rise to leadership positions. As the graphic above shows 60 years after independence, we are still to have a Lok Sabha in which women constitute even 10 per cent of the house. Of course, the gender skew in the legislature is only representative of a larger malaise. Successive governments have paid lip service to the idea of one-third of legislative seats being reserved for women, but the idea has not moved one step closer to fruition.

Reservation for women in Parliament has been long overdue. But reserving seats in Parliament is not the only way to change the unfortunate lot of women in our country. The discrimination that has been noted out to them for centuries cannot be wiped out by a single act of reservation. Unless we overhaul our mindset towards women, nothing can really change. And this can happen only be spreading education across the length and breadth of our country. The 33 per cent reservation for women is already on paper, but it has not yet been legitimized. No political party is interested in giving the required push to the women's reservation bill. They are scared that men may lose their supremacy in Parliament, and how could their fragile egos handle that?

The status of women in Indian society is full of contradictions. Deified on one hand, they are also shackled by the dictates of patriarchy on the other. India is a democratic country where laws and policies are made by politicians, who are elected representative to the people. They are supposed to be carrying out people's will. Unfortunately these laws and rules are interpreted by the judiciary and implemented by the executives. Under law women have equality with men, but the problems are with the administration. Therefore, if women need to be represented properly, there should be reservation in the judiciary and executive.

Women are still left on the periphery of the political process, and political participation remains elusive to most of them, in spite of their voting and election, and capturing few seats of power and influence. As amply brought out by various scholars, the most crucial problem in any attempt to measure women's political participation simply by studying official or organization membership and voting, is the finding that much of the Third World Politics occurs outside conventional political institutions.

In conclusion, it may be said that during the Women's Decade, there has been some achievement in making women visible in the political sphere. There has been more positive action on the part of the government to integrate women in the decision making process. It appears that the operation of larger politico-economic forces generate a political culture that women find difficult to get involved in. Women through the Constitution have been allowed to enter politics but there is a vast difference between allowing and integrating. As a scholar puts it "Toleration is not an active principle, it is a passive one. It places a premium on the elimination of tangible barriers but makes no commitment to a positive value of inclusion and membership. Political liberation of women, therefore would mean that women would be seen not as deviants or even as welcome strangers".

In short, women's real active political participation will necessitate changes both in value and in the social structure. Fresh strategies have to be evolved, not only for formal political activities but also for full involvement and participation in non-formal mass action. The pro-active strategies that would be beneficial are listed below:

1. To spread legal literacy not only among the general community but also amongst the elected representatives.
2. Modules can be included in existing non-formal educational programmes for this purpose.
3. Men and women in positions of power should be sensitized to women's issues.
4. Particular attention must be paid to the development of inter-personal communication skills amongst the community leaders.
5. The Planning Commission and all ministries and government departments must have a Women Cell.
6. Arrangements must be made for child care and other domestic responsibilities so that women can take part in public sphere and active politics.
7. NGOs can play a very important role in generating awareness about participation in the political system:

- NGOs can provide training for future women leaders.
- Can organize legal literacy programmes.
- Can work as pressure groups to press for the fulfillment of promises.

8. Media can play very productive role in enhancing women's participation in politics through:

- Wider coverage of activities and measures taken by women politicians.
- Highlighting the problems of women in politics.
- Projecting women issues and achievements.
- Alternate media can portray women's struggles and experiences which will help in generating values which encourage gender equality and build up a positive image of women participating in public life.

9. Increasing women's political representation requires reviewing the process of selection of candidates within the political parties.
10. Women in senior positions in politics can act as role models and mentors.
11. Campaigns and large scale mass movements must be initiated to change the perceptions and mindset of both the decision-makers and public at large.
12. Women must be brought in from the grassroot level and should be given position of power in the decision making processes.
13. There should be an increase in the numerical strength of women at different levels from lower to higher - the concept of women as a critical mass.
14. Education plays an important role as entry of women legislators into politics is concerned. Women have to be educated so as to bring them into the mainstream of national politics.
15. More number of minor/major studies is essential to investigate the various issues at various levels from Gram Sabha to District Panchayat.

All women members of panchayats and other executive bodies must be trained and empowered to exercise their authority. Both men and women members must be sensitized to women's issues. A committee should be formed to look into the training needs of women panchayat members and to help in designing modules. Particular attention must be paid to the development of interpersonal communication skills amongst the community leaders.

It has been observed though various studies that education of citizens not only builds up knowledge and information but also helps the citizens understand the complexities of the political process. The courses of studies and the text books should inculcate values of gender equality, self-respect, courage, independence etc. which would help in empowerment of women.

Working for women's development through their participation in setting the agenda for their own and others development and not merely to get on to such agenda requires immediate attention. This would lead to women's empowerment. There is thus, a close interaction and dialectical relationship between women's empowerment on the one hand and their role in politics and decision making on the other. Such a participation in making public choices would lead to a qualitative change not merely in women's lives but in the functioning of public institutions and nature of politics. A set of strategies and actions that would take care of the deficiencies and empower women in multiple ways and help them play the political role effectively can be evolved.

References

Ahuja. R., Rights of Women (A Feminist Perspective) Rawat Publication, Jaipur and New Delhi. 1992.

Alva M., Role of Women Political Leaders, Women in Politics in Asia and Pacific United Nations, New York. 1993.

Bhatt S., Women Parliamentarians of India, Shiva Publishers and Distributor, Udaipur. 1995.

Chopra J.K., Women in the Indian Parliament, Mittal Publication, New Delhi. 1993.

Gopalan S., Shiva M. National Profile on Women, Health and Development, Voluntary Health Association of India and WHO, Delhi. 2000.

Jeyapal P. and Dravidamani K., Women Panchayat Presidents Social Welfare, Vol. 40 No. 2, May 1997.

Kishwar M., Off the Beaten Track, Oxford University Press, New Delhi. 1999.

Kumari A. and Kidwai S., Crossing the Sacred Line... Women's search for political power, Orient Langman, New Delhi. 1998.

Menon, N., Gender and Politics in India, Oxford University Press, New Delhi. 1997.

Panwar P., "Women Sarpanches" in Verma S.B. (ed) status of women in Modern India Deep and Deep Publication, New Delhi. 2005.

Rajasekharan, K., Researvation : Boon or Bane ? Social Welfare Vol. 47 No. 1, April 1996.

Rasul B.Q.A., Purdah to Parliament Ajanta Book International, New Delhi. 2001.

Roy K., Women in Indian Politics. Rajat Publications, New Delhi. 1999.

Swarup H. and Bisaria S., Women Politics and Religion A.C. Brothers, New Delhi. 1991.

Ujwala H., Women in Grassroots Politics, Social Welfare Vol. 44, No. 2, May 1997.

Vidya K.C., Political empowerment of women at the grassroots, Kanishka Publishers and Distributors. New Delhi. 1997.

41

Women Stone-Breakers: Violation of Human Rights

Mausumi Majumdar

Domination, oppression, exploitation and subjugation of the weak are inherent characteristics of human society that have existed ever since society as a system came into existence. The conflicts that were the inevitable outcome, and the need to counteract the forces that lead to conflict in society, was what led people to build institutions to prevent atrocities on the weaker and vulnerable sections by the powerful. These institutions obtained a legal character when they became part of the state. The basic principle underlying these state institutions is to eliminate all forms of dominance in human society. They ensure individuals to live with dignity, equality, security, liberty and freedom, which are universal natural rights of all humans regardless of age, sex, nationality or religion. They are based on inherent human dignity which is the right of each individual since the time of his or her birth.

However, in spite of the existence of myriad state institutions that are meant to ensure the protection of human rights, violation of rights by both state institutions and powerful private individuals is a universal phenomenon. In order to check these infringements of the rights of individuals, the Universal Declaration of Human Rights was adopted and proclaimed on December 10, 1948, in the General Assembly of the United Nations, that was based on the notion that rights belong to a person by nature and because he is a human being and not by virtue of his citizenship in a particular country or membership in a particular religious or ethnic group.

Following this historic Act the Assembly called upon all Member countries to publicise the text of the Declaration and to cause it to be disseminated, displayed, read and expounded principally in schools and other educational institutions, without distinction based on the political status of countries or territories. The General Assembly has proclaimed this Declaration as a common standard of achievement for all peoples and all nations, to the end that every individual and every organ of the society keeping this Declaration constantly in mind, shall strive by teaching and education to promote respect for these rights and freedoms and by progressive measures, national and international, to secure their universal and effective recognition and observance, both among the peoples of Member

States themselves and among the peoples of territories under their jurisdiction. The rights included in the charter have been ratified by almost all nations of the world including India, and not allowing these rights and freedoms to be exercised amounts to violation of human rights that are punishable under the constitution of each country.

In addition to the rights guaranteed to all individuals under the Universal Declaration of Human Rights, India also guarantees rights to Indian citizens through the Constitution of India, adopted in 1950. The Indian Constitution is a social document that includes not only several human rights enlisted by the United Nations but also attempted to bring social revolution by resolving and balancing political and civil rights on the one hand, and social and economic rights on the other. The need for this arose from the fact that the social fabric of our country is highly fragmented and fractured, leading to discrimination and oppression of one powerless section by another more powerful section of the society. Women in particular suffer the most since they are discriminated against on the basis of their gender irrespective of whether they belong to a powerful or to a weak section of the society. The Constitution, when it was framed, guaranteed both rights and privileges to women through the Fundamental Rights and Directive Principles of State Policy. Alongside it not only ensured equality before law and equal protection of law but also prohibited discrimination against any citizen on the grounds of sex.

However the human rights situation in India still remained precarious because of the very nature of Indian society, which firmly refused to accept the legislative norms meant to create an egalitarian society. This compelled the passing of the Protection of Human Rights Act, which was passed in 1993. Under Section 2(d) of this Act, "human rights" means the rights relating to life, liberty, equality and dignity of the individual guaranteed under the Constitution or embodied in the International Covenants and enforceable by courts in India. "International Covenants" means the International Covenant on Civil and Political Rights and the International Covenant on Economic, Social and Cultural Rights adopted by the General Assembly of the United Nations on the December 16, 1966. The National Human Rights Commission (NHRC) was also set up in October 1993 as an expression of India's concern for the protection and promotion of human rights.

Among its other duties, the National Human Rights Commission has been authorized to inquire, on its own initiative or on a petition presented to it by a victim or any person on his behalf, into complaint of violation of human rights or abetment or negligence in the prevention of such violation by a public servant and if the enquiries of the National Human Rights Commission discloses the violation of human right or negligence in the prevention of violation of human rights by a public servant, or that men and women are not being treated as equal, it may recommend to the concerned Government or authority the initiation of proceedings for prosecution or such other action as the Commission may deem fit against the concerned person or persons (Majumder op cit).

From the above facts it appears that India is highly concerned about ensuring equality between men and women and is also committed to ensuring protection of human rights by public servants who represent the state. Every Indian citizen seems to be safeguarded against discrimination of any kind and the state appears to stringently care for the human rights of all individuals. The ground reality however presents an entirely different picture. In spite of the passage of so many years since the ratification of the Universal Declaration of Human Rights, the adoption of the Constitution and the passing of the Protection of Human Rights Act, the economic, social and cultural status of women has remained unchanged and they are being systematically bypassed from the development processes of the country although empowerment of women was one of the major objectives of the Ninth Five-Year Plan (1997-2002). The persistence of sharp gender-based inequality in many different forms is one of the most striking aspects of Indian society and it yields disparities in well-being as well as differences in power and decision-making authority (Dreze and Sen, 2002: 18). Comparative studies of different states of India have shown that the regions where women's participation in both the public and private domain is high, e.g., in Kerala and Himachal Pradesh, are rapidly rising both economically and socially since women's decisions and actions have a profound impact on the policies the government decides to pursue and the lives that people can lead. On the other hand the suppression of women's active and liberated participation in the economy and the society, e.g, in the northern states particularly UP, has been the cause of the economic and social backwardness of these states.

It is however a truism that woman in general are more homebound and concerned about their families than men, because of which their responsibilities and anxieties are different from those of men even if they are forced to participate equally with their men folk in earning livelihood for supporting their families. This can be observed in the case of women labourers who work along with their husbands at various kinds of jobs like brick making, as construction workers, as stone breakers and so on. Although they work with their husbands as family units rather than individually, the problems faced by them are grossly different from their husbands' because of their biological difference. This difference makes them vulnerable to other kinds of difficulties that their husbands don't need to face. Alongside they also have to perform their social roles as caretakers of their families and ensure the well-being of their husbands, children and other family members. This responsibility puts an added burden on their shoulders since they have to guarantee the availability of drinking water and ration and also look after the health of all the family members, especially their children. Since one duty of the state is to provide access to these basic needs to all the citizens of the country as a matter of right, not providing these necessities for human existence amounts to violation of the human rights of the people who are not getting them. By not providing these basic needs, the state is also obstructing the path of empowerment of women since most of their time is spent on ensuring these needs, which could have been spent on doing more constructive activities that could have enhanced their progress and development. This is also coming in the way of the construction of their self-esteem and is violating their basic right to lead a life filled with human dignity and respect.

We will study how the state is violating the human rights of the women stone breakers of the Shankargarh region by not providing access to the basic needs like food, clothing and shelter. The study is an ethnographic one in which women stone breakers themselves narrate how the state machinery is increasing their misery, both by not preventing the exploitations by the contractors who exploit and oppress them, and by not providing access to their basic needs. The paper is divided into three parts. The first part presents a brief description of the Shankargarh region, why it is important commercially and a general description of the condition of the stone breakers. The second part gives the narratives of the women stone workers. And the third part gives the conclusions of the study based on the narratives.

Shankargarh: A Brief Description

The Shankargarh region, also known as the Kaimur Mountain Range, is a part of the Vindhya Ranges. The name Shankargarh has a historical origin since the mountains forming part of the Vindhya Ranges are supposed to be the fort of Lord Shiva or Shankar. That is why the name of the region is Shankargarh. The thirteenth day of both full moon and new moon are dedicated to Lord Shiva and on those two days the labourers do not break stones. Although Shankargarh lies to the east of Vindhyanagar in Mirzapur, it is a part of three districts of Allahabad namely Bara, Meja and Koraon. Earlier this region was a part of the Bara Paragana in the Karchhana district under the rule of king Shankargarh. In 1981 Sri Hemvati Nandan Bahuguna created the Bara district and Shankargarh was made a part of it. In terms of development blocks, within the Bara district there are two development blocks, Shankargarh and Jasra. There are 108 revenue villages in the Shankargarh region, each having stone quarries and silica mines where the labourers living in the villages work. The total land area of these villages is 33,134 hectares. At the time of the1981 Census all the revenue villages in this stony region were under the Shankargarh Development Block but in 1996 when a new block called Kaudhiyara was created in this region, 10 villages, i.e., 3656 hectares or 11 per cent was transferred to the Jasra block during the reallocation. Thus 89 per cent of the 108 villages in Shankargarh are in the Shankargarh block while 11 per cent are under the Jasra block.

The major resource found in Shankargarh is silica sand, a natural resource that is highly useful for industrial purposes. It is found in great abundance in the rocky mountains of this region. This sand is used for the construction of blast furnaces in steel plants. In addition it is used for making glass, fiberglass, plastic, soap, kinds of cloth and as an ingredient in the making of cosmetics. Silica sand is of two kinds namely white silica and brown silica. The white silica extracted from this is famous all over the world and is also very expensive. Silica is present in the upper layer of the stones of Shankargarh. It is usually found in the soft and relatively newer stones, which are 93 per cent sand stone. After breaking up these sand stones they are taken by bullock carts to plants located in a place called Shivrajpur, which is 2-3 kilometers from Shankargarh. There they are thoroughly washed with chemicals and are then taken for processing to government factories located in Biharia, which is further down the road to Shivrajpur. The silica sand that is produced is then transported to industrial cities and towns in India like Raipur, Bhillai, Durg, Nagpur, Jabalpur, Gwalior, Kolkata, Mumbai, Firozabad and also exported to some places in Europe.

Besides silica, the rocky terrain of Shankargarh also makes it abundant in various kinds of stones like building stone, slabs, and sand stone including *patiya* and road ballast. These stones have multifold uses and are thus in great demand commercially. In addition, the stones covering the mountain ranges are broken down into ballast or 'gitti', which are used for laying railway tracks and for the construction of roads. The entire region is located on the banks of river Yamuna that makes it very rich in sand, which is an essential component for the construction of houses. Earlier most of the labourers were employed in the silica mines to extract silica but in the recent period there has been a marked shift towards stone breaking. The increasing use of 'gitti' by the government for constructing roads ever since the launching of the Fifth Five Year Plan has generated a massive demand for this commodity. Under this plan each village having a population of 1500 and fifty per cent of the villages having a population of 1000 to 1500 were decided to be connected by *pucca* roads. During the Eighth Five Year Plan nearly 10,000 new roads were constructed, which was 400 times more than the target. Today the gitti produced in Shankargarh is being used for fulfilling the demands in Allahabad, Pratapgarh, Sultanpur, Rae Bareli, Faizabad, Basti, Gonda, Lucknow, Gazipur, Balia, Jaunpur, Fatehpur and Barabanki. This is the reason why stone breaking has become the major source of employment of labour in the Shankargarh region (Singh 2000).

The stones which are broken to make gitti are found abundantly in the Shankargarh region. These stones are of various kinds. From the top layer of the hills that are around 100 and 200 meters above sea level are extracted *patiya* and from the hills which are hard, are extracted *gitti, sil, jora, chakiya* and so on. Earlier, there was not much problem in getting leases on these hills and the people asking for lease had to give only a token sum to the king of Shankargarh. But today the scenario has completely changed. The increasing demand for 'gitti' due to the expansion of railway network and roadways has led to a sharp increase in the demand for labourers. In addition to the original residents of the region of Shankargarh, the demand for extra labourers is fulfilled by bringing in a large number of people belonging to the Kol tribe from the adjoining regions and from the neighbouring state of Madhya Pradesh. Thus there are two kinds of stone breakers in Shankargarh, one, the original residents of the Shankargarh, and two, the migrant Kol labourers. Most of the labourers work as family units and women work shoulder to shoulder with their husbands to break stone. The payment is also not made to an individual but to the family.

The condition of the stone breakers in the Shankargarh region is quite miserable. More than 70 per cent of the people live below the poverty line but the Panchayat has secured BPL cards to only three or four families. Thus although the village has a PDS shop but the labourers have to buy all their essential necessities at high rates from the ration shop owner. Most of the stone breakers live in huts which they had built on plots of land belonging to the Gram Sabha. However only a few residents had leases on the land; many of them live there illegally since they had not been leased the land although they were entitled to obtain lease. The original residents of Shankargarh who work as stone breakers are mostly dalits like Chamar, Harijan etc., while some migrant labourers belonging to the Kol tribe who were brought in from Madhya Pradesh when the demand for labourers increased, also live there. Since the Kols do not belong to the region they do not live in the Gram Sabha land. The contractors had allowed them to live on land on the hilly tracts adjoining the quarries. Each of the workers had built 'marhai' or straw huts for their families, which were so small that they could barely accommodate one person. These marhais can be seen scattered on the slopes of the hills. One corner of the marhai is a tiny cooking space with an oven that is fuelled by firewood or kanda (cow dung cake), while the rest of the space is used for sleeping. The houses of the local people of Shankargarh were much better than those of the Kols although they were also quite small and built with straw or stones. Plastic sheets were used as roofs to cover the tops.

The settled population of Shankargarh who had been living there for many years are more aware and articulate about the problems facing the labourers than the Kol labourers. The uprooting of the Kols from their local environs by the labour contractors had rendered them very vulnerable and helpless and totally dependent on the contractors who had brought them. Being illiterate and extremely poverty stricken, hardly any of the Kols had the voice to express their pathetic condition. The local villagers on the other hand were full of rage against the gross violation of their human rights in all domains but were helpless to protest against these atrocities because of their lack of bargaining power. They revealed that the majority of the residents of the village were dependent on breaking stones for their livelihood and almost all of them were bonded to the contractors from whom they had taken loans for marriages and to cover medical expenses during illnesses.

Usually in the family units the men broke stone slabs from the slopes with powerful blows of their heavy hammers while their wives broke them into smaller pieces with their lighter hammers. The official rate to be paid to labourers for extracting and breaking 1000 stone slabs of the right size is around Rs. 1,000 for which the labourers have to put in between eight to ten days of hard labour. Sometimes they also have to make their children, especially boys of the age of ten or eleven years, work with them in order to reduce the time period. These stone slabs are then sold to the contractors, who load them on trucks to transport them to the city for selling to other agents for further processing. However, the labourers told us that they receive only Rs. 600 to Rs. 700 and sometimes even Rs. 500 for selling 1,000 pieces since most of them were mortgaged to the contractors for having taken loans. The repayment of their loans was not in cash but in kind in the form of bonded labour till the loans was repaid. The labourers had no option but to comply since they were always in need of lump sum cash to tide over one need after the other in the absence of savings. Their main requirement was for meeting the medical needs of their family members. Stone breaking being an extremely laborious work, which required a large quantity of nutritious food that none of them could afford, all of them were prone to illness and diseases. The continuous inhalation of stone dust often led to TB and other forms of lung infections among the labourers.

Outbreak of malaria, cholera, plague, typhoid and other kinds of water borne and viral diseases was also a frequent occurrence in the village. These illnesses entailed a lot of money since the patients had to be transported to the nearest city of Jari to private practitioners who fleeced them dry. Thus the stonebreakers, who ensure so much revenue to both the state and to private individuals are themselves leading lives of misery and destitution with no one to listen to their problems and ameliorate their condition.

Narratives of Women Stonebreakers of Shankargarh

The condition of women labourers of Shankargarh was worse than their male counterparts since they also had to face the constant burden of childbearing and other problems related with being women. Some of the women respondents told us that the minimum number of children that most women had was five. At the time of pregnancy they were not provided any medical care by either the contractor or the government. Although an ANM is supposed to regularly visit the village to check the pregnant women and new mothers and their babies and vaccinate them, the village women reported on the contrary. Neither they nor their children had been given of the vaccines as prescribed by the government since it was not possible for them to visit the nearest primary health centre which is quite far from their residence. Traveling there entailed both transport cost and loss of income for not working on that day. The women said that they were forced to work even at the extreme end of their pregnancy; sometimes some women even gave birth at the quarries. If any complication arose they had to be transported to Jari, where the nearest health centre was located, on public vehicles. A few women and children even lost their lives in this process but the contractors did not pay any compensation since he asserted that it was their own need that drove them to the work site in their precarious condition.

The women labourers narrated that they had to face many other kinds of problems since they had to also look after their families and ensure their basic needs. None of the families there had ration cards that enabled them to buy essential commodities at subsidized rates. All of them were living below the poverty line and were entitled to BPL cards, but the Pradhan, who was supposed to make sure that the district administration issued them cards, did not do so. They were thus forced to buy foodstuff from the local shops, often on credit. Many of them sent their children to the local school where they were supposed to be provided mid-day meals but they alleged that the food was of both poor quality and inadequate. Instead of 'khichri' the children were given poor quality rice with a little turmeric added to it to make it yellow. There was also hardly any teaching in the school since the teachers were mostly absent. Most of the villagers withdrew their children after class V because girls were needed to look after the households and younger siblings when their mothers were at work, while the boys had to start working with their parents to supplement the family income. The girls were married off at the age of sixteen or seventeen. Fortunately till then there had been no incident of physical harm to the girls in the village in the form of rape or physical violence from the contractor or other male members of the village, so the women did not have to worry about their daughters on that account. However overall the lives of the women were quite miserable on all domains and there was no one whom they could turn to for help.

The women narrated that although there were many NGOs working in the region, notably an organization called Sanchetna, they claimed that none of them had been able to curb their exploitation by the contractors or improve their lot. Rather they exploited the plight of the labourers to earn projects from funding agencies. Some of the labourers said that they had been taken to Delhi to narrate their woes to a funding agency while the NGO was negotiating for a project, but while the NGO secured the project, the condition of the labourers did not change. Some NGOs had also helped them to form Self-Help Groups so that they could sell their stones directly to agents without the help of contractors, but these groups usually fell apart under pressure from the contractors to break them. The Panchayat too was indifferent to the condition of the poor people of the village. Some of the labourers had joined the Communist Party active in that region in the hope that their condition would be alleviated.

The major problem facing the people of this region, especially the women whose responsibility it is to look after the needs of the family, is that of obtaining drinking water. In the center of the main village there is a handpump that was installed by the government but it is now dysfunctional. There are five wells in the village but only two have drinking water, which is grossly insufficient for the entire village. The government has installed only two hand pumps for 400-500 persons and if they are pumped for more than one hour they dry up. The villagers say that if the water of the canal is there then there is water in the hand pumps and small wells too but if the canal dries up then the water in the hand pumps and wells also dry up. Sometimes during summers tankers are called in to supply water to the residents but one tanker is not enough for the entire village. The people then walk more than one kilometer on the hilly terrain to fetch water.

The narratives of a few individual women are presented below:

Respondent's Name: **Pushpa Devi:** Pushpa Devi age 40 years is a widow with a 14 year old son. Her son is studying in class eight in the local government school. Pushpa Devi previously used to work as an agricultural labourer in another village, but the work opportunity was limited there and hence the earning was inadequate for survival. She had no land there and used to live in other's house. A few years back she left the village and constructed her hut on Gram Sabha land. Her husband died two years back because of TB. Pushpa Devi is illiterate and cannot count even rupees. She works as a load carrier whose job is to load stone pieces in trucks. She reports that she gets Rs. 50 per day as wage and all of it is spent on food. Since she is cardless, she has no access to subsidized food grains supplied to poor people by the government. If for some reason she is unable to work either she goes hungry or goes to the nearby shop to get vegetables and cereals on loan. This loan carries no interest, but is repaid after she earns money. She hopes her only son will not be engaged as stone crusher in the mines but will get some job elsewhere after his studies. Since her hut is on Gram Sabha land, hence she has to leave it if she is told to go. But where will she go? She has no answer.

Respondent's Name: Manraja Devi Kol: Manraja devi is a middle aged woman working as stone breaker, who is unable to tell her actual age. There are 5 members in her family including a son whose children she looks after. In November 2004 her daughter-in-law died of cancer. When Manraja devi learnt that her daughter-in-law had cancer, she borrowed a sum of Rs. 20,000 from the contractor for whom she worked. She took her daughter-in-law to private doctors in neighbouring regions of Jari, Gauhaniya etc., but she did not survive. When taking the loan, Manraja Devi's husband had promised the contractor that till the loan was repaid neither he nor his wife would work for any other contractor, would not sell their gitti to any one else, and would sell their gitti to this contractor at Rs. 100 to Rs. 200 less per truck. These are the conditions under which contractors, taking advantage of the needs of the poor labourers, manage to buy gitti from them at much lower rates and sell them at very high rates.

Manraja devi and her family originally hail from village Mudariya, Riva Janpad, Mauganj, in Madhya Pradesh. They came to Shankargarh 25 to 30 years earlier in search of work after their relatives from their village informed them that work as labourers was available. Initially they worked as agricultural labourers when canals had just been constructed for irrigation but they shifted to breaking stones when the demand for stone breaking labourers increased. After coming here they gradually set up a hut in the Gram Samaj land with stones and straw. Now in her middle age, Manraja devi's only concern is that she and her husband have to look after her wayward son's children since he refuses to work unless he is married for a second time. Manraja devi however cannot afford to get him married again since she still has to repay the outstanding loan she incurred for her daughter-in-law's treatment.

Like all the other families in this region, Manraja's family too is deprived of any government benefits. She is also unable to educate her grand children due to lack of financial resources. The family also does not have a ration card although their names on the voter's list. Manraja says ironically that they are free to cast their votes for anyone they like but otherwise they are forced to lead a life of bondage.

Respondent's Name: Ram Pyari Bind: Ram Pyari is a 40 year old widow whose husband died of TB, which he contracted by continuously inhaling stone dust, a few years ago. Ram Pyari was forced to break stones in place of her husband, but now her body has become so weak that she cannot do this work any more. She now earns money by working as an agricultural labourer to feed her six children and herself. She also sends some of her children to school. She is financially assisted by her oldest son who pulls a trolley in the city. Ram Pyari's twelve year old daughter also supplements the family income by working as a field labourer with her mother.

Ram Pyari's main grudge is against the Panchayat. She says that till today she has not been given any widow pension and neither does she have a ration card for buying necessities at subsized rates. Sometimes if she is lucky the ration shop owner gives her kerosene oil cheaply but mostly she has to buy at the open market rate. The predicament of obtaining a regular supply of clean water which is faced by the rest of the village is also faced by her. She complains that neither the Panchayat nor the government is concerned about this problem. Another problem facing Ram Pyari is that she does not get regular work in the village but has to go to neighbouring villages to look for work. Her continuous anxieties about her children' s education, daughters' marriage and ensuring the survival of her children have weakened her so much physically and mentally that she is afraid that she too might fall ill and die one day leaving her children orphaned.

Respondent's Name: Vitnidevi: Vitnidevi is a 65 year old widow who sold all her jewellery to buy 1 bigha of land after she became a widow. Three years ago however the Forest department forcibly took away the land saying that it was part of the forest area. The department even filed a case against her which she lost and was made to pay a fine of Rs. 1000. Vitnidevi says that the source of exploitation is not the upper castes but the administration or government. The stone breaking labourers somehow manage to save money to buy small plots of land for their children's future but the forest department takes them away. She had invested all her lifetime savings and her jewellery to buy the land. She succeeded in doing this even though she had to earn money by breaking stones and looking after her children single-handedly when her husband fell ill and subsequently died. Her children were also compelled to help her in breaking stones because of which they could not attend school. But after buying the land after overcoming so many difficulties the forest department took away the land. Vitnidevi says that the poor people cannot protest against the highhandedness of the authorities since they do not have the voice to do so. Today Vitnidevi is once again back to breaking stones.

Respondent's Name: Gulabkali, Age 55 Years, Kol Tribe, Village Bargari: Gulabkali age 55 years, used to live in Shankargarh earlier but thirty years ago she had to leave her house and settle in Bargari, a hamlet in Shankargarh, which is her natal house. After her marriage her house was burnt down in communal riots. With great difficulty she managed to build another house but thieves entered into it and stole all her belongings. She then left her house and came back to Bargari. Misfortune did not stop chasing her and after a hard life of breaking stones in Bargari she fell ill. In spite of her ill health she has to continue breaking stones in order to survive. She is full of complaints against the government and the administration which took away the 2 bighas of land whose lease she had obtained, claiming it to be a part of the forest area. Gulabkali sends her 15-16 year old daughter to school seven kilometers away. Twenty years ago her husband took a loan of Rs. 5,000 from a contractor which has now increased to Rs. 35,000. Being unable to repay the loan he was sent to jail. He is now out but has contracted TB for which he is undergoing treatment and cannot break stones any longer. Gulabkali's anxiety for her daughter's marriage and her own and her husband's ill health for which she cannot afford to buy medicines, is causing her to slowly decline. She laments that poor people have no voice and cannot make themselves heard in the Panchayat or in front of government officials. She was given a small house by the government after undergoing a sterilization operation, where she is now living, but she has to continue breaking stones to earn a living.

Conclusion

From the narratives of the poor women of Shankargarh it is obvious that they live in a condition of misery and wretchedness. Because of their pathetic financial condition they are forced to take loans from the contractors and they are afraid to speak out about the exploitation faced by them by the contractors as they might be further exploited by them. The various government departments functioning in the village work in collusion with the contractors and instead of helping the labourers, help the contractors to further exploit them. Thus, the labourers including the women are totally at the mercy of the contractors for their survival with no-one to help them out. They are deprived of the basic minimum necessities like water, electricity, education, health, roads, housing and so on. Theoretically they are free to work and earn but in practice, because of landlessness, ill health and no provision of social security by the administration, the families of all the women become attached/bonded to the contractors operating in the locality. The women are the worst sufferers since on the one hand they have to break stones to supplement the family income, while on the other they have to ensure the fulfillment of the basic needs of their families. In addition they have their own gender related problems stemming from biological reasons like pregnancy, child birth, protecting themselves from males, and so on.

This study showed that the human rights of the workers including the women are being violated the most by the very people who are supposed to ensure them, i.e. the various wings of the administration like the Panchayat, the Forest Department, the Tehsil office, the Mining Office and so on. This is obstructing the path to their empowerment since their entire life cycle is being spent in somehow surviving and ensuring the minimum subsistence level for their families. The human rights violations by the government functionaries are also preventing them from leading a life of dignity and self-respect and with basic human dignity. But there is no one to listen to their tales of misery and wretchedness and they are totally at the mercy of the contractors for their survival. Thus their right to live as human beings is being grossly violated.

References

Dreze, J. and A. Sen, *India: Development and Participation*, Oxford University Press, New Delhi. 2002

Majumder, B, *State Protection of Human Rights in UP*, project report submitted to G.B. Pant Social Science Institute, Allahabad (mimeo). 2006

Singh, S. *Shankargarh ke patthar torte mazdoor*, project report submitted to G. B. Pant Social Science Institute, Allahabad (mimeo). 2000

42

Women and Mass Media

Poonam Tiwari

Women constitute almost half of the country's population, which has been deprived of self-respect and subjugated into existence at the whim and mercy of the male. The past two decades have witnessed great efforts for human development contributing greatly to rapid progress in building women's capabilities and in closing gender gaps. More recently however, protest movements on global scale have brought out the concern that empowerment of women as a part of major transformation. This is one of the significant needs of the political development of women that can be successfully met by the mass media.

In the developing countries, mass media has a critical role in sharing information resources with the community, acting representatives to voice the opinions and experiences of the large mass of illiterate women and reshaping the communication agenda in gender equitable direction.

Media is a vast field today. Media today sets the trends for socio cultural life in society. The media not only give us information they guide our very experiences. People don't in other words trust their own experiences, until the media mirrors it. Media has not only filled our experiences of external reality, it has also entered into our way to experience our own selves. It has provided us with new identities and aspiration of what we should be.

Media has been the reflector of dominant values and works as an active agency, among reinforcing and strengthening dominant value structure. A platform when various interests can be brought together exists in the form of media in today's democratic society.

Media is a "Power Pressure" in terms of exerting influence in society, they are played out, they are 'source' of varied definitions of social reality, changing culture and values and most important, they are source of the 'public meaning system'. Media is the carrier of public opinion and plays a crucial role in giving voice to the people. All the content of the media is important to our national life, not just what frankly and directly relate to public affairs. To some extent, it sounds true that the T.V. reflects the reality, somehow, it does not stop at the depiction of reality but tries to step forward. It serves as an indicator of what is believed to do desirable and undesirable. It constantly evaluates the reality and points out the ideal picture of the world.

A mass medium, says Wilbur Schramm, is essentially a working group organized around some device for circulating the same message, at about the same time, to a large number of people. Such a definition excludes the folk media, group media and natural communication such as in rumour education and preaching. As generally interpreted the mass media are the press, cinema, radio, and television. But books, magazines, journals also need to be included in the label. Further, media have been playing major roles in our daily lives. In its various forms, the media informs us, reduces us, confuses us and programmes everything from what we should think, feel, smell, see, taste and hear.

Status of Women in Indian Society

India is a country of heterogeneous culture. The position of women in society is still influenced by social and cultural factors like traditions and customs, religion, caste, class and income-strata. All these factors are influential determinants of social perception of women. According to Manu Smriti, a woman must remain all her life under the male protection. The patriarchal ideology of 'pativrata' deems an Indian wife to make her own life, talent and interest secondary to the needs of her husband and family.

Status of Women in Media

In the battle for equal status and fair treatment of women an important role is generally attributed to the mass media and in particular to television because it has become a significant part of life, in a developing country like ours. The presentation of women and men in films and television is contradictory to reality. It misrepresents the real proportion of men versus women in the population or in the work force of the extent to which social class, age, occupational status are ascribed to the two sexes. It is generally observed that consistently and systematically women are being exploited to the advantage of man's self esteem. One important reason, one can assume is that its production, direction and other facts are controlled by men.

Mill's (1956:90) assessment of media's impact still holds true after fifty years. 'The media not only give us information they guide our very experiences. Our standards of credulity, our standards of reality tend to be set by these media rather then by own fragmentary experience. People do not in other words; trust their own experience, until it is mirrored by the media'. Media has not only filled our experience of external reality, it has also entered into our way to experience our own selves. It has provided us with new identities and aspiration of what we should be.

Media is not an exception to the fact of having a discriminatory attitude towards women. It is difficult to ascertain whether it is done intentionally or out of common habit. The point is not to pin the blame but to see the reality afresh. Media practitioners and academicians are of the view that media portrayal of women, both in and outside the family, project the negative and amazingly stereotypical images of women influenced by patriarchy.

Global Media Monitoring Project (GMMP)

The Global Media Monitoring Project mapped the representation of women and men in news media worldwide. On 16th February 2005, hundreds of women and men in 76 countries around he world participated in the third ever GMMP. They monitored almost 13,000 news items on television, radio and in newspapers-the monitoring was done by a wide range of groups from media professionals to media and gender advocacy groups. According to the India coordinators of GMMP, 17 electronic media organizations across English and regional electronic media were monitored.

The GMMP first began in 1995 as the first extensive research based tool to study gender in media, little has changed. Let take a look at the number of all, 76 countries surveyed, in 1995, the percentage of news subjects devoted to women in all media, print and electronic, was jut 17 per cent, which rose marginally to 18 per cent in 2000. However at the turn of the century, between 2000 and 2005, statistically there is a significant up-trend in the number of women subjects from 18 to 21 per cent.

Television for the same period (for all 76 countries) has stayed fairly static with 21 to 22 per cent of stories covering women related issues over the last ten years. It is also interesting to note that celebrities, culture, legal-social and crime and violence issues make up the bulk of the stories related to women.

Women, therefore, continue to be slotted in categories flowing from gender and the mainstreaming of half the globe's population is yet to be reflected in the media across the world. As the report points out if media is a mirror of society then this mirror is flawed reflecting back only a small percentage of the world.

Says Margaret Gallagher, the GMMP 2005 consultant and the author of the 2005 report (released in February 2006), "The overall reason for women's low representation in the news is linked with perceptions of women's status in society as a whole. These perceptions are mirrored in journalistic practice. Women's views are not considered as important as men's-even when these women are decision-makers or are in influential positions. To take the example of politicians: in almost every country in the survey, the percentage of female politicians in the news is lower than the actual percentage of female politicians in the country".

Generally it is shown in advertisements, a women's goal in life is to attract and attain man.

- Women are shown in advertising as always young and attractive.
- They are frequently depicted as sexual objects.
- Women in Advertisements are restricted to the home and isolated from other women. Outside the home man is her favourite companion.

The advertising world continues to use women to peddle its products, and to present women as a sexual object. Advertising also reinforces housework as the sole responsibility of women, with household equipment advertisements addressed only to women.

Notwithstanding various directives, woman's image has gone through several unjust projections at the hands of the media. The passivity of female characters in film/television is a major cause for concern. Notwithstanding various directives, woman's image has gone through several unjust projections at the hands of the media. The passivity of female characters in film/television is a major cause for concern. Rarely is a woman shown as capable of solving her problems, standing up to indignities or violence, facing challenges on her own, or taking decisions. The image of the educated woman is typecast as insensitive, self centre and uncaring. The economically independent woman is shown as domineering and ruthless. The woman is ideal only when she is in her nurturing roles and as a supportive supplement to man. Girls are always shown as cooking and looking after the younger siblings and imitating the nurturing role of their mothers, where as boys seek adventure, solve problems, and follow the role model of their fathers.

This is because for the most part men control the media from press, radios and T.V. to advertising, films and publishing. They use their influence to project ideas, attitudes and values of a patriarchal order. This mindset tends to deny women their rightful place in various ways, viz.

- Under representation of women in Media.
- Stereotypical portrayal, reinforcing their traditional roles
- Neglecting to portray those images that reflect their new socio-economic status.

As it is, the reach of mass media among women is much less due to factors like illiteracy, inaccessibility, lack of respite from household chores and traditionally imposed inhibitions restricting the movement of women. Thus, the distance between women and media not only deprives women of their right to information and knowledge but also keep them in the dark regarding the blatant misuse of female identity and distortion of the truth.

A number of studies made in different countries lead to the conclusion that the image of women as it is shown in the films and television is either of a housewife, a mother or as a sexual object. Women are shown, as dependent and she must remain all her life under male protection. In media men are always shown as confident, strong, brave, daring, independent, handsome and on the other side women are shown as 'plastic dolls', tall, lean, fair, with glowing skin and flowing hair.

Very often women are shown as 'soft toys' for men the way they are positioned emphasizing their subservience and dependence. They wear revealing clothes and take leading and yearning postures - signs of incompleteness. The media is flooded with fashion, lifestyle, beauty aids, entertainment, travel attracting by colourfully over-dressed or underdressed women.

Another typical observation is comodification and stereotyping of women in advertising. Women are the dominant targets for most advertised products with commercial involving domesticity emphasizing the traditional role of women. Most advertisement address women between the ages of 18-35, where models of 18-27 age wear jeans and cosmetics and 30-35 wear sari and buy detergent, cooking oil or masala.

The reason for distortion of a women's image in media, is that women find their identity with stereotype images outside the film and television too. It is the marginality of women in cultural and social activities generally which contributes to their subordination in life.

All these facts are hardly recognized and whenever women as a group or an individual have tried to protest, against the studied facts, they have had to face the argument which is often raised from all levels of society that women themselves willingly participate in such films, plays and television. Therefore it can be said that to some extent women themselves are responsible for their distorted picture in media.

Gender codes are pervasive in all language system, whether we are talking of print, visual or audiovisual media. They do not reflect biologically determined positions, but are embedded none the less in social hegemonies.

Media is not an isolated entity but is fashioned by a social context. Media must not selectively address certain sectorial concerns while ignoring some equally important ones. The contents of communication are reflective of the values of society which, in turn, are nurtured and sustained through communication. The treatment noted to women and girls in different modes of human communication, mirror the prevailing attitudes and values towards women in a particular society. Image portrayed through communication reinforces reality. In India, the dominant stereotype images of women and girls are that of:

- Less competent human beings
- Instruments for exploitation by men
- Key to commercial success in this age of advertising

It is a fact that advertisements are important in individual's life today as they provide the right to choose the product according to their choice. But there is an urgent need to change the portrayal of women, the stereotype in ages of women in advertisement to make this medium more effective and positive as far as women's portrayal is concerned.

To break the vicious circle of existing 'undesirable' images and project the reality of the lives of women and girl's would need an overhaul of the content of existing communication messages through a well thought out National Communication Policy on Women and Girls.

The role of media in empowerment of women is two folds:

- Empowerment through exposure to media by way of programmes and printed material. This is a consumer-oriented function and by the consumer, we mean women.
- Development through the active participation of women in production of media messages by participating in the decision-making process regarding programme content, policies and the projection of a balanced image of women.

Women have been recognized by India's policy makers as the largest oppressed group in Indian society. Broadly assessed, this oppression has the effect of limiting their capabilities, both in the conventional roles of home-maker, wife and mother and in the wider roles of productive resources and responsible citizens of a free nation. Poor access to knowledge social and cultural barriers to a choice of options, and law level of confidence in seeking and using knowledge have inhibited and continue to inhibit, women's potential to overcome these limitation.

Margaret Gallagher, the GMMP 2005 consultant, suggests the following four points to work at rectifying the situation;

1. Training and awareness rising for journalists and media managers. They need to become aware of the existence of bias - i.e. the fact that the news is so completely skewed towards male opinions, subjects and points of view. Frequently, stories needlessly overlook women's voices and points of view, and indeed very often the inclusion of such viewpoints would add an extra dimension to the story, make it more interesting and give it a wider appeal.
2. Media organizations need to adopt policies aimed at ensuring gender balance

in their output, and need to set numerical targets so as to achieve that balance.

3. Advocacy groups and NGOs need to monitor their media regularly, so as to have up-to-date facts and figures they can use in discussions with journalists, media managers and policy-makers.
4. Advocacy groups and NGOs can try to build up working relationships with media practitioners, so that they can input the names of female experts on particular topics. One strategy often used is to build up a database of women experts - but the creation of this kind of database is not enough by itself. Its use needs to be monitored, and data bases need to be constantly updated".

Challenges Ahead and Recommendations

- A conscious strategic change is required in national media and communication efforts to uplift the status of women in media.
- Expert group to work towards operationalizing a communication policy for women particularly on drawing up a framework on roles / images projection of women.
- The assumption is that women audiences needed information and once this was provided they would take to newer practices. It was soon realized that mere information was not enough. Motivation is very crucial for the audience to take action.
- Development Communication is primarily purpose communication for planned charge. It is intended to promote human development, which basically means communication that will help reduce poverty, unemployment and social inequality.
- In development communication assessing the communication needs is important before designing any social programme because information needs differ depending on the location and the dynamics within the workplace keeping women in focus.
- Small and low cost media can promote better interaction among the women folk. Moreover, the current development communication model lays lot more emphasis on participatory approach, so plan programmes in collaboration with women.
- The mainstream mass media are rarely seen taking up the agenda of women's development seriously. Women can successfully use alternate media strategies to promote gender justice and equality.
- One particular day or time slot can be declared as a "Women's Zone" where only the women will operate the equipment, compare and discuss issues that are relevant to their lives. Such programmes would lead to an increased

awareness among women and help them to be empowered.

- More and more women to be involved in mass communication so that women perspectives, issues and solutions gains ground.
- A strong censor board for monitoring the programmes and printed matter.
- Women in the mass media should be shown in a positive and constructive manner and in a wide variety of roles.
- Policy makers must urgently address the question of new media influence and its cultural implication.
- More critical thinking awareness of women's issues and careful planning among producers, directors and script writers can lead to the portrayal of women as strong capable professionals, as healthy, independent and innovative housewives, mothers and as a strong willed, responsible citizens. Husbands and wives could be shown as equal partners, nurturing and respective each other.
- Community radio projects and audio initiatives can become successful in promoting women's empowerment in rural India.
- T.V. is exciting and has captured the people's imagination. Its potential as a tool of mass communication is unquestionable. The increased variety of programming and competition among networks indicate greater opportunities for positive portrayal of women in Indian television.
- Text books in use in the formal and non-formal education system and at other levels of education and training should be carefully assessed for removing negative images and references to women.
- Information and communication need to become integral to grassroots initiatives particularly for women's empowerment to draw the active participation of women in development strategies. So that women get engaged in the new media initiative to reach the community which will strengthen their cause for development.
- There are key challenges that women in electronic media have to be true to their inner calling and job requirement report the news as it happens without discrimination and that also naturally tends to swing towards not having any specific gender focus while reporting.
- It is extremely important to set the agenda immediately for at least conducting media stock taking of what is the position of news in India and how much space does it allow to women's issues.
- Apart from commercial advertising television throughout the world also carriers out 'socially relevant and public services ads'. These are intended to educate and inform people and raise social awareness. Women issues should

also be made part of such socially relevant telecasting.

- Challenges to include women's issues in News. There are two ways in which women can contribute as part of the media - as executive decision-makers and as news editors and bureau chiefs setting the news agenda.
- Radio and television can offer better scope and facilities for women professionals. Women have been appointed to the post of announcers, news readers and feature and document producers in Broadcasting. Women can take initiatives in specialized work like interviewing and discussions they can be called upon to participate in prestigious programmes. Television has opened up a large area for women not only as announcers, newsreaders etc. but also as important programme producers in creating various serials and shows which are women oriented.
- Media personnel, including originators of information in all media forms including AIR, Doordarshan, Print Media etc. must be sensitized to women's issues particularly to the projection of positive images of women.
- More sensitized women need to be inducted for producing information programmes, films etc. in the national media. Positive role models of women as cultivators, producers, managers etc. must be forcefully projected.
- In order to change the attitudes towards women and girls and raise the social consciousness of the country, a conscious strategic change is required in national media and communication efforts.
- Folk media like puppetry theatre need to be widely encouraged, especially where electronic and print media have no outreach. Jathas can also be organized to reach poor women.
- Research and analysis should be undertaken to assess the ways in which the various communication channels reach and affect women and girls.
- There should be "Resource Centres" at the Centre and State levels for identification, collection, dissemination and documentation of material related to women's issues.

Conclusion

The people of today's world have to think deeply on these most important areas and take some action to improve the status of women in media and save the women, media as well as the world. Some of the organization are working for issues that are United Nation Development Fund for Women (UNIFEM), Global Media Monitoring Project (GMMP), etc. The role of all agencies is very important and effective in uplifting the images of women presented by media. By using some guidelines this can be improved.

- Making those who control media, aware of the need for a balanced workplace for both sexes.
- Creating positive attitude among mass communications towards the integration of women in the mainstream of social life.
- Developing mass media material, which portrays women in a positive and constructive manner and in a wide variety of roles.
- So, all the people of our society have to be aware and should take part in helping women, society and nation.

References

Bhatia, Sonia, "Women, Democracy and the Media" Sage Publications, New Delhi, 1998.

Chakraborty, S., "Mother India" Outlook Nov. 1, 2004.

Development and Educational Communication Unit. The Direction: Jhabua Development Communication Project, Ahmedabad : ISRO, DECU.

Gupta M,. "Women, Child Welfare and Media" Sarup and Sons New Delhi, 2000.

Gupta, V.S., Communication Technology Media Policy and National Development. Concept Publishing Company, New Delhi, 1999.

Jain, J. and Rai, S., "Films and Feminism : Essay an Indian Cinema (ed) Rawat Publications. Jaipur 2002.

Jha, Rana, "Woman and the Indian Bunt Media : Portrayal and Performance". Chanakya Publication Delhi, 1992.

Johnson Kirk, Television and Social change in Rural India, Sage Publication, New Delhi, 2000.

Joshi Ila, "India Towards Women-Friendly Communication Technologies", Asian Women in the Information Age. Singapore.

Mouli, Chandra., "Stree Shakti Come-Powers Women". The New Indian Express Nov. 27, 2002.

Ninan, S., Tune in to Quality, The Hindu July 29, 2001.

Prasad Kiran, "Women, Media and Society : Recasting Communication Policy". The Women's Press, New Delhi 2005.

Singh U., "New Women and Mass Media" Surabhi Publication Jaipur, 2000.

Singh, U., "New Women and Mass Media" Surabhi Publication Jaipur 2001.

Verma S.B., "Status of Women in Media" Deep and Deep Publication Pvt. Ltd., 2006.

Index